T0336733

# Soft Computing Applications for Database Technologies:
## Techniques and Issues

K. Anbumani
*Karunya University, India*

R. Nedunchezhian
*Sri Ramkrishna Engineering College, India*

**INFORMATION SCIENCE REFERENCE**

Hershey · New York

| | |
|---|---|
| Director of Editorial Content: | Kristin Klinger |
| Director of Book Publications: | Julia Mosemann |
| Acquisitions Editor: | Lindsay Johnston |
| Development Editor: | Joel Gamon |
| Typesetter: | Michael Brehm |
| Production Editor: | Jamie Snavely |
| Cover Design: | Lisa Tosheff |
| Printed at: | Yurchak Printing Inc. |

Published in the United States of America by
Information Science Reference (an imprint of IGI Global)
701 E. Chocolate Avenue
Hershey PA 17033
Tel: 717-533-8845
Fax: 717-533-8661
E-mail: cust@igi-global.com
Web site: http://www.igi-global.com/reference

Library of Congress Cataloging-in-Publication Data

Soft computing applications for database technologies : techniques and issues
/ K. Anbumani and R. Nedunchezhian, editors.
    p. cm.
  Includes bibliographical references and index.
  Summary: "This book investigates the advent of soft computing and its
applications in database technologies"--Provided by publisher.
  ISBN 978-1-60566-814-7 (hardcover) -- ISBN 978-1-60566-815-4 (ebook)  1.
Databases. 2.  Soft computing.  I. Anbumani, K. II. Nedunchezhian, R.
  QA76.9.D32S64 2010
  006.3--dc22
                          2010000636

British Cataloguing in Publication Data
A Cataloguing in Publication record for this book is available from the British Library.

# List of Reviewers

# Table of Contents

**Chapter 14**

# Detailed Table of Contents

*Angélica Urrutia, Universidad Católica del Maule, Chile*
*José Galindo, Universidad de Málaga, Spain*

In this chapter the authors present an overview of different fuzzy database modeling definitions by different authors. They highlight the FuzzyEER model, which is an extension of an EER model incorporating fuzzy semantics and notation. FuzzyEER is probably the most complete modeling tool. It has numerous characteristics, and in this chapter the authors list the main components and enhance some definitions relative to fuzzy attributes, fuzzy degrees associated to one or more attributes or with an independent meaning, fuzzy entities, as well as the definition of multivalued disjunctive attributes.

*Pierre Collet, Université de Strasbourg, France*

Evolutionary computation is an old field of computer science, that started in the 1960s nearly simultaneously in different parts of the world. It is an optimization technique that mimics the principles of Darwinian evolution in order to find good solutions to intractable problems faster than a random search. Artificial Evolution is only one among many stochastic optimization methods, but recently developed hardware (General Purpose Graphic Processing Units or GPGPU) gives it a tremendous edge over all the other algorithms, because its inherently parallel nature can directly benefit from the difficult to use Single Instruction Multiple Data parallel architecture of these cheap, yet very powerful cards.

*Bohumil Šulc, Czech Technical University in Prague, Czech Republic*
*David Klimanek, Czech Technical University in Prague, Czech Republic*

Evolutionary algorithms are well known as optimization techniques, suitable for solving various kinds of problems (Ruano, 2005). The new application of evolutionary algorithms represents their use in the detection of biased control loop functions caused by controlled variable sensor discredibility (Klimanek, Sulc, 2005). Sensor discredibility occurs when a sensor transmitting values of the controlled variable provides inexact information, however the information is not absolutely faulty yet. The use of discredible sensors in control circuits may cause the real values of controlled variables to exceed the range of tolerated differences, whereas zero control error is being displayed. However, this is not the only negative consequence. Sometimes, sensor discredibility is accompanied with undesirable and hardly recognizable side effects. Most typical is an increase of harmful emission production in the case of combustion control, (Sulc, Klimanek, 2005). We have found that evolutionary algorithms are useful tools for solving the particular problem of finding a software-based way (so called software redundancy) of sensor discredibility detection. Software redundancy is a more economical way than the usual hardware redundancy, which is otherwise necessary in control loop protection against this small, invisible control error occurrence. New results from a long-term tracking residuum trends show that credibility loss can be forecasted. Operators can be warned in advance that the sensor measuring the controlled variable needs to be exchanged. This need can be effectively reflected in maintenance plans. Namely, the standard genetic algorithm and the simulated annealing algorithm have been successfully applied and tested to minimize the given cost function. By means of these algorithms, a newly developed method is able to detect controlled variable sensor discredibility. When applied to combustion processes, production of harmful emissions can be kept within accepted limits. The application of the used evolutionary algorithms inclusive terminology transfer in this application area can serve as an explanatory case study to help readers gain a better understanding of the how the evolutionary algorithms operate.

**Chapter 4**

Spatial database systems and geographical information systems are currently only able to support geographical applications that deal with only crisp spatial objects, that is, objects whose extent, shape, and boundary are precisely determined. Examples are land parcels, school districts, and state territories. However, many new, emerging applications are interested in modeling and processing geographic data that are inherently characterized by spatial vagueness or spatial indeterminacy. Examples are air polluted areas, temperature zones, and lakes. These applications require novel concepts due to the lack of adequate approaches and systems. In this chapter, the authors show how soft computing techniques can provide a solution to this problem. They give an overview of two type systems or algebras that can be integrated into database systems and utilized for the modeling and handling of spatial vagueness. The first type system, called Vague Spatial Algebra (VASA), is based on well known, general, and exact models of crisp spatial data types and introduces vague points, vague lines, and vague regions. This enables an exact definition of the vague spatial data model since we can build it upon an already existing theory of spatial data types. The second type system, called Fuzzy Spatial Algebra (FUSA), leverages fuzzy set theory and fuzzy topology and introduces novel fuzzy spatial data types for fuzzy points, fuzzy lines, and fuzzy regions. This enables an even more fine-grained modeling of spatial objects that do not have sharp boundaries and interiors or whose boundaries and interiors cannot be precisely determined. This chapter provides a formal definition of the structure and semantics of both type systems. Further, the authors introduce spatial set operations for both algebras and obtain vague and fuzzy versions of geometric intersection, union, and difference. Finally, they describe how these data types can be embedded into extensible databases and show some example queries.

# Chapter 5

Artificial Neural Network (ANN) based systems are bio-inspired mechanisms for intelligent decision support with capabilities to learn generalized knowledge from the large amount of data and offers high degree of self-learning. However, the knowledge in such ANN system is stored in the generalized connection between neurons in implicit fashion, which does not help in providing proper explanation and reasoning to users of the system and results in low level of user friendliness. On the other hand, fuzzy systems are very user friendly, represent knowledge in highly readable form and provide friendly justification to users as knowledge is stored explicitly in the system. Type-2 fuzzy systems are one step ahead while computing with words in comparison to typical fuzzy systems. This chapter introduces a generic framework of type-2 fuzzy interface to an ANN system for course selection process. Resulting neuro-fuzzy system offers advantages of self-learning and implicit knowledge representation along with the utmost user friendliness and explicit justification.

# Chapter 6

Microarray studies and gene expression analysis have received significant attention over the last few years and provide many promising avenues towards the understanding of fundamental questions in biology and medicine. In this chapter the authors show that a combined GA-fuzzy classification system can be employed for effective mining of gene expression data. The applied classifier consists of a set of fuzzy if-then rules that allow for accurate non-linear classification of input patterns. A small number of fuzzy if-then rules are selected through means of a genetic algorithm, and are capable of providing a compact classifier for gene expression analysis. Experimental results on various well-known gene expression datasets confirm the good classification performance of our approach.

# Chapter 7

This chapter considers the soft computing approach called fuzzy decision trees (FDT), a form of classification analysis. The consideration of decision tree analysis in a fuzzy environment brings further interpretability and readability to the constructed 'if .. then ..' decision rules. Two sets of FDT analyses are presented, the first on a small example data set, offering a tutorial on the rudiments of one FDT technique. The second FDT analysis considers the investigation of an e-learning database, and the elucidation of the relationship between weekly online activity of students and their final mark on a university course module. Emphasis throughout the chapter is on the visualization of results, including the fuzzification of weekly online activity levels of students and overall performance.

Bayesian Belief Networks (BBNs) are increasingly used for understanding and simulating computational models in many domains. Though BBN techniques are elegant ways of capturing uncertainties, knowledge engineering effort required to create and initialize the network has prevented many researchers from using them. Even though the structure of the network and its conditional & initial probabilities could be learned from data, data is not always available and/or too costly to obtain. Further, current algorithms that can be used to learn relationships among variables, initial and conditional probabilities from data are often complex and cumbersome to employ. Qualitative-based approaches applied to the creation of graphical models can be used to create initial computational models that can help researchers analyze complex problems and provide guidance/support for decision-making. Once created, initial BBN models can be refined once appropriate data is obtained. This chapter extends the use of BBNs to help experts make sense of complex social systems (e.g., social capital in virtual communities) using a Bayesian model as an interactive simulation tool. Scenarios are used to update the model and to find out whether the model is consistent with the expert's beliefs. A sensitivity analysis was conducted to help explain how the model reacted to different sets of evidence. Currently, we are in the process of refining the initial probability values presented in the model using empirical data and developing more authentic scenarios to further validate the model. We will elaborate on how database technologies were used to support the current approach and will describe opportunities for future database tools needed to support this type of work.

Preserving the accuracy and the integrity of information in a database is extremely important for the organization that is maintaining that database. Such an organization is likely to rely heavily upon that accuracy. Applications that consult and use the database expect a warranty that the database is supplying the correct information. Critical business decisions may be made assuming that information extracted from the database is correct. Thus, incorrect data can lead to incorrect business decisions which can have serious implications for the people and organizations using it (Codd, 1990).

Due to the diffusion of multimedia databases and new ways of communication, there is an urgent need for developing more effective search systems capable of retrieving information by specifying directly in user queries elements strictly related to the multimedia content. This is the main rationale behind the flourishing area of Content-Based Multimedia Information Retrieval (CB-MIR), that finds in Soft Computing (SC) techniques a valid tool to handle uncertainty and vagueness underlying the whole information retrieval process. The main reason for this success seems to be the synergy resulting from SC paradigms, such as fuzzy logic, neural networks, rough sets and genetic algorithms. Each of these computing paradigms provides complementary reasoning and searching methods that allow the use of domain knowledge and empirical data to solve complex problems. In this chapter, the authors emphasize the potential of SC techniques, also combined in hybrid schemes, for the development of effective CB-MIR systems. As an example, the authors describe a content-based image retrieval system that employs SC techniques in its working scheme.

This chapter considers, and elucidates, the general methodology of rough set theory (RST), a nascent approach to rule based classification associated with soft computing. There are two parts of the elucidation undertaken in this chapter, firstly the levels of possible pre-processing necessary when undertaking an RST based analysis, and secondly the presentation of an analysis using variable precision rough sets (VPRS), a development on the original RST that allows for misclassification to exist in the constructed "if … then …" decision rules. Throughout the chapter, bespoke software underpins the pre-processing and VPRS analysis undertaken, including screenshots of its output. The problem of US bank credit ratings allows the pertinent demonstration of the soft computing approaches described throughout.

The purpose of this chapter is to demonstrate the possibility of transforming a large class of machine learning algorithms into commonsense reasoning processes based on using well-known deduction and induction logical rules. The concept of a good classification (diagnostic) test for a given set of positive examples lies in the basis of our approach to the machine learning problems. The task of inferring all good diagnostic tests is formulated as searching the best approximations of a given classification (a partitioning) on a given set of examples. The lattice theory is used as a mathematical language for constructing good classification tests. The algorithms of good tests inference are decomposed into subtasks and operations that are in accordance with main human commonsense reasoning rules.

The demand for rehabilitation increases daily as a result of diseases, occupational and traffic accidents and population growth. In the present time, some important problems occur regarding the rehabilitation period: the transportation of patients, the acquisition and storage of treatment data and the need to support the physiotherapists with intelligent devices. In order to overcome these challenges, the authors hereby propose a human machine interface to control an intelligent rehabilitation robot system designed for the lower limbs. The human machine interface has a structure that is created with a rule-based intelligent controlling structure, combined with conventional controller and an easy-to-use graphical user interface. By means of this interface, the rehabilitation sessions can be stored and members of the rehabilitation team can reach to this stored data via internet. Additionally, the patient can receive treatment in his house. One physiotherapist is able to treat several patients at a time by utilizing this system. The system's capacity has been elaborated through the test results.

In the recent Internet era the queue management in the routers plays a vital role in the provision of Quality of Service (QoS). Virtual queue-based marking schemes have been recently proposed for Active Queue Management (AQM) in Internet routers. In this chapter, the authors propose Fuzzy enabled AQM (F-AQM) scheme where the linguistics variables are used to specify the behavior of the queues in the routers. The status of the queue is continuously monitored and decisions are made adaptively to drop or mark the packets as is done in Random Early Discard (RED) and Random Early Marking (REM) algorithms or schemes. The authors design a fuzzy rule base represented in the form of matrix indexed by queue length and rate of change of queue. The performance of the proposed F-AQM scheme is compared with several well-known AQM schemes such as RED, REM and Adaptive Virtual Queue (AVQ).

# Preface

The digital revolution and the explosive growth of the Internet have helped create collection of huge amounts of useful data of diverse characteristics. Data is a valuable and intangible asset in any business today. Databases and database technologies play a crucial role in maintaining and manipulating data. Various database models exist such as relational, hierarchical, network, flat, and object-oriented. Each model organizes data in a different way to make them suitable for the intended application.

Real world data are diverse and imprecise in nature. They are growing at a phenomenal rate. As the application needs are diverse they demand a completely different set of requirements on the underlying models. The conventional relational database model is no longer appropriate for heterogeneous data. The diverse characteristics of data and its huge volume demand new ways of carrying out data analysis. Soft computing is a new, emerging complementary discipline for traditional computing principles. It exploits the tolerance for imprecision and uncertainty to achieve solutions for complex problems.

Soft computing methodologies include fuzzy sets, neural networks, genetic algorithms, Bayesian belief networks and rough sets. Fuzzy sets provide a natural framework for dealing with uncertainty. Bayesian belief networks, neural networks, and rough sets are widely used for classification and rule generation. Genetic algorithms handle various optimization and search processes like query optimization and template selection. Rough sets handle uncertainty arising from granules in the domain of discourse.

The advent of soft computing marks a significant paradigm shift in computing. Currently it has a wide range of application. The various techniques of soft computing and their applications in database technologies are discussed in the chapters of this book.

The first chapter, titled *"Fuzzy Database Modeling: An Overview and New Definitions,"* by Angélica Urrutia and José Galindo gives an overview of fuzzy database modeling. Much of data in real world is not precise, but fuzzy. Zadeh's fuzzy logic gives a tool to handle fuzzy data in decision making. Modeling of fuzzy data has been studied by a number of researchers. The authors of this chapter discuss further extensions in the field of fuzzy database modelling. This chapter starts with a review of contributions of previous authors with respect to fuzzy database modeling, particularly the FuzzyEER model. The chapter then proceeds to introduce and explain their proposed newly definitions pertaining to the FuzzyEER Model regarding fuzzy attributes, fuzzy degrees, and fuzzy entities. The newly introduced concepts are amply illustrated through suitable examples. The authors hope that the new definitions will further enhance FuzzyEER model to facilitate fuzzy queries and fuzzy data mining.

The author Pierre Collet, in the chapter *"A Quick Presentation of Evolutionary Computation,"* gives an easy-to-grasp exposition of generic evolutionary computation paradigm. After giving a brief historical perspective, the author presents a unified evolutionary algorithm. The various concepts involved are lucidly explained with examples. This chapter will be quite useful to get a gentle introduction and survey of generic evolutionary computation.

The third chapter, "*Evolutionary Algorithms in Supervision of Error-Free Control*," by Bohumil Šulc and David Klimanek, reports application of certain soft computing techniques in combustion control. Specifically, genetic and simulated annealing algorithms have been employed in a model-based controlled variable sensor discredibility detection. The authors outline procedure of incorporating genetic and simulated annealing algorithms in the control loop. They claim that such application of these soft computing techniques has a great importance in industrial practice because a timely predicted sensor malfunction helps to save additional costs resulting from unplanned shutdowns.

In the next chapter titled "*Soft Computing Techniques in Spatial Databases*," its author Markus Schneider explains how two different soft computing techniques with different expressiveness can be used for spatial data handling in the context of spatial databases and Geographic Information Systems. The focus of this chapter is the design of the algebra systems named Vague Spatial Algebra (VASA) and Fuzzy Spatial Algebra (FUSA). A formal definition of the structure and semantics of both types of systems are also provided. Further, spatial set operations for both the algebras have also been discussed. Finally, a description of how these data types can be embedded into extensible databases is explained with sample queries.

In the fifth chapter, "*Type-2 Fuzzy Interface for Artificial Neural Network*", the author Priti Srinivas Sajja introduces another hybrid soft computing technique. The field of applications of soft computing technique discussed by the author is the process of course selection performed by students. The author introduces a generic framework of type-2 fuzzy interface to an Artificial Neural Network system. The author covers the introduction of fuzzy logic, fuzzy membership functions, type-1 and type-2 fuzzy systems and Artificial Neural Networks (ANN) for novice readers. Also, the author gives the need for hybridization of ANN and fuzzy logic. Next, the author illustrates an experimental prototype with fuzzy interface and base ANN. In this system, the author uses type-2 fuzzy interface to feed input to the base ANN. The author claims that with sufficient amount of good quality input data, the system performs well and with minor modification, the system may be used for HR Management, aptitude testing and general career counseling.

In chapter 6, "*A Combined GA-Fuzzy Classification System for Mining Gene Expression Databases*," the authors Gerald Schaefer and Tomoharu Nakashima introduce yet another hybrid soft computing technique. The field of application of soft computing technique discussed by the authors is gene expression database. After explaining fuzzy rule generation and fuzzy rule classification, the authors point out the very many fuzzy if-then rules that would result. The number of generated rules increases exponentially with the number of attributes involved and with the number of partitions used for each attribute. The genetic algorithm technique is employed to reduce the number of rules to a compact set. The authors discuss genetic operations employed and give their algorithm in detail and ways of improving its performance. The authors demonstrate their hybrid technique on three gene expression data sets that are commonly used in the literature, viz., Colon dataset, Leukemia dataset and Lymphoma dataset. Exhaustive simulation results are given. The authors state that their technique yields good results.

The chapter on "*Fuzzy Decision Rule Construction Using Fuzzy Decision Trees: Application to E-Learning Database*" by Malcolm J.Beynon and Paul Jones (Chapter 7) discusses an application of fuzzy logic–specifically fuzzy decision tree. The authors give two sets of extensive FDT analysis. The first analysis deals with a small example dataset to illustrate the concepts. The second FDT analysis is in the field of E-Learning and considers the student's weekly online activities and subsequent performance in a university course. The authors emphasize visualization of results throughout the chapter.

Chapter 8, "*A Bayesian Belief Network Methodology for Modeling Social Systems in Virtual Communities: Opportunities for Database Technologies*," is contributed by the authors Ben K. Daniel, Juan-Diego Zapata-Rivera, and Gordon I. McCalla. Bayesian belief networks are used to model situations involving uncertainty arising in fields like social sciences. A Bayesian model encodes domain knowledge, showing relationships, interdependencies, and independencies among variables. However, knowledge engineering effort is required to create conditional probability for each variable in the network. This chapter describes an approach that combines both qualitative and quantitative techniques to elicit knowledge from experts without worrying about computing initial probabilities for training the model. The authors demonstrate their technique on a computational model of social capital in virtual communities.

The importance of preserving the accuracy and integrity of data in a database is highlighted in the chapter titled "*Integrity Constraints Checking in a Distributed Database*" by Hamidah Ibrahim. This chapter discusses checking integrity constraints in distributed databases. The author describes different integrity constraint tests that could be conducted in distributed databases. A review of the integrity constraints available in the literature is clearly given. Finally the author explains several strategies for checking the integrity constraints in distributed databases. The author also discusses important criteria for evaluating the integrity tests.

Authors G. Castellano, A. M. Fanelli, and M. A. Torsello in chapter 10, "*Soft Computing Techniques in Content-Based Multimedia Information Retrieval*," clearly explain the basic concepts of the four techniques coming under the purview of softcomputing, viz., Fuzzy Logic, Neural Networks, Rough Sets, and Genetic Algorithm. They give a good literature survey on the application of each soft computing technique to Content Based Multimedia Information Retrieval(CB-MIR). They also give a good survey of the applicaiton of hybrid, neuro-fuzzy technique to CB-MIR. Next, the authors discuss in detail about applying hybrid neuro-fuzzy techniques to CB-MIR. They have contributed a system called VIRMA(Visual Image Retrieval by Shape MAtching) that enables users to search for images having a shape similar to the sketch of a submitted sample image. The neuro-fuzzy strategy enables one to extract a set of fuzzy rules that classify image pixels for the extraction of contours included in the processed image, so that this can be stored in the database. The authors show how the neuro-fuzzy technique is useful for CB-MIR.

Chapter 11, "*An Exposition of Feature Selection and Variable Precision Rough Set Analysis: Application to Financial Data*," by Malcolm J. Beynon and Benjamin Griffiths presents a Variable Precision Rough Sets (VPRS) analysis of certain Fitch Individual Bank Rating (FIBR) datasets. There are two parts of elucidation undertaken in this chapter. First, the levels of possible pre-processing necessary for undertaking a Rough Set based Theory (RST) analysis and then the presentation of an analysis using VPRS. The vein graph software enables one to select a single $\beta$-reduct and derive the rules associated with the $\beta$-reduct. Two algorithms are used for feature selection namely ReliefF and RST_FS. The predictions based on the training and validation sets are displayed in the 'Predictive Summary Stat's panel.

Xenia Nadenova introduces the concept of Good Diagnostic Test (GDT) as the basis of her approach in "*Interconnection of Class of Machine Learning Algorithms with Logical Commonsense Reasoning Operations*" in chapter 12. This chapter explains the possibility of transforming a large class of machine learning algorithms into a commonsense reasoning processes by using well-known deduction and induction logical rules. The lattice theory is used for constructing a good classification test. The rules for implementing variant transitions have been constructed such as rules of generalization and specialization, inductive diagnostic rules, and dual inductive diagnostic rules. The commonsense reasoning rules have been divided into two classes. An algorithm DIAGaRa for inferring GMRTs has been proposed for incremental inferring of good diagnostic tests. The algorithm for inferring good tests is decomposed into subtasks and operations that are in accordance with main human common sense reasoning rules.

In chapter 13, the authors Erhan Akdoğan, M. Arif Adlı, Ertuğrul Taçgın, and Nureddin Bennett propose a human-machine interface (HMI) to control a robot manipulator that has three-degrees of freedom for the rehabilitation of the lower limbs. This system uses a rule-based intelligent controller structure, combined with conventional control algorithms. It also has a user friendly GUI which can be used on the Internet, thereby allowing the patients to receive treatment at home. With HMI, the progress and the current state of a patient's rehabilitation can be stored in the database. The system proposed in this chapter can handle common problems such as the transportation of patients, storage of data and availability of data of the progress of patient's rehabilitation. The authors claim that by utilizing this system physiotherapists can treat several patients at the same time.

In the last chapter, "Congestion Control Using Soft Computing", the authors T. Revathi, and K. Muneeswaran discuss the phenomenon of network congestion. They recapitulate some of the important existing techniques for congestion control. Then they take up the congestion avoidance problem and explain the need for Active Queue Management (AQM). They review some of the AQM techniques available in the literature. Then the authors propose a soft computing technique called Fuzzy-enabled Active Queue Management (F-AQM) which addresses the influence of the queuing behavior in handling the traffic in a network. They design a fuzzy rule base represented in the form of a matrix indexed by queue length and rate of change of queue. They have studied the performance of their scheme by suitable simulation and compared the performance with that of Adaptive Virtual Queue (AVQ) techniques. It is claimed that the proposed method outperforms AVQ in reducing the number of dropped packets for different settings of Explicit Congestion Notification (ECN) and queue size.

*K. Anbumani*
*Karunya University, India*

*R. Nedunchezhian*
*Sri Ramkrishna Engineering College, India*

# Chapter 1
# Fuzzy Database Modeling:
## An Overview and New Definitions

**Angélica Urrutia**
*Universidad Católica del Maule, Chile*

**José Galindo**
*Universidad de Málaga, Spain*

## ABSTRACT

*In this chapter the authors present an overview of different fuzzy database modeling definitions by different authors. They highlight the FuzzyEER model, which is an extension of an EER model incorporating fuzzy semantics and notation. FuzzyEER is probably the most complete modeling tool. It has numerous characteristics, and in this chapter the authors list the main components and enhance some definitions relative to fuzzy attributes, fuzzy degrees associated to one or more attributes or with an independent meaning, fuzzy entities, as well as the definition of multivalued disjunctive attributes.*

## INTRODUCTION

On occasions the term *"imprecision"* embraces several meanings between which we should differentiate. For example, the information we have may be incomplete or *"fuzzy"* (diffuse, *vague*), or we may not know if it is certain or not (*uncertainty*), or perhaps we are totally ignorant of the information (*unknown*), we may know that that information cannot be applied to a specific entity (*undefined*), or we may not even know if the data can be applied

or not to the entity in question (*"total ignorance"* or value *"null"*) (Umano and Fukami, 1994). Each of these terms will depend on the context in which they are applied and these concepts have been widely studied in the database context in many papers, such as (Galindo et al., 2006; Galindo, 2008; Zadrożny et al., 2008).

The management of uncertainty in database systems is a very important problem (Motro, 1995) as the information is often vague. Motro states that fuzzy information is content-dependent, and he classifies it as follows:

DOI: 10.4018/978-1-60566-814-7.ch001

- **Uncertainty**: We cannot know whether the information is true or false. For example, "John may be 38 years old".
- **Imprecision:** The information available is not specific enough. For example, "John may be between 37 and 43 years old", — disjunction — "John is 34 or 43 years old", — negative — "John is not 37 years old", or even unknown.
- **Vagueness:** The model includes elements (predicates or quantifiers) which are inherently vague, for example, "John is in his early years", or "John is at the end of his youth". However, once these concepts have been defined, this case would match the previous one (imprecision).
- **Inconsistency:** It contains two or more pieces of information, which cannot be true at the same time. For example, "John is 37 and 43 years old, or he is 35 years old"; this is a special case of disjunction.
- **Ambiguity:** Some elements of the model lack a complete semantics (or a complete meaning). For example, "It is not clear whether they are annual or monthly salaries".

**Zadeh** (1965) introduces the fuzzy logic in order to deal with this type of data. Traditional logic, because it is bi-valued, can only operate with concepts like: yes or no, black or white, true or false, 0 or 1, which allowed just for a very limited knowledge representation. Although there are other logics which take more truth values, namely multi-valued logics, fuzzy logic is one extension which takes endless truth levels (or degrees), associating the concept of membership degree or truth degree in an interval [0,1] within the fuzzy logic theory.

**Fuzzy databases** have also been widely studied (Galindo, 2008), with little attention being paid to the problem of conceptual modeling (Chaudhry et al., 1999) and focusing the research mainly in fuzzy queries (Zadrożny et al., 2008). This does not mean that there are no publications, however, but that they are sparse and with no standard. Therefore, there have also been advances in modeling uncertainty in database systems (Buckles and Petry, 1985; Kerre and Chen, 1995; Chen, 1998; Yazici and George, 1999) including object-oriented database models (Van Gyseghem et al., 1993; George et al., 1996; Caluwe, 1997; Bordogna et al., 1999; Yazici and George, 1999; Ma et al., 2004). Probably, the most complete approach was published in (Galindo et al., 2006) in the so-called FuzzyEER model.

At the same time, the extension of the ER model for the treatment of fuzzy data (with vagueness) has been studied in various publications (Zvieli and Chen, 1986; Ruspini, 1986; Vandenberghe, 1991; Chaudhry et al., 1994 and 1999; Chen and Kerre, 1998; Chen 1998; Kerre and Chen, 2000; Vert et al., 2000; Ma et al., 2001), but none of these refer to the possibility of expressing constraints by using the tools by fuzzy sets theory. In (Kerre and Chen, 1995) a summary of some of these models can be found. On the other hand, the main methodologies of databases design, such as (Elmasri and Navathe, 2000), have not paid attention to the modeling of data with uncertainty, although the intent of uncertainty modeling of the real world is rarely absent.

Based on these concepts, in this chapter we will discuss different approaches, by various authors, related to the uncertainty conceptual modeling problem in database models. After, we summarize the FuzzyEER model, a tool for fuzzy database modeling with many advantages with respect to the previous modeling tools. Some of its characteristics are: fuzzy values in the attributes, degree in each value of an attribute, degree in a group of values of diverse attributes, as well as, fuzzy entities, fuzzy relationships, fuzzy aggregation, fuzzy constraints. Furthermore, we include here some new definitions for the FuzzyEER model.

## THE ZVIELI AND CHEN APPROACH (1986)

Zvieli and Chen (1986) is the first great approach in ER modeling. They allow fuzzy attributes in entities and relationships and introduced three levels of fuzziness in the ER model:

1. At the first level, entity sets, relationships and attribute sets may be fuzzy, namely, they have a membership degree to the model. For example, a fuzzy entity "Company" may have a 0.9 membership degree, a relationship "To Accept" may have a 0.7 membership degree and a fuzzy attribute "Electronic mail" may have a 0.8 membership degree.
2. The second level is related to the fuzzy occurrences of entities and relationships. For example, an entity Young_Employees must be fuzzy, because its instances, its employees, belong to the entity with different membership degrees.
3. The third level concerns the fuzzy values of attributes of special entities and relationships. For example, attribute Quality of a basketball player may be fuzzy (bad, good, very good...).

The first level may be useful, but at the end we must decide whether such an entity, relationship or attribute will appear or will not appear in the implementation. The second level is useful too, but it is important to consider different degree meanings (membership degree, importance degree, fulfillment degree...). A list of authors using different meanings may be found in (Galindo et al., 2001). The third level is useful, and it is similar to writing the data type of some attributes, because fuzzy values belong to fuzzy data types.

## PROPOSAL OF VAN GYSEGHEM AND DE CALUWE (1997)

Van Gyseghem and **De Caluwe** (1997) discussed two types of imperfect information, appearing in database applications: fuzzy information representing information with inherent gradations, for which it is impossible to define sharp or precise borders, and uncertain or imprecise information, representing information which is (temporarily) incomplete due to a lack of sufficient or more precise knowledge. Dealing with this kind of imperfect information within the formal and crisp environment of a computer, is based in this paper upon the fuzzy set theory and its related possibility theory, which offers a formal framework to model imperfect information, and upon the object-oriented paradigm, which offers flexible modeling capabilities. The result is the UFO database model, a "fuzzy" extension of a full-fledged object-oriented database model (Van Gyseghem et al., 1993).

This research discusses the UFO database model in detail in three steps. First, it is shown how fuzzy information is handled: meaningful fuzzifications of several object-oriented concepts are introduced in order to store and maintain fuzzy information, and to allow a flexible or "soft" modeling of database application. Then, it is discussed how uncertainty and imprecision in the information are handled: possible alternatives for the information are stored and maintained by introducing role object, which are tied like shadows to regular objects in the database; they allow the processing of uncertainty and imprecision in a, to the user, implicit and transparent way, and they also allow the modeling of tentative behaviour and of hypothetical information in the database application. Both the static and the dynamic aspects of (imperfect) information are developed in the UFO database model, and imperfect information is considered at the data level as well as at the metalevel of a database application. The process of "extending" an object-oriented database model to the UFO database model, as discussed here, adheres, as closely as possible, to the original principles of the object-oriented paradigm, to allow a flexible and transparent, but semantically sound modeling of imprecise information. The object-oriented database model, which the extension process starts off from, adheres to the standard proposal ODMG-93, to allow for practical implementations of the UFO database model. For the same purpose, this paper also discusses an interface of the UFO database model to an extended relation database model, capable of handling some imperfect information, and for which some prototypes are already available.

## PROPOSAL BY YAZICI ET AL. (1996 AND 1999)

**Yazici** and Merdan (1996) proposed an extension of the IFO model, for the processing of imprecise data, and special treatment of data where similarity exists in a label. They call this extension ExIFO, and by means of examples they explain the implementation and validation of the representation of a fuzzy conceptual scheme by looking at a representation of uncertain attributes. In the model, three new constructors are added and using these new constructors it is possible to represent explicitly attributes that have uncertain values.

The ExIFO conceptual model (Yazici et al., 1999) allows imprecision and uncertainty in database models, based on the IFO conceptual model (Yazici and Merdan, 1996; Yazici and George, 1999). They use fuzzy-valued attributes, incomplete-valued attributes and null-valued attributes. In the first case, the true data may belong to a specific set or subset of values, for example the domain of this attribute may be a set of colors {red, orange, yellow, blue} or a subset {orange, yellow} where there is a similarity relation between the colors. In the second case, the true data value is not known, for example, the domain of this attribute may be a set of years between 1990

and 1992. In the third case, the true data value is available, but it is not expressed precisely, for example the domain of this attribute may be the existence or not of a telephone number. For each of these attribute types, there is a formal definition and a graphical representation. In this study, the authors introduce a high-level primitives to model fuzzy entity type whose semantics are related to each other with logic operators OR, XOR or AND. The main contribution of this approach is the use of an extended $NF^2$ relation (Non First Normal Form) to transform a conceptual design into a logical design. Consequently, the strategy is to analyze the attributes that compose the conceptual model in order to establish an $NF^2$ model.

## THE CHEN AND KERRE APPROACH (1998 AND 2000)

In (Chen and Kerre, 1998; Chen, 1998; Kerre and Chen, 2000) the authors introduced the fuzzy extension of several major EER concepts (superclass, subclass, generalization, specialization, category and shared subclass) without including graphical representations. The basic idea is that if E1 is a superclass of E2 and e∈E2, then E1(e) ≤ E2(e), where E1(e) and E2(e) are the membership functions of e to E1 and E2, respectively. They discussed three kinds of constraints with respect to fuzzy relationships but they do not study fuzzy constraints: a) The inheritance constraint means that, a subclass instance inherits all relationship instances in which it has participated as a superclass entity. b) The total participation constraint for entity E is defined when for any instance in E, $\exists \alpha_i$ such that $\alpha_i > 0$, where $\alpha_i$ is one membership degree in the fuzzy relationship. c) The cardinality constraints 1:1, 1:N and N:M are also studied with fuzzy relationships.

The fuzzy ER model (Chen, 1998) proposes a model generated by $M = (E, R, A)$ expressed by E as entity type, R as interrelation type, and A as attributes, also including label types which generate, at the first level, L1(M) = $(E, R, A_E, A_R)$, and proposes four set types, with a corresponding graphic notation, and where $\mu_X$ is the membership function to the set X (one Entity, one Relationship or one Attribute) and $D_E$ is the domain of $E$ composed of all possible entity types concerned:

- $E$ = $\{\mu_E (E)/E: E \in D_E \text{ and } \mu_E (E) \in [0,1]\}$.
- $R$ = $\{\mu_R (R)/R: R \text{ is a relationship type involving entity types in } D_E \text{ and } \mu_R (E) \in [0,1]\}$.
- $A_E$ = $\{\mu_{AE} (A)/A: A \text{ is an attribute type of entity type E and } \mu_{AE} (A) \in [0,1]\}$.
- $A_R$ = $\{\mu_{AR} (B)/B: B \text{ is an attribute type of relationship type R and } \mu_{AR} (B) \in [0,1]\}$.

The participation constraint is modeled setting that an entity E $\lambda$-participates in R if for every e of E, there exists a f in F such that $\mu_R(e,f) >= \lambda$. The cardinality constraint is set using two fuzzy numbers N and M. The concept of fuzzy quantifier is not used in this approach.

At the second level, for each entity type E and relationship type R, the sets of their values can be fuzzy sets, reflecting possible partial belonging of the corresponding values to their types. The third level of fuzzy extensions concerns with attributes and their values. For each attribute type A, any of its values can be a fuzzy set.

Later on, in another section, an attribute-defined specialization is defined with $FS_i \in F(Dom(A))$, where all the $FS_i$ are fuzzy sets on Dom(A), the domain of the attribute A. He also includes the fuzzy definition for categories and shared subclass, i.e. union and intersection. This proposal, makes always reference to linguistic labels, and to the trapezoidal function over an attribute or specific entity, not to a set of different attributes or different entities. This author, just like Yazici and Merdan (1998), establishes his data models from the attributes, and creates the object class or entity by using generalization and specialization tools.

Chen (1998) defines that a linguistic variable X is composed of the tuple (T, U, G, M) where:

T is the set of linguistic terms of X, U is the universe of discourse, G is the set of syntactic rules that generate the element T, and M is the set of semantic rules translated from T that correspond to the fuzzy subset of U. With this, he defines a conceptual model and its mathematical representation. For example, let X = Age, T is generated via G by the set {Young, Middle-Aged, Old}. Each term of T is specifically handled by M by fuzzy sets. The type of correspondence between an entity and a fuzzy entity is also established, as well as the set of values that a membership degree obtains from a fuzzy set: 1:1, 1:N, N:M, incorporating fuzziness to the ER model.

## THE CHAUDHRY ET AL. APPROACH (1999)

Chaudhry, Moyne and Rundensteiner (1994 and 1999) proposed a method for designing Fuzzy Relational Databases (FRDB) following the extension of the ER model of Zvieli and Chen (1986) taking special interest in converting crisp databases into fuzzy ones. The way to do so is to define *n* linguistic labels as *n* fuzzy sets over the universe of an attribute. After, each tuple in the crisp entity is transformed up to *n* fuzzy tuples in a new entity (or *n* values in the same tuple). Each fuzzy tuple (or value) does not store the crisp value but a linguistic label and a grade of membership giving the degree to which the corresponding crisp entity belongs to the new entity. Finally, the crisp entity and the new fuzzy entity are mapped to separate tables.

Their ER model includes fuzzy relationships as relationships with at least one attribute as membership grade. They propose FERM, a design methodology for mapping a fuzzy ER data model to an crisp relational database in four steps (constructing a fuzzy ER data model, transforming it to relational tables, normalization and ensuring correct interpretation of the fuzzy relational operators). They also presented the application of

FERM to build a prototype of a fuzzy database for a discreet control system for a semiconductor manufacturing process.

Chaudhry et al. (1999) expand the model presented in Chaudhry et al. (1994), focusing on their proposal for the *control processes* example. In each process imprecise values are observed, associated to linguistic labels, and every value involves a process called "DBFuzzifier construct".

## PROPOSAL OF MA ET AL. (2001, 2004 AND 2007)

**Ma** et al., (2001) worked with three levels of **Zvieli and Chen**, (1986), and incorporated in the Fuzzy Extended Entity-Relationship model (FEER model) a way of managing complex objects in the real world at a conceptual level, associating an importance degree of each of the components (attributes, entities, etc.) to the scheme. However, their definitions (of generalization, specialization, category, and aggregation) impose very restrictive conditions. They also provide an approach to mapping a FEER model to a Fuzzy Object-Oriented Database scheme (FOODB). They define graphic representation for: single-valued attribute type, multivalued attribute type, disjunctive fuzzy attribute type, conjunctive fuzzy attribute type, null attribute type, open or null attribute type, disjunctive imprecise attribute type, conjunctive imprecise attribute type, entity with grade of membership, relationship with grade of membership, attribute with grade of membership, fuzzy total and disjoint specialization, fuzzy total and overlapping specialization, fuzzy partial and disjoint specialization, fuzzy partial and overlapping specialization, fuzzy subclass with fuzzy multiple superclasses, fuzzy category, and fuzzy aggregation.

Ma et al. (2004) introduce an extended object-oriented database model to handle imperfect as well as complex objects. They extend some major notions in object-oriented databases such as objects, classes, objects-classes relationships, subclass/superclass, and multiple inheritances.

The proposal Ma and Yan (2007) focuses on fuzzy XML data modeling, which is mainly involved in the representation model of the fuzzy XML, its conceptual design, and its storage in databases. This fuzzy XML data model is developed based on "possibility distribution theory". The fuzzy UML data model is developed to design the fuzzy XML model conceptually. They investigated the formal conversions from the fuzzy UML model to the fuzzy XML model and the formal mapping from the fuzzy XML model to the fuzzy relational databases.

## APPROACHES BY OTHER AUTHORS

Ruspini (1986) proposed an extension of the ER model with fuzzy values in the attributes, and a truth value can be associated with each relationship instance. In addition, some special relationships such as same-object, subset-of, member-of... are also introduced.

Vandenberghe (1991) applied **Zadeh's extension principle** to calculate the truth value of propositions. For each proposition, a possibility distribution is defined on the doubleton true, false of the classical truth values. In this way, the concepts such as entity, relationship and attribute as well as subclass, superclass, category, generalization and specialization... have been extended.

The proposal of Vert et al. (2000) is based on the notation used by Oracle and uses the fuzzy sets theory to treat data sets as a collection of fuzzy objects, applying the result to the area of Geospatial Information Systems (GIS).

Other proposal of Vert et al. (2002) extended the data model notation ERD with some new entities from the initial model: a new entity and element was added. The initial model was extended with new fuzzy notation and this extended model, primarily can become ambiguous when managing sets of GIS data. The first extended relation is between Temporal Location and Set View. This has a fuzzy D() symbol.

Another line of work in fuzzy conceptual data modeling (without using the Entity-Relationship model) is reported in (Fujishiro et al., 1991), using a graph-oriented schema for modeling a fuzzy database. Fuzziness is handled by defining various links between records of the value database (actual data values) and the explanatory database (semantic interpretation of fuzzy attributes, symmetries...).

Other proposal in XML is in (Damiani et al., 2001). They reviewed the main problems related to the processing and restructuring of large amounts of XML databases, and propose some solutions in the framework of flexible query and processing model for well-formed documents. This authors incorporated grade to data.

Some other interesting approaches may be found in (Chen et al., 2007; Oliboni and Pozzani, 2008a and 2008b).

## THE FUZZYEER MODEL

The FuzzyEER model, is an extension of an EER model to create a model with fuzzy semantics and notations, presented in (Galindo et al., 2006). In the same book, authors study other aspects of fuzzy databases, such as a logic model for fuzzy relational databases, a mapping algorithm from FuzzyEER to relations and the definition of **FSQL (Fuzzy SQL)**, a complete fuzzy extension to **SQL**, widely analyzed also in (Urrutia et al., 2008).

The main characteristics of FuzzyEER are, firstly, different **fuzzy attributes** (including different kind of fuzzy values and fuzzy degrees as we explain below and summarize in Table 1). We can also define a **fuzzy degree** to the model, and use fuzzy entities, fuzzy weak entities (of two types: existence and identification), fuzzy **relationships,** fuzzy **aggregation** of entities and of attributes, fuzzy degree in **specializations** and in the subclasses, and a great variety

of fuzzy **constraints** using absolute or relative **fuzzy quantifiers**: fuzzy participation constraint, fuzzy cardinality constraint, the fuzzy (min,max) notation, fuzzy completeness constraint, fuzzy cardinality constraint on overlapping specializations, fuzzy disjoint and overlapping constraints on specializations, fuzzy attribute-defined specializations, fuzzy constraints in **union types** or categories and also in intersection types or shared subclasses (participation and completeness in both of them). A graphic and CASE tool for this model has been developed.

## Fuzzy Attributes

**Fuzzy attributes** are attributes of an entity or relationship which may have fuzzy values and it is possible to operate with these values (queries, updates, insertions, data mining processes...). There are two categories of fuzzy attributes depending on whether the underlying domain, within which the measure for each attribute lies, is inherently ordered or not ordered. In an ordered referential domain we can express any type of possibility distribution or fuzzy set: trapezoidal, linguistic labels (associated to specific possibility distributions), approximate values (triangular distributions) and intervals of possibility. A non-ordered referential domain contains measures such as simple "scalars" (or labels) and possibility distributions over "scalars". In both contexts, the values Unknown, Undefined, and Null are allowed and are as defined by Umano and Fukami (1994).

With these concepts, FuzzyEER considers four types of fuzzy attributes, taking into account the type of referential domain:

- **Type 1**: These are attributes with "*precise data*", classic or crisp (i.e. traditional, with no imprecision). Such attributes can have linguistic labels defined over them. This type of attribute is represented in the database system in the same way as precise data, but can be transformed or manipulated

*Table 1. Fuzzy attribute types in FuzzyEER and FSQL (Galindo et al., 2006; Urrutia et al., 2008)*

| Fuzzy Attribute Type: | Type 1 | Type 2 | Type 3 | Type 4 | Type 5 | Type 6 | Type 7 | Type 8 |
|---|---|---|---|---|---|---|---|---|
| Fuzzy Queries (labels, fuzzy comparators…) | × | × | × | × | × | × | × | × |
| Store Crisp Values (Numbers) | × | × | | | | | | |
| Ordered Domain | × | × | | | × | × | × | × |
| Store Fuzzy Sets and Labels | | × | × | × | | | | |
| Store Possibility Distributions on Numbers | | × | | | | | | |
| Store Possibility Distributions on Labels | | | × | × | | | | |
| Define Labels with a Similarity Relationship | | | × | | | | | |
| Store Only One Fuzzy Degree in [0,1] | | | | | × | × | × | × |
| Degree Associated to One Attribute | | | | | × | | | |
| Degree Associated to a Set of Attributes | | | | | | × | | |
| Degree Associated to the Whole Instance | | | | | | | × | |
| Non-Associated Degree | | | | | | | | × |

using fuzzy conditions. This type of attribute is useful for extending traditional databases, allowing fuzzy queries on classic data. However, databases containing this type of attribute do not inherently store imprecision, and therefore, strictly speaking, they are not fuzzy, although they do allow fuzzy queries or manipulations to be carried out. For example, queries of the kind "Give me employees that earn a lot more than the minimum salary", can be made.

- **Type 2**: These are attributes that gather *"imprecise data over an ordered referential domain"*. These attributes admit both crisp and fuzzy data, in the form of possibility distributions over an underlying ordered domain. This is therefore an extension of the Type 1 attribute that additionally allows the storage of imprecise information, such as "he is approximately 2 meters tall".

- **Type 3**: These are attributes over *"data of discrete non-ordered domain with analogy"*. In these attributes some labels are defined (for example "blond", "ginger", "brown"…) that are "scalars" with a similarity relationship (or proximity) defined

over them. This fuzzy relation indicates the extent to which each pair of labels is similar. Possibility distributions are also able to be applied over this domain (for example, the value {1/dark, 0.4/brown}, expressing that a certain person is more likely to be dark than brown-haired, but is definitely neither blond nor ginger).

- **Type 4**: These attributes are defined in the same way as Type 3 attributes, without it being necessary for a similarity relationship to exist between the labels (or values) of the domain. In this case, the defining element is the degree associated to each individual label, without evaluating the similarity between labels. This kind of attribute will often have measures associated with non-ordered referential domains. A possible example could be the type of role played by a client in a real estate agency, where the degree measures the importance with which a client is "seeking for" or "offering" a property, without taking into account the "similarity" between the two roles.

## Fuzzy Degrees

There is a basic way of incorporating uncertainty in a database, which consists of using "**fuzzy degrees**". The domain of these degrees may be the interval [0,1], although other values are also permitted, such as possibility distributions (usually over this unit interval), which, in turn, may be related to specific linguistic labels (such as "a lot", "normal", etc.). The following are some of the most important ways of using fuzzy degrees:

- **Associated degrees**: These degrees are associated to a specific being. These fuzzy degrees incorporate imprecision into the associated value. These degrees may be associated to different concepts:
    - **Type 5, degree in each value of an attribute**: An instance can have several attributes. In turn, some of these attributes may have a fuzzy degree associated to them. This implies that each value of this attribute has an associated degree, which measures the level of fuzziness of that value.
    - **Type 6, degree in a set of values of different attributes**: This is an intermediate case between the previous and subsequent cases. Here, the degree is associated to a subset of attributes. Whilst this is an unusual case, it can sometimes be very useful.
    - **Type 7, degree in the whole instance of the entity**: This is similar to the previous case, but here the degree is associated to the whole instance of the entity and not exclusively to the value of a specific attribute of the instance. It can measure to what degree this tuple (or instance) belongs to this table (or entity) of the database.
- **Type 8, non-associated degrees**: There are cases in which we wish to express imprecise information which can be represented by using only the degree, without associating this degree to another specific value or values.

These degrees may have different meanings. The following are the most important possible meanings:

- **Fulfillment Degree**: A property can be fulfilled with a certain degree between two extremes: the property has total fulfillment (usually degree 1) and the property has no fulfillment at all (usually degree 0). This is usually used in fuzzy queries, when a condition has been established over the values of an entity or relationship (i.e. a selection with a fuzzy condition).
- **Uncertainty Degree**: the uncertainty degree expresses the certainty with which a specific piece of data is known. When certainty exists regarding the truth of the value, then the degree will be 1 and, if certainty exists that the value is false the degree will be 0. The values between 0 and 1 express different levels of uncertainty.
- **Possibility Degree**: This measures the possibility of an attribute having a particular value. This meaning is similar to the previous one, but it can be seen to be a weaker degree, because it contains information that is more or less possible and not more or less certain.
- **Importance Degree**: Different objects (instances, attributes, etc.) can be of different relative importance, and this can be represented using an importance degree.

These degrees may also have linguistic labels defined in their own context. These labels are defined over the [0,1] interval, and the user is able to make fuzzy queries using these graded attributes.

*Figure 1. Graphic representation in FuzzyEER for: a) Fuzzy attribute Type 1 (simple), b) Fuzzy attribute Type n, with n∈{2,3,4} (simple), c) Derived fuzzy attribute, d) Optional multivalued fuzzy attribute, e) Multivalued fuzzy attribute with a minimum compulsory value, f) Generic example of a composite attribute with a fuzzy component, g) and h) compulsory and optional multivalued disjunctive attribute, respectively*

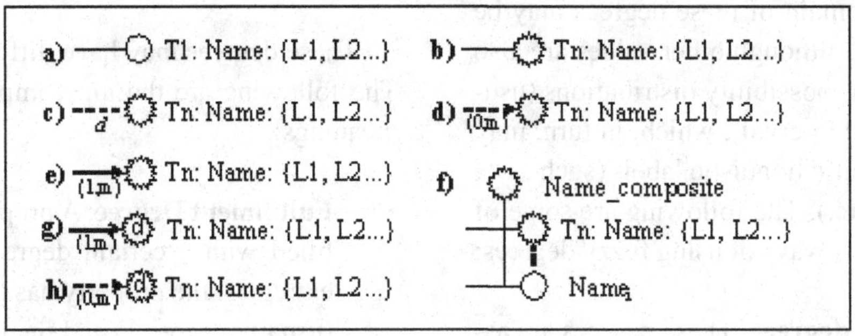

## DEFINITION OF FUZZY ATTRIBUTES IN THE FUZZYEER MODEL

In this section, we extend the definition of **fuzzy attributes** in the **FuzzyEER model**. We also define the graphical representation of these fuzzy concepts.

### Fuzzy Values in Fuzzy Attributes

Attributes in this model are represented graphically by a circle, labeled with the name of the attribute and joined by a line to the entity or relationship to which it belongs. The following definition ascribes graphical representations to types of fuzzy attribute.

**Definition 1:** *A type of entity or relationship E has attributes $A_1, A_2,..., A_n$ with $D_1, D_2,..., D_n$ being their respective domains. A **fuzzy attribute** is represented graphically in the FuzzyEER model depending on its type:*

- *A fuzzy attribute of Type 1 is represented in the same way as a classic attribute, by a plain circle with a line joining it to the entity, and with the name of the attribute T1 followed by a colon. See Figure 1 a).*

- *Fuzzy attributes Type 2, 3 and 4 have a similar representation except that a circle of stars is used and the label T2, T3 or T4 is placed before the name of the corresponding attribute. See Figure 1 b).*

*Another option is to include next to the name of the attribute a list in brackets with the linguistic labels that are defined for this attribute: {L1, L2...}. These labels must be defined in the Data Dictionary of the model.*

The graphical representations for the attributes defined in the FuzzyEER model are:

1. An **identifying attribute,** or **primary key**, is denoted by a bold black circle. The simple attribute is denoted by a bold white circle, in order to avoid problems such as ambiguity, or distinguish ability, the primary key cannot be represented by fuzzy values.

2. A **simple attribute** only takes a single value in a domain for each instance. This is the most common kind of attribute. For example, for simple attributes of a person are weight and height, as only single values are possible for each, although the value itself may or may not be fuzzy.

3. A **derived attribute** is derived from existing ones, which may or may not be fuzzy. For example, age can be obtained from the date of birth and if that date is fuzzy then age will be fuzzy. These attributes may be associated to a rule "*d*" for derivation that defines how to make the calculation. Graphically a derived attribute is represented using a dashed or broken line on the line that joins the circle of the attribute with the entity or relationship to which it belongs to. This dashed line may also be labelled with the rule of the derivation "*d*".

4. A **multivalued attribute** is one that takes more than one value in a domain for each instance. For example, a person can have several values for the attribute "telephone". Graphically, this is expressed by replacing the line joined to the attribute with an arrow, which points towards the circle. This arrow is labelled with two whole numbers, between round brackets and separated by commas, that define the minimum and maximum number of possible values, taking into account that:
   ◦ If the minimum value is 0, it indicates that this attribute is optional and that it cannot take any value. In this case the line of the arrow may be dashed (broken).
   ◦ If at least a value is compulsory then the minimum value will take a whole number that is equal to or greater than 1, and the line of the arrow will be continuous (not dashed).
   ◦ If the minimum or maximum number is unknown a letter is used.

5. A **composite attribute** is one that is composed of other attributes that can be of any type. For example, an address can be composed of a street, number, city, etc. A composite attribute is denoted by a normal circle with a line that crosses all the lines of attributes that compose it. All components of a composite attribute are represented normally (i.e. joined to the type of entity or relationship to which it belongs to).

The following two definitions assign graphical representations to additional aspects of fuzzy attributes. Example 1 illustrates an application of these fuzzy aspects.

**Definition 2:** *Simple or straightforward fuzzy attributes(Definition 1), and derived and multivalued attributes (optional and compulsory) preserve the same definition and graphic representation when they are fuzzy. That is to say, it is only necessary to place before the name of the attribute, the mark that distinguishes the type of fuzzy attribute (T1, T2, T3, or T4) and change the circle to a circle of stars (except for T1). See Figures 1 a), b), c), d) and e) respectively.*

*Incomposite attributes, when one of the components is fuzzy, this component is represented according to its type. See a generic example in Figure 1 f).*

**Definition 3:** *A multivalued disjunctive attribute is one attribute that takes only one value but we want to allow some stored values. The real value is one of the stored values, but we do not know which value is the correct one. Graphically, this is expressed like multivalued attributes but with the letter "d" inside the circle or the circle of stars. See a generic example in Figure 1 g) and h).*

**Definition 4:** *A graded multivalued disjunctive attribute is one multivalued disjunctive attribute whose values may have an associated fuzzy degree, which gives some information about which one is the more correct. Graphically, this is expressed like multivalued attributes but with "gd" inside the circle or the circle of stars.*

**Example 1:** In a theatrical company let us take the entity Actor, which represents the actors of the company. In this entity, we can consider in a simplified form the following attributes: Employee_ID, Height, Age, Hair-Color_hair and Color_skin. Some of these attributes can be characterized as fuzzy attributes:

- **Actor_ID:** This is a classic attribute consisting of a unique numerical identifier for each employee. This attribute is defined as a primary key for the entity Employee.
- **Height:** This is characterized as a fuzzy attribute of Type 1 with its domain defined to be the set of values in the interval (0, 2.5). This is understood to be measurable as a *precise attribute*, but we can define linguistic labels such as "short", "medium_ height" and "tall" to be used when manipulating these data (in queries, for example). In this case, it is assumed that the exact height of an employee is known and that if we do not know the height, the null value is stored (even though we know something about it). Note that this attribute would be of Type 2 if we stored fuzzy information about the height of an actor, such as "about 1.72 meters tall", or "tall", for example.
- **Date_of_Birth:** This is a fuzzy attribute of Type 2 with a date domain.
- **Age:** This is derived fuzzy attribute of Type 2 with a domain corresponding to a fuzzy set of ages, allowing one of three linguistic labels, "young", "mature" or "elderly", to be ascribed to each employee with a degree of confidence of between 0 and 1. These labels are represented and defined as *possibility distributions*. For example, the label "young" is defined as a trapezoidal function with the four characteristic values (0/15, 1/20, 1/25, 0/30), and where the age 26 belongs to the label "young" with a degree of 0.8.
- **Color_hair:** This is characterized as a fuzzy attribute of Type 3. Its underlying domain corresponds to the set: {"blond",

"dark", "ginger"}; each of these labels must be associated to a value of resemblance or similarity in the interval [0,1]. It should be noted that the values of this domain are not ordered. The referential domain is made up of simple values (for example 1/blond) or possibility distributions (for example {1/blond, 0.6/ginger}).

- **Ethnicity:** This is characterized as a fuzzy attribute of Type 4 and its underlying domain comprises the labels: {"caucasian", "asian", "latino", "african-american"}. The fuzzy domain is formed by adding a single degree to one or several labels of the underlying domain. For example, a valid value is {0.8/caucasian, 0.6/asian, 0.4/latino, 0.1/african-american}. This differs from the previous case as in this attribute there is no table of similarity, since we assume that we are not interested in establishing the similarity between labels, but rather, for each actor, we wish to store as precisely as possible information regarding his/her own ethnicity.
- **Clothing_Size:** It is a multivalued disjunctive attribute based on Type 3, because each actor may wear only one size, but possibly we do not know it. In that case, we can store some different sizes, among the different standard sizes {XS, S, M, L, XL, XXL}. Besides, the system may compare de similarity between sizes.

Figure 2 represents the entity Employee with the notation of the FuzzyEER model. It represents fuzzy attributes Type 1, Type 2, Type 3, and Type 4, as described in this Example 1.

## Fuzzy Degree Associated to Each Value of an Attribute

In this case, each value of an attribute (for each instance) can have an associated degree, generally

*Figure 2. Example 1: Entity Employee for the actors of a theatrical company, with fuzzy attributes Type 1, Type 2, Type 3, and Type 4*

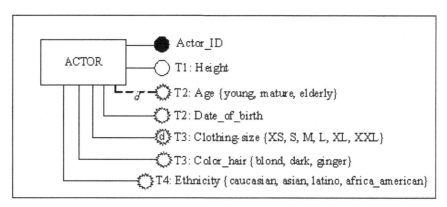

in the interval [0,1]. The degree measures the level of imprecision of that value, as explained above.

Definitions 5 and 6 assign graphical representations in cases where fuzzy degrees are associated to fuzzy attributes. Example 2 illustrates the way the definitions are applied in practice.

**Definition 5:** *Let E be an entity or a relationship with attributes ($A_1, A_2,...,A_n$). For each attribute $A_i$ where $i \in \{1,..., n\}$ (whether fuzzy or not), there may be one or several fuzzy degrees **Type 5** associated to each value of each instance of E. These degrees are represented as simple attributes but with a circle with a dashed outline, joined by a line to the object E to which it belongs. This degree will be placed next to the attribute that has that degree associated to it, and in order to indicate it, an arrow originating from its line points towards the line of the degree.*

*Furthermore, this degree may have different meanings that are expressed by labeling the dotted circle with the expression $G^n$, or $G^{Meaning}$, where "n", or its meaning is one of those that are later defined or other new ones. This expression can be optionally followed by the name of the attribute $A_i$ and, between brackets, any type of expression that can help to clarify the meaning of that degree in each specific context and/or its use. Generically we can define the following meanings:*

- **Membership Degree**: *The membership of a value to a specific instance can be quantified by a degree. It is represented by $G^0$ or $G^{Membership}$.*

- **Fulfilment Degree**: *In an instance, a property can be satisfied in an attribute with a certain degree between two extremes. It is represented by $G^1$ or $G^{Fulfillment}$.*

- **Uncertainty Degree**: *The uncertainty degree expresses to what degree we are certain or sure that we know a specific piece of data for a specific instance. It is represented by $G^2$ or $G^{Uncertainty}$.*

- **Possibility Degree**: *It measures the possibility of the information that is being modeled for each piece of data. It is represented by $G^3$ or $G^{Possibility}$.*

- **Importance Degree**: *Different values of an attribute can have different importance, so that certain values of certain attributes are more important than others. This importance may or may not depend on the instance. It is represented by $G^4$ or $G^{Importance}$.*

If the meaning is not defined as 0, 1, 2, 3, or 4, by default the attribute will represent the membership degree $G^0$.

Any fuzzy degree, from Type 5 to Type 8 may be derived or non-derived, multivalued, multivalued disjunctive or graded multivalued disjunctive:

*Figure 3. Example 2 case b): fuzzy derived degree and associated to the fuzzy attribute Type 2 Quality, with meaning of membership degree ($G^0$)*

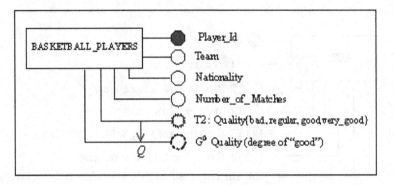

**Definition 6:** *Two types of fuzzy degrees according to the origin of the information:*

1. ***Derived fuzzy degree:*** *If a function $Q(x)$ exists that defines the calculus of those degrees. That is, the function allows the degrees to be automatically calculated based on the value of other attributes or on any other information stored or available in the database. In this case the function $Q$ will be used by labelling the dashed line that joins the dashed circle to its owner.*

2. **Non-derived fuzzy degree:** In this case a function for automatically calculating the degrees has not been defined. This case includes the cases in which those degrees are introduced manually by the user.

It is important to distinguish between the value of the fuzzy attribute and the value of the degree associated to that value. For example, if for a certain person, hair color is of importance, that importance degree is independent of the hair color of that person. It is also independent of the type of attribute. Furthermore, it is important to point out that this attribute can have a fuzzy value. It can be considered as a double attribute, because it has two related values (the value of the attribute, whether fuzzy or not, and the degree associated to it).

**Example 2:** Consider an entity for representing Basketball Players (Figure 3). Each player has certain attributes, such as Player_Id, Team, Nationality, Number_of_Matches, etc. Suppose one attribute is a Type 2 fuzzy attribute, "Quality", measured by the average number of points scored per match (which means the attribute values are members of the set of positive real numbers). The labels (Bad, Regular, Good, Very_Good) can be defined for this attribute. Moreover, a degree that can have different aspects can be associated to this attribute. The meanings may be as follows:

1. If we consider a derived degree where the function $Q(x)$ is the membership function of a label, such as "Good", then this degree represents the membership degree of each player to the fuzzy set composed of the "Good" players. In this case, the dashed circle could be labeled as $G^0$ Quality (degree of "Good"). If we need these degrees with regards to the other labels, then, we must add new derived degrees.

2. The known quality of a player will be less uncertain if the player has played a lot of matches. For example, if this degree is labeled as $G^2$ Quality, we are referring to the fact that this measure of the attribute Quality is of varying uncertainty. This can also be characterized as a derived degree if

we define the function $Q$, to depend on the attribute Number_of_Matches. This case is represented in Figure 3.

3. For each player this evaluation of Quality may be more or less important depending on his usual position in the team. We can express this by labeling the degree with: $G^4$ Quality, indicating that its importance may vary.

## Fuzzy Degree Associated to Values of Some Attributes

In this case a degree associated to a set of attributes belonging to an entity is required. This is an unusual case but it can add expressiveness if it is incorporated into a data model. An example of this association of a degree with a set of attributes can be found in the concept of fuzzy dependence proposed by Raju and Majumdar (1988).

Definition 7 assigns a graphical representation where a fuzzy degree is associated to a set of attributes, and Example 3 applies this definition.

**Definition 7:** *Let E be an entity or relationship with attributes ($A_1$, $A_2$,...,$A_n$), and X a subset of these attributes: $X = \{A_i: i \in I\}$, with 1 being a set of indices so that $I \subset \{1,..., n\}$. We can define a fuzzy degree Type 6 associated to each value that the attributes of X take in each instance of E. In a FuzzyEER model this type of attribute is represented in a similar way to that explained in Definition 5, but now the arrow crosses all the attributes of X which are associated with this degree. To make it clearer the attributes of X can be placed after the $G^n$ symbol denoting the degree as per Definition 5. In general, this degree is derived from the values of those attributes.*

**Example 3:** Consider the attributes (Employee_ID, Job, Ability, Experience) of an entity Employee. In this case, the attribute Job is considered to be classic, or ordinary, (alphabetical), and the attributes Ability and Experience are fuzzy

attributes of Types 2 and 3 respectively. Labels {Clumsy, Normal, Skilled} are assigned for the attribute Ability, and labels {Apprentice, Normal, Expert} for Experience.

Now we add a fuzzy grade to the group of attributes $X = \{$Experience, Ability$\}$. We may call this degree "degree of competence or expertise" and its meaning can be varied depending on the characteristic the model is intended to represent. For example:

1. **Uncertainty degree $G^2$:** This represents the extent to which the values of the attributes {Experience, Ability} are true reflections of the employee's actual experience and ability. Depending on how the two values have been calculated (whether they have been based on much or little evidence) they can be more or less reliable. Figure 4 represents this case, where "$d$" expresses the formula for the automatic calculation of the fuzzy degrees.

2. **Importance degree $G^4$:** For a kind of employee the attributes of experience and ability may be more important than others. For example, a surgeon requires more experience and ability than an administrative worker.

## Fuzzy Degree with its Own Meaning

Another way of using degrees is to consider the case in which a determined degree has no reason to be associated with any other attribute, but instead it can be fuzzy and have its own value (or meaning).

**Definition 8:** *An entity or a relationship E may have a fuzzy degree Type 8 with its own meaning. This degree is graphically represented by a dashed circle, labeled with the name of the degree, and having a "G" inside it, joined to its entity E. The meaning of the degree should be expressed as well as possible in its name.*

*Figure 4. Example 3: Fuzzy degree associated with two fuzzy attributes*

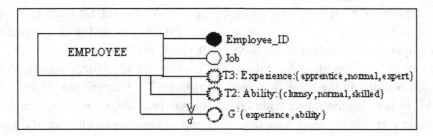

*Figure 5. Example 4: Fuzzy degree associated with the fuzzy attribute Type 3 Color, with meaning of Intensity degree, and one degree with its own meaning, known as Toxicity*

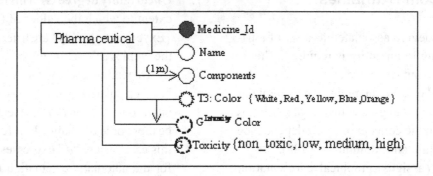

**Example 4:** The entity Pharmaceutical in Figure 5 has some attributes from which we can highlight Components, which is a multivalued (not fuzzy) attribute, Color which is a fuzzy attribute Type 3, and two degrees:

- The Color attribute has a degree associated with each value that measures to what extent that color is "intense".
- The Toxicity attribute measures how toxic that substance is. It is not a degree associated with any other attribute. It is a fuzzy degree with its own meaning.

## FUZZY ENTITIES

As we know, an entity is a real or abstract object about which we want to store information in the database. On the other hand, an instance (occurrence) of the entity is each one of the concrete realizations (objects or values) of that type of entity. The graphic representation of the type of entities is a rectangle labeled with the name of the type of entity it represents.

In the FuzzyEER model, in a fuzzy entity each instance has a different degree for measuring the relationship between this instance and the entity (its degree of pertinence to this type of entity, or its importance degree, its certainty degree...).

**Definition 9:** *A (regular) **fuzzy entity** is defined in a FuzzyEER model, as an entity with an attribute, which expresses a **Type 7** degree (with any meaning). In other words: If E is a fuzzy entity, with n instances, $e_1, e_2, ..., e_n$ then there is at least one $\mu_E$ function defined about these instances so that, $\forall e_i \in E$ with i = 1, 2,..., n, $\mu_E (e_i) \in [0,1]$. The expression $\mu_E (e_i)$ can measure the degree with which the instance $e_i$ "belongs" to E, although it can have other meanings, like those expressed in Definition 5.*

*The notation of a type of fuzzy entity is represented with a rectangle with dashed lines. The fuzzy attribute representing the degree must also be added with its meaning. This attribute is represented by a dashed circle with a dashed line (which distinguishes it from other degrees). The circle of that degree should be labeled with the symbol $G^n$, explained in Definition 5. Optionally, the function that allows this degree to be calculated can also be added.*

As a quick example of fuzzy entity with a derived membership degree, we can imagine an entity Employee, where membership (or importance) degree of each employee is derived using the Weekly_hours attribute. Note that we can allow an entity to have several degrees associated with it. The semantic concept becomes more complicated, but it would not make sense to limit each entity to only one degree. Furthermore, constraints could be established between different degrees (for example, the importance of each employee in his department should be greater than his degree of capacity for a certain task).

## CONCLUSION

**Fuzzy databases** have been widely studied with the aim of allowing the storage of imprecise or fuzzy data and the formulating of imprecise queries about the data. Two of the most recent and complete publications about it are (Galindo et al., 2006) and (Galindo, 2008).

However, in the application of fuzzy logic to databases, relatively little attention has been paid to the problem of representing or depicting the conceptual model. Few investigations study a complete and exhaustive means of incorporation and representation of the many characteristics of a model which may be "fuzzy". We have presented here an overview of different fuzzy database modeling definitions by different authors. We highlight the **FuzzyEER model**, which is an extension of an EER model incorporating fuzzy semantics and notation. FuzzyEER is probably the most complete modeling tool.

The FuzzyEER has many characteristics and in this study we have focused on the following: types of fuzzy attributes (T1, T2, T3 and T4), fuzzy degrees associated or not with different items and with different meanings and with useful labels in each context, fuzzy entities and the definition of multivalued disjunctive attributes. All the other proposals by other authors analyzed in this paper only use partial **fuzzy datatypes**, or **fuzzy degrees** in attributes, **relationships** or in other element.

The presented definitions and the whole FuzzyEER promote fuzzy databases and all their advantages: fuzzy queries (Zadrożny et al., 2008), fuzzy data mining (Feil and Abonyi, 2008). Some of the FuzzyEER notations may be used in a **FSQL (Fuzzy SQL)** language, which is an extension of SQL for permitting fuzzy queries and operations (Galindo et al., 2006; Urrutia et al., 2008). Future directions for research include extending the FSQL language with new concepts based on the Fuzzy-EER definitions, and use these characteristics for Data Mining applications.

## ACKNOWLEDGMENT

This work was partially supported by the Ministry of Education and Science of Spain (projects TIN2006-14285 and TIN2006-07262) and the Andalusian government (project P06-TIC-01570).

## REFERENCES

Bordogna, G., Lucarella, D., & Pasi, G. (1999). A Fuzzy Object-Oriented Data Model Managing Vague and Uncertain Information. *International Journal of Intelligent Systems*, *14*(7), 623–651. doi:10.1002/(SICI)1098-111X(199907)14:7<623::AID-INT1>3.0.CO;2-

Buckles, B. P., & Petry, F. E. (1985). Uncertainty Models in Information and Database Systems. *Information Sciences, 11*, 77–87. doi:10.1177/016555158501100204Chaudhry, N., & Moyne, J., E.A. & Rundensteiner, E.A. (1999). An Extended Database Design Methodology for Uncertain Data Management. *Information Sciences, 121*, 83–112. doi:10.1016/S0020-0255(99)00066-3

Chaudhry, N., Moyne, J., & Rundensteiner, E. (1994). A Design Methodology for Databases with Uncertain Data. In *7th International Working Conference on Scientific and Statistical Database Management, Charlottesville,* VA, (pp. 32-41). (www.mitexsolutions.com).

Chen, G., Ren, M., Yan, P., & Guo, X. (2007). Enriching the ER model based on discovered association rules. *Information Sciences, 177*, 1558–1566. doi:10.1016/j.ins.2006.07.001

Chen, G. Q. (1998). *Fuzzy Logic in Data Modeling, Semantics Constraints, and Databases Design.* Amsterdam: The Kluwer International Series on Advances in Database Systems.

Chen, G. Q., & Kerre, E. E. (1998). Extending ER/EER Concepts Towards Fuzzy Conceptual Data Modeling. *IEEE International Conference on Fuzzy Systems, 2*, 1320-1325.

Damiani, E., Oliboni, B., & Tanca, L. (2001). Fuzzy Techniques for XML Data Smushing. In B. Reusch (Ed.), 7th Fuzzy Days on Computational Intelligence, Theory and Applications, (LNCS 2206, pp. 637-652). Berlin: Springer Verlag.

De Caluwe, R. (Ed.). (1997). *Fuzzy and Uncertain Object-Oriented Databases, Concepts and Models. Advances in Fuzzy System – Application and Theory, 13*. Singapore: World Scientific.

Elmasri, R., & Navathe, S. B. (2000). Fundamentals of Database Systems, (3rd. Ed.). Reading, MA: Addison Wesley.

Feil, B., & Abonyi, J. (2008). Introduction to Fuzzy Data Mining Methods. In J. Galindo, (Ed.), *Handbook of Research on Fuzzy Information Processing in Databases,* (Vol. I, pp. 55-95). Hershey, PA, USA: Information Science Reference. Retrieved from http://www.info-sci-ref.com

Fujishiro, I., et al. (1991). The Design of a Graph-Oriented Schema for the Management of Individualized Fuzzy Data. *Japanese journal of Fuzzy Theory and System, 3*(1), 1-14.

Galindo, J. (Ed.). (2008). *Handbook of Research on Fuzzy Information Processing in Databases.* Hershey, PA: Information Science Reference. Retrieved from http://www.info-sci-ref.com

Galindo, J., Medina, J. M., Cubero, J. C., & García, M. T. (2001). Relaxing the Universal Quantifier of the Division in Fuzzy Relational Databases. *International Journal of Intelligent Systems, 16*, 713–742. doi:10.1002/int.1032

Galindo, J., Urrutia, A., & Piattini, M. (2006). *Fuzzy Databases: Modeling, Design and Implementation.* Hershey, PA: Idea Group Publishing.

George, R., Srikanth, R., Petry, F. E., & Buckles, B. P. (1996). Uncertainty Management Issues in the Object-Oriented Data Model. *IEEE Transactions on Fuzzy Systems, 4*(2), 179–192. doi:10.1109/91.493911

Gyseghem, N. Van, & De Caluwe, R. (1997). The UFO Model: dealing with Imperfect Information. In Fuzzy and uncertain Object-oriented databases, concepts and Models, (Advances in Fuzzy Systems: Vol. 13, pp. 123-185).Singapore: World Scientific Publishing Co. Pte. Ltd.

Kerre, E. E., & Chen, G. (1995). An Overview of Fuzzy Data Models. In Bosc, P., & Kacprzyk, J. (Eds.), *Studies in Fuzziness: Fuzziness in Database Management Systems* (pp. 23–41). Heidelberg, Germany: Physica-Verlag.

Kerre, E. E., & Chen, G. (2000). Fuzzy Data Modeling at a Conceptual Level: Extending ER/EERConcepts. In Pons, O., Vila, M. A., & Kacprzyk, J. (Eds.), *Knowledge Management in Fuzzy Databases* (pp. 3–11). Heidelberg, Germany: Physica-Verlag.

Ma, Z.M., & Yan, Li. (2007). Fuzzy XML data modeling with the XML and relation data model. *Data & Knowledge Engineering, 64,* 972–996. doi:10.1016/j.datak.2007.06.003

Ma, Z. M., Zhang, W. J., & Ma, W. Y. (2004). Extending Object-Oriented Databases for Fuzzy Information Modeling. *Information Systems, 29,* 421–435. doi:10.1016/S0306-4379(03)00038-3

Ma, Z. M., Zhang, W. J., Ma, W. Y., & Chen, Q. (2001). Conceptual Design of Fuzzy Object-Oriented Databases Using Extended Entity-Relationship Model. *International Journal of Intelligent Systems, 16*(6), 697–711. doi:10.1002/int.1031

Motro, A. (1995). Management of Uncertainty in Database System. In W. Kim, (Ed.), Modern Database System the Object Model, Interoperability and Beyond. Reading, MA: Addison-Wesley publishing Company.

Oliboni, B., & Pozzani, G. (2008a). Representing Fuzzy Information by using XML Schema. In *Proc. 19th Int. Conference on Database and Expert Systems Application,* (pp. 683-687).

Oliboni, B., & Pozzani, G. (2008b). *An XML Schema for managing fuzzy documents.* Technical Report RR 64/2008, Department of Computer Science of the University of Verona, Italy. Retrieved on December 2008 at http://profs.sci.univr.it/~pozzani/pub.html

Raju, K., & Majumdar, A. (1988). Fuzzy Functional Dependencies and Lossless Join Decomposition of Fuzzy Relational Database System. *ACM Transactions on Database Systems, 13*(2), 129–166. doi:10.1145/42338.42344

Ruspini, E. (1986). Imprecision and Uncertainty in the Entity-Relationship Model. In Prade, H., & Negoita, C. V. (Eds.), *Fuzzy Logic in Knowledge Engineering* (pp. 18–22). Köln, Germany: Verlag TUV Rheinland.

Umano, M., & Fukami, S. (1994). Fuzzy Relational Algebra for Possibility-Distribution-Fuzzy-Relation Model of Fuzzy Data. *Journal of Intelligent Information Systems, 3,* 7–28. doi:10.1007/BF01014018

Urrutia, A., Tineo, L., & Gonzalez, C. (2008). FSQL and SQLf: Towards a Standard in Fuzzy Databases. In J. Galindo (Ed.), *Handbook of Research on Fuzzy Information Processing in Databases,* (Vol. I, pp. 270-298). Hershey, PA: Information Science Reference (http://www.info-sci-ref.com).

Van Gyseghem, N., De Caluwe, R., & Vandenberghe, R. (1993, March). UFO: Uncertainty and Fuzziness in an Object-Oriented Model. In *Proc. IEEE 2nd. International Conference Fuzzy Systems,* San Francisco, CA, (pp. 773-778).

Vandenberghe, R. M. (1991). An Extended Entity-Relationship Model for Fuzzy Databases Based on Fuzzy Truth Values. In *Proceeding of 4th International Fuzzy Systems Association World Congress, IFSA'91,* Brussels, (pp. 280-283).

Vert, G., Morris, A., Stock, M., & Jankowski, P. (2000, July). Extending Entity-Relationship Modelling Notation to Manage Fuzzy Datasets. In *8th International Conference on Information Processing and Management of Uncertainty in Knowledge-Based Systems, IPMU'2000,* (pp. 1131-1138), Madrid, Spain.

Vert, G., Stock, M., & Morris, A. (2002). Extending ERD Modeling Notation to Fuzzy Management of GIS Data Files. *Data & Knowledge Engineering, 40,* 163–179. doi:10.1016/S0169-023X(01)00049-0

Yazici, A., Buckles, B. P., & Petry, F. E. (1999). Handling Complex and Uncertain Information in the ExIFO and NF2 Data Models. *IEEE Transactions on Fuzzy Systems*, 7(6), 659–675. doi:10.1109/91.811232

Yazici, A., & George, R. (1999). Fuzzy Database Modeling. New York: Physica-Verlag (Studies in Fuzziness and Soft Computing).

Yazici, A., & Merdan, O. (1996). Extending IFO Data Model for Uncertain Information. In *4th International Conference on Information Processing and Management of Uncertainty, IPMU'96.* (vol. III, pp. 1283-1282), Granada, Spain.

Zadeh, L. A. (1965). Fuzzy Sets. *Information and Control*, 8, 338–353. doi:10.1016/S0019-9958(65)90241-X

Zadrożny, S., de Tré, G., De Caluwe, R., & Kacprzyk, J. (2008). An Overview of Fuzzy Approaches to Flexible Database Querying. In J. Galindo (Ed.), *Handbook of Research on Fuzzy Information Processing in Databases,* (Vol. I, pp. 34-54). Hershey, PA, USA: Information Science Reference (http://www.info-sci-ref.com).

Zvieli, A., & Chen, P. (1986). ER Modeling and Fuzzy Databases. In *2nd International Conference on Data Engineering,* (pp. 320-327).

## KEY TERMS AND DEFINITIONS

**Fuzzy Attribute:** In a database context, a fuzzy attribute is an attribute of a row or object in a database, with a fuzzy datatype, which allows storing fuzzy information and/or a fuzzy processing (Galindo, 2008). Sometimes, if a classic attribute allows fuzzy queries, then it is also called fuzzy attribute, because it has only some of the fuzzy attribute characteristics.

**Fuzzy Degrees:** Fuzzy attributes, whose domain is usually the interval [0,1], although other values are also permitted, such as possibil-

ity distributions (usually over this unit interval), which, in turn, may be related to specific linguistic labels (like "a lot", "normal"...). In order to keep it simple, usually only degrees in the interval [0,1] are used, because the other option offers no great advantages and a greater technical and semantic complexity.

**Fuzzy Database:** If a regular or classical database is a structured collection of information (records or data) stored in a computer, a fuzzy database (Galindo, 2008) is a database which is able to deal with uncertain or incomplete information using fuzzy logic. There are many forms of adding flexibility in fuzzy databases. The simplest technique is to add a fuzzy membership degree to each record, i.e. an attribute in the range [0,1]. However, there are other kinds of databases allowing fuzzy values to be stored in fuzzy attributes using fuzzy sets, possibility distributions or fuzzy degrees associated to some attributes and with different meanings (membership degree, importance degree, fulfillment degree...). Of course, fuzzy databases should allow fuzzy queries using fuzzy or non-fuzzy data and there are some languages that allow this kind of queries, like FSQL or SQLf (Urrutia et al., 2008). In synthesis, the research in fuzzy databases includes the following areas: flexible querying in classical or fuzzy databases, extending classical data models in order to achieve fuzzy databases (fuzzy relational databases, fuzzy object-oriented databases...), fuzzy conceptual modeling, fuzzy data mining techniques, and applications of these advances in real databases.

**Fuzzy Logic:** Fuzzy logic is derived from fuzzy set theory by Zadeh (1965) dealing with reasoning that is approximate rather than precisely deduced from classical predicate logic. It can be thought of as the application side of fuzzy set theory dealing with well thought out real world expert values for a complex problem.

**FSQL (Fuzzy SQL):** Extension of the popular language **SQL** that allows the management of fuzzy relational databases using the fuzzy logic. Basically, FSQL define new extensions for fuzzy queries, extending the SELECT statement, but it also defines other statements. One of these fuzzy items is the definition of fuzzy comparators using mainly the possibility and necessity theory. Besides, FSQL allows the definition of linguistic labels (like hot, cold, tall, short...) and fuzzy quantifiers (most, approximately 5, near the half...). The more recent publications about FSQL is the book *Fuzzy databases: modeling, design and implementation* by Galindo et al. (2006), and (Urrutia et al., 2008).

**Fuzzy Query:** Query with imprecision in the preferences about the desired items. These preferences may be set usually using fuzzy conditions in the queries. These fuzzy conditions include many possible forms, like, fuzzy preferences (e.g. I prefer bigger than cheaper), fuzzy labels (e.g. hot and cold), fuzzy comparators (e.g. approximately greater or equal than), fuzzy quantifiers (e.g. most or approximately the half), etc. One basic target in a fuzzy query is to rank the resulting items according to their fulfillment degree (usually a number between 0 and 1).

**Fuzzy Comparators:** They are different techniques to compare two values using fuzzy logic. FSQL define fuzzy comparators like FEQ (fuzzy equal), NFEQ (necessarily fuzzy equal), FGT (fuzzy greater than), NFGT (necessarily fuzzy greater than), etc.

**FuzzyEER model:** Conceptual modeling tool, which extends the Enhanced Entity Relationship (EER) model with fuzzy semantics and fuzzy notations to represent imprecision and uncertainty in the entities, attributes and relationships. The basic concepts introduced in this model are fuzzy attributes, fuzzy entities, fuzzy relations, fuzzy degrees, fuzzy degrees in specializations, and fuzzy constraints. The first complete definition of this model was published in the book *Fuzzy databases: modeling, design and implementation* (Galindo et al., 2006).

# Chapter 2
# A Quick Presentation of Evolutionary Computation

**Pierre Collet**
*Université de Strasbourg, France*

## ABSTRACT

*Evolutionary computation is an old field of computer science, that started in the 1960s nearly simultaneously in different parts of the world. It is an optimization technique that mimics the principles of Darwinian evolution in order to find good solutions to intractable problems faster than a random search. Artificial Evolution is only one among many stochastic optimization methods, but recently developed hardware (General Purpose Graphic Processing Units or GPGPU) gives it a tremendous edge over all the other algorithms, because its inherently parallel nature can directly benefit from the difficult to use Single Instruction Multiple Data parallel architecture of these cheap, yet very powerful cards.*

## INTRODUCTION AND HISTORY

The development of evolutionary algorithms almost dates back to the dark ages of computers. To put back everything in perspective, Computer Science really started when John von Neumann designed the EDVAC (Electronic Discrete Variable Automatic Computer) in 1945, but the first prototype was actually implemented in 1949 with Wilkes' EDSAC (Electronic Delay Storage Automatic Calculator). Then, for a while, the only commercially available machines used valves and were therefore not that

reliable (IBM 650 in 1953). A quantum leap was made when transistors became available around the 1960s and finally, Integrated Circuits in 1964.

By that time, evolutionary computation had about ten independent beginnings in Australia, United States and Europe, starting in 1953, traced by David Fogel's excellent Fossil Record (Fogel, 1998): Alex Fraser had evolved binary strings using crossovers (Fraser, 1957), Friedberg had already thought of self-programming computers through mutations (Friedberg, 1958; Friedberg, Dunham, & North, 1958), and Friedman of how evolution could be digitally simulated (Friedman 1959). However, the main evolutionary trends that survived are:

DOI: 10.4018/978-1-60566-814-7.ch002

- Evolutionary Strategies (continuous optimization), by Rechenberg and Schwefel, best described in Rechenberg (1973) and Schwefel (1995),
- Genetic Algorithms, by Holland, later popularised by Goldberg on the US East Coast (Michigan) (Holland, 1975; Goldberg, 1989},
- Genetic Programming, by Cramer (1985) and later developed by John Koza (1992).

Evolutionary computation cannot, therefore, be seen as a recent development of computer science, or even classified as artificial intelligence, which is a different concept that can also be traced back to the mid 1950s, with John Mc Carthy and many others.

However, until the principles of evolutionary computation were clearly understood, these techniques necessitated a larger amount of computer power than was available until the beginning of the 1990s.

Thus, although evolutionary computation really started in the late 1960s it only came of age when computers had enough power to make it competitive with other (posterior) stochastic optimization paradigms such as simulated annealing (Kirkpatrick, 1983) or Tabu Search (Glover, 1977, 1989, 1990).

Now that the field is mature, a second drastic change is taking place with the advent of General Purpose Graphic Processing Units (GPGPUs) which are massively parallel cards developed by the billions of dollars of the gaming industry. Announced for the first quarter of 2010, NVidia's GeForce GTX395 card based on 40nm Fermi chips should give 5 TeraFlops for less than $1000. This tremendous power is directly usable by evolutionary programs, that share the very same parallel workflow than the graphic pixel and vertex shaders for which these cards have been designed.

## SHORT PRESENTATION OF THE EVOLUTIONARY COMPUTATION PARADIGM

The general idea comes from the observation that animals and plants are very well adapted to their environment. Back in 1859, Charles Darwin came with an explanation for this called *natural selection*, that is now widely accepted (Darwin, 1859) and shown at work in a wonderful recent book by Neil Shubin (2008): *Your Inner Fish*. The rationale is that *individuals* that are not well adapted to their environment do not survive long enough to reproduce, or have less chances to reproduce than other individuals of the same species that have acquired beneficial traits through *variations* during the *reproduction* stage. Adaptation to the environment is also called *fitness*.

Artificial evolution grossly copies these natural mechanisms in order to optimise solutions to difficult problems. All optimisation techniques based on Darwinian principles are *de facto* members of the evolutionary computation paradigm, even though a distinction must be made between two different kinds of algorithms. "Standard" evolutionary algorithms evolve a fixed string of bits or reals that is passed to an evaluation function that assesses the "fitness" of the individual, while genetic programming evolves individuals that are evaluated on a number of *fitness cases*. This distinction may seem tenuous, but one will see in the end of this chapter that that it is important.

## A UNIFIED EVOLUTIONARY ALGORITHM

Kenneth DeJong has been giving a GECCO tutorial on the unification of evolutionary algorithms for several years now and has come up with a recent book on the subject (DeJong 2005). Indeed, the previously quoted trends (Evolutionary Strategies, Genetic Algorithms, Evolutionary Programming,

Genetic Programming) all share the same principles copied from natural selection.

Rather than describing each algorithm, this chapter will describe a generic and complete version that can emulate virtually any paradigm, depending on chosen parameters. We will mainly focus on "standard" evolutionary algorithms. Genetic programming will be shortly evoked when necessary.

## Representation of Individuals

Due to the similarities between artificial evolution and natural evolution that was the source of its inspiration, a good part of the vocabulary was borrowed to biologists. In artificial evolution, a potential solution to a problem is called an *individual*.

Using a correct representation to implement individuals is a very essential step, that is trivial for some kinds of problems, and much less for others. The American trend (genetic algorithms) advocates using a representation that is as generic as possible, *i.e.* a bit string (even to code real values). The German trend (evolutionary strategies) that was designed to optimise continuous problems advocates using real variables. Genetic Programming evolves programs and functions that are typically (but not exclusively) implemented as trees.

Although using bitstrings makes sense for combinatorial problems or for theoretical studies, representing real values with bits, while feasible, has many drawbacks (Hinterding, Gielewski, & Peachey, 1995). It seems much more reasonable to use an appropriate representation tailored to the problem at hand.

If one tries to optimise a recipe for French *crêpes* (pancakes) that are made using flour, milk, eggs and salt, a reasonable encoding for an individual can be four "genes," namely:

*(float cupsFlour, float pintMilk, int nbEggs, int pinchSalt)*

This example will be used throughout this chapter because even though it is very simple and easy to grasp, it is complete enough to explain most of the problems encountered in artificial evolution. For instance, in this case, the fitness function will consist of measuring the width of the smile of the person who tastes the *crêpes*. This makes it easy to understand the essential point that individuals are not evaluated on their *genotype* (*i.e.* the ingredients) but on their *phenotype* (the cooked *crêpe*).

In many problems, the relationship between genotype and phenotype is not very clear, and there can be some intercorrelation between genes. In the *crêpes* example, one can understand that the *salt* ingredient is independent from the others. If the *crêpe* tastes too salty, the problem is simple to solve: put less salt in the next experiment. However, an essential characteristic of *crêpes* is that the texture of the batter should be such that it is both liquid enough to be poured into the saucepan, and thick enough so that when cooked, a *crêpe* becomes solid enough to be eaten with your fingers (the most enjoyable way to eat them). The solution for this problem is not as easy as for salt. The quantity of flour definitely plays a role, but moisture can be controlled by both the number of eggs and the volume of milk that makes the batter. So one can see that there is not a single gene that is coding for "liquidity." Eggs and milk are intercorrelated since both bring moisture, and to make things more complex, the amount of flour must also be taken into account to make crêpes that are not too gooey, not too brittle, and have the correct pleasant texture. The biology term to describe this correlation between genes is *epistasis*.

Choosing the good representation for the genotype is important, because it materialises the search space in which the best solution is sought. The representation of a *crêpe* batter uses both discrete and continuous variables.

Note that evolutionary algorithms are not limited to bits, integers or real values. Genetic programming uses binary trees (Koza 1992), or a linear representation (Brameier & Banzhaf 2007) for a program, or a grammar, or even stranger concepts, like Cartesian GP (Miller, J. 2000).

To each his own. The conclusion is that common sense should prevail: one should use the representation that is best suited to the problem at hand.

## Evaluation (or Fitness) Function

As for the individual representation, the fitness function is problem-dependent. It usually implements or simulates the problem to be solved, and should be able to evaluate the phenotype of the individuals proposed by the evolutionary engine.

What is nice with EAs is that fitness does not need to be represented by a mathematical function: anything can do, provided that it guides the evolution (such as the smile on the face of the *crêpe*-tester. The fact that EAs use a population to explore the search space means that they can even deal with evaluators that do not implement a total order on the space of solutions. In this case, the fitness function can simply be a comparison function, that can tell which of two individuals is the best. Some stochastic selection operators can then cope with such situations where individual $i_{32}$ is better than $i_{27}$, which is better than $i_{343}$, which is itself better than $i_{32}$. Only population-based stochastic optimizers such as EAs can do this. Others could circle round for a long time.

Then, most real-world problems must optimize several objectives at the same time, that can be antagonistic, such as the mass and resistance of a metallic structure. Here again, EAs have an edge over their competitors, because thanks to their population, they can calculate a complete Pareto-front in one run. In this case, several fitness functions must be provided (one for each objective) and a special ranking operator (such as NSGA-II (Deb 2000), or SPEA2 (Zitzler 2001)) must be used. Multi-objective ranking operators usually rank the individuals of the population according to their distance to the current Pareto-front and

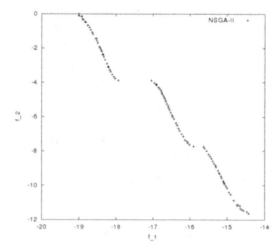

*Figure 1. Complex Pareto front*

in a second step refine the fitness value with a crowding operator, in order to favour individuals situated into sparse areas of the Pareto front. Figure 1 shows a complex Pareto front obtained in one run by NSGA-II, on a benchmark function.

Finally, one last point to take into account is that some selection schemes (roulette wheel, for instance) require that the fitness function always returns positive values.

## Individuals Initialisation

Initialisation is another very important step. Most evolutionary paradigms advocate starting with a population of random individuals, in order to sample the fitness landscape as uniformly as possible. The reason for this is that one must be aware that "helping" the evolutionary algorithm by initialising individuals with "good" values, may actually prevent it from finding very good solutions if these are unconventional. Back to the French *crêpes* example: some recipes do already exist, so one could initialise the population of *crêpes* with values varying around 2 cups of flour, 1.0 pint of milk, 3 eggs, 4 pinches of salt.

Doing so will sure help to find *crêpes* recipes, but did you realise that this would exclude something made of 0.01 cups of flour, 0.01 pint of milk, 4 eggs, 4 pinches of salt ? Baking this recipe may bring a large smile to the tester if he likes omelettes. Now, for sure, this is not a *crêpes* recipe, but was the aim of the algorithm to find French *crêpes* recipes, or to maximise the smile on the face of the taster ?

History is full of examples where progress was slowed down because some really good ideas had been rejected by people who refused to think differently. Flying has been the dearest dream of mankind for millenia. When one thinks of what is needed to build a hangglider (a couple of sticks, some canvas and rope) the only thing that prevented humans from flying ever since canvas was invented was that everyone until Otto von Lilienthal wanted to make *crêpes*, rather than a good recipe out of flour, milk, eggs and salt. In aeronautical terms, they all wanted to fly like birds, using flapping wings, while a flying solution using a fixed wing was within reach for ages.

This shows both the limits and interest of EAs. They may find something that works, but that is not exactly what you want.

Now, widening the search space as much as possible must not prevent the designer to restrict it to feasible solutions. Suppose we want to evolve our *crêpes* recipe, but only have a bowl containing 50 fluid ounces to mix our ingredients. What would be the point of creating an individual whose genome would require 60 fl.oz. jar to mix ? Does it make sense to create a recipe with 3,243 eggs ? In our example, making sure that the volume of the recipe is within lower and upper bounds can be considered as a restriction of the search space to feasible solutions.

In order to start the algorithm, the initialisation function is called repeatedly to create new individuals until the required initial population size is reached.

Each individual must then be evaluated by the fitness function in order to begin the evolutionary loop (it is necessary to know the fitness of all individuals in order to choose the parents that will create the first generation). If, by pure chance, a stopping criterion is met by an individual (error below 1%, for instance) of the initial population, there is no point in going on. The algorithm can stop there.

## A Generic Evolutionary Loop

At this point, a certain number of necessary parameters (discussed below) must have been chosen, among which the number of children per generation (which may go from 1, to the population size, to any number *n*, possibly greater than the population size). (see Figure 2)

While (Stopping criterion not met):

1. While(NbChildren<NbChildrenPerGeneration):
   a. Select a variation operator (following Darwin's vocabulary), usually either unary or *n*-ary. The *n*-ary variation operator is often called with a 80-100% probability and is also often a binary crossover. The unary operator (called with a 20-0% probability is a cloning operator (that also preserves the fitness value without needing to recalculate it in static environment systems).
   b. Pick up the correct number of parents, using an appropriate *selection operator*. To the opposite of a *replacement operator* (cf. below), picked up individuals are put back in the parents pool and can be selected more than once.
   c. Call the variation operator, thereby creating one or several children (usually one, in modern algorithms).
   d. Call a mutation operator on the created child with a *p* probability (usually 100%)[1]}.
   e. Variation operators can be followed by a *validation operator* that makes sure that newly created children are valid. Invalid individuals can be either deleted

*Figure 2.*

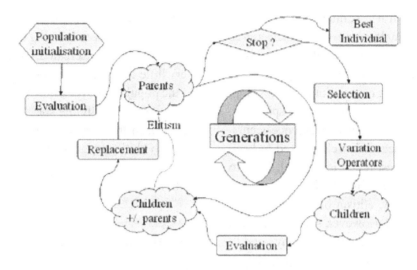

(in which case another individual needs to be created) or "repaired," or given a very low fitness without even being evaluated by the fitness function. This last method is very interesting in Constraints Satisfaction Problems (such as timetables) because it is very quick: in very constrained problems, one can spend a lot of time finding 100 individuals that do not violate a single hard constraint. It is also very fast because it does not call the evaluation function to give a fitness to the child. In problems with fast fitness functions, it is often more efficient to give a bad mark, and let artificial evolution deal with the problem.

2.  Call the evaluation function on all children who do not already have a fitness. Children may already have a fitness if they are clones of their parents or if they were given a bad mark by the validation operator.

3.  Strong/weak elitism: the algorithm now needs to deal with two populations: a population of already evaluated parents and a population of evaluated children. In algorithms with a constant population size

(the overwhelming majority) the number of individuals needs to be reduced back to the original population size in order to constitute the next generation.

There remains however a last step before replacement: Holland's original Genetic Algorithm uses a *generational* replacement, meaning that the population of children brutally replaces the population of parents to create the next generation. In this process, it is possible to lose a very good solution if, for instance, none of the children did better than the best of their parents.

The solution that was found to overcome this problem is called *elitism*. Generational GAs with elitism simply take the best parent and put it in the new generation.

This method is called *strong elitism* since it is a bit brutal. A more subtle form of elitism used in non-generational engines is *weak elitism*, that moves into the next generation the best individual from both the parent and children populations.

One must be aware that elitism may lead to premature convergence, as the best found individual will always make it to the next generation. Unfortunately, it may reside on a local optimum that is not the one that is desired, but if it is much better than the other individuals, it will often be selected as a parent, and its genes will therefore spread into the population along with the generations, preventing better solutions to develop. Elitism should therefore be used sparingly, especially if premature convergence occurs. If it is not used, it is well advised to keep track of the best found individual, so as to be sure that it does not get lost.

Finally, usually, elitism only concerns the best individual. However, some paradigms such as the Parisian approach may need to use elitism on up to 50% of the population (Collet & Louchet 2009).

4.  The final step of the evolutionary loop is the replacement operator. If elitism was used, one or several individuals are already part of the new generation. The replacement operator will pick up other individuals among parents and children until the new generation is complete, *i.e.* for constant size population algorithm, until a number of individuals equal to the original population size are selected.

The difference between the *selection* and the *replacement* operators is that the latter cannot choose individuals more than once, as it would not make any sense to have duplicates in a parent population. This would reduce diversity, which is what all EAs strive to maintain.

Note that in standard evolutionary algorithms, as with the millions of pixels or vertices of an image that are all shaded with identical algorithms, individuals of the population are evaluated using the very same evaluation function, meaning that general purpose highly parallel SIMD graphic cards that can be reprogrammed can be used at full speed to run artificial evolution algorithms (Maitre, Baumes, Lachiche, Corma, & Collet 2009).

In practice, the whole algorithm does not need to be embedded in the graphics card, since most of the time, evaluation is the big CPU consumer. So once all children are created, (which usually takes very little time) one can distribute the evaluation of the population over a network of machines, or CPU cores. Usually the speed-up ratio is nearly linear with the number of machines because in most evolutionary algorithms (but genetic programming) evaluation time is identical for all individuals.

## VARIATION OPERATORS

In *The Origin of Species*, Charles Darwin suggested that individuals evolved because they inherited traits from their parents with variations. Biological and physical constraints do not apply in evolutionary computation, meaning that virtually any kind of variation operators can be imagined, from unary operators (mutation), binary operators (crossover), to n-ary operators. Orgies are also possible, where all individuals of a population can share their genes to create a new individual (Mühlenbein & Paass, 1996), and of course, it is possible to implement Lamarckian variation operators (where a quick local search improves the parent's genome).

The most traditional way to create children is the one described above in the evolutionary loop, even though a more generic way is to have a number of variation operators, each associated with a probability to be applied to the parent population until the right number of children is generated (Keijzer, Merelo, Romero, & Schoenauer, 2002).

### Crossover: A (Usually) Binary Variation Operator

The way two (or *n*) parents' genotypes are mixed in order to create one or two children is highly dependent on the problem being solved. Then, Holland's genetic algorithms usually use a bitstring representation and rely heavily on crossover, while Rechenberg and Schwefel's Evolutionary Strategies, that use a vector of real values, originally only relied on mutation only. Genetic Programming uses a tree representation where crossover is implemented by swapping subtrees between parents. All in all, the guidelines for a good crossover operator are difficult to establish due to the variety of representations and evolutionary engines. One can however bear in mind that crossover is considered as an exploitation operator, so it is in the crossover operator that expertise in the target domain can be used. Some people even include into the crossover a local search method in order to rapidly improve the created child (*cf.* meta-heuristics, also called "memetic" algorithms (Hart, Krasnogor & Smith, 2005; Kruger, Baumes, Corma & Collet 2010)).

Typical crossover operators depend on the genotype:

- **Bitstring (cf. Figure 2):** one or several crossover points (called *loci*) are selected in both parents. The child is created by alternating genes from the first and second parent whenever a locus is reached (cf. multipoint crossover Figure 3).

- **Real values:** Many people are tempted by a barycentric crossover, where genes of the resulting child are the mean of the parent's genes. This crossover is rather problematic, because it tends to create children that are always "in between" their parents, which tends to reduce diversity in the population. In order to fight against this tendency, the BLX-$\alpha$ crossover was introduced (Eshelman & Schaffer 1993), that has a nice self-adaptation property: the distance between created children and their parents will depend on the distance between the two parents. In 1995, the SBX (Simulated Binary Crossover (Deb & Agrawal 1995)) operator was developed, that simulates the working principle of a single point cross-

*Figure 3. Multipoint crossover*

over on binary strings. The probability distribution for a child is high around each parent, but low elsewhere, including in between the two parents. This prevents the population from converging too quickly, and preserves the characteristics of good individuals.

- **Tree structure:** The standard Genetic Programming crossover consists in swapping subtrees selected in both parents. Note that since (in binary trees) there are as many leafs than there are nodes, subtree selection is usually made on a node with 90% probability and a leaf with 10% probability. This also applies to mutation.

Concerning multi-point crossovers, if individuals are made of $n$ genes, an $n-1$ points crossover is called a uniform crossover (Syswerda 1987). One should avoid many-point crossovers in problems that show a high degree of epistasis because interrelated genes (called building blocks) will be disrupted. Again, the *crêpes* example can very easily show what epistasis is about: Supposing evolution was at a stage where it still tried to obtained "feasible" *crêpes* batter, *i.e.* batter that is liquid enough to be poured into the pan, but containing enough flour to solidify while cooking. As was said above, "liquidity" is determined by both the volume of milk and the number of eggs. Supposing parent $P_1$ obtains the required texture with virtually no milk (i.e. thanks to eggs only), and parent $P_2$ obtains the same texture thanks with 0 eggs (i.e. thanks to milk only).

If a crossover point comes in between the milk and egg genes, it is then possible to have a child that will inherit the volume of milk of parent $P_1$ and the number of eggs of parent $P_2$. Even though both parents of this child poured well into the frying pan, the child will have a very different texture from its parents, since it will contain neither milk nor eggs ! On the opposite, a brother who has inherited the number of eggs of his $P_1$ parent and the volume of milk of his $P_2$ parent will be much more liquid than any of his parents.

These strange effects can happen if correlated genes are separated by a crossover point. Most of the time, one does not know how correlated are the variables of the problem to solve, and sometimes, correlation can be complex and involve more than two genes. However, without knowing the exact correlation between parameters, one can understand that using a many-point crossover will be more "disruptive" than a single point crossover, as it will increase the chances of "cutting" in between two related genes so generally speaking, it is better to use single-point crossovers in highly epistatic problems.

Interestingly enough, this observation can be used to somehow evaluate whether parameters of a problem are independent or not: if an algorithm using a single point crossover works as well as the same algorithm with a uniform crossover, this could be a hint that the parameters are independent and can be tuned one by one.

## Mutation

Note that here too, the *crêpes* example can easily show why mutation is an important operator. Suppose that the best *crêpes* recipe in a 50 fl.oz. bowl uses 4 eggs, but suppose also that in the original population, it happens so that no individual has the value 4 in gene 3 (number of eggs). If a multipoint crossover operator (like the one described in fig. 1) is used, it is impossible for the 4 value to appear in gene 3 without a mutation operator.

Mutation depends on the problem to be solved. As an exploration operator, it should ideally be *ergodic* in a strong sense, meaning that the probability of reaching any point of the search space from the current position through a single mutation should be greater than 0.

If the construction of such a mutation operator is not feasible, it should be ergodic in a weaker sense, meaning that it should be possible to reach any point of the search space in a *finite* number of mutations.

On a bitstring genome, mutation is simple: it merely consists in flipping a chosen bit. On a real genome, mutations can be done in several ways, the simplest being to add some gaussian noise to a selected real value. On a tree genome, mutation of a single node is usually not strong enough to have an important impact, so the standard mutation is to select a node (with 90% chance *vs* a leaf), delete its subtree and regrow it randomly.

Note that the effect of mutation increases with the elapsed number of generations: In the beginning of the algorithm, individuals mostly contain random values, so mutating a gene will not have much effect. On the contrary, after several hundred generations, all individuals do not contain random values anymore, so mutation will most likely have adverse effects.

This explains why one often decreases the probability of calling a mutation operator as the number of generations is increasing. Some *self-adaptive mutation* methods have been devised, such as the one used in Evolutionary Strategies (Schwefel, 1995; Beyer, 1995; Bäck, 1995; Bäck, Hammel, & Schwefel, 1997). The idea (inspired from nature) is that to each real value should be associated a variance value σ that is also subject to mutation and recombination just as the other genes of the genome.

This self-adaptive mutation is comparable to what happens with repair enzymes and mutator genes that are coded onto the DNA, thus providing partial control by the DNA of its own mutation rate.

In the first generation, σ values are initialised with random values between 0 and 0.5. If a mutation occurs on a gene, one starts by updating the σ value associated with this gene along a log-normal distribution, *i.e.* by multiplying it by exp($G$/sqrt($n$)), where $n$ is the number of genes in the genome and $G$ is a gaussian normally distributed random value with variance 1 and mean 0. One then adds to the real gene a gaussian value multiplied by the updated σ value associated to the gene.

Self adaptive mutation uses a bit more CPU time and resource, but allows one to achieve comparable results in fewer evaluations (Collet et al. 2002).

Finally, one of the most efficient real value mutation method is the Covariance Matrix Adaptation Evolutionary Strategy (CMA-ES) (Hansen et al. 2003). The idea is that an individual spawns a handful of children in a direction determined by a covariance matrix computed on previous results. This method was shown to perform very well on "turned problems," where variables are highly correlated.

## SELECTION AND REPLACEMENT OPERATORS

It has often been said that the force driving biological evolution was *natural selection*. In evolutionary computation, selection operators are also extremely important, as they can lead to premature or very slow convergence, depending on selection pressure.

Selection occurs at two stages: when choosing parents for breeding, and when choosing survivors for the next generation. In this chapter, *selection* chooses parents, and *replacement* chooses survivors. The main difference between *selection* and *replacement* is that the first operator allows a same individual to be chosen several times, while the latter removes the chosen individual from the pool of candidates.

In his original description of genetic algorithms, John Holland chose to use a *RouletteWheel* selector for theoretical purposes (Holland 1975). Unfortunately, in practice, this was probably the worst choice to make. This operator selects individuals proportionately to their fitness, which has several important drawbacks:

- Selection pressure totally depends on the fitness landscape, which is usually unknown. It is not translation invariant: on a population of 10 individuals, if the best has a fitness of 11 and the worst a fitness of 1, the probability for the best individual to be chosen is 16.6% and 1.5% for the worst. If one adds 100 to all fitness values, the best and worst individuals have nearly identical probabilities to be chosen (10.4% and 9.5%) !
  Things can be partially improved thanks to *linear scaling* of fitness values, or a *sigma truncation*, but with the cost of increased complexity (additional parameters to adjust).
- Roulette wheel is cpu-consuming, because the population needs to be sorted beforehand, leading to an $O(n \log n)$ complexity.
- Roulette requires the sum of the fitness values of all the individuals. This is problematic if the evolutionary computation is distributed over several machines. (This is the case for all other selection algorithms but Tournament selection.)
- The fitness function needs to yield positive values (which is not really problematic, but due to the fact that Roulette is not translation invariant, shifting the values so that they are all positive has consequences).

Other selection methods have been devised in order to mainly circumvent problem number 1:

- **Ranking (Baker, 1985):** Selection is based on rank, not fitness. One also needs to sort the population, leading to an $O(n \log n)$ complexity. Problem 1 is solved, but the others remain.
- **Stochastic Universal Sampling (Baker, 1987):** Individuals are assigned slots of a weighted roulette wheel, as for the Roulette

selection. *n* markers are then placed equally around the wheel and the wheel is spun once. The complexity of this algorithm is also *O(n* log *n)* and it requires the sum of the fitness values of all the individuals.

- **Selection in Genitor (Whitley, 1989):** Genitor is an evolutionary paradigm that is of the *Steady State* kind, in which only one individual is created per "generation." The population is initially ranked, after which each new child is inserted at its place and the worst individual of the population is discarded. This requires *O(*log *n)* steps, that need to be repeated n times in order to simulate the creation of a whole population, so the complexity of the algorithm is *O(n* log *n)*. The Genitor selection and replacement scheme may lead to premature convergence, which is why large population sizes are suggested.

- **Truncation selection (Mühlenbein & Schlierkamp-Voosen 1993):** This is the selection method used by breeders. Only the T best individuals are considered, and all of them have the same selection probability (random selection among T individuals). The population needs to be sorted first, so complexity is *O(n* log *n)*. Bad individuals (below threshold T) cannot be selected, so loss of diversity can be important.

- **Deterministic selection:** Only the *n* best individuals are selected. This method requires sorting the individuals. Loss of diversity is important (as for Truncation selection), and this selection method may lead to premature convergence.

- **Random:** Quick, but no selection pressure.

Then, there is n-ary **Tournament** selection (Brindle, 1981; Blickle & Thiele, 1995). Unless there is a good reason for using any other method, Tournament selection is most certainly the best of all. Binary tournament consists in picking two individuals at random, and comparing their fitness.

The individual with the highest fitness wins the tournament and is selected. Selection pressure can be increased by organising a tournament between three or more individuals. In contrast, if premature convergence occurs with a binary tournament, it is possible to decrease selection pressure by using a *stochastic Tournament* that uses a variable *p*. A stochastic tournament is a binary tournament where the best of the two individuals is chosen with a probability *p*. If *p*=0.5, then, this is equivalent to a random selection. If *p*=1, the stochastic tournament is not stochastic anymore, and becomes equivalent to a binary tournament.

Therefore, in comparison with Roulette wheel selection:

- Selection pressure does not depend on the fitness landscape, and can be very finely adjusted. This is a very important parameter to tune in a genetic algorithm: all other parameters being equal, if the algorithm does not converge rapidly enough (the best fitness curve was still increasing when a stopping criterion was met), one can increase the selection pressure *ad libitum* by increasing the number of participants in the tournament (n-ary tournament). Alternately, if premature convergence occurs (plateau on the best fitness many generations before the stopping criterion is met), it is possible to decrease pressure by reducing the number of participants. If it is already as low as two, one can switch to stochastic tournament which allows to further decrease selection pressure, possibly down to a purely random selection.

Loss of diversity represents the proportion of individuals of a population that are not selected. Some computed values for different tournament sizes are the following: 25% loss of diversity for size 2, 40% loss for size 3, 47% for size 4, 53% for size 5, 60% size 7, 70% size 10, 80% for size 20.

- Tournament complexity is simply $O(n)$, as one only needs $n$ tournaments to create a population of $n$ individuals. This method is therefore one of the fastest.
- Tournament is the method of choice for parallel evolutionary algorithms, as it does not require any global knowledge of individuals fitness. Tournament selection can be implemented locally on parallel machines, with pairwise or $s$-wise communication between different processors being the only requirement (Mühlenbein 1989; Harvey 1993).
- The fitness function needs not yield only positive values, and no scaling or post-processing of any kind is needed.

Finally, Tournament does not require an absolute evaluation of individuals. Only a comparison is necessary, meaning that evolutionary algorithms using Tournament as selection or replacement operators can work on problems where only a partial order between solutions exist.

A good study on selection schemes can be found in Blickle & Thiele (1997) and Goldberg and Deb (1991).

## STOPPING CRITERIA

Most users choose to stop evolution after $n$ generations and use this number as an evaluation of CPU-consumption. This only makes sense for generational replacement algorithms, where the number of individuals created per generation is equivalent to the population size.

Unfortunately, this is not the case for Evolutionary Strategies (see below) that use a $(\mu+\lambda)$ replacement scheme, were the number of created children is not correlated to the population size. A much better metric is therefore the number of *evaluations* and not the number of *generations*.

Run time can also be a stopping criterion (stop after one hour). When such fixed criteria (duration or number of evaluations) are used, parameters of the algorithm should be tweaked so that the algorithms converges at the end of the run, and not before or after. If the algorithm converges before the stopping criterion is met (plateau on the best fitness individual), one can either reduce selection pressure or increase population size and do the opposite if the algorithm had not converged yet.

This triggers another idea: why not use fitness convergence as stopping criterion ? One way of doing this is to stop if a plateau is too long: if $F_k$ is the fitness of the best individual at generation $k$ and $F_c$ is the current best fitness, one can stop if $F_c - (\sum_1^p F_k)/p \leq \varepsilon$, with $p$, the length of the plateau in number of generations.

Generally, a population that has converged is stuck in a local optimum, and does not evolve anymore (which is why it is very important to not let it converge, and to implement diversity preserving schemes to this effect). If a metrics is available that can determine the distance between two individuals' genotype, one can use loss of diversity over the population as a stopping criterion.

Finally, the ultimate stopping criterion is fitness value. If the problem is to find an individual with a fitness beyond 1000, the algorithm can stop once this value is met (possibly on the first generation if one is very lucky !).

## PARAMETERS

A reasonably complete list of parameters for an evolutionary algorithm is the following:

- **Population size/number of generations:** These two parameters go together: for a same number of evaluations, one can use a small population and evolve it for a large number of generations, or use a large population and evolve it for a smaller number of generations. Common sense says that using a larger population will preserve diversity and help fight against premature convergence.

- **Crossover and mutation probabilities:** Usage of unary or n-ary variation operators depends on people and paradigms (Evolution Strategies use nearly exclusively mutations, and Genetic Programming nearly exclusively crossovers, for instance). In fact, this is very problem-dependent. Without prior experience and a good reason for putting forward crossover or mutation, the most standard choice is to create offspring thanks to a binary crossover called with a probability of 80 to 90%, followed by a mutation function called on each child, with a mutation rate that will change a gene once in a while (one mutation every 10 children is a good starting base). Too many mutations (exploration operator) will lead to non-converging algorithms. A high (resp. low) mutation rate is therefore usually associated with a strong (resp. weak) selection pressure.

- **Number of children per generation:** If the population size is $n$, many people create $n$ children, although there is no real reason behind this choice, other than the fact that this is how Holland's genetic algorithms were working. Evolutionary Strategies use a $(\mu+\lambda)$ or $(\mu,\lambda)$ replacement scheme. In the first strategy, the replacement operator picks $n$ individuals for the new generation from a pool of individuals made of $\mu$ parents and $\lambda$ children, while the second strategy only picks individuals of the new generation in the $\lambda$ children population (with $\lambda \geq n$). Finally, steady-state algorithms create only one child per generation ! Choosing the number of children per generation generally depends on how fast one wants the algorithm to converge. Allowing parents to compete with children is a powerful form of elitism that can be countered by creating many children per generation.

## GENETIC PROGRAMMING

In this chapter, Genetic Programming has often been opposed to "standard evolutionary algorithms." Genetic Programming is an evolutionary algorithm where:

1. genes do not represent a fixed list of parameters, but a variable succession of instructions or functions (very often represented as a tree) that implements a program or a complex function, and
2. rather than passing the genome to an evaluation function, the genome is *executed* on learning cases in order to be evaluated.

The first point means that GP can be used to determine the structure and size of an unknown problem. Supposing that one wants to use GP for machine learning, to evolve a function on some data. How does one know how many nodes this function should contain ? If this function can call sub-functions, how many sub-functions are needed, and when should they be called ? Genome structure altering techniques have been shown to be efficient, and to lead to major human-competitive results in (Koza, 1999; Koza, 2003).

The second point is of importance if one wants to run the evaluation on GPGPUs. These cards are mostly SIMD (Single Instruction Multiple Data), meaning that pixel and vertex shaders (cores) are coupled together in such a way that a bunch of them must execute the very same instruction at the very same time.

If this is not much of a problem in standards EAs, where a single identical function is used to evaluate possibly thousands of different individuals, in GP, it is often the opposite that is done: individuals represent different functions, that are tested on a learning set.

SIMD cores cannot execute different functions at the same time, so using GPUs on Genetic Programming would seem an impossible task. However, fortunately, GPU cards are not strictly SIMD. A modern card such as the NVidia GTX395 contains as many as 1000 cores, but in practice, they are grouped by 8, meaning that it is possible to load a group of 8 cores with the same individual, and have them evaluate in parallel 8 different learning cases. Due to implementation reasons (instruction fetch latency,...), maximum speedup can be reached on GP with as few as 32 fitness cases (Maitre, Lachiche & Collet 2010).

Genetic Programming is clearly a different paradigm from fixed length genome evolutionary algorithms. Typically, incontrollable code growth (called bloat) must be avoided, meaning that parsimony operators should be introduced in order to favour generic solutions and fight against overfitting. Even though many GP paradigms have been developed over the years, John Koza's tree representation for individuals remains widely used (Koza, 1992; Koza, 1994; Koza, 1999; Koza, 2003).

## CONCLUSION

All the existing evolutionary paradigms have not been described because it was not possible to do so within a single chapter. Instead, a generic algorithm was presented that can emulate any of the different historical paradigms, should anyone wish to do so.

These paradigms correspond to different trends. It seems however that parameter choice should be made in order to solve a particular problem, rather than to follow a particular trend. Evolutionary computation has now come of age, with very impressive achievements, so it is high time that this domain be unified in a pragmatic way. Books such as DeJong (2005) are certainly going in the right direction.

Finally, the advent of GPGPU hardware is very promising for the future of Evolutionary Algorithms, simply because it is probably the only generic technique that can make full use of these massively parallel cards.

Our team in Strasbourg regularly obtains speedups of up to x100 on a $250 NVidia GTX260 card (Maitre et al. 2009) that, according to NVidia, is supposed to yield around 800 GFlops. Using the recently announced Fermi technology, the future GTX395 card is supposed to give around 5 Teraflops, for $750. Since on EAs, speedup is linear with parallel processing power, this means that speedups of more than x500 could be obtained with one of these cards.

Knowing that a PC could host as many as four of these cards, such a PC could give speedups of around x2000 compared to a standard PC, meaning that a one day optimization on GPGPUs would be equivalent to 5.5 years' calculation on a standard PC.

Even if an optimisation algorithm $B$ goes 10 times faster to obtain a similar result as an evolutionary algorithm $A$ on a particular problem, if algorithm $B$ cannot be parallelized, algorithm $A$ running on GPUs will still be 200 times faster than algorithm $B$...

This is why evolutionary algorithms will probably have a tremendous edge over most other algorithms in a short future

## REFERENCES

Bäck, T. (1995). *Evolutionary algorithms in theory and practice*. New York: Oxford University Press.

Baker, J. E. (1985). Adaptive selection methods for genetic algorithms. In *Proceedings of the International Conference on Genetic Algorithms and Their Applications,* (pp. 100-111).

Baker, J. E. (1987). Reducing bias and inefficiency in the selection algorithm. In J. J. Grefenstette (Ed.), *Proceedings of the 2 nd International Conference on Genetic Algorithms* (pp. 14-21). San Francisco: Morgan Kaufmann.

Blickle, T., & Thiele, L. (1995). A mathematical analysis of tournament selection. In L. J. Eshelman (Ed.), *Proceedings of the 6th International Conference on Genetic Algorithms* (pp. 9-16). San Francisco: Morgan Kaufmann.

Blickle, T., & Thiele, L. (1997). A comparison of selection schemes used in genetic algorithms. In Evolutionary Computation, (pp. 361-394).

Brameier, M., & Banzhaf, W. (2007). *Linear Genetic Programming*. Berlin: Springer.

Brindle, A. (1981). *Genetic algorithms in search, optimization*. Technical Report No. TR81-2, Department of Computer Science, University of Alberta, Canada.

Collet, P., & Louchet, J. (2009). Artificial Evolution and the Parisian Approach: Applications in the Processing of Signals and Images. In Siarry, P. (Ed.), *Optimization in Signal and Image Processing, iSTE*. Chichester, UK: John Wiley & Sons. doi:10.1002/9780470611319.ch2

Collet, P., Louchet, J., & Lutton, E. (2002). Issues on the optimization of evolutionary algorithms code. In D. B. Fogel, et al. (Eds.), *Proceedings of the 2002 Congress on Evolutionary Computation* (pp. 1103-1108). Washington, DC: IEEE Press.

Cramer, N. L. (1985). A representation for the adaptive generation of simple sequential programs. In *Proceedings of the International Conference on Genetic Algorithms and Their Applications* (pp.183-187).

Darwin, C. (1859). *On the origin of species by means of natural selection or the preservation of favored races in the struggle for life*. London: John Murray.

Deb, K., & Agrawal, R. B. (1995). Simulated binary crossover for continuous search space. *Complex Systems*, *9*, 115–148.

Deb, K., Agrawal, S., Pratab, A., & Meyarivan, T. (2000). A Fast Elitist Non-Dominated Sorting Genetic Algorithm for Multi-Objective Optimization: NSGA-II, (LNCS Vol 1917, pp. 849-858). Berlin: Springer.

DeJong, K. (2005). *Evolutionary computation: A unified approach*. Cambridge, MA: MIT Press.

Eshelman, L. J., & Schaffer, J. D. (1993). Real-coded genetic algorithms and interval-schemata. In Whitley, L. D. (Ed.), *Foundations of Genetic Algorithms 2* (pp. 187–202). San Mateo, CA: Morgan Kaufmann.

Fogel, D. B. (1992). An analysis of evolutionary programming. In D. B. Fogel & W. Atmar (Eds.), *Proceedings of the 1st Annual Conference on Evolutionary Programming*, (pp. 43-51).

Fogel, D. B. (1998). *Evolutionary computation: The fossil record*. New York: Wiley-IEEE Press.

Fogel, L. J., Owens, A. J., & Walsh, M. J. (1966). *Artificial intelligence through simulated evolution*. New York: John Wiley & Sons.

Fraser, A. S. (1957). Simulation of genetic systems by automatic digital computers. *Australian Journal of Biological Sciences*, *10*, 484–491.

Friedberg, R., Dunham, B., & North, J. (1958). A learning machine: Part II. *IBM Research Journal*, *3*(3).

Friedman, G. (1959). Digital simulation of an evolutionary process. *General Systems Yearbook*, *4*, 171–184.

Glover, F. (1977). Heuristics for integer programming using surrogate constraints. *Decision Sciences*, *8*, 156–166. doi:10.1111/j.1540-5915.1977.tb01074.x

Glover, F. (1989). Tabu search—part I. *ORSA Journal on Computing*, *1*(3), 190-206.

Glover, F. (1990). Tabu search—part II. *ORSA Journal on Computing*, *2*(3), 4–32.

Goldberg, D., & Deb, K. (1991). *A comparative analysis of selection schemes used in genetic algorithms* (pp. 416–421). Foundations of Genetic Algorithms.

Goldberg, D. E. (1989). *Genetic algorithms in search, optimization and machine learning.* Boston: Addison-Wesley.

Hansen, N., Müller, S. D., & Koumoutsakos, P. (2003). Reducing the time complexity of the derandomized evolution strategy with covariance matrix adaptation (CMA-ES). *Evolutionary Computation, 11*(1), 1–18. doi:10.1162/106365603321828970

Hart, W. E., Krasnogor, N., & Smith, J. E. (2005). *Recent advances in memetic algorithms.* Berlin: Springer. doi:10.1007/3-540-32363-5

Harvey, I. (1993). Evolutionary robotics and saga: The case for hill crawling and tournament selection. *Artificial Life III. Santa Fe Institute Studies in the Sciences of Complexity, XVI*, 299–326.

Hinterding, R., Gielewski, H., & Peachey, T. C. (2000), On the Nature of Mutation in Genetic Algorithms, In L. Eshelman (Ed), *Genetic Algorithms, Proceedings of the 6th International Conference*, (pp. 65-72). Morgan Kaufmann, San Francisco CA.

Holland, J. H. (1975). *Adaptation in natural and artificial systems.* Ann Arbor: University of Michigan Press.

Keijzer, M., Merelo, J. J., Romero, G., & Schoenauer, M. (2002). Evolving objects: A general purpose evolutionary computation library. In P. Collet, E. Lutton, M. Schoenauer, C. Fonlupt, & J.-K. Hao (Eds.), *Artificial Evolution '01* (pp. 229-241). Berlin: Springer (LNCS 2310).

Kirkpatrick, S., Gellat, C. D., & Vecchi, M. P. (1983). Optimization by simulated annealing. *Science, 220*(4598), 671–680. doi:10.1126/science.220.4598.671

Koza, J. R. (1992). *Genetic programming: On the programming of computers by means of natural evolution.* Cambridge, MA: MIT Press.

Koza, J. R. (1994). *Genetic programming II: Automatic discovery of reusable programs.* Cambridge, MA: MIT Press.

Koza, J. R. (1999). *Genetic programming III: Automatic synthesis of analog circuits.* Cambridge, MA: MIT Press.

Koza, J. R. (2003). *Genetic programming IV: Routine human-competitive machine intelligence.* Kluwer Academic.

Kruger F, Maitre, O., & Collet., P. (2010). Speedups between x70 and x120 for a generic local search (memetic) algorithm on a single GPGPU chip. To appear in the *Proceedings of EvoApplications '10*, Istanbul, Turkey.

Louchet, J. (2001). Using an individual evolution strategy for stereovision. *Genetic Programming and Evolvable Machines, 2*(2), 101–109. doi:10.1023/A:1011544128842

Maitre, O. Lachiche. N. & Collet., P. (2010). Maximizing speedup of GP trees execution on GPGPU cards for as few as 32 fitness cases. To appear in the Proceedings of EuroGP'10, Istanbul, Turkey.

Maitre, O., & Baumes, L. A. Lachiche. N., Corma. A., & Collet., P. (2009). Coarse grain parallelization of evolutionary algorithms on GPGPU cards with EASEA. *Proceedings of the 11th Annual conference on Genetic and evolutionary computation* (pp. 1403-1410). Montreal, Quebec, Canada.

Miller, J. (2000). Cartesian genetic programming. In R. P. et al. (Eds.), *Proceedings of EUROGP '00* (pp. 121-131). Edinburgh: Springer.

Mühlenbein, H. (1989). Parallel genetic algorithms, population genetics and combinatorial optimization. *Proceedings of the 3rd International Conference on Genetic Algorithms* (pp. 416-421).

Mühlenbein, H., & Paass, G. (1996). From recombination of genes to the estimation of distributions. *Parallel Problem Solving from Nature, 1411*, 178–187.

Mühlenbein, H., & Schlierkamp-Voosen, D. (1993). The science of breeding and its application to the breeder genetic algorithm (BGA). *Evolutionary Computation, 1*(4), 335–360. doi:10.1162/evco.1993.1.4.335

Rechenberg, I. (1973). *Evolutionstrategie: Optimierung technisher systeme nach prinzipien des biologischen evolution.* Stuttgart: Fromman-Hozlboog Verlag.

Schwefel, H.-P. (1995). Numerical optimization of computer models (2nd ed.). New-York: John Wiley & Sons.

Shubin, N. (2008). *Your inner fish: a journey into the 3.5-billion-year history of the human body.* New York: Pantheon Books.

Spears, W. M., & De Jong, K. A. (1990). An analysis of multi-point crossover. *Proceedings of the Foundations of Genetic Algorithms Workshop.*

Syswerda, G. (1987). Uniform crossover in genetic algorithms. In J. Schaffer (Ed.), *Proceedings of the 3 rd International Conference on Genetic Algorithms* (pp. 2-9). San Mateo: Morgan Kaufmann.

Whitley, D. (1989). The GENITOR algorithm and selection pressure: Why rank-based allocation of reproductive trials is best. In J.D. Schaffer (Ed.), *Proceedings of the 3 rd International Conference on Genetic Algorithms* (pp. 116-121). San Francisco: Morgan Kaufmann.

Zitzler, E., Laumanns, M., & Thiele, L. (2001). Spea2: Improving the strength pareto evolutionary algorithm. *Technical Report 103*, Gloriastrasse 35, CH-8092 Zurich, Switzerland.

## ENDNOTE

[1]   Please note that calling the mutation operator with a 100% probability does not mean that all children are mutated: mutation operators usually go through all the genes of the individual, and mutate each gene with a $q$ probability. If the genotype of an individual contains 10 genes, and $q=0.01$, then, if this operator is called on 100% of the children ($p=1$), in average, one children out of ten will undergo a mutation. Authors are generally not clear on the $p$ and $q$ values they use, making it difficult to reproduce their results.

# Chapter 3
# Evolutionary Algorithms in Supervision of Error– Free Control

**Bohumil Šulc**
*Czech Technical University in Prague, Czech Republic*

**David Klimanek**
*Czech Technical University in Prague, Czech Republic*

## ABSTRACT

*Evolutionary algorithms are well known as optimization techniques, suitable for solving various kinds of problems (Ruano, 2005). The new application of evolutionary algorithms represents their use in the detection of biased control loop functions caused by controlled variable sensor discredibility (Klimanek, Sulc, 2005). Sensor discredibility occurs when a sensor transmitting values of the controlled variable provides inexact information, however the information is not absolutely faulty yet. The use of discredible sensors in control circuits may cause the real values of controlled variables to exceed the range of tolerated differences, whereas zero control error is being displayed. However, this is not the only negative consequence. Sometimes, sensor discredibility is accompanied with undesirable and hardly recognizable side effects. Most typical is an increase of harmful emission production in the case of combustion control, (Sulc, Klimanek, 2005). We have found that evolutionary algorithms are useful tools for solving the particular problem of finding a software-based way (so called software redundancy) of sensor discredibility detection. Software redundancy is a more economical way than the usual hardware redundancy, which is otherwise necessary in control loop protection against this small, invisible control error occurrence. New results from a long-term tracking residuum trends show that credibility loss can be forecasted. Operators can be warned in advance that the sensor measuring the controlled variable needs to be exchanged. This need can be effectively reflected in maintenance plans. Namely, the standard genetic algorithm and the simulated annealing algorithm have been successfully applied and tested to minimize the given cost function. By means of these algorithms, a newly developed method is able to*

DOI: 10.4018/978-1-60566-814-7.ch003

*detect controlled variable sensor discredibility. When applied to combustion processes, production of harmful emissions can be kept within accepted limits. The application of the used evolutionary algorithms inclusive terminology transfer in this application area can serve as an explanatory case study to help readers gain a better understanding of the how the evolutionary algorithms operate.*

## INTRODUCTION

Evolutionary algorithms are well known as optimization techniques, suitable for solving various kinds of problems (Ruano, 2005). The new application of evolutionary algorithms represents their use in the detection of biased control loop functions caused by controlled variable sensor discredibility (Klimanek, Sulc, 2005). *Sensor discredibility* occurs when a sensor transmitting values of the controlled variable provides inexact information, however the information is not absolutely faulty yet. The use of discredible sensors in control circuits may cause the real values of controlled variables to exceed the range of tolerated differences, whereas zero control error is being displayed. However, this is not the only negative consequence. Sometimes, sensor discredibility is accompanied with undesirable and hardly recognizable side effects. Most typical is an increase of harmful emission production in the case of combustion control, (Sulc, Klimanek, 2005).

We have found that evolutionary algorithms are useful tools for solving the particular problem of finding a software-based way (so called software redundancy) of sensor discredibility detection. Software redundancy is a more economical way than the usual hardware redundancy, which is otherwise necessary in control loop protection against this small, invisible control error occurrence.

New results from a long-term tracking residuum trends show that credibility loss can be forecasted. Operators can be warned in advance that the sensor measuring the controlled variable needs to be exchanged. This need can be effectively reflected in maintenance plans.

Namely, the standard genetic algorithm and the simulated annealing algorithm have been successfully applied and tested to minimize the given cost function. By means of these algorithms, a newly developed method is able to detect controlled variable sensor discredibility. When applied to combustion processes, production of harmful emissions can be kept within accepted limits.

The application of the used evolutionary algorithms inclusive terminology transfer in this application area can serve as an explanatory case study to help readers gain a better understanding of the how the evolutionary algorithms operate.

## BACKGROUND

The above-mentioned controlled variable sensor discredibility detection represents a specific part of the fault detection field in control engineering. According to some authors (Venkatasubramanian, Rengaswamy, 2003, Korbic, 2004), fault detection methods are classified into three general categories: quantitative model-based methods, qualitative model-based methods, and process history based methods. In contrast to the mentioned approaches, where prior knowledge about the process is needed, for the controlled variable sensor discredibility detection it is useful to employ methods of evolutionary algorithms. The main advantage of such a solution is that necessary information about the changes in controlled variable sensor properties can be obtained with the help of evolutionary algorithms based on the standard process data – this is, in any case, acquired and recorded for the sake of process control.

*Figure 1. Principle of extrapolation of the development of sensor model parameters and the approximate time until control variable sensor discredibility evaluation*

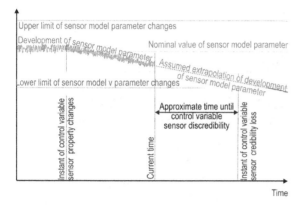

In order to apply evolutionary algorithms to controlled variable sensor discredibility detection, a cost function was designed as a *residual function e* defined by the absolute value of difference between the sensor model output ($y_m$) and the real sensor output ($y_{real}$),

$$e = |y_{real} - y_m| \qquad (1)$$

The design of residual function $e$ has been explained in detail (e.g. in Sulc, Klimanek, 2005).

In most sensor models it is assumed that the sensor output is proportional only to one input (Koushanfar, 2003), so that the sensor model equation is

$$y_m = k_m x_{est} + q_m, \qquad (2)$$

where parameter $k_m$ represents the gain of the sensor model, parameter $q_m$ expresses the shift factor, and $x_{est}$ is the estimated sensor model input, which represents the physical (real) value of the control variable. The physical value of the control variable is not available for us because we expect that the sensor is not reliable and we want to detect this stage. However, we can estimate this value from the other process data that are acquired usually for the purposes of the information system. This

estimation is usually based on steady-state data, so that it is important to detect the steady state of the process.

Basically, the underlying idea of applying the evolutionary algorithm is then based on finding a vector of the sensor model parameter for which the value of residual function $e$ is minimal.

The idea underlying control variable sensor discredibility detection consists of two parts (Figure 1):

1.  Indirect detection of changes in the sensor properties via adaptation of the sensor model parameters so that the residuum is minimal. Our method aims to minimize the residuum using evolutionary algorithms (simulated annealing algorithm, or standard genetic algorithms);

2.  Interpretation of the changes in the sensor model parameters (evaluation of the development of the sensor model parameters). This decides whether the changes have already reached the stage where the control variable sensor is regarded as discredible. The algorithm of the evaluation block can be described as follows:

    ◦   **Initialization stage**. At the beginning, when the control variable sensor is providing correct data, the nominal vector sensor of the model parameters is obtained. Based on the nominal values of the sensor model parameters, the maximum acceptable changes for each of the parameters are designated (as a percentage of the value of the given parameter).

    ◦   **Working stage**. When the initialization stage is processed, the block provides an evaluation of the development of the sensor model parameter vector. This means that the regression coefficients of the vector development are computed. Using the extrapolation function, we obtain

*Figure 2. A flow chart of the standard genetic algorithm applied for discredibility detection*

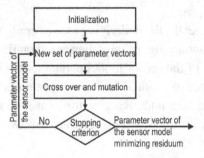

the assumed development of the sensor model parameter vector, as well as the approximate time until control variable sensor discredibility.

○ **Warning stage.** If the development of the sensor model parameter vector indicates that the time is shorter than the given time (usually n times the sampling period), the operator is warned about this situation.

## Advantages of the Evolutionary Algorithm Applied to Discredibility Detection

In principle, any optimization method could be used for the mentioned optimization task. The problem is that the sensor model input is an unknown, dynamically-changing variable. Therefore, the choice and the parameter selection must include certain element of a random selection from many alternatives, which is fulfilled in the case of evolutionary algorithms. The higher computational time requirements do not matter in the case of sensor discredibility detection, because the loss of credibility is the result of a gradual development.

## Problem Statement

A particular task of evolutionary algorithms in the solved problem is e.g. a finding extreme of a given cost function. We have utilized the evo-

lutionary algorithms to minimize the given cost function (in fault detection terminology a residual function). Based on this minimization, it is possible to detect that the control variable sensor is providing biased data.

## THE STANDARD GENETIC ALGORITHM AND THE SIMULATED ANNEALING ALGORITHM IN DESCREDIBILITY DETECTION

Both methods have been tested and proved to be legitimate for use. Unlike general genetic presentations of the methods, we will present the methods in a transformed way, based on the use of terms from the field of fault detection. From the engineering view point this should facilitate understanding of both procedures (Klimanek, Sulc, 2006). In our text, the terms introduced in the theory of evolutionary algorithms are indicated by the abbreviation "ET".

### The Standard Genetic Algorithm

In controlled variable sensor discredibility detection that uses genetic algorithm methods, the following steps are required (procedure by Fleming & Purshouse, 1995) (Figure 2):

1. **Initialization:** during initialization, the *evolutionary time* is set to zero and an initial *set of vectors* containing the sensor model parameters (called *population* in ET) is randomly generated within an expected range of reasonable values for each of the parameters. For each of the parameter vectors of the sensor model (in ET, individuals of the population), the value of the residual function (1) is evaluated. Also, the average value of the residual function values is computed.

2. **New set of parameter vectors:** after starting the *iteration* process, a new *set of parameter vectors* is generated (in ET, new population)

*Figure 3. A flow chart of the simulated annealing algorithm applied for dis-credibility detection*

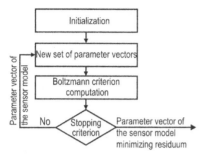

when the selection operator is employed. Selecting a set of the new parameter vectors, the following algorithm is used: the parameter vector of the sensor model that provides residual values lower than the average value is replicated into the next subset for generating new parameter candidates in more copies than in the original set, and the individuals with below-average residual values are rejected (Witczak, Obuchowicz, Korbicz, 2002).

3. **Crossover and mutation (ET):** next comes the crossover operation over the randomly selected pairs of the parameter vector of the sensor model of the topical set. In the presenting application of the standard genetic algorithm, the selected sensor model parameters are coded into binary strings and the standard one point crossover operator is used. The mutation operator mimics random mutations (Fleming, Purshouse, 1995). The newly created parameters are coded into binary strings and one bit of each string is switched with random probability. The value of the residual function (1) for the current run is evaluated. Also, the average value of the residual function values is computed.

4. **Stopping-criterion decision:** if the stopping criterion is not met, a return to step 2 repeats the process. The stopping criterion is met, e.g. when the size of the difference between the average of the residual values from the current run and the average of the residual values from the previous run is lower than the given size (Fleming, Purshouse, 2002).

## Simulated Annealing Algorithm

Controlled variable sensor discredibility detection via simulated annealing can be described by the following steps (Figure 3):

1. **Initialization:** an initial control parameter is set (in ET, initial annealing temperature). The control parameter is used to evaluate the Boltzmann criterion (King, 1999), which affects the acceptance of the current parameter vector of the sensor model in step 3. A vector of random values of the sensor model parameters is selected and the value of the residual function is computed.

2. **New set of parameter vectors:** the iteration index is increased and, using a stochastic strategy, a new vector of the sensor model parameters is randomly generated (in ET it is spoken about generating new individuals) and the corresponding value of the residual variable is obtained (in ET, value of the cost function).

3. **Boltzmann criterion computation:** the difference between the residual value obtained in step 2 and the residual value from the previous iteration is evaluated. If the difference is negative, then the new parameter vector is accepted automatically. Otherwise, the algorithm may accept the new parameter vector based on the Boltzmann criterion. The control parameter is weighted with a coefficient $\lambda$ (in ET, gradual temperature reduction). If the control parameter is less than or equal to the given final control parameter, then the stop criterion is met and the current vector of the sensor model parameters is accepted. Otherwise, returning to step 3 repeats the process of optimizing search.

*Figure 4. Detection of gradual changes of the level sensor gain via genetic algorithm and the simulated annealing algorithm*

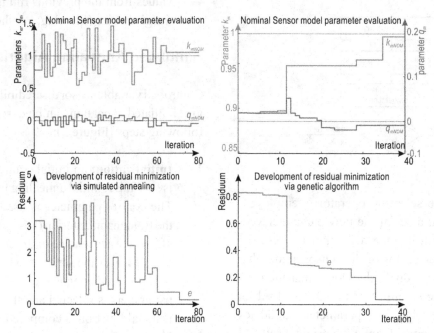

## Comparison of Usability of the Algorithms for Discredibility Detection

The comparison of both evolutionary algorithms applied to controlled variable sensor discredibility detection is shown by Figure 4. This comparison represents a part of results form paper Sulc, Klimanek. (2006). It is evident, that the simulated annealing algorithm needs more evaluation time for one evaluation period – a period for simulated annealing required 80 iterations, while genetic algorithm needed 40 iterations. This difference is because genetic algorithm works with a group of potential solutions, while simulated annealing compares only two potential solutions and accepts better one.

No difference was found between the two evolutionary algorithms used here; their good convergence depends mainly on the algorithm settings. Although evolutionary algorithms are generally much more time consuming than other optimizing procedures, this consideration does not matter in control variable sensor discredibility detection. This is because control variable sensor discredibility has no conclusive impacts on the control results and the time needed for the detection does not affect the control process.

## Testing Model-based Sensor Discredibility Detection Method

The model-based control variable sensor discredibility detection method using evolutionary algorithms was tested to find whether the method is able to detect the control variable sensor properties changes via presented evolutionary algorithms. The simulation experiments are more describes in (Klimanek, Sulc 2006). Results from the simulated experiments were summarized and they can be graphically demonstrated in the next paragraph.

## Results and Findings from the Tests

Figure 5 depicts a simulation run during which the sensor gain has been gradually decreased from a

*Figure 5. Detection of gradual changes of the level sensor gain via genetic algorithm*

*Figure 6. Detection of the step change of the level sensor gain via simulated annealing method*

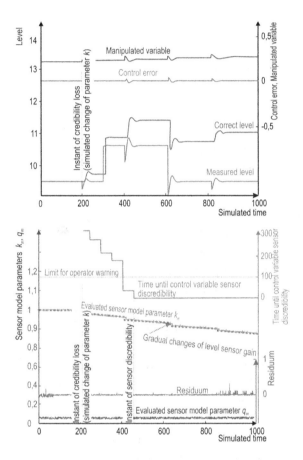

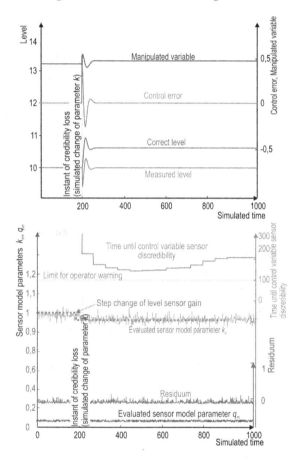

starting (correct) value. It can be seen that after the sensor properties has been changed, the measured value of the controlled variable (in this case the water level) is different from the correct value.

It is apparent that the algorithm used for sensor model parameter detection (in this case the genetic algorithm) is able to find the sensor model gain $k_m$, because the sensor model parameter development corresponds to the simulated real sensor parameter changing. By the experiment

The sensor level discredibility detection results obtained using the simulated annealing algorithm, were similar. Figure 6 shows results obtained when the model-based method using the simulated annealing algorithm was tested. A step change of

sensor gain was simulated and it is obvious that the algorithm was able to capture the change.

By this method the operator is informed about the estimated time remaining before sensor discredibility occurs. If the time is critical, the operator also receives timely a warning about the situation.

## APPLICATION OF EVOLUTIONDY ALGORITHMS

The importance of discredibility detection can be illustrated by the case of combustion process control. Figure 7 shows an illustrative example of a combustion process. The aim of the temperature

*Figure 7. Illustrative depiction of control loops in a combustion process*

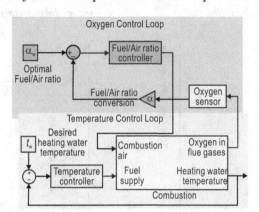

control loop is to maintain the heating water temperature at the desired value by changing the fuel supply; and the oxygen control loop represents maintaining the air factor (fuel/air ratio) $\alpha$ at its desired value (in an attempt to produce minimal gaseous emissions and steady fuel combustion.

The influence of changes in oxygen sensor properties on the control process is depicted in Figure 8. It is apparent that when the oxygen sensor starts to provide biased data, the oxygen control loop reacts to incorrect information about the fuel/air ratio by attempting to remove (unreal) the control error.

The main loop of the heating water temperature control works properly, because it returns the control error back to zero. The desired temperature value can be achieved at the cost of increasing the fuel supply, because the oxygen control loop has changed the combustion air delivery, so environmental impacts will occur but they will remain unrecognized.

## CONCLUSION

Implementation feasibility of the evolutionary algorithms in a model-based controlled variable sensor discredibility has been demonstrated here. In two variations of the standard evolutionary algorithms - the genetic algorithm and the simulated annealing algorithm, designed procedure of sensor discredibility detection was presented.

In both cases, the time needed for the evaluation was several minutes. In the case of the application for discredibility detection, this time demand does not matter because such small malfunctions do not lead to fatal errors in control loop operation and discredibility is usually a long developing process.

Evolutionary algorithms have become a useful tool in discovering hidden inaccuracy in the control loops. Discredibility detection saves costs on redundant controlled variable sensors, which are required if the controlled variable sensor discredibility is detected via hardware redundancy on the assumption that the costs for additional sensors are not negligible, of course.

The importance of discredibility detection using evolutionary algorithms can be found, e.g. in biomass combustion processes (due to the penalties for overstepped limits in harmful emissions), and also in the food-processing industry, where side effects may not be harmful, but rather unpleasant (i.e. bad odors).

In the planned continuation of the future research will be directed at optimizing the combustion process, special attention will be paid to the promising way of anticipating the instant when the controlled variable sensor credibility is lost. This newly developed second important feature of the discredibility detection using evolutionary

*Figure 8. Impacts of changes in the oxygen sensor on the control loop signals*

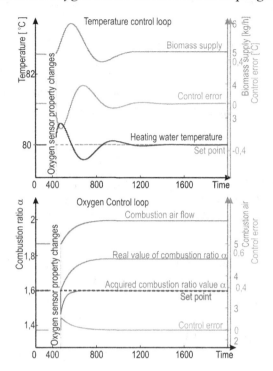

algorithms has a great importance in industrial practice because a timely predicted sensor malfunction helps to save additional costs resulting from unplanned shutdowns, e.g.-. An experiment will investigate ways of verifying oxygen probe credibility. This will be an important step toward non-simulated applications.

## REFERENCES

Chen, Z., He, Y., Chu, F., & Huang, J. (2003). Evolutionary Strategy for Classification Problems and its Application in Fault Diagnosis. *Engineering Applications of Artificial Intelligence*, *16*(1), 31–38. doi:10.1016/S0952-1976(03)00027-7

Fleming, P., & Purshouse, C. (1995). *The Matlab Genetic Algorithm Toolbox*. Sheffield, England: IEE Colloquium on Applied Control Technology Using Matlab.

Fleming, P., & Purshouse, C. (2002). Evolutionary Algorithms in Control Systems Engineering: A survey. *Control Engineering Practice*, *10*(11), 1223–1241. doi:10.1016/S0967-0661(02)00081-3

King, R. (1999). *Computational Methods in Control Engineering*. Amsterdam: Kluwer Academic Publishers.

Klimanek, D. (2007). *Detection of a Biased Control Loop Function via Evolutionary Algorithms*. PhD. Thesis, Czech Technical University, Prague, Czech Republic.

Klimanek, D., & Sulc, B. (2005). Evolutionary Detection of Sensor Discredibility in Control Loops, In *Proceedings of the 31st Annual Conference IEEE*, (pp. 136–141).

Klimanek, D., & Sulc, B. (2006). Sensor Discredibility Detection by Means of Software Redundancy. In *Proceedings of the 7th International Carpathian Control Conference*, (pp. 249–252).

Korbicz, J. (2004). *Fault Diagnosis: Models, Artificial Intelligence, Applications*. Berlin: Springer.

Koushanfar, R. (2003). On-line fault detection of sensor measurements. In. *Proceedings of IEEE Sensors, 2*(8), 974–979.

Ruano, A. E. (Ed.). (2005). *Intelligent Control Systems Using Computational Intelligence Techniques*. London: The IEE Press.

Saloky, T., & Piteľ, J. (2005). Adaptive control of heating process with outdoor temperature compensation. 30. *Proceedings of ASR Seminar, Instruments and Control, 51*(2), 113-116.

Sulc, B., & Klimanek, D. (2006). Enhanced Function of Standard Controller by Control Variable Sensor Discredibility Detection. In *Proceedings of the WSEAS International Conferences: ACS06, EDU06, REMOTE06, POWER06, ICOSSSE06*, (pp. 119–124).

Venkatasubramanian, V., & Rengaswamy, R. (2003). A Review of Process Fault Detection and Diagnosis. *Quantitative Model-based Methods. Computers & Chemical Engineering, 27*(3), 293–311. doi:10.1016/S0098-1354(02)00160-6

Witczak, M. (2003). *Identification and Fault Detection of Non-Linear Dynamic Systems*. Poland: University of Zielona Gora Press.

Witczak, M. (2006). Advances in model-based fault diagnosis with evolutionary algorithms and neural networks. *International Journal of Applied Mathematics and Computer Science, 16*, 85–99.

Witczak, M. (2009). *Modelling and Estimation Strategies for Fault Diagnosis of Non-Linear Systems*. Berlin: Springer.

Witczak, M., Obuchowicz, A., & Korbicz, J. (2002). Genetic Programming Based Approaches to Identification and Fault Diagnosis of Non-linear Dynamic Systems. *International Journal of Control, 75*(13), 1012–1031. doi:10.1080/00207170210156224

## KEY TERMS AND DEFINITIONS

*The following key terms and definitions introduce a fault detection engineering interpretation of the terms usual in the evolutionary algorithm vocabulary. This should facilitate orientation in the presented engineering problem.*

**Sensor Discredibility:** A stage of the controlled variable sensor at which the sensor is not completely out of function yet, but its properties have gradually changed to the extent that the data provided by the sensor are so biased that the tolerated inaccuracy of the controlled variable is over-ranged and usually linked with possible side effects.

**Cost Function:** A criterion evaluating level of the congruence between the sensor model output and the real sensor output. In the fault detection terminology, the cost function corresponds to the term residuum (or residual function).

**Individual:** A vector of the sensor model parameters in a set of possible values (see population).

**Evolutionary Time:** The number assigned to steps in the sequence of iteration performed during a search for sensor model parameters based on evolutionary development.

**Population:** A set of the vectors of the sensor model parameters with which the sensor model has a chance to approach the minimum of the residual function.

**Population Size:** The number of the sensor model parameter vectors taken into the consideration in population.

**Chromosome:** A particular sensor model parameter vector (a term for individuals used in evolutionary terminology).

**Initial Annealing Temperature:** An initial algorithm parameter. Annealing temperature is used as a measure of evolutionary progress during the simulated annealing algorithm run.

# Chapter 4
# Soft Computing Techniques in Spatial Databases

**Markus Schneider**
*University of Florida, USA*

## ABSTRACT

*Spatial database systems and geographical information systems are currently only able to support geographical applications that deal with only crisp spatial objects, that is, objects whose extent, shape, and boundary are precisely determined. Examples are land parcels, school districts, and state territories. However, many new, emerging applications are interested in modeling and processing geographic data that are inherently characterized by spatial vagueness or spatial indeterminacy. Examples are air polluted areas, temperature zones, and lakes. These applications require novel concepts due to the lack of adequate approaches and systems. In this chapter, the authors show how soft computing techniques can provide a solution to this problem. They give an overview of two type systems or algebras that can be integrated into database systems and utilized for the modeling and handling of spatial vagueness. The first type system, called Vague Spatial Algebra (VASA), is based on well known, general, and exact models of crisp spatial data types and introduces vague points, vague lines, and vague regions. This enables an exact definition of the vague spatial data model since we can build it upon an already existing theory of spatial data types. The second type system, called Fuzzy Spatial Algebra (FUSA), leverages fuzzy set theory and fuzzy topology and introduces novel fuzzy spatial data types for fuzzy points, fuzzy lines, and fuzzy regions. This enables an even more fine-grained modeling of spatial objects that do not have sharp boundaries and interiors or whose boundaries and interiors cannot be precisely determined. This chapter provides a formal definition of the structure and semantics of both type systems. Further, the authors introduce spatial set operations for both algebras and obtain vague and fuzzy versions of geometric intersection, union, and difference. Finally, they describe how these data types can be embedded into extensible databases and show some example queries.*

DOI: 10.4018/978-1-60566-814-7.ch004

# INTRODUCTION

*Spatial database systems* (*SDBS*) are full-fledged database systems which, in addition to the functionality of standard database systems for alphanumeric data, provide special support for the storage, retrieval, management, and querying of spatial data, that is, objects in space. In particular, SDBS are used as the data management foundation of *Geographic Information Systems* (*GIS*). In the literature, the common consensus prevails that special data types are necessary to adequately model geometry and to efficiently represent geometric data in database systems. These data types are commonly denoted as *spatial data types* (Schneider 1997) such as *point*, *line*, and *region*. We speak of *spatial objects* as instances of these data types. So far, the mapping of spatial phenomena of the real world leads almost exclusively to precisely defined spatial objects. Spatial data modeling implicitly assumes that the positions of points, the locations and routes of lines, and the extent and hence the boundary of regions are precisely determined and universally recognized. This leads to *exact object models*. Examples are especially man-made spatial objects representing engineered artifacts (like monuments, highways, buildings, bridges) and predominantly immaterial spatial objects exerting social control (like countries, districts, and land parcels with their political, administrative, and cadastral boundaries). We denote this kind of entities as *crisp* or *determinate spatial objects*.

But for many geometric applications, the mapping into crisp spatial objects is an insufficient abstraction process since many geographic objects show the inherent feature of *spatial vagueness* or *spatial indeterminacy* (Burrough & Frank 1996). Current GIS and spatial database systems are not capable of supporting applications based on vague geometric data. In these applications, the positions of points are not exactly known, the locations and routes of lines are unclear, and regions do not have sharp boundaries, or their boundaries cannot be precisely determined. Examples are natural phenomena (like soil quality, vegetation, oceans, valleys, mountains, oil fields, biotopes, deserts, clouds, temperature zones, air pressure, sandbanks), cultural phenomena (like a Rhaeto-Romanic language speaking area) and social phenomena (like population density, unemployment rate, air pollution emission, terrorists' refuges and escape routes). We denote this kind of entities as *vague* or *indeterminate spatial objects*.

This chapter shows that and how different soft computing techniques can be leveraged to represent spatial vagueness. It gives an overview of two different type systems that can be integrated into database systems and whose types can be employed as attribute types in the same way as standard data types like *integer* or *string*. A fundamental design concept is that these new types are *not* represented through a database model (for example, relational, object-oriented, complex data model) but through *abstract data types* that encapsulate and hide the internal complexity of their values. This implies that a database model and its underlying theoretical framework (for example, relational database theory) does not have to be modified in any manner. The first type system, called *Vague Spatial Algebra* (*VASA*), is based on well known, general, and exact models of *crisp spatial data types* and introduces *vague points*, *vague lines*, and *vague regions*. This enables an exact definition of the vague spatial data model since we can build it upon an already existing theory of spatial data types. The second type system, called *Fuzzy Spatial Algebra* (*FUSA*), leverages fuzzy set theory and fuzzy topology and introduces novel *fuzzy spatial data types* for *fuzzy points*, *fuzzy lines*, and *fuzzy regions*. This enables an even more fine-grained modeling of spatial objects that do not have sharp boundaries and interiors or whose boundaries and interiors cannot be precisely determined.

The "Background" section discusses related work. The section "VASA: An Algebra for Vague Spatial Data in Databases" presents the Vague Spa-

*Figure 1. Examples of a simple point object (a), a simple line object (b), a simple region object (c), a complex point object (d), a complex line object (e), and a complex region object (f)*

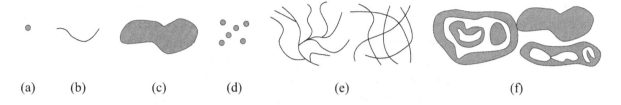

    (a)      (b)       (c)       (d)         (e)             (f)

tial Algebra, and the section "FUSA: An Algebra for Fuzzy Spatial Data in Databases" introduces the Fuzzy Spatial Algebra. We provide a formal definition of the structure and semantics of both type systems. Further, we introduce spatial set operations for them and thus obtain vague and fuzzy versions of the geometric intersection, union, and difference operations. Finally, the section "Querying with VASA and FUSA" describes how these data types can be embedded into extensible databases and their query languages, and shows some example queries. This chapter concludes with some future research directions and conclusions.

## BACKGROUND

We discuss related work that is relevant for the design and construction of VASA and FUSA. First we deal with crisp, determinate spatial data types and operations that serve as the basis of both algebras. Then we characterize spatial vagueness, give a classification of current models for representing spatial indeterminacy, and provide an overview of other models that are related to both algebras.

## Crisp Spatial Data Types and Operations

In the spatial database and GIS community, *spatial data types* like *point*, *line*, or *region* have found wide acceptance as fundamental abstractions for modeling the structure of geometric entities, their relationships, properties, and operations. They form the basis of a large number of data models and query languages for processing spatial data and have gained access into commercial software products. The literature distinguishes *simple* spatial data types (for example, Egenhofer 1994, Güting 1988) and *complex* spatial data types (for example, Clementini & Di Felice 1996a, Schneider 1997, Schneider & Behr 2006), depending on the spatial complexity they are able to model. Simple spatial data types (Figure 1(a)-(c)) only provide simple object structures like single points, continuous lines, and simple regions. However, from an application perspective, they are insufficient to cope with the variety and complexity of geographic reality. From a formal perspective, they are not closed under the geometric set operations *intersection*, *union*, and *difference*. Complex spatial data types (Figure 1(d)-(f)) solve these problems. They provide universal and versatile spatial objects with multiple components, permit regions with holes, that are closed under geometric set operations, and form the basis of our vague spatial data types.

## A Classification of Models for Vague Spatial Objects

So far, spatial data modeling has represented spatial objects as entities with sharply determined boundaries emphasizing abrupt changes of spatial phenomena. Hence, in the past, there has been a tendency to force geographical reality into determinate spatial objects. In practice, however, there is no apparent reason for the whole contour of a line or the boundary or interior of a region to be determinate. Numerous geographical application examples illustrate that the extent and the boundaries of spatial objects can be indeterminate. For instance, boundaries of geological, soil, and vegetation units are often crisp in some places and vague in others; concepts like the "Indian Ocean", "South England", or a biotope are intrinsically vague.

In the real, non-artifactual world, we can essentially find two categories of indeterminate boundaries: sharp boundaries whose position and shape are unknown or cannot be measured precisely, and boundaries which are not well defined or which are useless (for example, between a mountain and a valley). Spatial objects with indeterminate boundaries are difficult to represent and are so far not supported in spatial database systems and GIS. *Spatial vagueness* describes the feature of a spatial object that we cannot be sure whether certain components belong completely or partially to the object or not. According to the two categories of boundaries, mainly two kinds of spatial vagueness can be identified: spatial uncertainty and spatial fuzziness. *Spatial uncertainty* is traditionally equated with randomness and chance occurrence and relates either to a lack of knowledge about the position and shape of a spatial object with an existing, real boundary (*positional* uncertainty) or to the inability of measuring such an object precisely (*measurement* uncertainty). *Spatial fuzziness* is an intrinsic feature of a spatial object itself and describes the vagueness of such an object which certainly has an extent but which inherently cannot or does not have a precisely definable boundary.

At least four alternatives are proposed as general design methods: exact object models, fuzzy set-based models, probabilistic models, and rough set-based models.

**Exact object models** transfer data models, type systems, and concepts for spatial objects with

sharp boundaries to objects with indeterminate boundaries. A benefit of this approach is that existing definitions, techniques, data structures, algorithms, etc. need not be redeveloped but only modified and extended, or simply used. The approaches in Clementini & Di Felice (1996b), Clementini & Di Felice (2001), Cohn & Gotts (1996), and Schneider (1996) propose a *zone concept*. The central idea is to consider determined zones surrounding the indeterminate boundaries of a region (*broad boundaries*) and expressing its minimal and maximal extent. The zones serve as a description and separation of the space that certainly belongs to the region, that perhaps belongs to the region, and that is certainly outside. The approaches in Erwig & Schneider (1997) and Pauly & Schneider (2004), which contribute to the VASA approach, generalize these concepts and introduce *vague spatial data types* for *vague points*, *vague lines*, and *vague regions*. A vague spatial object is modeled as a pair of two meeting or disjoint crisp spatial objects. For example, a vague region is given as a pair of two meeting or disjoint crisp regions. The first object is the *kernel part* and models the part that definitely belongs to the vague spatial object. The second object is the *conjecture part* from which we can only assume that it or parts of it belong to the vague object. Designs of vague topological predicates, which are not discussed in this chapter, have been described in Clementini & Di Felice (1996b), Clementini & Di Felice (2001), Pauly & Schneider (2005a), Pauly & Schneider (2005b), and Pauly & Schneider (2006).

**Fuzzy set-based models** are based on *fuzzy set theory* (Zadeh 1965). It describes the *admission of the possibility* (given by a so-called *membership function*) that an individual is a member of a set or that a given statement is true. Hence, the vagueness represented by fuzziness is not the uncertainty of expectation. It is the vagueness resulting from the imprecision of meaning of a concept. Examples of fuzzy spatial objects include mountains, valleys, biotopes, and oceans, which cannot be rigorously bounded by a sharp line. The usefulness of fuzzy concepts in geoscience applications from a modeling standpoint has, for example, been demonstrated in Burrough, van Gaans & Macmillan (2000) for modeling geomorphological units, De Gruijter, Walvoort & Vangaans (1997), Lagacherie, Andrieux & Bouzigues (1996) for representing soil types and boundaries, Cheng, Molenaar & Lin (2001) for designing landscape objects, Brown (1998) for describing forest types, Hendricks Franssen, van Eijnsbergen & Stein (1997) for determining soil pollution classes in environmental applications, and Bogàrdi, Bárdossy & Duckstein (1990) for performing hydrological studies. Approaches nearer to computer science have been given by Burrough (1996) introducing fuzzy geographical objects for modeling natural objects with indeterminate boundaries, Dutta (1989, 1991) and Kollias & Voliotis (1991) dealing with qualitative spatial and temporal reasoning using fuzzy logic, Edwards (1994) and Wang & Hall (1996) dealing with fuzzy representations of geographical boundaries in GIS, Usery (1996) defining concepts like core and boundary of a fuzzy region, and Wang, Hall & Subaryono (1990) and Wang (1994) presenting a fuzzy query approach in order to introduce more natural language expressions into GIS user interfaces. Approaches that deal with the issue of representing, storing, retrieving, and querying fuzzy spatial objects in *fuzzy spatial databases* are rare. However, there is an increasing interest in applying fuzzy theory to spatial topics. Examples are given by Altman (1994) presenting fuzzy set theoretic approaches for handling imprecision in spatial analysis and introducing *fuzzy regions* in $N^2$, Schneider (1999) providing the foundation of FUSA in terms of *fuzzy spatial data types* for *fuzzy points*, *fuzzy lines*, and *fuzzy regions* together with some *fuzzy spatial operations*, Dilo, de By & Stein (2007) introducing a similar type system of fuzzy (called "vague") spatial data types with a more comprehensive set of operations, Schneider (2003) proposing a conceptual model and an

implementation model of fuzzy spatial objects that are not defined on the Euclidean plane but on a discrete geometric domain called *grid partition*, and Schneider (2000) presenting metric operations on fuzzy spatial objects like the area of a fuzzy region or the length of a fuzzy line. Different models of fuzzy topological predicates, which are not discussed in this chapter and which characterize the relative position of two fuzzy spatial objects towards each other, are discussed in Petry et al. (2002), Schneider (2001a, 2001b), Shi & Guo (1999), Tang & Kainz (2002), and Zhan (1997, 1998).

**Probabilistic models** are able to represent positional and measurement uncertainty. Their basis is *probability theory* which defines the grade of membership of an entity in a set by a statistically defined probability function and deals with the expectation of a future event, based on something known now. As examples of a large amount of literature, we mention the approaches in Blakemore (1984), Burrough (1996), Finn (1993), Shibasaki (1993), and Zinn, Bosch & Gertz (2007).

**Rough set-based models** are based on *rough set theory* (Pawlak 1982) and model vague spatial objects by a lower and an upper spatial approximation. As examples, Beaubouef, Ladner, & Petry (2004) and Worboys (1998) show how rough sets can be used for vague spatial data modeling.

## VASA: AN ALGEBRA FOR VAGUE SPATIAL DATA IN DATABASES

VASA comprises a set of *vague spatial data types* designed as abstract data types and equipped with a set of operations between these types. A few operations are applicable to several types and are thus overloaded. Due to space restrictions, regarding operations, we confine ourselves to geometric set operations. The VASA approach belongs to the class of exact models. One of its main benefits is that its formal framework is based on well known and general crisp spatial data types. That is, vague spatial data types and operations are based on their crisp counterparts and can be expressed by them so that we obtain *executable specifications*. These specifications can be directly used as implementations and minimize the needed implementation effort since available implementations of crisp spatial algebras can be utilized. Moving from an exact to a vague domain does not necessarily invalidate conventional (computational) geometry; in our case, it is merely an extension. Thus, VASA provides the advantage of conceptual simplicity, ease of understanding, ease of use, ease of implementation, and efficiency. However, VASA is conservative and restrictive in the sense that it makes only use of a three-valued (and not a multi-valued) logic with the values *true*, *false*, and *maybe*. Therefore, VASA cannot capture all potential applications dealing with indeterminate spatial data. For example, fuzzy approaches allow the distinction and consideration of different degrees of spatial vagueness due to their multi-valued logic. However, this requires more and especially precise knowledge about uncertainty distributions that is frequently not available.

First, we describe and illustrate our concept of vague spatial objects. Then we formally define *vague spatial data types* for *vague points*, *vague lines*, and *vague regions*. Next we motivate vague spatial operations, and finally provide the formal definition of vague spatial set operations.

## What are Vague Spatial Objects?

The central idea of *vague spatial objects* is to base their definition on already well defined, geometric modeling techniques. VASA leverages general exact object models incorporating the crisp spatial data types *point2D*, *line2D*, and *region2D*, as they have been reviewed before. We assume that these data types are closed under (appropriately defined) geometric union, intersection, and difference operations.

Vague spatial objects can, for example, represent the uncertainty about the precise paths or the spatial extent of phenomena in space; that is, objects can shrink and extend and hence have a minimal and maximal extent. An example is a lake whose water level depends on the degree of evaporation and on the amount of precipitation. High evaporation implies dry periods and thus a minimal water level. High precipitation entails rainy periods and thus a maximal water level. Islands in the lake are less flooded by water in dry periods and more flooded in rainy periods. If an island can never be completely flooded by water, it forms a "hole" in the lake. But if an island like a sandbank can be flooded completely, it belongs to the vague part of the lake. Hence, we have confident information about the minimal and maximal extent of a lake. But the actual extent of a lake, which is somewhere between these two extreme limits, is vague. Figure 2 illustrates this spatial constellation. Dark-gray shading shows areas that definitely belong to the lake. Light-gray shading indicates areas that perhaps belong to the lake. White color indicates areas that do definitely not belong to the lake.

As a further illustrating example, which we also use to introduce our terminology deployed in VASA, we consider a homeland security scenario. Secret services (should) have knowledge of the whereabouts of terrorists. For each terrorist, some of their refuges are precisely known; some others are assumed and thus only conjectures. We can model all these locations as a single *vague point* object where the precisely known locations are called the *kernel point* object and the assumed locations are denoted as the *conjecture point* object. Secret services are also interested in the routes a terrorist takes to move from one refuge to another. These routes can be modeled as a single *vague line* object. Some routes collected in a *kernel line* object have been identified with certainty. Other routes can only be assumed to be taken by a terrorist; they are gathered in a *con-*

*Figure 2. The extent of a lake depending on the degree of evaporation and on the amount of precipitation*

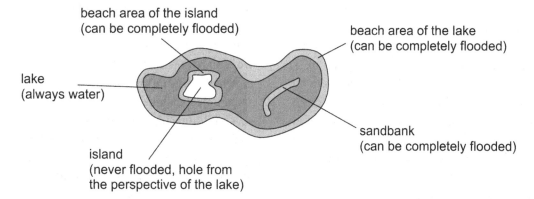

*Figure 3. Examples of a (complex) vague point object (a), a (complex) vague line object (b), and a (complex) vague region object (c). The term "complex" indicates that each collection of components forms a single vague spatial object*

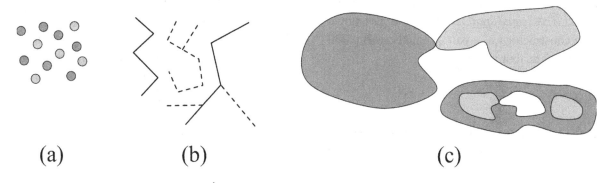

(a)          (b)                    (c)

*jecture line* object. Knowledge about areas of terroristic activities is also important for secret services. From some areas it is well known that a terrorist operates in them; we summarize them in a *kernel region* object. From other areas we can only assume that they are the target of terroristic activity; we denote them as a *conjecture region* object. Figure 3 gives some examples. Dark-gray shaded areas, straight curves, and dark-gray points indicate kernel parts. Areas with light-gray interiors, dashed lines, and light-gray points refer to conjecture parts. White areas describe exterior parts. In this sense, many application scenarios can be found that could leverage this concept of vague spatial objects.

## A Generic Definition of Vague Spatial Data Types

Based on the motivation in the previous subsection, we now give formal definitions of *vague spatial data types*. An interesting observation is that these definitions can be given in a generic manner in the sense that type-specific considerations and distinctions are unnecessary. For the definition of vague points, vague lines, and vague regions we make use of the data types *point2D* for (complex) crisp points, *line2D* for (complex) crisp lines, and *region2D* for (complex) crisp regions, which are defined as special point sets (Schneider & Behr 2006) and closed under the geometric set operations $\oplus$ (*union*), $\otimes$ (*intersection*), $\ominus$ (*difference*), and ~ (*complement*). Given a type α ∈ {*point2D*, *line2D*, *region2D*}, the signatures of the operations are ⊕, ⊗, ⊖: α × α → α and ~: α → α. Each type α together with the operations ⊕ and ⊗ forms a Boolean algebra. We denote the identity of ⊗ by **1**, which corresponds to IR². We represent the identity of ⊕ by **0**, which corresponds to the empty spatial object (empty point set ∅). The use of an exact model for constructing vague spatial data types leads to the benefit that existing definitions, techniques, data structures, and algorithms need not be redeveloped but can simply be used or in the worst case slightly modified or extended as necessary. This leads to the following generic definition of vague spatial data types:

**Definition 1.** Let α ∈ {*point2D*, *line2D*, *region2D*}, and let $A°$ denote the interior of a spatial object $A$. A *vague spatial data type* is given by a type constructor $v$ as a pair of equal crisp spatial data types α, that is,

$$v(α) = α × α$$

such that for $w = (w_k, w_c) ∈ v(α)$ and an auxiliary function *points*: $v(α) → 2^{IR×IR}$, which yields the (unknown) point set of a vague spatial object, holds:

1. $w_k° ∩ w_c° = ∅$
2. $w_k ⊆ points(w) ⊆ w_k ⊕ w_c$
3. $points(w) ∈ α$

We call $w ∈ v(α)$ a (two-dimensional) vague spatial object with **kernel part** $w_k$ and **conjecture part** $w_c$. Further, we call $wo := ~(w_k ⊕ w_c)$ the *outside part* of $w$. If α = *point2D* holds, an element of $v(point2D) = point2D × point2D =: vpoint2D$ is called a *vague point* object. Correspondingly, an element of $v(line2D) =: vline2D$ is called a *vague line* object, and an element of $v(region2D) =: vregion2D$ is called a *vague region* object. If $w_k = **0**$ and $w_c = **0**$, we call $w = (**0**, **0**)$ the *empty vague spatial object*.

Syntactically, a vague spatial object is described as a pair of crisp complex spatial objects of the same type. Semantically, the following constraints have to be satisfied. In condition (i) we require that the kernel part and the conjecture part have disjoint interiors since a point of the same object cannot belong to both parts.

Condition (ii) makes two statements. First, it states that the kernel part $w_k$ describes the determinate component of the vague spatial object, that is, the component that definitely and always belongs to the vague spatial object. Second, it states that the conjecture part $w_c$ describes the vague component of the vague spatial object, that is, the component from which we cannot say with any certainty whether it or pieces of it belong to the vague spatial object or not. *Maybe* the conjecture part or pieces of it belong to the vague object; *maybe* this is not the case. We could also say that this is *unknown*. Another, related view is to regard $w_k$ as a *lower* (minimal, guaranteed) *approximation* of $w$ and $w_k ⊕ w_c$ as an *upper* (maximally possible, speculative) *approximation* of $w$. This brings us near to a rough set theoretical view.

Condition (iii) requires that even if we do not know the exact point set of $w$, the actual point set *points*($w$) may not be arbitrary but must be compatible to type α. A direct conclusion from this requirement is that $points(w) ⊖ w_k ∈ α$ since $w_k ∈ α$.

Finally, we give the definition of the *characteristic function* of a vague spatial object. This function decides about existence or non-existence of a point in a vague spatial object.

**Definition 2.** The *characteristic function* $χ_w(p)$ for a point $p ∈ IR²$ and a vague spatial object $w ∈ v(α)$ is defined as shown in Box 1.

*Box 1.*

$$χ_w(p) = \begin{cases} \{1\} & \text{if } p ∈ w_k \\ \{0\} & \text{if } p ∈ IR² - (w_k ∪ w_c) \\ \{0, 1\} & \text{if } p ∈ w_c - w_k \end{cases}$$

*Figure 4. Example scenarios with a focus on the intersection between two kernel parts (a), a kernel part and a conjecture part (b), and two conjecture parts (c) of two vague regions*

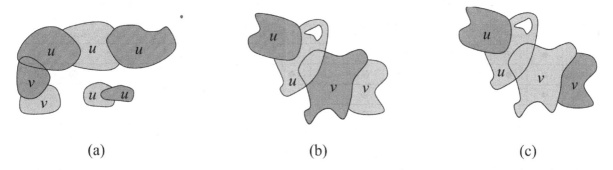

(a)                                        (b)                                        (c)

Note in Box 1. the deliberate use of set-theoretic operations. Especially the common boundary points of $w_k$ and $w_c$ ($w_k \cup w_c \neq \emptyset$) are mapped to 1. Further, we obtain that $\chi_w(p) = 1$ for all $p \in points(w)$.

## What are Vague Spatial Operations?

Unsurprisingly, *vague spatial operations* are spatial operations operating on vague spatial objects. That is, these operations take vague spatial objects as arguments and yield vague objects as a result. It is common consensus in the spatial database field that a spatial algebra is never complete since always new operations can be designed and added to it. Hence, we take an extensible approach and assume that VASA will be extended if necessary.

We now briefly present two real life applications and motivate the use of vague spatial operations. The first example is taken from the animal kingdom. We view the living spaces of different animal species and distinguish kernel parts where they mainly live and conjecture parts like peripheral areas or corridors where they in particular hunt for food or which they cross in order to migrate from one kernel part to another one. We consider the following example queries regarding their living spaces: (1) Find the animal species that (partially) share their living spaces. (2) Determine hunters that penetrate into the living space of other animals. (3) Ascertain the areas

where two species can only meet by accident. For two animal species *u* and *v*, the interesting situations for the queries are illustrated in Figure 4. The common task of all three queries is to compute the common living spaces of two animal species, that is, to calculate the intersection of two vague regions. But the nature of the intersection is different in all three cases. The first query asks for an intersection between two kernel parts (Figure 4(a)). The (non-empty) result is definitely a kernel part. The second query amounts to an intersection between a kernel part and a conjecture part but not between two kernel parts (Figure 4(b)). Since a conjecture part is involved that describes a vague part, we cannot make a definite statement whether this intersection belongs to the kernel part. It only remains to regard this intersection as a conjecture part. The third query exclusively asks for an intersection between two conjecture parts (Figure 4(c)); it is definitely a conjecture part. In total, we see that the "strength of intersection" decreases from left to right in Figure 4. Last but not least, we mention that the intersection of an exterior part with anything else is an exterior part.

The second example refers to our homeland security scenario from before. Taking into account spatial vagueness, we are able to pose interesting queries. We can ask for the locations where any two terrorists have definitely, perhaps, and/or never taken the same refuge. We can determine those terrorists that definitely, perhaps, and/or

Table 1. Components resulting from intersecting kernel parts, conjecture parts, and outside parts of two vague spatial objects with each other for the four vague geometric set operations vunion (a), vintersection (b), vdifference (c), and vcomplement (d)

| (a)vunion |  |  |  | (b)vintersection |  |  |  | (c)vdifference |  |  |  | (d)vcomplement |  |  |
|---|---|---|---|---|---|---|---|---|---|---|---|---|---|---|
|  | ● | ⊙ | ○ |  | ● | ⊙ | ○ |  | ● | ⊙ | ○ | ● | ⊙ | ○ |
| ● | ● | ● | ● | ● | ● | ⊙ | ○ | ● | ○ | ⊙ | ● | ○ | ⊙ | ● |
| ⊙ | ● | ⊙ | ⊙ | ⊙ | ⊙ | ⊙ | ○ | ⊙ | ○ | ⊙ | ⊙ |  |  |  |
| ○ | ● | ⊙ | ○ | ○ | ○ | ○ | ○ | ○ | ○ | ○ | ○ |  |  |  |

never operated in the same area. We can compute the locations where routes taken by different terrorists definitely, perhaps, and/or never crossed each other. We can find out the sphere of a number of terrorists on the basis of their locations as a ***vague convex hull***.

Many further application scenarios and queries are conceivable. Vague concepts offer a greater flexibility and more nuances for modeling and computing properties of spatial phenomena in the real world than determinate "black or white" concepts do. Still, vague concepts comprise the modeling power of determinate concepts as a special case.

## A Generic Definition of Vague Spatial Operations

Due to space limitations, we confine our consideration of vague spatial operations to the vague geometric set operations *vunion*, *vintersection*, and *vdifference* that have all the same signature $v(\alpha) \times v(\alpha) \to v(\alpha)$ with $\alpha \in \{point, line, region\}$ in a type-independent and thus generic manner. In addition, we define the operation *vcomplement* with the signature $v(\alpha) \to v(\alpha)$. In order to define them for two vague spatial objects $u$ and $w$, it is helpful to consider meaningful relationships between the kernel part, the conjecture part, and the outside part of $u$ and $w$ (Table 1). For each operation we give a table where a column/row labeled by ●, ⊙, or ○ denotes the kernel part, conjecture part, or outside part of $u$ and $w$ respectively. Each entry of the table denotes a possible combination, i.e., non-empty intersection, of kernel parts, conjecture parts, and outside parts of both objects, and the label in each entry specifies whether the corresponding intersection belongs to the kernel part, conjecture part, or outside part of the operation's result object.

Regarding the *union* operation (Table 1(a)), the intersection component of a kernel part with any other part belongs to the kernel part of the resulting vague spatial object $r$ since the union operation asks for the definite membership in either part only. Likewise, the intersection component of the two conjecture parts or the intersection component of a conjecture part with an outside part belongs to the conjecture part of $r$, and only the intersection component of the two outside parts belongs to the outside part of $r$. Regarding the *intersection* operation (Table 1(b)), the intersection component of an outside part with any other part belongs to the outside part of $r$ because intersection requires at least potential membership in both parts. The kernel part of $r$ only contains components which definitely belong to the kernel parts of both operand objects. The intersection component of both conjecture parts or of a conjecture part and a kernel part contribute to the conjecture part of $r$. Obviously, the *complement* (Table 1(d)) of the kernel part is the outside part, and vice versa. With respect to the conjecture part, anything inside the vague part of an object might or might not belong to the object; hence, the result is the conjecture part itself. The *differ-*

*ence* (Table 1(c)) between any two parts is equal to the intersection of the first part with the complement of the second part.

Table 1 enables us now to formally define the four operations. An interesting aspect is that these definitions can be based solely on already known crisp geometric set operations on well-understood exact spatial objects. Hence, we are able to give *executable specifications* for the vague geometric set operations. That is, by employing the geometric set operations of an available crisp spatial algebra, we can directly *execute* the vague geometric set operations without being forced to design and implement new algorithms for them.

**Definition 3.** Let $u, w \in v(\alpha)$, and let $u_k$ and $w_k$ denote their kernel parts and $u_c$ and $w_c$ their conjecture parts. We define:

1.  *u vunion w*$:= (u_k \oplus w_k, (u_c \oplus w_c) \ominus (u_k \oplus w_k))$
2.  *u vintersection w*$:= (u_k \otimes w_k, (u_c \otimes w_c) \oplus (u_k \otimes w_c) \oplus (u_c \otimes w_k))$
3.  *u vdifference w*$:= (u_k \otimes (\sim(w_k \oplus w_c)), (u_c \otimes w_c) \oplus (u_k \otimes w_c) \oplus (u_c \otimes (\sim(w_k \oplus w_c))))$
4.  *vcomplement u*$:= (\sim(u_k \oplus u_c), u_c)$

If $u$ and $v$ are vague spatial objects with empty conjecture parts, that is, $u_c = 0$ and $w_c = 0$, the operations behave exactly like their crisp counterparts.

One can show (not done here) that the specifications of Definition 3 fit to the specifications in Table 1.

## FUSA: AN ALGEBRA FOR FUZZY SPATIAL DATA IN DATABASES

FUSA comprises a set of *fuzzy spatial data types* designed as abstract data types and equipped with a set of operations between these types. The FUSA approach belongs to the class of fuzzy set-based models. The formal framework of the algebra design is based on *fuzzy set theory* (Zadeh 1965, Buckley & Eslami 2002) and *fuzzy topology* (Liu

& Luo 1997). FUSA makes use of a multi-valued logic and has the great advantage of providing a fine-grained view and distinction of spatial indeterminacy. However, this requires much more and especially precise data and knowledge about uncertainty distributions.

First, we describe and illustrate our concept of fuzzy spatial objects. Then we formally define *fuzzy spatial data types* for *fuzzy points*, *fuzzy lines*, and *fuzzy regions*. Finally we provides the formal definition of fuzzy spatial set operations.

## What are Fuzzy Spatial Objects?

Points are the simplest geometric abstraction. They are the atoms, that is, the elements, of the Euclidean space $IR^2$. Each element of a crisp point set $X$ of $IR^2$ belongs definitely and totally to this set. For each point of $IR^2$, we can definitely say whether it belongs to $X$ or not. A crisp point object, as it has been defined, for example, in Schneider 1997 and Schneider & Behr 2006, includes a finite set of points in order to ensure the closure of set operations. In the fuzzy domain, a fuzzy point set $\tilde{X}$ also represents a subset of $IR^2$ but each point of $\tilde{X}$ only has a certain partial membership in this set. It can also partially belong to another fuzzy set, that is, multiple set membership is possible. For example, if we consider an air-polluted area (which is a fuzzy region), then each point of this area is fuzzy since the concentration of air pollution at this point is not 100 percent. That is, the degree of membership of this fuzzy point in the air-polluted area is less than 1 and larger than 0. Fuzzy points can also arise as the result of two fuzzy lines.

Lines are the one-dimensional, geometric abstraction for linear features like rivers, boundaries, and transportation routes. Each crisp line is a subset of the Euclidean plane $IR^2$ with particular properties. Each element of a single crisp line is a crisp point that definitely and totally belongs to the line. A crisp line object (Schneider

*Figure 5. Example of a fuzzy region consisting of two fuzzy faces as components*

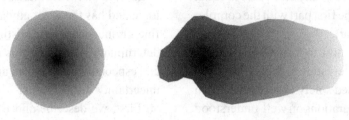

1997; Schneider & Behr 2006) includes a finite set of blocks. Each block consists of a finite set of simple lines (curves) such that each pair of simple lines is either disjoint or meets in a common end point. Fuzzy lines are supposed to adopt the fundamental structure of crisp lines. That is, a fuzzy line $\tilde{X}$ has the same linear geometry as a crisp line and is hence a subset of $IR^2$; however, each point of $\tilde{X}$ may only be to some degree a member of $\tilde{X}$. For example, the pollution of a river can be represented by the line geometry of the river where each point represents the degree or concentration of pollution at that location. The concentration is larger than 0 for all points of the fuzzy line but usually different at different locations.

A crisp region is defined as a set of disjoint, connected areal components, called *faces*, possibly with disjoint *holes* (Clementini & Di Felice 1996a, Schneider 1997, Schneider & Behr 2006) in the Euclidean space $IR^2$. This model has the nice property that it is closed under (appropriately defined) geometric union, intersection, and difference operations. Hence, we would like to transfer the structural definition of crisp regions (that is, the component view) to fuzzy regions and allow partial membership of a point in a region. There are at least three possible, related interpretations for a point in a fuzzy region. First, this situation may be interpreted as the *degree of belonging* to which that point is *inside* or *part of* some areal feature. Consider the transition between a mountain and a valley and the problem to decide which points have to be assigned to the valley and

which points to the mountain. Obviously, there is no strict boundary between them, and it seems to be more appropriate to model the transition by partial and multiple membership. Second, this situation may indicate the *degree of compatibility* of the individual point with the attribute or concept represented by the fuzzy region. An example are "warm areas" where we must decide for each point whether and to which grade it corresponds to the concept "warm". Third, this situation may be viewed as the *degree of concentration* of some attribute associated with the fuzzy region at the particular point.

An example is air pollution where we can assume the highest concentration at power stations, for instance, and lower concentrations with increasing distance from them. The distribution of attribute values within a region and transitions between different regions may be *smooth* or *continuous*. Application examples are air pollution, temperature zones, magnetic fields, storm intensity, and sun insolation. Figure 5 demonstrates a possible visualization of a fuzzy region object which could model the expansion of air pollution caused by two nearby power stations. The left image shows a radial expansion of the first power station where the degree of pollution concentrates in the center (darker locations) and decreases with increasing distance from the power station (brighter locations). The right image shows the distribution of air pollution of the second power station that is surrounded by high mountains to the north, the south, and the west. Hence, the pollution cannot escape in these directions and finds its way out of the valley in eastern direction.

## A Formal Definition of Fuzzy Spatial Data Types

We now provide formal definitions of data types for fuzzy points, fuzzy lines, and fuzzy regions. We assume that the reader is familiar with the fundamentals of fuzzy set theory and fuzzy topology. We begin with a definition of a single fuzzy point that can be used as a foundation for a definition of the type *fpoint*. This definition views a fuzzy point as a point in the two-dimensional Euclidean space with a membership value greater than 0, since 0 documents the non-existence of a point.

**Definition 4.** A *fuzzy point* $\tilde{p}$ at $(a, b)$ in $IR^2$, written $\tilde{p}(a, b)$, is a fuzzy singleton in $IR^2$ defined in box 2.

In Box 2 $0 < m \leq 1$. Point $\tilde{p}$ is said to have *support* $supp(\tilde{p}(a, b)) = \{(a, b)\}$ and value $m$. Let $P_f$ be the set of all fuzzy points. $P_f$ is a proper superset of $P_c$, the set of all crisp points in $IR^2$. For $\tilde{p} = p = (a, b) \in P_c$, we obtain $\mu_{p\sim(a,b)}(x, y) = \chi p(x, y) = 1$, if $(x, y) = (a, b)$, and 0 otherwise.

Next, we define three *geometric primitives* on fuzzy points.

**Definition 5.** Let $\tilde{p}(a, b)$, $\tilde{q}(c, d) \in P_f$ with $a, b, c, d \in IR$. Then

1. $\tilde{p}(a, b) = \tilde{q}(c, d) :\Leftrightarrow a = c \wedge b = d \wedge \mu_{p\sim(a,b)}$ $= \mu_{q\sim(a,b)}$

2. $\tilde{p}(a, b) \neq \tilde{q}(c, d) :\Leftrightarrow \neg(\tilde{p}(a, b) = \tilde{q}(c, d))$

3. $\tilde{p}(a, b)$ and $\tilde{q}(c, d)$ are *disjoint* $:\Leftrightarrow supp(\tilde{p}(a, b)) \cap supp(\tilde{q}(c, d)) = \emptyset$

*Box 2.*

$$\mu_{p\sim(a,b)}(x, y) = \begin{cases} m \text{ if } (x, y) = (a, b) \\ 0 \text{ otherwise} \end{cases}$$

In contrast to crisp points, for fuzzy points we also have a predicate for disjointedness.

**Definition 6.** The fuzzy spatial data type *fpoint* is defined as

$$fpoint = \{Q \subseteq P_f \mid \forall \ \tilde{p}, \tilde{q} \equiv Q : \tilde{p}(a, b) \text{ and } \tilde{q} \\ (c, d) \text{ are } disjoint \wedge Q \text{ is finite}\}$$

Disjointedness of the single fuzzy points of a fuzzy point object is required since the membership degree of each single fuzzy point should be unique.

Next, we specify the fuzzy spatial data type *fline* for **fuzzy lines**. For that, we first introduce a *simple* fuzzy line as a continuous curve with smooth transitions of membership grades between neighboring points of the line (Figure 6(a)). We assume a total order on $IR^2$ which is given by the lexicographic order "<" on the coordinates (first $x$, then $y$) of the points of $IR^2$.

**Definition 7.** The membership function of a *simple fuzzy line* $\tilde{l}$ is defined by

- $\mu_{\tilde{l}} : f_{\tilde{l}} \rightarrow [0, 1]$ with $f_{\tilde{l}} : [0, 1] \rightarrow IR^2$ such that
  1. $\mu_{\tilde{l}}$ is continuous
  2. $f_{\tilde{l}}$ is continuous
  3. $\forall a, b \in {]}0, 1[ : a \neq b \Rightarrow f_{\tilde{l}}(a) \neq f_{\tilde{l}}(b)$
  4. $\forall a \in \{0, 1\} \ \forall b \in {]}0, 1[ : f_{\tilde{l}}(a) \neq f_{\tilde{l}}(b)$
  5. $f_{\tilde{l}}(0) < f_{\tilde{l}}(1) \vee (f_{\tilde{l}}(0) = f_{\tilde{l}}(1) \wedge \forall a \in {]}0, 1[ : f_{\tilde{l}}(0) < f_{\tilde{l}}(a))$

Function $f_{\tilde{l}}$ on its own models a continuous, simple *crisp* line (a *curve*). The points $f_{\tilde{l}}(0)$ and $f_{\tilde{l}}(1)$ are called the *endpoints* of *f*. The definition allows loops ($f_{\tilde{l}}(0) = f_{\tilde{l}}(1)$) but prohibits equality of interior points and thus self-intersections (condition (iii)). The reason is that self-intersec-

*Figure 6. Example of a simple fuzzy line (a) and a (complex) fuzzy line (b). Fuzziness is indicated by shading. The complex fuzzy line consists of two fuzzy blocks that are made up of seven fuzzy simple lines*

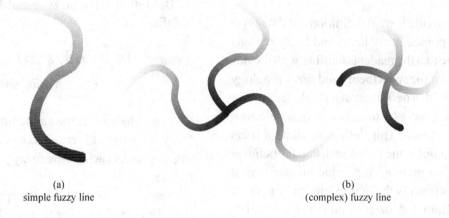

(a)
simple fuzzy line

(b)
(complex) fuzzy line

tions do not occur in spatial reality; hence, our model excludes them. Condition (iv) disallows the equality of an interior point with an end point. Condition (v) requires that in a *closed simple line* $f_{\tilde{l}}(0)$ must be the leftmost point, that is, the smallest point with respect to the lexicographic order "<". The main reason of the conditions (iii) to (v) is to ensure the uniqueness of representation of a simple fuzzy line. For example, consider a simple line that intersects itself one time and is not closed. An alternative to model this configuration is to model the intersection point explicitly with three incident simple lines from which one line forms a closed loop. This alternative concept leads to a unique representation.

All conditions together define a fuzzy line $\tilde{l}$ as the fuzzy point set $\tilde{l} = \{(p, \mu_{\tilde{l}}(p)) \mid p \in f_{\tilde{l}}([0, 1])\}$.

**Definition 8.** Let $SL_f$ be the set of fuzzy simple lines, and let $\tilde{l}_1, \tilde{l}_2 \in SL_f$. Then we define:

1. $\tilde{l}_1, \tilde{l}_2$ are *disjoint*: $\Leftrightarrow supp(\tilde{l}_1) \cap supp(\tilde{l}_2) = \emptyset$
2. $\tilde{l}_1, \tilde{l}_2$ *meet*: $\Leftrightarrow f_{\tilde{l}_1}(]0, 1[) \cap f_{\tilde{l}_2}(]0, 1[) = \emptyset \wedge \{f_{\tilde{l}_1}(0), f_{\tilde{l}_1}(1)\} \cap \{f_{\tilde{l}_2}(0), f_{\tilde{l}_2}(1)\} \neq \emptyset$

**Definition 9.** A *fuzzy block* $\tilde{b}$ is the fuzzy set $\tilde{b} = \bigcup_{i=1}^{n} \tilde{l}_i$ such that[1]

1. $n \in N, 1 \leq i \leq n$: $\tilde{l}_i \in SL_f$
2. $\forall 1 \leq i < j \leq n$: $f_{\tilde{l}_i}(]0, 1[) \cap f_{\tilde{l}_j}(]0, 1[) = \emptyset$
3. $\forall 1 \leq i < j \leq n$: $\{f_{\tilde{l}_i}(0), f_{\tilde{l}_i}(1)\} \cap f_{\tilde{l}_j}(]0, 1[) = \emptyset \wedge f_{\tilde{l}_i}(]0, 1[) \cap \{f_{\tilde{l}_j}(0), f_{\tilde{l}_j}(1)\} = \emptyset$
4. $\forall 1 \leq i \leq n \, \exists 1 \leq j \leq n, j \neq i$: $f_{\tilde{l}_i}(0), f_{\tilde{l}_i}(1)\} \cap \{f_{\tilde{l}_j}(0), f_{\tilde{l}_j}(1)\} \neq \emptyset$
5. $\forall 1 \leq i, j \leq n \, \forall a, k \in \{0, 1\}$ let $V_{\tilde{l}_i}^a = \{(j, k) \mid f_{\tilde{l}_i}(a) = f_{\tilde{l}_j}(k)\}$. Then we require: $\forall 1 \leq i \leq n \, \forall a \in \{0, 1\}$: $(|V_{\tilde{l}_i}^a| = 1) \vee (|V_{\tilde{l}_i}^a| > 2)$
6. $\forall 1 \leq i \leq n \, \forall a \in \{0, 1\} \, \forall (j, k) \in V_{\tilde{l}_i}^a$: $\mu_{\tilde{l}_i}(f_{\tilde{l}_i}(a)) = \mu_{\tilde{l}_j}(f_{\tilde{l}_j}(k))$

Intuitively, a fuzzy block is a maximal, connected fuzzy line component (Figure 6(b)). Condition (i) states that a fuzzy block consists of a finite set of fuzzy simple lines. Condition (ii) requires that the elements of a fuzzy block do not intersect or overlap within their interior. Moreover,

*Figure 7. Example of a fuzzy set that is not fuzzy region due to lower-dimensional, geometric anomalies like cuts, punctures, and dangling lines*

they may not be touched within their interior by an endpoint of another element (condition (iii)). The main reason for both conditions is again their uniqueness of representation. Condition (iv) ensures the property of connectivity of a fuzzy block; isolated fuzzy simple lines are disallowed. Condition (v) expresses that each endpoint of an element of $\tilde{b}$ must belong to exactly one or more than two incident elements of $\tilde{b}$ (note that always $(i, a) \in V_{\tilde{l}_i}^a$). This condition supports the requirement

of "maximal elements" and hence achieves uniqueness of representation. Condition (vi) requires that the membership values of more than two elements of $\tilde{b}$ with a common end point must have the same membership value; otherwise we get a contradiction saying that a point of a fuzzy block has more than one different membership value.

**Definition 10.** Let $B_f$ be the set of fuzzy blocks over $SL_f$. The disjointedness of any two fuzzy blocks $\tilde{b}_1$, $\tilde{b}_2 \in B_f$ is defined as follows:

$\tilde{b}_1$ and $\tilde{b}_2$ are *disjoint*: $\Leftrightarrow supp(\tilde{b}_1) \cap supp(\tilde{b}_2) = \emptyset$

We are now able to define the fuzzy spatial data type *fline* for **fuzzy line**s in Definition 11 and give an example of a fuzzy line object in Figure 6(b).

**Definition 11.** The fuzzy spatial data type *fline* is defined as

$$fline = \{ \bigcup_{i=1}^{n} \tilde{b}_i \mid n \in \mathbb{N} \land \forall 1 \leq i \leq n: \tilde{b}_i \in B_f \land$$
$$\forall 1 \leq i < j \leq n: \tilde{b}_i \text{ and } \tilde{b}_j \text{ are } disjoint\}$$

Finally, we specify the fuzzy spatial data type *fregion* for **fuzzy regions**. Since our objective is to model two-dimensional fuzzy areal objects for spatial applications, we consider a fuzzy topology T on the Euclidean plane IR². In this spatial context, we denote the elements of T as *fuzzy point sets*. The membership function for a fuzzy point set $\tilde{A}$ in the plane is then described by $\mu_{\tilde{A}}$: IR² → [0, 1]. From an application point of view, there are two observations that prevent a definition of a fuzzy region simply as a fuzzy point set.

The first observation refers to a necessary *regularization* of fuzzy point sets. The first reason for this measure is that fuzzy (as well as crisp) regions that actually appear in spatial applications in most cases cannot be just modeled as arbitrary point sets but have to be represented as point sets that do not have "geometric anomalies" (Figure 7) and that are in a certain sense *regular*. Geometric anomalies relate to isolated or dangling line or point features and missing lines and points in the form of cuts and punctures. Spatial phenomena with such degeneracies never appear as entities in reality. The second reason is that, from a data type point of view, we are interested in fuzzy spatial data types that satisfy closure properties for (appropriately defined) geometric union, intersection, and difference.

We are, of course, confronted with the same problem in the crisp case where the problem can be avoided by the concept of *regularity* (Tilove 1980; Schneider 1997). It turns out to be useful to appropriately transfer this concept to the fuzzy case.

**Definition 12.** Let $\tilde{A}$ be a fuzzy set of a fuzzy topological space (IR$^2$, T). Then $\tilde{A}$ is called a *regular open fuzzy set* if $\tilde{A} = int_T(cl_T(\tilde{A}))$. Whereas crisp regions are usually modeled as **regular closed crisp sets**, we will use **regular open fuzzy sets** due to their vagueness and their usual lack of boundaries. Regular open fuzzy sets avoid the aforementioned geometric anomalies, too. Since application examples show that fuzzy regions can also be partially bounded, we admit *partial boundaries* with a crisp or fuzzy character and call them *frontiers*.

**Definition 13.** The *frontier* of a fuzzy set is defined as

$$frontier_T (\tilde{A}):= \{((x, y), \mu_{\tilde{A}}(x, y)) \mid (x, y) \in supp(\tilde{A}) - supp(int_T (\tilde{A}))\}$$

The term $supp(\tilde{A}) - supp(int_T (\tilde{A}))$ determines the crisp locations of all fuzzy points of $\tilde{A}$ that are not interior points. However, these locations do not necessarily all belong to the boundary of $\tilde{A}$ since $\tilde{A}$ has not been constrained so far. This is done in the following definition.

**Definition 14.** A fuzzy set $\tilde{A}$ is called a *spatially regular fuzzy set* if, and only if,

1. $int_T (\tilde{A})$ is a regular open fuzzy set
2. $frontier_T (\tilde{A}) \subseteq frontier_T (cl_T (int_T (\tilde{A})))$
3. $frontier_T (\tilde{A})$ is a partition of $n \in N$ connected boundary parts (fuzzy sets)

Not every set $\tilde{A}$ is a spatially regular fuzzy set. Therefore, condition (i) ensures that the interior of $\tilde{A}$ is without any geometric anomalies. The other two conditions arrange for a correct (partial) boundary if it exists. Condition (ii) works as follows: On the right side of "⊆", the set $\tilde{A}' = cl_T (int_T$

$(\tilde{A}))$ is a *regular closed fuzzy set*, that is, the interior of $\tilde{A}$ is complemented by its boundary without any geometric anomalies. Hence, the *frontier*$_T$ operator applied to $\tilde{A}'$ yields the boundary of $\tilde{A}'$. The condition now requires that the frontier of $\tilde{A}$ is a subset of the frontier of $\tilde{A}'$ and does not contain other fuzzy points. Condition (iii) states that the frontier of $\tilde{A}$ has to consist of a finite number of connected pieces due to the "finite component assumption" explained before. Infinitely many boundary pieces cannot be represented in an implementation.

From the definition of *frontier*$_T$, we can conclude that $frontier_T(\tilde{A}) = \emptyset$ if $\tilde{A}$ is regular open. We will base our definition of fuzzy regions on spatially regular fuzzy sets and define a *regularization* function $reg_f$ which associates the interior of a fuzzy set $\tilde{A}$ with its corresponding regular open fuzzy set and which restricts the partial boundary of $\tilde{A}$ (if it exists at all) to a part of the boundary of the corresponding regular closed fuzzy set of $\tilde{A}$.

**Definition 15.** The *fuzzy regularization function* $reg_f$ applied to a fuzzy set $\tilde{A}$ is defined as

$$reg_f (\tilde{A}) = int_T (cl_T (\tilde{A})) \cup (frontier_T(\tilde{A}) \cap frontier_T(cl_T (int_T (\tilde{A}))))$$

The different components of the regularization process work as follows: the *interior* operator $int_T$ eliminates dangling point and line features since their interior is empty. The *closure* operator $cl_T$ removes cuts and punctures by appropriately adding points. Furthermore, the *closure* operator introduces a fuzzy boundary (similar to a crisp boundary in the ordinary point-set topological sense) separating the points of a closed set from its exterior. The operator *frontier*$_T$ supports the restriction of the boundary.

The second observation is that, according to the application cases shown before, the mapping $\mu_{\tilde{A}}$ itself may not be arbitrary but must take into account the intrinsic smoothness of fuzzy regions. This property can be modeled by the well known mathematical concept of *continuity*. Here, we employ the concept of a piecewise continuous function for modeling the smooth membership distribution in a single fuzzy face. A function is *piecewise continuous* if it is made of a finite number of continuous pieces. Hence, it has only a finite number of *discontinuities* (*continuity gaps*), and its left and right limits are defined at each discontinuity. The only possible kinds of discontinuities for a piecewise continuous function are removable and step discontinuities. A *removable discontinuity* represent a hole in the function graph. It can be repaired by filling in a single point. A *step discontinuity* (also called *semi-continuity*) is a location in the function graph where the graph steps or jumps from one connected piece of the graph to another. Formally, it is a discontinuity for which the limits from the left and right both exist but are not equal to each other.

We are now able to give the definition of the fuzzy spatial data type *fregion* for **fuzzy regions**.

**Definition 16.** Let *SRFS* be the set of spatially regular fuzzy sets. The fuzzy spatial data type *fregion* is defined as

- *fregion* = { $\tilde{R} \in SRFS$ |
    1. $\tilde{R} = \bigcup_{i=1}^{n} \tilde{R}_i$, $n \in \mathrm{N}$
    2. $\forall 1 \leq i \leq n$: $R_i$ is a connected component (*fuzzy face*)
    3. $\mu_{\tilde{R}} = \bigcup_{i=1}^{n} \mu_{\tilde{R}_i}$
    4. $\forall 1 \leq i \leq n$: $\mu_{\tilde{R}_i}$ is a piecewise continuous function}

Since different connected components of a set are disjoint (except for single common boundary points perhaps), the fuzzy faces of a fuzzy region object are disjoint too.

## Fuzzy Spatial Set Operations

The **fuzzy spatial set operation**s *funion*, *fintersection*, and *fdifference* have all the same signature

$\alpha \times \alpha \rightarrow \alpha$ with $\alpha \in$ {*fpoint, fline, fregion*}. In addition, we define the operation *fcomplement* with the signature $\alpha \rightarrow \alpha$. The definition of these operations for $\alpha =$ *fpoint* corresponds to the ones on fuzzy sets.

**Definition 17.** Let $\tilde{A}$, $\tilde{B} \in$ *fpoint*. Then

1. $\tilde{A}$ *funion* $\tilde{B} := \tilde{A} \cup \tilde{B} = \{((x, y), \mu_{\tilde{A} \cup \tilde{B}}((x, y))) \mid (x, y) \in \mathrm{R}^2 \wedge \mu_{\tilde{A} \cup \tilde{B}}((x, y)) = \max(\mu_{\tilde{A}}((x, y)), \mu_{\tilde{B}}((x, y)))\}$

2. $\tilde{A}$ *fintersection* $\tilde{B} := \tilde{A} \cap \tilde{B} = \{((x, y), \mu((x, y))) \mid (x, y) \in \mathrm{R}^2 \wedge \mu((x, y)) = \min(\mu_{\tilde{A}}((x, y)), \mu_{\tilde{B}}((x, y)))\}$

3. $\tilde{A}$ *fdifference* $\tilde{B} := \tilde{A} - \tilde{B} = \tilde{A} \cap \neg \tilde{B}$

4. *fcomplement* $\tilde{A} := \neg \tilde{A} = \{((x, y), \mu_{\neg \tilde{A}}((x, y))) \mid (x, y) \in \mathrm{R}^2 \wedge \mu_{\neg \tilde{A}}((x, y)) = 1 - \mu_{\tilde{A}}((x, y))\}$

These operations are defined in a similar manner for $\alpha =$ *fline*. However, since the result of such an operation can consist of linear and punctual parts, the punctual parts have to be removed by a corresponding regularization function.

For $\alpha =$ *fregion*, we first, informally and without proof, make some statements about set operations on regular open fuzzy sets. The intersection of two regular open fuzzy sets is regular open. The union, difference, and complement of two regular open fuzzy sets are not necessarily regular open since they can produce anomalies. Correspondingly, this also holds for spatially regular fuzzy sets. Hence, we introduce *regularized set operations* on spatially regular fuzzy sets that preserve regularity.

**Definition 18.** Let $\tilde{A}$, $\tilde{B} \in$ *fregion*, and let $a \dot{-} b = a - b$ for $a \geq b$ and $a \dot{-} b = 0$ otherwise ($a$, $b \in \mathbb{R}_0^+$). Then we define the following *regularized set operations*:

1. $\tilde{A} \cup_r \tilde{B} := reg_f(\tilde{A} \cup \tilde{B})$
2. $\tilde{A} \cap_r \tilde{B} := reg_f(\tilde{A} \cap \tilde{B})$

3.  $\tilde{A} -_r \tilde{B} := reg_f(\{((x,y), \mu_{\tilde{A}-_r\tilde{B}}((x,y))) \mid (x,y)$

$\in supp(\tilde{A}) \wedge \mu_{\tilde{A}-_r\tilde{B}}((x,y)) = \mu_{\tilde{A}}((x,y)) \dot{-} \mu_{\tilde{B}}$

$((x,y))\})$

4.  $\neg_r \tilde{A} := reg_f(\neg \tilde{A})$

Note that we have changed the meaning of difference, that is, $\tilde{A} -_r \tilde{B} \neq \tilde{A} \cap_r \neg \tilde{B}$, since the right side of the inequality is not meaningful in the spatial context. Regular open fuzzy sets, spatially regular fuzzy sets, and regularized set operations express a natural formalization of the desired closure properties of fuzzy geometric set operations.

## Querying with VASA and FUSA

The design of the data types provided by VASA and FUSA as abstract data types whose internal structure is hidden from the user enables us to embed these types as attribute types in all known database models (for example, relational, object-oriented, object-relational, complex models). Information about objects of these types can only be obtained by high-level operations and predicates and not by direct access to object components. Assuming an available implementation, we look at two example queries. Note that the query capabilities are restricted since we have not presented the full algebras with all operations and especially predicates.

Our first scenario makes use of VASA and assumes an ecological database with the following relations:

- weather(climate: *string*; area: *vregion*)
- soil(quality: *string*, area: *vregion*)

The relation *weather* has a column named *area* containing vague region values for various climatic conditions given by the column *climate*. The relation *soil* describes the soil quality for certain regions.

The query considered is supposed to find out all regions of bad ecological conditions, that is, all locations where a lack of water or a bad soil quality is a hindrance for cultivation.

- **select vunion**(dry area, bad soil) **as** bad region
- **from select vsum**(area) **as** dry area **from** weather **where** climate = "dry"; **select vsum**(area) **as** bad soil **from** soil **where** quality = "bad"

In the *from* clause, the function *vsum* is a *spatial aggregation* function that here computes the geometric union of a collection of selected vague point objects of the column *area*. We obtain two temporary relations that contain the aggregated areas of dry climate and bad soil quality respectively. Each relation contains a single tuple with a single attribute value of type *vregion*. In the *select* clause, we compute the union of the two attribute values of both tuples and obtain a result relation with a single attribute *bad region* of type *vregion* and a single tuple.

Our second scenario makes use of FUSA and takes an example from the animal kingdom. Information about animals species and their habitats is assumed to be stored in the following relation:

- animal(name: *string*, habitat: *fregion*)

The fact that the habitat of an animal is modeled as a fuzzy region indicates that the extent of such a habitat is not clearly known; it is fuzzy. We consider the query that asks about the common living space of each pair of animal species. For this purpose, we use the special fuzzy modifier *at all* that represents the existential modifier and checks whether a predicate like *overlaps* can be fulfilled to any extent.

- **select** A.name, B.name, **fintersection**(A. habitat; B.habitat)

- **from** animals A, animals B
- **where** A.habitat **at all overlaps** B.habitat

## FUTURE RESEARCH DIRECTIONS

Future research will first have to focus on an extension and completion of the available models VASA for vague spatial objects and FUSA for fuzzy spatial objects. This refers to comprehensive collections of vague and fuzzy spatial operations and predicates. In terms of predicates, especially vague and fuzzy topological and directional relationships are of interest.

Second, an interesting question is how VASA and especially FUSA can be implemented. While we can implement VASA on available software implementations of crisp spatial data types, the implementation of FUSA seems to be more difficult since the membership values within a fuzzy spatial object can change. For example, if we consider a point in a fuzzy region and a small circle around it, it could be that all points in the circle have a different membership value. Since the number of these points is infinite, this leads to a collision with the finiteness of computers. Appropriate finite approximations have to be found that enable us to represent such objects.

Third, VASA and FUSA as type systems have to be integrated into extensible database systems to make their functionality available to the user.

Fourth, a vague spatial query language for VASA and a fuzzy spatial query language for FUSA have to be designed and embedded into database systems.

## CONCLUSION

In this chapter, we have demonstrated how two different soft computing techniques with different expressiveness can be leveraged for spatial data handling in the context of spatial databases and Geographic Information Systems. Two type systems or algebras named Vague Spatial Algebra (VASA) and Fuzzy Spatial Algebra (FUSA) have been sketched whose types are modeled as abstract data types and can be integrated as attribute data types in any (extensible) database system. The focus of this chapter has been on the design of the data types. The description of spatial operations and predicates as well as implementation issues have been neglected due to space limitations. However, references given below will lead the reader to the respective literature.

## ACKNOWLEDGMENT

This work was partially supported by the National Science Foundation under grant number NSF-CAREER-IIS-0347574.

## REFERENCES

Altman, D. (1994). Fuzzy Set Theoretic Approaches for Handling Imprecision in Spatial Analysis. *International Journal of Geographical Information Systems, 8*(3), 271–289. doi:10.1080/02693799408902000

Beaubouef, T., Ladner, R., & Petry, F. (2004). Rough Set Spatial Data Modeling for Data Mining. *International Journal of Geographical Information Science, 19*, 567–584.

Blakemore, M. (1984). Generalization and Error in Spatial Databases. *Cartographica, 21*(2/3), 131–139.

Bogàrdi, I., Bárdossy, A., & Duckstein, L. (1990). Risk Management for Groundwater Contamination: Fuzzy Set Approach. In Khanpilvardi, R., & Gooch, T. (Eds.), *Optimizing the Resources for Water Management* (pp. 442–448). ASCE.

Brown, D. G. (1998). Mapping Historical Forest Types in Baraga County Michigan, USA as Fuzzy Sets. *Plant Ecology, 134*, 97–111. doi:10.1023/A:1009796502293

Buckley, J. J., & Eslami, E. (2002). *An Introduction to Fuzzy Logic and Fuzzy Sets*. Advances in Soft Computing. Physica-Verlag.

Burrough, P. A. (1996). Natural Objects with Indeterminate Boundaries. In Burrough, P. A., & Frank, A. U. (Eds.), *Geographic Objects with Indeterminate Boundaries* (pp. 3–28). Boca Raton, FL: Taylor & Francis.

Burrough, P. A., van Gaans, P. F. M., & Macmillan, R. A. (2000). High-Resolution Landform Classification Using Fuzzy k-Means. *Fuzzy Sets and Systems, 113*, 37–52. doi:10.1016/S0165-0114(99)00011-1

Cheng, T., Molenaar, M., & Lin, H. (2001). Formalizing Fuzzy Objects from Uncertain Classification Results. *International Journal of Geographical Information Science, 15*, 27–42. doi:10.1080/13658810010004689

Clementini, E., & Di Felice, P. (1996a). A Model for Representing Topological Relationships between Complex Geometric Features in Spatial Databases. *Information Sciences, 90*(1-4), 121–136. doi:10.1016/0020-0255(95)00289-8

Clementini, E., & Di Felice, P. (1996b). An Algebraic Model for Spatial Objects with Indeterminate Boundaries. In Burrough, P. A., & Frank, A. U. (Eds.), *Geographic Objects with Indeterminate Boundaries* (pp. 153–169). Boca Raton, FL: Taylor & Francis.

Clementini, E., & Di Felice, P. (2001). A Spatial Model for Complex Objects with a Broad Boundary Supporting Queries on Uncertain Data. *Data & Knowledge Engineering, 37*, 285–305. doi:10.1016/S0169-023X(01)00010-6

Cohn, A. G., & Gotts, N. M. (1996). The 'Egg-Yolk' Representation of Regions with Indeterminate Boundaries. In Burrough, P. A., & Frank, A. U. (Eds.), *Geographic Objects with Indeterminate Boundaries* (pp. 171–187). Boca Raton, FL: Taylor & Francis.

De Gruijter, J., Walvoort, D., & Vangaans, P. (1997). Continuous Soil Maps-a Fuzzy Set Approach to Bridge the Gap between Aggregation Levels of Process and Distribution Models. *Geoderma, 77*, 169–195. doi:10.1016/S0016-7061(97)00021-9

Dilo, A., de By, R. A., & Stein, A. (2007). A System of Types and Operators for Handling Vague Spatial Objects. *International Journal of Geographical Information Science, 21*(4), 397–426. doi:10.1080/13658810601037096

Dutta, S. (1989). Qualitative Spatial Reasoning: A Semi-Quantitative Approach Using Fuzzy Logic. In *1st International Symposium on the Design and Implementation of Large Spatial Databases* (LNCS 409, pp. 345-364). Berlin: Springer Verlag.

Dutta, S. (1991). Topological Constraints: A Representational Framework for Approximate Spatial and Temporal Reasoning. In *2nd International Symposium on the Design and Implementation of Large Spatial Databases* (LNCS 525, pp. 161-180). Berlin: Springer Verlag.

Edwards, G. (1994). Characterizing and Maintaining Polygons with Fuzzy Boundaries in GIS. In *6th International Symposium on Spatial Data Handling* (pp. 223-239).

Egenhofer, M. J. (1994). Spatial SQL: A Query and Presentation Language. *IEEE Transactions on Knowledge and Data Engineering, 6*(1), 86–94. doi:10.1109/69.273029

Erwig, M., & Schneider, M. (1997). Vague Regions. In 5th *International Symposium on Advances in Spatial Databases,* (LNCS 1262, pp. 298-320). Berlin: Springer Verlag.

Finn, J. T. (1993). Use of the Average Mutual Information Index in Evaluating Classification Error and Consistency. *Int. Journal of Geographical Information Systems, 7*(4), 349–366. doi:10.1080/02693799308901966

Güting, R. H. (1988). Geo-Relational Algebra: A Model and Query Language for Geometric Database Systems. In *International Conference on Extending Database Technology*, (pp. 506-527).

Hendricks Franssen, H., van Eijnsbergen, A., & Stein, A. (1997). Use of Spatial Prediction Techniques and Fuzzy Classification for Mapping Soil Pollutants. *Geoderma, 77*, 243–262. doi:10.1016/S0016-7061(97)00024-4

Kollias, V. J., & Voliotis, A. (1991). Fuzzy Reasoning in the Development of Geographical Information Systems. *International Journal of Geographical Information Systems, 5*(2), 209–223. doi:10.1080/02693799108927844

Lagacherie, P., Andrieux, P., & Bouzigues, R. (1996). Fuzziness and Uncertainty of Soil Boundaries: From Reality to Coding in GIS. In Burrough, P. A., & Frank, A. U. (Eds.), *Geographic Objects with Indeterminate Boundaries* (pp. 275–286). Boca Raton, FL: Taylor & Francis.

Liu, Y.-M., & Luo, M.-K. (1997). *Fuzzy Topology. Advances in Fuzzy Systems — Applications and Theory* (*Vol. 9*). Singapore: World Scientific.

Pauly, A., & Schneider, M. (2004). Vague Spatial Data Types, Set Operations, and Predicates. In 8th *East-European Conference on Advances in Databases and Information Systems,* (pp. 379-392).

Pauly, A., & Schneider, M. (2005a). Identifying Topological Predicates for Vague Spatial Objects. In *20th ACM Symposium on Applied Computing*, (pp. 587-591).

Pauly, A., & Schneider, M. (2005b). Topological Predicates between Vague Spatial Objects. In *9th International Symposium on Spatial and Temporal Databases,* (pp. 418-432).

Pauly, A., & Schneider, M. (2006). Topological Reasoning for Identifying a Complete Set of Topological Predicates between Vague Spatial Objects. In *19th International FLAIRS Conference* (pp. 731-736).

Pawlak, Z. (1982). Rough Sets. Basic Notions. *International Journal of Computer and Information Science, 11*, 341–356. doi:10.1007/BF01001956

Petry, F. E., Cobb, M., Ali, D., Angryk, R., Paprzycki, M., Rahimi, S., et al. (2002). Fuzzy Spatial Relationships and Mobile Agent Technology in Geospatial Information Systems. In P. Matsakis & L.M. Sztandera (Eds.), Soft Computing in Defining Spatial Relations (pp. 123-155), volume in series: Soft Computing. Heidelberg, Germany: Physica-Verlag.

Schneider, M. (1996). Modelling Spatial Objects with Undetermined Boundaries Using the Realm/ROSE Approach. In Burrough, P. A., & Frank, A. U. (Eds.), *Geographic Objects with Indeterminate Boundaries* (pp. 141–152). Boca Raton, FL: Taylor & Francis.

Schneider, M. (1997). *Spatial Data Types for Database Systems — Finite Resolution Geometry for Geographic Information Systems*, (LNCS 1288). Berlin: Springer-Verlag.

Schneider, M. (1999). Uncertainty Management for Spatial Data in Databases: Fuzzy Spatial Data Types. In *6th International Symposium on Advances in Spatial Databases* (LNCS 1651, pp. 330-351). Berlin: Springer Verlag.

Schneider, M. (2000). Metric Operations on Fuzzy Spatial Objects in Databases. In *8th ACM Symposium on Geographic Information Systems* (pp. 21-26). New York: ACM Press.

Schneider, M. (2001a). A Design of Topological Predicates for Complex Crisp and Fuzzy Regions. In *20th International Conference on Conceptual Modeling,* (pp. 103-116).

Schneider, M. (2001b). Fuzzy Topological Predicates, Their Properties, and Their Integration into Query Languages. In *9th ACM Symposium on Geographic Information Systems* (pp. 9-14). New York: ACM Press.

Schneider, M. (2003). Design and Implementation of Finite Resolution Crisp and Fuzzy Spatial Objects. *Data & Knowledge Engineering, 44*(1), 81–108. doi:10.1016/S0169-023X(02)00131-3

Schneider, M., & Behr, T. (2006). Topological Relationships between Complex Spatial Objects. *ACM Transactions on Database Systems, 31*(1), 39–81. doi:10.1145/1132863.1132865

Shi, W., & Guo, W. (1999). Modeling Topological Relationships of Spatial Objects with Uncertainties. In *International Symposium on Spatial Data Quality* (pp. 487-495).

Shibasaki, R. (1993). *A Framework for Handling Geometric Data with Positional Uncertainty in a GIS Environment. GIS: Technology and Applications* (pp. 21–35). Singapore: World Scientific.

Tang, X., & Kainz, W. (2002). Analysis of Topological Relations between Fuzzy Regions in a General Fuzzy Topological Space. In *Joint International Symposium on Geospatial Theory, Processing and Application.*

Tilove, R. B. (1980). Set Membership Classification: A Unified Approach to Geometric Intersection Problems. *IEEE Transactions on Computers, C-29,* 874–883. doi:10.1109/TC.1980.1675470

Usery, E. L. (1996). A Conceptual Framework and Fuzzy Set Implementation for Geographic Features. In Burrough, P. A., & Frank, A. U. (Eds.), *Geographic Objects with Indeterminate Boundaries* (pp. 71–85). Boca Raton, FL: Taylor & Francis.

Wang, F. (1994). Towards a Natural Language User Interface: An Approach of Fuzzy Query. *International Journal of Geographical Information Systems, 8*(2), 143–162. doi:10.1080/02693799408901991

Wang, F., & Hall, G. B., & Subaryono. (1990). Fuzzy Information Representation and Processing in Conventional GIS Software: Database Design and Application. *International Journal of Geographical Information Systems, 4*(3), 261–283. doi:10.1080/02693799008941546

Wang, F., & Hall, G. B. (1996). Fuzzy Representation of Geographical Boundaries in GIS. *International Journal of Geographical Information Systems, 10*(5), 573–590.

Worboys, M. (1998). Computation with Imprecise Geospatial Data. *Computers, Environment and Urban Systems, 22*(2), 85–106. doi:10.1016/S0198-9715(98)00023-4

Zadeh, L. A. (1965). Fuzzy Sets. *Information and Control, 8,* 338–353. doi:10.1016/S0019-9958(65)90241-X

Zhan, B. F. (1997). Topological Relations between Fuzzy Regions. In *ACM Symposium on Applied Computing* (pp. 192-196). New York: ACM Press.

Zhan, B. F. (1998). Approximate Analysis of Topological Relations between Geographic Regions with Indeterminate Boundaries. *Soft Computing, 2,* 28–34. doi:10.1007/s005000050032

Zhan, B. F. (1998). Approximate Analysis of Topological Relations between Geographic Regions with Indeterminate Boundaries. *Soft Computing, 2,* 28–34. doi:10.1007/s005000050032

Zinn, D., Bosch, J., & Gertz, M. (2007). Modeling and Querying Vague Spatial Objects Using Shapelets. *International Conference on Very Large Data Bases,* (pp. 567-578).

## KEY TERMS AND DEFINITIONS

**Abstract Data Type:** A data type whose internals are hidden and whose components are only accessible though high-level methods.

**Fuzzy Spatial Data Type:** A spatial data type either for fuzzy points, fuzzy lines, or fuzzy regions that are based on an infinite logic

**Spatial Data Type:** A data type like for representing geometries like points, lines, and regions in a database system.

**Spatial Vagueness:** The feature of spatial objects that their boundary and/or interior is vague or indeterminate and cannot be precisely described.

**Vague Spatial Algebra:** (VASA): A type system that comprises vague spatial data types, vague spatial operations, and vague spatial predicates.

**Vague Spatial Data Type:** A spatial data type either for vague points, vague lines, or vague regions that are based on a three-valued logic with the truth values *true*, *false*, and *maybe*.

## ENDNOTE

[1] The application of a function $f$ to a set $X$ of values is defined as $f(X) = \{f(x) \mid x \in X\}$.

# Chapter 5
# Type-2 Fuzzy Interface for Artificial Neural Network

**Priti Srinivas Sajja**
*Sardar Patel University, India*

## ABSTRACT

*Artificial Neural Network (ANN) based systems are bio-inspired mechanisms for intelligent decision support with capabilities to learn generalized knowledge from the large amount of data and offers high degree of self-learning. However, the knowledge in such ANN system is stored in the generalized connection between neurons in implicit fashion, which does not help in providing proper explanation and reasoning to users of the system and results in low level of user friendliness. On the other hand, fuzzy systems are very user friendly, represent knowledge in highly readable form and provide friendly justification to users as knowledge is stored explicitly in the system. Type-2 fuzzy systems are one step ahead while computing with words in comparison to typical fuzzy systems. This chapter introduces a generic framework of type-2 fuzzy interface to an ANN system for course selection process. Resulting neuro-fuzzy system offers advantages of self-learning and implicit knowledge representation along with the utmost user friendliness and explicit justification.*

## INTRODUCTION

Artificial Neural Network (ANN) is a step towards simulation of human brain, where knowledge is stored in the interconnected processing elements called neurons. ANN systems have been widely used for classification, pattern recognition, forecasting, and learning. These systems can learn automatically from large number of data sets and hence overcome need of documenting knowledge manually. One of the major limitations of ANN is that, they operate on crisp data. Preparation of such large crisp data sets is a tedious and time consuming procedure, which can be avoided by facilitating an interface that directly inputs the environmental fuzzy data. This chapter describes design of a fuzzy interface system which enables users to input environmental

DOI: 10.4018/978-1-60566-814-7.ch005

linguistic values of the input parameters to a base ANN instead of crisp data.

The fuzzy interface system proposed here is based on type-2 fuzzy sets. Traditional fuzzy logic i.e. type-1 fuzzy logic operates on fuzzy membership functions, mapping fuzzy to crisp values whereas type-2 fuzzy system has grades of membership that are fuzzy. There are some perceptions which can not be modeled by traditional mathematical techniques, not even with traditional fuzzy logic. The type-2 fuzzy membership grades can be used to model perceptions like health, comfort, etc. more effectively than the type-1 fuzzy sets. Type-2 fuzzy system offers significant improvement on type-1 fuzzy system where data is more imprecise or vague. Second section of the chapter covers introduction of fuzzy logic, fuzzy membership functions, and type-1 and type-2 fuzzy systems for the benefit of novice readers to provide conceptual clarity. The second section elucidates related work in fuzzy systems and introduces type-2 fuzzy logic. Third section presents the concept of ANN and discusses structure, advantages and applications of ANN. Fourth section elaborates need of hybridization of ANN and Fuzzy Logic (FL) and discusses the approaches available for modeling of neuro-fuzzy system. To facilitate fuzzy vague linguistic parameters to a base ANN, a general structure of the interface with detailed methodology of the type-2 fuzzy interface is discussed in the fifth section.

Sixth section illustrates an experimental prototype with fuzzy interface and base ANN. ANN system used in the experiment is meant for course selection process assisting users in taking effective and timely decision while selecting suitable course. The course selection process is basically an advisory and counseling type of system, in which critical decisions are to be taken in timely and effective fashion. There are plenty of students and professionals who select study courses every academic year. However, the relevant data are not available in a desired manner to come to a generalized conclusion. That is, from the bulk of

domain transactions it is difficult to derive generalized logic and rules which aid future decision making and provide necessary guidelines to the candidate users/students. The situation becomes more complex as every academic year results in increased number of institutes and novel study courses at national and international level. The ANN used here as a base system help in generalizing logic from the large training sets and help in determining broad aptitude category of the user. The decision is further fine tuned by the fuzzy interface system. The type-2 fuzzy interface is used to feed the input to the base ANN system. That is, the system operates with fuzzy inputs and output advices in user friendly (fuzzy) fashion. In the sixth section the ANN system design, heuristic used for the hidden layers, and learning paradigm are discussed in detail for the application of course selection. Apart from fuzzy interface system design and ANN methodology, the input and output design along with a few sample screens from the experiment are also shown in sixth section.

The next section discusses the output and findings of the experiment to develop the neuro-fuzzy system at the Department of Computer Science, Sardar Patel University, India. The concluding section discusses future enhancement and enlists different multi disciplinary application areas where such interfaces are critically required and increases the effectiveness of the system to which the interface is integrated.

## FUZZY LOGIC AND FUZZY INTERFACE SYSTEM

### Fuzzy Logic

**Fuzzy logic**, in comparison to traditional crisp logic, is a flexible machine-learning technique. Crisp logic is a bi-valued logic representing two possible solution states, often represented by yes/no, 0/1, black/white, or true/false. Fuzzy logic is a multi-valued logic that attempts at mimicking the logic of human thoughts. Human logic is flexible and less rigid as compared to crisp logic. Fuzzy logic allows intermediate values to be defined between the two usual extreme points.

Fuzzy logic is based on fuzzy set introduced by Zadeh (1965) to represent/manipulate data and information having non-statistical uncertainties and vagueness. According to Zadeh (1965), some of the essential characteristics of fuzzy logic relate to the following:

- Exact reasoning is viewed as a limiting case of approximate reasoning.
- Everything is a matter of degree.
- Knowledge is interpreted as a collection of elastic or, equivalent, fuzzy constraint on a collection of variables.
- Inference is viewed as a process of propagating elastic constraints.
- Any logical system can be fuzzified.

Humans routinely and subconsciously place things into classes whose meaning and significance are well understood but whose boundaries are not well defined.

*Hot season, large car, young boy,* and *rich people* are few such examples. With crisp logic, it is difficult to represent notions like *rather warm* or *pretty cold* mathematically and have them processed by machines. Such linguistic terms help in applying a more humanlike way of thinking to the programming of computers. Using fuzzy logic makes the system more flexible, transparent, and user-friendly. Fuzzy logic is based on a fuzzy set. An element of a fuzzy set is a number, which defines the degree to which it is contained in a set.

Fuzzy sets offer an opportunity for a member to possess flexible belongingness into the set, which is measured in a degree. That means member X is either belongs to a typical crisp set C or does not. On the other hand, member X belongs to the fuzzy set F partially with a specific truth value (degree). Consider an example of set of young persons, say 'Y'. If person X is 30 years old, then

*Figure 1. Fuzzy sets and fuzzy membership*

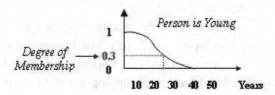

he is a member of set of young person 'Y' with the degree 0.65. If the person X is 18 years old then the degree is 0.8. This situation is demonstrated in Figure 1.

The fuzzy set can be defined as follows:

Let $X$ be a nonempty set. A fuzzy set A in $X$ is characterized by its **membership function** $\mu A: X \to [0, 1]$, where $\mu A(x)$ is the degree of membership of element $x$ in fuzzy set A for each $x \in X$.

Here, $X$ is treated as a universe of discourse, which is a set with a reference to a context that contains all possible elements of the set. It is obvious that all the elements posses the same properties. For example, all numbers, all books in a library, and all cars in the world.

The function which maps fuzzy linguistic value to an appropriate crisp value between the interval [0,1] is called a fuzzy membership function. Usage of such membership functions facilitate FL systems to represent and reason with linguistic type of knowledge. Fuzzy logic enables expression of knowledge in verbal form and provides means to manipulate it using a computer. The curve representing the mathematical function in Figure 1 is nothing but a membership function that determines the degree of belonging of member $x$ to the fuzzy set of Young people. Mathematically, it is represented as follows:

$$\mu A: X \to [0, 1],$$

where X is the set of all possible temperatures and $\mu A$ is the fuzzy membership function.

The membership function shown in Figure 1 yields value $\mu A(x) = \mu A(27^0\ C) = 0.3$.

The process of transforming crisp input values into linguistic values is called '**fuzzification**'. It has two major steps as follows:

- **Step 1:** Input values are translated into linguistic concepts, which are represented by fuzzy sets.
- **Step 2:** Membership functions are applied to the measurements and the degree of membership is determined.

**Defuzzification** converts the fuzzy value into a "crisp" value. It is the process of producing a quantifiable result from the fuzzy linguistic variable used. Defuzzification is necessary because a fuzzy set might not translate directly into crisp values. Example methods of defuzzification are:

1. *Max-Membership Method:* This method chooses the element with the maximum value.
2. *Centroid Method:* The centroid defuzzification method finds the "center" point of the targeted fuzzy region by calculating the weighted mean of the output fuzzy region.
3. *Weighted Average Method:* The weighted average method assigns weights to each membership function in the output by its respective maximum membership value.

On the crisp set, operations like intersection, union and complement are well defined. On the fuzzy sets also, such operations are possible. Zadeh (1965) suggested the minimum operator for the intersection and the maximum operator for the union of two fuzzy sets. These operators are defined as follows:

The intersection of A and B is defined as $(A \cap B)(x) = \min\{A(x), B(x)\} = A(x) \cap B(x)$, for $x \in X$.

The union of A and B is defined as $(A \, 4 \, B)(x) = \max\{A(x), B(x)\} = A(x) \, 4 \, B(x)$, for $x \in X$.

The complement of a fuzzy set A is defined as $(\sim A)(x) = 1 - A(x)$, for $x \in X$.

Let A and B be fuzzy sets on a classical set $X$. A and B are said to be equal, denoted A = B, if A _ B and B _ A. That is A = B if and only if $A(x) = B(x)$, for $x \in X$.

It is obvious that these operators coincide with the crisp unification, and crisp intersection functions if we consider the specific membership degrees 0 and 1.

## Fuzzy Inference System

**Fuzzy inference system** provides a powerful framework for reasoning with imprecise and uncertain information. The inference procedures are known as Generalized Modus Ponens (GMP) and Generalized Modus Tollens (GMT).

GMP is described as follows:

Given: X is A, then Y is B

X is A'

One may conclude that Y is B'.

GMT is described as follows:

Given: X is A, then Y is B

Y is B'

One may conclude that X is A'.

The power and flexibility of simple 'if… then…else' logic rules are enhanced by adding the linguistic parameter in it. Fuzzy rules are usually expressed in the form:

*IF variable IS set THEN action.*

Some examples are as follows:

- IF temperature IS very cold THEN stop Air Conditioner

*Figure 2. Triangular MFs for T2FS*

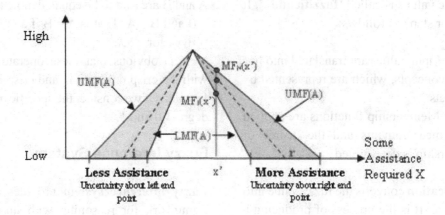

- IF temperature IS hot THEN start Air Conditioner

The AND, OR, and NOT operators (also known as Zadeh's operators) are also applicable on these rules.

A fuzzy rule-based system (FRBS) is an application of fuzzy logic to rule based systems. Generally, two models are available: the Mamdani model (Mamdani, 1974) and the Takagi-Sugeno-Kang model (Takagi & Sugeno, 1985). Mamdani (1974) was the first to model Zadeh's (1965) fuzzy logic concept in a structure, resulting in a fuzzy rule-based system for a control problem.

## Type-2 Fuzzy Systems

Most of the Type-1 Fuzzy Systems (T1 FS) have less customized mechanisms to deal with vague parameters. According to John and Coupland (2007), **Type-2 Fuzzy Systems** (T2 FS) takes a step closer to the goal of 'computing with words' or the use of computers to represent human perception. Zadeh (1999) presents that perceptions of size, health, and comfort cannot be modeled by traditional mathematical techniques and fuzzy logic is more suitable for the same. Since T2 FS are based on fuzzy sets whose membership grades are non-crisp fuzzy membership functions, they

can model perceptions more effectively than the T1 FS (John & Coupland 2007; Mendal, 2007). That is, a T1 FS has a grade of membership that is crisp; whereas a T2 FS has grades of membership that are fuzzy. Such sets are useful when it is difficult to model the exact membership function. For more imprecise or vague data, T2 FS offers a significant improvement on T1 FS fuzzy sets.

To improve understanding of perceptions in more human friendly way, a fuzzy system needs some measures of dispersion to capture more about linguistic uncertainties than just a single **Membership Function** (MF). T1 FS deals with a single MF. A T2 FS provides these measures of dispersion (Mendal, 2007). For example, suppose the variable of interest is '*assistance required*' to complete the course, denoted by x, where x∈[0, 10], where 0 means no assistance required and 10 means maximum assistance required. The term 'some assistance required' can be interpreted in different ways to different people, which is denoted in Figure 2 (Sajja, 2008).

In Figure 2, X-Axis denotes the assistance required to learn or revise subject topics. In the type-1 fuzzy sets the X-Axis shows the universe of discourse showing crisp units. In this example, it may be number of hours required to complete the subject revision. Here, as stated earlier, the type-2 fuzzy system maps fuzzy values to fuzzy values for human like decision processing, hence, the X-Axis has the linguistic fuzzy values like 'less assistance required' and 'more assistance required'. The region 'r' on X-Axis represents uncertainty about the right point and the region 'l' on X-Axis represent uncertainty about the left point. The Y-Axis represents the fuzzy degrees as usual. Precisely the uncertainty region is specified by lower and upper membership functions as LMF(A) and UMF(A). For each data point, x, there can be many different membership functions within the interval. From the Figure 2, it is clear that, if all uncertainty disappears, the T2 FS lowers to a T1 FS.

**Defuzzification** can be performed by taking the average as follows (Mendal, 2007):

1.  Compute the centroid of each rule consequent. Call it $c^l$ (I=1,…,M).
2.  Compute the firing level for each fired rule. Call it $f^l$ (I=1,…,M).
3.  Compute $y_{cos}(x) = \sum c^l f^l / \sum f^l$.

Use of T2 FS is promoted by Gorzalczany (1987), Turksen (1995; 2002), Schwartz (1985), and Klir and Folger (1988) after its introduction by Zadeh (1975). Later on Karnik and Mendal (1998; 2001) gave a complete description of the fuzzy inference process. With this background and work of Wu and Mendal (2002) on minimax uncertainty fast execution of type-2 fuzzy systems, complex and multi-variable control application begun. Figueroa, Soriano, and Rojas (2005) used a type-2 interval control for non-autonomous robots for a robot football game. Recently a Real Time T-2 Neuro-Fuzzy Controller (RT2NFSC) was developed by Lynch, Hagras, and Callaghan (2006) based on Wu and Mendal (2002) uncertainty bound model resulting in considerable improvement in its performance in comparison with type-1 systems. Similar type of performance can be achieved in advisory systems regarding important decision-making in human oriented way. In fact this is one

of the few areas where a generalized T2 FS can be used in preference to T1 FS.

Fuzzy systems are easy to implement, even if the designer has little knowledge of formal fuzzy logic theory. Fuzzy systems can deal with crucial parameter changes and broadly unstable load conditions. Fuzzy logic is appropriate for industrial processes where the control cycle time may operate over an extended period. Fuzzy systems help in reducing complexity and increasing user-friendliness. Fuzzy systems manage imprecise data and information used.

Fuzzy logic becomes trivial for complex procedures that are nonlinear by nature, lacks a mathematical model, and requires expert knowledge. The candidate areas of applications include automatic control; prediction, diagnostic, and advisory systems; user interface; Very Large Scale Integrated circuits (VLSI) microcontroller; fuzzy expert system and fuzzy inference, etc.

Fuzzy systems lack the capabilities of machine learning, as well as a neural network-type memory and pattern recognition. Therefore, hybrid systems (e.g. neuro fuzzy systems) are becoming more popular for specific applications. Another important factor that leads to such hybridization is the requirement of verification and validation support. Verification and validation of a fuzzy knowledge-based system typically requires extensive testing. This is an expensive affair. In addition to this, determining exact fuzzy rules and membership functions is a tedious task. One cannot predict how many membership functions are required even after wide testing.

## INTERFACING ANN SYSTEM

### Artificial Neural Network

**Artificial Neural Network** (ANN) is a bio-inspired system that is loosely modeled on the human brain. Each processing element called

*Figure 3. Biological Neuron and Artificial Neuron*

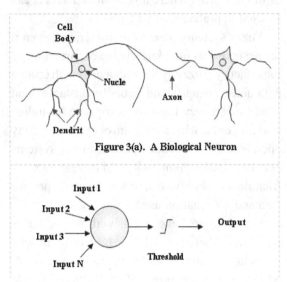

Figure 3(a). A Biological Neuron

neuron is connected with one or more other neurons. The neuron itself is far poorer in terms of processing efficiency and empowered with less complex logic. The actual knowledge is stored in the connections between the neurons. Biological neuron uses biochemical reactions to receive, process, and transmit information. In the human brain, neuron collects signals through a host of fine structures called *dendrites*. After processing the signals in desired way, dendrites sends out spikes of electrical activity through a long, thin stand known as an *axon* to one or more connected neurons utilizing thousands of branches. At the end of each branch, a structure called a *synapse* converts the activity from the axon into electrical effects that inhibit or excite activity in the connected neurons (Stergiou & Siganos, 1996). When a neuron receives excitatory input that is sufficiently large compared to its inhibitory input, it sends a spike of electrical activity down its axon. Learning happens by changing the effectiveness of the synapses so that the influence of one neuron on another changes. The biological neuron can be perceived as shown in Figure 3 (a).

In similar way, an artificial neuron receives inputs, possesses capability to process the input

according to the stored function in it and outputs the result. Refer Figure 3 (b) for simulation of artificial neuron. The inputs to the artificial neurons are biased with positive or negative weights. The mathematical function within the neuron sums up each input after multiplying it with the concerned weight factor and outputs the result. If the result is significant in comparison to the threshold value provided, the neuron is allowed to fire output further.

## Structure of Multi-Layer ANN

Real world problems cannot be solved with single neuron. Large number of neurons is the basic requirement to solve complex problem. There are different models and structures available for formulating network of such neurons. The concept of artificial neural network was first conceived by McCulloch and Pitts (1943). An ANN is an architecture of consisting of a large number of neurons organized in a different way. Hopfield model (1982), Perceptron model (URL, 2008) and Kohonen model (Kohonen, 1995) are a few architectures to name. Figure 4 shows a multilayer neural network with N input, M output and 2 layers of hidden nodes with k nodes in each layer. These nodes are connected in forward direction with weights assigned to them. The input layer nodes receive input, process it and send internal output to the every node of the adjacent layer. The receiving layer nodes further process it and send output forward. Hence, this type of network is known as feed forward network. Initially, the weights are decided in random fashion. The network requires training data to learn and generalize weights to solve real problems. Training involves the process of modifying a neural network by updating its weights and other parameters. Learning may be either supervised or un-supervised in nature. In supervised learning with every input training data, a sample output data set is also available. The network first calculates what it thinks during the forward pass (from input to output) and then

*Figure 4. Multi Layer Perceptron and Back Propagation Learning*

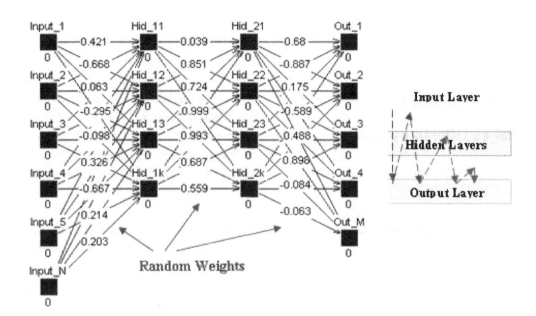

the calculated output is compared with the provided output. Difference between the calculated output and desired output is used to determine the change in weight and error calculated is propagated backwards i.e. from output to input layers. To get expected result for just one training data set, many such forward and backward passes are required (Rumelhart, Hinton, & Williams, 1988). This process continues for every training data set and at end the network is supposed to have learned generalized weights in such a way that, if actual input is given, it can calculate the output at single pass. The creditability of such multilayer back-propagation feed-forward neural network depends on the amount and quality of training set provided to it. Rather, this is also the way how human learns!

The training procedure for a multilayer perceptron encompasses the following phases:

## Phase 1: Creation of a Structure

Create a structure of an artificial neural network with at least one input layer and one output layer.

For the input layer, one should consider the major parameters that affect the decision to be taken and take that many neurons as input nodes. That is, each node represents a parameter. For the output layer, consider all the opportunities and let each output neuron represent an opportunity. Create a few (two to three) hidden layers and create neurons in each layer.

## Phase 2: Initialization

Initialize random weights and thresholds.

## Phase 3: Training (Forward Pass and Backward Pass)

Apply a training pattern consisting of the desired input with the output. For a multilayer feed-forward perceptron, back-propagation can be one of the choice under supervised environment. Calculate output for the training data provided, compute the output error, and adjust weights accordingly. Continue training till training data are available. If the training set is exhausted, evaluate the average system error. If the evaluated error is acceptable, the network is considered as trained and connections weights are generalized.

## Phase 4: Utilization

Apply real data and calculate the actual output.

## Advantages Offered by ANN

**Artificial Neural Networks** have got remarkable ability to learn and derive meaning from large amount of domain data. In reality, it is difficult to document generalized rules and detect patterns from enormous amount of complicated or imprecise data for humans or through other computer techniques. A trained neural network can be considered as a tool for the same. Besides the capability to learn generalized pattern from large amount of data, ANN offers following advantages:

- Ability to learn automatically from the training.
- Ability to organize itself from the information it receives during learning time.
- Ability to work in parallel, without support of special hardware organization.
- Ability to tolerate faults and distributed control. In a typical ANN, large number of neurons are working in parallel, every single neuron in the network adds up to a global solution, and hence, even if some neurons are not working, the performance of the network will not be affected much.

Connectionist systems are very popular because of many reasons. Some of the application areas are classification, pattern matching, recognition, novelty detection and sequential decision making. ANN systems are also applicable in system identification, game-playing, medical diagnosis and financial applications.

## NEURO-FUZZY MODELING

As stated earlier in this chapter, the Fuzzy Logic provides benefits of explicit knowledge representation, explanation and reasoning in friendly manner using linguistic variables as knowledge is stored in machine readable form. In case of Artificial Neural Network, the knowledge is stored in the generalized connections between the neurons, hence, it can not provide the facility of interface and justification along with documentation of knowledge. However, the ANN system is fault tolerant and capable to learn on its own. To get combined advantages of self-learning and explicit knowledge representation, it is necessary to follow a hybrid approach called neuro-fuzzy approach.

There are four major approaches of the hybrid neuro-fuzzy computing namely:

1.  Fuzzy neural network model
2.  Concurrent neuro-fuzzy model
3.  Co-operative neuro-fuzzy model
4.  Hybrid neuro-fuzzy model

First model, Fuzzy Neural Network is an example of enhanced learning capabilities of neural network by fuzzy system. This approach is useful in creating neural network that operates on fuzzy inputs. This approach utilized by Sajja (2006a; 2006b; 2006c; 2006d; 2008) offers dual advantages of FL and ANN technologies with utmost simplicity and ease of implementation in a distributed way. That is, both the FL and ANN agents can be developed and tested independently and integrated further. This approach is also useful in creating neural network that operates on fuzzy inputs (Sajja 2006a; Abraham 2001) as shown in Figure 5(a).

Second model, Co-operative Neuro-Fuzzy, as shown in Figure 5(b) first uses the neural net to decide and enhance parameters of fuzzy system. Once parameters and rules are defined, the fuzzy system takes the charge and solves problem more efficiently (Nauck, 1995; Abraham, 2001).

*Figure 5. Approaches of Neuro-Fuzzy Computing*

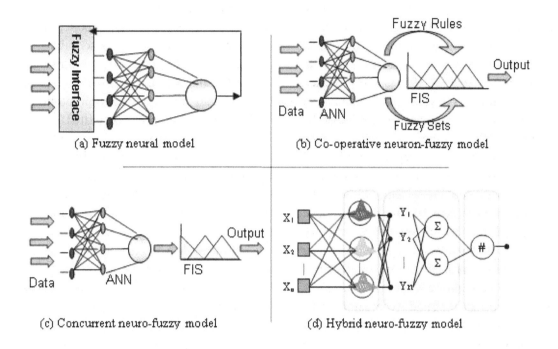

(a) Fuzzy neural model

(b) Co-operative neuron-fuzzy model

(c) Concurrent neuro-fuzzy model

(d) Hybrid neuro-fuzzy model

In the third model, Concurrent Neuro-Fuzzy, ANN assists the FL system continuously to determine the required parameters especially if the input variables of the controller cannot be measured directly. According to Abraham (2001), in some cases the FL system outputs might not be directly applicable to the process. In that case ANN can act as a post-processor of FL system outputs as shown in Figure 5(c).

Hybrid neuro-fuzzy model supports special neural network with fuzzy parameters. Neural network in multi-layer architecture can extract fuzzy rules. Alternatively, the fuzzy system can be implemented using distributed approach in layers. The multipurpose models like ANFIS (Jang, 1992) NFECLASS (Nauck & Kruse, 1995), Fuzzy Rule Net (Tschichold-Gurman, 1995) have been developed using this approach. Rutkowski and Cpalka (2003) designed a flexible neuro-fuzzy system using the same approach. Figure 5(d) shows input and fuzzification layer, rule layer, output layer, and defuzzification layer respectively in a general framework for hybrid neuro-fuzzy model.

## FRAMEWORK OF THE SYSTEM

As discussed earlier, ANN system lacks explicit explanation and reasoning facility, as knowledge is stored in the connections. Moreover, input values to ANN needs to be crisp and normalized unlike in real practice. For most of the user-friendly knowledge-based systems, the values of the input parameters from users and domain experts are vague and in the form of linguistic variables like '*good resources*', '*competent faculty*' etc. The output of the system is also appreciated much if it uses native language and style of users. This leads to the difficulty that neural network-based systems have capability to learn from data (self-learning) but cannot provide explicit justification of the decision made and documentation of the knowledge for future use. Hence, it is necessary to have an intermediate system which helps to fuzzify and normalize the input parameters to the base ANN system (Gunadi et al, 2003) as well as provide fine tuning and justification of the results of the base ANN system (Cordon & Herrera, 2003; Takagi & Sugeno, 1985). The proposed system here utilizes a **type-2 fuzzy system** as an interface to the ANN. The basic objective of the fuzzy rule-based system is to map user's vague parameters into the both fuzzy and normalized crisp values through membership functions and type reducer facility of the system. This way, the fuzzy rule-based system becomes an interface to the base neural network and helps to receive results from the network and to present it to user after fine tuning and justification. The received output is also in linguistic form which increases the level of understanding and acceptability of the system. The fuzzy system here also keeps track of history, user profile and tries to document some domain knowledge in 'if…then…else' rule form. The detailed structure of the proposed system is depicted in Figure 6 (Sajja, 2008).

## AN EXPERIMENT

### An Advisory for Course Selection

The **course selection** process is an important area as it has serious impact on the overall quality of students' satisfaction with the education received, and on the career students take. Selection of the 'right' course may be considered as a high involvement, high risk decision-making situation because the cumulative effect of the series of selection students make every time may impact the selection of the major in their college, their ability to take additional coursework, as well as their career direction, and future employment opportunities.

A greater understanding of course selection may help students to make better choices and thus lead to greater student satisfaction with the educational experience. There are many sources of information available to assist students in selecting a course. These include college bulletins, academic advisors, course descriptions, course syllabus, published course guides for students or Web sites, and informal word of mouth. However, it was found that a significant proportion of the students were not firmly committed to their field of study, and many had decided to enroll under time pressures. The existing system of providing information and advice to prospective students is not satisfactory. The following observations may be concluded from the current scenario.

- Critical decision is to be taken within limited time period.
- Parents and students are not exposed to high number of opportunities though educated.
- All alternatives are not available at one place.
- Non availability of updated information on continuously changing data about courses and job opportunities.
- Too many choices v/s. shortfall in specific stream syndrome leads to gap in industry demand and supply resulting imbalance in trained personnel etc.

There is a strong need of a systematic effort to provide an advisory to the student community in a consistent well documented form to meet information needs. Advances in technology help in providing effective decision-making and problem solving in many aspects of life. Information Technology can be effectively utilized to take 'right decision' at 'right time' by evaluating multi-dimensional constraints.

There is a need of technology which offers self-learning from the collected data sets implicitly and interacts with users for their need and advice in friendly and customized manner. For implicit learning, Artificial Neural Network based systems

*Figure 6. Type-2 Fuzzy Interface for the Proposed System with Base ANN*

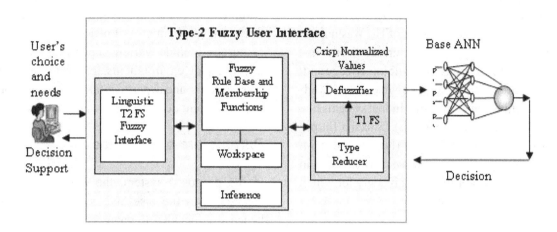

are useful; and for explicit knowledge management, explanation, handling uncertainty and more human like working Fuzzy Logic based systems are useful. To get the best of both the worlds, neuro-fuzzy decision support system for course selection is proposed here.

## Objectives of the Proposed System

The main objectives of the system are as follows:

1. To develop fuzzy system that
   - Facilitates user friendly interaction;
   - Facilitates fuzzy inputs to the base neural network system through fuzzy membership functions after converting the values into crisp values;
   - Gives the output of the base neural network to the users in friendly way;
   - Refines and fine tunes the broad career guidelines provided through base neural network; and
   - Documents the domain knowledge in the form of 'if…then…else' rules.
2. To develop and train an artificial neural network
   - With input nodes categorized into educational, economical, family background, personal interest etc.
   - To output broad career guidelines.

## Review of Research and Development in the Area

Much research has been carried out to help students in course selection. However, the area of research is limited to the native areas like Education and Psychology and the work is in manual form. It is observed that expertise offering decision support is a limited commodity in the field and not easily available to the advice seekers. The present form of advisory include college bulletins, academic advisors, course descriptions, course syllabus, published course guides for students or Web sites, and informal word of mouth (Wilhelm, Wendy & Charles, 2004).

Many automated systems in foreign countries have been developed such as 'Course Selector' at the University of Edinburg, UK (http://www.aiai.ed.ac.uk/project/courseselector/); 'Course Advisor Expert System' at the Griffith University (http://www.cit.gu.edu.au/~noran/Docs/

ES-Course_Advisor.pdf); 'Course Advisor' at Massatusets, USA (http://www.kellysearch.com/us-company-301093566.html); 'An Advisor' by courseadvisor Inc., a subsidiary of The Washington Post Company (http://www.courseadvisor.com/) etc. Most of the systems use static knowledge and/or information and meant for course selection advisory within their University. Indian systems like 'Antya' (http://www.antya.com), 'Shiksha' (http://www.shiksha.com) and goIIT (http://www.goiit.com) offers static material and expert advisory in a limited proportion for the University for which they have been developed.

## Location of the Experiment

At present there is no such system which can help and guide students in their effective course selection process at the Sardar Patel University, India. The other examples mentioned in the earlier section are also limited in scope and not knowledge-based. Hence, a decision support system is being developed for the Sardar Patel University which interacts with parents, students and academicians in a friendly manner and provides advisory in knowledge based fashion.

The major activities of the surveyed department are as follows:

- MCA, PGDCA, MS, M Phil, and Ph.D. programs;
- Research and Development;
- Training programs entrusted by academic institutes and industries;
- Extension services - providing software development on need basis; and
- Providing consultancy on need basis etc.

The department is located in three-storied building and has computing facility supported by 10 servers and 300 workstations amongst which few are high graphics workstations for total 475 students, teachers, and supporting staff. The department has two multimedia auditoriums, 8 classrooms out of which, 6 are equipped with multimedia projectors, 2 laboratories, a workshop, a multimedia seminar hall, conference rooms, server farm, and faculty and staff offices. The software resources include various operating systems, development environments, programming languages, tools, and departmental application along with e-content developed for various courses.

## Parameters of the Case

In the proposed system, the input parameters considered by the base ANN systems are many, hence it is decided to categorize the input into various categories like educational background, economical, family background etc. The output nodes are also planned to be categorized into technical, scientific, management, etc. Here the base ANN is used to determine the suitable career opportunities according to the aptitude of the user based on the training data provided. Major inputs of the system are as follows:

The administrator inputs information on course, institute, faculty, infrastructure, market trends, and job opportunities etc.

Users input values of parameters as follows:

1. **Personal Information:** Name, Gender, Birth date, City, Nationality, Contact details, etc.
2. **Education:** SSC, HSC and Degree Results, Discipline, Scholarships, Achievements, Category (handicap, SC/BC), etc.
3. **Economical and Family Background:** Father's occupation, Mother's occupation, Annual income of family, Siblings, etc.
4. **Personal Interest:** Area of interest, Hobbies, Skills, Long term goal, etc.

These parameters are accepted as direct crisp values or in the form of fuzzy linguistic variables to make the interaction with the system more user-friendly. For example, the economical background

*Figure 7. Linguistic Variable 'Economic Background'*

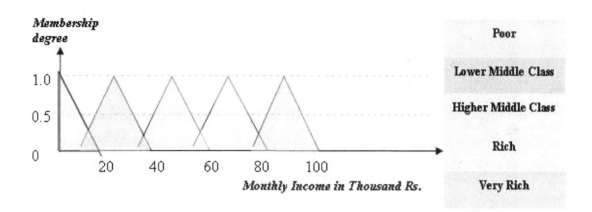

of family of a user can be acquired using the linguistic values 'High', "Poor", "Middle Class", etc. The fuzzy membership function used for this can be given as in Figure 7.

## Design of the Base ANN

The parameters collected through the fuzzy interface system are sent to the base ANN after necessary processing and categorization. The major categories of inputs are personal details, educational, economical, and personal interests, etc. These values are now crisp normalized values between the [0,1]. The output layer contains 6 nodes to specify the 6 different categories like further studies, business, technical, management, etc. At the early stage of the experiment it was decided to fix three hidden layers each with 7 nodes. Hence, the ANN structure is 8 input nodes, 6 output categories and 3 hidden layers each with 7 nodes. The heuristic used for selection of the hidden layer nodes is as follows:

$$N_h = 1/2\{N_i + N_o\} \tag{1}$$

where $N_h$ = Number of neurons in hidden layers
$N_i$ = Number of neurons in an input layer
$N_o$ = Number of neurons in an output layer

Figure 8 presents the visual structure of the neural network used in the experiment.

## Sample Input/Output and Process Design

There are two categories of users namely administrator and user in the proposed **course selection system**. The administrator inputs data such as information on course, institute, faculty, infrastructure, market trends, and job opportunities etc. Users input values of different parameters like personal information, educational information, economical, family back ground, and personal interest etc.

After successful *log-in* into the system, users can input their information and choices and obtain guidance with regard to course selection opportunities. As stated earlier, there is at least one administrative type of user along with simple users for the system. The process flow of the proposed system can be presented as shown in Figure 9.

Administrator first creates different users, assigns access rights to the created users and manages the user profile. The administrator also update information regarding institutes which includes courses available, maximum number of students

*Figure 8. Visual Structure of the Neural Network*

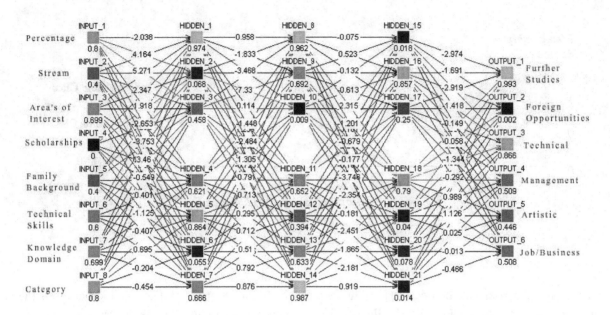

*Figure 9. Process Flow of the System*

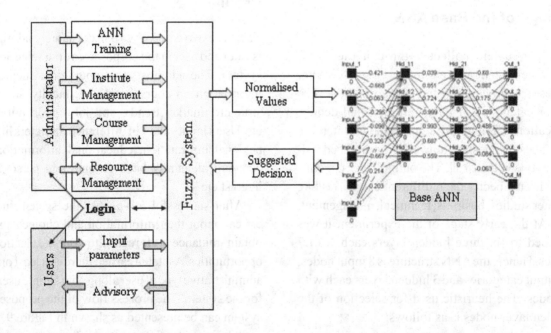

to be enrolled, accreditation of the institute by governing bodies like UGC, AICTE, ISTE, etc., faculty and other resources, placement information, admission history, etc.

Besides creating and managing users and other administrative trouble shooting, the administrator of the system is supposed to train the base neural network with suitable training data. The data are

*Figure 10. Feeding input in fuzzy fashion*

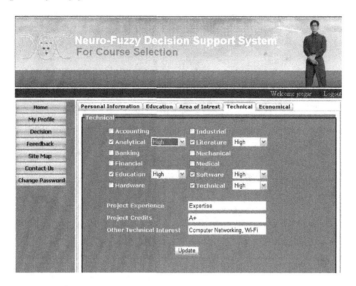

collected using the fuzzy interface of the system. These data are automatically converted using the script (written at the backend) embedding heuristic provided by the field experts as discussed in the section on parameters of the case. Some sample training sets are collected using data entry screens as shown in Figure 10(a). There are many input screens which collect input data regarding academic qualification, personal information, family background, etc., as the training set data. The same interface screens are used to collect user's actual data when system is in execution. The collected data for training set or actual data are first to be converted into equivalent crisp values. An example of fuzzy **training** data is shown in Table 1.

The training set also requires output to generalize the weights of ANN and learning in supervised fashion. For the above input sample, the output data is shown in Table 2.

The screen shown in Figure 10 collects user's technical information. There are 4 other input screens similar to the one shown in the Figure 10(a), which collects personal information, academic qualification information, information about area of interests, and information regarding

*Table 1.*

| Input category | Converted Crisp Data |
|---|---|
| Percentage | 0.7 |
| Stream | 0.6 |
| Area of interest | 0.3 |
| Scholarship | 0.4 |
| Family background | 0.6 |
| Technical skills | 0.6 |
| Knowledge domain | 0.4 |
| Category | 0.4 |

*Table 2.*

| Output category | Value |
|---|---|
| Further studies | 0.46 |
| Foreign opportunities | 0.30 |
| Technical aptitude | 0.48 |
| Managerial aptitude | 0.41 |
| Artistic aptitude | 0.42 |
| Job / business | 0.60 |

*Figure 11. Analytical advices through the system*

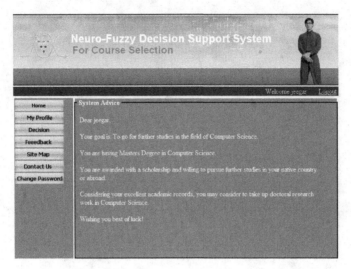

technical abilities and economical background of the user.

As stated earlier, the input user interface developed for the system is simple and requires a few key strokes. It also permits to enter some loose words like 'average family income', 'high knowledge skills', etc. The system first finds out the broad aptitude category of the user and fine tune it before presenting an analytical report and counseling advices.

The Figure 11 shows the way in which the output is presented with supporting information.

## CONCLUSION

The proposed hybrid approach incorporates dual advantages of both the techniques. The ANN offers advantages of implicit knowledge representation and self learning. The type-2 fuzzy interface offers advantages of user-friendliness and explicit knowledge representation for better justification of the decision suggested. Such system describes an application of a neuro-fuzzy technique for student community and adds value to the University services by enhancing friendly advisory to users anytime, anywhere.

The proposed system once implemented offers following major advantages:

- It provides advisory to parents, students, and academicians to select proper course within a University;
- It provide advantages like justification and partial learning along with all the opportunities presented in user friendly way;
- It provides documentation of the various courses, institutes, and resources available with learned market value and job opportunities readily, on-line;
- It provides base for further research in neuro-fuzzy techniques. The proposed system learns from the data generated from real cases through a neural network; hence effort needed for documentation of generalized rules would be minimum. The system also overcomes limitation of neural network-based system by providing explicit justification of the decisions suggested to the users.

The proposed system needs training prior to execution. The system can perform well, provided sufficient amount of good quality data is made available. Automatic on-line learning and an interactive editor to input/update domain knowledge need to be designed in future to accompany the system. Such addition leads the proposed system toward a generic product on the Internet platform. With minor modifications, the system can be used for HR management, aptitude testing, and general career counseling.

## ACKNOWLEDGMENT

Author is grateful to the University Grants Commission, New Delhi, India for funding this research work [File No. 36-203/2008 (SR)].

## REFERENCES

Abraham, A. (2001). Neuro-fuzzy systems: State-of-the-art modeling techniques. In *proceedings of the 6th International Work-Conference on Artificial and Natural Neural Networks: Connectionist Models of Neurons, Learning Processes and Artificial Intelligence* (pp.269-276). Granada, Spain.

Cordon, O., & Herrera, F. (2003). Author's reply. *IEEE Transactions on Fuzzy Systems, 11*(6), 866–869.

Figueroa, J. P., Soriano, M. M., & Rojas, S. (2005). A type-2 fuzzy controller for tracking mobile objects in the context of robotic soccer games. In proceedings of the FUZZ-IEEE 2005 (pp.359-364), USA.

Gorzalczany, M. B. (1987). A method of inference in approximate reasoning based on interval-valued fuzzy sets. *Fuzzy Sets and Systems, 21*, 1–17.

Gunadi, W. N., Shamsuddin, S. M., Alias, R. A., & Sap, M. N. (2003). Selection of defuzzification method to obtain crisp value for representing uncertain data in a modified sweep algorithm. *Journal of Computer Science & Technology, 3*(2), 22–28.

Hopfield, J. J. (1982). Neural networks and physical systems with emergent collective computational abilities. *Proceedings of the National Academy of Sciences of the United States of America, 79*(8), 2554–2558.

Jang, R. (1992). *Neuro-fuzzy modeling: Architectures, analyses and applications*. PhD Thesis, University of California, Berkeley, CA.

John, R. I., & Coupland, S. (2007). Type-2 fuzzy logic: A historical view. *IEEE Computational Intelligence Magazine, 2*, 57–62.

Karnik, N. N., & Mendal, J. M. (1998). Introduction to type-2 fuzzy logic systems. In *proceedings of the IEEE World Congress and Computational Intelligence* (pp.915-920), AK.

Karnik, N. N., & Mendal, J. M. (2001). Centroid of a type-2 fuzzy sets. *Information Sciences, 132*, 195–220.

Klir, G. J., & Folger, T. A. (1988). *Fuzzy Sets, Uncertainty, and Information*. Englewood Cliffs, NJ: Prentice-Hall.

Kohonen, T. (1995). *Self Organizing Maps*. Heidelberg, Germany: Springer-Verlag.

Lynch, C., Hagras, H., & Callaghan, V. (2006). Using uncertainty bounds in the design of an embedded real-time type-2 neuro-fuzzy speed controller for machine diesel engines. In *Proceedings of the 2006 IEEE International Conference on Fuzzy Systems* (pp.7217-7224), Vancouver, Canada.

Mamdani, E. H. (1974). Applications of fuzzy algorithm for control a simple dynamic plant. *Proceedings of the IEEE, 121*(12), 1585–1588.

McCulloch, W. S., & Pitts, W. (1943). A logical calculus of the ideas immanent in nervous activity. *The Bulletin of Mathematical Biophysics, 5*, 115–133.

Mendal, J. M. (2007). Type-2 fuzzy sets and systems: An overview. *IEEE Computational Intelligence Magazine, 2,* 20–29.

Nauck, D. (1995). Beyond neuro-fuzzy: Perspective and directions. In *proceedings of the 3rd European Congress on Intelligent Techniques and Soft Computing* (pp.1159-1164), Aachen, France.

Nauck, D., & Kruse, R. (1995). NEFCLASS, A neuro-fuzzy approach for the classification of data. In *Proceedings of 1995 ACM Symposium on Applied Computing* (pp.461-465), New York.

Rumelhart, D. E., Hinton, G. E., & Williams, R. J. (1988). Learning representation of back-propagation errors. *Nature, 323,* 321–355.

Rutkowski, L., & Cpałka, K. (2003). Flexible neuro-fuzzy systems. *IEEE Transactions on Neural Networks, 14*(1), 554–574.

Sajja, P. S. (2006a). Deliberative fuzzy agent for distributed systems. In *Proceedings of the National Seminar on ICT for Productivity,* India.

Sajja, P. S. (2006b). Multi-layer connectionist model of expert system for an advisory system. In proceedings of the National Level Seminar - Tech Symposia on IT Futura, India.

Sajja, P. S. (2006c). A fuzzy agent to input vague parameters into multi-layer connectionist expert system: An application for stock market. *ADIT Journal of Engineering, 3*(1), 30–32.

Sajja, P. S. (2006d). Fuzzy artificial neural network decision support system for course selection. *Journal of Engineering and Technology, 19,* 99–102.

Sajja, P. S. (2008). Type-2 fuzzy user interface for artificial neural network based decision support system for course selection. *International Journal of Computing and ICT Research, 2*(2), 96–102.

Schwartz, D. G. (1985). The case for an interval-based representation of linguistic truth. *Fuzzy Sets and Systems, 17,* 153–165.

Stergiou, C., & Siganos, D. (1996). *Neural Networks.* Retrieved November 6, 2008 from http://www.doc.ic.ac.uk/~nd/surprise_96/journal/vol4/cs11/report.html#Introduction to neural networks

Takagi, T., & Sugeno, M. (1985). Fuzzy identification of systems and its applications to modeling and control. *IEEE Transactions on Systems, Man, and Cybernetics, 15*(1), 116–132.

Tschichold-Gürman, N. N. (1995). Generation and improvement of fuzzy classifiers with incremental learning using fuzzy RuleNet. In proceedings of the ACM symposium on Applied computing (pp. 466-470), Nashville, TN.

Turksen, I. B. (1995). Fuzzy normal functions. *Fuzzy Sets and Systems, 69,* 319–346.

Turksen, I. B. (2002). Type-2 representation and reasoning for CWW. *Fuzzy Sets and Systems, 127,* 17-36. Retrieved November 6, 2008 from http://en.wikipedia.org/wiki/Frank_Rosenblatt

Wilhelm, W. B., & Charles, C. (2004). Course selection decisions by students on campuses with and without published teaching evaluations. *Practical Assessment. Research Evaluation, 9*(16).

Wu, H., & Mendal, J. M. (2002). Uncertainty bounds and their use in the design of interval type-2 fuzzy logic system. *IEEE Transactions on Fuzzy Systems, 10*(5), 622–639.

Zadeh, L. A. (1965). Fuzzy sets. *Journal of Information and Control, 8,* 338–353.

Zadeh, L. A. (1975). The concept of linguistic variable and its application to approximate reasoning. *Information Sciences, 8,* 199–249.

Zadeh, L. A. (1999). From computing with numbers to commuting with words-from manipulation of measurement to manipulation of perceptions. *IEEE Transactions on Circuits and Systems. I, Fundamental Theory and Applications, 45,* 105–119.

## ADDITIONAL READING

Akerkar, R. A., & Sajja, P. S. (2009). *Knowledge-Based Systems. ISBN:9780763776473*. Sudbury, MA, USA: Jones & Bartlett Publishers.

John, R. I., & Coupland, S. (2007). Type-2 fuzzy logic: A historical view. *IEEE Computational Intelligence Magazine, 2*, 57–62.

Klir, G. J., & Folger, T. A. (1988). *Fuzzy Sets, Uncertainty, and Information*. New Jersey: Prentice-Hall.

Mamdani, E. H. (1974). Applications of fuzzy algorithm for control a simple dynamic plant. *Proceedings of the IEEE, 121*(12), 1585–1588.

McCulloch, W. S., & Pitts, W. (1943). A logical calculus of the ideas immanent in nervous activity. *The Bulletin of Mathematical Biophysics, 5*, 115–133.

Mendal, J. M. (2007). Type-2 fuzzy sets and systems: An overview. *IEEE Computational Intelligence Magazine, 2*, 20–29.

Nauck, D. (1995). Beyond neuro-fuzzy: Perspective and directions. In *proceedings of the 3rd European Congress on Intelligent Techniques and Soft Computing* (pp.1159-1164). Aachen.

Nauck, D., & Kruse, R. (1995). NEFCLASS, A neuro-fuzzy approach for the classification of data. In *proceedings of 1995 ACM Symposium on Applied Computing* (pp.461-465). New York.

Rich, E., & Knight, K. (1991). *Artificial Intelligence. ISBN: 9780070522633*. NY, USA: McGraw-Hill.

Russell, S., & Norvig, P. (1995). *Artificial Intelligence: A Modern Approach. ISBN: 9780131038059*. NJ, USA: Prentice Hall.

Rutkowski, L., & Cpałka, K. (2003). Flexible neuro-fuzzy systems. *IEEE Transactions on Neural Networks, 14*(1), 554–574.

Sajja, P. S. (2006). Deliberative fuzzy agent for distributed systems. In proceedings of the National Seminar on ICT for Productivity, India.

Sajja, P. S. (2006). Multi-layer connectionist model of expert system for an advisory system. In proceedings of the National Level Seminar - Tech Symposia on IT Futura, India.

Sajja, P. S. (2006). A fuzzy agent to input vague parameters into multi-layer connectionist expert system: An application for stock market. *ADIT Journal of Engineering, 3*(1), 30–32.

Sajja, P. S. (2006). Fuzzy artificial neural network decision support system for course selection. *Journal of Engineering and Technology, 19*, 99–102.

Sajja, P. S. (2008). Type-2 fuzzy user interface for artificial neural network based decision support system for course selection. *International Journal of Computing and ICT Research, 2*(2), 96–102.

Takagi, T., & Sugeno, M. (1985). Fuzzy identification of systems and its applications to modeling and control. *IEEE Transactions on Systems, Man, and Cybernetics, 15*(1), 116–132.

Turksen, I. B. (2002). Type-2 representation and reasoning for CWW. *Fuzzy Sets and Systems, 127*, 17–36.

Wilhelm, Wendy, B. & Charles, C. (2004). Course selection decisions by students on campuses with and without published teaching evaluations. *Practical Assessment. Research Evaluation, 9*(16).

Wu, H., & Mendal, J. M. (2002). Uncertainty bounds and their use in the design of interval type-2 fuzzy logic system. *IEEE Transactions on Fuzzy Systems, 10*(5), 622–639.

Zadeh, L. A. (1965). Fuzzy Sets. *Journal of Information and Control, 8*, 338–353.

Zadeh, L. A. (1975). The concept of linguistic variable and its application to approximate reasoning. *Information Sciences, 8*, 199–249.

Zadeh, L. A. (1999). From computing with numbers to commuting with words-from manipulation of measurement to manipulation of perceptions. *IEEE Transactions on Circuits and Systems. I, Fundamental Theory and Applications, 45,* 105–119.

## KEY TERMS AND DEFINITIONS

**Knowledge-Based System:** Knowledge-Based Systems (KBS) are productive tools of Artificial Intelligence (AI) working in a narrow domain to impart quality, effectiveness, and knowledge-based approach in decision-making process. The major components of a KBS are knowledge base – to document domain and control knowledge; inference engine – to refer and generate new knowledge; self-learning – to learn from cases and outcomes; explanation and reasoning – to justify the actions taken by the system; and user friendly interface.

**Fuzzy Logic:** Fuzzy logic is a multi-valued logic based on fuzzy sets. This type of logic is very nearer to the way how humans identify and categorize things into the classes whose boundaries are not fixed.

**Fuzzy Membership Functions:** The function which maps fuzzy linguistic value to an appropriate crisp value between the interval [0,1] is called a fuzzy membership function. Usage of such membership functions facilitate FL systems to represent and reason with linguistic type of knowledge.

**Type-2 Fuzzy System:** Type-2 Fuzzy Systems are based on fuzzy sets whose membership grades are non-crisp fuzzy membership functions; hence they can model perceptions more effectively than Type-1 Fuzzy Systems.

**Artificial Neural Network:** Artificial Neural Network (ANN) is a bio-inspired system that is loosely modeled on the human brain.

**Neuro-Fuzzy Approaches:** To get combined advantages of self-learning and explicit knowledge representation, neuro-fuzzy approach is used. The Fuzzy Logic provides benefits of explicit knowledge representation, explanation, and reasoning in friendly manner using linguistic variables as knowledge is stored in machine readable form. The Artificial Neural Network is fault tolerant and capable to learn on its own.

**Course Selection System:** The automated course selection/counseling system designed using neuro-fuzzy approach and discussed in this work help students to make better choices and thus lead to greater student satisfaction with the educational experience.

# Chapter 6
# A Combined GA–Fuzzy Classification System for Mining Gene Expression Databases

**Gerald Schaefer**
*Loughborough University, UK*

**Tomoharu Nakashima**
*Osaka Prefecture University, Japan*

## ABSTRACT

*Microarray studies and gene expression analysis have received significant attention over the last few years and provide many promising avenues towards the understanding of fundamental questions in biology and medicine. In this chapter, the authors show that a combined GA-fuzzy classification system can be employed for effective mining of gene expression data. The applied classifier consists of a set of fuzzy if-then rules that allow for accurate non-linear classification of input patterns. A small number of fuzzy if-then rules are selected through means of a genetic algorithm, and are capable of providing a compact classifier for gene expression analysis. Experimental results on various well-known gene expression datasets confirm good classification performance of our approach.*

## INTRODUCTION

**Microarray** expression studies use a hybridisation process to measure the levels of **genes** expressed in biological samples. Knowledge gained from these studies is deemed increasingly important as it will contribute to the understanding of fundamental questions in biology and clinical medicine. Microarray experiments can either monitor each gene several times under varying conditions, or can be used to analyse genes in the same environment but in dif-

ferent types of tissue. In this chapter, we focus on the latter, that is on the classification of the recorded samples. This classification can be used to either categorise different types of cancerous tissues as in (Golub *et al.*, 1999*)* where different types of leukemia are identified, or to discriminate cancerous tissue from normal tissue as done in (Alon *et al.*, 1999) where tumor and normal colon tissues are analysed.

One of the main challenges in classifying **gene expression** data is that the number of genes is typically much higher than the number of analysed samples. Furthermore, it is difficult to determine

DOI: 10.4018/978-1-60566-814-7.ch006

which of the genes are important and which can be omitted without reducing the classification performance. Many pattern classification techniques have been employed to analyse microarray data. For example, Golub *et al.* (1999) used a weighted voting scheme, Fort and Lambert-Lacroix (2005) employed partial least squares and logistic regression techniques, whereas Furey *et al.* (2000) applied support vector machines (SVMs). Dudoit *et al.* (Dudoit, Fridlyand, & Speed, 2002) investigated nearest neighbour classifiers, discriminant analysis, classification trees and boosting, while Statnikov *et al.* (2005) explored several support vector machine techniques, nearest neighbour classifiers, neural networks and probabilistic neural networks. In several of these studies it has been found that no single classification algorithm is performing best on all datasets (although for several datasets SVMs seem to perform best) and that hence the exploration of several classifiers is useful. Similarly, no universally ideal gene selection method has yet been found as several studies (Liu, Li, & Wong, 2002; Statnikov *et al.*, 2005) have shown.

In this chapter we apply a hybrid GA-fuzzy classification scheme to analyse microarray expression data. Our classifier consists of a set of fuzzy if-then rules that allow for accurate non-linear classification of input patterns. A small number of fuzzy if-then rules are then selected by means of a genetic algorithm to arrive at a compact yet effective rule base. Experimental results on several gene expression datasets show that this approach affords classification performance comparable with that of a fuzzy classifier (Schaefer *et al.*, 2007) where a much larger rule base is used.

## FUZZY RULE-BASED CLASSIFICATION

**Pattern classification** is a process where, based on a set of training samples with known classifi-

cations, a classifier is derived that performs automatic assignment to classes based on unseen data. Let us assume that our pattern classification problem is an $n$-dimensional problem with $C$ classes (in microarray analysis $C$ is often 2) and $m$ given training patterns $\mathbf{x}_p = (x_{p1}, x_{p2}, ..., x_{pn})$, $p = 1, 2, ..., m$. Without loss of generality, we assume each attribute of the given training patterns to be normalised into the unit interval $[0,1]$; the pattern space is hence an $n$-dimensional unit hypercube $[0,1]^n$. In this study we use **fuzzy if-then rule**s of the following type as a base of our classification systems:

Rule $R_j$: If $x_1$ is $A_{j1}$ and ... and $x_n$ is $A_{jn}$
    then Class $C_j$ with $CF$, $j = 1, 2, ..., N$

$$(1)$$

where $R_j$ is the label of the $j$-th fuzzy if-then rule, $A_{j1}, ..., A_{jn}$ are antecedent fuzzy sets on the unit interval $[0,1]$, $C_j$ is the consequent class (i.e., one of the $C$ given classes), and $CF_j$ is the grade of certainty of the fuzzy if-then rule $R_j$. As antecedent fuzzy sets we use triangular fuzzy sets as in Figure 1 where we show the partitioning into a number of fuzzy sets.

Our fuzzy rule-based classification system consists of $N$ rules each of which has a form as in Equation (1). There are two steps in the generation of fuzzy if-then rules: specification of antecedent part and determination of consequent class $C_j$ and the grade of certainty $CF_j$. The antecedent part of fuzzy if-then rules is specified manually. Then, the consequent part (i.e., consequent class and the grade of certainty) is determined from the given training patterns (Ishibuchi, Nozaki & Tanaka, 1992). In (Ishibuchi & Nakashima, 2001) it was shown that the use of the

*Figure 1. Example triangular membership function (L=3)*

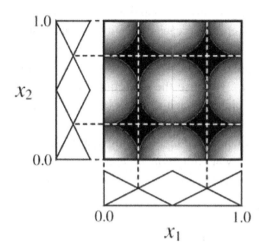

grade of certainty in fuzzy if-then rules allows the compilation of comprehensible fuzzy rule-based classification systems with high classification performance.

## Fuzzy Rule Generation

Let us assume that $m$ training patterns $\mathbf{x}_p = (x_{p1}, ..., x_{pn})$, $p=1,...,m$, are given for an $n$-dimensional $C$-class pattern classification problem. The consequent class $C_j$ and the grade of certainty $CF_j$ of the if-then rule are determined in the following two steps:

1.  Calculate $\beta_{Class}(j)$ for Class $h$ as

$$\beta_{Class\ h}(j) = \sum_{x_p \in Class\ h} \mu_j(x_p) \qquad (2)$$

where

$$\mu_j(x_p) = \mu_{j1}(x_{p1}) \cdot ... \cdot \mu_{jn}(x_{pn}), \qquad (3)$$

and $\mu_{jn}(\cdot)$ is the membership function of the fuzzy set $A_{jn}$. We use triangular fuzzy sets as in Figure 1.

2.  Find Class $\hat{h}$ that has the maximum value of $\beta_{Class\ h}(j)$:

$$\beta_{Class\ \hat{h}}(j) = \max_{1 \le k \le C}\{\beta_{Class\ k}(j)\}. \qquad (4)$$

If two or more classes take the maximum value, the consequent class $C_j$ of the rule $R_j$ cannot be determined uniquely. In this case, specify $C_j$ as $C_j = \varphi$. If a single class $\hat{h}$ takes the maximum value, let $C_j$ be Class $\hat{h}$. The grade of certainty $CF_j$ is determined as

$$CF_j = \frac{\beta_{Class\ \hat{h}}(j) - \bar{\beta}}{\sum_h \beta_{Class\ h}(j)} \qquad (5)$$

with

$$\bar{\beta} = \frac{\sum_{h \ne \hat{h}} \beta_{Class\ h}(j)}{C - 1}. \qquad (6)$$

## Fuzzy Reasoning

Using the rule generation procedure outlined above we can generate $N$ fuzzy if-then rules as in Equation (1). After both the consequent class $C_j$ and the grade of certainty $CF_j$ are determined for all $N$ rules, a new pattern $\mathbf{x} = (x_1, ..., x_n)$ can be classified by the following procedure:

1.  Calculate $\alpha_{Class\,h}(\mathbf{x})$ for Class $h$, $j=1,...,C$, as

$$\alpha_{Class\,h}(\mathbf{x}) = \max\{\mu_j(\mathbf{x}) \cdot CF_j \mid C_j = h\}, \quad (7)$$

2.  Find Class $h'$ that has the maximum value of $\alpha_{Class\,h}(\mathbf{x})$:

$$\alpha_{Class\,h'}(\mathbf{x}) = \max_{1 \le k \le C}\{\alpha_{Class\,h}(\mathbf{x})\}. \quad (8)$$

If two or more classes take the maximum value, then the classification of $\mathbf{x}$ is rejected (i.e. $\mathbf{x}$ is left as an unclassifiable pattern), otherwise we assign $\mathbf{x}$ to Class $h'$.

## GA-FUZZY CLASSIFICATION

While the basic fuzzy rule based system detailed above provides a reliable and accurate classifier, it suffers - as do many other approaches - from the curse of dimensionality. In the case of our fuzzy classifier, the number of generated rules increases exponentially with the number of attributes involved and with the number of partitions used for each attribute. We are therefore interested in arriving at a more compact classifier that affords the same classification performance while not suffering from the problems.

In a previous work (Schaefer *et al.*, 2007), we applied a rule splitting step to deal with the problem of dimensionality. By limiting the number of attributes in each rule to 2, a much smaller rule base was developed. In this chapter however we present a different approach to arrive at an even more compact rule base by developing a **hybrid fuzzy classification** system through the application of a **genetic algorithm** (GA). The fuzzy if-then rules used do not change and are still of the same form as the one given in Equation (1), i.e., they contain a number of fuzzy attributes and a consequent class together with a grade of certainty.

Our approach of using GAs to generate a fuzzy rule-based classification system is a Michigan style algorithm (Ishibuchi & Nakashima, 1999) which represents each rule by a string and handles it as an individual in the population of the GA. A population consists of a pre-specified number of rules. Because the consequent class and the rule weight of each rule can be easily specified from the given training patterns as shown above, they are not used in the coding of each fuzzy rule (i.e., they are not included in a string). Each rule is represented by a string using its antecedent fuzzy sets.

## Genetic Operations

First, the algorithm randomly generates a pre-specified number $N_{rule}$ of rules as an initial population (in our experiments we set $N_{rule} = 20$). Next, the fitness value of each fuzzy rule in the current population is evaluated. Let $S$ be the set of rules in the current population. The evaluation of each rule is performed by classifying all the given training patterns by the rule set $S$ using the single winner-based method described above. The winning rule receives a unit reward when it correctly classifies a training pattern. After all the given training patterns are classified by the rule set $S$, the fitness value $fitness(R_q)$ of each rule $R_q$ in $S$ is calculated as

$$fitness(R_q) = NCP(R_q), \quad (9)$$

where $NCP(R_q)$ is the number of correctly classified training patterns by $R_q$. It should be noted that the following relation holds between the classification performance $NCP(R_q)$ of each rule $R_q$ and the classification performance $NCP(S)$ of the rule set $S$ used in the fitness function:

$$NCP(S) = \sum_{R_q \in S} NCP(R_q). \qquad (10)$$

The algorithm is implemented so that only a single copy is selected as a winner rule when multiple copies of the same rule are included in the rule set $S$. In GA optimisation problems, multiple copies of the same string usually have the same fitness value which often leads to undesired early convergence of the current population to a single solution. In our algorithm, only a single copy can have a positive fitness value and the other copies have zero fitness which prevents the current population from being dominated by many copies of a single or few rules.

Then, new rules are generated from the rules in the current population using genetic operations. As parent strings, two fuzzy if-then rules are selected from the current population and binary tournament selection with replacement is applied. That is, two rules are randomly selected from the current population and the better rule with the higher fitness value is chosen as a parent string. A pair of parent strings is chosen by iterating this procedure twice.

From the selected pair of parent strings, two new strings are generated by a crossover operation. We use a uniform crossover operator where the crossover points are randomly chosen for each pair of parent strings. The crossover operator is applied to each pair of parent strings with a pre-specified crossover probability $p_c$. After new strings are generated, each symbol of the generated strings is randomly replaced with a different symbol by a mutation operator with a pre-specified mutation probability $p_m$. Usually the same mutation probability is assigned to every position of each string. Selection, crossover, and mutation are iterated until a pre-specified number $N_{replace}$ of new strings are generated.

Finally, the $N_{replace}$ strings with the smallest fitness values in the current population are removed, and the newly generated $N_{replace}$ strings added to form a new population. Because the number of removed strings is the same as the number of added strings, every population consists of the same number of strings. That is, every rule set has the same number of rules. This generation update can be viewed as an elitist strategy where the number of elite strings is $(N_{rule} - N_{replace})$.

The above procedures are applied to the new population again. The generation update is iterated until a pre-specified stopping condition is satisfied. In our experiments we use the total number of iterations (i.e., the total number of generation updates) as stopping condition.

## Algorithm Summary

To summarise, our hybrid fuzzy rule-based classifier works as follows:

- **Step 1:** *Parameter Specification:* Specify the number of rules $N_{rule}$, the number of replaced rules $N_{replace}$, the crossover probability $p_c$, the mutation probability $p_m$, and the stopping condition.
- **Step 2:** *Initialisation:* Randomly generate $N_{rule}$ rules (i.e., $N_{rule}$ strings of length $n$) as an initial population.
- **Step 3:** *Genetic Operations:* Calculate the fitness value of each rule in the current population. Generate $N_{replace}$ rules using selection, crossover, and mutation from existing rules in the current population.
- **Step 4:** *Generation Update (Elitist Strategy):* Remove the worst $N_{replace}$ rules from the current population and add the

newly generated $N_{replace}$ rules to the current population.

- **Step 5:** *Termination Test:* If the stopping condition is not satisfied, return to Step 3. Otherwise terminate the execution of the algorithm.

During the execution of the algorithm, we monitor the classification rate of the current population on the given training patterns. The rule set (i.e., population) with the highest classification rate is chosen as the final solution.

## Improving Classification Performance

Randomly generated initial rules with fine fuzzy partitions usually do not classify many training patterns in high-dimensional pattern classification problems such as those encountered when analysing gene expression data. This is because each rule covers only a very small portion of the pattern space.

A simple method for expanding the covered area by each initial rule is to increase the selection probability $p_{don't\ care}$ of "*don't care*" attributes, that is attributes that are not partitioned into several fuzzy sets, among the antecedent fuzzy sets. In turn, this simple trick has a significant positive effect on the search ability of the hybrid fuzzy classifier.

Another method for generating initial rules with high classification ability is to use training patterns for specifying their antecedent fuzzy sets (Ishibuchi & Nakashima, 1999). To generate an initial population of $N_{rule}$ fuzzy rules, we first randomly select $N_{rule}$ training patterns. Next, we choose the combination of the most compatible terms with each training pattern. Note that *don't care* is not used in this stage because any attribute values are fully compatible with *don't care* (i.e.,

because *don't care* is always chosen as the most compatible antecedent fuzzy set for any attribute values). Each term in the selected combination is replaced with *don't care* using the selection probability $p_{don't\ care}$. The combination of the terms after this replacement is used as the antecedent part of an initial rule. This procedure is applied to all the randomly selected $N_{rule}$ training patterns for generating an initial population of $N_{rule}$ rules.

The specification of antecedent fuzzy sets from training patterns can be utilised not only for generating an initial population but also for updating the current population. When a training pattern is misclassified or its classification is rejected by the current population, the generation of a new fuzzy rule from the misclassified or rejected training pattern may improve the classification ability of the current population. We can modify the generation update procedure as follows. We generate a single rule using the genetic operations and another rule from a misclassified or rejected training pattern. When all the training patterns are correctly classified, two rules are generated using the genetic operations.

Another extension to the hybrid fuzzy algorithm is the introduction of a penalty term with respect to the number of misclassified training patterns to the fitness function in Equation (9) as follows:

$$fitness(R_q) = NCP(R_q) - w_{NMP} \times NMP(R_q),$$

$$(11)$$

where $NMP(R_q)$ is the number of misclassified training patterns and $w_{NMP}$ is a positive constant. The fitness function in Equation (9) can be viewed as a special case of Equation (11) with $w_{NMP} = 0$. In Equation (11), $NCP(R_q)$ and $NMP(R_q)$ are calculated by classifying all the training patterns by the current population $S$ including the rule $R_q$.

To understand the effect of the second term of on the evolution of rules, let us consider a rule that correctly classifies ten patterns and misclassifies three patterns. If the misclassification penalty is zero (i.e., if $w_{NMP} = 0$), the fitness value of this rule is 10. Thus this rule is not likely to be removed from the current population. As a result, the three misclassified patterns will also be misclassified in the next population. On the other hand, the fitness value of this rule is negative (i.e., -5) when $w_{NMP} = 5$. In this case, the rule will be removed from the current population. As a result, the three misclassified patterns may be correctly classified by other rules or their classification may be rejected in the next population. From this we can see that the introduction of the misclassification penalty to the fitness function may improve the search ability of the algorithm to identify rule sets with high classification ability.

## EXPERIMENTAL RESULTS

We evaluated our proposed method on three gene expression data sets that are commonly used in the literature. In the following we characterise each dataset briefly:

- **Colon dataset (Alon *et al.*, 1999):** This dataset is derived from colon biopsy samples. Expression levels for 40 tumor and 22 normal colon tissues were measured for 6500 genes using Affymetrix oligonucleotide arrays. The 2000 genes with the highest minimal intensity across the tissues were selected. We pre-process the data following (Dudoit, Fridlyand, & Speed, 2002), i.e. perform a thresholding [floor of 100 and ceil of 16000] followed by filtering [exclusion of genes with max/min <5 and (max-min) <500] and $\log_{10}$ transformation.

- **Leukemia dataset (Golub *et al.*, 1999):** Bone marrow or peripheral blood samples were taken from 47 patients with acute lymphoblastic leukemia (ALL) and 25 patients with acute myeloid leukemia (AML). The ALL cases can be further divided into 38 B-cell ALL and 9 T-cell ALL samples and it is this 3-class division that we are basing our experiments on rather than the simpler 2-class version which is more commonly referred to in the literature. Each sample is characterised by 7129 genes whose expression levels where measured using Affymetrix oligonucleotide arrays. The same preprocessing steps as for the Colon dataset are applied.

- **Lymphoma dataset (Alizadeh *et al.*, 2000):** This dataset contains gene expression data of diffuse large B-cell lymphoma (DLBCL) which is the most common subtype of non-Hodgink's lymphome. In total there are 47 samples of which 24 are of germinal centre B-like" and the remaining 23 of activated B-like subtype. Each sample is described by 4026 genes, however there are many missing values. For simplicity we removed genes with missing values from all samples.

Not all genes are equally important for the classification task at hand. We therefore sort the significance of genes according to the BSS/WSS (the ratio of between group to within group sum of squares) criterion used in (Dudoit, Fridlyand, & Speed, 2002) and consider only the top 50 respectively 100 genes as input for our classification problem.

We perform standard leave-one-out cross-validation where classifier training is performed on all available data except for the sample to be classified and this process is performed for all samples (the top 50 respectively 100 genes were selected solely based on the training set). Fuzzy rule based classifiers as in (Schaefer *et al.*, 2007) and hybrid fuzzy classifiers as presented in this chapter, based on partition sizes $L$ between 2 and 5 partitions for each gene, were constructed. We furthermore implemented nearest neighbour and CART classifiers. The **nearest neighbour classifier** we employ searches through the complete training data to identify the sample which is closest to a given test input and assigns the identified sample's class. **CART** (Breiman *et al.*, 1984) is a classical rule based classifier which builds a recursive binary decision tree based on misclassification error of subtrees.

The results on the three datasets are given in Figures 2, 3, and 4. In each table we give the number of correctly classified samples (CR), the number of incorrectly classified or unclassified samples (FR), and the classification accuracy (Acc.), i.e. the percentage of correctly classified samples.

Looking at the results for the Colon dataset which are given in Figure 2, for the case of 50 selected features the fuzzy classifier with 3 partitions performs best with a classification accuracy of 85.48% which corresponds to 9 incorrectly classified cases while nearest neighbour classification and CART produce 13 and 14 errors respectively. However, when selecting the 100 top genes the nearest neighbour classifier performs slightly better than the fuzzy system. It is interesting to compare the performance of the fuzzy rule-based classifier when using different numbers of partitions for each attribute. It can be seen that on this dataset the best performance is achieved when using 3 partitions (although on training data alone more partitions afford better performance). In particular it can be observed that the case with $L=2$ as used in the work of Vinterbo *et al.* (Vinterbo, Kim, & Ohno-Machado, 2005) produces the worst results and hence confirms that increasing the number of fuzzy intervals improves the classification performance. However, it can also be seen that applying too many partitions can decrease classification performance as is apparent in the case of $L=5$ on test data. For the hybrid fuzzy classifier we ran the experiment 10 times

*Figure 2. Classification performance on Colon dataset given in terms of number of correctly classified samples (CR), falsely classified or unclassified samples (FR), and classification accuracy (Acc)*

| n | classifier | CR | FR | Acc. |
|---|---|---|---|---|
| 50 | fuzzy $L = 2$ | 50 | 12 | 80.65 |
| | fuzzy $L = 3$ | **53** | **9** | **85.48** |
| | fuzzy $L = 4$ | 52 | 10 | 83.87 |
| | fuzzy $L = 5$ | 48 | 14 | 77.42 |
| | hybrid fuzzy $L = 2$ | 49.7 | 12.3 | 80.11 |
| | hybrid fuzzy $L = 3$ | 52.0 | 10.0 | 83.87 |
| | hybrid fuzzy $L = 4$ | 49.0 | 13.0 | 79.03 |
| | hybrid fuzzy $L = 5$ | 50.0 | 12.0 | 80.64 |
| | nearest neighbour | 49 | 13 | 79.03 |
| | CART | 48 | 14 | 77.42 |
| 100 | fuzzy $L = 2$ | 44 | 18 | 70.97 |
| | fuzzy $L = 3$ | 51 | 11 | 82.26 |
| | fuzzy $L = 4$ | 50 | 12 | 80.65 |
| | fuzzy $L = 5$ | 46 | 16 | 74.19 |
| | hybrid fuzzy $L = 2$ | 48.4 | 13.6 | 78.01 |
| | hybrid fuzzy $L = 3$ | 49.7 | 12.3 | 80.11 |
| | hybrid fuzzy $L = 4$ | 47.7 | 14.3 | 76.88 |
| | hybrid fuzzy $L = 5$ | 48.0 | 14.0 | 77.42 |
| | nearest neighbour | **52** | **10** | **83.87** |
| | CART | 45 | 17 | 72.58 |

with different, random, initial populations and list the average of the 3 best runs. We can see that the hybrid fuzzy approach performs only slightly worse than the full fuzzy rule-based system which, considering that classification is performed based only on 20 selected rules, proves the potential of this method.

Turning our attention to the results on the Leukemia dataset which are given in Figure 3 we see a similar picture. Again, the worst performing fuzzy classifier is that which uses only two partitions per gene while the best performing one as assessed by leave-one-out cross validation is the case of $L=3$. CART performs fairly poorly on this dataset with classification accuracies reaching only about 65% while nearest neighbour classification performs well again confirming previous observations that despite its simplicity nearest neighbour classifiers are well suited for gene

*Figure 3. Classification performance on Leukemia dataset, laid out in the same fashion as Figure 2*

| n | classifier | CR | FR | Acc. |
|---|---|---|---|---|
| 50 | fuzzy $L = 2$ | 66 | 6 | 91.67 |
| | fuzzy $L = 3$ | 68 | 4 | 94.44 |
| | fuzzy $L = 4$ | 67 | 5 | 93.06 |
| | fuzzy $L = 5$ | 66 | 6 | 91.67 |
| | hybrid fuzzy $L = 2$ | 69.3 | 2.7 | 96.29 |
| | hybrid fuzzy $L = 3$ | 69.3 | 2.7 | 96.29 |
| | hybrid fuzzy $L = 4$ | 67.7 | 4.3 | 93.98 |
| | hybrid fuzzy $L = 5$ | 65.7 | 6.3 | 91.20 |
| | nearest neighbour | **70** | **2** | **97.22** |
| | CART | 47 | 25 | 65.28 |
| 100 | fuzzy $L = 2$ | 63 | 9 | 87.50 |
| | fuzzy $L = 3$ | **71** | **1** | **98.61** |
| | fuzzy $L = 4$ | 69 | 3 | 95.83 |
| | fuzzy $L = 5$ | 67 | 5 | 93.06 |
| | hybrid fuzzy $L = 2$ | 68.0 | 4.0 | 94.44 |
| | hybrid fuzzy $L = 3$ | 67.3 | 4.7 | 93.52 |
| | hybrid fuzzy $L = 4$ | 63.9 | 8.1 | 88.74 |
| | hybrid fuzzy $L = 5$ | 63.0 | 9.0 | 87.50 |
| | nearest neighbour | 70 | 2 | 97.22 |
| | CART | 45 | 27 | 62.50 |

*Figure 4. Classification performance on Lymphoma dataset, laid out in the same fashion as Figure 2*

| n | classifier | CR | FR | Acc. |
|---|---|---|---|---|
| 50 | fuzzy $L = 2$ | 45 | 2 | 95.74 |
| | fuzzy $L = 3$ | 46 | 1 | 97.87 |
| | fuzzy $L = 4$ | **47** | **0** | **100** |
| | fuzzy $L = 5$ | 44 | 3 | 93.62 |
| | hybrid fuzzy $L = 2$ | 46.0 | 1.0 | 97.88 |
| | hybrid fuzzy $L = 3$ | 43.3 | 3.7 | 92.20 |
| | hybrid fuzzy $L = 4$ | 42.3 | 4.7 | 90.07 |
| | hybrid fuzzy $L = 5$ | 43.0 | 4.0 | 91.49 |
| | nearest neighbour | 45 | 2 | 95.74 |
| | CART | 36 | 11 | 76.60 |
| 100 | fuzzy $L = 2$ | 44 | 3 | 93.62 |
| | fuzzy $L = 3$ | 44 | 3 | 93.62 |
| | fuzzy $L = 4$ | 44 | 3 | 93.62 |
| | fuzzy $L = 5$ | 39 | 8 | 82.98 |
| | hybrid fuzzy $L = 2$ | 44.0 | 3.0 | 93.61 |
| | hybrid fuzzy $L = 3$ | 42.1 | 4.9 | 89.65 |
| | hybrid fuzzy $L = 4$ | 37.7 | 9.3 | 80.14 |
| | hybrid fuzzy $L = 5$ | 34.7 | 12.3 | 73.76 |
| | nearest neighbour | **47** | **0** | **100** |
| | CART | 38 | 9 | 80.85 |

expression classification (Dudoit, Fridlyand, & Speed, 2002). The best classification results are achieved by the fuzzy classifier with $L=3$ for the case of 100 selected genes with a classification accuracy of 98.61% and the nearest neighbour classifier with 97.22% for 50 selected genes. For the case of 50 features, the hybrid fuzzy classifier outperforms the conventional fuzzy classification system in most cases while for classification based on 100 features it is more accurate only for the case of $L=2$.

Figure 4 lists the results obtained from the Lymphoma dataset. Here, perfect classification is achieved by the fuzzy classifier with $L=4$ for 50 selected genes and by nearest neighbour classification based on 100 genes. The hybrid fuzzy approach performs slightly worse in most cases but is significantly worse for $L=4$ and $L=5$ and

100 features. The reason for this performance is probably that during the run, the genetic algorithm was unable to explore sufficiently all of the search space.

## CONCLUSION

In this chapter we have shown that a hybrid GA-fuzzy classifier can be successfully employed for the problem of analysing gene expression data. The presented classifier consists of a set of fuzzy if-then rules that allow for accurate non-linear classification of input patterns. A compact yet effective rule base is constructed through the application of a genetic algorithm to select useful rules. Experimental results have shown this approach to be useful for gene expression classification. Also, the classification performance of the hybrid method was shown to be comparable to that of full fuzzy rule-based classifier.

# REFERENCES

Alizadeh, A. A., Eisen, M. B., Davis, E. E., Ma, C., & Lossos, I. S. (2000). Different types of diffuse large B-cell lymphoma identified by gene expression profiles. *Nature, 403*, 503–511. doi:10.1038/35000501

Alon, U., Barkai, N., Notterman, D. A., Gish, K., Ybarra, S., Mack, D., & Levine, A. J. (1999). Broad patterns of gene expression revealed by clustering analysis of tumor and normal colon tissues probed by oligonucleotide arrays. *Proceedings of the National Academy of Sciences of the United States of America, 96*, 6745–6750. doi:10.1073/pnas.96.12.6745

Breiman, L., Friedman, J. H., Olshen, R., & Stone, R. (1984). *Classification and Regression Trees.* New York: Wadsworth.

Dudoit, S., Fridlyand, J., & Speed, T. P. (2002). Comparison of discrimination methods for the classification of tumors using gene expression data. *Journal of the American Statistical Association, 97*(457), 77–87. doi:10.1198/016214502753479248

Fort, G., & Lambert-Lacroix, S. (2005). Classification using partial least squares with penalized logistic regression. *Bioinformatics (Oxford, England), 21*(7), 1104–1111. doi:10.1093/bioinformatics/bti114

Furey, T. S., Cristianini, N., Duffy, N., Bednarski, D. W., Schummer, M., & Haussler, D. (2000). Support vector machine classification and validation of cancer tissue samples using microarray expression data. *Bioinformatics (Oxford, England), 16*(10), 906–914. doi:10.1093/bioinformatics/16.10.906

Golub, T. R., Slonim, D. K., Tamayo, P., Huard, C., Gaasenbeek, M., & Mesirov, J. P. (1999). Molecular classification of cancer: class discovery and class prediction by gene expression monitoring. *Science, 286*, 531–537. doi:10.1126/science.286.5439.531

Ishibuchi, H., & Nakashima, T. (1999). Improving the performance of fuzzy classifier systems for pattern classification problems with continuous attributes. *IEEE Transactions on Industrial Electronics, 46*(6), 1057–1068. doi:10.1109/41.807986

Ishibuchi, H., & Nakashima, T. (2001). Effect of rule weights in fuzzy rule-based classification systems. *IEEE Transactions on Fuzzy Systems, 9*(4), 506–515. doi:10.1109/91.940964

Ishibuchi, H., Nozaki, K., & Tanaka, H. (1992). Distributed representation of fuzzy rules and its application to pattern classification. *Fuzzy Sets and Systems, 52*(1), 21–32. doi:10.1016/0165-0114(92)90032-Y

Liu, H., Li, J., & Wong, L. (2002). A comparative study on feature selection and classification methods using gene expression profiles and proteomic patterns. *Gene Informatics, 13*, 51–60.

Schaefer, G., Nakashima, T., Yokota, Y., & Ishibuchi, H. (2007). Fuzzy classification of gene expression data. In *IEEE Int. Conference on Fuzzy Systems*, (pp. 1090–1095).

Statnikov, A., Aliferis, C., Tsamardinos, I., Hardin, D., & Levy, S. (2005). A comprehensive evaluation of multicategory classification methods for microarray expression cancer diagnosis. *Bioinformatics (Oxford, England), 21*(5), 631–643. doi:10.1093/bioinformatics/bti033

Vinterbo, S. A., Kim, E.-Y., & Ohno-Machado, L. (2005). Small, fuzzy and interpretable gene expression based classifiers. *Bioinformatics (Oxford, England), 21*(9), 1964–1970. doi:10.1093/bioinformatics/bti287

## KEY TERMS AND DEFINITIONS

**Pattern Classification:** Automatic assignment of input data to categories (classes).

**Fuzzy Logic:** A form of logic where attributes can take on variable degrees of truth.

**Fuzzy Set:** An extension of the classical set to allow for a representation of variable degrees of truth.

**Membership Function:** A function that describes the degree of an element's membership in a fuzzy set.

**Rule-Based Classifier:** A pattern classification system in which the classification is expressed as a set of rules.

**Genetic Algorithm:** An intelligent search and optimisation technique based on the ideas of natural selection and genetics.

# Chapter 7
# Fuzzy Decision Rule Construction Using Fuzzy Decision Trees:
## Application to E-Learning Database

**Malcolm J. Beynon**
*Cardiff University, UK*

**Paul Jones**
*University of Glamorgan, UK*

## ABSTRACT

*This chapter considers the soft computing approach called fuzzy decision trees (FDT), a form of classification analysis. The consideration of decision tree analysis in a fuzzy environment brings further interpretability and readability to the constructed 'if.. then..' decision rules. Two sets of FDT analyses are presented, the first on a small example data set, offering a tutorial on the rudiments of one FDT technique. The second FDT analysis considers the investigation of an e-learning database, and the elucidation of the relationship between weekly online activity of students and their final mark on a university course module. Emphasis throughout the chapter is on the visualization of results, including the fuzzification of weekly online activity levels of students and overall performance.*

## INTRODUCTION

In 1998, Bonissone (1998) perceived soft computing to be a recently coined term, describing the symbiotic use of many emerging computing disciplines, amongst these Fuzzy Logic (introduced by Zadeh, 1965). They suggested that fuzzy logic gives us a language, with syntax and local semantics, in which we can translate our qualitative knowledge about the problem to be solved, with its main characteristic the robustness of its interpolative reasoning mechanism (see Bonissone, 1998).

The association of fuzzy logic with soft computing is regularly perceived. Mitra *et al.* (2002) consider the role of soft computing in data mining (viewing data mining as a step in knowledge discovery in databases) (p. 6):

DOI: 10.4018/978-1-60566-814-7.ch007

*Fuzzy logic is capable of supporting, to a reasonable extent, human type reasoning in natural form. It is the earliest and most widely reported constituent of soft computing.*

It is this characteristic of fuzzy logic, including the potential to perceive qualitative observations and calibration of commonsense rules, in an attempt to establish meaningful and useful relationships between system variables, that allows it to be a pertinent tool to be encompassed in knowledge discovery in databases, which itself is mainly concerned with identifying interesting patterns and describing them in a concise and meaningful manner (Fayyad *et al.*, 1996).

An ability to construct 'commonsense' rules, which are readable and so easily interpretable, is considered here through the employment of a fuzzy decision tree approach (FDT). Amongst the FDT techniques previously constructed, include, fuzzy versions of crisp decision techniques, such as fuzzy ID3 (see Ichihashi *et al.*, 1996; Pal and Chakraborty, 2001), and other versions (see Yuan and Shaw, 1995; Olaru and Wehenkel, 2003). Like the original crisp algorithms, such as the ID3 algorithm (Quinlan, 1979), the general approach involves the repetitive partitioning of the objects in a data set through the augmentation of attributes down a tree structure from a root node, through a series of branches ending in a number of leaf nodes, where each subset of objects is associated with the same decision class or no attribute is available for further decomposition.

With the operation of FDTs in a fuzzy environment (Zadeh, 1965), it is closely associated with the analysis of uncertain and imperfect information. Further, as previously hinted at, the fuzzy environment offers a linguistic domain, within which an analysis can be undertaken and subsequent results expressed (Herrera *et al.*, 2000). This domain is determined through the utilisation of membership functions (MFs), which define fuzzy based analyses (Sancho-Royo and Verdegay, 1999). FDT analyses have further been praised

for comprehensibility in Janikow (1998), who goes on to state Quinlan (1993), when discussing decision trees in general:

*This appeals to a wide range of users who are interested in domain understanding, classification capabilities, or the symbolic rules that may be extracted from the tree.*

The rudiments of FDTs are, as an inductive learning technique, for the fuzzy classification of objects that are described by a number of characteristic attributes. The results from using FDTs are a set of fuzzy '*if.. then..*' decision rules (see Dubois and Prade, 1996). The fuzziness associated with these rules brings with it the pertinent qualities of readability and interpretability to any analysis, offering an efficient insight into the considered problem, a further facet of soft computing (Bodenhofer *et al.*, 2007).

In this chapter, the FDT approach of Yuan and Shaw (1995) is utilised, which attempts to include the cognitive uncertainties evident in data values (for alternative FDT approaches see also Umano *et al.* (1994) and Pal and Chakraborty (2001)). Particularly pertinent to its applicability in areas such as business, but appropriate here, Chen and Chiou (1999, pp. 408) highlight:

*In practical business, economic data are usually imprecise and fuzzy. The assessment level of a criterion often depends on judgement or approximation. A sharp classification or unnatural approximating values results in unreasonable or incorrect outcomes.*

The FDT approach described in this chapter is initially demonstrated on a small data set, where explicit analytic calculations are given, for when different numbers of MFs are employed to define the linguistic terms formulating the linguistic variables of attributes. This, almost tutorial based exposition, should allow a reader of this chapter the opportunity to follow the rudiments of a

FDT technique. Further, a pertinent application is considered, namely the analysis of a database formulated from the student activity on an e-learning based university course.

E-learning represents a rapidly evolving frontier of Higher Education (HE) provision, enabling enhanced delivery of curricula through the use of information communication technology (Gunasekaran *et al.*, 2002; Romano *et al.*, 2005). However, academic debate is ongoing as to what constitutes effective pedagogical design (Bangert, 2004). Indeed, there is an emergent body of literature recording significant high dropout rates from such courses due to problems in course design, delivery and implementation (Packham *et al.*, 2004; Doherty, 2006).

With respect to e-learning, the importance of student online activity within the virtual learning environment (VLE), as a determinant of student success, remains questionable and is the focus of ongoing research via a range of techniques (Davies and Graff, 2005; Jones and Beynon, 2007). In this study, a single module is considered, part of a Business undergraduate degree run by a UK university, which is managed and evaluated online. Moreover, the problem investigated is on the association between the students' weekly activity, database of online pages viewed, with respect to the module and their final mark.

The use of FDTs in this study is to discern between those students with a final module mark described linguistically as either an indifferent or good performance (each represented by an MF). This classification is conditional on the activity of the students, based on the level of concomitant online pages viewed (Jones and Beynon, 2007), over the twelve weeks of the module's duration. Two FDT analyses are presented, which utilise different numbers of linguistic terms (MFs) to describe the students' weekly online activities. It follows, at the technical level, a comparison is also made here when different levels of fuzzifica-

tion of the known weekly online activity of the students are undertaken.

## FUZZY SET THEORY

In this section, the rudiments of fuzzy set theory are briefly presented. In classical set theory, an element (value) either belongs to a certain set or it does not, thus a two-valued membership function (MF), with values 0 or 1, defines membership or non-membership to the set, respectively. In fuzzy set theory (Zadeh, 1965), a grade of membership exists to characterise the association of a value $x$ to a set $S$, the MF, defined $\mu_S(x)$, has range [0, 1]. The domain of a numerical attribute can be described by a finite series of MFs, which each offers a grade of membership to describe a value $x$ to a linguistic term, which form its concomitant fuzzy number (see Kecman, 2001). The finite set of MFs defining a numerical attribute's domain can be denoted a linguistic variable (Herrera *et al.*, 2000).

Different types of MFs have been proposed to describe fuzzy numbers, including triangular and trapezoidal functions (Zeidler *et al.*, 1996). Yu and Li (2001) highlight that MFs may be (advantageously) constructed from mixed shapes, supporting the use of piecewise linear MFs. The functional forms of two piecewise linear MFs, including the type utilised here (in the context of the $j$th linguistic term $T_j^k$ of a linguistic variable $A_k$), are given by;

$$\mu_{T_j^k}(x) = \begin{cases} 0 & \text{if } x \leq \alpha_{j,1} \\ \dfrac{x - \alpha_{j,1}}{\alpha_{j,2} - \alpha_{j,1}} & \text{if } \alpha_{j,1} < x \leq \alpha_{j,2} \\ 1 & \text{if } x = \alpha_{j,2} \\ 1 - \dfrac{x - \alpha_{j,2}}{\alpha_{j,3} - \alpha_{j,2}} & \text{if } \alpha_{j,2} < x \leq \alpha_{j,3} \\ 0 & \text{if } \alpha_{j,3} < x \end{cases}$$

*Figure 1. Fuzzification of C using two MFs (labeled $C_L$ and $C_H$)*

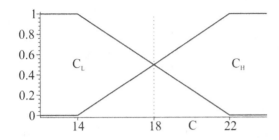

and

$$\mu_{T_j^k}(x) = \begin{cases} 0 & \text{if } x \leq \alpha_{j,1} \\ 0.5\dfrac{x - \alpha_{j,1}}{\alpha_{j,2} - \alpha_{j,1}} & \text{if } \alpha_{j,1} < x \leq \alpha_{j,2} \\ 0.5 + 0.5\dfrac{x - \alpha_{j,2}}{\alpha_{j,3} - \alpha_{j,2}} & \text{if } \alpha_{j,2} < x \leq \alpha_{j,3} \\ 1 & \text{if } x = \alpha_{j,3} \\ 1 - 0.5\dfrac{x - \alpha_{j,3}}{\alpha_{j,4} - \alpha_{j,3}} & \text{if } \alpha_{j,3} < x \leq \alpha_{j,4} \\ 0.5 - 0.5\dfrac{x - \alpha_{j,4}}{\alpha_{j,5} - \alpha_{j,4}} & \text{if } \alpha_{j,4} < x \leq \alpha_{j,5} \\ 0 & \text{if } \alpha_{j,5} < x \end{cases}$$

with the respective *defining values* in list form, $[\alpha_{j,1}, \alpha_{j,2}, \alpha_{j,3}]$ and $[\alpha_{j,1}, \alpha_{j,2}, \alpha_{j,3}, \alpha_{j,4}, \alpha_{j,5}]$. The implication of the defining values is also illustrated, including the idea of associated support, the domains $[\alpha_{j,1}, \alpha_{j,3}]$ in Figure 1a and $[\alpha_{j,1}, \alpha_{j,5}]$ in Figure 1b. Further, the notion of **dominant support** can also be considered where a MF is most closely associated with an attribute value, the domain $[\alpha_{j,2}, \alpha_{j,4}]$ in Figure 1b.

## DESCRIPTION OF A FUZZY DECISION TREE METHOD (YUAN & SHAW, 1995)

This section outlines the technical details of the fuzzy decision tree approach introduced in Yuan and Shaw (1995). With an inductive fuzzy decision tree, the underlying knowledge related to a decision outcome can be represented as a set of fuzzy '*if.. then..*' decision rules, each of the form;

If $(A_1$ is $T_{i_1}^1)$ and $(A_2$ is $T_{i_2}^2)$ ... and $(A_k$ is $T_{i_k}^k)$ then $C$ is $C_j$,

where $A_1, A_2, ..., A_k$ and $C$ are linguistic variables for the multiple antecedents ($A_i$'s) and consequent ($C$) statements used to describe the considered objects, and $T(A_k) = \{T_1^k, T_2^k, ... T_{S_i}^k\}$ and $\{C_1, C_2, ..., C_L\}$ are their respective linguistic terms. Each linguistic term $T_j^k$ is defined by the MF $\mu_{T_j^k}(x)$, which transforms a value in its associated domain to a grade of membership value to between 0 and 1. The MFs, $\mu_{T_j^k}(x)$ and $\mu_{C_j}(y)$, represent the grade of membership of an object's antecedent $A_j$ being $T_j^k$ and consequent $C$ being $C_j$, respectively.

A MF $\mu(x)$ from the set describing a fuzzy linguistic variable $Y$ defined on $X$, can be viewed as a possibility distribution of $Y$ on $X$, that is $\pi(x) = \mu(x)$, for all $x \in X$ the values taken by the objects in $U$ (also normalized so $\max_{x \in X} \pi(x) = 1$). The possibility measure $E_\alpha(Y)$ of ambiguity is defined by $E_\alpha(Y) = g(\pi) = \sum_{i=1}^{n} (\pi_i^* - \pi_{i+1}^*) \ln[i]$, where $\pi^* = \{\pi_1^*, \pi_2^*, ..., \pi_n^*\}$ is the permutation of the normalized possibility distribution $\pi = \{\pi(x_1), \pi(x_2), ..., \pi(x_n)\}$, sorted so that $\pi_i^* \geq \pi_{i+1}^*$ for $i = 1, ..., n$, and $\pi_{n+1}^* = 0$ (Zadeh, 1978). In the limit, if $\pi_2^* = 0$, then $E_\alpha(Y) = 0$, indicates no ambiguity, whereas if $\pi_n^* = 1$, then $E_\alpha(Y) = \ln[n]$, which indicates all values are fully possible for $Y$, representing the greatest ambiguity.

The ambiguity of attribute $A$ (over the objects $u_1, ..., u_m$) is given as: $E_\alpha(A) = \dfrac{1}{m}\sum_{i=1}^{m} E_\alpha(A(u_i))$, where $E_\alpha(A(u_i)) = g\left(\mu_{T_s}(u_i)\Big/\max_{1 \le j \le s}(\mu_{T_j}(u_i))\right)$, with $T_1, ..., T_s$ the linguistic terms of an attribute (antecedent) with $m$ objects. When there is overlapping between linguistic terms (MFs) of an attribute or between consequents, then ambiguity exists.

For all $u \in U$, the intersection $A \cap B$ of two fuzzy sets is given by $\mu_{A \cap B} = \min[\mu_A(u), \mu_B(u)]$. The fuzzy subsethood $S(A, B)$ measures the degree to which $A$ is a subset of $B$, and is given by, $S(A, B) = \sum_{u \in U}\min(\mu_A(u),\mu_B(u))\Big/\sum_{u \in U}\mu_A(u)$. Given fuzzy evidence $E$, the possibility of classifying an object to the consequent $C_i$ can be defined as, $\pi(C_i|E) = S(E, C_i)/\max_j S(E, C_j)$, where the fuzzy subsethood $S(E, C_i)$ represents the degree of truth for the classification rule ('if $E$ then $C_i$'). With a single piece of evidence (a fuzzy number for an attribute), then the classification ambiguity based on this fuzzy evidence is defined as: $G(E) = g(\pi(C|E))$, which is measured using the possibility distribution $\pi(C|E) = (\pi(C_1|E), ..., \pi(C_L|E))$.

The classification ambiguity with fuzzy partitioning $P = \{E_1, ..., E_k\}$ on the fuzzy evidence $F$, denoted as $G(P|F)$, is the weighted average of classification ambiguity with each subset of partition: $G(P|F) = \sum_{i=1}^{k} w(E_i|F)G(E_i \cap F)$, where $G(E_i \cap F)$ is the classification ambiguity with fuzzy evidence $E_i \cap F$, and where $w(E_i|F)$ is the weight which represents the relative size of subset $E_i \cap F$ in $F$: $w(E_i|F) = \sum_{u \in U}\min(\mu_{E_i}(u),\mu_F(u))\Big/\sum_{j=1}^{k}\left(\sum_{u \in U}\min(\mu_{E_j}(u),\mu_F(u))\right)$

In summary, attributes are assigned to nodes based on the lowest level of classification ambiguity. A node becomes a leaf node if the level of subsethood is higher than some truth value $\beta$ assigned to the whole of the fuzzy decision tree. The

*Table 1. Example small data set*

| Object | T1 | T2 | T3 | C |
|--------|----|----|----|----|
| $u_1$ | 30 | 52 | 26 | 14 |
| $u_2$ | 40 | 56 | 20 | 16 |
| $u_3$ | 36 | 38 | 16 | 10 |
| $u_4$ | 24 | 22 | 30 | 20 |

classification from the leaf node is to the decision group with the largest subsethood value. The truth level threshold $\beta$ controls the growth of the tree; lower $\beta$ may lead to a smaller tree (with lower classification accuracy), higher $\beta$ may lead to a larger tree (with higher classification accuracy).

## FUZZY DECISION TREE ANALYSES OF EXAMPLE DATA SET

In this section two analyses are described that form different FDTs for the same small example data set, consisting of four objects described by three condition (T1, T2 and T3) and one decision (C) attribute, see Table 1.

Using the data set presented in Table 1, the two FDT analyses are next exposited, in each case starting with the fuzzification of the individual attribute values. The two analyses are different in the levels of fuzzification employed; the first analysis uses two MFs to describe each condition attribute, whereas in the second analysis three MFs are employed. For consistency, two MFs are used to fuzzify the single **decision attribute** C, see Figure 1.

In Figure 1, two MFs, $\mu_L(C)$ (labelled $C_L$) and $\mu_H(C)$ ($C_H$), are shown to cover the domain of the decision attribute C, the concomitant defining values are, for $C_L$: $[-\infty, -\infty, 14, 18, 22]$ and $C_H$: $[14, 18, 22, \infty, \infty]$. An interpretation could then simply be the association of a decision attribute value to being low (L) and/or high (H), with the two MFs showing the linguistic partition.

*Figure 2. Fuzzification of condition attributes using two MFs*

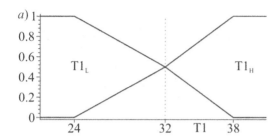

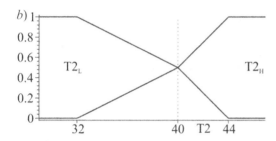

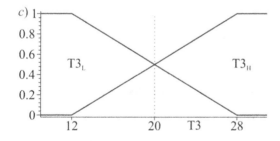

## Analysis with Two MF Based Fuzzification of Condition Attributes

This section analyses the example data set using two MFs to fuzzify each condition attribute, see Figure 2.

The MFs described in Figure 2 are each found from a series of defining values, in this case for; T1 - [[−∞,−∞, 24, 32, 38], [24, 32, 38, ∞, ∞]], T2 - [[−∞,−∞, 32, 40, 44], [32, 40, 44, ∞, ∞]] and T2 - [[−∞,−∞, 12, 20, 28], [12, 20, 28, ∞, ∞]]. Applying these MFs on the example data set achieves a fuzzy data set, see Table 2.

In Table 2, each condition attribute, T1, T2 and T3, is described by two values associated with two fuzzy labels. For the construction of a FDT, the classification ambiguity of each condition attribute with respect to the decision attribute is first considered, namely the evaluation of the $G(E)$ values. Further, a threshold value of $\beta = 0.95$ was used throughout this construction process. The evaluation of a $G(E)$ value is shown for the attribute T1 $(= g(\pi(C|T1)))$, where it is broken down to the fuzzy labels L and H, so for L; $\pi(C|T1_L) = S(T1_L, C_i) / \max_j S(T1_L, C_j)$, considering $C_L$ and $C_H$ with the information in Table 1:

$$S(T1_L, C_L) =$$
$$\sum_{u \in U} \min(\mu_{T1_L}(u), \mu_{C_L}(u)) / \sum_{u \in U} \mu_{T_L}(u)$$
$$= (\min(0.625, 1.000) + \min(0.000, 0.750)$$
$$+ \min(0.167, 1.000) + \min(1.000, 0.250))$$
$$/ (0.625 + 0.000 + 0.167 + 1.000)$$

$$= (0.625 + 0.000 + 0.167 + 0.250)/1.792 =$$

$$1.042/1.792 = 0.581,$$

whereas $S(T1_L, C_H) = 0.419$. Hence $\pi = \{0.581, 0.419\}$, giving $\pi^* = \{1.000, 0.720\}$, with $\pi_3^* = 0$, then:

$$G(T1_L) = g(\pi(C|T1_L)) = \sum_{i=1}^{2} (\pi_i^* - \pi_{i+1}^*) \ln[i]$$

$$= (1.000 - 0.720) \ln[1] + (0.720 - 0.000) \ln[2]$$
$$= 0.499,$$

with $G(T1_H) = 0.088$, then $G(T1) = (0.499 + 0.088)/2 = 0.294$. Compared with $G(T2) = 0.338$ and $G(T3) = 0.248$. It follows, the T3 attribute, with the least classification ambiguity, forms the root node in this case. The subsethood values

*Table 2. Fuzzy data set using two MFs for each condition attribute*

| Object | T1 = [T1$_L$, T1$_H$] | T2 = [T2$_L$, T2$_H$] | T3 = [T3$_L$, T3$_H$] | C = [C$_L$, C$_H$] |
|--------|----------------------|----------------------|----------------------|--------------------|
| $u_1$ | [**0.625**, 0.375] | [0.000, **1.000**] | [0.125, **0.875**] | [**1.000**, 0.000] |
| $u_2$ | [0.000, **1.000**] | [0.000, **1.000**] | [**0.500, 0.500**] | [**0.750**, 0.250] |
| $u_3$ | [0.167, **0.833**] | [**0.625**, 0.375] | [**0.750**, 0.250] | [**1.000**, 0.000] |
| $u_4$ | [**1.000**, 0.000] | [**1.000**, 0.000] | [0.000, **1.000**] | [0.250, **0.750**] |

in this case are; for T3: $S(T3_L, C_L) = 1.000$ and $S(T3_L, C_H) = 0.182$; $S(T3_H, C_L) = 0.714$ and $S(T3_H, C_H) = 0.381$. In each case the linguistic term with largest subsethood value (in bold), indicates the possible augmentation of the path. For $T3_L$, this is to $C_L$, with largest subsethood value above the desired truth value of 0.95, so a leaf node is establlished. For $T3_H$, its largest subsethood value is 0.714 ($S(T3_H, C_L)$), hence it is not able to be a leaf node and further possible augmentation needs to be considered.

With only three condition attributes considered, the possible augmentation of $T3_H$ is with T1 or T2, where with $G(T3_H) = 0.370$, the ambiguity with partition evaluated for T1 ($G(T3_H$ and T1| C)) or T3 ($G(T3_H$ and T2| C)) has to be less than this value. In the case of T1:

$$G(T3_H \text{ and } T1| C) =$$
$$\sum_{i=1}^{k} w(T1_i | T3_H) G(T3_H \cap T1_i).$$

Starting with the weight values, in the case of $T3_H$ and $T1_L$, it follows:

$$w(T1_L| T3_H) =$$
$$\sum_{u \in U} \min(\mu_{T1_L}(u), \mu_{T3_H}(u)) / \sum_{j=1}^{k} \left( \sum_{u \in U} \min(\mu_{T1_j}(u), \mu_{T3_H}(u)) \right)$$
$$= (\min(0.625, 0.875) + \min(0.000, 0.500)$$
$$+ \min(0.167, 0.250) + \min(0.000, 0.000)),$$
$$/ \sum_{j=1}^{k} \left( \sum_{u \in U} \min(\mu_{T1_j}(u), \mu_{T3_H}(u)) \right)$$

where $\sum_{j=1}^{k} \left( \sum_{u \in U} \min(\mu_{T1_j}(u), \mu_{T2_H}(u)) \right) = 2.917$, so $w(T2_L| T1_H) = 1.792/2.917 = 0.614$. Similarly $w(T3_H| T1_H) = 0.386$, hence:

$$G(T3_H \text{ and } T1| C) = 0.614 \times G(T3_H \cap T1_L) + 0.386 \times G(T3_H \cap T1_H)$$

$$= 0.614 \times 0.499 + 0.386 \times 0.154$$

$$= 0.366.$$

Similarly, $G(T3_H$ and T2| C) = 0.261. With $G(T3_H$ and T2| C) = 0.261, the lowest of these two values, and lower than the concomitant $G(T3_H) = 0.370$ value, so less ambiguity would be found if the T2 attribute was augmented to the T3 = H path.

The subsequent subsethood values in this case for each new path are; $T2_L$; $S(T3_H \cap T2_L, C_L) = 0.400$ and $S(T3_H \cap T2_L, C_H) = \mathbf{0.600}$; $T2_H$: $S(T3_H \cap T2_H, C_L) = \mathbf{1.000}$ and $S(T3_H \cap T2_H, C_H) = 0.154$. These subsethood results show one path $T3_H \cap T1_H$ ends in a leaf node, the other $T3_H \cap T2_L$ would require the possible further augmentation of other condition attribute linguistic terms. This process continues until; either all paths end at a leaf node, or no further augmentation will reduce classification ambiguity, or there are no further condition attributes to augment. The resultant FDT in this case is presented in Figure 3.

The tree structure in Figure 3 clearly demonstrates the visual form of the results described previously. Only shown in each node box is the truth level associated with the highest subsethood value to a decision attribute class. There are three

*Figure 3. FDT for example data set with two MFs describing each condition attribute*

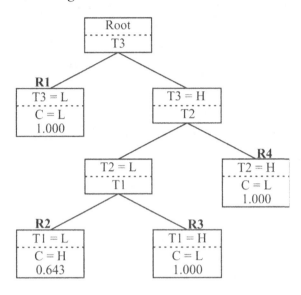

*Figure 4. Fuzzification of condition attributes using three MFs*

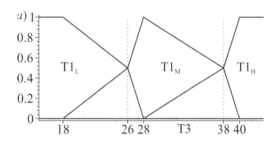

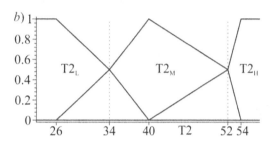

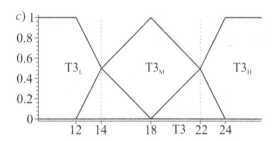

levels of the tree showing the use of all the considered condition attributes. There are four leaf nodes which each have a defined decision rule associated with them.

## Analysis with Three MF Based Fuzzication of Condition Attributes

This section analyses the example data set using three MFs to fuzzify each condition attribute, see Figure 4.

The MFs described in Figure 4 are each found from a series of defining values, in this case for; T1 - [[$-\infty,-\infty$, 18, 26, 28], [18, 26, 28, 38, 40], [28, 38, 40, $\infty$, $\infty$]], T2 - [[$-\infty,-\infty$, 26, 34, 40], [26, 34, 40, 52, 54], [40, 52, 54, $\infty$, $\infty$]] and T2 - [[$-\infty,-\infty$, 12, 14, 18], [12, 14, 18, 22, 24], [18, 22, 24, $\infty$, $\infty$]]. Applying these MFs on the example data set achieves a fuzzy data set, see Table 3.

In Table 3, each condition attribute, T1, T2 and T3, describing an object is itself described by three values associated with three fuzzy labels. A similar process is then undertaken to construct a

FDT, as was performed for the previous fuzzy data set (in Table 2). The resultant FDT is shown in Figure 5.

The tree structure in Figure 5 shows two levels of the tree, using only the T2 and T3 condition attributes. There are five leaf nodes, which each have a defined decision rule associated with them. In R3, the *, along with $S(T2_L \cap T3_H) = 0.750 < 0.95 = \beta$, indicates that there was insufficient improvement in classification ambiguity to warrant augmentation with the T1 attribute, not previously utilised.

*Table 3. Fuzzy data set using three MFs for each condition attribute*

| Object | T1 = [T1$_L$, T1$_M$, T1$_H$] | T2 = [T2$_L$, T2$_M$, T2$_H$] | T3 = [T3$_L$, T3$_M$, T3$_H$] | C = [C$_L$, C$_H$] |
|--------|-------------------------------|-------------------------------|-------------------------------|---------------------|
| $u_1$ | [0.000, **0.900**, 0.100] | [0.000, **0.500**, 0.500] | [0.000, 0.000, **1.000**] | [**1.000**, 0.000] |
| $u_2$ | [0.000, 0.000, **1.000**] | [0.000, 0.000, **1.000**] | [0.000, **0.750**, 0.250] | [**0.750**, 0.250] |
| $u_3$ | [0.000, **0.600**, 0.400] | [0.167, **0.833**, 0.000] | [0.250, **0.750**, 0.000] | [**1.000**, 0.000] |
| $u_4$ | [**0.625**, 0.375, 0.000] | [**1.000**, 0.000, 0.000] | [0.000, 0.000, **1.000**] | [0.250, **0.750**] |

*Figure 5. FDT for example data set with three MFs describing each condition attribute*

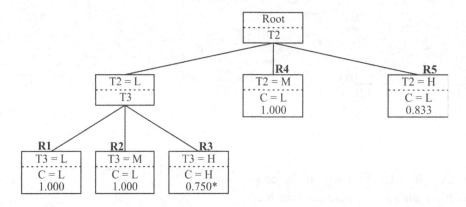

## APPLICATION OF FUZZY DECISION TREES TO E-LEARNING DATA SET

This section applies the fuzzy decision tree approach outlined and demonstrated in the previous sections. The area of application concerns a database of student activity on a university course, the collection of this data being part of the concomitant e-learning based course considered.

## E-Learning

E-learning has been defined as education learning enabled via the Internet utilizing digital media such as computers, web pages, video conferencing and CD-ROMs (Keller and Cernerud, 2002). The module under investigation entitled "Entrepreneurial Competencies (EC)" represents one module of an undergraduate business degree run by a UK university, developed specifically for e-learning delivery. The module was supported by "Blackboard" software, utilising synchronous and asyn-

chronous communication mechanisms including discussion boards, e-mail and virtual classrooms, with module materials all held within an associated Content Management System (CMS).

The pedagogical design meant, students were expected to access relevant pages of content on a weekly basis, completing associated tasks and participating in regular discussions with fellow classmates and tutor. In this case the online tasks represented the assessment regime for the module. A total of 66 students were analyzed, who participated during the duration of the module. The "EC" module represented the initial module of study upon the degree. The rationale for the module was to provide students with the appropriate range of study skills to be successful as a distance learner. This study analyses student activity on the "EC" module using the number of online pages within the CMS viewed each week. Students are encouraged to actively participate within the weekly activities by the online tutor.

The data available within the CMS provides the opportunity to evaluate student performance and engagement on a daily, weekly and individual task basis using a variety of techniques. Such analysis should enable programme designers to enhance the quality of the learning experience within the VLE and also act as a reactive system to effectively monitor student performance. Such a system could be automated via a database providing e-mail responses to non-performing or non-participating members of the student cohort which could potentially improve retention and individual performance.

To initially gauge the variation in the weeks' online activity, certain summary measures are presented in Table 4. The mean values in Table 4 show different levels of activity of the online pages accessed over the different weeks, as do the standard deviation ($\sigma$) values. Also reported are the minimum and maximum values associated with each week's activity, again supporting the variation in activity. Indeed, it is this inherent variation in the utilization of the e-learning facilities by the students over the different weeks that is a motivation for this study, as well as the exposition of the FDT system for performance analysis.

The performance classification of the students considered here is based on their final module mark, with the threshold defined between 'less than 60%' and 'greater than or equal to 60%', described exclusively here as indifferent and good performance, respectively (in summary it is based on students 'not attaining' and 'attaining' a UK 2–1 class or above). Of the 66 students who completed the module ($s_i$, $i = 1, ..., 66$), 23 and 43 students are classified as indifferent and good, respectively, with marks (termed Mrk) spread over a continuous domain from a minimum of 32.8% to a maximum of 78.2%. The fuzzification of the general level of mark performance is reported in Figure 6.

In Figure 6, there are two MFs shown to fuzzify the final module mark performances of the individual students, each into a linguistic

*Table 4. Descriptive details of weekly student 'online activity' levels*

| Week | Mean | Min | Max | σ |
|---|---|---|---|---|
| $c_1$ | 285.92 | 0 | 1114 | 245.77 |
| $c_2$ | 284.44 | 0 | 1427 | 298.70 |
| $c_3$ | 230.97 | 0 | 838 | 175.16 |
| $c_4$ | 118.21 | 0 | 358 | 100.37 |
| $c_5$ | 72.74 | 0 | 466 | 99.73 |
| $c_6$ | 113.88 | 0 | 505 | 110.99 |
| $c_7$ | 326.73 | 0 | 1519 | 244.65 |
| $c_8$ | 188.18 | 0 | 894 | 169.71 |
| $c_9$ | 132.00 | 0 | 575 | 122.48 |
| $c_{10}$ | 117.20 | 0 | 561 | 120.55 |
| $c_{11}$ | 176.32 | 0 | 825 | 165.49 |
| $c_{12}$ | 207.48 | 0 | 791 | 192.46 |

variable, with the linguistic terms of Indifferent (Mrk = I) and Good (Mrk = G). The associated pairs of defining values with these MFs are; I - [0, 0, 52. 5, 60.0, 68.2] and G - [52. 5, 60.0, 68.2, 100, 100]. Understandably, the boundary between where these MFs have dominant support is either side of the 60% mark. The 52.5 and 68.2 values included in these sets of defining values are the mean values of the respective equivalence classes of students' marks, associated separately with students with marks below or above (or equal) the partition value of 60%, respectively.

## FDT Analysis E-Learning Data Set Using Two MFs for Each Condition Attribute

In this section the construction of a FDT to describe the efficacy of the e-learning module is undertaken for the first time. Included in this process is the initial fuzzification of the condition attributes, namely the weekly levels of online activity of students during the twelve weeks of the module. This fuzzification is similar to that for the decision attribute as undertaken previously (see Figure 6),

*Figure 6. Membership functions describing students' module marks to indifferent and good performance*

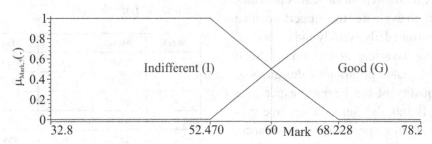

where each condition attribute is described by two MFs, see Figure 7.

In Figure 7, the doublets of MFs for each condition attribute are denoted linguistically, as; low (L) and high (H), in terms of separate week's online activity by the students. To demonstrate, for the case of the week 1's online activity by students, the associated two sets of defining values are; L - [0, 0, 102, 202, 470] and H - [102, 202, 470, ∞, ∞].[1] These doublets of MFs are then used to directly fuzzify the online activity of each student over the twelve weeks of the module, from now on labelled Wk1, Wk2, ..., Wk12 for brevity. This fuzzification process is demonstrated for the student $s_{11}$, see Table 5.

The fuzzification demonstrated in Table 5 shows how the original crisp activity levels of a student can be described in linguistic terms. To demonstrate, in week 1 (Wk1) the student viewed 372 online pages, through fuzzification this is high (H), but the actual MF values show a level of ambiguity in this statement. For the week 4 (Wk4), its level of activity, 93 online pages viewed, creates a fuzzification with equal membership to being low and high activity (see week 4 graph in Figure 3). The final mark for the student was 68.2%, hence from Figure 6, its fuzzification confers a good performance (Mrk = G), with very little ambiguity.

The fuzzification presented in Table 5, for the student $s_{11}$, along with the linguistic labeling, when employed on all the 66 students, form the data for an analysis using FDTs. The full description of the FDT approach employed here was described

in a previous section, on the example data set. In this study, a truth value of $\beta = 0.75$ is employed. The calculation of the classification ambiguity of each condition attribute (weekly online activity), namely the evaluation of the $G(E)$ values, is first considered. For the twelve weeks of the module, the respective $G(E)$ values are reported in Table 6.

In Table 6, the least $G(\cdot)$ value is associated with week 5 ($G$(Wk5) = 0.397), hence the Wk5 attribute, with the least classification ambiguity, forms the root node in this case. The subsethood values associated with the branches from the Wk5 attribute to each of the decision classes of, indifferent (I) and good (G), performance are; for Wk5 = L, $S$(Wk5 = L, Mrk = I) = 0.436 and $S$(Wk5 = L, Mrk = G) = **0.614**; and for Wk5 = H, $S$(Wk5 = H, Mrk = I) = 0.322 and $S$(Wk5 = H, Mrk = G) = **0.741**. In each case, the linguistic term with largest subsethood value (in bold) is less than the imposed truth value of 0.75 ($\beta$), indicating the possible 'necessary' augmentation of the path from the respective node partition, next considered.

For Wk5 = L, its possible augmentation is with any of the other weeks' activities, where with $G$(Wk5 = L) = 0.492, the concomitant ambiguity with partition evaluated with each other weeks' activities has to be less than this value. It is found, with $G$(Wk5 = L and Wk2| Mrk) = 0.479 < 0.492 = $G$(Wk5 = L), the augmentation is with the Wk2 activity. The associated subsethood values are $S$(Wk5 = L and Wk2 = L, Mrk = I) = 0.436 and $S$(Wk5 = L and Wk2 = L, Mrk = G) = **0.614**, so further augmentation is still needed in

*Figure 7. Doublets of membership functions describing students' weekly online activity*

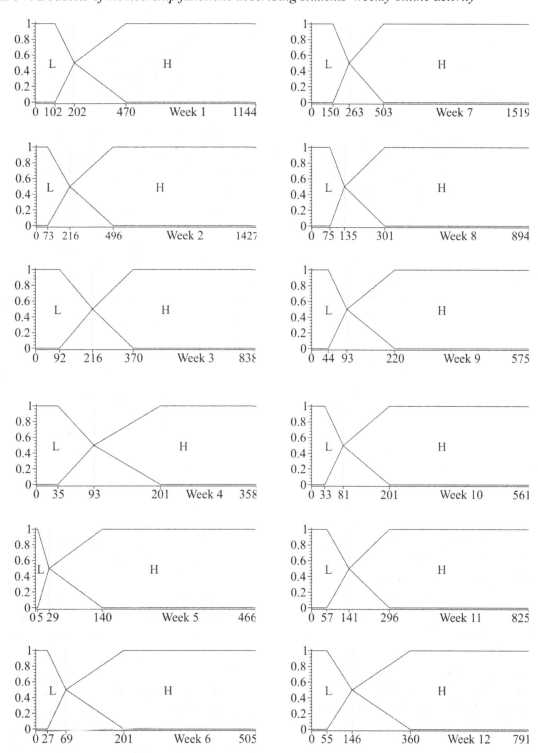

*Table 5. Attribute values and fuzzification with linguistic labels presented for the student $s_{11}$.*

| Week | Crisp Activity | Fuzzy values | Label |
|------|----------------|--------------|-------|
| Wk1 | 372 | [0.183, **0.817**] | H |
| Wk2 | 333 | [0.291, **0.709**] | H |
| Wk3 | 209 | [**0.528**, 0.472] | L |
| Wk4 | 93 | [**0.500**, **0.500**] | L, H |
| Wk5 | 0 | [**1.000**, 0.000] | L |
| Wk6 | 0 | [**1.000**, 0.000] | L |
| Wk7 | 485 | [0.038, **0.962**] | H |
| Wk8 | 227 | [0.223, **0.777**] | H |
| Wk9 | 0 | [**1.000**, 0.000] | L |
| Wk10 | 134 | [0.279, **0.721**] | H |
| Wk11 | 199 | [0.312, **0.688**] | H |
| Wk12 | 157 | [0.474, **0.526**] | H |
| Mrk | 68.2 | [0.002, **0.998**] | G |

both branches. For Wk5 = H, with $G$(Wk5 = H) = 0.301, there was found no ambiguity with partition evaluated was less than this value, so the node became a leaf node. This process was continued with the subsequent FDT fully constructed, see Figure 8.

The resultant FDT presented in Figure 8, is made up of a root (top) node, here the activity in week 5 (Wk5), from which branches are created through the nodes down to a number of leaf (end) nodes. Here, the FDT has a maximum depth of seven non-leaf nodes. That is, upto a maximum of seven condition attributes (weeks' levels of online activities), make up a branch from the root node to a leaf node. In total there are 16 leaf nodes, indicating 16 fuzzy '*if.. then..*' decision rules, **R1**, **R2**, …, **R16**, are included in the concomitant fuzzy decision rule set.

To demonstrate the type of rule included, the case of the rule **R12** is considered. A direct representation of this rule from the FDT, in Figure 8, is:

*If Wk5 = L and Wk2 = H and Wk8 = H and Wk9 = L then Mrk = G, with truth level 0.761.*

A more linguistic version of this rule is:

*If week 5 activity is low and week 2 activity is high and week 8 activity is high and week 9 activity is low then the student's performance mark is good, with truth level 0.761.*

Finally, using the defining values associated with the doublets of MFs for each condition attribute expressed in Figure 7 and the notion of dominant support, a more quantitative (crisp) version of the rule is of the form:

*If week 5 activity is below 29 pages viewed, week 2 activity is above or equal to 216 pages viewed and week 8 activity is above or equal to 135 pages viewed and week 9 activity is below 93 pages viewed then mark is above or equal to 60%, with truth level 0.761.*

Each of these three forms of the fuzzy decision rules, described in Figure 8, can be used to match students to a rule, using the matching procedure given in Wang *et al*. (2000), namely:

1. Matching starts from the root node and ends at a leaf node along the branch of the maximum membership of an object to each node (condition) met,

2. If the maximum membership at the node is not unique, matching proceeds along several branches,

3. The decision class with the maximum degree of truth from the leaf nodes is then assigned the classification for the associated rule (for example I or G).

It follows, each fuzzy rule is associated with a number of objects, for which it affords their predicted performance classification, in this case, an indifferent (I) or good (G) module mark (Mrk). For the rule **R12**, considered earlier, it matches with four students online activity, amongst these is the student $s_{11}$ considered earlier (see Table 5).

*Table 6. Classification ambiguity values (G(E)) for each week's online activity*

| | **Wk1** | **Wk2** | **Wk3** | **Wk4** | **Wk5** | **Wk6** |
|---|---|---|---|---|---|---|
| $G(\cdot)$ | 0.414 | 0.410 | 0.409 | 0.414 | 0.397 | 0.414 |
| | **Wk7** | **Wk8** | **Wk9** | **Wk10** | **Wk11** | **Wk12** |
| $G(\cdot)$ | 0.410 | 0.415 | 0.411 | 0.415 | 0.414 | 0.406 |

*Figure 8. Fuzzy decision tree for e-learning efficacy, described by low or high weekly online activity*

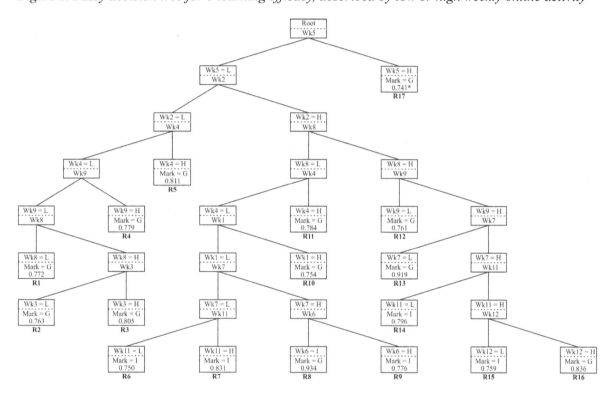

Indeed, each of the original crisp online activity levels and fuzzy labels can be used with the different forms of the **R12** fuzzy decision rule to verify its path down the FDT and its subsequent final predicted performance mark classification.

Indepth interpretation of this FDT is left until the second FDT analysis is undertaken (in the next section). However, there is some reasoning for the presence of the week 5 activity level as the root node, since in week 6 students are working towards the completion of an important piece of coursework associated with the module. Using this week's activity level there is no further activity needed to be considered if a student's activity was high (Wk5 = H), since the predicted classification of such students is to a good performance. There is noticeable further activity needed to be considered when a low level of activity in week 5 is undertaken. Poor performance within this week was typically indicative of a lack of engagement with the online learning experience and under performance within the module as a whole.

*Figure 9. Triplets of membership functions describing students' weekly online activity*

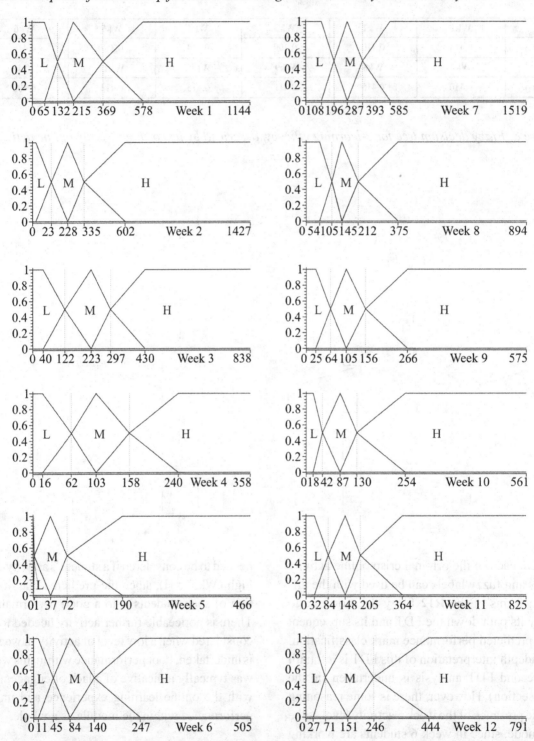

*Table 7. Attribute values and fuzzification with linguistic labels presented for the student $s_{11}$.*

| Week | Crisp | Fuzzy | Label |
|------|-------|-------|-------|
| Wk1 | 372 | [0.000, 0.493, **0.507**] | H |
| Wk2 | 333 | [0.000, **0.509**, 0.491] | M |
| Wk3 | 209 | [0.069, **0.931**, 0.000] | M |
| Wk4 | 93 | [0.125, **0.875**, 0.000] | M |
| Wk5 | 0 | [**1.000**, 0.000, 0.000] | L |
| Wk6 | 0 | [**1.000**, 0.000, 0.000] | L |
| Wk7 | 485 | [0.000, 0.260, **0.740**] | H |
| Wk8 | 227 | [0.000, 0.454, **0.546**] | H |
| Wk9 | 0 | [**1.000**, 0.000, 0.000] | L |
| Wk10 | 134 | [0.000, 0.484, **0.516**] | H |
| Wk11 | 199 | [0.000, **0.557**, 0.443] | M |
| Wk12 | 157 | [0.000, **0.971**, 0.029] | M |
| Mark | 68.2 | [0.002, **0.998**] | G |

## FDT Analysis E-Learning Data Set Using Three MFs for Each Condition Attribute

This section elucidates the construction of another FDT to describe the efficacy of the considered e-learning module. The reason for the further analysis is to see the effect of changing the level of fuzzification of the condition attribute, namely increasing the number of linguistic terms that describe each week's activity level. This is an ongoing technical issue when working in a fuzzy environment, for example, DeOliveria (1999) considers the implication of principle of incompatibility (Zadeh, 1973), whereby, as the number of MFs increase, so the precision of the system increases, but at the expense of relevance decreasing.

Here, each weeks' online activity by a student is described by three fuzzy based linguistic terms (MFs), denoting low (L), medium (M) and high (H) levels of their online activity, see Figure 9.

The construction process for these sets of triplets of MFs follows the process for the MFs employed in the FDT analyses given previously.

In summary, each week's activity level was partitioned into three groups using the criteria of equal-frequency. The respective cut-point between each group are retained as defining values, as well as the concomitant means of the activity levels included in each identified group.

For the week 1's activity, the sets of defining values that define the three linguistic terms, for; L - [0, 0, 65, 132, 215], M - [65, 132, 215, 369, 578] and H - [215, 369, 578, ∞, ∞]. Inspection of these sets shows there are only five different defining values necessary to describe the three linguistic terms (not including the general 0 and ∞ values used). The effect of these defining values is shown in the fuzzification of the weekly online activity of the student $s_{11}$, see Table 7.

In Table 7, each crisp value of the weekly online activity of the student $s_{11}$ is now represented by three fuzzy values associated with the linguistic terms, low (L), medium (M) and high (H). For each week's activity, the linguistic term it is most associated with is also given (label column). The fuzzification of each of the considered 66 students using three linguistic terms for each week's activity allows a concomitant FDT to be constructed, see Figure 10.

An inspection of the FDT presented in Figure 10 shows up to six weeks' online activity levels of students are used as conditions in the included fuzzy decision rules from the root node, again Wk5, to the individual leaf nodes. There are 27 rules (leaf nodes), **R1, R2, …, R27**, shown to be present in the FDT, noticeably more than in the FDT presented in Figure 8.

With respect to the student $s_{11}$, considered in the previous section and its newly fuzzified weekly online activity described in Table 7, it can be found that it is described by rule **R14**, in words:

*If Wk5 = L and Wk3 = M and Wk7 = H then Mrk = G, with truth level 0.871.*

*Figure 10. Fuzzy decision tree for e-learning efficacy, described by low, medium or high weekly online activity*

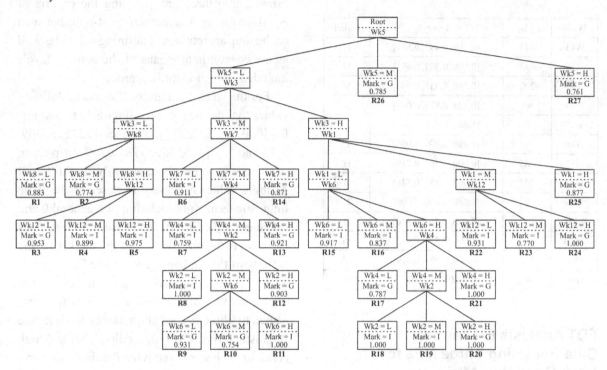

*If week 5 activity is low and week 3 activity is medium and week 7 activity is high then performance mark is good, with truth level 0.871.*

*If week 5 activity is below 1 page viewed and week 3 activity is greater than or equal to 122 pages viewed and less than 297 pages and week 7 activity is above or equal to 393 pages viewed then performance mark is good, with truth level 0.871.*

Comparisons between the two FDTs constructed, starts with the increase in the number of fuzzy decision rules associated with the increased fuzzification of the weekly online activity. That is, 27 fuzzy decision rules included in the FDT in Figure 10, compared to the lesser number of 16 in the FDT in Figure 8. In contrast, the maximum number of conditions in a fuzzy decision rule decreases as the level of fuzzification increases. That is, the FDT in Figure 10 has a depth of six

different week's activity, compared to a depth of seven with the FDT in Figure 8.

## FUTURE RESEARCH DIRECTIONS

An interesting feature of soft computing based techniques is the associated added realism that may be associated with it. In the case of fuzzy decision trees (FDTs), the development, over traditional decision tree approaches is the added interpretability and readability associated with the decision rules constructed. Fundamental to the added interpretability and readability is the linguistic variables form using different numbers of membership function (in fuzzy set theory) to fuzzy numerical attributes. How these are chosen, their number and possibly different types, is an ongoing research question.

## CONCLUSION

This chapter has considered the utilisation of the methodology of fuzzy decision trees (FDTs). Reasons for the utilisation of a FDT based analysis include; the understood belief in its comprehensibility, as well as the linguistic interpretability the analysis in a fuzzy environment can confer. These and other positive characteristics associated with fuzzy logic and subsequently FDTs, make fuzzy logic one of the most pertinent of general methodologies to be associated with soft computing.

The specific FDT technique employed here is closely associated with the inclusivity of the concomitant cognitive uncertainties. At the technical level, the results produced in this study were based on creating an optimal FDT, through minimising ambiguity. The FDTs constructed on the example data set, made up of only four objects, elucidates the intricacies of the FDT technique, allowing the reader the clearest of opportunities to follows the required construction process (its operations).

The larger application concerns two FDTs, each constructed to describe the relationship between students' weekly online activity and subsequent performance on a university course. There is an important underlying issue exhibited by the study given here, namely the ability to have worked with data created through the recording of the online activity of students and utilised it in a way that produced readable inference on the e-learning efficacy problem (in this case). However, the efficacy described needs to be understood by individuals using the information that is available. If the information is available in readable form, as is the case with fuzzy decision trees, then the appropriate inference can be gained.

## REFERENCES

Bangert, A. W. (2004). The Seven Principles of Good Practice: A framework for evaluating online teaching. *The Internet and Higher Education*, *7*(3), 217–232. doi:10.1016/j.iheduc.2004.06.003

Bodenhofer, U., Hüllermeier, E., Klawonn, F., & Kruse, R. (2007). Special issue on soft computing for information mining. *Soft Computing, 11*, 397–399. doi:10.1007/s00500-006-0105-3

Bonissone, P. P. (1998). Soft Computing: The Convergence of Emerging Reasoning Technologies. *Soft Computing, 1*, 6–18. doi:10.1007/s005000050002

Chen, L.-H. & Chiou, T.-W. (1999). A fuzzy credit-rating approach for commercial loans: a Taiwan case. *OMEGA - International Journal of Management Science, 27*, 407-419.

Davies, J., & Graff, M. (2005). Performance in e-learning: online participation and student grades. *British Journal of Educational Technology, 36*(4), 657–663. doi:10.1111/j.1467-8535.2005.00542.x

DeOliveria, J. V. (1999). Semantic constraints for membership function optimization. *IEEE Transactions on Systems, Man, and Cybernetics. Part A, Systems and Humans, 29*(1), 128–138. doi:10.1109/3468.736369

Doherty, W. (2006). An analysis of multiple factors affecting retention in Web-based community college courses. *The Internet and Higher Education, 9*(4), 245–255. doi:10.1016/j.iheduc.2006.08.004

Dubois, D., & Prade, H. (1996). What are fuzzy rules and how to use them. *Fuzzy Sets and Systems, 84*, 169–185. doi:10.1016/0165-0114(96)00066-8

Dubois, D., & Prade, H. (1998). Soft Computing, Fuzzy Logic, and Artificial Intelligence. *Soft Computing, 2*, 7–11. doi:10.1007/s005000050025

Fayyad, U. M., Piatetsky-Shapiro, G., Smyth, P., & Uthurusamy, R. (1996). *Advances in Knowledge Discovery and Data Mining*. Menlo Park, CA: AAAI/MIT Press.

Gunasekaran, A., McNeil, R., & Shaul, D. (2002). E-learning: research and applications. *Industrial and Commercial Training, 34*(2), 44–53. doi:10.1108/00197850210417528

Herrera, F., Herrera-Viedma, E., & Martinez, L. (2000). A fusion approach for managing multi-granularity linguistic term sets in decision making. *Fuzzy Sets and Systems, 114*(1), 43–58. doi:10.1016/S0165-0114(98)00093-1

Ichihashi, H., Shirai, T., Nagasaka, K., & Miyoshi, T. (1996). Neuro-fuzzy ID3: a method of inducing fuzzy decision trees with linear programming for maximising entropy and an algebraic method for incremental learning. *Fuzzy Sets and Systems, 81*(1), 157–167. doi:10.1016/0165-0114(95)00247-2

Janikow, C. Z. (1998). Fuzzy decision trees: Issues and methods. *IEEE Transactions of Systems. Man and Cybernetics Part B, 28*(1), 1–14. doi:10.1109/3477.658573

Jones, P., & Beynon, M. J. (2007). Temporal Support in the identification of e-learning efficacy: an example of object classification in the presence of ignorance. *Expert Systems: International Journal of Knowledge Engineering and Neural Networks, 24*(1), 1–16. doi:10.1111/j.1468-0394.2007.00417.x

Kecman, V. (2001). *Learning and Soft Computing: Support Vector Machines, Neural Networks, and Fuzzy Logic*. London: MIT Press.

Keller, C., & Cernerud, L. (2002). Students' perceptions of e-learning in university education. *Journal of Educational Media, 27*(1-2), 55–67. doi:10.1080/0305498032000045458

Mitra, S., Pal, S. K., & Mitra, P. (2002). Data Mining in Soft Computing Framework: A Survey. *IEEE Transactions on Neural Networks, 13*(1), 3–14. doi:10.1109/72.977258

Olaru, C., & Wehenkel, L. (2003). A complete fuzzy decision tree technique. *Fuzzy Sets and Systems, 138*, 221–254. doi:10.1016/S0165-0114(03)00089-7

Packham, G., Jones, P., Miller, C. & Thomas, B. (2004). E-learning and Retention: Key factors influencing Student withdrawal, *Education + Training*, (6/7), 335-342.

Pal, N. R., & Chakraborty, S. (2001). Fuzzy Rule Extraction From ID3-Type Decision Trees for Real Data. *IEEE Transactions on Systems, Man, and Cybernetics B, 31*(5), 745–754. doi:10.1109/3477.956036

Quinlan, J. R. (1979). Discovery rules from large examples: A Case Study. In Michie, D. (Ed.), *Expert Systems in the Micro Electronic Age*. Edinburgh, UK: Edinburgh University Press.

Quinlan, J. R. (1993). *C4.5: Programs for Machine Learning*. San Mateo, CA: Morgan Kaufmann.

Romano, J., Wallace, T. L., Helmick, I. J., Carey, L. M., & Adkins, L. (2005). Study procrastination, achievement, and academic motivation in web-based and blended distance learning. *The Internet and Higher Education, 8*(4), 299–305.

Sancho-Royo, A., & Verdegay, J. L. (1999). Methods for the Construction of Membership Functions. *International Journal of Intelligent Systems, 14*, 1213–1230. doi:10.1002/(SICI)1098-111X(199912)14:12<1213::AID-INT3>3.0.CO;2-5

Umano, M., Okamoto, H., Hatono, I., Tamuri, H., Kawachi, F., Umedzu, S., & Kinoshita, J. (1994). Fuzzy decision trees by fuzzy ID3 algorithm and its application to diagnosis systems. In *Proc. of 3rd IEEE International Conference on Fuzzy Systems*, Orlando, FL, (pp. 2113-2118).

Wang, X., Chen, B., Qian, G., & Ye, F. (2000). On the optimization of fuzzy decision trees. *Fuzzy Sets and Systems, 112*, 117–125. doi:10.1016/S0165-0114(97)00386-2

Yu, C.-S., & Li, H.-L. (2001). Method for solving quasi-concave and non-cave fuzzy multiobjective programming problems. *Fuzzy Sets and Systems, 122*(2), 205–227. doi:10.1016/S0165-0114(99)00163-3

Yuan, Y., & Shaw, M. J. (1995). Induction of fuzzy decision trees. *Fuzzy Sets and Systems, 69*, 125–139. doi:10.1016/0165-0114(94)00229-Z

Zadeh, L. A. (1965). Fuzzy Sets. *Information and Control, 8*(3), 338–353. doi:10.1016/S0019-9958(65)90241-X

Zadeh, L. A. (1973). Outlined of a new approach to the analysis of complex systems and decision processes. *IEEE Transactions on Systems, Man, and Cybernetics. Part A, Systems and Humans, SMC-3*, 28–44.

Zadeh, L. A. (1978). Fuzzy sets as a basis for a theory of possibility. *Fuzzy Sets and Systems, 1*, 3–28. doi:10.1016/0165-0114(78)90029-5

Zeidler, J., Schlosser, M., Ittner, A., & Posthoff, C. (1996). Fuzzy Decision Trees and Numerical Attributes. *IEEE International Conference on Fuzzy Systems, 2*, 985-990.

## ADDITIONAL READING

Abdel-Galil, T. K., Sharkawy, R. M., Salama, M. M. A., & Bartnikas, R. (2005). Partial Discharge Pattern Classification Using the Fuzzy Decision Tree Approach. *IEEE Transactions on Instrumentation and Measurement, 54*(6), 2258–2263. doi:10.1109/TIM.2005.858143

Bouchon-Meunier, B., & Marsala, C. (1997). Fuzzy Decision Trees and Databases. In Andreasen, T., Christiansen, H., & Larsen, H. L. (Eds.), *Flexible query answering systems* (pp. 277–288). Norwell, MA, USA: Kluwer Academic Publishers.

Breiman, L., Friedman, J. H., Olshen, R. A., & Stone, C. J. (1984). *Classification and Regression Trees*. Monterey, CA: Wadsworth and Brooks/Cole.

Chang, R. L. P., & Pavlidis, T. (1977). Fuzzy decision tree algorithms. *IEEE Transactions on Systems, Man, and Cybernetics, SMC-7*(1), 28–35. doi:10.1109/TSMC.1977.4309586

Clark, R. (2003). *Building expertise. Cognitive methods for training and performance improvement*. Washington, DC, USA: Book of International Society for Performance Improvement.

Crockett, K., Bandar, Z., Mclean, D., & O'Shea, J. (2006). On constructing a fuzzy inference framework using crisp decision trees. *Fuzzy Sets and Systems, 157*, 2809–2832. doi:10.1016/j.fss.2006.06.002

Derouin, R., Fritzsche, B., & Salas, E. (2005). E-Learning in Organizations. *Journal of Management, 31*, 920–940. doi:10.1177/0149206305279815

Galindo, J., Urrutia, A., & Piattini, M. (2006). *Fuzzy Databases: Modelling, Design and Implementation*. Hershey, USA: Idea Group Publishing.

Govindasamy, T. (2002). Successful implementation of e-Learning pedagogical considerations. *The Internet and Higher Education, 4*, 287–299. doi:10.1016/S1096-7516(01)00071-9

Lim, C. P. (2004). Engaging learners in online learning environments. *TechTrends, 48*, 16–23. doi:10.1007/BF02763440

Mitra, S., Konwar, K. M., & Pal, S. K. (2002). Fuzzy Decision Tree, Linguistic Rules and Fuzzy Knowledge-Based Network: Generation and Evaluation. *IEEE Transactions on Systems, Man and Cybernetics. Part C, Applications and Reviews, 32*(4), 328–339. doi:10.1109/TSMCC.2002.806060

Moallem, M. (2003). An interactive online course: A collaborative design model. *Educational Technology Research and Development, 51*, 85–103. doi:10.1007/BF02504545

Safavian, S. R., & Landgrebe, D. (1991). A survey of decision tree classifier methodology. *IEEE Transactions on Systems, Man, and Cybernetics, 21*, 660–674. doi:10.1109/21.97458

## KEY TERMS AND DEFINITIONS

**Condition Attribute:** An attribute that describes an object. Within a decision tree it is part of a non-leaf node, so performs as an antecedent in the decision rules used for the final classification of an object.

**Decision Attribute:** An attribute that characterises an object. Within a decision tree is part of a leaf node, so performs as a consequent, in the decision rules, from the paths down the tree to the leaf node.

**Decision Tree:** A tree-like way of representing a collection of hierarchical decision rules that lead to a class or value, starting from a root node ending in a series of leaf nodes.

**Dominant Support:** The domain of the linguistic variable where there is majority association of an object to the respective linguistic term.

**Leaf Node:** A node not further split - the terminal grouping – in a classification or decision tree. A path down the tree to a leaf node contains the complements for the respective decision rule.

**Linguistic Term:** One of a set of linguistic terms, which are subjective categories for a linguistic variable, each described by a membership function.

**Linguistic Variable:** A variable made up of a number of words (linguistic terms) with associated degrees of membership.

**Membership Function:** A function that quantifies the grade of membership of a variable to a linguistic term.

**Node:** A junction point down a path in a decision tree that describes a condition in an if-then decision rule. From a node, the current path may separate into two or more paths.

**Root Node:** The node at the tope of a decision tree, from which all paths originate and lead to a leaf node.

## ENDNOTE

[1] The defining values presented in Figure 7 are rounded to the nearest integer value, and were found from two group equal-frequency based grouping of the students' activity over the separate weeks. The associated cut-point value to facilitate these groupings form the respective $\alpha_{L,4}$, and $\alpha_{H,2}$ defining values, for the low and high linguistic terms. The two remaining defining values necessary are the respective mean activity values in each group (equivalence classes) of activity levels.

# Chapter 8
# A Bayesian Belief Network Methodology for Modeling Social Systems in Virtual Communities:
## Opportunities for Database Technologies

**Ben K. Daniel**
*University of Saskatchewan, Canada*

**Juan-Diego Zapata-Rivera**
*Educational Testing Service, USA*

**Gordon I. McCalla**
*University of Saskatchewan, Canada*

## ABSTRACT

*Bayesian Belief Networks (BBNs) are increasingly used for understanding and simulating computational models in many domains. Though BBN techniques are elegant ways of capturing uncertainties, knowledge engineering effort required to create and initialize the network has prevented many researchers from using them. Even though the structure of the network and its conditional & initial probabilities could be learned from data, data is not always available and/or too costly to obtain. Further, current algorithms that can be used to learn relationships among variables, initial and conditional probabilities from data are often complex and cumbersome to employ. Qualitative-based approaches applied to the creation of graphical models can be used to create initial computational models that can help researchers analyze complex problems and provide guidance/support for decision-making. Once created, initial BBN models can be refined once appropriate data is obtained. This chapter extends the use of BBNs to help experts make sense of complex social systems (e.g., social capital in virtual communities) using a Bayesian model as an interactive simulation tool. Scenarios are used to update the model and to find out whether the model is consistent with the expert's beliefs. A sensitivity analysis was conducted to help explain how the model reacted to different sets of evidence. Currently, we are in the process of refining the initial probability values presented in the model using empirical data and developing more*

DOI: 10.4018/978-1-60566-814-7.ch008

*authentic scenarios to further validate the model. We will elaborate on how database technologies were used to support the current approach and will describe opportunities for future database tools needed to support this type of work.*

## INTRODUCTION

Bayesian networks, Bayesian models or Bayesian belief networks (BBNs) can be classified as part of the probabilistic graphical model family. Graphical models provide an elegant and mathematically sound approach to represent uncertainty. It combines advances in graph theory and probability. BBNs are graphs composed of nodes and directional arrows (Pearl 1988). Nodes in BBNs represent variables and directed edges (arrows) between pairs of nodes indicate relationships between variables. The nodes in a BBN are usually drawn as circles or ovals. Further, BBNs offer a mathematically rigorous way to model a complex environment that is flexible, able to mature as knowledge about the system grows, and computationally efficient (Druzdzel & Gaag, 2000; Rusell & Norvig, 1995).

Research shows that BBN techniques have significant power to support the use of probabilistic inference to update and revise belief values (Pearl, 1988). In addition, they can readily permit qualitative inferences without the computational inefficiencies of traditional joint probability determinations (Niedermayer, 1998). Further more, the causal information encoded in BBNs facilitates the analysis of actions, sequences of events, observations, consequences, and expected utility (Pearl, 1988).

Despite the relevance of BBNs, the ideas and techniques have not spread into the social sciences and humanities research communities. The goal of this chapter is to make Bayesian networks more accessible to a wider community in the social sciences and humanities, especially researchers involved in many aspects of social computing. The common problems, which can prevent the wider use of BBN in other domains, include:

- Building BBNs requires considerable knowledge engineering effort, in which the most difficult part of it is to obtain numerical parameters for the model and apply them in complex, which are the kinds of problems social scientists are attempting to address.
- Constructing a realistic and consistent graph (i.e., the structure of the model) often requires collaboration between knowledge engineers and subject matter experts, which in most cases is hard to establish.
- Combining knowledge from various sources such as textbooks, reports, and statistical data to build models can be susceptible to gross statistical errors and by definition are subjective.
- The graphical representation of a BBN is the outcome of domain specifications. However, in situations where domain knowledge is insufficient or inaccurate, the model's outcomes are prone to error.
- Acquiring knowledge from subject matter experts can be subjective.

Despite the problems outlined above, BBNs still remain a viable modelling approach in many domains, especially domains which are quite imprecise and volatile such as weather forecasting, stock market etc. This chapter extends the use of BBN approaches to complex and imprecise constructs. We use social capital as an example of showing the modeling procedures involved. The approach presented in the chapter help experts and researchers build and explore initial computational models and revise and validate them as more data become available. We think that by providing appropriate tools and techniques, the process of building Bayesian models can be extended to address social issues in other domains in the social sciences and the humanities. We also believe that database technologies provide enormous opportunities to access diverse data sources that can be used for creating robust BBNs. For example learning BBNs from data and informing expert opinions using data, some of the latter will be discussed in this chapter.

The rest of the chapter is described as follows. In section 2, basic Bayesian concepts are presented. The goal is to provide the reader with some of the fundamental principles underlying Bayesian probabilities and the modeling process. Section 3 briefly describes the role of computational models in the area of Artificial Intelligence in Education. In section 4, we provide procedures for building Bayesian models and illustrate them with a model of social capital in virtual communities, which is described in section 5. In section 6, various stages of model construction, updating, and validation are described. Section 7 discusses and summarizes the chapter. It also describes future research directions.

## BACKGROUND

Graphical models draw upon probability theory and graph theory. Graphical models provide a natural way of dealing with two major problems—uncertainty and complexity. In addition, they provide intuitive ways in which both humans and machine can model a highly interactive set of random variables as well as complex data structures to enable them to make logical, useful and valid inferences from data. In mathematical notation, a graph $G$ is simply a collection of vertices $V$ and edges $E$ i.e. $G = (V, E)$ and a typical graph $G$ is associated with a set of variables (nodes) $N = \{X_1, X_2, X_3 ... X_n\}$ and by establishing one-to-one relationships among the variables in $N$. Each edge in a graph can be either directed or undirected.

Directed graphs in particular consist only of directed edges. Acyclic directed graphs (ADGs)

are special kinds of directed graphs that do not include cycles. One of the advantages of directed graphs over undirected graphs is that ADGs can be used to represent causal relationships among two or more variables, for example an arc from A to B indicates that A causes B. Such a property can be used to construct a complex graph with many variables (a causal graph). In addition, directed graphs can encode deterministic as well as probabilistic relationships among variables. BBNs are examples of acyclic directed graphs, where nodes represent random variables and the arcs represent direct probabilistic dependencies among the variables (Pearl, 1988).

Building on graph theory and conditional probability, Bayesian modelling is the process of using initial knowledge and updating beliefs using Bayes' Theorem in relation to probability theory, resulting in Bayesian belief networks (a.k.a belief networks, Bayesian belief networks, causal probabilistic networks, or causal networks). The Bayesian interpretation of probability is based on the principles of conditional probability theory. In Bayesian statistics, conditional probabilities are used with partial knowledge about an outcome of an experiment. For example, such knowledge is conditional on relationships between two related events A and B such that the occurrence of one will affect the occurrence of the other. Suppose event B is true, i.e., it has occurred, the probability that A is true given the knowledge about B is expressed by: $P(A|B)$. This notation suggests the following two assumptions:

1.  Two events A and B are independent of each other if $P(A) = P(A|B)$
2.  Two events A and B are conditionally independent of each other given C if $P(A|C) = P(A|B, C)$

Drawing from these two assumptions, Bayes' Theorem swaps the order of dependence between events. For instance:

$$P(A|B) = \frac{P(A,B)}{P(B)} \qquad (1)$$

And Bayes' Theorem states that:

$$P(A|B) = \frac{P(B|A)P(A)}{P(B)} \qquad (2)$$

$$P(A|B) = \frac{P(B|A)P(A)}{P(B)} = \frac{P(B|A)P(A)}{\sum_j P(B|A_j)P(A_j)} \qquad (3)$$

Where j indicates all possible states of A.

From the above equations, the following can be stated about BBN models relationships to conditional probability:

- **P (A|B)** is posterior probability given evidence **B**
- **P (A)** is the initial probability of **A**
- **P (B|A)** is the likelihood probability of the evidence given **A**
- **P (B)** is the initial probability of the evidence **B**

## Modeling Process

Models are useful tools for representing abstractions and concrete realities in any domain. They provide various ways of organizing, analyzing and understanding logical relationships among data, objects, or classes. There are several kinds of models used in a variety of contexts and domains. Computational models are tools use by researchers to understand social and technical aspect of systems, and provide systems designers and analysts with rich insights to build processes, procedures and tools to support systems' operations.

In artificial intelligence in education (AIED) models are used to capture characteristics of learners that can themselves be used by tools to support learning (McCalla, 2000). Models can also be used for representing various educational systems. Baker (2000) summarized three major uses of models within AIED: models as scientific tools for understanding learning problems; models as components of educational systems; and models as educational artifacts. Baker (2000) further observed that the future of artificial intelligence in education (AIED) would involve building models to support learners in learning communities and to help educators manage learning under distributed circumstances.

The process of building models is an iterative one, involving organization of data, establishing logical relationships among the data and coming up with a knowledge representation scheme. The process involves interaction of data, observation of a phenomenon, a knowledge representation scheme and an emergent model (see Figure 1). Data can be drawn from diverse database source, using various mechanisms for accessing and integrating distributed data (i.e., distributed and fragmented databases).

A fundamental assumption underlying most of model building process is that data is available in which a researcher can be able to infer logical relationships and draw logical and concrete conclusions from the model. There are modelling approaches that do not allow the introduction of prior knowledge during the modelling process. These approaches normally prevent the introduction of extraneous data to avoid skewing the experimental results. However, there are times when the use of prior knowledge would be a useful contribution to the modelling and evaluation processes and the overall observation of the behaviour of a model.

## Related Research and Building Bayesian Models

BBN techniques are increasingly used in a variety of domains, including medical diagnostic systems (Pradhan, Provan, Middleton, & Henrion, 1994;

*Figure 1. Modelling process*

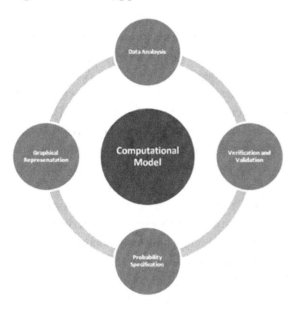

Niedermayer, 1998); student modeling (Conati, Gertner, & VanLehn, 2002; Reye, 2004; VanLehn et al. 1998; Vomlel, 2004; Zapata-Rivera & Greer, 2004); troubleshooting of malfunctioning systems (Finn, & Liang, 1994); and intelligent help assistant in Microsoft Office (Heckerman and Horvitz, 1998). Daniel, Zapata-Rivera, and McCalla (2003) extended the use of BBNs to model social interactions in virtual learning communities.

The construction of BBNs consists of several phases (see Figure 2). The first step involves identifying and defining the problem domain, followed by the identification of the relevant variables constituting the problem being modelled. Further, once the variables are established, variable states and their relevant initial probabilities are assigned (Druzdzel & Gaag, 2000). Probability values are normally estimated or appropriated based on certain sources of evidence (empirical data, expert's belief, literature review or intuition). Clearly, this is an opportunity for applying database technology to inform BBN models. The second step is to determine the relationships among the variables and establish the graphical structure of the model. The third step then is to apply Bayesian

rules to compute conditional probability values for each of variables in the model. The fourth stage of model building requires development of scenarios to update and train the model. Once a model is updated, the fifth phase is to run sensitivity analysis to assess the performance of the model against its parameters.

Model validation takes place during the sixth and the last phase of the model development. Validation ensures that the model is useful and valid and that it reflects real world phenomenon. The modelling phases are normally conducted to reach a stable computational model. In some circumstances these are only shown in three steps, we extended this to 7 phases shown in Figure 2. The different phases are elaborated and shown with an example of modelling social capital discussed in section 5.

The joint probabilities in Bayesian models can grow exponentially given two or more states of sets of variables. For instance, assuming a binary set of variables with no graphical structure specified, the number of probability values needed to determine the joint probability distribution in a BBN model is $2^n$, where n = number of variables. In other words if there are 10 variables in a model, then their joint probability distribution is $2^{10} = 2048$ probability values. But it is seldom necessary that all these numbers be elicited and stored in the model.

This combinatorial problem can be reduced through factorization and exploring independencies among variables through techniques of "explaining away". The notion of "explaining away" suggests that there are two competing causes **A** and **B** which are conditionally dependent given that their common child, **C**, is observed, even though they are marginally independent. For example, suppose the grass is wet, but that we also know that it is raining. Then the posterior probability that the sprinkler is on goes down.

The inherent structure of a Bayesian model can be defined in terms of dependency/independency assumptions between variables and it

*Figure 2. Fundamental phases and procedures in building Bayesian Belief Network models*

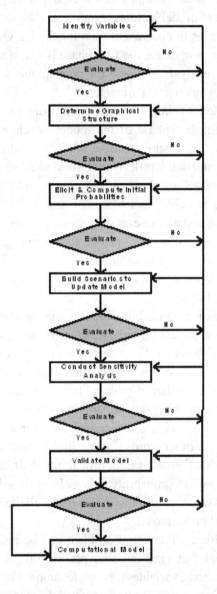

mon effect. Figure 3 shows a scenario in which, **A** acts as a common cause for **B** and **C**. If there is no evidence about **A**, knowing about B could change the probability of **C** (by propagating new evidence through **A**). However, if **A** is observed (i.e., evidence of **A** is available), knowing about **B** will not change the probability of **C** (i.e., the path between **B** and **C** is blocked given **A** – **B** and **C** are d-separated by **A**). D-separation is a Bayesian rule describing relationships between two nodes X and Y with respect to another node Z. X and Y are d-separated by Z if no information can flow between them when Z is observed. More information about conditional independence and d-separation can be found in (Neapolitan, 2004), Korb & Nicholson (2003) and Finn (1996). Additional information regarding learning Bayesian networks can be found in Heckerman (1996) and Neapolitan (2004).

Though initial probabilities can be obtained from many sources these sources seldom offer the requirements for the quantitative aspect of the model. As a result several algorithms are required to compute the values needed, most of which are time consuming and difficult to apply in some domains as noted in section 1 in this chapter. Nonetheless, there are generally two approaches for learning BBNs from data. The first is based on constraint-search (Pearl and Verma, 1991), the second uses Bayesian search for graphs with highest posterior probability (Copper & Herskovits, 1992).

In building Bayesian graphs, knowledge obtained from human experts is normally determined by drawing causal links among nodes and probabilities are based on subject estimates. As described in section 1, the most daunting task of building models is to translate experts' knowledge into numerical values. Subsequently, combinations of quantitative and qualitative approaches are sometimes required. Eliciting probabilities from experts has some drawbacks. For instance, it has been found that common problems can arise such as overconfidence, adjustment of probability

greatly simplifies the representation of the joint probability distribution capturing any dependencies, independences, conditional independences and marginal independences between variables.

A Bayesian model is usually composed of n variables and each variable is deliberately associated with those variables that lie under its influence. This is known as conditional independence (see equation 2), and it can be represented in different ways, e.g., causal chain, common cause, and com-

*Figure 3. Example of a conditional independence*

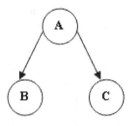

estimates up and down based on an initial estimate (anchoring problem), disagreement among experts, assignment of high probability values to easy to remember events (availability problem) (Morgan & Henrion, 1990). All these issues are likely to affect the quality of the probabilities elicited.

Wellman (1999) introduced a qualitative abstraction of BBNs known as qualitative Bayesian networks (QBN), which uses the concept of positive and negative influences between variables to determine causal relationships between variables in a graph. It assumes an ordered relationship between variables. Qualitative propagation is based on the premise that each variable in a network is provided a sign either positive (+) or negative (-) and that the effect of an observation **e** on **n** variables in a network propagates the sign of change throughout the network.

Zapata-Rivera (2002) described a case-based approach that makes use of data to document various interesting cases and facilitate elicitation of probabilities from experts. Drawing from QBN approaches, Daniel, Zapata-Rivera and McCalla (2003) used a qualitative and quantitative approach of eliciting knowledge from experts (i.e., structure and initial and conditional probabilities) based on the descriptions of the strength of the relationship among variables in a network. This approach takes into account the number of states of a variable, the number of parents, the degree of strength (e.g., strong, medium, weak) and the kind of relationship/influence (e.g., positive or

negative influence) to produce initial and conditional probabilities.

Once an initial model is elicited, particular scenarios are used to refine and document the network. In contrast to QBN, which makes use of its own qualitative propagation algorithms, this approach uses standard Bayesian propagation algorithms. Initial probabilities can also be refined when data becomes available. This approach is illustrated with the help of an example of modelling social capital in virtual communities discussed in section 4. In choosing a probabilistic approach to modelling, BBNs offer a number of advantages over other methods:

- BBN models are powerful tools both for graphically representing the relationships among a set of variables and for dealing with uncertainties in expert systems.
- The graphical structure of BBNs provides a visual method of relating relationships among variables in a simple way.
- Graphs in probabilistic modelling are convenient means of expressing substantial assumptions and they facilitate economical representation of a joint probability function to enhance making efficient inferences from observations.
- The BBN approach to modelling permits qualitative inferences without the computational inefficiencies of traditional joint probability determinations (Niedermayer, 1998).
- In BBNs, a network can be easily refined i.e. additional variables can be easily added and mapping from the mathematics to common understanding or reference points could be quickly done.
- The BBN approach allows for evidence to be entered into the network, and for updating the network to propagate the probabilities to each node; the resulting probabilities tend to reflect common sense notions

including effects such as "explaining away" and "pooling of evidence."

- BBNs offer an interactive graphical modeling mechanism that researchers can use to understand the behavior of a system or situation, (e.g., it is possible to add evidence/observe variables and propagate it throughout the whole graphical model to see/inspect the effects on particular variables of interest).

- The fact that BBNs have a qualitative and quantitative part gives them advantages over other methods.

## FUNDAMENTAL COMPONENTS OF SOCIAL CAPITAL

There are numerous variables that constitute social capital in geographical communities, some of which can be extended to virtual communities. This is evident in the various definitions available in the literature. Examining the various definitions available in the literature, it became apparent that some definitions have shared variables. These shared variables became the loci for building the model of social capital in virtual communities.

The definitions in the literature with shared variables refer to social capital as a function of positive engagement. It suggests that when people have positive engagement on issues of mutual concerns, they are more likely to get to know one another and together, they can derive value from positive engagement. Typically, engagement involves sharing of personal experiences with others, endorsing positive behaviors or discouraging negative ones, sharing information, recommending resources, and providing companionship and hospitality.

A psychological attitude simply refers to a state of mind or a feeling. It is a disposition often manifested in explicit behavioral tendencies. In other words, an attitude arises from attempts to

account for observed regularities in the behavior of individual persons. For example, one can have an impression about someone as trustworthy, warm, emotional or scary. Such an impression can be used to build an attitude and the attitude is often externalized into observerable behavior, although some attitudes are hidden inside the individual.

People can hold complex relationships with other people, the environments and the world around them based on their attitudes and their behavioral tendencies. In almost everything we do, attitude and behavior are intertwined into the fabric of our daily life. Attitude has been a central topic of behavioral psychologists. Much of the work on attitudes tends to revolve around two schools of thought. One school believes that people are born into the world with certain inherited biological attitudes; emotional tendencies such as anger, patience etc. Another school believes that attitudes are learned from others, their environments or experiences, and thus are socialized or enculturalised to individuals. For examples, religious social systems that tend to educate calmness, patience and forgiveness in their followers are typical examples in this regard.

Regardless of any school of thought, people can form attitudes almost instantaneously at their first encounter with certain individuals, objects or circumstances. It follows that some of the attitudes people formed in a first encounter last for a long time and in fact, they become permanently inculcated within individuals to an extent that they become the basis for establishing the order of social relationships.

Irrespective of how an attitude is manifested, a person's attitude can directly affect the way they interact with other people and their ability to carry out productive engagement, which is central to building social capital. Productive engagement does not automatically happen; it occurs when people have a common set of expectations that are mediated by a set of shared social protocols. It also takes place when people are willing to identify with each other as members of one community.

Shared understanding is another key component of social capital. Similar to engagement, shared understanding represents an amicable platform for smooth interaction and engagement. It is also achieved when people are willing to interact with each other long enough to identify shared attributes, understand the language and symbolic representations of the community and effectively resolve any differences that are detrimental to communication and engagement in the community to which they belong.

The process involved in establishing shared understanding in any community often draws upon a set of shared beliefs, shared goals and values, experiences and knowledge. Within the context of virtual communities, shared understanding is enhanced by various forms of awareness; for example, when people become aware of each other, they identify shared interests which are a basis for establishing shared understanding. In the event of possible disagreement, resolution can be achieved through effective negotiation mechanisms. This argument is substantiated by research in computer-supported collaborative learning which asserts that meaning is constructed by social interaction until people share a common understanding (Stahl, 2000). In addition, for many years, researchers in Human Computer Interactions have established that awareness is critical to effective interactions and productive social relationships in virtual settings (Gutwin, at al., 1998).

Awareness can also help in enforcing productive engagement. Moreover, maintaining different forms of awareness in a virtual community can lubricate and increase the value of engagement and possibly increase shared understanding. In other words, in a virtual community, people need to be aware of the people they are interacting with. They want to know where others are located (demographic awareness) and what they are up

to (activity awareness). In more professional settings or in distributed communities of practice, people are often curious about what others do for a living (professional awareness) or are interested in what others know (knowledge awareness) or what they are able to do (capability awareness) (Daniel, Sarkar & O'Brien, 2003).

In addition to engagement, interaction, attitudes, shared understanding and various types of awareness, trust is another critical ingredient and component of social capital. In many instances, trust acts as an accelerating lever to many forms of social interaction whether online or in face-to-face settings. Trust enables people to work together, collaborate and smoothly exchange information and share knowledge without time worsted on negotiations (Cohen & Prusak, 2000). Trust can also be treated as an outcome of positive attitudes among individuals in a community. Further, in virtual communities, trust can only be created and sustained when individuals are provided with an environment that can support different forms of awareness.

These variables serve as basic components of social capital in virtual communities. The data sources were used to inform the identification of variables were obtained from the literature but they could equally be obtained from databases. In Bayesian modelling, once variables are identified, the second step is to map the variables into a graphical structure based on solid qualitative reasoning. In particular, the knowledge of the structure of the model and the qualitative reasoning of the causal relationships among variables are grounded in research into social capital and virtual communities. For example, in previous research, Daniel, Zapata-Rivera and McCalla (2007) observed that people's attitudes in virtual learning communities can strongly influence the level of their engagement with each other and consequently their ability to know various issues about themselves. Such information is viewed as influential in building trusting relationships.

*Table 1. Social capital variables and their definitions*

| Variable Name | Variable Definition | Variable States |
|---|---|---|
| Attitudes | Individuals' general perception about each other and others' actions and beliefs. | *Positive/Negative* |
| Shared Understanding | A mutual agreement/consensus between two or more agents about the meaning of an object or idea. | *High/Low* |
| Knowledge Awareness | Knowledge of people, tasks, or environment and or all of the above. | *Present/Absent* |
| Demographic Awareness | Knowledge of an individual: country of origin, language and location. | *Present/Absent* |
| Professional Awareness | Knowledge of people's background training, affiliation etc. | *Present/Absent* |
| Engagement | An extended period of interaction between two or more people that goes beyond exchange of words but important and meaningful social connections. | *positive/negative* |
| Social protocols | The mutually agreed upon, acceptable and unacceptable ways of behavior in a community. | *Present/Absent* |
| Trust | A particular level of certainty or confidence with which an agent use to assess the action of another agent. | *High/Low* |

According to Bayesian Belief Network principles, causal relationships among variables (see Figure 4), is shown by the direction of the arrow. For example in our case attitudes influence different forms of awareness and the strength of the influence suggests strongly positive relationship among the variables. Further, since awareness can contribute to trust and distrust, the strength of the relationships is set to medium positive, medium weak, etc. Depending on the type of awareness, demographic awareness is set as a positive influence, with a medium effect on trust, meaning that it is more likely that people will trust others regardless of their demographic backgrounds and in fact this is the case with distributed communities of practice (Daniel, Sarkar & O'Brien, 2003). In this type of qualitative reasoning nodes (variables) that contribute to higher nodes align themselves in "child" to "parent" relationships, where parent nodes are super-ordinate to child nodes (e.g. trust is the child of shared understanding; different forms of awareness and social protocols, are children of interaction and attitudes).

The graph (Figure 4) presented here relates to the context of only two kinds of virtual communities (virtual learning communities and distributed communities of practice). This graph topology enables one to run different forms of experiments, with results only interpreted within the evidences used and communities described. After the development of a Bayesian graph, the third stage is to obtain initial probability values to populate the graph (network).

Initial probabilities can be obtained from different sources, but in the Bayesian modeling practice obtaining accurate initial numbers that can yield valid and meaningful posteriors (resulting probability values) is sometimes a difficult undertaking. Nonetheless, the approach presented in the chapter is intended to simplify the procedure although it entails a great deal of cross validation and tuning of the model over a period of time against various new evidence.

## Computing Conditional Probabilities

In construction of any Bayesian network model, every stage of situation assessment requires assigning initial probabilities to the hypotheses made or the assumptions driving the construction of the model. In a typical situation, initial probabilities are obtained from knowledge of a particular situation prevailing at a particular time. However, converting a state of knowledge to probability

*Figure 4. Graphical Model of Social Capital*

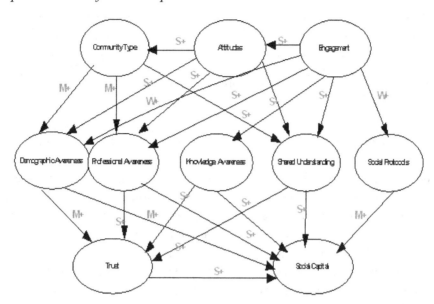

values is a challenge facing Bayesian modellers, and if not accurately done it can result in models that are inadequate and in some cases invalid. The initial conditional probabilities for the social capital model discussed in this chapter were obtained by examining qualitative descriptions of the influence between two or more variable. This is supported by database technologies by providing methods for extracting the data that helps experts make sense of particular situations (e.g., see Zapata-Rivera 2002). Database and visualization technologies are instrumental in supporting this task. Each probability value describes strength of relationships and the letters **S (strong)**, **M (medium)**, and **W (weak)** represent different degrees of influence among the variables in the model are (Daniel, Zapata-Rivera & McCalla, 2003). The signs + and - represent positive and negative relationships among the variables.

Once, the initial probabilities were determined, a fully specified joint probability distribution was computed. In the process, each node, **X** (where **X** implies any variable in the graph), the probability distribution for **X** conditional upon **X**'s parents was specified. Moreover, the criterion

used to obtain the conditional probability values was based on adding weights to the values of the variables depending on the number of parents and the strength of the relationship between the parents and the children. For example, Attitudes and Engagement have positive and strong (S+) relationships with Knowledge Awareness; the evidence of positive engagement and positive attitudes, produce a conditional probability value for Knowledge Awareness **0.98** (a threshold value for strong = **0.98**).

These weights were obtained by subtracting a base value (**1 / number of states**, **0.5** in this case) from the threshold value associated to the degree of influence and dividing the result by the number of parents (i.e. **(0.98 - 0.5) / 2 = 0.48 / 2 = 0.24**), which follows from the fact that in the graph knowledge awareness is a child of both interactions and attitudes. Table 2, shows the threshold values and weights used in this example. Since it is more likely that no situation is exhaustive and perfect, i.e. a certain degree of uncertainty might exist, the value $\alpha = 0.02$ leaves some room for uncertainty, considering evidence coming from positive and strong relationships among variables.

*Table 2. Threshold values and weights with two parents*

| Degree of influence | Thresholds | Weights |
|---|---|---|
| Strong | 1-α = 1 - 0.02 = 0.98 | (0.98-0.5) / 2 = 0.48 / 2 = 0.24 |
| Medium | 0.8 | (0.8-0.5) / 2 =0.3 / 2 = 0.15 |
| Weak | 0.6 | (0.6-0.5) / 2 =0.1 / 2 = 0.05 |

These threshold values can be adjusted based on new evidence or expert opinion.

Using this approach it is possible to generate conditional probability tables (CPTs) for each node (variable) regardless of the number of parents and this immensely simplifies the complexity of constructing models based on partial knowledge of a domain (Zapata-Rivera, 2002). Of course the accuracy of this approach is dependent on how the consistency, coherence and validity of the initial knowledge gathered from experts and the decisions the knowledge engineer makes to transform the knowledge gathered into initial probabilities.

## Querying the Model

A Bayesian model can contain many variables each of which can be relevant for some kind of reasoning but rarely are all variables in a Bayesian model relevant for all kinds of reasoning at once. To make models practical and useful, researchers need to identify a subset of variables in a model that is relevant to their needs. In other words, it is sometimes the case that the modeller only enters evidence for a few variables in order to observe changes in certain variables. In general, the mechanism for drawing conclusions in Bayesian models is based on probability propagation of evidence.

Probability propagation refers to model updating based upon known evidence entered into the model. Probability propagation is normally carried out through querying a Bayesian model. Querying a Bayesian model refers to a process of updating the conditional probability table and making inferences based on new evidence entered

into a model. There are several ways to update a model, one which is to develop a detailed number of scenarios that can be used to query the model.

A scenario can generally be described as a set of written stories or synopsis of acts in stories built around carefully constructed events. It is a written synopsis of inferences drawn from observed phenomenon or empirical data. In a scientific and technical sense a scenario describes a vision of the future state of a system. Such a description can be based on current assessment of the system, of the variables and assumptions, and the likely interaction between system variables in the progression from current conditions to a future state (Collion, 1989).

Druzdzel and Henrion (1993) describe a scenario as an assignment of values to those variables in Bayesian network which are relevant for a certain conclusion, ordered in such a way that they form a coherent story—a causal story which is compatible with the evidence of the story. The use of scenarios as an approach in updating Bayesian network models is based on psychological research (Pennington & Hastie, 1988). This research shows that humans tend to interpret and explain any social situation by weighing the most credible stories to test and understand social phenomena.

In order to update the model presented in the chapter, scenarios were developed underlying various events based on either evidence or an expert's knowledge. These scenarios were intended to test and tune the model over time. The construction and presentation of the scenarios followed an approach which is at best described as "scenario-based modelling". Scenario-based modeling in this context is essentially a set of procedures for describing specific sequences of behaviours within a model representing actual interactions within a virtual community. These scenarios are supported by data – database technologies play an important role here. For example, querying the Bayesian model could result not only on new posterior probabilities but also on the data used to support a particular scenario/prior/conditional probability or qualitative relationship.

The goal is to understand and explain the interactions of variables or set of events within a model and how these might possible influence direction of interaction patterns, and subsequently the level of social capital within a community.

Scenario based modelling is a powerful approach for updating initial Bayesian Models. While a hypothesis normally refers to a set of unproven ideas, beliefs, and arguments, a scenario can describe proven states of events, which can be used to understand future changes within a model. When several scenarios are used together to describe possible outcomes of events within a model, they can exceed the power of predictions based on a single hypothesis or a set of propositions drawn from a single data set.

The use of a scenario-based approach to query a model also offers with a common vocabulary and an effective basis for communicating complex and sometimes paradoxical conditions. In the context of this chapter, this provides opportunity for incorporating strategies from qualitative perspectives and to avoid the potential for any sharp discontinuities between quantitative and qualitative approaches.

## CASE SCENARIOS

During the process of updating the Bayesian model various sources of evidence was collected and compiled as scenarios to simplify the process and to enhance clarity of the stories. Although the

stories presented here are authentic and taken from real world virtual communities, these scenarios are intended only to emulate but not to replace experimental data. They were intended only to illustrate the process of updating an initial Bayesian model. However, it is possible that the results of the model predictions could change, in the face of further empirical data. Some of the data used for creating scenarios were extracted from electronic (i.e. community forums and web-logs).

## Case 1: A Virtual Learning Community of Graduate Students

Community **A** was a formal virtual learning community of graduate students learning fundamental concepts and philosophies of E-Learning. The members of this community were drawn from diverse cultural backgrounds and different professional training. In particular, participants were practising teachers teaching in different domains at secondary and primary schools levels. Some individuals in the community had extensive experiences with educational technologies, while others were novices but had extensive experience in classroom pedagogy. These individuals were not exposed to each other before and thus were not aware of each other's talents and experiences.

Since the community was a formal one, there was a formalized discourse structure and the social protocols for interactions were explained to participants in advance. The social protocols required different forms of interactions including posting messages, critiquing others, providing feedback to others' postings, asking for clarifications, etc. As the interactions progressed in this community, intense disagreements were observed in the community. Individuals began to disagree more on the issues under discussion and there was little shared understanding among the participants in most of the discourse. Given the description of this scenario, one wonders about the strength of social capital in this community.

## Case 2: A distributed Community of Practice of Software Engineers

Community **B** was a distributed community of practice for software engineers who gathered to discuss issues around software development. The main goals of this community were to facilitate exchange of information and knowledge, and for members to provide peer-support to each other in the community. Members of this community shared common concerns. Membership skills in this community varied, ranging from highly experienced software developers to novice computer programmers. In addition, members were globally distributed and came from diverse organisations, including researchers at the university and software support groups.

After a considerable period of interaction, individuals were exposed to each other long enough to trust each other and started exchanging personal information among themselves. It was also observed that individuals offered a lot of help to each other throughout their interactions. Though no formal social protocols were explained to the participants, members interacted as if there were social protocols guiding their interactions. Further, there were no visible roles of community leaders. In this highly professional community, with no visible social protocols, and limited prior exposure, members were able to initiate useful interaction and trust each other to the extent of exchanging sensitive personal information. The most interesting question is whether or not the presence or absence of social capital played a role.

## Case 3: A Distributed Community of Practice of Programmers

Community **C** consisted of a group of individuals learning fundamentals of programming in Java. It was an open community whose members were

geographically distributed and had diverse demographic backgrounds and professional cultures. They did not personally know each other; they used different aliases from time to time while interacting in the community. Diverse programming experiences, skills and knowledge were also observed among the participants.

It was interesting to observe that although these individuals did not know each other in advance, they were willing to offer help and to support each other in learning Java. Though there were no formal social protocols of interaction, individuals interacted as if there were clear set social protocols to be followed in the community. Can it be possible that the high spirit of community collaboration and peer-support are attributed to the underlying power of social capital? How can one determine if the social capital of this community is indeed high given the observed description of events?

## Case 4: A Distributed Community of Practice of Biomedical and Clinicians

This case for community **D** is extracted from a recent phenomenon observed within health system research. The continuous demand for understanding of complex human diseases, the solutions to chronic diseases and preventative measures will most likely lie within many disciplines with the biomedical sciences and clinicians, all coming together to participate in a distributed community of practice. Increasing complexity of clinical problems and the difficulty of engaging all health professionals to do research, coupled with failure to rapidly move research into new clinical methodologies have created a need for new approaches to clinical research, practice and policy interface. The hallmark of these new approaches is embedded in the conceptual understanding of the framework of distributed communities of practice, with members operating as an interdisciplinary unit, drawing membership from nurses, clinicians, policy analysts and academic researchers to move research findings into patient care.

Members of this community are highly distributed in terms of both epistemological stances towards addressing health problems as well as the organizations in which they work. And so for them to effectively work together, it is imperative that knowledge required for solving problems draw from theories, concepts or models that are integral to two or more disciplines. It is also required that methods of problem solving need to be developed from multiple perspectives. Throughout the collaborative process, shared understanding and awareness of what people could bring to the table were definitely crucial factors that could leverage collaboration in this community. Though diversity in this community allowed a variety of views, methods, approaches and procedures to enrich problem solving, specific problem solving protocols seemed to be difficult to carry out due to lack of shared understanding. In this unique distributed community of practice what happens to social capital?

## UPDATING THE MODEL

The scenarios described above all represent typical situations where the model can be applied in real world settings. In updating the initial Bayesian model of social capital, each case scenario was analysed looking for various evidence regarding the impact of individual variables in the model. Once a piece of evidence was added to the model, typically through tweaking a state of one or more variables (i.e. observing a particular state of a variable) or a process commonly known as variable initialisation, the model was updated and results were propagated to the rest of variables in the Bayesian model. This process generated a set of new marginal probabilities for the variables in the model. In the four case scenarios, the ultimate purpose was to observe changes in probability values for trust and social capital.

The outcomes of the model prediction were limited to the nature of the cases described in the chapter. It is important to note that these cases themselves represent some abstraction of the actual interactions in these virtual communities. However, this was an important exercise, with outcomes intended to train the model and prepare fruitful grounding for conducting empirical experiments to further validate the model. This exercise in Bayesian modelling helps experts to examine their beliefs about the domain being modelled and the accuracy of the knowledge representation scheme. The whole endeavour, therefore, serves as an interactive tool that enables experts to create a probabilistic model, simulate scenarios and reflect on the results of the predictions.

## Community A

Community **A** is a virtual learning community (Community Type = VLC.) Based on the case description, shared understanding was set to low and professional knowledge awareness set to "does not exist". Individuals in this community were familiar with their geographical diversity and so demographic awareness was set to "exists". Further, there was a well-established formal set of social protocols and so social protocols were initiated to "known". Figure 5 shows the Bayesian model and the posterior probabilities after the evidence from the scenario described in community A were added (see shaded nodes/variables).

The results of the predictions showed a relatively low probability that trust was high (P (Trust=*high*) =41.0%) and a correspondingly low probability that SC was high (P (SC=*high*) =36.2%). Several explanations were provided for the drop in the levels of social capital and trust. First, there was an observed negative interaction in the community, which might have eventually negatively affected the level of engagement. Second, there was lack of shared understanding which might have negatively skewed the level of trust and consequently social capital, since social

*Figure 5. Community A showing updated probabilities*

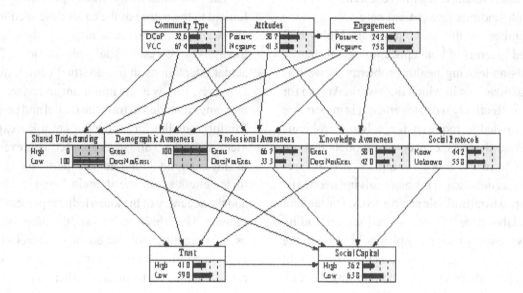

capital is directed influenced by trust. It was also possible that negative interactions and negative attitudes, negatively affected the levels of task knowledge awareness and individual capability awareness.

## Community B

The variables observed in the scenario described in community **B** included community type which was initialized to distributed community of practice (DCoP); professional awareness set to *"exists"*. It was observed that individuals in this community became aware of their individual talents and skills after some form of interactions, so knowledge awareness was set to *"exists"*. Further, individuals in this community shared common concerns and frames of reference; consequently shared understanding was set to *high*. Figure 6 shows the Bayesian model after evidence was added (shaded nodes).

Propagating the evidence showed high levels of trust and SC (P (Trust=*high*) =93.1% and P (SC=*high*) = 74%). It was also observed that interactions and attitudes had positively influenced demographic cultural awareness and social pro-

tocols. Further, the presence of shared understanding and the high degree of different types of awareness and the explicit exposition of social protocols in the community, contributed to a rise in the levels of trust and social capital.

In spite of the evidence entered, demographic cultural awareness had little influence on the level of trust in this community; as a result social capital was not significantly affected. This was attributed to the fact that professionals in most cases are likely to cherish their professional identity more than their demographic backgrounds. This is in line with a previous study, which suggested most people in distributed communities of practice mainly build and maintain social relations based on common concerns other than geographical distribution (Daniel, O'Brien & Sarkar, 2003).

## Community C

The variables extracted from this case scenario included community type (*VLC*), shared understanding, professional awareness, demographic awareness, knowledge awareness that were all set to *exists*. Figure 7 shows the Bayesian model after the evidence from community C has been added

*Figure 6. Community B showing updated probabilities*

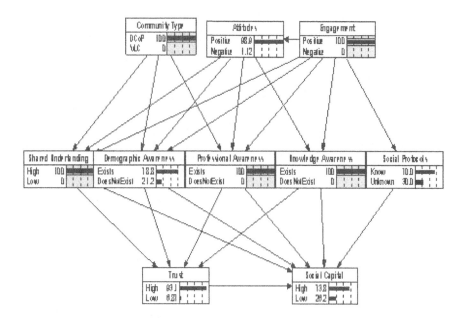

(shaded nodes) and propagated through the model.

The results showed high levels of trust and SC (P(Trust=high)=92.7% and P(SC=high)=78.4%). The high levels of trust and social capital were attributed to the fact that the community was based on an explicit and focused domain. Though members might have participated anonymously, they were positively interacting with each other and vibrantly participated in order to learn the domain. Further the observed increase in the levels of trust and social capital was attributed to the presence of shared understanding. In other words, people in that community were able to get along well with each other, since they used the same frame of reference and shared common goals of learning a domain (programming in Java).

## Community D

Community D showed all the features of a distributed community of practice. This community had an explicit identified need for collaboration across domains. It occurred that social capital would be a good tool to understand the platform needed to forge collaboration. However, most of the variables critical to the development of social capital were lacking. Consequently variables critical for collaboration within distributed communities of practice such as shared understanding were set to low, social protocols not observed, professional and knowledge awareness were similarly all set to low. The results are shown in Figure 8.

After the evidence was entered, the results of the model's prediction revealed a relatively low level of trust (P (Trust=high) = 59.6%) and an even lower probability of high social capital (P (SC=high) = 35%). This was expected since core the variables constituting social capital were lacking and consequently were not observed or instantiated.

## OPPORTUNITIES AND CHALLENGES

In theory computational models are expected to be fully verified and valid but in practice, no computational model will ever be fully verified,

*Figure 7. Community C showing updated probabilities*

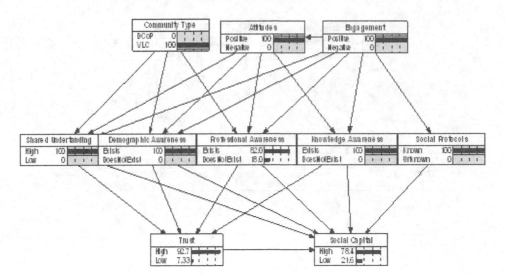

guaranteeing 100% error free accuracy. But a high degree of statistical certainty is still required to demonstrate the usefulness of a model. One of greatest challenges of building a computational model is making it valid, relevant and useful, which implies for the most part establishing model credibility. Establishing model credibility requires a lot of work. It involves gathering empirical data, subjecting the model to undergo several rigorous verification and validation stages and building an argument that the model has produced sound insights based on a wide range of tests comparable to data in real world settings.

The development of the social capital model would probably not pass rigorous model validation. But in many social systems, modelling social issues is not so much about gaining 100% error free models but rather it is about gaining insights required to identifying and understanding a problem and addressing it using alternative methods. In addition, most of the approaches used for building models of social systems make use of qualitative inferences rather than quantitative predictions about the future state of systems. Besides, most social systems or constructs such as social capital cannot easily be captured with one approach at single point in time since they are more dynamic.

The input variables used for building the model of social capital were extracted from the literature, which might not necessarily be empirically based, or situated within virtual communities. In addition, the assumptions made during the modelling process, might be susceptible to errors. Furthermore, research into social capital in virtual communities is still in its infancy and more still is required to fully gain an understanding of the nature of the fundamental components of the model and how these interact with each other.

In terms of technical design and construction of Bayesian belief network models, there are two ways to construct Bayesian models. One way is to learn a graphical structure from data and the other is to initially propose a graphical structure based on some logical reasoning and train the graph to learn probability values from the structure using new evidence. The latter is the approach taken and reported in the chapter. It should be noted that such an approach, though appealing and useful, is not necessarily consistent all the time. But validation of the structure is inevitable to demonstrate accuracy and relevance.

*Figure 8. Community D showing updated probabilities*

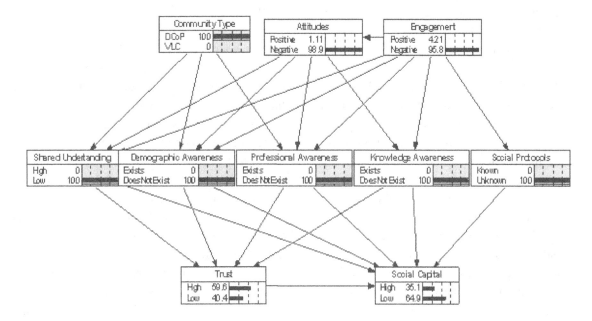

Validation of reasoning or assumptions is normally conducted through sensitivity analysis (see Appendix A). The results of the sensitivity analysis conducted to validate the structure confirmed some of the assumptions made during the graphical construction of the model. But it will still be interesting to investigate the predictions of the model or formulate questions that can be pursued using an alternative method of study such as survey or Delphi technique.

The need for database tools for supporting the creation of BBN scenarios. These database tools include: (a) tools used that provide the data needed to support decisions made in the modeling process at various levels of granularity (e.g., qualitative relationship between variables, prior and conditional probabilities, strength of relationships); (b) tools that combine database and visualization technologies to facilitate elicitation of BBNs scenarios; and (c) tools for integrating data from distributed and fragmented virtual communities and using these data to create computational models.

## Limitation of Bayesian Belief Network

Despite the relevance of Bayesian belief networks, ideas and techniques derived from BBNs have not spread into the social sciences and humanities research communities. Daniel, Zapata-Revera & McCalla (2007) summarized the main problems, which prevented the wider use of BBN in other domains as follows:

- Building Bayesian Belief Networks requires considerable knowledge engineering effort, in which the most difficult part is to obtain numerical parameters for the model and apply them in complex situations, which are the kinds of situations social scientists are attempting to address.
- Constructing a realistic and consistent graph (i.e., the structure of the model) often requires collaboration between knowledge engineers and subject matter experts, which in most cases is hard to establish.

- Combining knowledge from various sources such as textbooks, reports, and statistical data to build models can be susceptible to gross statistical errors and by definition are subjective.
- The graphical representation of a Bayesian belief network is the outcome of domain specifications. However, in situations where domain knowledge is insufficient or inaccurate, the model's outcomes are prone to error.
- Acquiring knowledge from subject matter experts can be subjective.
- Finding the prior probabilities or a threshold weights is often complicated
- In an event where there are many values representing belief, the nuisance parameters [1] have to be arranged in sequence of importance, even though none of them is of intrinsic interest.
- If a parameter of interest changes the whole prior distribution table might change as well as the structure of the model.
- If a sampling rule or design changes in an experiment or the people involved are different, the prior values of variables generally will change.

Despite the problems outlined above, Bayesian belief networks still remain a viable modelling approach in many domains, especially domains which are quite imprecise and volatile such as weather forecasting, stock market etc. The BBN approach helps experts and researchers build and explore initial computational models and revise and validate them as more data become available. Further, by providing appropriate tools and techniques, the process of building Bayesian models can be extended to address social issues in other domains in the social sciences and the humanities.

## Model Validation and Sensitivity Analysis (SA)

Further, approximating probabilities elicited from experts and experts' judgments can be prone to errors, and sometimes due to uncertainty of the properties of an event their accuracy is not guaranteed. For example, if one is asked to toss a coin and estimate the probability that the coin can either land head or tail, one would suggest that the probability value to be 0.5, assuming that the coin is a fair. But in a situation where one has never seen the coin and is uncertain whether it is fair or not, then a degree of belief can be used as initial knowledge. In other words, initial assumptions are made that the coin is fair, and sometimes such assumptions can be biased or wrong.

Sensitivity analysis is primarily used to validate the quantitative part of a Bayesian model. There are two approaches to sensitivity analysis; one approach tests how sensitive the network model is to changes in overall findings and the other approach aims to find changes in each variable in the model. In the former case the influence of each of the nodes in the network on a query node can be measured, using a measure such as entropy, and ranked (http://www.norsys.com). The results of a sensitivity analysis can be used for initializing the portions of the model for later iterations in the development cycle (Haddaway, 1999). In the latter case the goal is to determine whether more precision in estimating variables is required and whether it can be useful in a later iteration of the model development cycle. Sensitivity analysis is a mathematical technique for investigating the effects of inaccuracies in the parameters of a mathematical model. It aims to study how variation in output of a model (numerical or otherwise) can be apportioned, qualitatively or quantitatively, to different sources of data (Morgan & Henrion, 1990). In general, SA is conducted by:

- Defining the model with all its input and output variables
- Assigning probability density functions to each input parameter
- Generating an input matrix through an appropriate random sampling method and evaluating the output
- Assessing the influences or relative importance of each input parameter on the output variable

Sensitivity analysis is relevant to the SC model since the states of the input variables are numerous and their individual influences on the model are not precisely known. Sensitivity analysis will also help to further refine the model and suggest further studies to validate the model (Chan & Darwiche, 2004). In order to identify which variables had dominating effects on the query variables, automated analysis on the sensitivity of each variable in the model was conducted (support for this type of analysis was provided in the Netica software package; https://www.norsys.com/ environment). The results of the sensitivity analysis (see Appendix A) show that those variables with a weak level of influence on social capital show low mutual information values. Trust, capability awareness and task awareness are relatively sensitive to social capital compared to professional awareness, demographic awareness, social protocols and shared understanding.

In general terms, results indicated that social capital is not sensitive to only one variable, but rather it is sensitive to a number of variables and even more so to variables that are on strong positive paths in the model, see Figure 4. The results of the sensitivity analysis reveal at least three relatively high levels of entropy reduction for the following variables: interactions and attitudes with the same entropy reduction of 0.1533, capability awareness with entropy reduction of 0.1494, shared understanding at 0.1112 and trust at 0.1175. Higher values of entropy reduction correspond to variables on strong paths and it

generally suggests that the qualitative reasoning used for deriving the initial probabilities presented in the social capital model is reasonable. Though results of the sensitivity analysis seem to suggest that different variables can affect social capital at different levels, at this point further studies are required to determine the effects of individual variables on social capital.

The results of the sensitivity analysis can be used to improve the model by changing the threshold initial probability values presented earlier in the chapter. Further, drawing from the results, one could speculate that the individual variations in values could be caused by partial knowledge of domain experts used for building the network and early assumptions made during the development of the model, both of which are common problems inherent the development of any Bayesian model.

Another possible way of rectifying inconsistency in a Bayesian model is to conduct model validation. Model validation in essence is post sensitivity analysis, which is performed by altering the parameters of query variable and observing the related changes in the posterior probabilities of the target variable. This is done with the help of evidence coming from empirical data (see last phase of Figure 2, building Bayesian networks). However, in a situation, where there are N-scenarios, a straightforward analysis can be extremely time consuming and difficult to maintain, especially on larger networks. Coupe and Van der Gaag (1998) addressed this difficulty by identifying a sensitivity set of a variable given evidence.

## DISCUSSIONS AND CONCLUSIONS

A Bayesian network is a tool that helps to model a situation involving uncertainty. In the social sciences and indeed in many other fields, uncertainty may arise due to a variety of causes. For instance it can be the result of gaps in knowledge, complexity and imprecision of domain knowledge, ignorance, or volatility of a knowledge domain. And so, by representing knowledge in graphical form, researchers can more effectively communicate results.

A Bayesian model encodes domain knowledge, showing relationships, interdependencies and independence among variables. The qualitative part of the model is represented by links showing direction of influence or independence among variables. The information describing the details of the quantitative relationships among the variables is often stored in conditional probability tables (CPTs). This enables the model to use probability theory, especially Bayesian statistics to calculate conditional dependencies among the variables in the network and resolve the uncertainties with probability inferences.

Though BBN techniques are elegant ways of capturing uncertainties, knowledge engineering effort is required to create conditional probability values for each variable in a network. This has prevented many researchers from using them in many domains. In addition, current algorithms that can be used to learn initial and conditional probabilities from data are often complex and cumbersome to employ and data is not always available. Even though initial probabilities can be elicited from experts, it sometimes raises the problems of accuracy in values.

In addition, translating experts' qualitative knowledge into numerical probabilistic values is a daunting and often complex task. Since Bayesian network modeling involves establishing cause and effects among variables, it is sometimes difficult to determine causal relationships or to adequately describe all the causes and effects. In such cases, Bayesian networks can be described using probabilities derived from what we know or believe is happening in a particular domain.

The ultimate goal of this chapter was to demonstrate a working example of a computational model of social capital in virtual communities and provide guidance to researchers and practitioners interested in exploring social issues in virtual communities. Moreover phenomena predicted by the model were intended to open up debate about social capital in virtual communities and its technical and social implications on knowledge. The chapter has extended the use of BBN techniques to complex domains, illustrating with an example of a social capital construct the different phases in which a model can be built. The approach described in the chapter combined both qualitative and quantitative techniques to elicit knowledge from experts without worrying about computing initial probabilities for training the model. A summary of the model predictions, showed that where there was a high degree of shared understanding and the fact that individuals were aware of each other's capabilities (knowledge awareness), there was potentially an increase in trusting relationships as well high levels of social capital. Similarly, when all forms of awareness were present, there tended to be an increased level of shared understanding, and correspondingly to levels of trust and social capital.

Based on the results of the predictions, it can be concluded that different forms of awareness, shared understanding and trust can variously influence our understanding of social capital in virtual communities. Although the scenarios presented in this chapter were inadequate to fully draw final conclusions about causal links between these variables and an overall level of social capital in a community, the predictions provided a starting point for understanding and perhaps establishing grounds for serious discourse on social capital in virtual communities and possibly more thinking in terms of how to enhance social capital in virtual communities. Database technologies offer promising opportunities for eliciting data that could be used for building Bayesian models as well as for developing concrete scenarios for updating Bayesian models.

## ACKNOWLEDGMENT

We would like to acknowledge the Natural Sciences and Engineering Research Council of Canada (NSERC) as well as the Social Sciences and Humanities Research Council of Canada (SSHRC) for their financial support towards Ben Daniel's research. We would also like to thank Educational Testing Service researchers David Williamson and Russell Almond for reviewing this chapter and providing very constructive feedback.

## REFERENCES

Baker, M. (2000). The Roles of Models in Artificial Intelligence and Education Research: A Prospective View. *International Journal of Artificial Intelligence in Education*, (11): 122–143.

Chan, H., & Darwiche, A. (2004). Sensitivity analysis in Bayesian Networks: From single to multiple parameters. In *Proceedings of the 20th conference on uncertainty in Artificial Intelligence (UAI)*, (pp. 67-75).

Cohen, D., & Prusak, L. (2001). *In good company: How social capital makes organizations work*. Cambridge, MA: Harvard Business School Press.

Cohen, D., & Prusak, L. (2001). *In good company: How social capital makes organizations work*. Cambridge, MA: Harvard Business School Press.

Collion, M. H. (1989). Strategic planning for national agricultural research systems: An Overview. *Working Paper, 26*. Retrieved November 24th 2008 from http://www.ifpri.org/divs/isnar.htm

Conati, C., Gertner, A., & VanLehn, K. (2002). Using bayesian networks to manage uncertainty in student modeling. *User Modeling and User-Adapted Interaction*, *12*(4), 371–417. doi:10.1023/A:1021258506583

Cooper, G. F., & Herskovits, E. (1992). A Bayesian method for the induction of Probabilistic networks from data. *Machine Learning*, *9*(4), 309–347. doi:10.1007/BF00994110

Coupé, V. M. H., & Van der Gaag, L. C. (1998). Practicable sensitivity analysis of Bayesian belief networks. In M. Huskova, P. Lachout, & J.A. Visek (Eds.), *Proceedings of the Joint Session of the 6th Praque Symposium of Asymptotic Statistics and the 13th Praque Conference on Information Theory, Statistical Decision Functions and Random Processes*, (p.81-86). Prague: Union of Czech Mathematicians and Physicists.

Daniel, B. K. Zapata-Rivera, D. J., & McCalla, G. I. (2003) A Bayesian computational model of social capital. In Huysman, M. Wenger, E. and Wulf, V. (Eds.). Communities and technologies (pp. 287-305). London: Kluwer Publishers.

Daniel, B. K., McCalla, G., & Schwier, R. (2003). Social capital in virtual learning communities and distributed, communities of practice. *The Canadian Journal of Learning Technology*, *29*(3), 113–139.

Daniel, B. K., McCalla, G. I., & Schwier, R. A. (2005). Data mining and modeling social capital in virtual learning communities. *Proceedings of the 12th International Conference on Artificial Intelligence in Education*, Amsterdam, 18-22 July, 2000-2008.

Daniel, B. K., O'Brien, D., & Sarkar, A. (2003). A design approach for Canadian distributed community of practice on governance and international development: A preliminary report. In Verburg, R. M., & De Ridder, J. A. (Eds.), *Knowledge sharing under distributed circumstances* (pp. 19–24). Enschede, The Netherlands: Ipskamps.

Daniel, B. K., Zapata-Rivera, D. J., & McCalla, G. I. (2003). A Bayesian computational model of social capital in virtual communities. In Huysman, M., Wenger, E., & Wulf, V. (Eds.), *Communities and technologies* (pp. 287–305). London: Kluwer.

Daniel, B. K., & Zapata-Rivera, J. D & McCalla, G. I. (2005, November). Computational framework for constructing Bayesian belief network models from incomplete, inconsistent and imprecise data in E-Learning (Poster). In *The Second LORNET International Annual Conference, I2LOR-2005, November 16 to 18*. Vancouver, Canada.

Daniel, B. K., Zapata-Rivera, J. D., & McCalla, G. I. (2007). A Bayesian Belief Network approach for modelling complex domains. In Mittal, A., Kassim, A., & Tan, T. (Eds.), *Bayesian Network Technologies: Applications and Graphical Models* (pp. 13–41). Hershey, PA: IGI Publishing.

Druzdzel, M. (1996). Qualitative verbal explanations in bayesian belief networks. *Artificial Intelligence and Simulation of Behaviour Quarterly*, *9*(4), 43–54.

Druzdzel, M. J., & Gaag, L. C. (2000). Building probabilistic networks: "Where do the numbers come from?" Guest editor's introduction. *Data Engineering*, *12*(4), 481–486. doi:10.1109/TKDE.2000.868901

Druzdzel, M. J., & Henri, J. S. (1994). *Relevance in probabilistic models: "backyards" in a "small world."* In Working notes of the AAAI-1994 Fall Symposium Series: Relevance, New Orleans, LA, (pp. 60-63).

Druzdzel, M. J., & Henrion, M. (1993). Efficient reasoning in qualitative probabilistic networks. In *Proceedings of the 11th National Conference on Artificial Intelligence,* (pp. 548-553).

Finn, J. (1996). *An introduction to Bayesian networks*. London: University College Press.

Finn, J., & Liang, J. (1994). drHugin: A system for value of information in Bayesian networks. In *Proceedings of the Fifth International Conference on Information Processing and Management of Uncertainty in Knowledge - based Systems (IPMU),* Paris, France, (pp. 178-183).

Goldman, R., & Charniak, E. (1990). Dynamic Construction of Belief Networks. In *Proceedings of the Sixth Conference on Uncertainty in Artificial Intelligence*, (pp. 90-97).

Gutwin, C., & Greenberg, S. (1998). Design for individuals, design for groups: Tradeoffs between power and workspace awareness. In *Proceedings of the ACM Conference on Computer Supported Cooperative Work* (pp. 207-216). New York: ACM Press.

Haddaway, P. (1999). An overview of some recent developments in Bayesian problem solving techniques. *AI Magazine*, (Spring Issue).

Heckerman, D. (1996). *A tutorial on learning with Bayesian networks.* Retrieved 22-06-06 from [ftp://ftp.research.microsoft.com/pub/tr/tr-95-06.pdf]

Heckerman, D., & Horwitz, E. (1998). Inferring informational goals from free-text queries: a bayesian approach. In *Proc 14th Conf on Uncertainty in AI*, (pp. 230-238).

Koller, D., & Pfeffer, A. (1996). Object Oriented Bayesian networks. In *Proceedings of the Thirteenth Conference on Uncertainty in Artificial Intelligence.*

Korb, K. B., & Nicholson, A. E. (2004). *Bayesian artificial intelligence.* Boca Raton, FL: Chapman & Hall/CRC.

Lacave, C., & Diez, F. J. (2002). Explanation for causal Bayesian networks in Elvira. In *Proceedings of the Workshop on Intelligent Data Analysis in Medicine and Pharmacology (IDAMAP-2002),* Lyon, France.

Lee, A., Danis, C., Miller, T., & Jung, Y. (2001). Fostering Social Interaction in Online Spaces. In M. Hirose, (ed.), *Human-Computer Interaction (INTERACT'01) — Eighth IFIP TC.13 Conference on Human-Computer Interaction,* (pp. 59-66). Amsterdam: IOS Press.

McCalla, G. (2000). The fragmentation of culture, learning, teaching and technology: Implications for Artificial Intelligence in Education Research. *International Journal of Artificial Intelligence,* *11*(2), 177–196.

McMillan, D. W., & Chavis, D. M. (1986). Sense of community: A definition and theory. *American Journal of Community Psychology, 14*(1), 6–23. doi:10.1002/1520-6629(198601)14:1<6::AID-JCOP2290140103>3.0.CO;2-I

Neapolitan, R. E. (2004). *Learning Bayesian Networks.* London: Prentice Hall.

Niedermayer, D. (1998). *An introduction to Bayesian networks and their contemporary applications.* Retrieved 6th January, 2006 from http://www.niedermayer.ca/papers/bayesian/

Pearl, J. (1988). *Probabilistic reasoning in intelligent systems: Networks of plausible inference.* San Mateo, CA: Morgan Kaufmann.

Pearl, J. & Verma, T. (1991). A theory of inferred causation, in Principles of Knowledge

Pennington, N., & Hastie, R. (1988). Explanation-based decision-making: Effects of memory structure on judgment. *Journal of Experimental Psychology. Learning, Memory, and Cognition, 14*(3), 521–533. doi:10.1037/0278-7393.14.3.521

Pradhan, M., Provan, G., Middleton, B., & Henrion, M. (1994). Knowledge engineering for large belief networks. In *Proceedings of the Tenth Conference on Uncertainty in Artificial Intelligence,* (pp. 484-490).

Putnam, R. (2000). *Bowling Alone: The Collapse and Revival of American Community.* New York: Simon Schuster.

Renooij, S., & Witteman, C. (1999). Talking probabilities: communicating probabilistic information with words and numbers. *International Journal of Approximate Reasoning, 2,* 169–194. doi:10.1016/S0888-613X(99)00027-4

Representation and Reasoning. Proceedings of the Second International Conference Morgan Kaufmann, San Mateo, CA.

Resnick, P. (2002). Beyond bowling together: sociotechnical capital. In J. M. Carroll (Ed), HCI in the new millennium (pp. 247 272). New York: Addison-Wesley.

Reye, J. (2004). Student modelling based on belief networks. *International Journal of Artificial Intelligence in Education, 14,* 63–96.

Russell, S., & Norvig, P. (1995). *Solution manual for "artificial intelligence: a modern approach.* Englewood Cliffs, NJ: Prentice Hall.

Schwier, R. A., & Daniel, B. K. (2007). Did we become a community? Multiple methods for identifying community and its constituent elements in formal online learning environments. In Lambropoulos, N., & Zaphiris, P. (Eds.), *User-Evaluation and Online Communities.* Hershey, PA: IDEA Group.

Stahl, G. (2000). A Model of collaborative knowledge-building. In B. Fishman & S. O'Connor-Divelbiss, (Eds.), *Fourth International Conference of the Learning Sciences* (pp.70-77). Mahwah, NJ: Erlbaum.

The World Bank. (1999). *Social capital research Group.* Retrieved from http://www.worldbank.org/poverty/scapital/

Van der Gaag, L. C., Renooij, S., Witteman, C., Aleman, B. M. P., & Taal, B. G. (1999). How to elicit many probabilities. In. *Proceedings of Incertainty in Artificial Intelligence, UI99,* 647–654.

VanLehn, K., Niu, Z., Siler, S., & Gertner, A. S. (1998). Student modeling from conversational test data: A bayesian approach without priors. In *ITS'98: Proceedings of the 4th International Conference on Intelligent Tutoring Systems,* (pp. 434–443).

Vomlel, J. (2004). Bayesian networks in educational testing. *International Journal of Uncertainty, Fuzziness and Knowledge Based Systems, 12* (Supplementary Issue 1), 83–100.

Wellman, M. P. (1990). Fundamental concepts of qualitative probabilistic networks. *Artificial Intelligence,* (44): 257–303. doi:10.1016/0004-3702(90)90026-V

Wong, S. K. M. (2001). The Relational Structure of Belief Networks. *Journal of Intelligent Information Systems, 16*(2), 117–148. doi:10.1023/A:1011237717300

Zapata-Rivera, J. D. (2002). cbCPT: Knowledge engineering support for CPTs in Bayesian networks. In *Canadian Conference on AI,* (pp. 368-370).

Zapata-Rivera, J. D. (2003) *Learning environments based on inspectable student models.* Ph.D. Thesis, University of Saskatchewan, Department of Computer Science, Canada.

Zapata-Rivera, J. D., & Greer, J. (2004). Interacting with Bayesian student models. *International Journal of Artificial Intelligence in Education, 142,* 127–163.

## ENDNOTE

[1] A nuisance parameter in Statistics is any parameter which is not of immediate interest but which must be accounted for in the analysis of parameters of interest.

## APPENDIX A: RESULTS OF THE SENSITIVITY ANALYSIS

Appendix A shows the spread of probabilities obtained from the sensitivity analysis (Tables 3, 4, 5, 6, 7, 8, 9, 10, 11, 12, and 13). Each variable was examined with respect to social capital, including social capital to itself. Overall findings are reported in percentages and each sensitivity value is measured in terms of its entropy reduction value.

*Probability of new finding = 100%, of all findings = 100%.*

*Table 3. Sensitivity of 'Social Capital' to findings at 'SocialCapital'*

| Probability ranges: | Min | Current | Max | RMS |
|---|---|---|---|---|
| Change | | | | |
| High | 0 | 0.5423 | 1 | 0.4982 |
| Low | 0 | 0.4577 | 1 | 0.4982 |

**Entropy reduction = 0.9948 (100%)**
**Belief Variance = 0.2482 (100%)**

*Table 4. Sensitivity of 'Social Capital' to findings at 'Engagement'*

| Probability ranges: | Min | Current | Max | RMS |
|---|---|---|---|---|
| Change | | | | |
| High | 0.3168 | 0.5423 | 0.7677 | 0.2255 |
| Low | 0.2323 | 0.4577 | 0.6832 | 0.2255 |

**Entropy reduction = 0.1534 (15.4%)**
**Belief Variance = 0.05083 (20.5%)**

*Table 5. Sensitivity of 'Social Capital' to findings at 'Attitudes'*

| Probability ranges: | Min | Current | Max | RMS |
|---|---|---|---|---|
| Change | | | | |
| High | 0.3169 | 0.5423 | 0.7676 | 0.2254 |
| Low | 0.2324 | 0.4577 | 0.6831 | 0.2254 |

**Entropy reduction = 0.1533 (15.4%)**
**Belief Variance = 0.05079 (20.5%)**

*Table 6. Sensitivity of 'Social Capital' to findings at 'Knowledge Awareness'*

| Probability ranges: | Min | Current | Max | RMS |
|---|---|---|---|---|
| Change | | | | |
| High | 0.3162 | 0.5423 | 0.764 | 0.2239 |
| Low | 0.236 | 0.4577 | 0.6838 | 0.2239 |

**Entropy reduction = 0.1511 (15.2%)**
**Belief Variance = 0.05012 (20.2%)**

*Table 7. Sensitivity of 'Social Capital' to findings at 'Capability Awareness'*

| Probability ranges: | Min | Current | Max | RMS |
|---|---|---|---|---|
| Change | | | | |
| High | 0.3174 | 0.5423 | 0.7628 | 0.2227 |
| Low | 0.2372 | 0.4577 | 0.6826 | 0.2227 |

**Entropy reduction = 0.1494 (15%)**
**Belief Variance = 0.04959 (20%)**

*Table 8. Sensitivity of 'Social Capital' to findings at 'Trust'*

| Probability ranges: | Min | Current | Max | RMS |
|---|---|---|---|---|
| Change | | | | |
| High | 0.3148 | 0.5423 | 0.7158 | 0.1987 |
| Low | 0.2842 | 0.4577 | 0.6852 | 0.1987 |

**Entropy reduction = 0.1175 (11.8%)**
**Belief Variance = 0.03948 (15.9%)**

*Table 9. Sensitivity of 'Social Capital' to findings at 'Shared Understanding'*

| Probability ranges: | Min | Current | Max | RMS |
|---|---|---|---|---|
| Change | | | | |
| High | 0.315 | 0.5423 | 0.7069 | 0.1934 |
| Low | 0.2931 | 0.4577 | 0.685 | 0.1934 |

Entropy reduction = 0.1112 (11.2%)
Belief Variance = 0.03742 (15.1%)

*Table 10. Sensitivity of 'Social Capital' to findings at 'Professional Awareness'*

| Probability ranges: | Min | Current | Max | RMS |
|---|---|---|---|---|
| Change | | | | |
| High | 0.3279 | 0.5423 | 0.7076 | 0.1883 |
| Low | 0.2924 | 0.4577 | 0.6721 | 0.1883 |

Entropy reduction = 0.1052 (10.6%)
Belief Variance = 0.03544 (14.3%)

*Table 11. Sensitivity of 'Social Capital' to findings at 'Demographic Awareness'*

| Probability ranges: | Min | Current | Max | RMS |
|---|---|---|---|---|
| Change | | | | |
| High | 0.4328 | 0.5423 | 0.6647 | 0.1157 |
| Low | 0.3353 | 0.4577 | 0.5672 | 0.1157 |

Entropy reduction = 0.03937 (3.96%)
Belief Variance = 0.0134 (5.4%)

*Table 12. Sensitivity of 'Social Capital' to findings at 'Social Protocols'*

| Probability ranges: | Min | Current | Max | RMS |
|---|---|---|---|---|
| Change | | | | |
| High | 0.4487 | 0.5423 | 0.6359 | 0.0936 |
| Low | 0.3641 | 0.4577 | 0.5513 | 0.0936 |

Entropy reduction = 0.02562 (2.58%)
Belief Variance = 0.008761 (3.53%)

*Table 13. Sensitivity of 'Social Capital' to findings at 'Community Type'*

| Probability ranges: | Min | Current | Max | RMS |
|---|---|---|---|---|
| Change | | | | |
| High | 0.4873 | 0.5423 | 0.5972 | 0.05493 |
| Low | 0.4028 | 0.4577 | 0.5127 | 0.05493 |

Entropy reduction = 0.008786 (0.883%)
Belief Variance = 0.003017 (1.22%)

# Chapter 9
# Integrity Constraints Checking in a Distributed Database

**Hamidah Ibrahim**
*Universiti Putra Malaysia, Malaysia*

## ABSTRACT

*Preserving the accuracy and the integrity of information in a database is extremely important for the organization that is maintaining that database. Such an organization is likely to rely heavily upon that accuracy. Applications that consult and use the database expect a warranty that the database is supplying the correct information. Critical business decisions may be made assuming that information extracted from the database is correct. Thus, incorrect data can lead to incorrect business decisions which can have serious implications for the people and organizations using it (Codd, 1990).*

## INTRODUCTION

Preserving the accuracy and the integrity of information in a database is extremely important for the organization that is maintaining that database. Such an organization is likely to rely heavily upon that accuracy. Applications that consult and use the database expect a warranty that the database is supplying the correct information. Critical business decisions may be made assuming that information extracted from the database is correct. Thus, incor-

rect data can lead to incorrect business decisions which can have serious implications for the people and organizations using it (Codd, 1990).

An important problem for a database system is to guarantee *database consistency*. Many techniques and tools have been devised to fulfill this requirement in many interrelated research areas, such as concurrency control, security control, reliability control and integrity control (Eswaran & Chamberlin, 1975; Grefen, 1993). Concurrency control deals with prevention of inconsistencies caused by concurrent access by multiple users or applications to a database. Security control deals with prevent-

DOI: 10.4018/978-1-60566-814-7.ch009

ing users from accessing and modifying data in a database in unauthorized ways. Reliability control deals with the prevention errors due to the malfunctioning of system hardware or software. Integrity control deals with the prevention of semantic errors made by the users due to their carelessness or lack of knowledge.

A database state is said to be consistent if the database satisfies a set of statements, called *semantic integrity constraints* (or simply *constraints*). Integrity constraints specify those configurations of the data that are considered semantically correct. Any update operation (insert, delete or modify) or transaction (sequence of updates) that occurs must not result in a state that violates these constraints. Thus, a fundamental issue concerning integrity constraints is *constraint checking*, that is the process of ensuring that the integrity constraints are satisfied by the database after it has been updated. Checking the consistency of a database state will generally involve the execution of *integrity tests* on the database which verify whether the database is satisfying its constraints or not.

In a database system, a semantic integrity subsystem (SIS) is responsible for managing and enforcing integrity constraints to ensure that these rules are not violated by the database and the database is in a consistent state. An early proposal by Eswaran and Chamberlin (1975) described the functionality requirements for an integrity subsystem. The main tasks of this subsystem are to determine which constraints are to be checked after each database change and to trigger the appropriate actions when a constraint violation is detected. The crucial problem encountered in designing a complete integrity subsystem is the difficulty of devising an efficient algorithm for enforcing database integrity when updates occur. Many proposals for designing an integrity subsystem can be found in the database literature. In Grefen (1993) and McCarroll (1995) three ways to couple the integrity subsystem to the DBMS are described.

The first approach is known as the *decoupled subsystem* approach. This adds the subsystem as an additional layer on top of an existing DBMS. It was employed by the AIM project (Cremers & Domann, 1983) and the KBDTA system (Wang, 1992). In this approach, the responsibility for ensuring the consistency of the database when a transaction occurs is part of the transaction design process. The transaction designers are responsible for ensuring that the transactions are *safe*, i.e. when executed, the transactions are guaranteed to bring the database from one consistent state to another consistent state. Consequently, as transactions can get complex, a *transaction design tool* is usually incorporated into the subsystem to assist the transaction designers to construct safe transactions. Hence, in this approach, little or no support within the DBMS is needed for automatically enforcing database integrity constraints.

The second approach is known as the *loosely coupled subsystem*. It adds the subsystem as an extension to the DBMS. This is employed by the SABRE (Simon & Valduriez, 1987) and the PRISMA (Grefen, 1990) projects. In this approach, transactions have integrity tests embedded in them to perform the necessary integrity checking. The modified transactions can then be executed by the standard transaction facilities. This approach is based on *query modification* and *transaction modification* strategies, where an arbitrary query or transaction that may violate the integrity of a database is modified, such that the execution of the modified query or transaction is assured to leave the database in a consistent state.

In the third approach which is known as the *tightly coupled subsystem*, the subsystem is seen as part of the basic functionality of a database system, and is fully integrated into it. This approach, initially proposed by Hammer and McLeod (1975) and Eswaran and Chamberlin (1975), is employed by the Starbust project (Ceri, Fraternali, Paraboschi & Tanca, 1994), SICSDD project (Ibrahim, Gray & Fiddian, 1998) and the latest versions of commercial DBMSs such as INGRES

*Table 1. Coupling integrity system to a DBMS*

| Approach | Decoupled Subsystem | Loosely Coupled Subsystem | Tightly Coupled Subsystem |
|---|---|---|---|
| Responsibility of ensuring database consistency: | Transaction designers | DBMS + SIS | SIS |
| DBMS support: | Little/No | Yes | Yes |
| Automatic enforcement: | Yes with transaction design tool | Yes | Yes |
| Type of transaction: | Specific | Specific | General |
| **Diagram:** | | | |
| Example: | AIM project, KBDTA system | SABRE, PRISMA project | Starbust project, SICSDD project, INGRESS, ORACLE |

and ORACLE. In this approach, integrity tests are general rather than transaction specific and thus no knowledge of the internal structure of a transaction is required. Typically, this requires rule mechanisms to implement integrity constraint enforcement (Ibrahim, 2002b).

Table 1 summarizes the three approaches for coupling the integrity subsystem to the DBMS.

## PRELIMINARIES

This chapter focuses on the relational databases, which can be regarded as consisting of two distinct parts, namely: an intensional part and an extensional part. A database is described by a database schema, $D$, which consists of a finite set of relation schemas, $<R_1, R_2, ..., R_m>$. A relation schema is denoted by $R(A_1, A_2, ..., A_n)$ where $R$ is the name of the relation (predicate) with $n$-arity and $A_i$'s are the attributes of $R$. Let $dom(A_i)$ be the domain values for attributes $A_i$. Then, an instance of $R$ is a relation R which is a finite subset of cartesian product $dom(A_1)$ x...x $dom(A_n)$. A database instance is a collection of instances for its relation schemas. A relational distributed database schema is described as a quadruple $(D, IC, FR, AS)$ where $IC$ is a finite set of integrity constraints, $FR$ is a

finite set of fragmentation rules and $AS$ is a finite set of allocation schemas.

Without loss of generality we assume that the database integrity constraints are expressed in prenex conjunctive normal form with the range restricted property (Nicolas, 1982). A conjunct (literal) is an atomic formula of the form $R(u_1, u_2, ..., u_k)$ where $R$ is a $k$-ary relation name and each $u_i$ is either a variable or a constant. A positive atomic formula (positive literal) is denoted by $R(u_1, u_2, ..., u_k)$ whilst a negative atomic formula (negative literal) is prefixed by $\neg$. An (in)equality is a formula of the form $u_1$ OP $u_2$ (prefixed with $\neg$ for inequality) where both $u_1$ and $u_2$ can be constants or variables and OP $\in \{<, \leq, >, \geq, \neq, =\}$.

A set of fragmentation rules, $FR$, specifies the set of restrictions, $C_i$, that must be satisfied by each fragment $R_i$. These rules introduce a new set of integrity constraints and therefore have the same notation as $IC$. For simplicity, our example will only consider horizontal fragmentation. We assume that the fragmentation of relations satisfies the completeness, the disjointness and the reconstructability properties. An allocation schema locates a fragment, $R_i$, to one or more sites. Throughout this chapter the example *company* database is used, as given in Box 1. This example is taken from Ibrahim, Gray & Fiddian (2001) and

*Box 1. The Company static integrity constraints*

---

*Schema:*
emp(eno, dno, ejob, esal); dept(dno, dname, mgrno, mgrsal); proj(eno, dno, pno)

*Integrity Constraints:*

'A specification of valid salary'

IC-1: $(\forall w \forall x \forall y \forall z)(emp(w, x, y, z) \rightarrow (z > 0))$

'Every employee has a unique eno'

IC-2: $(\forall w \forall x1 \forall x2 \forall y1 \forall y2 \forall z1 \forall z2)(emp(w, x1, y1, z1) \wedge emp(w, x2, y2, z2) \rightarrow (x1 = x2) \wedge (y1 = y2) \wedge (z1 = z2))$

'Every department has a unique *dno*'

IC-3: $(\forall w \forall x1 \forall x2 \forall y1 \forall y2 \forall z1 \forall z2)(dept(w, x1, y1, z1) \wedge dept(w, x2, y2, z2) \rightarrow (x1 = x2) \wedge (y1 = y2) \wedge (z1 = z2))$

'The *dno* of every tuple in the *emp* relation exists in the *dept* relation'

IC-4: $(\forall t \forall u \forall v \forall w \exists x \exists y \exists z)(emp(t, u, v, w) \rightarrow dept(u, x, y, z))$

'The *eno* of every tuple in the *proj* relation exists in the *emp* relation'

IC-5: $(\forall u \forall v \forall w \exists x \exists y \exists z)(proj(u, v, w) \rightarrow emp(u, x, y, z))$

'The *dno* of every tuple in the *proj* relation exists in the *dept* relation'

IC-6: $(\forall u \forall v \forall w \exists x \exists y \exists z)(proj(u, v, w) \rightarrow dept(v, x, y, z))$

'Every manager in *dept* 'D1' earns > £4000'

IC-7: $(\forall w \forall x \forall y \forall z)(dept(w, x, y, z) \wedge (w = `D1') \rightarrow (z > 4000))$

'Every employee must earn ≤ to the manager in the same department'

IC-8: $(\forall t \forall u \forall v \forall w \forall x \forall y \forall z)(emp(t, u, v, w) \wedge dept(u, x, y, z) \rightarrow (w \leq z))$

'Any department that is working on a project $P_1$ is also working on project $P_2$'

IC-9: $(\forall x \forall y \exists z)(proj(x, y, P_1) \rightarrow proj(z, y, P_2))$

*Fragmentation Rules:*

FR-1: $(\forall w \forall x \forall y \forall z)(emp_1(w, x, y, z) \rightarrow (z > 0) \wedge (z \leq 10000))$

FR-2: $(\forall w \forall x \forall y \forall z)(emp_2(w, x, y, z) \rightarrow (z > 10000))$

FR-3: $(\forall w \forall x \forall y \forall z)(dept_1(w, x, y, z) \rightarrow (w = `D1'))$

FR-4: $(\forall w \forall x \forall y \forall z)(dept_2(w, x, y, z) \rightarrow (w = `D2'))$

FR-5: $(\forall x \forall y \forall z)(proj_i(x, y, z) \rightarrow (z = Pi))$ for $i = \{1, 2\}$

---

Alwan, Ibrahim & Udzir (2008). Here we assume that the relation *emp* is horizontally fragmented into two fragments, $emp_1$ and $emp_2$ with predicates $(esal > 0) \wedge (esal \leq 10000)$ and $(esal > 10000)$; *dept* is horizontally fragmented into two fragments, $dept_1$ and $dept_2$ with predicates $dno = `D1'$ and $dno = `D2'$; and *proj* is horizontally fragmented into two fragments, $proj_1$ and $proj_2$ with predicates $pno = `P1'$ and $pno = `P2'$.

In the database literature, many types and variations of integrity tests have been described. The classifications of integrity tests are based on some of their characteristics, as presented in Table 2 (Alwan, Ibrahim & Udzir, 2008). This is explained below:

1. **Based on when the integrity test is evaluated:**

   a.  *post-tests:* allow an update operation to be executed on a database state, which changes it to a new state, and when an inconsistent result is detected undo this update. The method that applies these integrity tests is called the detection method.

   b.  *pre-tests:* allow an update to be executed only if it changes the database state to a consistent state. The method that applies these integrity tests is called the prevention method.

2. **Based on region:**

   a.  *local tests:* verify the consistency of a database within the local region, i.e. by accessing the information at the local site. The method that adopts these integrity tests is called the *local method.*

   b.  *global tests:* verify the consistency of a database outside the local region, i.e. by accessing the information at the remote site(s). The method that adopts

*Table 2. Types of integrity tests in distributed databases*

| Integrity test based on input | Integrity test based on region | Integrity test based on detection/ prevention methods | Integrity test based on its properties |
|---|---|---|---|
| Non-support test | *Global test: spans remote sites* | Post-test: evaluated after an update is performed | Sufficient test |
| | | | Necessary test |
| | | | Complete test |
| | | Pre-test: evaluated before an update is performed | Sufficient test |
| | | | Necessary test |
| | | | Complete test |
| | Local test: spans local sites | Post-test: evaluated after an update is performed | Sufficient test |
| | | | Necessary test |
| | | | Complete test |
| | | Pre-test: evaluated before an update is performed | Sufficient test |
| | | | Necessary test |
| | | | Complete test |
| Support test | Global test: spans remote sites | Post-test: evaluated after an update is performed | Sufficient test |
| | | | Necessary test |
| | | | Complete test |
| | | Pre-test: evaluated before an update is performed | Sufficient test |
| | | | Necessary test |
| | | | Complete test |
| | Local test: spans local sites | Post-test: evaluated after an update is performed | Sufficient test |
| | | | Necessary test |
| | | | Complete test |
| | | Pre-test: evaluated before an update is performed | Sufficient test |
| | | | Necessary test |
| | | | Complete test |

these integrity tests is called the *global method*.

3. **Based on its properties (McCarroll, 1995):**
   a. *sufficient tests:* when the test is satisfied, this implies that the associated constraint is satisfied and thus the update operation is safe with respect to the constraint.
   b. *necessary tests:* when the test is not satisfied, this implies that the associated constraint is violated and thus the update operation is unsafe with respect to the constraint.

   c. *complete tests:* has both the sufficiency and the necessity properties.

4. **Based on the input used to generate the test:**
   a. *non-support tests:* these integrity tests are generated based on the update operation and the integrity constraint to be checked.
   b. *support tests:* any tests that are derived using other integrity constraints as the support to generate the tests. Both the non-support tests and support tests can have the characteristics as mentioned above, namely: pre-test or post-test,

depending on when the test is evaluated, local-test or global test, depending on the region it covers during the evaluation, and complete, sufficient or necessary depending on the properties of the test.

Table 3 summarizes the integrity tests generated for the integrity constraints listed in Box 1 using the simplification methods proposed by Nicolas (1982), Ibrahim, Gray & Fiddian (2001), and Alwan, Ibrahim & Udzir (2008). It is not the intention of this chapter to present the simplification methods as readers may refer to Nicolas (1982), Ibrahim, Gray & Fiddian (2001), and Alwan, Ibrahim & Udzir (2008). Based on Table 3, integrity tests 1, 2, 5, 8, 11, 12, 15, 16, 19, 20, 21, 23, 24 and 26 are the complete tests (generated using the simplification method proposed by Nicolas (1982)), while integrity tests 9, 13, 17, 22, 25 and 27 are the sufficient tests (generated using the simplification method proposed by Ibrahim, Gray & Fiddian (2001)), where these tests are derived using the update operation and the integrity constraint to be checked as the input. Thus, they are the non-support tests. Support tests are 3, 4, 6, 7, 10, 14 and 18, where these tests are generated based on the update operation and other integrity constraint as the support (generated using the simplification method proposed by Alwan, Ibrahim & Udzir (2008)). For example test 3 and test 18 are generated using *IC*-5 as the support.

Once integrity constraints have been specified for a database, maintaining a database's integrity whenever the database state changes to a new state involves checking that these constraints are not violated by the operations that caused the transition. Two types of information are required, namely: (i) *when* to enforce the constraints, and (ii) *what* to do when a constraint is violated by the database. Thus, a more operational form of an integrity constraint is required. This form is called an *integrity rule*. In this chapter, an integrity rule has the following template, which is based on the Event-Condition-Action (ECA) rules.

- WHEN triggering operation
- IF NOT integrity test
- THEN then-action
- [ELSE else-action]

A rule is triggered when its triggering operation is verified by some database modification (Event part). Once a rule is triggered, the integrity test is checked (Condition part). This is the test generated by the simplification methods. If a test is not satisfied, an action is executed (Action part). Example: the following are the integrity rules for the integrity constraint *IC*-4:

*R*-4*a*: WHEN insert($emp(a, b, c, d)$) IF NOT $(\exists x \exists y \exists z)(dept(b, x, y, z))$ THEN abort

*R*-4*b*: WHEN insert($emp(a, b, c, d)$) IF NOT $(\exists t \exists v \exists w)(emp(t, b, v, w))$ THEN *R*-4*a*

*R*-4*c*: WHEN insert($emp(a, b, c, d)$) IF NOT $(\exists y \exists z)(proj(y, b, z))$ THEN *R*-4*a*

## BACKGROUND

The growing complexity of modern database applications plus the need to support multiple users has further increased the need for a powerful integrity subsystem to be incorporated into these systems. Therefore, a complete integrity subsystem is considered to be an important part of any modern DBMS (Grefen, 1993). The crucial problem in designing a complete integrity subsystem is the difficulty of devising an efficient algorithm for enforcing database integrity against updates. Thus, it is not surprising that much attention has been paid to the maintenance of integrity in centralized databases over the last decade. A naive approach is to perform the update and then check whether the integrity constraints are satisfied in the new database state. This method, termed *brute force checking*, is very expensive,

*Table 3. Integrity tests of the integrity constraints of Box 1*

| IC-i | Update template | Integrity test |
|------|-----------------|----------------|
| IC-1 | insert($emp(a, b, c, d)$) | 1. $d > 0$ |
| IC-2 | insert($emp(a, b, c, d)$) | 2. $(\forall x2 \forall y2 \forall z2)(\neg emp(a, x2, y2, z2) \vee (x2 \neq b) \vee (y2 \neq c) \vee (z2 \neq d))$ |
|      |                 | 3. $(\forall y \forall z)(\neg proj(a, y, z))$ |
|      |                 | 4. $(\forall x \forall y \forall z)(\neg dept(x, y, a, z))$ |
| IC-3 | insert($dept(a, b, c, d)$) | 5. $(\forall x2 \forall y2 \forall z2)(\neg dept(a, x2, y2, z2) \vee (x2 \neq b) \vee (y2 \neq c) \vee (z2 \neq d))$ |
|      |                 | 6. $(\forall x \forall y \forall z)(\neg emp(x, a, y, z))$ |
|      |                 | 7. $(\forall y \forall z)(\neg proj(y, a, z))$ |
| IC-4 | insert($emp(a, b, c, d)$) | 8. $(\exists x \exists y \exists z)(dept(b, x, y, z))$ |
|      |                 | 9. $(\exists t \exists v \exists w)(emp(t, b, v, w))$ |
|      |                 | 10. $(\exists y \exists z)(proj(y, b, z))$ |
|      | delete($dept(a, b, c, d)$) | 11. $(\forall t \forall v \forall w)(\neg emp(t, a, v, w))$ |
| IC-5 | insert($proj(a, b, c)$) | 12. $(\exists x \exists y \exists z)(emp(a, x, y, z))$ |
|      |                 | 13. $(\exists v \exists w)(proj(a, v, w))$ |
|      |                 | 14. $(\exists x \exists y \exists z)(dept(x, y, a, z))$ |
|      | delete($emp(a, b, c, d)$) | 15. $(\forall v \forall w)(\neg proj(a, v, w))$ |
| IC-6 | insert($proj(a, b, c)$) | 16. $(\exists x \exists y \exists z)(dept(b, x, y, z))$ |
|      |                 | 17. $(\exists u \exists w)(proj(u, b, w))$ |
|      |                 | 18. $(\exists x \exists y \exists z)(emp(x, b, y, z))$ |
|      | delete($dept(a, b, c, d)$) | 19. $(\forall u \forall w)(\neg proj(u, a, w))$ |
| IC-7 | insert($dept(a, b, c, d)$) | 20. $(\forall x \forall y \forall z)(\neg dept(a, x, y, z) \vee (a \neq \text{'}D1\text{'}) \vee (d > 4000))$ |
| IC-8 | insert($emp(a, b, c, d)$) | 21. $(\forall x \forall y \forall z)(\neg dept(b, x, y, z) \vee (d \leq z))$ |
|      |                 | 22. $(\exists t \exists v \exists w)(emp(t, b, v, w) \wedge (w \geq d))$ |
|      | insert($dept(a, b, c, d)$) | 23. $(\forall t \forall v \forall w)(\neg emp(t, a, v, w) \vee (w \leq d))$ |
| IC-9 | insert($proj(a, b, P1)$) | 24. $(\exists z)(proj(z, b, P2))$ |
|      |                 | 25. $(\exists z)(proj(z, b, P1))$ |
|      | delete($proj(a, b, P2)$) | 26. $(\forall x)(\neg proj(x, b, P1))$ |
|      |                 | 27. $(\exists z)(proj(z, b, P2) \wedge (z \neq a))$ |

impractical and can lead to prohibitive processing costs (Embury, Gray & Bassiliades, 1993; Hsu & Imielinski, 1985; Mazumdar, 1993; Plexousakis, 1993; Qian, 1989; Qian 1988; Sheard & Stemple, 1989). Enforcement is costly because the evaluation of integrity constraints requires accessing large amounts of data which are not involved in the database update transition (Simon & Valduriez, 1987). Hence, improvements to this approach have been reported in many research papers (Bernstein & Blaustein, 1981; Blaustein, 1981; Henschen, McCune & Naqvi, 1984; Hsu & Imielinski, 1985; McCune & Henschen, 1989; Nicolas 1982; Qian 1989). Although this research effort has yielded fruitful results that have given centralized systems a substantial level of reliability and robustness with respect to the integrity of their data, there has so far been little research carried out on integrity issues for distributed databases. The problem of devising an efficient enforcement mechanism is more crucial in a distributed environment. This is due to the following facts (Barbara & Garcia-Molina, 1992; Mazumdar, 1993; Qian 1989; Simon & Valduriez, 1987):

- Integrity constraints are general statements about sets of data elements which may spread over several sites in a distributed database. A large amount of data may therefore need to be transferred around the network in order to determine the truth of such statements.

- Owing to the possibility of fragmentation of relations with the fragments stored at different locations, the integrity constraints must be transformed into constraints on the fragments so that they can be straightforwardly used for constructing efficient enforcement algorithms. Thus there are usually more integrity constraints in an equivalent distributed database than a centralized database, all of which need to be maintained. In addition, replication of data imposes an additional constraint that the replicas must have equivalent values at all times.

- Frequent updates can lead to frequent executions of expensive violation testing operations.

- If some constraints are violated, the whole update transaction which causes the state transition must be aborted and the database must be restored to the previous state, which can be a very costly operation in a distributed system.

The brute force strategy of checking constraints is worse in the distributed context since the checking would typically require data transfer as well as computation leading to complex algorithms to determine the most efficient approach. Allowing an update to execute with the intention of aborting it at commit time in the event of constraint violation is also inefficient since rollback and recovery must occur at all sites which participated in the update. Thus, the question of interest is *how to efficiently check integrity constraints in a distributed environment.*

Many researchers have studied the problem of maintaining the consistency of a database and not surprisingly many different approaches have been proposed. For centralized databases, researchers have suggested that constraint checking can be optimized by exploiting the fact that the constraints are known to be satisfied prior to an update, and by *reducing the number of integrity constraints that need checking* by only checking the sub-set of integrity constraints that may be violated by the current update or transaction. This is based on the following observation by Nicolas (1982). Given a valid database state, a new state is obtained when it is updated either by a single update operation or by a transaction. Depending on the operation leading to the new state, some integrity constraints remain necessarily satisfied in this new state, while others have to be evaluated to determine whether they are actually satisfied or not (Nicolas, 1982). Thus an integrity testing strategy which avoids redundantly checking constraints that are satisfied in the database before and are not affected by the update operation is better (more efficient) than a basic strategy which checks all the constraints. This revised strategy known as *incremental integrity checking* (Gupta, 1994; Plexousakis, 1993) or constraint filtering (Grefen, 1990) is the basis of most current approaches to integrity checking in databases. In Gupta (1994), this strategy is also referred to as a brute force strategy because by default it uses all the underlying relations.

Another strategy is to simplify the constraint formulae so that *less data are accessed* in order to determine the truth of the constraint. With the assumption that the set of initial constraints, *IC*, is known to be satisfied in the state before an update, simplified forms of *IC*, say *IC'*, are constructed such that *IC* is satisfied in the new state if and only if *IC'* is satisfied, and the evaluation cost of *IC'* is less than or equal to the evaluation cost of *IC*.

This strategy is referred to as *constraint simplification* and the simplified forms of these constraints are referred to as *integrity tests* (Ibrahim, 2002a; Ibrahim, Gray & Fiddian, 1996; McCarroll, 1995) or *constraint protectors* (Stemple, Mazumdar & Sheard, 1987). This approach conforms to the admonition of Nicolas (1982) to concentrate on the problem of finding *good* constraints. Various simplification techniques have been proposed where integrity tests are derived from the syntactic structure of the constraints and the update operations (Bernstein & Blaustein, 1981; Blaustein, 1981; Gupta, 1994; Henschen, McCune & Naqvi, 1984; Hsu & Imielinski, 1985; McCarroll, 1995; McCune & Henschen, 1989; Nicolas, 1982; Qian, 1989; Simon & Valduriez, 1987). These techniques are referred to as *constraint simplification by update analysis*. Researchers in this area have focused solely on the derivation of efficient integrity tests, claiming that they are cheaper to enforce and reduce the amount of data accessed, thus reducing the cost of integrity constraint checking. Many types and variations of integrity tests have been described in the database literature as presented in the *Preliminaries* section. An important property desired of an integrity test of any of these types is that the test will be cheaper to execute than the initial constraint from which it is derived. Thus, it is important to ensure that such integrity tests are as efficient as possible in order to reduce the performance overheads imposed by integrity enforcement. The issue addressed here is *how to derive an efficient set of tests to prove that an update operation will guarantee the semantic integrity of the database with respect to each and every constraint defined on the database.*

Furthermore, to avoid undoing the updates, these tests must be evaluated before the database state transition caused by the update occurs. The introduction of inconsistencies in the database is therefore prevented by committing only those update operations that result in a consistent database state. Methods following this approach are term *preventive methods* and are favoured over *detective methods* which allow an update operation to be executed on a database state and when an inconsistent result state is detected undo this update.

For distributed database environments, most of the strategies proposed for centralized systems are used, in particular the incremental integrity checking strategy and the constraint simplification method strategy, which aim to reduce the number of integrity constraints to be evaluated and the amount of data accessed. In addition, new strategies appropriate to a distributed environment have been proposed which aim to reduce the number of sites involved and thus reduce the amount of data transferred across the network (Barbara & Garcia-Molina, 1992; Gupta, 1994; Ibrahim, Gray & Fiddian, 1998; Mazumdar, 1993; Qian, 1989). These strategies try to avoid remote accesses to the update sites (target sites) and are invaluable in a situation where it is impossible to access data located at other sites in the distributed system, for example in situations where network failure is detected, or a high-security database is involved. This means identifying *how to simplify the integrity constraints so that evaluation is more local and at best is entirely local to the sites involved in the update.*

Although the performance of constraint checking in a distributed database system has been improved by adopting the centralized strategies, with respect to the amount of data accessed or transferred, these strategies are still inefficient for distributed environments since:

1. In these strategies, most of the simplified forms are derived from the initial constraints as specified by the user. These derivations do not exploit knowledge about the database application, especially its data fragmentation and allocation, which can be used to:

   a. Derive a set of simplified constraints that can be straightforwardly used for constructing efficient enforcement algorithms with respect to the distributed environment.

b. Infer the information stored at different sites of the network and so minimize the support from remote sites required when checking the constraints.

2. Complete tests, which are the tests used most often in centralized systems, are usually expensive in a distributed environment. However, sufficient tests are useful in a distributed environment (Mazumdar, 1993) since their checking space often only spans a single site and therefore they can be performed at a reasonable cost as the number of sites involved and the amount of data transferred across the network are reduced. Thus, most of the previous works in the area of constraint checking for distributed databases concentrate on improving the performance of the checking mechanism by executing the complete and sufficient tests when necessary. Recent study by Alwan, Ibrahim & Udzir (2008) observed that most of the previous works proposed an approach to derive simplified form of the initial integrity constraint with the sufficiency property, since the sufficient test is known to be cheaper than the complete test and its initial integrity constraint as it involved less data to be transferred across the network and always can be evaluated at the target site, i.e. only one site will be involved during the checking process. The previous approaches assume that an update operation will be executed at a site where the relation specified in the update operation is located, which is not always true. For example, consider a relation $R$ that is located at site 1. An insert operation into $R$ is assume to be submitted by a user at site 1 and the sufficient test generated is used to validate the consistency of the database with respect to this update operation, which can be performed locally at site 1. But if the same update operation is submitted at different site, say 2, the sufficient test is no longer appropriate as it will definitely access information from site 1 which is now remote to site 2.

The problem of choosing a good set of constraints for better enforcement which has been explored intensively in centralized systems has been relatively neglected for distributed systems. In addition, an approach is needed so that local checking can be performed regardless the location of the submitted update operation. Also, the approach must be able to cater the important and frequently used integrity constraint types.

Constraint simplification methods in a distributed environment can be classified into two types of approach. Both approaches are targeted at deriving integrity tests/conditions but they use different information. The first approach uses knowledge about the application domain and data fragmentation (Mazumdar, 1993; Qian, 1989). This approach is referred to as *constraint simplification by reformulation*. The second approach analyses the syntactic structure of the constraints and the update operations in order to generate the integrity tests, as reported in Gupta (1994), and is referred to as *constraint simplification by update analysis*.

## STRATEGIES FOR CHECKING INTEGRITY CONSTRAINTS IN A DISTRIBUTED DATABASE

In order to improve and to generate an efficient integrity constraint checking in a distributed environment the following circumstances should be undertaken.

1. **Constraint Filtering:** It assumes that the database is consistent prior to an update and an incremental integrity checking strategy is adopted which *reduces the number of*

*constraints evaluated*. For each update request, only those constraints that may be violated by it are selected for further evaluation. This can be performed by observing the following rules (Nicolas, 1982) where integrity constraints are specified in prenex conjunctive normal form:

a.  Whenever an update operation is dealing with the extension of a relation $R$, integrity constraints in which $R$ does not occur are unaffected. Example, inserting or deleting a tuple into/from the relation *emp* will only affect the *IC*-1, *IC*-2, *IC*-4, *IC*-5, and *IC*-8 while other integrity constraints are not affected.

b.  Integrity constraints which do not contain $R$ in negated atomic formula are unaffected when a tuple is inserted into the extension of $R$. Example, inserting a tuple into the relation *emp* will only affect the *IC*-1, *IC*-2, *IC*-4, and *IC*-8 while other integrity constraints are not affected.

c.  Integrity constraints which do not contain $R$ in a nonnegated atomic formula are unaffected when a tuple is deleted from the extension of $R$. Example, deleting a tuple from the relation *emp* will only affect the *IC*-5 while other integrity constraints are not affected.

Also, by rescheduling the execution of the integrity rules, early update abortion in the case of constraint violation is affected. Detecting constraint violation as early as possible is important since it eliminates the execution of further integrity rules and thus reduces the execution time of the process. Some heuristic rules can be applied, such as:

a.  Choose an integrity constraint (rule) whose violation implies that no other integrity constraints are triggered, i.e. an isolated node in the triggering graph (a triggering graph is a graph generated to present the relationships

between integrity rules). For example, an integrity rule for a key constraint with an ABORT action. This is because inserting a new tuple which violates a key constraint implies that no insertion should be made at all.

b.  Choose a local rule, i.e. an integrity rule that can be performed at a local site.

c.  An integrity rule with test $Ti$ which subsumes another integrity rule with test $Tj$ is preferred since the truth of test $Ti$ implies the truth of test $Tj$. Example: consider the following integrity rules;

    $R$-4$b$: WHEN insert($emp(a, b, c, d)$) IF NOT ($\exists t \exists v \exists w$)($emp(t, b, v, w)$) THEN $R$-4$a$

    $R$-8$b$: WHEN insert($emp(a, b, c, d)$) IF NOT ($\exists t \exists v \exists w$)($emp(t, b, v, w) \wedge (w \geq d)$) THEN $R$-8$a$

It is obvious that if the integrity test of the integrity rule $R$-8$b$ is true then this implies that the integrity test of the integrity rule $R$-4$b$ is also true.

2.  **Constraint Optimization:** Since the enforcement of the constraints takes place at the fragment level, the constraints specified in terms of global relations should be transformed into constraints specified in terms of fragment relations so that they can be straightforwardly used for constructing efficient enforcement algorithms. Here, efficient means a set of fragment constraints which is semantically equivalent to the initial set, does not contain any semantic or syntactically redundant fragment constraints/constructs, eliminates any fragment constraints whose evaluation is proven to be true, eliminates any fragment constraints which contradict already existing fragmentation rules and whose derived constraints are either more local (less distributed) or are entirely local when compared with the initial set. Thus, the properties that one should look for in

the derived fragment constraints are that they are *more efficient* and *more local* than the initial set of constraints. Most of the previous approaches/methods proposed for finding/deriving a good set of constraints concentrate on deriving simplified forms of the constraints by analyzing both the syntax of the constraints and their appropriate update operations. These methods are based on syntactic criteria. In fact, an improved set of constraints (fragment constraints) can be constructed by applying both the semantic and syntactic methods. Also, the knowledge about the data distribution and the application domain can be used to create algorithms which derive using this knowledge an efficient set of fragment constraints from the original constraints. In order to derive an integrity tests from a given initial constraint, the following steps can be followed (Ibrahim, Gray & Fiddian, 2001):

a.  Transform the initial constraint into a set of logically equivalent fragment constraints which reflect the data fragmentation. At this stage, the transformations are restricted to logically equivalent transformations, without considering any reformulation of the original constraints. The transformation is one to many, which means that given an integrity constraint, the result of the transformation is a logically equivalent set of fragment constraints. There are six transformation rules that are applied during this process (Ibrahim, Gray & Fiddian 2001) which cover the horizontal, vertical, and mixed fragmentation. Example: $\vee^{i=2}_{i=1}(\forall w \forall x \forall y \forall z)(\neg dept_i(w, x, y, z) \vee \neg(w = `D1') \vee (z > 4000))$ are the fragment constraints which are logically equivalent to its initial constraint *IC*-7 based on the fragmentation rules given in Box 1.

b.  Optimize the derived set of fragment constraints. There are several types of optimization technique that can be applied to constraints at the fragment level, such as techniques for optimizing query processing (Chakravarthy, 1990), reformulation techniques (Qian, 1989) and theorem based techniques (McCarroll, 1995; McCune & Henschen, 1989). Constraint optimization can be performed before (pre-optimization) or after (post-optimization) compilation. The constraint optimization process should utilize both syntactic and semantic information about the database integrity constraints. Example: $(\forall w \forall x \forall y \forall z)$ $(\neg dept_1(w, x, y, z) \vee (z > 4000))$ is the optimized fragment constraint for the *IC*-7 and the fragmentation rules given in Box 1.

c.  Distribute the set of fragment constraints to the appropriate site(s). Because the complexity of enforcing constraints is directly related to both the number of constraints in the constraint set and the number of sites involved, the objective of this phase is to reduce the number of constraints allocated to each site for execution at that site. Distributing the whole set of fragment constraints to every site is not cost-effective since not all fragment constraints are affected by an update and so sites may not be affected by particular updates. The decision of the distribution is based on the site allocation of the fragment relations specified in the constraint. Example: if $dept_1$ is allocated only at site 1, then the fragment constraint $(\forall w \forall x \forall y \forall z)$ $(\neg dept_1(w, x, y, z) \vee (z > 4000))$ should be allocated at site 1 only.

d.  Generate the integrity tests. There are a lot of techniques proposed by previous researchers to generate integrity tests (simplified forms) as discussed in the previous section. As mentioned in the *Preliminaries* section, there are many types of integrity tests. Recent study by Alwan, Ibrahim & Udzir (2008) confirmed that for distributed database, not only sufficient test should be the main test for evaluation but tests such as complete and support should also be considered depending on the allocation of the relations and the site where the update operation is submitted.

These four steps utilize: the assumption that the database is consistent prior to an update operation, the fragmentation strategies used, the allocation of the fragment relations, the specification of the fragment constraints, and the generated update templates.

3.  **Localizing Integrity Checking:** It assumes efficient integrity tests can be generated. Here, efficiency is measured by analyzing three components, namely: *the amount of data that needs to be accessed, the amount of data that needs to be transferred across the network* and *the number of sites that are involved* in order to check a constraint. The intention is to derive local tests whose evaluation is local to a site. Constraint simplification by update analysis is preferred to constraint simplification by reformulation, since reformulation will generally require an unbounded search over all possible constraints when generating the integrity tests. Using heuristics to minimize this search may mean some optimal reformulations are not found. The fragment constraints derived by the transformation process can be classified as either local or non-local fragment constraints. The evaluation of a local fragment constraint is performed at a single site, thus it is similar to the evaluation of a constraint in a centralized system. Therefore, the constraint simplification techniques proposed by previous researchers can be adopted for constructing integrity tests for local fragment constraints. For non-local fragment constraints, a process which derives local tests from these constraints is more attractive than one which derives global tests whose evaluation spans more than one site. This means exploiting the relevant general knowledge to derive local tests. This will involve using, for example, techniques that can infer the information stored at different sites of the network. Example: given the following allocation; *emp* at site 1 and *dept* at site 2 and an insert operation into the *emp* relation submitted at site 1 then the test $(\exists t \exists v \exists w)(emp(t, b, v, w))$ which can be evaluated locally is preferable than the test $(\exists x \exists y \exists z)(dept(b, x, y, z))$ which is global when evaluating the integrity constraint *IC*-4.

4.  **Pre-test Evaluation:** It adopts an evaluation scheme which avoids the need to undo the update in the case of constraint violation, i.e. pre-test evaluation is preferred as it avoids the undoing process.

5.  **Test Optimization:** Integrity test evaluation costs can be further reduced by examining the semantics of both the tests and the relevant update operations. An integrity test for a modify operation can be simplified if the attribute(s) being modified is not the attribute(s) being tested. Also, in some cases it is more efficient to construct transition tests. These simplified tests further reduce the amount of data needing to be accessed or the number of sites that might be involved, and they are more selective as more constants are being substituted for the variables in these tests, which make them easier and cheaper to evaluate than the generated initial tests. Example: given an update operation, modify($emp(a, b, c, d1)$:$emp(a, b, c, d2)$). This is equivalent to delete($emp(a, b, c, d1)$)

followed by insert($emp(a, b, c, d2)$). For the first update operation, $IC$-5 is affected and as for the second update operation, $IC$-1, $IC$-2, $IC$-4, and $IC$-8 are affected. Analyzing further the modify operation one noticed that the only value changed by the modify operation is salary, i.e. from $d1$ to $d2$. Thus, the integrity constraints that need to be checked are reduced to $IC$-1 and $IC$-8 while others are proven to be true.

6.  **History of Constraint Violations:** Soumya, Madiraju & Ibrahim (2008) proposed a constraint optimization technique that analyzes the constraints based on their history. History of constraints is maintained in metadatabase. An optimized ranked list of constraints is generated based on number of constraint violations, number of sites affected, and local constraint checking time. This has achieved optimization in terms of time.

## FUTURE TRENDS

From the above sections, it is obvious that a constraint checking mechanism for a distributed database is said to be efficient if it can minimize the number of sites involved, the amount of data accessed and the amount of data transferred across the network during the process of checking and detecting constraint violation in addition to the number of constraints to be checked and the time optimized during the checking. Thus, five main components can be identified with respect to a given integrity constraint which affect the efficiency of its evaluation. These components are: (i) the number of sites involved in verifying the truth of the integrity constraint, $\sigma$, (ii) the amount of data accessed (or the checking space), $A$, (iii) the amount of data transferred across the network, $T = \Sigma^n_{i=1} dt_i$ where $dt_i$ is the amount of data transferred from site $i$ and $n$ is the number of remote sites involved in verifying the truth of the integrity constraint, (iv) the number of constraints

to be checked, and (v) the time taken to check a constraint.

A constraint checking mechanism is said to be more efficient if in most cases it is able to allocate the responsibility of verifying the consistency of a database to a single site, i.e. the site where the update operation is to be performed. Thus, the number of sites involved, $\sigma = 1$. As the checking operation is carried out at a single site, no transferring of data across the network is required (Gupta, 1994), so $T = 0$. The evaluation of local tests involves a checking space and an amount of data accessed (assumed $A = a_i$) which are always smaller than the checking space and the amount of data accessed by the initial constraints since these tests are the simplified forms of those constraints so these are minimized as well.

Although the topic of checking integrity constraints has been explored since the middle of 1970s (Eswaran & Chamberlin, 1975), it is still one of the main topics discussed in today's conferences and workshops (e.g. the International Conference on Database and Expert Systems Applications – the Second International Workshop on Logical Aspects and Applications of Integrity Constraints (LAAIC'06), Krakow (Poland), 8 September 2006). The issues as discussed in the previous section are still debated. New technologies especially those employed in the Artificial Intelligent field such as agents, data mining and fuzzy set are now being investigated to examine their potential in enhancing the performance of deriving and checking constraints.

Mobile agents which are autonomous active programs that can move both data and functionality (code) to multiple places in a distributed system are now getting popular as a technique for checking databases' constraints. It is believed that mobile agents can be used to speed up the process of checking integrity constraints. Data mining, on the other hand, can be used to identify the pattern that occurs in a database to derive the relationships between the data. Based on these relationships, integrity constraints can be generated automatically. This can reduce the burden of the user in specifying the correct and complete set of business rules. While, fuzzy set is adopted to identify the range of possible consistent values in which consistency of the database is flexible and not as rigid as the traditional approach.

We believe that the capabilities and the characteristics of the artificial intelligence technologies especially in deducing (inferring) new information based on the current or incomplete information, handling incomplete data and fuzzy conditions will be greatly explored in the future, and can significantly improve the performance of the database systems, especially when dealing with the processes of maintaining the consistency and checking the integrity of the database regardless the environments.

## CONCLUSION

An important aim of a database system is to guarantee database consistency, which means that the data contained in a database is both accurate and valid. There are many ways which inaccurate data may occur in a database. Several issues have been highlighted with regards to checking integrity constraints. The main issue is *how to efficiently check integrity constraints in a distributed environment*. Several strategies can be applied to achieve efficient constraint checking in a distributed database such as constraint filtering, constraint optimization, localizing constraint checking, pre-test evaluation, and test optimization. Here, efficiency is measured by analyzing five components, namely: *the amount of data that needs to be accessed*, *the amount of data that needs to be transferred across the network*, *the number of sites that are involved*, *the number of constraints to be checked*, and *the time taken*, in order to check a constraint.

## REFERENCES

Alwan, A. A., Ibrahim, H., & Udzir, N. I. (2008). Integrity Constraints Checking in Distributed Databases with Complete, Sufficient, and Support Tests. In *Proceedings of the IADIS International Conference Applied Computing,* (pp. 49-58).

Barbara, D., & Garcia-Molina, I. I. (1992). The Demarcation Protocol: A Technique for Maintaining Linear Arithmetic Constraints in Distributed Database Systems. In *Proceedings of the Conference on Extending Database Technology (EDBT'92)*, (pp. 373-388).

Bernstein, P. A., & Blaustein, B. T. (1981). A Simplification Algorithm for Integrity Assertions and Concrete Views. In *Proceedings of the 5th International Computer Software and Applications Conference (COMPSAC'81),* (pp. 90-99).

Blaustein, B. T. (1981). *Enforcing Database Assertions: Techniques and Applications*. PhD Thesis, Harvard University, Cambridge, MA.

Ceri, S., Fraternali, P., Paraboschi, S., & Tanca, L. (1994). Automatic Generation of Production Rules for Integrity Maintenance. *ACM Transactions on Database Systems*, *19*(3), 367–422. doi:10.1145/185827.185828

Chakravarthy, U. S. (1990). Logic-Based Approach to Semantic Query Optimization. *ACM Transactions on Database Systems*, *15*(2), 162–207. doi:10.1145/78922.78924

Codd, E. F. (1990). *The Relational Model for Database Management*. Reading, MA: Addison-Wesley Publishing Company, Inc.

Cremers, A. B., & Domann, G. (1983). AIM – An Integrity Monitor for the Database System INGRES. In *Proceedings of the 9th International Conference on Very Large Data Bases (VLDB 9),* (pp. 167-170).

Embury, S. M., Gray, P. M. D., & Bassiliades, N. D. (1993). Constraint Maintenance using Generated Methods in the P/FDM Object-Oriented Database. In *Proceedings of the 1ˢᵗ International Workshop on Rules in Database Systems,* (pp. 365-381).

Eswaran, K. P., & Chamberlin, D. D. (1975). Functional Specifications of a Subsystem for Data Base Integrity. *Proceedings of the 1ˢᵗ International Conference on Very Large Data Bases (VLDB 1),* 1(1), 48-68.

Grefen, P. W. P. J. (1990). *Design Considerations for Integrity Constraint Handling in PRISMA/DB1. Prisma Project Document* (p. 508). Twente, The Netherlands: University of Twente.

Grefen, P. W. P. J. (1993). Combining Theory and Practice in Integrity Control: A Declarative Approach to the Specification of a Transaction Modification Subsystem. In *Proceedings of the 19ᵗʰ International Conference on Very Large Data Bases (VLDB 19),* (pp. 581-591).

Gupta, A. (1994). *Partial Information Based Integrity Constraint Checking.* PhD Thesis, Stanford University, Stanford, CA.

Hammer, M. M., & McLeod, D. J. (1975). Semantic Integrity in a Relational Data Base System. In *Proceedings of the 1ˢᵗ International Conference on Very Large Data Bases (VLDB 1),* 1(1), 25-47.

Henschen, L. J., McCune, W. W., & Naqvi, S. A. (1984). Compiling Constraint-Checking Programs from First-Order Formulas. *Advances in Database Theory, 2,* 145–169.

Hsu, A., & Imielinski, T. (1985). Integrity Checking for Multiple Updates. In *Proceedings of the 1985 ACM SIGMOD International Conference on the Management of Data,* (pp. 152-168).

Ibrahim, H. (2002a). A Strategy for Semantic Integrity Checking in Distributed Databases. In *Proceedings of the Ninth International Conference on Parallel and Distributed Systems (ICPADS 2002),* (pp. 139-144). Washington, DC: IEEE Computer Society.

Ibrahim, H. (2002b). Extending Transactions with Integrity Rules for Maintaining Database Integrity. In *Proceedings of the International Conference on Information and Knowledge Engineering (IKE'02),* (pp. 341-347).

Ibrahim, H., Gray, W. A., & Fiddian, N. J. (1996). The Development of a Semantic Integrity Constraint Subsystem for a Distributed Database (SICSDD). In *Proceedings of the 14ᵗʰ British National Conference on Databases (BNCOD 14),* (pp. 74-91).

Ibrahim, H., Gray, W. A., & Fiddian, N. J. (1998). SICSDD – A Semantic Integrity Constraint Subsystem for a Distributed Database. In *Proceedings of the 1998 International Conference on Parallel and Distributed Processing Techniques and Applications (PDPTA'98),* (pp. 1575-1582).

Ibrahim, H., Gray, W. A., & Fiddian, N. J. (2001). Optimizing Fragment Constraints – A Performance Evaluation. *International Journal of Intelligent Systems – Verification and Validation Issues in Databases. Knowledge-Based Systems, and Ontologies, 16*(3), 285–306.

Mazumdar, S. (1993). Optimizing Distributed Integrity Constraints. In *Proceedings of the 3ʳᵈ International Symposium on Database Systems for Advanced Applications, 4,* 327-334.

McCarroll, N. F. (1995). *Semantic Integrity Enforcement in Parallel Database Machines.* PhD Thesis, University of Sheffield, Sheffield, UK.

McCune, W. W., & Henschen, L. J. (1989). Maintaining State Constraints in Relational Databases: A Proof Theoretic Basis. *Journal of the Association for Computing Machinery, 36*(1), 46–68.

Nicolas, J. M. (1982). Logic for Improving Integrity Checking in Relational Data Bases. *Acta Informatica, 18*(3), 227–253. doi:10.1007/BF00263192

Plexousakis, D. (1993). Integrity Constraint and Rule Maintenance in Temporal Deductive Knowledge Bases. In *Proceedings of the 19th International Conference on Very Large Data Bases (VLDB 19),* (pp. 146-157).

Qian, X. (1988). An Effective Method for Integrity Constraint Simplification. In *Proceedings of the 4th International Conference on Data Engineering (ICDE 88),* (pp. 338-345).

Qian, X. (1989). Distribution Design of Integrity Constraints. In *Proceedings of the 2nd International Conference on Expert Database Systems,* (pp. 205-226).

Sheard, T., & Stemple, D. (1989). Automatic Verification of Database Transaction Safety. *ACM Transactions on Database Systems, 14*(3), 322–368. doi:10.1145/68012.68014

Simon, E., & Valduriez, P. (1987). Design and Analysis of a Relational Integrity Subsystem. MCC *Technical Report DB-015-87.*

Soumya, B., Madiraju, P., & Ibrahim, H. (2008). Constraint Optimization for a System of Relational Databases. In *Proceedings of the IEEE 8th International Conference on Computer and Information Technology (CiT 2008),* (pp. 155-160).

Stemple, D., Mazumdar, S., & Sheard, T. (1987). On the Modes and Measuring of Feedback to Transaction Designers. In *Proceedings of the 1987 ACM-SIGMOD International Conference on the Management of Data,* (pp. 374-386).

Wang, X. Y. (1992). *The Development of a Knowledge-Based Transaction Design Assistant.* PhD Thesis, University of Wales College of Cardiff, Cardiff, UK.

## KEY TERMS AND DEFINITIONS

**Distributed Database:** A collection of multiple, logically interrelated databases distributed over a computer network.

**Integrity Control:** Deals with the prevention of semantic errors made by the users due to their carelessness or lack of knowledge.

**Database Consistency:** Means that the data contained in the database is both accurate and valid.

**Sufficient Test:** Verifies that an update operation leads a consistent database state to a new consistent database state.

**Necessary Test:** Verifies if an update operation leads a consistent database state to an inconsistent database state.

**Complete Test:** Verifies if an update operation leads a consistent database state to either a consistent or inconsistent database state.

**Local Test:** Verifies if an update operation violates an integrity constraint by accessing data at the local site.

**Global Test:** Verifies if an update operation violates an integrity constraint by accessing data at remote sites.

**Data Fragmentation:** Refers to the technique used to split up the global database into logical units. These logical units are called *fragment relations* or simply *fragments.*

# Chapter 10
# Soft Computing Techniques in Content–Based Multimedia Information Retrieval

**G. Castellano**
*University of Bari, Italy*

**A. M. Fanelli**
*University of Bari, Italy*

**M. A. Torsello**
*University of Bari, Italy*

## ABSTRACT

*Due to the diffusion of multimedia databases and new ways of communication, there is an urgent need for developing more effective search systems capable of retrieving information by specifying directly in user queries elements strictly related to the multimedia content. This is the main rationale behind the flourishing area of Content-Based Multimedia Information Retrieval (CB-MIR), that finds in Soft Computing (SC) techniques a valid tool to handle uncertainty and vagueness underlying the whole information retrieval process. The main reason for this success seems to be the synergy resulting from SC paradigms, such as fuzzy logic, neural networks, rough sets and genetic algorithms. Each of these computing paradigms provides complementary reasoning and searching methods that allow the use of domain knowledge and empirical data to solve complex problems. In this chapter, the authors emphasize the potential of SC techniques, also combined in hybrid schemes, for the development of effective CB-MIR systems. As an example, the authors describe a content-based image retrieval system that employs SC techniques in its working scheme.*

## INTRODUCTION

In the last years, the growing dissemination of digital information and the consequent need to improve the retrieval of this information have given rise to a strong interest for the research in Information Retrieval (IR), a field that is expanding along with the challenges related to the explosion of the Web and the development of information and communication technologies. The diffusion of new ways of com-

DOI: 10.4018/978-1-60566-814-7.ch010

munication and information sharing has led to the so-called digital convergence. Today, the key role of multimedia documents combined with the tools offered by digital technologies have promoted the creation of multimedia databases characterized by a complexity level higher than traditional databases. This is mainly due to the need to equip the modern multimedia databases with integrated methods of management and access to heterogeneous documents through specific systems for indexing, search and automatic extraction of data representing the complex content of multimedia documents (images, videos, audios,...) which support the traditional manual systems of analysis and indexing term-based (terminological) of textual or audiovisual documents. Whereas in databases of textual documents a search based on key words encoding the textual descriptors extracted from documents seems to be sufficient and appropriate, in multimedia databases the assignment of textual descriptions to multimedia contents reveals to be very limited and subjective.

The retrieval approach for multimedia databases needs to be improved through the definition of queries based on multimedia content, including not only textual data but also visual and audio data. Today, to achieve a good precision level in the retrieval from a multimedia database, IR systems are directing towards the possibility to combine term-based queries with content-based queries. In this way, term-based queries could be conveniently used to preliminary select a portion of the huge quantity of documents that can be potentially retrieved from a multimedia collection and to hit the search according to data such as membership domains, types, classes, titles, authors, etc. Successively, content-based queries can improve and refine search results. In this way, the traditional textual database interfaces that allow the search on the basis of an index exclusively composed of keywords extracted from documents or also inserted in textual metadata are replaced with new interfaces that enable the formulation of queries in different dimensions, not only on the basis of

textual key words but also specifying multimedia contents of the same nature of the information to be searched. In this way, it is possible to realize a search based on heterogeneous indexes composed of texts extracted from captions or spoken language, key images from a sequence, simple figures, melodies, shapes, colours and sounds, without excluding the importance of textual data, descriptive or classificatory, that can be related to aspects not specifically audiovisual of the document.

A wider criterium of IR has been defined reflecting the evolution of a more visual culture, leading to so-called Content-Based Multimedia Information Retrieval (CB-MIR) (Lew et al., 2006). In CB-MIR, each kind of digital document is managed, stored and retrieved through the elements of the language, or metalanguage, own of the specific digital object, hence referred to the content of the object itself. In the last years, CB-MIR has been investigated in a growing number of research projects and applications at international level, showing that various communities working in the field of multimedia document management are interested in the new chances of exploitation of archives and professional activities: from biomedicine applications to architecture and archaeology, from film and video collections to journalism, from cultural heritage to design, from education to e-commerce and entertainment, from GIS (Geographical Information Systems) to remote sensing systems, from medical sector to identification and surveillance systems. However, due to their augmented potential, CB-MIR systems require a more advanced consideration about the intrinsic characteristics of digital documents, the semantic and the structuration of the elements included in a document, the way of interaction and presentation of query results to the user. Hence, today, the content-based approach underlying CB-MIR, represents a border field arising many challenges that the current research has only partially addressed up to now.

In a CB-MIR system, the information retrieval is not an easy task due to different factors strictly related to the nature of queries and objects to be retrieved, such as the vagueness of a content-based query, the complexity of multimedia data representation, the approximation and the flexibility in the comparison between the query content and the information included in the database. In particular, this last issue introduces the need of defining adequate similarity metrics, not based on a hard matching among the requested object and those retrieved, but able to realize more flexible kinds of matching that provide similarity degrees to be shown as relevance feedback together with the search results. Soft Computing (SC) (John & Birkenead, 2001) provides valid tools to cope with the complexity in the mechanisms underlying CB-MIR (Hassanien et al., 2008; Herrera-Viedma et al., 2005). In fact, SC embraces a variety of computing paradigms that work synergistically to exploit the tolerance for imprecision, uncertainty, approximate reasoning, and partial truth in order to provide flexible information processing capabilities and obtain low-cost solutions and close resemblance to human-like decision making.

This chapter is intended to investigate the benefits and the potential of SC techniques in the retrieval of multimedia information based on the content analysis. In particular, in the following section, we explain the main phases of a typical CB-MIR system. Next section provides a review of recent works that adopt the different SC techniques (Neural Networks, Fuzzy Logic, Genetic Algorithms, Rough Sets and combination schemas of these ones) for the development of different tasks involved in the overall CB-MIR process. Then we present an example of content-based image retrieval system that exploits a SC strategy in its working scheme. Finally, a conclusive section closes the chapter by drawing open challenges in the CB-MIR field and some future directions.

## CONTENT BASED-MULTIMEDIA INFORMATION RETRIEVAL

Recently, the rapid growth in the use of digital media such as images, video and audio has prompted an urgent need for the development of new retrieval strategies able to facilitate the effective searching and browsing of large multimedia databases.

Traditional retrieval systems exploit the keyword-based indexing approach (also known as text-based search). According to this approach, multimedia objects are annotated with a number of keywords or descriptive texts stored together with media in the database. In particular, retrieval is performed by matching the user query expressed in the form of keywords with the stored media keywords. However, this approach is not satisfactory because the textual descriptions of media reveal to be incomplete, imprecise and often inconsistent. Moreover, text-based search approach suffers from further limitations such as the long time required by manual annotations, the expensive implementation costs, the discrepancy between manual annotations and subjective perception, the difficulty to describe in words the media contents.

To overcome limitations and difficulties of traditional text-based retrieval systems, many research efforts have been addressed to the development of novel retrieval systems that exploit the content information expressed in a form that better encodes the same nature of the media to be searched in order to automatically index and search media without costly human interventions. Retrieval systems based on this approach fall in the area of CB-MIR systems that are aimed to automatically index media and to allow their retrieval via a more appropriate search engine reflecting the nature of the media objects to be retrieved.

CB-MIR systems can be classified into three main approaches according to the information used to represent the media content (Mittal, 2006):

- **Keyword based:** the content is described through annotations provided by users

*Figure 1. The architecture of a typical CB-MIR system*

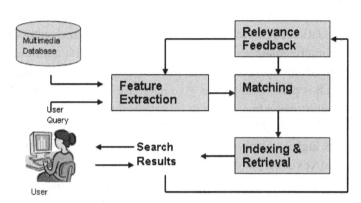

such as free text or keywords within a limited vocabulary.

- **Feature based:** the content is represented by a set of features generally extracted in automatic manner. Typical features represent either general information (colour, shape, position, note, pitch, melody, etc.) or specific information for a particular application (i.e. face recognition, medical images, etc.).

- **Concept based:** media content is obtained through the application of the domain knowledge that derives concepts that can be used in the retrieval process. This approach is usually domain specific and it requires the user intervention.

In a typical CB-MIR system, the contents of media stored in the database are extracted and described by multi-dimensional feature vectors, also called descriptors. The set of media feature vectors are collected to form a feature database. To retrieve the desired media, users provide query examples to the CB-MIR system that represents such examples trough specific feature vectors. The distances (or similarities) between the feature vectors of the query and those of the media contained in the feature database are then computed. Generally, the retrieval of media is performed by applying an index scheme that

enables an efficient way to search for the media in the database. As a final step, the system may rank the search results in order to return a list of the top matching search results corresponding to the most similar to the query contents. Recent CB-MIR systems have also incorporated the user relevance feedback useful to refine the retrieval process so as to generate more meaningful search results. A diagram of the architecture of a typical CB-MIR system is depicted in figure 1. As can be observed, in the design of a CB-MIR system, the main modules that can be distinguished are: feature extraction and representation, matching, indexing or retrieval, and relevance feedback. The following subsections provide a description of each module.

## Feature Extraction and Representation

The aspect concerning the representation of media in database is strongly related to the choice of features describing the contents of media and the definition of the approaches employed to model these contents.

In particular, multimedia contents can be modelled by a hierarchy of different levels of abstraction. At the lowest level, content is described by features directly extracted from media such as raw pixels with unprocessed information. In this level, comparison between media objects is performed on a pixel-by-pixel basis using similarity measures such as the correlation coefficient and Euclidean distance. At the intermediate level, the description of content consists in objects and attributes. In this case, search is performed on the basis of the descriptive object attributes (e.g. colour histogram, shape, texture, pitch, duration, rhythm signature). Finally, at the highest level, media content representation involves concepts such as the interpretation of the objects and perceptual emotion. Features are grouped into meaningful objects and semantic descriptions are also defined for the objects. Retrieval is performed on entities with well defined spatio-temporal properties.

Based on this hierarchy, descriptive features are categorized into syntactic or low-level features and semantic or high-level features (Wei & Li, 2005). Low-level features such as object motion, colour, shape, texture, loudness, power spectrum, bandwidth, and pitch are extracted directly from media in the database (Djeraba, 2002). These kinds of features are generally derived from media without considering any external semantic. High-level features such as rhythm, events, timbre involve different semantic degrees contained in media. However, the use of this kind of features leads to the "semantic gap" problem, i.e. the lack of coincidence between the information that can be extracted from media and the interpretation that the same media have for a user in a given situation (Wang & Ma, 2005). The semantic gap existing between the concepts derived by the external knowledge and the description of low-level features makes difficult the processing of queries including high-level features. To minimize the semantic gap, two possible solutions have been proposed in literature (Marques & Furht, 2002). The first solution consists in the automatic generation of metadata (Jeon et al., 2003). The second one concerns the incorporation of the user relevance feedback that enables the retrieval system to learn the semantic context of a query operation.

Another problem that has to be addressed in the media feature extraction is the dimension reduction of feature vectors. In fact, many applications dealing with multimedia database extract a wide number of features to analyze and query the database. High dimensionality of feature vectors causes the "curse of dimension" problem, where the complexity and computational cost of the query increase exponentially with the number of dimensions (Egecioglu et al., 2004). Dimension reduction is a popular technique to overcome this problem and support efficient retrieval in large-scale databases. However, the tradeoff between the efficiency obtained through dimension reduction and the completeness obtained through the information extracted has to be taken into account. In effect, if each data is represented by a smaller number of dimensions, the speed of retrieval is increased but inevitably some information is lost.

## Matching

Matching is another important task that has to be addressed in a typical CB-MIR system. This task is devoted to find the most similar multimedia objects with respect to the query formulated by the user. A general approach used to measure the similarity between media objects consists in representing media features as multi-dimensional points and then calculate the distances existing among the corresponding multi-dimensional points (Feng et al., 2003).

In literature, many measures have been proposed to estimate the similarity between multimedia data. Euclidean distance represents one of the most employed measures. However, this measure has not appeared effective in some applications because it revealed to be not compatible with the similarity concept as perceived by humans. Other distance/similarity measures such as Mahalonobis distance, Minkowski-Form Distance, Quadratic-Form Distance, Kullback-Leibler Divergence and Jeffrey-Divergence have been employed to evaluate similarity among media taking into account the specific application purposes. Jolion (2001) provided an exhaustive review of the similarity measures commonly employed in the CB-MIR context. Moreover, the use of nonmetric distances has been investigated by Jacobs et al. (2000). In their work, they have also evaluated the performances obtained by the investigated measures.

The choice of the similarity measure to be used in the matching task is central in the design of a CB-MIR system since it significantly affects the effectiveness and the performance of the overall retrieval process.

## Indexing and Retrieval

Multi-dimensional indexing is a mechanism used to facilitate and to accelerate the processing of user queries in the search process. In the early multimedia database systems, media objects such as images, audio, video were files in a directory or also entries in a SQL database table. From a computational perspective, both options have shown poor performances because most of filesystems use the method of linear search within directories. Consequently, as the size of multimedia databases increases, applications are not able to answer to the user queries in an acceptable time period. Although there was an attempt to design SQL databases providing higher performances, here, the search keys have to be exact as in text-based search. In the case of media objects, they were stored as blobs that cannot be indexed effectively by using these kinds of approaches. Moreover, the retrieval of media often exploits not only the value of certain features but also the location of the corresponding feature vectors within a feature space (Fonseca & Jorge, 2003). To obtain faster execution of search operations, an appropriate multi-dimensional access method has to be used to index the high dimensional feature vectors. In this context, research has focused on the development of similarity-based databases that employ tree-based indexing schema able to achieve logarithmic performances (Lew, 2000). Lo &

Chen (2002) proposed an approach to transform music into numeric forms and developed an index structure based on R-tree for effective retrieval. K-d tree methods have been implemented in the case of multimedia oriented databases that show to be effectiveness in the context of feature-based similarity searches. Vector quantization is another media representation proposed in (Ye & Xu, 2003) to realize an effective search in large multimedia databases.

To search for a set of media objects, a CB-MIR system requires to users to formulate queries. In general, these systems employ two main kinds of queries to interface with the users: "query by example" and "query through the dialog box". As the name implies, this last kind of queries are specified by the users in the apposite dialog box. This method requires that users know the exact details of features and their implementation as well as the details of the search strategy. The alternative method consists in specifying queries containing an example or series of examples. The retrieval system determines the most similar objects to the given example. The retrieval of media objects through the specification of query by example presents some limitations. In fact, since there is no matching of exactly defined fields, a larger similarity threshold is required. The retrieved media are often so many that the task is tedious and meaningless. Dependently on the type of media, in content-based retrieval systems other types of queries can be specified such as query by sketch, query by painting for video and images, query by singing for audio.

## Relevance Feedback

Relevance feedback (also known as query refinement, interactive search or active learning) refers to the interactive process characterizing the most recent **CB-MIR** systems attempted to integrate continuous feedback from the users in order to understand their information needs. In particular, the relevance feedback process consists in asking the user a sequential set of questions after each round of search results in order to learn more about the user queries.

The fundamental idea behind the relevance feedback process is to show a list of candidate objects and to ask the user to select relevant and/or irrelevant (positive and/or negative) media with respect to the specified query. Then, the retrieval system analyzes the user feedback and, by applying a learning process, it modifies the parameter space or the feature space in order to reflect the relevant and irrelevant examples. Finally, results can be refined and returned to the user. Hence, the key issue in relevance feedback approaches is how to incorporate positive and/or negative objects in query and/or the similarity refinement.

Relevance feedback is a powerful technique in **CB-MIR** and it has become an active research area in recent years. In literature, a variety of relevance feedback approaches have been proposed that can be classified into the following categories (Petrakis et al., 2006):

- The query point movement (query refinement) method: this method essentially tries to improve the estimation of the "ideal query point" by moving it towards positive examples and away from negative ones (Rocchio, 1971).
- The re-weighting (similarity measure refinement) method: this is the most intuitive and simple method. Such method adjusts the relative importance (weights) of terms in media representations. Terms that vary less in the set of positive examples are more important and should weigh more in retrievals. The inverse of the standard deviation is usually used for re-weighting the query terms (Ishikawa et al., 1998).
- The query expansion method: this method attempts to find an ideal query by adding new terms into the user's query (Chen et al., 2001).

- The similarity adaptation method: this method approximates the ideal matching method by substituting the system similarity (or distance) function with one that better captures the user's notion of similarity (Wu et al., 2000).

## SC FOR CB-MIR

**Soft Computing** (**SC**) refers to a collection of computational paradigms (such as Artificial Neural Networks, Fuzzy Logic, Genetic Algorithms, Rough Set Theory) that attempt to find acceptable solutions at low cost by searching for approximate solutions to imprecisely/precisely formulated real-world problems.

Main characteristics of such paradigms are their ability to evaluate, decide, check, and calculate within a vague and imprecise domain, emulating the human capacities in the execution of such activities taking advantage from their past experience. Though these common abilities, **SC** paradigms differ for some aspects (see figure 2):

- the capacity to learn complex functional relations, proper of Artificial Neural Networks (ANNs);
- the possibility to model and check uncertain and complex systems together with the capacity to represent knowledge in efficient manner through linguistic representations, typical of the Fuzzy Logic (FL);
- the ability of Rough Sets (RSs) to automatically convert data into knowledge by offering useful mechanisms for analyzing and selecting essential attributes and rules from data dealing with vagueness and uncertainty in decision situations.
- the optimization ability proper of Genetic Algorithms (GAs) that are inspired to the mutation and selection laws of human beings.

*Figure 2. The fundamental paradigms of soft computing*

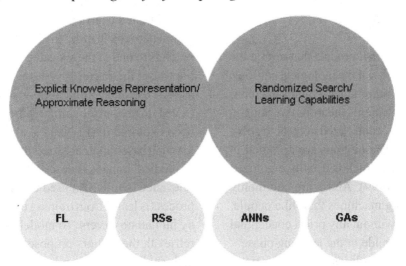

Unlike traditional computing paradigms (hard-computing), **SC** focuses on adapting to the pervasive imprecision of the real world. Its principle guide consists in exploiting the tolerance for imprecision, uncertainty and partial truth to achieve tractability, robustness, low cost solutions and a better rapport with reality. Hence, these paradigms, that should be complementary and not competitive with the traditional ones, represent the central core of **SC** and a new way to address the topic of machine intelligence. In fact, key features of **SC** are the possibility to deal with uncertain, ambiguous or incomplete data and to provide approximate solutions and adaptive capacities.

Due to these characteristics, techniques based on **SC** paradigms are valid tools to deal with the imprecision and vagueness inherent a IR process based on the content analysis. In the last few years, many researchers have drawn their interest towards the investigation about the potential of **SC** paradigms for the development of **CB-MIR** systems based on the content analysis, as also indicated in a recent review (Hassanien et al., 2008).

The employment of **SC** techniques in **CB-MIR** systems to model the subjectivity and the complex-

ity intrinsic in the retrieval process represents a promising direction to improve their effectiveness and to make them adaptive (i.e. able to learn the concept of user relevance) and more flexible. Specifically, the vagueness and the uncertainty underlying the content-based IR process can be properly addressed by the knowledge representation abilities of fuzzy logic and rough set theory. Concretely, FL can be applied to realize advanced and more flexible mechanisms of matching that can improve the search results. RS theory may offer suitable mechanisms to reduce the dimensionality of feature set describing media without significantly affecting the retrieval accuracy. ANNs can be conveniently employed to retrieval tasks such as feature extraction, classification of features, interpretation of queries by example and relevance feedback. GAs can be mainly used for efficient search and retrieval of information in large multimedia databases.

In the following subsections, we provide an overview of works that propose the use of **SC** techniques to develop different tasks involved in **CB-MIR** systems.

## Artificial Neural Networks for CB-MIR Tasks

ANNs are computational models that mimic the fundamental properties of the biological neurons. They are composed by a number of highly interconnected processing elements (neurons) working in parallel, without any centralized control to solve specific problems. The neurons are arranged in a particular structure which is usually organized in layers (Haykin, 1999). ANNs are commonly regarded as learning machines that, like people, learn by examples without any priori conceptual patterns that could guide in the learning phase.

These learning capabilities make ANNs powerful tools to face predictive and classification problems in a **CB-MIR** process typically involved in the management of the user relevance feedback as well as in the interpretation of queries.

In (Lee et Yoo, 2001), the authors proposed a Neural-Network based image retrieval system for the content-based retrieval of images from a large database. By using Radial Basis Function (RBF) Networks, especially appropriate because they do not require a large training set, the authors are able to better reflect the user feedback. In this system, a set of retrieved images are returned and, if the user is not satisfied by the obtained results, he marks the retrieved images with tags such as 'similar', 'alike', or 'different'. These tags are used by the retrieval system to incrementally refine the employed RBF network so that the search process starts again.

Research has investigated on the combination of ANNs with wavelet transforms for the efficient retrieval of images from database in terms of their contents (Park et al., 2004), (Zhang & Salari, 2005). In (Gonzalez-Garcia et al., 2007), wavelets and ANNs are used to retrieve images from a database taking into account the object shape and the image colour distribution. In particular, the indexing procedure applies a Daubechies 4 wavelet transform to get the descriptive features. These features are represented by the wavelet

coefficients encoding the semantic of images. The obtained coefficients are used for training a neural network in order to recognize if an airplane belongs to one of the six categories employed for the test of the retrieval system.

The use of NNs and Support Vector Machines (SVM) to predict the similarity notion of users has been explored in (El-Naqa et al., 2004), where a learning based approach to content-based retrieval of medical images is described. In this work, the relevance (similarity) used to guide the retrieval process is learnt from training examples provided by human observers. To model the similarity for retrieval, the authors proposed a two-stage hierarchical learning network consisting in a cascade of a binary classifier and a regression stage for predicting similarity coefficients between a query image and the images in the database. In the first stage, images that are very different from the query image are eliminated and, in the next stage, the survived images are compared to the query for obtaining a numerical similarity coefficient for retrieval.

In (Park et al., 2005), a modified version of the Fuzzy Adaptive Resonance Theory (Fuzzy-ART), a clustering technique based on ANNs, is adopted to find images from a large database. According to this scheme, similar images are clustered based on the image features. When the query is presented, similar images to the query are retrieved only from the most similar cluster to the query, thus full-database searches are not necessary.

An approach based on neural learning is also employed in the PicSOM system aimed at video retrieval. In such a system, video and the parts extracted from these are arranged on a tree structure where the main video is the parent object and the extracted media types are child objects. Features are extracted from each media type and these are given in input to Self-Organizing Maps (a kind of feed-forward neural network) for the training.

In (Shen et al., 2006), a hybrid architecture based on principal component analysis and a neural network is used to support efficient content-based music retrieval and classification.

In (Doulamis et al., 1999), ANNs are employed for the management of the relevance feedback within an adaptive video indexing and retrieval system. In this framework, a feed-forward neural network structure is proposed as a parametric distance for retrieval and an adaptation mechanism is also proposed for updating the neural weights whenever a user selects a new image.

## Fuzzy Logic for CB-MIR Tasks

FL defines a framework in which the inherent ambiguity of real-world data can be captured, modeled and used to reason under uncertainty. The FL theory is based on the key concept of fuzzy set which expresses the degree of membership of an element in that set. This degree can take continuous values between [0,1]. This characteristic allows capturing the uncertainty inherent in real data. An introduction to FL can be found in (Klir & Yuan, 1995) and (Yan et al., 1994).

Due to its characteristics, FL may be adopted in the context of **CB-MIR** to cope different tasks such as feature extraction and representation, matching and query representation.

In (Nepal et al., 1998), a fuzzy system for content based retrieval is proposed. Such a system models the imprecision using fuzzy data models and it allows users to express their preferences using linguistic terms such as 'few' and 'many' rather than numeric weights. In addition, a fuzzy linguistic language is defined to model queries.

FL has been proposed for mapping database in many works. In (Vertan & Boujemaa, 2000) an investigation on the use of colour histograms by adopting FL is presented. In (Han & Ma, 2002), a fuzzy colour histogram that permits to consider colour similarity across different bins is proposed. In (Sugano, 2001), the author describes a method for the conversion of colour into words by using fuzzy membership functions. A FL approach is used in (Chen & Wang, 2002) for region-based

image retrieval. Here, an image is represented by a set of segmented regions. Each region is characterized by a fuzzy feature (fuzzy set) indicating color, shape properties, etc. Hence, an image consists of a family of fuzzy features and, consequently, the resemblance of two generic images is defined as the similarity between the two corresponding families of fuzzy features. This similarity is evaluated using the UFM (Unified Feature Matching) similarity measure derived from fuzzy set operations that provides a very intuitive quantification by integrating properties of all regions in images.

In (Kulkarni, 2007), the author proposed an approach for the fuzzy mapping of the image database. In particular, instead of having numerical values, the colour feature values are expressed in linguistic terms such as 'large', 'small', 'medium', etc. representing the fuzzy colour content of images. Hence, weights assigned to fuzzy contents are used by a distance measure based on FL to calculate the similarity between the query image and the images in database. Fuzzy aggregator operators are employed in (Kushki et al., 2002) to perform object similarity matching by combining similarities of individual features in order to obtain a single value which indicates the overall similarity among two objects.

Mesadani and Khrishnapuram (1999) use a fuzzy graph matching algorithm for content-based retrieval. In (Khrishnapuram et al., 2004), the authors describes FIRST, an image retrieval system that employs FL to handle the vagueness inherent the retrieval tasks. FIRST uses Fuzzy Attributed Relational Graphs (FARG) to represent images where each node in the graph represents an image region and each edge represents a relation between two regions. The given query is converted to a FARG and a low-complexity fuzzy graph matching algorithm is used to compare the query graph with the FARGs in the database.

Vereb (2003) presents a hierarchical indexing fuzzy approach to content based image retrieval where FL is employed to define the distance between two generic objects.

## Rough Sets for CB-MIR Tasks

RS theory is a model of approximate reasoning that allows to convert the available data into knowledge by working under imprecise conditions characterized by vagueness and uncertainty. Methodologies underlying this theory are especially used to discover data dependencies and to evaluate the relevance of data attributes for the identification of the minimum subset of these. Such methodologies are particularly useful for their ability to derive readable if-then rules from data included in databases. An exhaustive analysis about RS theory can be found in (Pawlak, 2001; Polkowsky, 2003).

The modelling capacities proper of RSs make this methodology appropriate to face different problems intrinsic a **CB-MIR** process such as the feature reduction, the classification and the effective retrieval of media.

Hassanien and Jafar (2003) presented a RS reduction technique to find all reducts of data containing the minimal subset of attributes that are associated to a class label for classification. In their work, they also exploited RSs to define a similarity distance measure.

In (Li et al., 2005), a feature selection algorithm based on RS theory is proposed to find the feature subset from audio stream. In another work, they constructed audio feature set by audio features, retrieve and match the audio clip in the approximate space of tolerances RS.

Wu et al. (2007) adopted RS for the extraction and selection of video features. In particular, the authors proposed a partition algorithm based on RS to deal with huge dataset; they used Rough classification to develop a motion information based video pre classification retrieval system. In addition, the paper propose an approach to shot boundary detection using RS which comprehen-

sively employs the motion features included in video sequence.

Zhao et al. (2005) proposed an interactive image retrieval system that realizes a relevance feedback method known as group-based relevance feedback. In this system, the intentions of users are learnt by a learning method that employs reduct from RS theory. The same authors in (Zhao et al., 2002) used the idea of RS theory to develop a retrieval algorithm for the automatic search of images. This algorithm is generated by learning features of images divided into two kinds: "Key images" (containing objects corresponding to the keywords that describe image contents) and "non-key images" (not containing the objects). It consists of a scalar quantizer that replaces the value of a region with a representative value and a discriminator that establishes the kind of the image using inclusive and exclusive rules. RS theory is used to generate the retrieval algorithm considering the image features as attributes and the quantized values as the values for these attributes.

RS theory is used in retrieval systems to realize a relevance feedback mechanism that can express objectively human perception (Wang et al., 2006).

## Genetic Algorithms for CB-MIR Tasks

GAs represent one of the most important variants of evolutionary algorithms within the evolutionary computing paradigm including a variety of computational strategies especially employed to find near optimal solutions to complex searching and optimization problems (Eiben & Smith, 2003). GAs are iterative probabilistic search algorithms inspired by the evolutionary theory of natural selection and genetic. These algorithms are particularly suitable for applications that require adaptive problem-solving strategies, because they are parallel in nature and they can offer a number of possible solutions. In fact, the basic idea of GAs consists in solving problems by simulating the evolutionary processes of natural systems. In this way, the solution to a problem faced with GAs evolves starting from an initial set of solutions called population. Given a fitness function to be maximized, at each iteration some of the better candidates are chosen to form the next population by applying recombination and/or mutation to them. Recombination of two selected candidates provides one or more new candidates. Mutation of a candidate results in a new candidate. The resulting new candidates compete, based on their fitness, with the old ones for a place in the new population. This process is iterated until a candidate with sufficient quality (solution) is found (Schwefel, 1995).

A natural employment of GAs in the development of **CB-MIR** systems concerns the search problem.

There exist several interactive image retrieval systems using GAs (Kato and Isaku, 1998), where minimum knowledge is needed for the prototype. These systems interactively search for the desired images while receiving subjective evaluations of images from the user according to the similarity with the prototype. GAs use the user's evaluations as feedback for the fitness value to converge towards the desired images. These systems also allow modifying the prototype during the search.

Papadias et al. (1999) used binary string encoding of spatial relations in their GA and they named the algorithm as Genetic Configuration Similarity Algorithm (GCSA). In the GCSA, each chromosome is an array S of n values, where S[i] is the instantiation of variable xi in solution S. The similarity measurement function, defined in the equation 6 above, is used to measure the quality of S. The GCSA uses proportionate selection, where an individual in a population is selected with a probability proportional to the individual's fitness.

Arkoumanis et al. (2002) applied a GA to process structural similarity queries.

Tran (2005) used Multi-Objective GA for the design of a content-based retrieval system. The proposed method is able to find multiple solutions in one run and to provide a natural way for integrating multiple image representation schemes

by formalizing representation schemes as a set of objective functions to be optimized by a Multi-Objective GA. A MOGA can find one or more optimal solutions and these solutions are tradeoff solutions based on constraints imposed by image representation schemes.

You and Cho (2007) proposed an emotion-based video scene retrieval algorithm that uses emotion information extracted from a video scene. The proposed method retrieves video scenes that a user has in mind trough the evolutionary computation known as interactive genetic algorithm. This algorithm performs the optimization by exploiting the human evaluation. The system displays a set of videos, obtains a relevance feedback from a human and selects the candidates based on the relevance. A genetic crossover operator is applied to the selected candidates.

## Hybrid SC Techniques for CB-MIR Tasks

The potential of **SC** techniques is mainly justified by their complimentary nature. In fact, rather than to be competitive, **SC** techniques work in synergistic way to find near optimal solution to imprecise and not well-defined problems. As a consequence, it is a natural practice to build up hybrid strategies derived from the combination of concepts underlying the different **SC** paradigms in order to overcome weaknesses and exploit strengths proper of each single paradigm (Tsakonas et al., 2002; Hildebrand, 2005).

In literature, many works provide examples of **CB-MIR** systems developed by adopting hybrid strategies based on the combination of different **SC** techniques, ranging from very simple combination schemas to more complicated ones.

One of the most representative combination schemas is represented by Neuro-Fuzzy strategy derived from the integration of principles of FL with NNs. In (Kulkarni et al., 1999), a **neuro-fuzzy** technique is proposed for content-based image retrieval. The adopted technique is based on fuzzy interpretation of natural language, neural network learning and search algorithms. In particular, firstly, FL is used to interpret natural expressions such as mostly, many, etc. Then, a neural network is designed to learn the meaning of these expressions. Finally, a binary search algorithm is used to match and display neural network's output and images from database. Kulkarni (2004) also proposed a similar neural-fuzzy based approach for retrieving a specific video clip from a video database. In this work, user queries were designed based on features such as colour and texture of scenes and objects in video clips. An error back propagation algorithm was proposed to learn the meaning of queries expressed in fuzzy terms such as very similar, similar and some-what similar.

Another example of hybrid strategy adopted in the **CB-MIR** context is in (Cordon et al., 2002) where simulated annealing and genetic programming are combined for relevance feedback within an extended Boolean (fuzzy) retrieval systems.

In (Maslov, 2003), the author proposes an approach that combines a hybrid genetic algorithm and a self-organizing neural network in a content-based retrieval system of distorted images with the aim to search for a set of parameters defining a correct mapping between images.

## A CONTENT-BASED IMAGE RETRIEVAL SYSTEM USING SC TECHNIQUES

In this section, we provide an example of content-based retrieval system that employs **SC** techniques to perform the content-based retrieval of images based on **shape matching**. The system, called VIRMA (Visual Image Retrieval by shape MAtching), (Castellano et al., 2006) provides a sample-based engine mechanism that enables the user to search an image in the available database by submitting a query that is simply represented by the sketch of a sample image. The search results to the formulated query are obtained through a

comparison between the submitted sample shape and the shapes of all objects appearing in the images stored into the database.

In the architecture of the system, two main modules can be distinguished (see figure 3):

*   **Database Filling**: this module allows to insert new images into the available image database. The main task of this module is Shape detection, that is, for each image, the shape content information is extracted and shapes of objects included in the image are stored in a separate database, called shape database;
*   **Search Engine**: this module enables the user to submit a query in the form of a sample sketch and to retrieve images containing objects whose shape matches the sketched shape on the basis of a defined similarity measure. Here, the main task is Shape matching.

## Shape detection

Images included in the database are stored as a set of shapes related to the objects included in each image. Hence, a processing phase has to be performed in order to store a new image in the database. This phase is devoted to the identification of objects appearing in the image. To this aim, firstly, an edge detection process is executed in order to extract all contours in the image.

In VIRMA, edge detection is performed through a neuro-fuzzy system that is able to classify image pixels into three classes: edge, texture and regular. The neuro-fuzzy strategy, founded on the correspondence between a fuzzy inference engine and a neural network, is able to learn a set of fuzzy rules that classify a single pixel $g_{ij}$ as contour, regular or texture point according to its edge strength values $E_{ij}^{(r)}$, $r = 1, ..., R$ in $R$ different scale representations. The use of different scale representations is introduced for texture

*Figure 3. The architecture of the developed content-based image retrieval system*

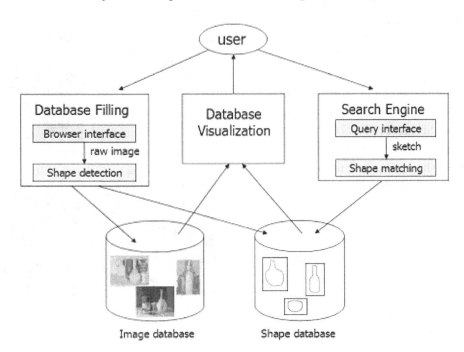

classification. Indeed, while the contour features may be easily extracted working in a single scale resolution, texture features need often to be identified using multiple scale. Perceptually, when an image is viewed from near to far, the edge strength of a pixel decreases in general, but the relative decreasing rates for contour, regular and texture points are different. Therefore the classification of pixels is based on the analysis of an image at different resolution levels and on the evaluation of the edge strength at each scale.

The k-th fuzzy rule is expressed in the form:

$$\text{IF } E_{ij}^1 \in A_k^1 \text{ AND ... AND } E_{ij}^R \in A_k^R \text{ THEN}$$

$$g_{ij} \in C_p \text{ with degree } b_{kp}$$

where $A_k^{(r)}$ are fuzzy sets defined over the variables $E_{ij}^{(r)}$ using Gaussian membership functions, and $b_{kp}$, ($p=1, 2, 3$) are fuzzy singletons representing the degree to which a pixel belongs to one of the

output classes: contour ($C_1$), regular ($C_2$) and texture ($C_3$). To classify image pixels, the neuro-fuzzy edge detection method employs a three-layer feed-forward neural network (the neuro-fuzzy network) reflecting the structure of the fuzzy rule base in its topology and the free parameters of the fuzzy rules in its adjustable weights. Further details about the adopted learning algorithms, can be found in (Castiello et al., 2003).

The result of the edge detection is a thin contour without spurious points. Nevertheless, for complex images containing many overlapping objects, human intervention is necessary to manually remove spurious edge points. Also, the problem of occlusion is not automatically solved in VIRMA, since the edge-detection algorithm is not able to reconstruct the whole contour in the case of occluded shapes. In these cases, contour reconstruction should be made manually by drawing missing parts of an object contour. This manual retouch of contours can be done through an Edge reconstruction tool integrated in VIRMA, that allows the user to manually intervene on an image.

The final edge pixels are analyzed to detect object shapes and represent them as polygonal curves. To this aim, a Shape identification tool based on a particular contour following algorithm (Kovesi, 2000) is implemented. Such algorithm, starting from a pixel on the edge, follows the contour by linking adjacent edge points into a single chain, so that an object shape is reconstructed. The final result of the Shape identification is a collection of closed curves, each curve represented by an ordered list of pixel coordinates. Hence, at the end of this process, each pixel is labeled with a number representing the curve it belongs to.

Finally, curves representing the shape of objects in the image are simplified. This is necessary not only to save space in the Shape database but also to make faster the shape matching process performed in the retrieval phase. Simplification of an object shape is achieved by reducing the number of vertices in the polyline by a simple curve evolution procedure (Latecki & Lakamper, 2000) that reduces vertices iteratively.

Finally, after shape simplification, each object shape identified in the image is stored in the Shape database as a list of vertices. Figure 4 shows the results of each processing step involved in the shape detection process.

## Shape matching

The Search Engine, representing the core of the VIRMA system, consists of a package of functions that allow the user to submit a sample image sketch as a query to interrogate the database. The presented sample image, which is assumed to contain just the contour of a shape, is processed by the Shape simplification tool described in the previous section, in order to be represented as a polygonal contour made of a reduced list of vertices.

Successively, a **shape matching** process is applied in order to evaluate similarity between

*Figure 4. Processing steps performed by VIRMA to detect object shapes in an image*

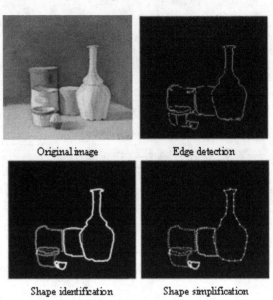

the sample shape and the shapes of all objects appearing in the stored images. Of course, to achieve efficient retrieval, the measure used to evaluate similarity (or dissimilarity) between two object shapes should be invariant under rotation, translation and scaling of the shapes.

The shape similarity measure adopted in VIRMA was proposed in (Arkin et al., 1991), where comparison of polygonal curves is based on the distance between their turn angle representations, also called turning functions. Given a curve A expressed as a list of vertices, its turning function $\Theta_A(s)$ measures the angle of the counterclockwise tangent as a function of the arc length s, measured from some reference point on A's boundary. By definition, the function $\Theta_A(s)$ is invariant under translation and scaling of the polygon A. Rotation of A corresponds to a shift of $\Theta_A(s)$ in the $\theta$ direction. Now, given two polygonal curves A and B (that are assumed to have the same length for simplicity), their dissimilarity can be measured by evaluating the distance between their turning functions $\Theta_A(s)$ and $\Theta_B(s)$:

*Figure 5. The results of the shape detection process*

Original image                    Canny edge detection                    N-F edge detection

$$\delta\left(a, B\right) = \left\| \Theta_A - \Theta_B \right\| = \left( \int_0^1 \left| \Theta_A\left(s\right) - \Theta_B\left(s\right) \right|^2 ds \right)^{\frac{1}{2}},$$

where $\left\| \cdot \right\|$ is the $L_2$ norm.

Since this distance function is sensitive to both the rotation of polygons and choice of reference point, it makes sense to consider as distance measure, the minimum over all possible rotation angles θ and all possible shifts t with respect to the reference point O:

$$d\left(A, B\right) = \left( \min_{\theta \in [o, 2\pi], t \in [0,1]} \int_0^1 \left| \Theta_A\left(s + t\right) - \Theta_B\left(s\right) + \theta \right|^2 ds \right)^{\frac{1}{2}}$$

To alleviate the computational burden required by the computation above, VIRMA computes a discretization of it by considering only some values of t and θ. Different tests have led to consider 25 equally spaced values $\theta_i = i \cdot \dfrac{\pi}{12}$ for i=0,...,24. As concerns possible values of t (choice of reference point), each vertex of the shape is considered as a possible reference point. Since, each shape, after the simplification process, is represented as a list of 30 vertices, 30 different reference points are considered.

## Application Example

As an example of application, VIRMA was applied on a collection of 20 digitalized images representing still-object paintings by the Italian artist Giorgio Morandi, used as test dataset in (Del Bimbo and Pala, 1997). Firstly, all the available digitalized images were subjected to the Shape detection process. In this way, the Image and Shape databases have been properly filled. For the sake of comparison, two distinct Shape databases have been initialized:

- the first Shape database has been derived by means of an edge detection tool based on the Canny operator, also available in VIRMA;
- the second Shape database has been derived by means of the edge detection tool based on the pixel classification performed by the **neuro-fuzzy** system.

The **neuro-fuzzy** tool for edge detection proved to be more effective in producing better results, thus affecting the overall shape detection process. The different quality results can be appreciated in figures 5 and 6: the shapes detected employing the Canny operator appear to be more scattered and inaccurate than those obtained by means of the **neuro-fuzzy** classification.

The difference among the two Shape databases reverberates also in the performance of the

*Figure 6. The results of the shape detection process*

Original image

Canny edge detection

N-F edge detection

*Figure 7. The results of the shape research process for a simple object sketch*

Object

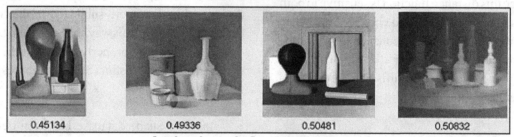

| 0.45134 | 0.49336 | 0.50481 | 0.50832 |

Search results over the Canny-originated Shape

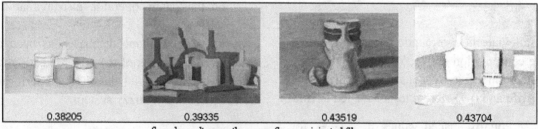

| 0.38205 | 0.39335 | 0.43519 | 0.43704 |

Search results over the neuro-fuzzy-originated Shape

search engine. In fact, experimental evidence shows how the image retrieval process is more accurate when performed over the second Shape database, at least in terms of immediate visual perception. In particular, figure 7 shows the retrieval results for a simple object sketch searched over both the databases. Even though the retrieved images are different, in both cases the results can be considered adequate to the sketched sample. In figure 8, instead, it can be noticed how the search for a more complicated object shape produced the most expected results over the **neuro-fuzzy**-originated database. In fact, as it can be observed also by referring to the reported dis-

*Figure 8. The results of the shape research process for a more complicated object sketch*

Object sketch

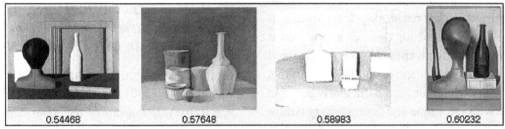

| 0.54468 | 0.57648 | 0.58983 | 0.60232 |

Search results over the Canny-originated Shape database

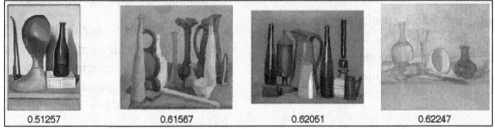

| 0.51257 | 0.61567 | 0.62051 | 0.62247 |

Search results over the neuro-fuzzy-originated Shape database

similarity measure values, the image with a higher visual resemblance is immediately retrieved from the **neuro-fuzzy** originated database, while it is classified as fourth best choice inside the Canny-originated database.

## CONCLUSION

In the **CB-MIR** context, **Soft Computing (SC)** techniques emerge as valid tools to cope with the ambiguity and uncertainty characterizing the complex mechanisms underlying the whole information retrieval process. An overview of recent approaches adopted for the design of **CB-MIR** systems employing **SC** techniques has been presented. This work advises the potential of **SC** techniques, often synergistically combined in hybrid schemas, for the development of tasks involved in a general **CB-MIR** system. As an example, in this chapter, we have described VIRMA, a system for the content-based image retrieval that enables users to search for images having a shape similar to the sketch of a submitted sample image. **SC** techniques are employed in VIRMA. Specifically, a **neuro-fuzzy** strategy permits to extract a set of fuzzy rules that classify image pixels for the extraction of contours included in the processed image so that this can be stored in the database. The presented system shows how **CB-MIR** systems can benefit from the integration of **SC** techniques as concerns the content feature extraction. Anyway other challenging problems can be successfully addressed by the use of **SC** such as matching, indexing and relevance feedback.

In addition, **SC** may offer a variety of advantages in the development of the so-called personalized content retrieval systems, i.e. systems that incorporate personalization functionalities in the overall retrieval process in order to return more desirable search results according to the user information needs. Today, many research efforts have been drawn to the investigation on personalized content retrieval systems leading to the growth of a promising research area aimed at improving the effectiveness of such systems and making them more adaptive and flexible. In this context, **SC** techniques are particularly suitable to cope with the vague and contradictory nature proper of personalization processes in **CB-MIR** systems.

In summary, we can conclude by saying that **SC** approaches reveal to be very profitable for **CB-MIR**, opening new important challenges and drawing a novel interesting investigation field in research.

# REFERENCES

Arkin, E., Chew, P., Huttenlocher, D., Kedem, K., & Mitchel, J. (1991). An efficiently computable metric for comparing polygonal shapes. *IEEE Transactions on Pattern Analysis and Machine Intelligence, 13*(3), 209–215. doi:10.1109/34.75509

Arkoumanis, D., Terrovitis, M., & Stamatogiannakis, L. (2002). Heuristic Algorithms for Similar Configuration Retrieval in Spatial Databases. In *proceeding of the 2nd Hellenic Conference on Artificial Intelligence (SETN)*, Thessalonica, Greece.

Castellano, G., Castiello, C., & Fanelli, A. M. (2006). Visual Image Retrieval by Shape Matching. In *Proceeding of ISMIS 2006* (pp. 208–217). VIRMA.

Castiello, C., Castellano, G., Caponetti, L., & Fanelli, A. M. (2003). Classifying image pixels by a neuro-fuzzy approach. In *Proceeding of International Fuzzy Systems Association World Congress (IFSA 2003)*, (pp. 253-256).

Chen, Y., & Wang, J. Z. (2002). A region based fuzzy feature matching approach to content based image retrieval. *IEEE Transactions on Pattern Analysis and Machine Intelligence, 24*(9), 1252–1267. doi:10.1109/TPAMI.2002.1033216

Chen, Z., Wenyin, L., Zhang, F., Li, M., & Zhang, H.-J. (2001). Web Mining for Web Image Retrieval. *Journal of the American Society for Information Science American Society for Information Science, 52*(10), 831–839.

Cordon, O., Moya, F., & Zarco, C. (2002). A new evolutionary algorithm combining simulated annealing and genetic programming for relevance feedbackin fuzzy information retrieval systems. *Soft Computing, 6*, 308–319. doi:10.1007/s00500-002-0184-8

Del Bimbo, A., & Pala, P. (1997). Visual image retrieval by elastic matching of user sketches. *IEEE Transactions on Pattern Analysis and Machine Intelligence, 19*, 121–132. doi:10.1109/34.574790

Djeraba, C. (2002). Content-based multimedia indexing and retrieval. *IEEE MultiMedia, 9*(2), 18–22. doi:10.1109/MMUL.2002.998047

Doulamis, A. D., Doulamis, N. D., & Kollias, S. D. (1999). Relevance feedback for content-based retrieval in video database: a neural network approach. In *Proceeding of International Conference on Electronic Circuit and Systems*, (Vol. 3, pp. 1745-1748).

Egecioglu, O., Ferhatosmanoglu, H., & Ogras, U. (2004). Dimensionality reduction and similarity computation by inner-product approximations. *IEEE Transactions on Knowledge and Data Engineering, 16*(6), 714–726. doi:10.1109/TKDE.2004.9

Eiben, A. E., & Smith, J. E. (2003). Introduction to Evolutionary Computing. In *Natural Computing Series*. Berlin: Springer.

El-Naqa, I., Yang, Y., Galatsanos, N. P., Nishikawa, R. M., & Wernik, M. N. (2004). A similarity learning approach to content-based image retrieval: application to digital mammography. *IEEE Transactions on Medical Imaging, 23*(10), 1233–1244. doi:10.1109/TMI.2004.834601

Feng, D., Siu, W. C., & Zhang, H. J. (Eds.). (2003). *Multimedia information retrieval and management: Technological fundamentals and applications.* Berlin: Springer.

Fonseca, M. J., & Jorge, J. A. (2003). Indexing high dimensional data for content-based retrieval in large database. In *Proceedings of the Eighth International Conference on Database Systems for Advanced Applications*, Kyoto, Japan.

Gonzalez-Garcia, A. C., Sossa-Azuela, J. H., Felipe-Riveron, & E. M., Pogrebnyak, O. (2007). Image retrieval based on Wavelet transform and neural network classification. *Computation Y Systemas, 11*(2), 143-156.

Han, J., & Ma, K. (2002). Fuzzy Colour Histogram and its Use in Colour Image Retrieval. *IEEE Transactions on Image Processing, 11*(8), 944–952. doi:10.1109/TIP.2002.801585

Hassanien, A.-E., Abraham, A., Kacprzyk, J., & Peters, J. F. (2008). Computational Intelligence in Multimedia Processing: Foundation and Trends. [SCI]. *Studies in Computational Intelligence, 96*, 3–49. doi:10.1007/978-3-540-76827-2_1

Hassanien, A.-E., & Jafar, A. (2003). Image classification and retrieval algorithm based on rough set theory. [SACJ]. *South African Computer Journal, 30*, 9–16.

Herrera-Viedma, E., Martin-B, M. J., Guadarrama, S., Sobrino, A., & Olivas, J. A. (2005). Soft Computing for Information Retrieval in the Web. *Eusflat-FLA 2005.*

Hildebrand, L. (2005). Hybrid Computational Intelligence Systems for Real World Application. In *Studies in Fuzziness and Soft Computing, 179* (pp. 165–195). Berlin: Springer.

Ishikawa, Y., Subramanya, R., & Faloutsos, C. (1998). Mindreader: Query Databases Through Multiple Examples. In *Proceeding of the 24th VLDB Conference*, New York, USA, (pp. 218–227).

Jacobs, D. W., Weinshall, D., & Gdalyahu, Y. (2000). Classification with nonmetric distances: Image retrieval and class representation. *IEEE Transactions on Pattern Analysis and Machine Intelligence, 22*(6), 583–600. doi:10.1109/34.862197

Jeon, J., Lavrenko, V., & Manmatha, R. (2003). Automatic image annotation and retrieval using crossmedia relevance models. In *Proceedings of the 26th Annual International ACM SIGIR Conference on Research and Development in Information Retrieval*, Toronto, Canada.

John, R., & Birkenead, R. (Eds.). (2001). *Developments in Soft Computing.* Heidelberg, Germany: Physica Verlag.

Jolion, J. M. (2001). Feature similarity. In Lew, M. S. (Ed.), *Principles of Visual Information Retrieval* (pp. 122–162). London: Springer-Verlag.

Kato, S., & Iisaku, S.-I. (1998). An Image Retrieval Method Based on a Genetic Algorithm. In *proceedings of the 13th International Conference on Information Networking (ICOIN '98).*

Klir, J., & Yuan, B. (1995). *Fuzzy sets and fuzzy logic: Theory and applications.* New York: Prentice Hall.

Kovesi, P. D. (2000). *MATLAB and Octave Functions for Computer Vision and Image Processing.* School of Computer Science and Software Engineering, The University of Western Australia. Available from: http://www.csse.uwa.edu.au/~pk/research/matlabfns/.

Krishnapuram, R., Mesadani, S., Jung, S. H., Choi, Y. S., & Balasubramaniam, R. (2004). Content based image retrieval based on a fuzzy approach. *IEEE Transactions on Knowledge and Data Engineering, 16*(10), 1185–1199. doi:10.1109/TKDE.2004.53

Kulkarni, S. (2004). Neural-fuzzy approach for content based retrieval of digital video. *Canadian on Electrical and Computer Engineering, 4,* 2235–2238.

Kulkarni, S. (2007). Image retrieval based on fuzzy mapping of image database and fuzzy similarity distance. In *Proceeding of the 6th International conference on computer and information science (ICIS 2007).*

Kulkarni, S., Verma, B., Sharma, P., & Selvaraj, H. (1999). Content based image retrieval using a neuro-fuzzy technique. In *Proceeding of the International Joint Conference on Neural Networks, 6,* (pp. 4304-4308).

Kushki, A., Androutsos, P., Plataniotis, K. N., & Venetsanopoulos, A. N. (2002). Fuzzy aggregation of image features in content based image retrieval. In *Proceedings of the IEEE International Conference on Image Processing (ICIP),* (pp. 115-118).

Latecki, L. J., & Lakamper, R. (2000). Shape similarity measure based on correspondence of visual parts. *IEEE Transactions on Pattern Analysis and Machine Intelligence, 22,* 1–6. doi:10.1109/34.879802

Lee, H. K., & Yoo, S. I. (2001). Intelligent Image Retrieval Using Neural Network. *IEICE Transactions on Information and Systems, E84*(12), 1810–1819.

Lew, M. S. (2000). Next Generation Web Searches for Visual Content. *IEEE Computing,* 46-53.

Lew, M. S., Sebe, N., Djeraba, C., & Jain, R. (2006). Content-Based Multimedia Information Retrieval. *ACM Transaction on Multimedia Computing. Communication and Application, 2*(1), 1–19.

Li, X.-L., Du, Z.-L., Wang, T., & Yu, D.-M. (2005). Audio Feature selection based on Rough Set. *International Journal of Information Technology, 11*(6), 117–123.

Lo, Y. L., & Chen, S. J. (2002). The numeric indexing for music data. In *Proceedings of the 22nd International Conference on Distributed Computing Systems Workshops,* Vienna, Austria.

Marques, O., & Furht, B. (2002). *Content-based image and video retrieval.* London: Kluwer.

Maslov, I. V. (2003). Content-based retrieval of distorted images using a hybrid genetic algorithm augmented by a self-organizing network. In Proceeding of Internet Multimedia Management systems, (Vol. 5242, pp. 125-136).

Mesadani, S., & Krishnapuram, R. (1999). A fuzzy approach to content-based image retrieval. In *Proceeding of the 1999 IEEE International Conference of Fuzzy systems,* (Vol. 3, pp. 1251-1260).

Mittal, A. (2006). An Overview of Multimedia Content-Based Retrieval Strategies. *Informatica, 30,* 347–356.

Nepal, S., Ramakrishna, M. V., & Thom, J. A. (1998). A fuzzy system for content based retrieval. IEEE International conference on Intelligent Processing System, Gold Coast, (pp. 335-339).

Papadias, D., Mantzourogiannis, M., Kalnis, P., Mamoulis, N., & Ahmad, I. (1999). Content-based retrieval using heuristic search. In *Proceedings of the 22th Annual International ACM SIGIR Conference on Research and Development in Information Retrieval,* (pp. 168-175).

Park, S. B., Lee, J. W., & Kim, S. K. (2004). Content-based image classification using a neural network. *Pattern Recognition Letters, 25,* 287–300. doi:10.1016/j.patrec.2003.10.015

Park, S. S., Seo, K.-K., & Jang, D.-S. (2005). Expert system based on artificial neural networks for content based image retrieval. *Expert Systems with Applications, 29,* 589–597. doi:10.1016/j.eswa.2005.04.027

Pawlack, Z. (1991). *Rough sets – Theoretical aspects of reasoning about data.* Dordrerecht, The Netherlands: Kluwer.

Petrakis, E. G. M., Kontis, K., & Voutsakis, E. (2006). Relevance feedback methods for logo and trademark image retrieval on the web. *SAC, 06,* 23–27.

Polkowski, L. (2003). *Rough sets: Mathematical foundation.* Heidelberg, Germany: Physica.

Rocchio, J. (1971). Relevance Feedback in Information Retrieval. In Salton, G. (Ed.), *The SMART Retrieval System - Experiments in Automatic Document Processing* (pp. 313–323). Englewood Cliffs, NJ: Prentice Hall.

Schwefel, H. P. (1995). *Evolution and optimum seeking.* New York: Wiley.

Shen, J., Stepherd, J., & Ngu, A. H. H. (2006). Towards effective content-based music retrieval with multiple acoustic feature combination. *IEEE Transactions on Multimedia, 8*(6), 1179–1189. doi:10.1109/TMM.2006.884618

Sugano, N. (2001). Colour Naming System using Fuzzy Set Theoretical Approach. In *Proceedings of 10th IEEE International Conference on Fuzzy Systems,* (Vol. 1, pp. 81-84).

Tran, K. D. (2005). Content-based Retrieval using a multi-objective genetic algorithm. In *proceeding of Southeast Conference,* (pp. 561-569).

Tsakonas, A., Dounias, G., Vlahavas, I. P., & Spyropoulos, C. D. (2002). Hybrid computational intelligence schemes in complex domains: An extended review. *Lecture Notes in Computer Science, 2308,* 494–511. doi:10.1007/3-540-46014-4_44

Vereb, K. (2003). On a hierarchical fuzzy content image retrieval approach. In *Proceeding of VLDB 2003 (Vol. 76).* Berlin, Germany: PhD Workshop.

Vertan, C., & Boujemaa, N. (2000). Embedding fuzzy logic in content based image retrieval. In Proceeding of CIR'2000, Brighton, UK.

Wang, D., & Ma, X. (2005). A Hybrid Image Retrieval System wit User's Relevance Feedback Using Neurocomputing. *Informatica, 29,* 271–279.

Wang, Y., Ding, M., Zhou, C., & Hu, Y. (2006). Interactive relevance feedback mechanisms for image retrieval using rough set. *Knowledge-Based Systems, 19,* 696–703. doi:10.1016/j.knosys.2006.05.005

Wei, C.-H., & Li, C.-T. (2005). *Content-Based Multimedia Retrieval* (pp. 116–122). Hershey, PA: Idea Group Inc.

Wu, L., Sycara, K., Payne, T., & Faloutsos, C. (2000). FALCON: Feedback Adaptive Loop for Content-Based Retrieval. In *Proc. 26th VLDB Conf.,* Cairo, Egypt, (pp. 297–306).

Wu, Y., Han, J., Li, H., & Li, M. (2007). Features Extraction and Selection Based on Rough Set and SVM in Abrupt Shot Detection. In *Proceeding of Intelligent Systems and Knowledge Engineering (ISKE 2007).*

Yan, J., Ryan, M., & Power, J. (1994). *Using fuzzy logic.* New York: Prentice Hall.

Ye, H., & Xu, G. (2003). Fast search in large scale image database using vector quantization. In *Proceedings of the 2nd International conference on image and video retrieval* [London: Springer-Verlag.]. *Urbana (Caracas, Venezuela), IL,* 477–487.

Yoo, H.-W., & Cho, S.-B. (2007). Video scene retrieval with interactive genetic algorithms. *Multimedia Tools Application, 3*(3).

Zhang, S., & Salari, E. (2005). Image denoising using a neural network based on non linear filter in wavelet domain Acoustics, speech and signal processing. In *Proceeding IEEE on international Conference ICASSP '05,* (Vol. 2, pp. 989-992).

Zhao, G., Kobayashi, A., & Sakai, Y. (2002). Image information retrieval using rough set theory. In. *Proceedings of the International Conference on Image Processing, 1,* 417–420.

Zhao, G., Kobayashi, A., & Sakai, Y. (2005). Group-based relevance feedback for interactive image retrieval. In proceeding of Databases and Applications.

# Chapter 11

# An Exposition of Feature Selection and Variable Precision Rough Set Analysis:
## Application to Financial Data

**Malcolm J. Beynon**
*Cardiff University, UK*

**Benjamin Griffiths**
*Cardiff University, UK*

## ABSTRACT

*This chapter considers, and elucidates, the general methodology of rough set theory (RST), a nascent approach to rule based classification associated with soft computing. There are two parts of the elucidation undertaken in this chapter, firstly the levels of possible pre-processing necessary when undertaking an RST based analysis, and secondly the presentation of an analysis using variable precision rough sets (VPRS), a development on the original RST that allows for misclassification to exist in the constructed "if ... then ..." decision rules. Throughout the chapter, bespoke software underpins the pre-processing and VPRS analysis undertaken, including screenshots of its output. The problem of US bank credit ratings allows the pertinent demonstration of the soft computing approaches described throughout.*

## INTRODUCTION

There are a number of types of information industries, providing information on a wide range of areas such as, scientific, technical, medical, media, and relevant to this chapter, business and financial information (Fayyad *et al.*, 1996). In his 1984 book Megatrends, Naisbitt (pp. 24) wrote, "We are drowning in information, but starved for

knowledge...", this is a sentiment which still holds true over 20 years later.

Utilising modern technology (computers), the process by which knowledge is extracted from databases of information is commonly known as data mining, and is seen as a major step of the broader discipline of Knowledge Discovery in Databases (KDD). Where knowledge management, in a business context, is the process by which companies organise, collect and assimilate this knowledge into their systems (Zorn and Taylor, 2003). Due to

DOI: 10.4018/978-1-60566-814-7.ch011

the volume of data available, and facilitated by the advances made in modern computers, new techniques are being developed, both in industry and academia, to exploit this increasing abundance of information. Tay *et al.* (2003, pp. 1) notes that:

*A new generation of techniques and tools is emerging to intelligently assist humans in analyzing mountains of data, finding useful knowledge and in some cases performing analysis automatically...*

This chapter considers one of the more nascent data mining methods, namely Variable Precision Rough Sets (VPRS) (Ziarko, 1993a), an extension of Rough Set Theory (RST) (Pawlak, 1982), within the field of quantitative financial analysis. The financial analysis in this case is with respect to the classification and prediction of banks to Fitch's Individual Bank Strength Ratings (Fitch, 2007).

Mitra *et al.* (2002) in a review of the impact of soft computing in data mining, state (pp. 3):

*Soft computing methodologies (involving fuzzy sets, neural networks, genetic algorithms, and rough sets) are most widely applied in the data mining step of the overall KDD process.*

Their review specifically suggests RST has emerged as a major mathematical tool for managing uncertainty, which arises from granularity in the domain of discourse, and has proved to be useful in a variety of KDD processes. Further, it (RST) offers mathematical tools to discover hidden patterns in data and therefore its importance, as far as data mining is concerned, can in no way be overlooked.

In this chapter, bespoke, software is described, which incorporates a suite of facilities capable of tackling some of the most relevant issues within the field KDD and data mining, and pertinently applies VPRS, to produce sets of decision rules associated with the data being analysed. Due to their contemporary nature, there are no strict definitions of KDD and data mining. Frawley *et*

*al.* (1992, pp. 58) described KDD as the, "nontrivial extraction of implicit, unknown, and potentially useful information from data". Although the terms, KDD and data mining, are often used synonymously (data mining is considered to be the more popular term, Piatetsky-Shapiro, 2000), a clear distinction can be drawn, as stated by Fayyad *et al.* (1996, pp. 39):

*KDD refers to the overall process of discovering useful knowledge from data, and data mining refers to a particular step in this process. Data mining is the application of specific algorithms for extracting patterns from data...*

Amongst the facilities considered is the *preprocessing* of the data (as a prerequisite for the later data mining stage), which includes methods for, handling missing data, tackling imbalanced data, and discretisation of continuous valued data into discrete data (a requirement of some data mining methods, including RST). Often, data sets contain variables (also described as features or attributes) that are redundant or irrelevant, hence, a *feature selection* facility may be required prior to data mining, considered here also

These facilities associated with KDD, could be described as supportive processes for the main stage (facility), that is, *data mining*, here undertaken through the employment of VPRS (an extension of RST). Developed by Pawlak (1982, 1991), RST is a set theoretical approach for dealing with imprecise or vague concepts within knowledge. With regards to data mining, it offered a new methodology for, construction and application of decision tables, based on inconsistent data sets (Ziarko, 2003). VPRS is an extension of RST, which relaxes an assumption that the given classifications within the data set are totally correct (Mi *et al.*, 2004). Hence, VPRS allows for a level of uncertainty, which may be inherent within some data sets (Ziarko, 1993a). This was an important development, since it enabled the construction of probabilistic decision rules when using VPRS, rather than the deterministic decision rules when using the original RST.

RST based approaches, have intrinsic aspects that make them attractive as a modern analytical method (Beynon *et al.*, 2004; Ilczuk and Wakulicz-Deja, 2007). RST is a non-parametric method, which makes no assumptions regarding the underlying distributions of the data variables, which is a limitation of other methods, such as regression (Johnson and Wichern, 2007). RST, when utilised in classification problems, provides the user with a list of readable, interpretable, decision rules.

With regards to feature selection (a facility of KDD), most data mining methods require feature selection to be performed prior to the data mining process (Liu and Motoda, 2002). However, to some extent, feature selection is integral to RST based methods, including VPRS, through what is known respectively as reducts and $\beta$-reducts. These are subsets of variables that maintain the data's semantics or 'meaning', whilst eliminating irrelevant or redundant variables from the data set.

The overall intention of this chapter is too offer insights into the soft computing methodology generally known as rough set theory. The primary vehicle to present this is through the presentation of results from bespoke software, enabling the employment of pre-processing and VPRS analyses required for pertinent data mining. It is hoped, a reader will appreciate the balance between technical detail and presented results (screenshots of software results) given in this chapter. The included references will allow a reader to look in more detail at the mechanisms involved in the data analysis able to be undertaken.

## BACKGROUND

The software considered in this chapter can be considered a specific type of KDD system, namely a Decision Support System (DSS). Introduced in the early 1960's (Raymond, 1966), a DSS supports an expert, or the analyst, with complex real world decision making. The system was developed to empower the analyst, allowing them choice and flexibility to choose from a range of facilities etc., including; pre-processing, feature selection and data mining; and setting certain parameters associated with these during the KDD process.

VPRS, described in detail later, requires a discrete data format; hence four discretisation methods were incorporated in the software, two basic methods, equal-width and equal-frequency, and two more advanced methods, Minimum Entropy and FUSINTER (Fayyad and Irani, 1992; Zighed *et al.*, 1998). Although the developed VPRS software incorporates a level of feature selection through $\beta$-reducts (certain subsets of the set of condition attributes describing the considered objects - Ziarko, 1993 - see later). However, a level of pre-feature selection may be required for when large data sets are being analysed. Here, two recent feature selection methods are implemented; ReleifF (Kononenko, 1994) and a development of an RST based feature selection method proposed by Beynon (2004). The results are augmented by a series of graphs which provide the analyst with further information to support their variable selection choice.

The VPRS vein graph software (see later), follows the approach introduced in Beynon (2001), and allows the analyst to select $\beta$-reducts using a novel point and click graphical interface, that is, the vein graph. The decision rules associated with the choice of $\beta$-reducts are derived, and displayed on a separate panel of information for inspection by the analyst. Using the VPRS vein graph software, the analyst has the choice to retain a certain percentage of the data as a validation set. Within the software, with regards to testing the classifier (set of rules), the predictions based on training and validation sets are comprehensively broken down into a number of panels of information. The panels viewed separately, and together, the ability of the rules to match objects, as well as only nearly match them.

*Table 1. Fitch's definition of its individual bank rating categories*

| FIBR | Recoded to | Description |
|------|-----------|-------------|
| A | 0 | A very strong bank. |
| B | 1 | A strong bank. |
| C | 2 | An adequate bank. |
| D | 3 | A bank, which has weaknesses of internal and/or external origin. |
| E | 4 | A bank with very serious problems |

## INTRODUCTION TO FIBR DATA, AND SOFTWARE PRE-PROCESSING AND FEATURE SELECTION RESULTS

### FIBR Data Set

As stated in the introduction to this chapter, the described software (including pre-processing, feature selection and VPRS analyses), will be applied to the prediction of bank ratings, specifically, Fitch's Individual Bank Strength Ratings (FIBRs) (Fitch, 2007), from the information in a number of descriptive bank financial attributes.

Fitch (2007) describe FIBRs as designed to assess a bank's exposure to, appetite for, and management of risk, and thus represent their view on the likelihood that it would run into significant difficulties such that it would require support. The five main FIBR categories are described below in Table 1, as given by Fitch (2007).

From Table 1, the five categories shown have FIBR descriptions which range from the strongest 'A very strong bank' to the weakest 'A bank with very serious problems'. To model these categories of bank, the target data used within this chapter has been taken form Bureau van Dijk's Bankscope Database (2007). This database provides information on banks and financial institutions world wide, with up to 16 years of detailed accounts, on ratios, ratings and rating reports, ownership, country risk and country finance reports.

In regard to the bank attributes (characteristics such as financial ratios etc.) to consider in the analysis of FIBRs which describe the banks considered, the CAMELS bank ratings systems in use by the U.S. Federal Reserve are indicative of the principle of implementing an economic rationale, made up of, Capital, Asset Quality, Management, Earnings, Liquidity and Sensitivity to market risk (Derviz and Podpiera, 2004). Within the related literature, the elements of the CAMELS model are typically captured using balance sheet data in the form of financial ratios (Sahajwala and Van Den, 2000). They are expressed as decimal values and are used by company managers, shareholders and financial analysts.

Table 2 lists the number of occurrences of 19 attributes (financial ratios etc.) that occurred twice or more, across twelve recent studies related to bank rating predictions (including Poon, 2003; Poon and Firth, 2005; Kosmidou *et al.*, 2006; Pasiouras *et al.*, 2006; Van Roy, 2006). These ratios have been separated into the appropriate CAMELS categories for which they are considered representative.

With the initial set of attributes identified, and banks (objects) from Bureau van Dijk's Bankscope Database (2007), associated with less than 5% missing data selected, resulted in the target data set containing 620 banks, broken down into the categories, A - 16, B - 319, C - 163, D - 107 and E - 15. The analysis in this chapter will involve the employment of VPRS on a training subset of the available data; the constructed rules are then tested on a validation set (the remains of the available data).

With regards to the number of objects taken for the training set, 405 objects were taken, using the sub-sampling method described in Israel (2007), broken down into, A - 15/16 (15 out of 16 in data), B - 177/319, C - 115/319, D - 115/163 and E - 14/15. This means 215 banks make up the validation set. The proportional split between the training and validation sets is around two thirds and one third respectively, which is in line with

*Table 2. Occurrence of attributes from 12 recent bank rating studies*

| CAMELS Category | Attribute Occurrence |
|---|---|
| **Capital Adequacy(C)** | |
| Tier 1 Ratio | 2 |
| Total Capital Ratio | 4 |
| Equity / Total Assets | 9 |
| Equity / Net Loans | 2 |
| Cap Funds / Tot Assets | 2 |
| **Asset Quality (A)** | |
| Loan Loss Reserve / Gross Loans | 2 |
| Loan Loss Prov / Net Int Rev | 4 |
| Loan Loss Res / Impaired Loans | 2 |
| Impaired Loans / Gross Loans | 3 |
| **Earnings (E)** | |
| Net Interest Margin | 3 |
| Net Int. Inc./ Aveg Assest | 3 |
| Non Int Exp / Avg Assets | 3 |
| Return on Average Assets | 11 |
| Return on Average Equity | 5 |
| Cost to Income Ratio | 4 |
| **Liquidity (L)** | |
| Net Loans / Total Assets | 5 |
| Net Loans / Customer & ST Funding | 3 |
| Liquid Assets / Cust & ST Funding | 5 |
| **Sensitivity to Market Risk (S)** | |
| Number of subsidiaries | 3 |

the recommendations quoted in the associated literature (Weiss and Kulikowski, 1991; Han and Kamber, 2006).

Having constructed the initial FIBR data set, made up of 620 banks, the pre-processing part of KDD is first undertaken, namely discretisation and feature selection, in this chapter.

## Data Discretisation Results

Here, the FUSINTER discretisation algorithm (see Zighed, 1994, for details of the bottom-up algorithm) has been applied to the training set of the FIBR data set (FUSINTER was used for all attributes), see Figure 1.

The first column in Figure 1, beyond the names of the attributes, displays the choice of discretisation method used to discretise the data. The second column displays the number of intervals associated with each attribute, and the interval ranges themselves are displayed in the proceeding columns. Taking the attribute Loan Loss Reserve/ Gross Loans as an example (highlighted in Figure 1), it has been discretised, using the FUSINTER algorithm, into three intervals [0.0, 1.09], (1.09, 2.55] and (2.55, 30.86]. Hence, the data associated with this attribute, is recoded into the discrete values '0', '1' and '2', respectively. The next two Figures show the impact of the aforementioned discretisation, see Figure 2 and 3, where a sample of the considered data set is shown pre and post discretisation, respectively.

The validation set is similarly discretised using the intervals calculated from the training set, shown previously (with values outside the limits of the first and last intervals given their labels).

## Feature Selection

This section presents the results of the two implemented feature selection algorithms employed on the training set part of the FIBR data set, namely ReliefF (see Kononenko, 1994, for details of the algorithm) and the more novel algorithm proposed by Beynon (2004) based on RST, referred to here as the RST_FS method (RST Feature Selection - see Beynon, 2004, for details of the algorithm).

Within the VPRS software, the ReliefF algorithm, is applied to both the pre-discretised (ReliefFC) training set and the post-discretised (ReliefFD) training set, see Figure 4 for the ReliefFD based results.

The colour coded legend to the right of the graph in Figure 4, indicates the final ranked positions of all the attributes based on the highest value of $m$ (number of iterations used in ReliefF - see Kononenko, 1994). Only the top ten ranked

*Figure 1. Data discretisation table of bank condition attributes (using FUSINTER)*

| | Method | Intervals | | | | | | | | |
|---|---|---|---|---|---|---|---|---|---|---|
| Loan Loss Reserve / Gross Loans | Fusinter | 3 | 0 | 1.09 | 2.55 | 30.86 | - | - | | |
| Loan Loss Prov / Net Int Rev | Fusinter | 4 | -47.98 | 9.69 | 17.02 | 20.85 | 213.7 | - | | |
| Loan Loss Res / Impaired Loans | Fusinter | 2 | 0 | 130.55 | 997.68 | - | - | | | |
| Impaired Loans / Gross Loans | Fusinter | 5 | 0 | 0.66 | 1.44 | 2.82 | 5.45 | 100.0 | | |
| Tier 1 Ratio | Fusinter | 5 | 0 | 5.5 | 8.66 | 9.2 | 11.61 | 72.4 | | |
| Total Capital Ratio | Fusinter | 5 | 0 | 9.3 | 11.09 | 13.7 | 16.5 | 102.7 | | |
| Equity / Total Assets | Fusinter | 3 | 0 | 4.21 | 8.88 | 49.06 | - | | | |
| Equity / Net Loans | Fusinter | 5 | 0 | 6.86 | 9.33 | 13.49 | 24.27 | 346.79 | | |
| Cap Funds / Tot Assets | Fusinter | 4 | 0 | 6.22 | 7.52 | 10.09 | 77.87 | - | | |
| Subord Debt / Cap Funds | Fusinter | 4 | 0 | 16.86 | 22.04 | 31.79 | 56.01 | - | | |
| Net Interest Margin | Fusinter | 3 | -3.51 | 1.68 | 4.75 | 12.97 | - | - | | |
| Non Int Exp / Avg Assets | Fusinter | 2 | -0.74 | 3.58 | 28.06 | - | - | | | |
| Return on Average Assets (ROAA) | Fusinter | 4 | -2.87 | 0.25 | 0.56 | 1.8 | 12.37 | - | | |
| Return on Average Equity (ROAE) | Fusinter | 3 | -64.75 | 7.13 | 11.2 | 102.08 | - | - | | |
| Cost to Income Ratio | Fusinter | 3 | 0 | 56.93 | 63.76 | 120.66 | - | - | | |
| Net Loans / Total Assets | Fusinter | 5 | 0 | 58.15 | 66.07 | 69.98 | 73.26 | 94.89 | | |
| Net Loans / Customer & ST Funding | Fusinter | 5 | 0 | 65.68 | 71.28 | 85.82 | 118.14 | 832.2 | | |
| Liquid Assets / Cust & ST Funding | Fusinter | 3 | 0 | 9.79 | 18.81 | 226.2 | - | | | |
| EIU Overall Country Risk | Fusinter | 4 | 0 | 1.0 | 2.0 | 3.0 | 6.0 | - | | |
| EIU Banking Sector Risk | Fusinter | 4 | 0 | 1.0 | 2.0 | 3.0 | 6.0 | - | | |
| EIU Banking Sector Risk Outlook | Fusinter | 1 | 0 | 2.0 | - | - | - | | | |
| Number of recorded subsidiaries | Fusinter | 5 | 0 | 0.0 | 5.0 | 14.0 | 33.0 | 4005.0 | | |
| GDP/head | Fusinter | 7 | 0 | 2348.0 | 13064.0 | 23264.0 | 27231.0 | 30506.0 | 32257.0 | 48625.0 |

*Figure 2. Sample of the training set, pre-discretisation*

| | Net Loan... | Net Loan... | Liquid As... | EIU Over... | EIU Bank... | EIU Bank... | Number ... | GDP/head | Decision |
|---|---|---|---|---|---|---|---|---|---|
| 11 | 54.8 | 103.29 | 1.04 | 1.0 | 1.0 | 1.0 | 374.0 | 28495.0 | 0.0 |
| 12 | 68.53 | 84.1 | 12.91 | 1.0 | 1.0 | 1.0 | 374.0 | 28495.0 | 0.0 |
| 13 | 65.43 | 97.61 | 8.27 | 1.0 | 1.0 | 1.0 | 1203.0 | 36355.0 | 0.0 |
| 14 | 72.86 | 103.73 | 7.3 | 1.0 | 1.0 | 1.0 | 1203.0 | 36355.0 | 0.0 |
| 15 | 91.45 | 99.48 | 5.18 | 1.0 | 1.0 | 1.0 | 38.0 | 28495.0 | 1.0 |
| 16 | 65.14 | 79.91 | 15.84 | 2.0 | 2.0 | 1.0 | 123.0 | 13723.0 | 1.0 |
| 17 | 57.76 | 90.86 | 4.72 | 2.0 | 2.0 | 1.0 | 123.0 | 13723.0 | 1.0 |
| 18 | 86.03 | 118.11 | 3.14 | 1.0 | 1.0 | 1.0 | 2.0 | 36355.0 | 1.0 |
| 19 | 53.92 | 128.24 | 26.89 | 1.0 | 1.0 | 1.0 | 290.0 | 36108.0 | 1.0 |
| 20 | 55.22 | 64.31 | 8.05 | 1.0 | 2.0 | 2.0 | 5.0 | 24213.0 | 1.0 |

*Figure 3. Sample of the training set, post-discretisation*

| | Net Loan... | Net Loan... | Liquid As... | EIU Over... | EIU Bank... | EIU Bank... | Number ... | GDP/head | Decision |
|---|---|---|---|---|---|---|---|---|---|
| 11 | 0 | 3 | 0 | 1 | 1 | 1 | 4 | 4 | 0 |
| 12 | 2 | 2 | 1 | 1 | 1 | 1 | 4 | 4 | 0 |
| 13 | 1 | 3 | 0 | 1 | 1 | 1 | 4 | 6 | 0 |
| 14 | 3 | 3 | 0 | 1 | 1 | 1 | 4 | 6 | 0 |
| 15 | 4 | 3 | 0 | 1 | 1 | 1 | 4 | 4 | 1 |
| 16 | 1 | 2 | 1 | 2 | 2 | 1 | 4 | 2 | 1 |
| 17 | 0 | 3 | 0 | 2 | 2 | 1 | 4 | 2 | 1 |
| 18 | 4 | 3 | 0 | 1 | 1 | 1 | 1 | 6 | 1 |
| 19 | 0 | 3 | 2 | 1 | 1 | 1 | 4 | 6 | |

*Figure 4. ReliefFD weights graph over the range of m values (Iterations of Algorithm)*

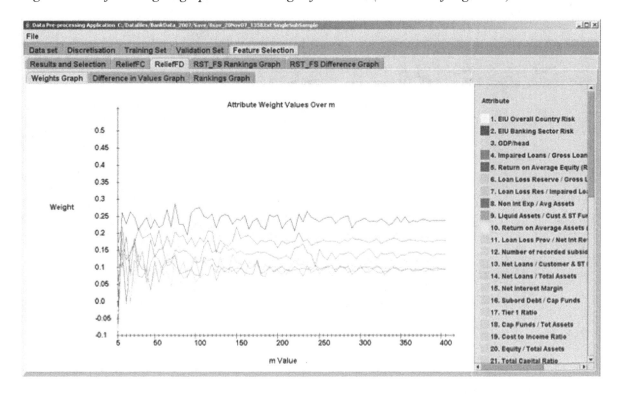

'contributing' attributes are plotted on the graph, and are coloured other than grey in the legend (described in more detail later in this section).

Continuing with the results of feature selection based on the FIBR data (the training set), this subsection describes two graphs that were developed in association with the RST_FS algorithm described by Beynon (2004), see Figure 5 (the technical details surrounding this approach are given in the next section).

The RST_FS graph, as shown in Figure 5, indicates the disparity, or notional distance between the Quality of Classification (QoC - measure defined in VPRS, described later) over the range of $\beta$ (from VPRS, defined later), for the selected attributes compared to the full set of attributes. The legend to the right of the graph, indicates the order in which the attributes were selected and hence ranked. Here, with GDP/head ranked as first (yellow) and Loan Loss Reserve/ Gross Loans ranked last (dark green).

The information from all the feature selection analyses was considered before a final selection of attributes was decided on. Beyond this level of feature selection, RST/VPRS itself has a form of feature selection embedded in it, through the identification of $\beta$-reducts (particular subsets of attributes, see their formal definition in the next section). The subsequent VPRS analyses based on attributes identified by the feature selection methods, tended to provide more of a varied range of $\beta$-reducts, in terms of the number of $\beta$-reducts, the number of attributes associated with those $\beta$-reducts, the QoC and $\beta$-ranges associated with the set of $\beta$-reducts. The final selected attributes to be considered in the subsequent VPRS analysis were decided, see Figure 6.

This legend of considered attributes in Figure 6 is available to the analyst during the analysis, for referencing the condition attribute names against their index numbers.

*Figure 5. RST_FS graph, depicting the difference in QoC over the range of β values for each subset of selected attributes*

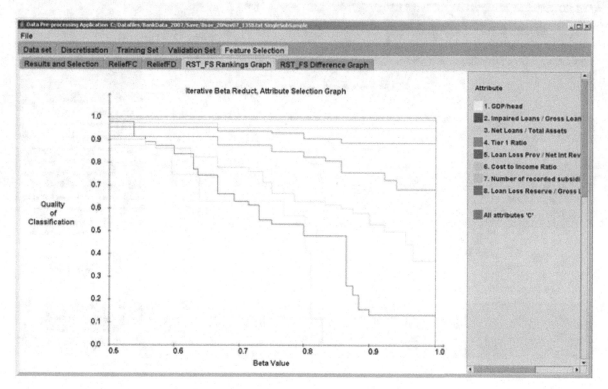

*Figure 6. Attribute legend for the considered FIBR data set (from training set)*

## VPRS ANALYSIS OF THE FIBR DATA SET

The main thrust of this chapter reports the VPRS analysis of the FIBR data set, through the VPRS 'vein graph' software, using the pre-processing details described previously, based on the vein graph described in Beynon (2001). Prior to the elucidation of the results, a brief technical description of VPRS is first given.

## Technical Description of VPRS

Ziarko (1993a, 1993b), proposed the Variable Precision Rough Set (VPRS) model as a generalisation of RST, that allows for a level of misclassification to exist in the constructed set of '*If... then...*' decision rules, and is more applicable to real world data (Dembczyński *et al.*, 2007). That is, the generalisation of the set inclusion relationship in RST, to a majority inclusion relationship, by means of introducing a probabilistic value $\beta$ in the range (0.5, 1.0] (see An *et al.*, 1996, and later), rather than the inherent deterministic notion of classification given with RST (and is a special case of VPRS when $\beta = 1$).

Central to RST (and so VPRS), and many other data mining methods, is the notion of an information system, which is defined as the universe of objects (observations) $U \{o_1, o_2,...\}$, characterised by the set of attributes $A \{a_1, a_2,...\}$. More appropriate here, is a specialised case of the information system known as the decision table, which further defines the universe of objects $U$ as being characterised by the set of condition attributes $C = \{c_1, c_2,...\}$ and classified to the set of decision attributes $D = \{d_1\}$ (here only one decision attribute is considered), where $A = C \cup D$. Hence, a decision table can be denoted as $S = (U, C, D)$. The value of an attribute associated with a particular object is referred to as an attribute value (Beynon and Peel, 2001; Ślęzak, 2004).

Considering the proportion of the objects within the condition class $X_i \in E(C)$ ($E(C)$ - equivalence class of $C$), that are also associated with a decision class $Z_j \in E(D)$, if that proportion is greater than the pre-defined $\beta$ value, then the condition class $X_i$ is said to be in, what is now termed, the $\beta$-positive region of $Z_j$. The $\beta$-positive region of $Z_j$, for the set of condition attributes $C$, is defined as:

$$POS_C^\beta (Z_j) = \bigcup_{\Pr(Z_j | X_i) \geq \beta} \{X_i \in E(C)\}.$$

Conversely, the $\beta$-negative region is defined as those objects belonging to the condition classes whose proportion within the associated decision class $Z_j$ is less than $1 - \beta$. Formally:

$$NEG_C^\beta (Z_j) = \bigcup_{\Pr(Z_j | X_i) \leq 1-\beta} \{X_i \in E(C)\}$$

The $\beta$-negative region can also be considered as the set of the condition classes which can be classified to the compliment of $Z_j$, namely $\neg Z_j$, with the proportion of objects greater than $\beta$, that is $POS_C^\beta (\neg Z_j) = NEG_C^\beta (Z_j)$.

The $\beta$-boundary region, refers to those condition classes whose proportion within the associated decision class $Z_j$ is less than $\beta$ but greater than $1 - \beta$. That is, the set of the condition classes that belongs neither to the decision class $Z_j$, nor its compliment $\neg Z_j$, with certainty greater than $\beta$. The $\beta$-boundary region is formally defined as:

$$BND_C^\beta (Z) = \bigcup_{1-\beta < \Pr(Z_j | X_i) < \beta} \{X_i \in E(C)\}$$

Beynon (2001) considered a visual representation of certain aspects of VPRS, aimed towards aiding the analyst in understanding the interim analysis, including a visualisation of the $\beta$-reducts over their respective domains of $\beta$. This visual representation has been titled here the "vein graph", as the lines resemble veins, and because of the connotations with veins of knowledge within a mountain of data, an analogy used by Linoff (1998).

The numbers of objects included in the condition classes that are contained in the respective $\beta$-positive regions for each of the decision classes, subject to the necessary $\beta$ value, make up a measure of the *quality of classification* (QoC). That is, the QoC, denoted $\gamma^\beta(P, D)$, is the proportion of those objects in a data set that is assigned a classification (correctly or incorrectly), defined by (Beynon, 2001):

$$\gamma^\beta(C, D) = \frac{\text{card}(\bigcup_{\forall Z_j \in E(D)} POS_C^\beta (Z_j))}{\text{card}(U)}.$$

There is an inverse relationship between the QoC and the $\beta$ value. That is, a lower $\beta$ value allows for a higher level of classification (majority inclusion). It is the QOC measure used in the RST_FS feature selection algorithm employed earlier.

Before considering the selection of $\beta$, a measure of the accuracy of the rules induced during VPRS can also be calculated. Following Pawlak (1991), here, the accuracy of the whole rule set is considered; hence, the number of objects given a correct classification, out of those objects given a classification, is defined as:

$$\alpha^\beta(C, D) = \frac{\text{card}(\bigcup_{\forall X_i, Z_j} \{X_i \cap Z_j : ((X_i \cap Z_j \,/\, card(X_i)) \geq \beta\})}{\text{card}(\bigcup_{\forall Z_j \in E(D)} POS_C^\beta(Z_j))}$$

Here, this expression is referred to as the Quality of Approximation (QoA) (Katzberg and Ziarko, 1996).

An integral part of VPRS is rule construction through the use of $\beta$-reducts which are particular subsets of condition attributes ($P$) providing the classification of objects with the same $\gamma^\beta(P, D)$ as the full set of attributes $C$ (Ziarko, 1993b). Ziarko (1993b) states that a $\beta$-reduct ($R$) of the set of conditional attributes $C$, with respect to a set of decision attributes $D$, is:

1. A subset $R$ of $C$ that offers the same quality of classification, subject to the $\beta$ value, as the whole set of condition attributes.
2. No proper subset of $R$ has the same quality of the classification as $R$, subject to the associated $\beta$ value.

Based on an identified $\beta$-reduct, a number of different sets of decision rules can be identified (maximal, minimal etc., see An *et al.*, 1996). Here the minimal rule set is constructed, found through the identification of prime implicants and then with further reduction in conditions in the individual rules. Only rules associated with condition classes within the $\beta$-positive regions are considered, because rules induced within VPRS, are based on the prime implicants, which are induced from the $\beta$-positive region (*ibid.*).

## VPRS Analysis of FIBR Data Set

The VPRS 'vein graph' software allows an analyst, via a simple point and click interface, to inspect and select the $\beta$-reduct, amongst the $\beta$-reducts associated with a data set, which they believe is most appropriate to their analysis. That is, selection of a $\beta$-reduct which has a low $\beta$ threshold value (near 0.5), allowing for a greater level of misclassification, but with a relatively high proportion of the objects given a classification; or selection of a $\beta$-reduct which has a high $\beta$ threshold value (near 1), allowing for a greater level of accuracy, but fewer objects given a classification. In Figure 7, the vein graph presented shows that there are six $\beta$-reducts identified when using the selected set of attributes making up the FIBR set, looking only at the training set currently.

Five out of the six identified $\beta$-reducts shown in Figure 7, have a QoC of 0.95 (lying in the $\beta$ sub-domain (0.5, 0.67] - full $\beta$ domain shown in red in top line), including the selected $\beta$-reduct $\{c_2, c_4, c_8\}$ to be further considered here. Where there is no $\beta$-reduct over a certain sub-domain of $\beta$, the system defaults to the full set of attributes $C$, that is, as shown by the sixth $\beta$-reduct $\{c_1, c_2, c_3, c_4, c_5, c_6, c_7, c_8\}$, with nine associated $\beta$ sub-domains ranging in (0.6667, 1.0].

Within Figure 7, the three condition attributes associated with the selected $\beta$-reduct $\{c_2, c_4, c_8\}$, belong to three of the five represented categories of the CAMELS model (the 'M' category was not considered). That is, attribute '2' (Impaired Loans / Gross Loans) belongs to the Asset quality category (A), attribute '4' (Non Int Exp / Avg Assets) belongs to the Earnings category (E), and attribute '8' (GDP/head) belongs to the Sensitivity to market risk category (S).

Returning to the selection of $\beta$-reduct $\{c_2, c_4, c_8\}$, Figure 8 displays the 13 rules associated with it (following the approach given in An *et al.*, 1996). The cross-hairs in the top half of the panel shown indicate that, the $\beta$ value is set to 0.5131, which is within the $\beta$-reduct's $\beta$ sub-domain of (0.5, 0.5238], and is associated with a QoC of 0.9506. Note that, the $\beta$-reduct $\{c_2, c_4, c_8\}$ has an upper $\beta$ threshold value equal to the lowest certainty value belonging to rule 8, shown in Figure 8.

*Figure 7. Vein graph representation of β-reducts associated with the FIBR data set*

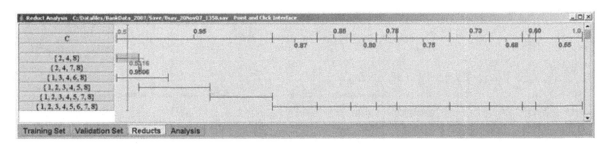

Giving some interpretation to the rules shown within Figure 8, of the 13 rules shown, rule 1 based only on the attribute GDP/head is the strongest (rule supported by 112 banks it classifies, giving a strength value of 112/405 or 0.2765) and has the second highest certainty value (correctly predicts 92 banks, giving a certainty value of 92/112 or 0.8214). It is interesting to note that almost a third of all the banks are given a classification based on just rule 1, associated with only one condition attribute, namely GDP/Head (but different intervals).

There are a number of rules within the rule set, which have relatively high support values but are associated with weak certainties, for example, rules 6 and 8. This is understandable since the β-reduct $\{c_2, c_4, c_8\}$ is associated with a low β threshold value, which therefore implies that the analysis is including rules associated with a high degree of misclassification. Furthermore, there are a number of rules with low support values (therefore low strength), but have high certainty values, for example, rules 7, 11 and 13. These rules tend to be associated with condition classes containing only a few banks (objects), or in the extreme case, such as rule 7, a single bank. In total, 385 out of the 405 banks in the training set were assigned a classification (from the 13 rules), with 287 of these correctly classified.

Here in terms of the FIBR, the general trend suggests that a bank domicile within a country that has a high GDP/head, is more likely to have a relatively high bank rating. Loan Loss Res/

Impaired Loans (index 2) and Non Int Exp/Avg Assets (index 4), appear to be important additional factors to a bank's final rating classification (grade) (as considered with regards to Figure 8). Where Loan Loss Res/Impaired Loans, is associated with a relatively high value (discrete value of 1) and Non Int Exp/Avg Assets is associated with a relatively low value (discrete value of 0), this could imply the difference between a bank being classified with a 'B' (1) rating, or a 'C' (2) rating (see rule 5).

Finally, it is pertinent to note, that the rule set associated with the β-reduct $\{c_2, c_4, c_8\}$ contains no rules capable of classifying banks to the 'A' (0) and 'E' (4) grades. It is hypothesised that the β-reduct $\{c_2, c_4, c_8\}$ does not contain enough condition attributes, hence enough detail, to produce a rule set capable of distinguishing between the three well represented bank ratings 'B' (1), 'C' (2) and 'D' (3), and the under-represented bank ratings 'A' (0) and 'E' (4).

In summary, it is reasonable to assume, that the threshold value associated with the selected β-reduct $\{c_2, c_4, c_8\}$ is too low, because it lacked the capability to predict banks belonging to all five rating grades. That is, 'A' and 'E' grade banks would be classified to the other three grades. Hence, it is presumable that selecting a β-reduct whose β sub-domain is associated with a higher β threshold value, may be inclusive of rules that predict the 'A' (0) and 'E' (4) grade banks, and in addition, removes the strong rules that are as-

*Figure 8. Analysis of the β-reduct {c₂, c₄, c₈}, which has 13 associated rules*

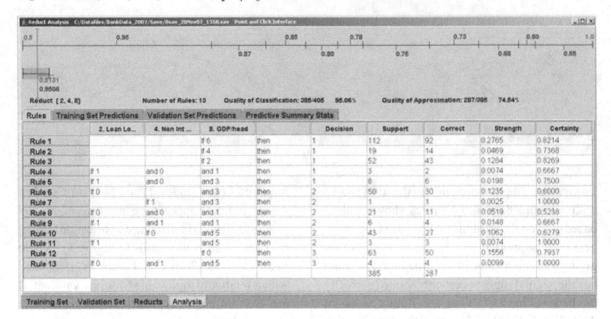

sociated with weak certainty values (such as rule 10 in Figure 8).

The developed VPRS vein graph software utilises the rules associated with a selected β-reduct, to predict both the training and the validation sets. This includes, amongst other aspects, informing the analyst to which banks were predicted by matching rules (matching their condition attribute values), and which were predicted using the nearest rule method, as described by Słowiński (1992). This section discusses these aspects in detail, beginning with the predictions made on the training set.

Within the developed VPRS software, exact values on the number of banks classified, and the predictive accuracies of the rule set on the training set, are presented through three additional information tables, within three selectable panels, namely, the 'Predictable Objects Summary Table', the 'Nearest Rule Objects Summary Table' and the 'Combined Summary Table', each of which are described next. Firstly, the 'Predictable Objects Summary Table', shown in Figure 9, displays summary information based on those banks predicted

by rules with matching values (both correctly and incorrectly).

Within Figure 9, the table shows the number of banks in the training set (405); the number of banks classified by matching rules (385), and of those banks, the number of them predicted correctly (287) and incorrectly (98). In addition, it displays as a percentage, the predictive accuracy of those 385 banks that have been predicted correctly, that is 74.54% (287/305). This 74.54% value, is equivalent to the displayed QoA (as a percentage), displayed below the "vein line" on the far right of the screenshot. This is understandable, because the predictive accuracy is based on applying the rules to the data they were constructed upon, namely the training set. Moreover, the predictive accuracy could be considered the apparent predictive accuracy on the banks that are predictable. This is an important point, because the QoA value is known prior to applying the rule set to the training set. Hence, with regards to the VPRS framework, the apparent predictive accuracy is known without the need for further calculations.

*Figure 9. Summary table for training set banks predicted by matching rules from the rule set associated with β-reduct {c₂, c₄, c₈}*

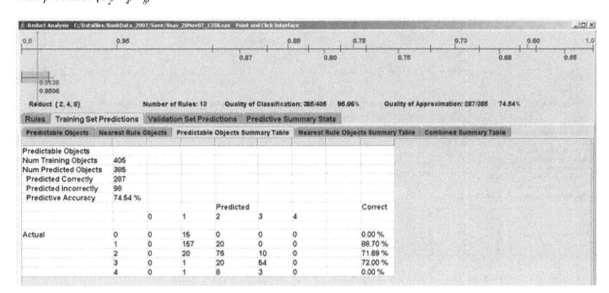

The lower portion of the table in Figure 9, displays information cross-referencing the 'Actual' decision classes (rating grades) of the banks, and the 'Predicted' decision classes of the banks, through the implementation of the confusion matrix. To describe further, 15 'A' (0) grade banks have been incorrectly classified as 'B' (1) grade banks; 157 'B' (1) grade banks have been correctly classified, but 20 have been incorrectly classified as 'C' (2) grade banks, and so forth.

The final column of this confusion matrix displays the predictive accuracies associated with each individual decision class. For example, 88.7% of the 'B' (1) grade banks have been classified correctly. These predictive accuracies play a key role in determining the performance (predictive capability) of the classifier (the β-reduct and its associated rules), because the predictive accuracy of 74.54% based on all the decision classes, does not reflect the fact that the predictive accuracies over the five individual decisions classes, predictable by the rule set, varies between 0.0% and 88.70%.

Displaying the range of predictive accuracies over all the decision classes (the confusion matrix), allows for a level of transparency which, may be lacking from, or not reported within many studies (Poon *et al.*, 1999; Oelericha and Poddig, 2006). Clearly, quoting the single overall predictive accuracy could be misleading and indeed with reference to the analysis based on the validation set (shown later), this variance between the predictive accuracies of the individual decision classes is magnified. Moreover, when dealing with an imbalanced data set, such as the FIBR data, there is a likelihood that, the well represented decision classes will be associated with a relatively high predictive accuracy, and the under-represented decision classes will be associated with a low predictive accuracy, but based on the overall predictive accuracy, the dominance of the larger well represented decision classes would mask the disparity.

A final pertinent observation, with regards to the distribution of the predicted banks within the confusion matrix shown in Figure 9, is that, 89.8% (88/98) of the incorrectly predicted banks are at most, only one decision class away from their actual decision class. This is also reflected in the later validation set analysis (see Figure 12). These banks could be border line cases, and by selecting

*Figure 10. Summary table for training set banks predicted by nearest rules from the rule set associated with β-reduct $\{c_2, c_4, c_8\}$*

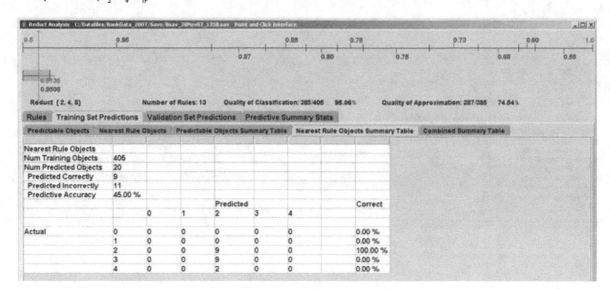

a β-reduct associated with a higher β threshold value (which typically implies the β-reduct is associated with more condition attributes, and hence, a larger more complex, potentially more accurate rule set), may allow for more banks to be correctly classified. Choosing a β-reduct with a higher β threshold value, appears to "thin out" these borderline cases, particularly with regards to the training set. This trend though, is not reflected in the later validation set analysis.

Considering next, the 'Nearest Objects Summary Table' panel as shown in Figure 10, it displays summary information based on those banks predicted, both correctly and incorrectly by the nearest rule method. The format of the table within Figure 10 is identical to that described in Figure 9. Here, there is less information displayed within the confusion matrix portion of the table, due to there being fewer banks predicted by the nearest rule method (bank which do not fit exactly the condition parts of a rule). The most interesting point to note here, is, the poor predictive performance, with only nine out of the 20 banks (45.0%) classified correctly (note they are all predicted 'B' grade banks).

With final reference to the training set predictions, the 'Combined Summary Table' panel, shown in Figure 11, displays summary information based on all the banks within the training set, that is, on both those groups of banks predicted correctly and incorrectly, by matching rules and by the nearest rule method, respectively.

The purpose of the information displayed in Figure 11 is to allow the analyst to compare the results of this VPRS analysis with other classifier methods, such as regression analysis. A major advantage the VPRS software has to offer over other classifier methods, is the ability to distinguish between, and report separately on, those banks that the rule set can and cannot predict (predicted by a matching rule and predicted by nearest rule, respectively).

Moreover, in the knowledge that the nearest rule method performs poorly on those banks the rule set does not have a matching rule for, it is likely that the analyst would rather discount those banks as unpredictable, and concentrate on those banks which the software indicates are predictable. To bring this notion back to the FIBR data, and the field of financial investments, this

*Figure 11. Summary table for training set banks predicted by matching and nearest rules from the rule set associated with β-reduct $\{c_2, c_4, c_8\}$*

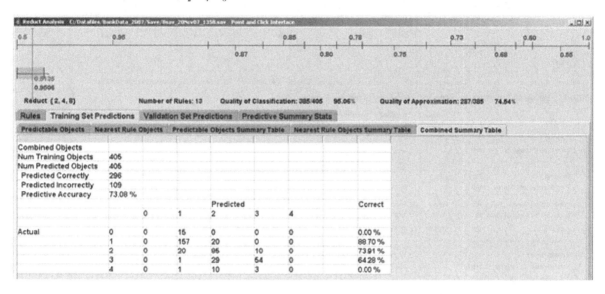

*Figure 12. Summary table for validation set banks predicted by matching rules from the rule set associated with β-reduct $\{c_2, c_4, c_8\}$*

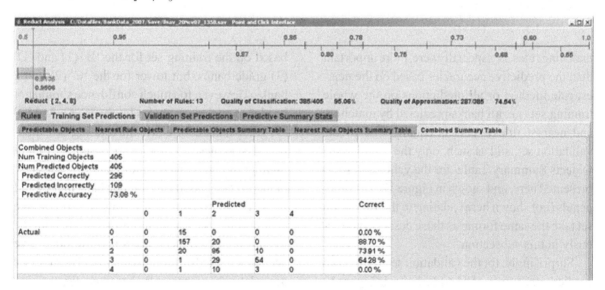

allows the analyst to "cherry pick" and invest in those banks that the VPRS systems indicates are predictable. Furthermore, having knowledge on the strength and certainty of a rule used to predict a bank, the analyst may steer away from predictions made by weaker or less certain rules. This of course, depends on the amount of risk the analyst

is willing to take and their investment strategy; for example, invest small amounts on high risk predictions, on a large scale, or large amounts on low risk predictions, on a relatively smaller scale (hedging).

As the above statement suggests, the predictive accuracies based only on the banks predicted by

*Figure 13. Summary statistics associated with the selected $\beta$-reduct $\{c_2, c_4, c_8\}$*

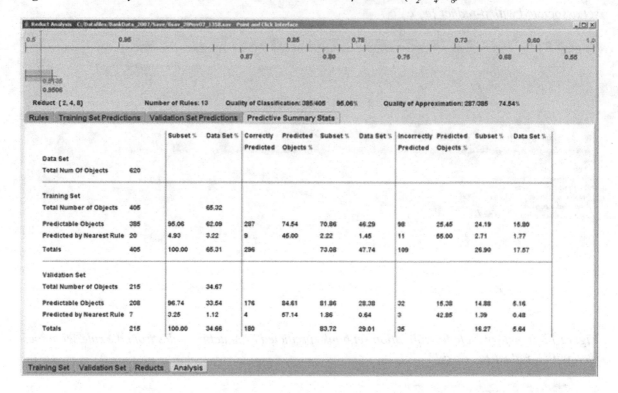

matching rules, is, especially here, more important than the predictive accuracies based on the nearest rule method or all predictions on the whole training set (i.e. all banks predicted by matching and nearest rules). This is equally true of the validation set, and as such, only the 'Predictable Objects Summary Table' for the validation set is presented here, and shown in Figure 12. The other panels (not shown here) relating to the validation set take the same format as those described previously in this subsection.

Surprisingly, for the validation set, the overall predictive accuracy of 84.61% shown in Figure 12 is higher than the predictive accuracy of 74.54% reported for the training set shown in Figure 9.

Comparing the individual predictive accuracies over the individual decision classes, between both the training and validation sets (Figures 9 and 12 respectively), based on the rule set associated with $\beta$-reduct $\{c_2, c_4, c_8\}$; the accuracies based on the validation set are higher than the accuracies

based on the training set for the 'B' (1) and 'D' (3) grade banks, but lower for the 'C' (2) grade banks. However, too much confidence should not be placed on the accuracies for the 'C' (2) and 'D' (3) grade banks, for either the training or validation sets, as these accuracies are based, on a small number of banks. That is, for example, correctly or incorrectly classifying a single bank that should be a 'D' grade bank can change the predictive accuracy by 5%. Encouragingly though, both the overall predictive accuracies and the predictive accuracies based on the individual decision classes are relatively respectable, based on the training and validation sets, and comparable with results of similar studies (Oelericha and Poddig, 2006).

Finally, as it can be observed throughout this subsection, based on the one selected $\beta$-reduct, there is a plethora of information (displayed on a number of panels), relating both to the training and validation sets for the analyst to digest. Hence, the final panel of information to be described here, summarises the more pertinent information presented within the other panels, such as, the sample sizes and overall predictive accuracies for the training and validation sets, shown here in Figure 13.

The 'Predictive Summary Stats' panel in Figure 13, allows the analyst to quickly observe the performance of a selected $\beta$-reduct, and to compare between the performance based on the training and validation sets. From experience, the summary panel is most useful at the initial stages of the analysis, when searching for $\beta$-reducts that have a good predictive accuracy on the validation set and can predict a large portion of the banks by matching rules (displayed as 'Predictable Objects' in the first column within the table in Figure 13). The analyst may then further investigate any $\beta$-reducts of interest, using the more comprehensive panels of information described throughout this section.

For the single $\beta$-reduct investigated, the predictive accuracies were as stated previously, quite respectable and comparable with other studies (Oelericha and Poddig, 2006). Although noticeably, the rule set lacked the capability to predict 'A' and 'E' grade banks.

## FUTURE RESEARCH DIRECTIONS

The level of continued research into rough set theory (RST) based analysis is clear testament to its inclusion as a constituent methodology associated with soft computing. It ability to be inclusive of uncertainty in the information in an information system, as in the case of using variable precision rough sets (VPRS), includes the allowance for misclassification of objects by rules, as well as the ability to simply not classify certain objects with any of the rules, due to the ambiguity of their classification etc.

Amongst the continued research on RST there are clear attempts to see where it fits in with other methodologies, such as fuzzy set theory (FST).

The combination of RST and FST, in theory, would certainly add increased readability to the constructed '*if.. then..*' decision rules, the result of an RST analysis. At the technical level, there is also developments on the relation type employed, away from the indiscernibility relation in RST and VPRS to a dominance relation (as in dominance based rough sets), which mitigates the level (and total need) for the 'pre-processing' discretisation often employed. Indeed, how impacting the employed pre-processing is in the RST based analyses, is an open question, requiring investigation in the future.

The presentation of results from bespoke software, enabling pre-processing and VPRS analysis does open up the question of usability of this form of analysis. Future employment of VPRS using software like this will start to answer the question about how well analysts can use this type of analysis methodology, and is a question that goes with many of the soft computing methodologies that exist.

## CONCLUSION

This chapter has presented a variable precision rough sets (VPRS) analysis of a certain Fitch Individual Bank Rating (FIBR) data set, and the accompanying pre-processing that is regularly used in this form of analysis. The developed software has been demonstrated through the selection of a single $\beta$-reduct (subset of bank attributes that classifies the banks to the same level as all the attributes), and the rules associated with that $\beta$-reduct applied to the respective training and validation sets. A number of panels of information were described (screenshots), which offered further breakdown, transparency and incite into the impact of the pre-processing undertaken and predictive accuracy results from the constructed decision rules.

The role and impact of the regularly undertaken pre-processing of data is very often understated, namely it is a stage (facility) of an analysis that an analyst would rather get through quickly to then concentrate on the real issue, in this case the employment of VPRS. There has to be an acknowledgment that the pre-processing stage(s) need to be thought through and for there to be checking instruments to see that their impact is in balance with the intended analysis which follows.

There is a clear advantage of using VPRS, or any RST based technique, namely the interpretability and readability of the constructed '*if.. then..*' decision rules, a facet of the type of non-standard analysis often associated with soft computing methodologies. It is facets like the interpretability and readability that makes the whole nuance of soft computing an exciting and evolving area within data analysis.

# REFERENCES

An, A., Shan, N., Chan, C., Cercone, N., & Ziarko, W. (1996). Discovering Rules for Water Demand Prediction: An Enhanced Rough-Set Approach. *Engineering Applications of Artificial Intelligence, 9*(6), 645–653. doi:10.1016/S0952-1976(96)00059-0

Bankscope. (2007). *Bureau van Dijk*. Retrieved from https://bankscope.bvdep.com

Beynon, M. (2001). Reducts Within the Variable Precision Rough Sets Model: A Further Investigation. *European Journal of Operational Research, 134*, 592–605. doi:10.1016/S0377-2217(00)00280-0

Beynon, M. J. (2004). The Elucidation of an Iterative Procedure to $\beta$-Reduct Selection in the Variable Precision Rough Sets Model. In S., Tsumoto, R., Slowinski, J. Komorowski, & J., W. Grzymala-Busse, (Eds.), *Rough Sets and Current Trends in Computing - Fourth International Conference on Rough Sets and Current Trends in Computing*, Uppsala, Sweden, (pp. 412-417). Berlin: Springer-Verlag.

Beynon, M., J., Clatworthy, M., A. & Jones, M., J. (2004). A Prediction of Profitability Using Accounting Narratives: A Variable Precision Rough Set Approach. *International Journal of Intelligent Systems in Accounting Finance & Management, 12*, 227–242. doi:10.1002/isaf.256

Dembczyński, K., Greco, S., Kotłowski, W., & Słowiński, R. (2007). *Statistical Model for Rough Set Approach to Multicriteria Classification* (pp. 164–175). Knowledge Discovery in Databases.

Derviz, A. & Podpiera., J. (2004). *Predicting Bank CAMELS and S&P Ratings: The Case of the Czech Republic*. Working Papers Series of the Czech National Bank.

Fayyad, M., U. & Irani B., K. (1992). Technical Note: On the Handling of Continuous-Valued Attributes in Decision Tree Generation. *Machine Learning, 8*(1), 87–102. doi:10.1007/BF00994007

Fayyad, M., U., Piatetsky-Shapiro, G. & Smyth, P. (1996). From Data Mining to Knowledge Discovery in Databases. *AI Magazine, 17*(3), 37–54.

Fitch. (2007). Retrieved from www.fitchratings.com

Frawley, W., J., Piatetsky-Shapiro, G. & Matheus, C. (1992). Knowledge Discovery In Databases: An Overview. *AI Magazine, 13*(3), 57–70.

Han, J., & Kamber, M. (2006). *Data Mining: Concepts and Techniques*. San Francisco: Morgan Kaufmann.

Ilczuk, G., & Wakulicz-Deja, A. (2007). Selection of Important Attributes for Medical Diagnosis Systems. In Peters, F. J., & Skowron, A. (Eds.), *Transactions on Rough Sets, 7* (pp. 70–84). Berlin: Springer-Verlag. doi:10.1007/978-3-540-71663-1_5

Israel, G. D. (2007). *Determining Sample Size. Institute of Food and Agricultural Sciences*. Gainesville, FL: University of Florida.

Johnson, R., & Wichern, D. (2007). *Applied Multivariate Statistical Analysis*. Upper Saddle River, NJ: Pearson.

Katzberg, J. D., & Ziarko, W. (1996). Variable Precision Extension of Rough Sets. *FundamentaInformaticae, 27*, 155–168.

Kononenko, I. (1994). Estimating Attributes: Analysis and Extensions of RELIEF. In *Proceedings of the 1994 European Conference on Machine Learning*, (pp. 171-182).

Kosmidou, K., Pasiouras, F., Zopounidis, C., & Doumpos, M. (2006). A Multivariate Analysis of the Financial Characteristics of Foreign and Domestic Banks in the UK. *Omega, 34*(2), 189–195. doi:10.1016/j.omega.2004.10.002

Linoff, G. (1998). *Which Way to the Mine?* (pp. 42–44). Systems Management.

Liu, H., & Motoda, H. (2000). *Feature Selection for Knowledge Discovery and Data Mining*. Amsterdam: Kluwer Academic Publishers.

Mi, J., Wu, W., & Zhang, W. (2004). Approaches to Knowledge Reduction Based on Variable Precision Rough Set Model. *Information Sciences, 159*, 255–272. doi:10.1016/j.ins.2003.07.004

Mitra, S., Pal, S. K., & Mitra, P. (2002). Data Mining in Soft Computing Framework: A Survey. *IEEE Transactions on Neural Networks, 13*(1), 3–14. doi:10.1109/72.977258

Naisbitt, J. (1984). *Megatrends: Ten New Directions Transforming Our Lives*. London: Macdonald & Co.

Oelericha, A., & Poddig, T. (2006). Evaluation of Rating Systems. *Expert Systems with Applications, 30*(3), 437–447. doi:10.1016/j.eswa.2005.10.004

Pasiouras, F., Gaganis, C., & Zopoundis, C. (2006). The Impact of Bank Regulations, Supervision, Market Structure, and Bank Characteristics on Individual Bank Ratings: A Cross-Country Analysis. *Review of Quantitative Finance and Accounting, 27*, 403–438. doi:10.1007/s11156-006-0045-0

Pawlak, Z. (1982). Rough Sets. *International Journal of Computer and System Sciences, 11*, 341–356.

Pawlak, Z. (1991). *Rough Sets: Theoretical Aspects of Reasoning about Data*. Amsterdam: Kluwer Academic Publishers.

Piatetsky-Shapiro, G. (2000). Knowledge Discovery in Databases: 10 Years After. *SIGKDD Explorations. Newsletter, 1*(2), 59–61.

Poon, W., P., H., Firth, M. & Fung, H. (1999). A Multivariate Analysis of the Determinants of Moody's Bank Financial Strength Ratings. *Journal of International Financial Markets, Institutions and Money, 9*(3), 267–283. doi:10.1016/S1042-4431(99)00011-6

Poon, W., P., H. (2003). Are Unsolicited Credit Ratings Biased Downward? *Journal of Banking & Finance, 27*(4), 593–614. doi:10.1016/S0378-4266(01)00253-9

Poon, W., P., H. & Firth, M. (2005). Are Unsolicited Credit Ratings Lower? International Evidence From Bank Ratings. *Journal of Business Finance & Accounting, 32*(9-10), 1741–1771.

Raymond, R., C. (1966). Use of the Time-sharing Computer in Business Planning and Budgeting. *Management Science, 12*(8), B363–B381. doi:10.1287/mnsc.12.8.B363

Sahajwala, R., & Van den Bergh, P. (2000). Supervisory Risk Assessment and Early Warning Systems. *BASEL Committee on Banking Supervision Working Papers Working papers 4,* Bank for International Settlements.

Tay, F., Shen, L., & Cao, L. (2003). *Ordinary Shares, Exotic Methods: Financial Forecasting Using Data Mining Techniques.* Singapore: World Scientific. doi:10.1142/9789812791375

Van Roy, P. (2006). Is There a Difference Between Solicited and Unsolicited Bank Ratings and if so, Why? *National Bank of Belgium, Research Series*, 200603-1.

Weiss, S. M. & Kulikowski, C., A. (1991). Computer Systems that Learn: Classification and Prediction Methods from Statistics, Neaural Nets, Machine Learning, and Expert Systems. San Francisco: Morgan Kaufmann.

Ziarko, W. (1993a). Variable Precision Rough Set Model. *Journal of Computer and System Sciences*, *46*, 39–59. doi:10.1016/0022-0000(93)90048-2

Ziarko, W. (1993b). Analysis of Uncertain Information in the Framework of Variable Precision Rough Set. *Foundations of Computing and Decision Sciences*, *18*, 381–396.

Ziarko, W. (2003). Evaluation of Probabilistic Decision Tables. In G. Wang, et al. (Eds.), *Rough Sets, Fuzzy Sets, Data Mining, and Granular Computing, 9th International Conference, RSFDGrC'03* (189-196). Berlin: Springer-Verlag.

Zighed, D. A., Rabaséda, S., & Rakotomalala, R. (1998). FUSINTER: A method for Discretization of Continuous Attributes. *International Journal of Uncertainty. Fuzziness and Knowledge-Based Systems*, *6*(3), 307–326. doi:10.1142/S0218488598000264

Zorn, T. E. & Taylor, J., R. (2003). Knowledge Management and/as Organizational Communication. In D. Tourish & O. Hargie (eds.), Key Issues in Organizational Communication. London: Routledge.

## ADDITIONAL READING

Altman, E., & Avery, R., B., Eisenbeis, R., A. & Sinkey, J., F., Jr. (1981). Application of Classification Techniques in Business, Banking and Finance. *Journal of Money, Credit and Banking*, *15*(4), 532–535.

Arabie, P., & Hubert, L. J. & De Soete, G. (1996). Clustering and Classification. World Scientific.

Bell, M., Z. (1985). Why Expert Systems Fail. *The Journal of the Operational Research Society*, *36*(7), 613–619.

Brachman, R., Khabaza, T., Kloesgen, W., Piatesky-Shapiro, G., & Simoudis, E. (1996). Mining Business Databases. *Communications of the ACM*, *39*(11), 42–48. doi:10.1145/240455.240468

Brachmann, R., Malsch, T., & Ziegler, S. (1993). Success and Failure of Expert Systems in Different Fields of Industrial Application. In: Ohlbach, H. J. (Ed.). *Proceedings of the 16th German Conference on Artificial intelligence: Advances in Artificial intelligence*, 671, 77-86.

Chmielewski, M., R. & Grzymala-Busse, J., W. (1996). Global Discretization of Continuous Attributes as Preprocessing for Machine Learning. *International Journal of Approximate Reasoning*, *15*, 319–331. doi:10.1016/S0888-613X(96)00074-6

Dietterich, T., G. (1997). Machine Learning Research: Four Current Directions. *AI Magazine*, *18*(4), 97–136.

Dougherty, J., Kohavi, R., & Sahami, M. (1995). Supervised and Unsupervised Discretization of Continuous Features. In: *Proceedings of the 12th International Conference on Machine Learning*, Morgan Kaufmann, Tahoe City, CA, 194-202.

Greco, S., Matarazzo, B., & Słowiński, R. (2001). Rough Sets Theory for Multicriteria Decision Analysis. *European Journal of Operational Research*, *129*, 1–47. doi:10.1016/S0377-2217(00)00167-3

Grzymala-Busse, J., Stefanowski, J., & Wilk, S. (2005). Comparison of Two Approaches to Data Mining from Imbalanced Data. *Journal of Intelligent Manufacturing, 16*(6), 565–573. doi:10.1007/s10845-005-4362-2

Holte, R., C. (1993). Very Simple Classification Rules Perform Well on Most Commonly Used Datasets. *Machine Learning, 11*, 63–91. doi:10.1023/A:1022631118932

Kantardzic, M. (2003). *Data Mining: Concepts, Models, Methods and Algorithms*. U.S.A.: Wiley-Interscience.

Larose, D. T. (2005). Discovering Knowledge in Data: An Introduction to Data Mining. Wiley, U.S.A.

Liu, H., Hussain, F., & Tan, C., L. & Dash, M. (2002a). Discretization: An Enabling Technique. *Data Mining and Knowledge Discovery, 6*(4), 393–423. doi:10.1023/A:1016304305535

Pal, S., K. & Skowron, A. (1999). *Rough Fuzzy Hybridization: A New Trend in Decision-Making*. Springer-Verlag Telos.

Robnik-Šikonja, M., & Kononenko, I. (2003). Theoretical and Empirical Analysis of ReliefF and RReliefF. *Machine Learning, 53*(1-2), 23–69. doi:10.1023/A:1025667309714

Ślęzak, D. (2004). The Rough Bayesian Model for Distributed Decision Systems. In: Tsumoto, S., Słowiński, R., Komorowski, J. and Grzymala-Busse, J., W. (eds.), *Rough Sets and Current Trends in Computing. Fourth International Conference on Rough Sets and Current Trends in Computing*, Uppsala, Sweden, Springer-Verlag, Berlin Heidelberg, 384-393.

Słowiński, R. (1992). *Intelligent Decision Support: Handbook of Applications and Advances in Rough Set Theory*. Dordrecht: Kluwer Academic Publishers.

Weiss, S. M. & Indurkhya, N. (1998). Predictive Data Mining: A practical Guide. Morgan Kaufmann, California U.S.A.

West, R., R. (1970). An Alternative Approach to Predicting Corporate Bond Ratings. *Journal of Accounting Research, 8*(1), 118–125. doi:10.2307/2674717

## KEY TERMS AND DEFINITIONS

**Discretisation:** The general stage of pre-processing that intervalises a continuous attribute, categorising the attribute values into a number of intervals. A number of techniques are available to perform this.

**Equivalence Classes:** The grouping of objects based on having the same condition (condition classes) or decision (decision classes) attribute values within an information system (decision table).

**Feature Selection:** The general stage of pre-processing that offers a quantification of the relative importance/relevance of condition attributes within an information system (decision table). A number of techniques are available to perform this.

**Indiscernibility Relation:** Within rough set theory, the mathematical relation used to group objects in an information system (decision table), based on their condition or decision attribute values.

**Reduct:** Within rough set theory, the subset of condition attributes which has the same classification level as the whole set of condition attributes (the same quality of classification)

**Rough Set Theory:** The general set-theoretical methodology for rule based object classification of objects in an information system (decision table).

**Variable Precision Rough Sets:** Development on rough set theory, which allows for misclassification in the decision rules constructed.

# Chapter 12

# Interconnecting a Class of Machine Learning Algorithms with Logical Commonsense Reasoning Operations

**Xenia Nadenova**
*Military Medical Academy, Russia*

## ABSTRACT

*The purpose of this chapter is to demonstrate the possibility of transforming a large class of machine learning algorithms into commonsense reasoning processes based on using well-known deduction and induction logical rules. The concept of a good classification (diagnostic) test for a given set of positive examples lies in the basis of our approach to the machine learning problems. The task of inferring all good diagnostic tests is formulated as searching the best approximations of a given classification (a partitioning) on a given set of examples. The lattice theory is used as a mathematical language for constructing good classification tests. The algorithms of good tests inference are decomposed into subtasks and operations that are in accordance with main human commonsense reasoning rules.*

## INTRODUCTION

### Background

The development of a full on-line computer model for integrating deductive and inductive reasoning is of great interest in machine learning. The main tendency of integration is to combine into a whole system some already well-known models of learning (inductive reasoning) and deductive reasoning. For instance, the idea of combining inductive learning

from examples with prior knowledge and default reasoning has been advanced in (Giraud-Carrier & Martinez, 1994). Obviously, this way leads to a lot of difficulties in knowledge representation because deductive reasoning tasks are often expressed in the classical first-order logic language (FOL) but machine learning tasks use a variant of simbolic-valued attribute language (AVL).

The principle of "aggregating" different models of human thinking for constructing intelligent computer systems leads to dividing the whole process into two separate modes: learning and execution or deductive reasoning. This division is used, for

DOI: 10.4018/978-1-60566-814-7.ch012

example, in (Zakrevskij, 2006). This approach is based on using finite spaces of Boolean or multi-valued attributes for modeling natural subject areas. It combines inductive inference used for extracting knowledge from data with deductive inference (the type of theorem proving) for solving pattern recognition problems. The inductive inference is reduced to looking for empty (forbidden) intervals of Boolean space of attributes describing a given set of positive examples. The deductive inference relates to the situation when an object is contemplated with known values of some attributes and unknown values of some others, including a goal attribute. The possible values of the latter ones are to be calculated based on implicative regularities in the Boolean space of attributes. The fundamental unified model for combining inductive reasoning with deductive reasoning is developed in the framework of Inductive Logic Programming (ILP). ILP is a discipline that investigates the inductive construction of first-order clausal theories from examples and background knowledge. ILP has the same goal as machine learning, namely, to develop tools and techniques to induce hypotheses from examples and to obtain new knowledge from experience. But the traditional theoretical basis of ILP is in the framework of first-order predicate calculus.

Inductive inference in ILP is based on inverting deductive inference rules; for example, inverting resolution (rules of absorption, identification, intraconstruction, and interconstruction), inverting implication (inductive inference under θ-subsumption).

There is a distinction between concept learning and program synthesis. Concept learning and classification problems, in general, are inherently object-oriented. It is difficult to interpret concepts as subsets of domain examples in the frameworks of ILP. One of the ways to overcome this difficulty has been realized in a transformation approach: an ILP task is transformed into an equivalent learning task in different representation formalism. This approach is realized in LINUS (Lavrâc

& Džeroski, 1994), (Lavrâc et al, 1999) which is an ILP learner inducing hypotheses in the form of constrained deductive hierarchical database (DHDB) clauses. The main idea of LINUS is to transform the problem of learning relational DHDB descriptions into the attribute-value learning task. This is achieved by the so-called DHDB interface. The interface transforms the training examples from the DHDB form into the form of attribute-value tuples. Some well known attribute-value learners can then be used to induce "if-then" rules. Finally, the induced rules are transformed back into the form of DHDB clauses. The LINUS uses already known algorithms, for example, the decision tree induction system ASSISTANT, and two rule induction systems: an ancestor of AQ15, named NEWGEM, and CN2.

A simple form of predicate invention through first-order feature construction is proposed by Lavrâc and Flash (2000). The constructed features are used then for propositional learning.

Another way for combining ILP with an attribute-value learner has been developed in (Lisi & Malerba, 2004). In this work, a novel ILP setting is proposed. This setting adopts AL-log as a knowledge representation language. It allows a unified treatment of both the relational and structural features of data. This setting has been implemented in SPADA, an ILP system developed for mining multi-level association rules in spatial databases and applied to geographic data mining.

AL-log is a hybrid knowledge representation system that integrates the description logic ALC (Schmidt-Schauss & Smolka, 1991) and the deductive database language DATALOG (Ceri & Tanca, 1990). Therefore it embodies two subsystems, called structural and relational, respectively.

The description logic ALC allows for the specification of structural knowledge in terms of concepts, roles, and individuals. Individuals represent objects in the domain of interest. Concepts represent classes of these objects, while roles represent binary relations between concepts. Complex concepts can be defined from primitive concepts and roles by applying constructors such as ∩ (conjunction), ∪ (disjunction), and ¬ (negation).

ALC knowledge bases have an intensional part and an extensional part. In the intensional part, relations between concepts are syntactically expressed as inclusion statements of the form $C \subseteq D$ where $C$ and $D$ are two arbitrary concepts. As for the extensional part, it is possible to specify instances of relations between individuals and concepts. Relations are expressed as membership assertions, for example concept assertions of the form "$a$: $C$" ("$a$ belongs to $C$").

The formal model of conceptual reasoning based on an algebraic lattice has been obtained in two independent ways. One way goes back to the works of great psychologist J. Piaget who introduced the concept of grouping (Piaget, 1959) to explain methods of object classification used mainly by 7-11 - years-old children.

The idea of concepts' classification as a lattice arose from practical tasks of developing information retrieval and pattern recognition systems. Boldyrev N. (1974) advanced the formalization of pattern recognition system as algebra with two binary operations of refinement and generalization defined by an axiom system including lattice axioms. The ideas of Boldyrev have been used often for minimization of Boolean partial functions with a large number of "Don't Care" conditions, but we have been interested, from the beginning of our investigation, in applying the lattice theory for feature extraction and classification of attribute-value's tuples, and later, -of concepts (symbols, names...).

The Formal Concept Analysis (FCA) based on the concept lattice has been advanced by Wille, R. (1992). The problems of the FCA have been extensively studied by Stumme et al. (2000), Dowling (1993), Salzberg (1991). Some algorithms for building concept lattices are considered in (Nourine & Raynaud, 1999), (Ganter, 1984), (Kuznetsov, 1993), and (Kuznetsov & Obiedkov, 2001).

A lot of experience has been obtained on the application of algebraic lattices in machine learning. From this point of view, the JSM-method of reasoning (Finn, 1984), (Finn, 1991), (Finn, 1988), (Finn, 1999) is interesting.

The JSM-method of hypotheses' automatic generation formalizes a special class of plausible reasoning. The technique of this method is a synthesis of several cognitive procedures: empirical induction based on modeling John S. Mill's joint rule of similarity-distinction (Mill, 1900), causal analogy and Charles S. Peirce's abduction.

Similarity in the JSM-method is both a relation and an operation that is idempotent, commutative and associative (i.e., it induces a semi-lattice on objects' descriptions and their generalizations). Being described in algebraic terms, the JSM-method can be implemented in the procedural programming languages.

In (Galitsky et al., 2005), the system JASMINE based on the JSM-method is presented. The system extends this methodology by implementing (i) a combination of abductive, inductive and analogical reasoning for hypotheses generation, and (ii) multivalued logic-based deductive reasoning for verification of their consistency. Formally, all the above components can be represented as deductive inference via logic programming (Anshakov et al., 1989), (Finn, 1999). In fact, JASMINE is based on the logic programming implementation (Vinogradov, 1999).

The purpose of this work is to show that one class of machine learning algorithms can be transformed into the process of integral reasoning, where different rules (deductive, inductive, abductive, traductive, etc.) alternate and support each other. These are mental acts that can be found in any reasoning: stating new propositions, choosing the relevant part of knowledge and/or data for further steps of reasoning, involving a new rule of reasoning (deductive, abductive, inductive, traductive, etc.).

The concept acts as the principal "atom" in commonsense reasoning. This reasoning is based on the knowledge system, with objects, properties (values of attributes) and classifications (attributes) being its elements. If we take into account that implications express relations between concepts (object ↔ class, object ↔ property, property ↔ class), we can assume that schemes of inferring and applying implications (rules of the "if → then" type) form the core of classification processes, which, in turn, form the basis of commonsense reasoning. Deductive steps of commonsense reasoning imply using known facts and statements of the "if → then" type to infer consequences from them. To do it, we apply deductive rules of inference, the main forms of which are modus ponens, modus tollens, modus ponendo tollens and modus tollendo ponens. Inductive steps imply applying known facts and existing knowledge to infer new implicational statements and correct those that turned out to be in contradiction with the existing knowledge. These steps rely on inductive rules of reasoning represented by inductive canons stated in (Mill, 1900). These canons are known as five inductive methods, viz. the Methods of Agreement, the Method of Difference, the Joint Method of Agreement and Difference, the Methods of Residues, and the Method of Concomitant Variations.

Our approach to machine learning problems is based on the concept of a good diagnostic (classification) test. This concept has been advanced firstly in the framework of inferring functional and implicative dependencies from relations (Naidenova & Polegaeva, 1986). But later, the fact has been revealed that the task of inferring all good diagnostic tests for a given set of positive and negative examples can be formulated as the search for the best approximation of a given classification on a given set of examples and that it is this task that some well- known machine-learning problems can be reduced to (Naidenova, 1996): finding keys and functional dependencies in data base relations, finding association rules, finding implicative dependencies, inferring logical rules (if-then rules, rough sets, "ripple down" rules),

decision tree construction, learning by discovering concept hierarchies, eliminating irrelevant features from the set of exhaustively generated features.

We consider the theory of mathematical lattices as a mathematical language for constructing algorithms of inferring good classification tests. The advantage of an algebraic lattice is that, being an algebraic structure, it can be described by algebraic expressions (by declarations) and, at the same time, by dual operations (procedures), which generate elements of the lattice and relations between them.

At present, many researchers use algebraic lattices to represent data or knowledge in algorithms. In this connection, the following works can be noted: inductive inference of concepts (Ganascia, 1989), conceptual clustering (Carpineto & Romano, 1996), mining conceptual knowledge (Stumme et al., 1998), (Nguifo & Njiwoua, 1998). The following works are devoted to the application of algebraic lattices for extracting functional and implicative dependencies from data: (Demetrovics & Vu, 1993), (Mannila & Räihä, 1992), (Mannila & Räihä, 1994), (Huntala, et al., 1999), (Cosmadakis, et al., 1986), (Naidenova & Polegaeva, 1986), (Megretskaya, 1988), (Naidenova, et al., 1995a), (Naidenova, et al., 1995b), (Naidenova, 1992), (Naidenova, 2001).

In this work, we use the concept of inductive transition introduced in (Naidenova, 2006) that helps generate all nearest elements for any element of the algebraic lattice. The detailed analysis of algorithms of searching for all good tests in terms of constructing the algebraic lattice allowed us not only to determine the structure of inferences but also to decompose algorithms into sub-problems and operations that represent known deductive and inductive modes of reasoning.

This chapter is organized as follows. In Section 2, we describe the forms of an expert's rules (rules of the first type). These rules can be represented with the use of only one class of logical rules based on implicative dependencies between concepts (names). Then we describe commonsense reasoning operations (deductive and inductive) or rules of the second type. In Section 3, the concept of a good diagnostic test is introduced and the problem of inferring all good diagnostic tests for a given classification on a given set of examples is formulated. Section 4 contains the description of the mathematical model underlying algorithms of inferring good tests from examples. This model allows demonstrating that the inferring of good tests entails applying deductive and inductive commonsense reasoning rules of the second type. Section 5 proposes a decomposition of learning algorithms into operations and subtasks with the use of which good diagnostic tests inferring is transformed into an incremental process. The concepts of an essential value and an essential example are also introduced. We describe an incremental learning algorithm DIAGaRa and an approach to incremental inferring good diagnostic tests. The paper ends with a brief summary section.

## THE LOGICAL REASONING RULES

We need the following three types of rules in order to realize logical inference (deductive and inductive):

- **Instances** or relationships between objects or facts really observed. Instance can be considered as a logical rule with the least degree of generalization. On the other hand, instances can serve as a source of a training set of positive and negative examples for inductive inference of generalized rules.
- **Rules of the First Type** or logical rules. These rules describe regular relationships between objects and their properties and between properties of different objects. The rules of the first type can be given explicitly by an expert or derived automatically from examples with the help of some learning

process. These rules are represented in the form "if-then" assertions.
- **Rules of the Second Type** or inference rules with the help of which rules of the first type are used, updated, and inferred from data (instances) and background or already inferred knowledge. The rules of the second type embrace both inductive and deductive reasoning rules.

## The Rules of the First Type

The rules of the first type can be represented with the use of only one class of logical statements, namely, the statements based on implicative dependencies between names. Names are used for designating concepts, things, events, situations, or any evidences. They can be considered as attributes' values in the formal representations of logical rules. In our further consideration, the letters A, B, C, D, a, b, c, d will be used as attributes' values in logical rules.

We consider the following rules of the first type:

- **Implication:** $a, b, c \rightarrow d$. This rule means that if the values standing on the left side of the rule are simultaneously true, then the value on the right side of the rule is always true.
- **Interdiction or forbidden rule:** (a special case of implication) $a, b, c \rightarrow false$ (*never*). This rule interdicts a combination of values enumerated on the left side of the rule. The rule of interdiction can be transformed into several implications such as $a, b \rightarrow$ not $c$; $a, c \rightarrow$ not $b$; $b, c \rightarrow$ not $a$.
- **Compatibility:** $a, b, c \rightarrow VA$, where $VA = \{$*very rarely, rarely, …, frequently, very frequently*$\}$ is the frequency of occurrence of the rule. Experts in many research areas use this rule to show the following observation: "values in the left-hand side of the rule do not always exist simultaneously but can occur rather frequently (seldom)".

Generally, the compatibility rule represents the most common combination of values characterized by an insignificant number of exceptions (contrary examples) from the regularity or the rule that is met always. Compatibility is equivalent to a collection of assertions as follows: $a, b \rightarrow c$ *VA*; $a, c \rightarrow b$ *VA*; $b, c \rightarrow b$ *VA*.

- **Diagnostic rule:** $x, d \rightarrow a$; $x, b \rightarrow$ not $a$; $d, b \rightarrow false$. For example, $d$ and $b$ can be two values of the same attribute. This rule works when the truth of '$x$' has been proven and it is necessary to determine whether '$a$' is true or not. If '$x$ & $d$' is true, then '$a$' is true, but if '$x$ & $b$' is true, then '$a$' is false.

- **Rule of alternatives:** $a$ or $b \rightarrow true$ (*always*); $a, b \rightarrow false$. This rule says that $a$ and $b$ cannot be simultaneously true, either $a$ or $b$ can be true but not both. This rule is a variant of interdiction.

## Deductive Reasoning Rules of the Second Type

Deductive steps of commonsense reasoning consist of inferring consequences from some observed facts with the use of statements of the form "if-then" (i.e. knowledge). For this goal, deductive rules of reasoning are applied the main forms of which are modus ponens, modus tollens, modus ponendo tollens, and modus tollendo ponens.

Suppose $x$ is a totality of true values of some attributes (or evidences) (values, in what follows) observed simultaneously. We consider first-type rules used in deductive inferences:

- **Using implication:** Let $r$ be an implication, left($r$) be the left part of $r$ and right($r$) be the right part of $r$. If left($r$) $\subseteq x$, then $x$ can be extended by right($r$): $x \leftarrow x \cup$ right($r$). Using implication is based on modus ponens: if $A$, then $B$; $A$; hence $B$.

- **Using interdiction:** Let $r$ be an implication $y \rightarrow$ not $k$. If left($r$) $\subseteq x$, then $k$ is a

forbidden value for all the extensions of $x$. Using interdiction is based on modus ponendo tollens: either $A$ or $B$ ($A$, $B$ – alternatives); $A$; hence not $B$; either $A$ or $B$; $B$; hence not $A$.

- **Using compatibility:** Let $r =$ '$a, b, c \rightarrow k$, *VA*', where *VA* is the value of a special attribute. If left($r$) $\subseteq x$, then $k$ can be used for an extension of $x$ along with the calculated value *VA* for this extension. Calculating the estimate *VA* requires special consideration. In any case, to do this, we need the function which would be monotonous, continuous and bounded above.

- Using compatibility is based on modus ponens.

- **Using diagnostic rules:** Let $r$ be a diagnostic rule such as '$x, d \rightarrow a$; $x, b \rightarrow$ not $a$', where '$x$' is true, and '$a$', 'not $a$' are hypotheses or possible values of some attribute. Using a diagnostic rule is based on modus ponens and modus ponendo tollens. There are several ways for refuting one of the hypotheses:

  1. To infer either $d$ or $b$ with the use of one's knowledge;

  2. To involve new known facts and/or statements for inferring (with the use of inductive reasoning rules of the second type) new rules of the first type for distinguishing the hypotheses '$a$' and 'not $a$'; to apply these new rules;

  3. To get, from an observation, which of the values $d$ or $b$ is true?

- **Using rule of alternatives:** Let '$a$' and '$b$' be two alternative hypotheses about the value of some attribute. If one of these hypotheses is inferred with the help of reasoning operations, then the other one is rejected. Using a rule of alternatives is based on modus tollendo ponens: either $A$ or $B$ ($A$, $B$ – alternatives); not $A$; hence $B$; either $A$ or $B$; not $B$; hence $A$. The operations enumerated can be named as "forward reasoning" rules. Experts also use implicative assertions in a different way. This way can be named as "backward reasoning".

- **Generating hypothesis or abduction rule**. Let $r$ be an implication $y \rightarrow k$. Then the following hypothesis is generated "if $k$ is true, then it is possible that $y$ is true".

- **Using modus tollens**. Let $r$ be an implication $y \rightarrow k$. If 'not $k$' is inferred, then 'not $y$' is also inferred.

Natural diagnostic reasoning is not any method of proving the truth. It has another goal: to infer all possible hypotheses about the value of some target attribute. These hypotheses must not contradict with the expert's knowledge and the situation under consideration (evidences). The process of inferring hypotheses is reduced to extending maximally a collection $x$ of attribute values such that none of the forbidden pairs of values would belong to the extension of $x$.

## Inductive Reasoning Rules of the Second Type

Inductive steps of commonsense reasoning consist of using already known facts and statements, observations, and experience for inferring new logical rules of the first type or correcting those that turn out to be false.

For this goal, inductive reasoning rules are applied. The main forms of induction are the canons of induction that have been formulated by English logician Mill (1900). These canons are known as the five induction methods of reasoning: the Method of Agreement, the Method of Difference, the Joint Method of Agreement and Difference, the Method of Residues, and the Method Concomitant Variations:

- **The Method of Agreement**: This rule means that if the previous events (values) $A$, $B$, $C$ lead to the events (values) $a$, $b$, $c$ and the events (values) $A$, $D$, $E$ lead to the events (values) $a$, $d$, $e$, then $A$ is a plausible reason of $a$.

- **The Method of Difference**: This rule means that if the previous events (values) $A$, $B$, $C$ lead to (or give rise to) the events (values) $a$, $b$, $c$ and the events (values) $B$, $C$ lead to the events (values) $b$, $c$, then $A$ is a plausible reason of $a$.

- **The Joint Method of Agreement and Difference**: This method consists of applying two previous methods simultaneously.

- **The Method of Residues**: Let $U$ be a complex phenomenon $abcd$ and we know that $A$ is the reason of $a$, $B$ is the reason of $b$, and $C$ is the reason of $c$. Then it is possible to suppose that there is an event $D$ that is a reason of $d$.

- **The Method of Concomitant Variations**: This rule means that if the change of a previous event (value) $A$ is accompanied by the change of an event (value) $a$, and all the other previous events (values) do not change, then $A$ is a plausible reason of $a$.

## THE CONCEPT OF A GOOD DIAGNOSTIC TEST

Our approach to machine-learning problems is based on the concept of a good diagnostic (classification) test. A good classification test can be understood as an approximation of a given classification on a given set of examples (Naidenova & Polegaeva, 1986; Naidenova, 1996).

Let $S = \{1, 2,..., N\}$ be the set of objects' indices (objects, for short) and $T = \{A_1, A_2, ..., A_j, ...A_m\}$ be the set of attributes' values (values, for short). Each object is described by a collection of values from $T$.

The definition of good tests is based on correspondences of Galois G on $S \times T$ and two relations $S \rightarrow T$, $T \rightarrow S$ (Ore, 1944; Riguet, 1948; Everett, 1944). Let $s \subseteq S$, $t \subseteq T$. Denote by $t_i$, $t_i \subseteq T$, $i = 1,..., N$ the description of object with index $i$. We define the relations $S \rightarrow T$, $T \rightarrow S$ as follows: $S \rightarrow T$: $t = \mathrm{val}(s) = \{$intersection of all $t_i$: $t_i \subseteq T$, $i \in s\}$ and $T \rightarrow S$: $s = \mathrm{obj}(t) = \{i: i \in S, t \subseteq t_i\}$. Of course, we have $\mathrm{obj}(t) = \{$intersection of all $s(A)$: $s(A) \subseteq S$, $A \in t\}$.

Operations $\mathrm{val}(s)$, $\mathrm{obj}(t)$ are reasoning operations related to discovering the general feature of objects the indices of which belong to $s$ and to discovering the indices of all objects possessing the feature $t$.

These operations possess the following properties (Birkhoff, 1954):

1. $s_1 \subseteq s_2 \Rightarrow \mathrm{val}(s_2) \subseteq \mathrm{val}(s_1)$ for all $s_1, s_2 \subseteq S$;
2. $t_1 \subseteq t_2 \Rightarrow \mathrm{obj}(t_2) \subseteq \mathrm{obj}(t_1)$ for all $t_1, t_2 \subseteq T$;
3. $s \subseteq \mathrm{obj}(\mathrm{val}(s))$ & $\mathrm{val}(s) = \mathrm{val}(\mathrm{obj}(\mathrm{val}(s)))$ for all $s \subseteq S$;
4. $t \subseteq \mathrm{val}(\mathrm{obj}(t))$ & $\mathrm{obj}(t) = \mathrm{obj}(\mathrm{val}(\mathrm{obj}(t)))$ for all $t \subseteq T$;
5. $\mathrm{val}(\cup s_j) = \cap \mathrm{val}(s_j)$ for all $s_j \subseteq S$; $\mathrm{obj}(\cup t_j) = \cap \mathrm{obj}(t_j)$ for all $t_j \subseteq T$.

The properties (1), (2) related to extending collections $s$, $t$ as reasoning operations.

Extending $s$ by an index $j^*$ of some new object leads to receiving a more general feature of objects:

$(s \cup j^*) \supseteq s$ implies $\mathrm{val}(s \cup j^*) \subseteq \mathrm{val}(s)$.

Extending $s$ by an index $j^*$ of some new object is an elementary step of generalization.

Extending $t$ by a new value $A$ leads to decreasing the number of objects possessing the general feature '$tA$' in comparison with the number of objects possessing the general feature '$t$':

$(t \cup A) \supseteq t$ implies $\mathrm{obj}(t \cup A) \subseteq \mathrm{obj}(t)$.

Extending $t$ by a new value $A$ is an elementary step of specialization.

Extending $t$ or $s$ is effectively used for finding classification tests, so the property (v) is very important to control the domain of searching for tests. In order to choose a new collection $(s_i \cup j)$

such that $\mathrm{val}(s_i \cup j) \neq \emptyset$ it is necessary to choose $j, j \in /s_i$ such that the condition $(\mathrm{val}(s_i) \cap t_j) \neq \emptyset$ is satisfied. Analogously, in order to choose a new collection $(t_i \cup A)$ such that $obj(t_i \cup A) \neq \emptyset$ it is necessary to choose $A$, $A \in /t_i$ such that the condition $(obj(t_i) \cap obj(A)) \neq \emptyset$ is satisfied.

The properties (iii), (iv) relate to the following generalization operations (functions):

$\mathrm{generalization\_of}(t) = t' = \mathrm{val}(\mathrm{obj}(t))$;
$\mathrm{generalization\_of}(s) = s' = \mathrm{obj}(\mathrm{val}(s))$.

The sequence of operations $t \rightarrow \mathrm{obj}(t) \rightarrow \mathrm{val}(\mathrm{obj}(t))$ gives that $\mathrm{val}(\mathrm{obj}(t)) \supseteq t$. This generalization operation gives the maximal general feature for objects the indices of which are in $\mathrm{obj}(t)$.

The sequence of operations $s \rightarrow \mathrm{val}(s) \rightarrow \mathrm{obj}(\mathrm{val}(s))$ gives that $\mathrm{obj}(\mathrm{val}(s)) \supseteq s$. This generalization operation gives the maximal set of objects possessing the feature $\mathrm{val}(s)$.

The generalization operations are actually closure operators (Ore, 1980). A set $s$ is closed if $s = \mathrm{obj}(\mathrm{val}(s))$. A set $t$ is closed if $t = \mathrm{val}(\mathrm{obj}(t))$.

These generalization operations are not artificially constructed operations. One can perform, mentally, a lot of such operations during a short period of time. We give an example of these operations. Suppose that somebody has seen two films ($s$) with the participation of Gerard Depardieu ($\mathrm{val}(s)$). After that he tries to know all the films with his participation ($\mathrm{obj}(\mathrm{val}(s))$). One can know that Gerard Depardieu acts with Pierre Richard ($t$) in several films ($\mathrm{obj}(t)$). After that he can discover that these films are the films of the same producer Francis Veber ($\mathrm{val}(\mathrm{obj}(t))$).

Namely these generalization operations are used for searching for good diagnostic tests.

Notes that these generalization operations are also used in FCA for concepts' definition (Wille, 1992; Stumme et al., 1998): a pair C = ($s$, $t$), $s \subseteq S$, $t \subseteq T$, is called a concept if $s = \mathrm{obj}(t)$ and simultaneously $t = \mathrm{val}(s)$, i. e. for a concept C = ($s$, $t$) both $s$ and $t$ are closed. Usually, the set $s$ is called the extent of C (in our notation, it is the set of indices of objects possessing the feature $t$) and the set of values $t$ is called the intent of C.

Let $R = R(+) \cup R(-)$ be the set of object descriptions $t_i$, $i \in S$ and $S(+)$ and $S(-) = S\backslash S(+)$ be the sets of indices of positive and negative objects respectively (or simply objects, for short).

A diagnostic test for $S(+)$, $R(+)$ is a pair $(s, t)$ such that $t \subseteq T$ $(s = \text{obj}(t) \neq \varnothing)$, $s \subseteq S(+)$ and $t \not\subset t'$, $\forall t'$, $t' \in R(-)$.

In general case, a set $t$ is not closed for diagnostic test $(s, t)$, i. e. the condition $\text{val}(\text{obj}(t)) = t$ is not always satisfied, consequently, a diagnostic test is not obligatory a concept of FCA. This condition is true only for the special class of tests called 'maximally redundant ones'.

- **Definition 1. A diagnostic test** $(s, t)$, $t \subseteq T$ $(s = \text{obj}(t) \neq \varnothing)$ is **good** for $S(+)$ if and only if any extension $s' = s \cup i$, $i \notin s$, $i \in S(+)$ implies that $(s', \text{val}(s'))$ is **not a test** for $S(+)$.
- **Definition 2. A good test** $(s, t)$, $t \subseteq T$ $(s = \text{obj}(t) \neq \varnothing)$ for $S(+)$ is **irredundant** (GIRT) if any narrowing $t' = t\backslash A$, $A \in t$ implies that $(\text{obj}(t'), t'))$ is **not a test** for $S(+)$.
- **Definition 3. A good test** for $S(+)$ is **maximally redundant** (GMRT) if any extension of $t' = t \cup A$, $A \notin t$, $A \in T$ implies that $(\text{obj}(t \cup A), t')$ is **not a good test** for $S(+)$.

Any object description $t$ in $R$ is a maximally redundant collection of values because for any value $v \notin t$, $v \in T$ $s(t \cup v)$ is equal to $\varnothing$.

For example, in Table 1 the collection '*Blond Bleu*' is a good irredundant test for Class 1 and, simultaneously, it is maximally redundant collection of values. The collection '*Blond Embrown*' is a test for Class 2 but it is not good and, simultaneously, it is maximally redundant collection of values.

The collection '*Embrown*' is a good irredundant test for Class 2. The collection '*Red*' is a good irredundant test for Class 1. The collection '*Tall Red Bleu*' is a good maximally redundant test for Class 1.

*Table 1. Example 1 of data classification (This example is adopted from Ganascia, 1989)*

| Index of example | Height | Color of hair | Color of eyes | Class |
|---|---|---|---|---|
| 1 | Low | Blond | Bleu | 1 |
| 2 | Low | Brown | Bleu | 2 |
| 3 | Tall | Brown | Embrown | 2 |
| 4 | Tall | Blond | Embrown | 2 |
| 5 | Tall | Brown | Bleu | 2 |
| 6 | Low | Blond | Embrown | 2 |
| 7 | Tall | Red | Bleu | 1 |
| 8 | Tall | Blond | Bleu | 1 |

Note to Table 1 and all the following tables: the values of attributes must not be considered as the words of English language, they are the abstract symbols only

Let $k$ be the name of a set $R(k)$ of examples. To say that a collection $t$ of values is a diagnostic test for $R(k)$ is equivalent to say that it does not cover any example $t^*$, $t^* \in R(k)$. At the same time, the condition $s(t) \subseteq S(k)$ implies that the following implicative dependency is true: 'if $t$, then $k$'. Thus a diagnostic test, as a collection of values, makes up the left side of a rule of the first type.

It is clear that the best tests for pattern recognition problems must be good irredundant tests. These tests allow constructing the shortest rules of the first type with the highest degree of generalization.

One of the possible ways for searching for good irredundant tests for a given class of positive examples is the following: first, find all good maximally redundant tests; second, for each good maximally redundant test, find all good irredundant tests contained in it. This is a convenient strategy as each good irredundant test belongs to one and only one good maximally redundant test with the same interpretation (Naidenova, 1999).

## GENERATION OF GOOD DIAGNOSTIC TESTS AS DUAL ELEMENTS OF INTERCONNECTED LATTICES

We shall consider two interconnected lattices OBJ $= (2^S, \cup, \cap) = (2^S, \subseteq)$ and VAL $= (2^T, \cup, \cap) = (2^T, \subseteq)$, where $2^S$, $2^T$ designate the set of all subsets of objects and the set of all subsets of values, respectively.

Inferring the chains of lattice elements ordered by the inclusion relation lies in the foundation of generating all diagnostic tests:

$$s_0 \subseteq \ldots \subseteq s_i \subseteq s_{i+1} \subseteq \ldots \subseteq s_m \ (\mathrm{val}(s_0) \supseteq \mathrm{val}(s_1) \supseteq \ldots \supseteq \mathrm{val}(s_i) \supseteq \mathrm{val}(s_{i+1}) \supseteq \ldots \supseteq \mathrm{val}(s_m)), \quad (1)$$

$$t_0 \subseteq \ldots \subseteq t_i \subseteq t_{i+1} \subseteq \ldots \subseteq t_m \ (\mathrm{obj}(t_0) \supseteq \mathrm{obj}(t_1) \supseteq \ldots \supseteq \mathrm{obj}(t_i) \supseteq \mathrm{obj}(t_{i+1}) \supseteq \ldots \supseteq \mathrm{obj}(t_m)). \quad (2)$$

The process of generating chains of form (1) is defined as an ascending process of generating lattice elements. The process of generating chains of form (2) is defined as a descending process of generating lattice elements. The process of generating lattice elements can be two-directional when chains (1) and (2) alternate.

The dual ascending and descending processes of lattice generating are determined as follows:

$$t_0 \supseteq t_1 \supseteq \ldots \supseteq t_i \supseteq t_{i+1} \supseteq \ldots \supseteq t_m \ (\mathrm{obj}(t_0) \subseteq \mathrm{obj}(t_1) \subseteq \ldots \subseteq \mathrm{obj}(t_i) \subseteq \mathrm{obj}(t_{i+1}) \subseteq \ldots \subseteq \mathrm{obj}(t_m)), \quad (3)$$

$$s_0 \supseteq s_1 \supseteq \ldots \supseteq s_i \supseteq s_{i+1} \supseteq \ldots \supseteq s_m \ (\mathrm{val}(s_0) \subseteq \mathrm{val}(s_1) \subseteq \ldots \subseteq \mathrm{val}(s_i) \subseteq \mathrm{val}(s_{i+1}) \subseteq \ldots \subseteq \mathrm{val}(s_m)). \quad (4)$$

### Inductive Rules for Constructing Elements of a Dual Lattice

We use the following variants of inductive transition from one element of a chain to its nearest element in the lattice:

1. from $s_q = (i_1, i_2, \ldots, i_q)$ to $s_{q+1} = (i_1, i_2, \ldots, i_{q+1})$;
2. from $t_q = (A_1, A_2, \ldots, A_q)$ to $t_{q+1} = (A_1, A_2, \ldots, A_{q+1})$;
3. from $s_q = (i_1, i_2, \ldots, i_q)$ to $s_{q-1} = (i_1, i_2, \ldots, i_{q-1})$;
4. from $t_q = (A_1, A_2, \ldots, A_q)$ to $t_{q-1} = (A_1, A_2, \ldots, A_{q-1})$.

Thus inductive transitions are the processes of extending or narrowing collections of values (objects). Inductive transitions can be smooth or boundary. Under smooth transition, the extending (narrowing) of collections of values (objects) is going with preserving a given property of them. These properties are, for example, "to be a test for a given class of examples", "to be an irredundant collection of values", "not to be a test for a given class of examples", "to be a good test for a given class of examples" and some others. A transition is said to be boundary if it changes a given property of collections of values (objects) into the opposite one.

We need the special rules for realizing these inductive transitions.

Note that reasoning begins with using a mechanism for restricting the space of searching for tests: (i) for each collection of values (objects), to avoid constructing all its subsets and (ii) to restrict the space of searching only to the subspaces deliberately containing the desired GMRTs or GIRTs. For this goal, admissible and essential values (objects) are used.

During the lattice construction, the deductive rules of the first type, namely, implications, interdictions, rules of compatibility (approximate implications), and diagnostic rules are generated and used immediately. The knowledge acquired during the process of generalization (specialization) is used for pruning the search space.

### The Generalization Rule

The generalization rule is used to get all the collections of objects $s_{q+1} = \{i_1, i_2, \ldots i_q, i_{q+1}\}$ from a collection $s_q = \{i_1, i_2, \dots i_q\}$ such that $(s_q, \text{val}(s_q))$ and $(s_{q+1}, \text{val}(s_{q+1}))$ are tests for a given class of objects.

The termination condition for constructing a chain of generalizations is: for all the extension $s_{q+1}$ of $s_q$, $(s_{q+1}, \text{val}(s_{q+1}))$ is not a test for a given class of positive examples.

The generalization rule uses, as a leading process, an ascending chain $(s_0 \subseteq \dots \subseteq s_i \subseteq s_{i+1} \subseteq \dots \subseteq s_m)$. The application of this rule for inferring GMRTs (Naidenova, 2006) requires using the generalization operation generalization_of($s$) $= s' = \text{obj}(\text{val}(s))$ for each obtained collection of objects.

The rule of generalization is an inductive extension rule meaning the choice of admissible objects for extending $s_q$. This rule realizes the Joint Method of Agreement and Difference.

The extending of $s$ results in obtaining the subsets of objects of more and more power with more and more generalized features (set of values). This operation is analogous to the generalization rule applied for star generation under conceptual clustering (Michalski, 1983).

## The Specification Rule

The specification rule is used to get all the collections of values $t_{q+1} = \{A_1, A_2, \dots, A_{q+1}\}$ from a collection $t_q = \{A_1, A_2, \dots, A_q\}$ such that $t_q$ and $t_{q+1}$ are irredundant collections of values and $(\text{obj}(t_q), t_q)$ and $(\text{obj}(t_{q+1}), t_{q+1})$ are not tests for a given class of objects.

The termination condition for constructing a chain of specifications is: for all the extensions $t_{q+1}$ of $t_q$, $t_{q+1}$ is either a redundant collection of values or a test for a given class of objects.

This rule has been used for inferring GIRTs (Megretskaya, 1988).

The specification rule uses, as a leading process, a descending chain $(t_0 \subseteq \dots \subseteq t_i \subseteq t_{i+1} \subseteq \dots \subseteq t_m)$.

The application of this rule for inferring GIRTs does not require using the generalization opera-

tion generalization_of($t$) $= t' = \text{val}(\text{obj}(t))$ for each obtained collection of values.

The rule of specification is an inductive extension rule meaning the choice of admissible values for extending a given collection of values. This rule realizes the Joint Method of Agreement and Difference.

In general case, the extending of $t$ results in obtaining the subsets of objects of less and less power with more and more specified features (set of values).

The dual generalization (specification) rules relate to narrowing collections of values (objects).

The dual generalization rule can be used to get all the collections of values $t_{q-1} = (A_1, A_2, \dots, A_{q-1})$ from a collection $t_q = (A_1, A_2, \dots, A_q)$ such that $(\text{obj}(t_q), t_q)$ and $(\text{obj}(t_{q-1}), t_{q-1})$ are tests for a given class of objects.

The dual specification rule can be used to get all the collections of objects $s_{q-1} = (i_1, i_2, \dots, i_{q-1})$ from a collection $s_q = (i_1, i_2, \dots, i_q)$ such that $(s_{q-1}, \text{val}(s_{q-1}))$ and $(s_q, \text{val}(s_q))$ are tests for a given set of positive examples.

All inductive transitions take their interpretations in human mental acts. The extending of a set of objects with checking the satisfaction of a given condition is a typical method of inductive reasoning. For example, Claude-Gaspar Bashet de Méziriak, a French mathematician (1581 – 1638) has discovered (without proving it) that apparently every positive number can be expressed as a sum of at most four squares; for example, $5 = 2^2 + 1^2$, $6 = 2^2 + 1^2 + 1^2$, $7 = 2^2 + 1^2 + 1^2 + 1^2$, $8 = 2^2 + 2^2$, $9 = 3^2$. Bashet has checked this for more than 300 numbers. It wasn't until the late 18th century that Joseph Lagrange gave a complete proof.

In pattern recognition, the process of inferring hypotheses about the unknown values of some attributes is reduced to the maximal expansion of a collection of the known values of some attributes in such a way that none of the forbidden pairs of values would belong to this expansion.

The contraction of a collection of values is used, for instance, in order to delete from it redundant or non-informative values.

The contraction of a collection of objects is used, for instance, in order to isolate a certain cluster in a class of objects. Thus, we distinguish lemons in the citrus fruits.

## The Boundary Induction Transitions

The boundary inductive transitions are used to get:

1. all the collections $t_q$ from a collection $t_{q-1}$ such that $(obj(t_{q-1}), t_{q-1})$ is not a test but $(obj(t_q), t_q)$ is a test, for a given set of objects;
2. all the collections $t_{q-1}$ from a collection $t_q$ such that $(obj(t_q), t_q)$ is a test, but $(obj(t_{q-1}), t_{q-1})$ is not a test for a given set of objects;
3. all the collections $s_{q-1}$ from a collection $s_q$ such that $(s_q, val(s_q))$ is not a test, but $(s_{q-1}, val(s_{q-1}))$ is a test for a given set of objects;
4. all the collections of $s_q$ from a collection $s_{q-1}$ such that $(s_{q-1}, val(s_{q-1}))$ is a test, but $(s_q, val(s_q))$ is not a test for a given set of objects.

All the boundary transitions are interpreted as human reasoning operations. Transition (1) is used for distinguishing two diseases with similar symptoms. Transition (2) can be interpreted as including a certain class of objects into a more general one. For instance, squares can be named parallelograms, all whose sides are equal. In some intellectual psychological texts, a task is given to remove the "superfluous" (inappropriate) object from a certain group of objects (rose, butterfly, phlox, and dahlia) (transition (3)). Transition (4) can be interpreted as the search for a refuting example.

The boundary inductive transitions realize the method of only distinction or the method of concomitant changes.

For their implementation, boundary transitions need special inductive reasoning rules, namely, inductive diagnostic ones.

Note that reasoning begins with using a mechanism for restricting the space of the search for tests: 1) for each collection of values (objects), to avoid constructing all its subsets, 2) for each step of reasoning, to choose a collection of values (objects) without which good tests can not be constructed. For this goal, admissible and essential values (objects) are determined. The search for the admissible or essential values (objects) uses inductive diagnostic rules.

## The Inductive Diagnostic Rule: The Concept of Essential Value

First, consider the boundary transition (1): getting all the collections $t_q$ from a collection $t_{q-1}$ such that $(obj(t_{q-1}), t_{q-1})$ is not a test but $(obj(t_q), t_q)$ is a test, for a given set of objects.

The concept of an essential value is determined as follows.

**Definition 4**. *Let t be a collection of values such that (obj(t), t) is a test for a given set of objects. We say that the value A is essential in t if (obj(t\A), (t\A)) is not a test for a given set of object.*

Generally, we are interested in finding the maximal subset $sbmax(t) \subset t$ such that $(obj(t), t)$ is a test but $(obj(sbmax(t)), sbmax(t))$ is not a test for a given set of positive objects. Then $sbmin(t) = t \setminus sbmax(t)$ is the minimal set of essential values in $t$.

We extend $t_{q-1}$ by choosing values that appear simultaneously with it in the objects of a given set $R(+)$ and do not appear in any object of a set $R(-)$. These values are to be said essential ones.

Let us examine an example of searching for essential values (see, please, Table 2).

Let $s$ be equal to $\{1,2,5,7,8\}$, then $val(s) =$ '*Bleu*', where $(s, val(s))$ is not a test for both Classes 1 and 2. We can extend $val(s)$ by choosing values which appear simultaneously with it

*Table 2. Example 1 of data. (this example is adopted fromGanascia, 1989)*

| Index of Example | Height | Color of Hair | Color of Eyes | Class |
|---|---|---|---|---|
| 1 | Low | Blond | Bleu | 1 |
| 2 | Low | Brown | Bleu | 2 |
| 3 | Tall | Brown | Embrown | 2 |
| 4 | Tall | Blond | Embrown | 2 |
| 5 | Tall | Brown | Bleu | 2 |
| 6 | Low | Blond | Embrown | 2 |
| 7 | Tall | Red | Bleu | 1 |
| 8 | Tall | Blond | Bleu | 1 |

in the objects of the first class and do not appear in any object of the second class and vice versa.

The objects 1, 7, 8 of Class 1 contain the values '*Bleu*' with the values '*Low*', '*Blond*', '*Tall*', and '*Red*'. The objects 2, 5 of Class 2 contain the values '*Bleu*' with the values '*Brown*', '*Low*', and '*Tall*'. The set of essential values for Class 1 is {*Blond, Red*}, the set of essential values for Class 2 is {*Brown*}. We have the following tests containing the value '*Bleu*': for Class 1 - '*Bleu Red*' (good but redundant one) and '*Bleu Blond*' (good and irredundant one), and only one test (although not a good one) for Class 2 – '*Bleu Brown*'.

The inductive diagnostic rule is a reasoning rule of the second type with the help of which the diagnostic assertions (rules of the firs type) are inferred. In our example, the following diagnostic assertions have been inferred: "if '*Bleu*' is true, then '*Brown*' → 'Class 2', ' *Blond*' → Class 1, '*Red*' → Class 1. These assertions can also be transformed into several interdictions: '*Bleu Brown*' → not Class 1, '*Bleu Blond*' → not Class 2, '*Bleu Red*' → not Class 2.

The inductive diagnostic rule is based on the inductive Method of Difference.

The diagnostic rule for extending a collection of values is analogous to the specialization rule defined in (Michalski, 1983), and (Ganascia, 1989). If a newly presented training example contradicts

an already constructed concept description, the specialization rule is applied to generate a new consistent concept description. A specialization method has been given in (Michalski and Larson, 1978).

In general case, the extended set $t_{q-1}$ is not a GIRT or GRMT, so we use the ascending (descending) process for inferring good tests contained in it.

## The Dual Inductive Diagnostic Rule: The Concept of Essential Object

Consider the boundary inductive transition (3): getting all the collections $s_{q-1}$ from a collection $s_q$ such that $(s_q, \mathrm{val}(s_q))$ is not a test, but $(s_{q-1}, \mathrm{val}(s_{q-1}))$ is a test for a given set of objects.

For realizing this transition, we use a method for choosing objects for deleting from $s_q$. By analogy with an essential value, we define an essential example (object).

**Definition 5.** *Let s be a subset of objects belonging to a given positive class of objects; assume also that (s, val(s)) is not a test. The object $t_j$, j ∈ s is to be said an essential in s if (s\j, val(s\j)) proves to be a test for a given set of positive objects.*

Generally, we are interested in finding the maximal subset sbmax(s) ⊂ s such that (s, val(s)) is not a test but (sbmax(s), val(sbmax(s))) is a test for a given set of positive objects. Then sbmin(s) = s\sbmax(s) is the minimal set of essential objects in s.

The dual inductive diagnostic rule can be used for inferring compatibility rules of the first type. The number of objects in sbmax(s) can be understood as a measure of "carrying-out" for an acquired rule related to sbmax(s), namely, val(sbmax(s)) → $k$(R(+)) frequently, where $k$(R(+)) is the name of the set R(+).

Next we describe the procedure with the use of which a quasi-maximal subset s of s* is obtained such that (s, val(s)) is a test for given set of objects.

*Table 3. Deductive rules of the first type obtained with the use of inductive rules for inferring diagnostic tests*

| Inductive rules | Action | Inferring deductive rules of the first type |
|---|---|---|
| Generalization rule | Extending *s* (narrowing *t*) | Implications |
| Specification rule | Extending *t* (narrowing *s*) | Implications |
| Inductive diagnostic rule | Searching for essential values | Diagnostic rules |
| Dual inductive diagnostic rule | Searching for essential objects | Compatibility rules (approximate implications) |

We begin with the first object $i_1$ of $s^*$, then we take the next object $i_2$ of $s^*$ and evaluate the function to_be_test ($\{i_1, i_2\}$, val($\{i_1, i_2\}$)). If the value of this function is "*true*", then we take the next object $i_3$ of $s^*$ and evaluate the function to_be_test ($\{i_1, i_2, i_3\}$, val($\{i_1, i_2, i_3\}$)). If the value of the function to_be_test ($\{i_1, i_2\}$, val($\{i_1, i_2\}$)) is "*false*", then the object $i_2$ of $s^*$ is skipped and the function to_be_test ($\{i_1, i_3\}$, val($\{i_1, i_3\}$)) is evaluated. We continue this process until we achieve the last object of $s^*$.

For instance, consider $s = \{1,7,8\}$ in Table 1. We have, after applying the procedure, described above, that ($\{1,7\}$, val($\{1,7\}$)) is not a test for Class 1 because of val($\{1,7\}$) = '*Bleu*', but ($\{1,8\}$, val($\{1,8\}$)) is a test for Class 1 because val($\{1,8\}$) = '*Blond Bleu*'. The object 7 is an essential one in $\{1, 7, 8\}$.

The dual inductive diagnostic rule is based on the inductive Method of Difference.

The inductive rules generate logical rules of the first type, as shown in Table 3.

In the sequel, we will see that the deductive rules of the first type, obtained by means of inductive reasoning rules of the second type are used immediately in the process of good tests construction.

## Reducing the Rules of Inductive Transitions to the Deductive and Inductive Rules of the Second Type

### Realization of the Generalization Rule for Inferring GMRTs

Any realization of this rule must allow the following actions for each element *s*:

- To avoid constructing the set of all its subsets,
- To avoid the repetitive generation of it.

Let S(test) be the partially ordered set of elements $s = \{i_1, i_2, \ldots i_q\}, q = 1, 2, \ldots, nt - 1$ obtained as a result of generalizations and satisfying the following condition: ($s$, val($s$)) is a test for a given class R(+) of positive objects. Here *nt* denotes the number of positive objects. Let STGOOD be the partially ordered set of elements *s* satisfying the following condition: ($s$, val($s$)) is a GMRT for R(+).

The function to_be_test($t$) is defined as follows: if $s(t) \cap S(+) = s(t)$ then *true* else *false*.

Consider some methods for choosing objects admissible for extending *s*.

**Method 1.** Suppose that S(test) and STGOOD are not empty and $s \in$ S(test). Construct the set V:

$$V = \{\cup s', s \subseteq s', s' \in \{S(test) \cup STGOOD\}\}.$$

The set V is the union of all the collections of objects in S(test) and STGOOD containing *s*, hence, *s* is in the intersection of these collections. If we want an extension of *s* not to be included in any element of $\{S(test) \cup STGOOD\}$, we must use, for extending *s*, the objects not appearing simultaneously with *s* in the set V. The set of objects, candidates for extending *s*, is equal to:

$$CAND(s) = nts \backslash V, \text{ where } nts = \{\cup s, s \in S(test)\}.$$

An object $j^* \in$ CAND($s$) is not admissible for extending *s* if at least for one object $i \in s$ the pair

$\{i, j^*\}$ either does not correspond to a test or it corresponds to a good test (it belongs to STGOOD).

Let Q be the set of forbidden pairs of objects for extending $s$: Q = $\{\{i, j\} \subseteq$ S(+): ($\{i, j\}$, val($\{i, j\}$)) is not a test for R(+)$\}$. Then the set of admissible objects is select($s$) = $\{i, i \in$ CAND($s$): ($\forall j$) ($j \in s$), $\{i, j\} \notin \{$STGOOD or Q$\}\}$.

The set Q can be generated in the beginning of searching all GMRTs for R(+).

Return to our current example (Table 1). Suppose that the set STGOOD contains an element $\{2,3,5\}$, for which ($\{2,3,5\}$, val($\{2,3,5\}$)) is a test for Class 2. Suppose that S(test) = $\{\{2,3\},\{2,5\}, \{3,4\}, \{3,5\} \{3,6\}\{4,6\}\}$ and Q = $\{\{2,4\},\{2,6\},\{4,5\}, \{5,6\}\}$. We try to extend $s = \{3, 4\}$. Then CAND($\{3,4\}$) = $\{2, 5, 6\}$ and select($\{3, 4\}$) = $\{6\}$. The collection $\{3, 4, 6\}$ is not extended and it corresponds to a good test – ($\{3,4,6\}$, «*Embrown*»).

An algorithm NIAGaRa based on this variant of generalization rule is used in (Naidenova, 2001), for inferring GMRTs.

**Method 2.** The set CAND($s$) is determined as described above. Index $j^* \in$ CAND($s$) can be used for extending $s$, if for any $i$ from $s$ the pair $\{i, j^*\}$ corresponds a test. But then $s$ must be in the union of all the collections containing $j^*$, with the exception of only the pairs which are in the set STGOOD (these pairs have no enlarging). Hence the following condition must be satisfied for $j^*$: $\{Q(j^*)$ contains $s\}$, where $Q(j^*) = \{\cup s': j^* \in s'$, $s' \in \{$S(test)$\cup$STGOOD$\backslash\{j^*, g\}\}\}$.

**Method 3.** In this method, the set CAND($s$) is determined as follows. Let $s^* = \{s \cup j\}$ be an extension of $s$, where $j \notin s$. Then val($s^*$) $\subseteq$ val($s$). Hence the intersection of val($s$) and val($j$) must be not empty. The set CAND($s$) = $\{j: j \in nts\backslash s$, val($j$) $\cap$ val($s$) $\neq \varnothing\}$.

For the previous example (Table 2) we have val($\{2\}$) $\cap$ val($\{3,4\}$) = $\varnothing$, val($\{5\}$) $\cap$ val($\{3,4\}$) $\neq \varnothing$, and val($\{6\}$) $\cap$ val($\{3,4\}$) $\neq \varnothing$. Hence we have that CAND ($\{3, 4\}$) = $\{5, 6\}$.

The set ext($s$) contains all the possible extensions of $s$ in the form $snew = (s \cup j), j \in$ select($s$)

*Table 4. Using deductive and inductive rules of the second type*

| Inductive rules | Process | Deductive and inductive rules of the second type |
|---|---|---|
| Generalization rule | | |
| | Forming *Q* | Generating forbidden rules |
| | Forming *CAND(s)* | The joint method of similarity-distinction |
| | Forming *select(s)* | Using forbidden rules |
| | Forming *ext(s)* | The method of only similarity |
| | Function_to_be test(*t*) | Using implication |
| | Generalization_ of(*snew*) | Closing operation |

and *snew* corresponds to a test for R(+). This procedure of forming ext($s$) executes the function generalization_of(*snew*) for each element *snew* $\in$ ext($s$).

The generalization rule is a complex process in which both deductive and inductive reasoning rules of the second type are performed (please, see Table 4). The knowledge acquired during the process of generalization (the sets Q, CAND($s$), S(test), STGOOD) is used for pruning the search in the domain space.

The generalization rule with searching only admissible variants of generalization is not an artificially constructed operation. A lot of examples of using this rule in human thinking can be given. For example, if your child were allergic to oranges, then you would not buy not only these fruits but also orange juice and also products that contain orange extracts. A good gardener knows the plants that cannot be adjacent in a garden. A lot of problems related to placing personnel, appointing somebody to the post, finding lodging for somebody etc., deal with partitioning a set of objects or persons into groups by taking into account forbidden pairs of objects or persons.

## Realization of the Specification Rule for Inferring GIRTs

Let TGOOD be the partially ordered set of elements $t$ satisfying the following condition: $(obj(t), t)$ is a good irredundant test for $R(+)$. We denote by SAFE the set of elements $t$ such that $t$ is an irredundant collection of values but $(obj(t), t)$ is not a test for $R(+)$.

Let us recall that we find all GIRTs contained in a given GMRT already obtained for $R(+)$.

**Method 1.** We use an inductive rule for extending elements of SAFE and constructing $t_{q+1} = \{A_1, A_2, ..., A_{q+1}\}$ from $t_q = (A_1, A_2, ..., A_q)$, $q = 1, 2, ..,$ $na - 1$, where $na$ is the number of values in the set $T$. This rule relies on the following consideration: if the collection of values $\{A_1, A_2, ..., A_{q+1}\}$ is an irredundant one, then all its proper subsets must be irredundant collections of values too and, consequently, they must be in SAFE. Having constructed a set $t_{q+1} = \{A_1, A_2, ..., A_{q+1}\}$, we determine whether it is the irredundant collection of values or not. If the collection $t_{q+1}$ is redundant, then it is deleted from consideration. If it corresponds to a test for $R(+)$, then it is transferred to TGOOD. If $t_{q+1}$ is irredundant but $(s(t_{q+1}), t_{q+1})$ is not a test for $R(+)$, then it is a candidate for extension and it is memorized in SAFE.

We use the function to_be_irredundant$(t) =$ if $(\forall A)\ (A \in t)\ obj(t) \neq obj(t \setminus A)$ then true else false.

An analogous method of extending collections of objects is used in an algorithm of inferring GMRTs given in (Naidenova and Polegaeva, 1991). The same principle of inductive extension of items' collections is also used in two algorithms *Apriory* and *AprioryTid* proposed in (Agrawal and Srikant, 1994) for mining association rules between items in a large database of sales transactions.

**Method 2.** This method is based on using the inductive diagnostic rule for searching directly for essential values of which consist GIRTs. We begin with the collection of values $Z = \{A_4, A_{12}, A_{14}, A_{15}, A_{24}, A_{26}\}$, for which obj$(\{A_4, A_{12}, A_{14}, A_{15},$ $A_{24}, A_{26}\}) = \{2, 3, 4, 7\}$ and $(s(Z), Z)$ is a GMRT for the set of positive objects.

We need the set of negative objects in which at least one value of $\{A_4, A_{12}, A_{14}, A_{15}, A_{24}, A_{26}\}$ appears. We may take only the projection of $Z$ on these negative objects (see, please, Table 5).

We find by means of the inductive diagnostic rule that the value $A_{26}$ is the only essential value in $Z$. Hence this value must belong to any GIRT. Next, select all the negative examples containing $A_{26}$ (Table 6).

Now we must find a maximal subset of $Z$ containing $A_{26}$ and not corresponding to a test for positive objects. This subset is $\{A_4, A_{14}, A_{15}, A_{26}\}$. Hence values $A_{24}$, or $A_{12}$ must belong to GIRTs containing $A_{26}$ because they are essential values in $Z$ with respect to the subset $\{A_4, A_{14}, A_{15}, A_{26}\}$.

Next, we form the collections $\{A_{24}, A_{26}\}$ and $\{A_{12}, A_{26}\}$. But these collections do not correspond to tests.

Now select the set of negative objects containing $\{A_{24}, A_{26}\}$ and the set of negative objects containing $\{A_{12}, A_{26}\}$ (Table 7). These sets are used for searching for essential values to extend collections $\{A_{24}, A_{26}\}$ and $\{A_{12}, A_{26}\}$.

Now we must find a maximal subset of $Z$ containing the collections $\{A_{24}, A_{26}\}$ and a maximal subset of $Z$ containing $\{A_{12}, A_{26}\}$ such that they do not correspond to tests for positive objects. These collections are $\{A_{24}, A_{26}\}$ and $\{A_4, A_{12}, A_{26}\}$, respectively.

In the first case, we have the set $\{A_4, A_{12}, A_{14}, A_{15}\}$ as the set of essential values in $Z$. Hence we can form the collections $\{A_4, A_{24}, A_{26}\}$, $\{A_{12}, A_{24}, A_{26}\}$, $\{A_{14}, A_{24}, A_{26}\}$, and $\{A_{15}, A_{24}, A_{26}\}$. All these collections correspond to GIRTs for positive objects.

In the second case, we have the set $\{A_{14}, A_{15}, A_{24}\}$ as the set of essential values in $Z$. Hence we can form the collections $\{A_{12}, A_{15}, A_{26}\}$, $\{A_{12}, A_{14}, A_{26}\}$. These collections correspond to GIRTs for positive objects. The essential value $A_{24}$ is not admissible for extending $\{A_{12}, A_{26}\}$ because the collection $\{A_{12}, A_{24}, A_{26}\}$ is included in the union

*Table 5. Initial set of negative examples*

| index of object | $R(-)$ |
|---|---|
| 17 | $A_{24}A_{26}$ |
| 23 | $A_{14}A_{15}$ |
| 38 | $A_4A_{12}$ |
| 30 48 | $A_{12}A_{14}A_{15}$ |
| 31 | $A_{14}A_{15}A_{26}$ |
| 42 | $A_4A_{12}A_{26}$ |
| 47 | $A_4A_{12}A_{14}$ |
| 37 40 41 43 44 45 | $A_4A_{12}A_{14}A_{15}$ |
| 39 | $A_4A_{14}A_{15}A_{26}$ |
| 46 | $A_4A_{12}A_{14}A_{15}A_{24}$ |

*Table 6. Current set of negative examples*

| index of object | $R(-)$ |
|---|---|
| 17 | $A_{24}A_{26}$ |
| 31 | $A_{14}A_{15}A_{26}$ |
| 42 | $A_4A_{12}A_{26}$ |
| 39 | $A_4A_{14}A_{15}A_{26}$ |

*Table 7. Current set of negative examples*

| Index of Object | $R(-)$ |
|---|---|
| 17 | $A_{24}A_{26}$ |
| 42 | $A_4A_{12}A_{26}$ |

*Table 8. Decision tree of tests*

| Level 1 | Level 2 | Level 3 |
|---|---|---|
| | | $A_4$ |
| | | $A_{12}$ |
| | $A_{24}$ | |
| | | $A_{14}$ |
| $A_{26}$ | | |
| | | $A_{15}$ |
| | | $A_{15}$ |
| | $A_{12}$ | |
| | | $A_{14}$ |

of all GIRTs already obtained and containing the collection $\{A_{12}, A_{26}\}$.

The algorithm builds a decision tree of tests (Table 8) and, in parallel, constructs also the appropriate tree of the subsets of negative objects used for searching for essential values.

The generalization operation generalization_ of$(t)$ = val(obj$(t)$) is not used with the search for irredundant tests. The algorithm uses the function to_be_test$(t)$ = if $t \subset t'$ for $\forall t'$, $t' \in$ R(-).

We see that the compatibility rules of the first type, obtained with the use of dual inductive di-

agnostic rule, are used immediately in the process of good tests construction.

## THE DECOMPOSITION OF INFERRING GOOD DIAGNOSTIC TESTS INTO SUBTASKS

To transform good diagnostic tests inferring into an incremental process we introduce two kinds of subtasks (Naidenova and Ermakov, 2001):

For a given set of positive examples:

1. Given a positive example $t$, find all GMRTs contained in $t$, more exactly, all $t' \subset t$, (obj$(t')$, $t'$) is a GMRT;
2. Given a non-empty collection of values $X$ (maybe only one value) such that it is not a test, find all GMRTs containing $X$, more exactly, all $Y$, $X \subset Y$, (obj$(Y)$, $Y$) is a GMRT.

Each example contains only some subset of values from $T$, hence each subtask of the first kind is simpler than the initial one. Each subset $X$ of $T$ appears only in a part of all examples; hence each subtask of the second kind is simpler than the initial one.

*Table 9. The intersections of $t_2$ with the objects of class 2*

| Index of Example | Height | Color of hair | Color of eyes | Test? |
|---|---|---|---|---|
| 2 | Low | Brown | Bleu | Yes |
| 3 | | Brown | | Yes |
| 4 | | | | No |
| 5 | | Brown | Bleu | Yes |
| 6 | Low | | | No |

There are the analogies of these subtasks in natural human reasoning. Having a set of features, describing a situation, one can conclude from different subsets of these features.

**The subtask of the first kind**. We introduce the concept of an object' (example's) projection proj(R)[$t$] of a given positive object $t$ on a given set R(+) of positive examples. The proj(R)[$t$] is the set $Z = \{z: (z$ is non empty intersection of $t$ and $t'$) & ($t' \in R(+))$ & (obj($z$), $z$) is a test for a given class of positive objects)}.

If the proj(R)[$t$] is not empty and contains more than one element, then it is a subtask for inferring all GMRTs that are in $t$. If the projection contains one and only one element equal to $t$, then (obj($t$), $t$) is a GMRT.

To make the operation of forming a projection perfectly clear we construct the projection of $t_2$ = '*Low Brown Bleu*' on the objects of the second class (see, please, Table 1). This projection includes $t_2$ and the intersections of $t_2$ with the examples $t_3$, $t_4$, $t_5$, $t_6$ Table 9 shows this projection.

For checking whether an element of the projection corresponds to a test or not we use the function to_be_test($t$) in the following form: to_be_test($t$) = if $obj(t) \subseteq s(+)$ then *true* else *false*, where $s(+)$ is the set of positive objects, $obj(t)$ is the set of all positive and negative objects the descriptions of which contain $t$. If $s(-)$ is the set of negative objects, then $S = s(+) \cup s(-)$ and $obj(t) = \{i: t \subseteq t_i, i \in S\}$.

The intersection $t_2 \cap t_4$ is the empty set. Hence the row of the projection with the number 4 is empty. The intersection $t_2 \cap t_6$ does not correspon

to a test for Class 2 because $obj(Low) = \{1,2,6\} \not\subset s(+)$, where $s(+)$ is equal to $\{2,3,4,5,6\}$. Finally, we have the projection of $t_2$ on the objects of Class 2 in Table 10.

The subtask turns out to be very simple because the intersection of all the rows of the projection is a test for Class 2: $val(\{2,3,5\}) = ($'*Brown*', $obj(Brown)) = \{2,3,5\}$ and $\{2,3,5\} \subseteq s(+)$.

**The subtask of the second kind.** We introduce the concept of an attributive projection proj($R$)[$A$] of a given value $A$ on a given set $R(+)$ of positive examples. The projection proj($R$)[$A$] = $\{t: (t \in R(+))$ & ($A$ appears in $t$)}. Another way to define this projection is: proj($R$)[$A$] = $\{t_i: i \in (obj(A) \cap s(+))\}$. If the attributive projection is not empty and contains more than one element, then it is a subtask of inferring all GMRTs containing a given value $A$. If $A$ appears in one and only one object $X$, then $A$ does not belong to any GMRT different from $X$. Forming the projection of $A$ makes sense if $A$ is not a test and the intersection of all positive objects in which $A$ appears is not a test too, i.e. $obj(A) \not\subset s(+)$ and $t' = t(obj(A))$ is not a test for a given set of positive examples.

Denote the set $\{obj(A) \cap s(+)\}$ by splus($A$). For example in Table 1, we have: obj(+) = $\{2,3,4,5,6\}$, splus(*Low*) → $\{2,6\}$, splus(*Brown*) → $\{2,3,5\}$, splus(*Bleu*) → $\{2,5\}$, splus(*Tall*) → $\{3,4,5\}$, splus(*Embrown*) → $\{3,4,6\}$, and splus(*Blond*) → $\{4,6\}$.

For the value '*Brown*' we have: obj(*Brown*) = $\{2,3,5\}$ and obj(*Brown*) = splus(*Brown*), i.e. obj(*Brown*) $\subseteq s(+)$. Analogously for the value

'*Embrown*' we have: obj(*Embrown*) = {3,4,6} and obj(*Embrown*) ⊆ s(+).

These values are irredundant and simultaneously maximally redundant tests for R(+) because *val*({2,3,5}) = '*Brown*' and *val*({3,4,6}) = '*Embrown*'. It is clear that these values cannot belong to any test different from the test obtained. We delete '*Brown*' and '*Embrown*' from further consideration with the following result as shown in Table 11.

Now none of the remaining rows of Class 2 is a test because obj(*Low, Bleu*) = {1,2}, obj(*Tall*) = {3,4,5,7,8}, obj(*Tall, Blond*) = {4,8}, obj(*Tall, Bleu*) = {5,7,8}, obj(*Low, Blond*) = {1,6} □ s(+).

The subtasks of the first and second kind form some **subcontexts** of an initial context. Choosing values or examples for subtasks we can manage the process of inferring good tests.

The decomposition of good classification tests inferring into subtasks of the first and second kinds implies introducing a set of special operations to realize the following acts: choosing an object (value) for a subtask, forming a subtask, deleting values or objects from a subtask and some other rules controlling the process of inferring good tests.

The following theorem gives the foundation for reducing projections both of the first and the second kind. The proof of this theorem can be found in (Naidenova et al., 1995b).

## THEOREM 1

Let *A* be a value from *T*, (obj(*X*), *X*), *X* ⊆ *T* be a maximally redundant test for a given set R(+) of positive objects and obj(*A*) ⊆ obj(*X*). Then *A* does not belong to any maximally redundant good test

for R(+) different from (obj(*X*), *X*).

It is convenient to choose essential values in an object and essential objects in a projection for the decomposition of inferring GMRTs into the subtasks of the first or second kind.

We give a small example for inferring all the GMRTs for the instances of Class 1 presented in Table 12, where we have: S(+) = {1,2,3}, obj(*Low*) → {1,2,6}, obj(*Brown*) → {2,3,5}, obj(*Bleu*) → {1,2,5,7,8}, obj(*Tall*) → {3,4,5,7,8}, obj(*Embrown*) → {3,4,6}, and obj(*Blond*) → {1,4,6,8}.

We discover that the value '*Low*' is essential in lines 1 and 2. Then it is convenient to form the subtask of the second kind for this value as shown in Table 13.

In Table 13, we have: S(+) = {1,2}, splus(*Low*) → {1,2}, splus(*Brown*) → {2}, splus(*Bleu*) → {1,2}, and obj(*Blond*) → {1}. Then we observe (val(splus(*Bleu*) = '*Low Bleu*' corresponds to a test for Class 1. Analogously, for the value '*Brown*', we have that val(splus(*Brown*) = '*Low Brown*' corresponds a test for Class 1 but not a good one because of splus(*Brown*) ⊆ splus(*Bleu*).

It is clear that these values cannot belong to any test different from the tests already obtained. We delete '*Brown*' and '*Bleu*' from further consideration in this subtask. But after deleting these values, line 1 and 2 do not correspond to tests for Class 1. Hence the subtask is over.

Return to the main problem. Now we can delete the value '*Low*' from further consideration because we have got all good tests containing this value for Class 1. But we know that the value '*Low*' is essential in lines 1 and 2, this fact means that

*Table 10. The projection of t₂ on the objects of class 2*

| Index of Example | Height | Color of hair | Color of eyes | Test? |
|---|---|---|---|---|
| 2 | Low | Brown | Bleu | Yes |
| 3 | | Brown | | Yes |
| 5 | | Brown | Bleu | Yes |

*Table 11. The result of reducing the projection after deleting the values 'brown' and 'embrown'*

| Index of Example | Height | Color of hair | Color of eyes | test? |
|---|---|---|---|---|
| 2 | Low | | Bleu | No |
| 3 | Tall | | | No |
| 4 | Tall | Blond | | No |
| 5 | Tall | | Bleu | No |
| 6 | Low | Blond | | No |

these lines do not correspond to tests for Class 1 after deleting this value.

A recursive procedure based on using attributive subtasks for inferring GMRTs has been described in (Naidenova et al., 1995b). In the following section of this chapter, we give an algorithm based on the subtasks of the first kind combined with searching for essential examples. This algorithm is used only for inferring GMRTs.

## AN ALGORITHM FOR INFERRING GMRTS WITH THE USE OF THE SUBTASK OF THE FIRST KIND

The algorithm DIAGaRa is the basic recursive algorithm for solving subtasks of the first kind.

The initial information for the algorithm of finding all the GMRTs contained in a positive object is the projection of this object on the current set $R(+)$. Essentially, the projection is simply a subset of objects defined on a certain restricted subset $t^*$ of values. Let $s^*$ be the subset of indices of positive objects producing the projection.

It is useful to introduce the characteristic $W(t)$ of any collection $t$ of values named by the weight of $t$ in the projection: $W(t) = \|obj(t) \cap s^*\|$ is the number of positive objects of the projection containing $t$. Let WMIN be the minimal permissible value of the weight.

Let *STGOOD* be the partially ordered set of elements $s$ satisfying the condition that $(s, val(s))$ is a good test for $R(+)$.

The basic algorithm consists of applying the sequence of the following steps:

- **Step 1.** Check whether the intersection of all the elements of projection corresponds to a test and if so, then $s^*$ is stored in *STGOOD* if $s^*$ corresponds to a good test at the current step; in this case, the subtask is over. Otherwise the next step is performed (we use the function to_be_test($t$): if obj($t$) $\cap$ $S(+)$ = obj($t$) (obj($t$) $\subseteq$ $S(+)$) then *true* else *false*).

- **Step 2.** For each value $A$ in the projection, the set $splus(A) = \{s^* \cap obj(A)\}$ and the weight $W(A) = \|splus(A)\|$ are determined and if the weight is less than the minimum permissible weight WMIN, then the value $A$ is deleted from the projection. We can also delete the value $A$ if $W(A)$ is equal to WMIN and val($splus(A)$) is not a test – in this case $A$ will not appear in a maximally redundant test (obj($t$), $t$) with $W(t)$ equal to or greater than WMIN.

- **Step 3.** The generalization operation is performed: $t' = val(splus(A))$, $A \in t^*$; if $t'$ correspond to a test, then the value $A$ is deleted from the projection and $splus(A)$ is stored in *STGOOD* if $splus(A)$ corresponds to a good test at the current step.

- **Step 4.** The value $A$ can be deleted from the projection if $splus(A) \subseteq s'$ for some $s'$ $\in$ *STGOOD*.

- **Step 5.** If at least one value has been deleted from the projection, then the reduction

*Table 12. Example 2 of data classification*

| Index of example | Height | Color of hair | Color of eyes | Class |
|---|---|---|---|---|
| 1 | Low | Blond | Bleu | 1 |
| 2 | Low | Brown | Bleu | 1 |
| 3 | Tall | Brown | Embrown | 1 |
| 4 | Tall | Blond | Embrown | 2 |
| 5 | Tall | Brown | Bleu | 2 |
| 6 | Low | Blond | Embrown | 2 |
| 7 | Tall | Red | Bleu | 2 |
| 8 | Tall | Blond | Bleu | 2 |

of the projection is necessary. The reduction consists of deleting the elements of projection that do not correspond to tests (as a result of previous eliminating values). If, under reduction, at least one element has been deleted from the projection, then Step 2, Step 3, Step 4, and Step 5 are repeated.

- **Step 6.** Check whether the subtask is over or not. The subtask is over when either the projection is empty or the intersection of all elements of the projection corresponds to a test (see Step 1). If the subtask is not over, then the choice of an essential object in this projection is performed and the new subtask is formed with the use of this essential object. The new subsets $s^*$ and $t^*$ are constructed and the basic algorithm runs recursively. The important part of the basic algorithm is how to form the set *STGOOD*.

We give in the Appendix an example of the work of this algorithm.

**An Approach for Forming the Set *STGOOD*.** Let $L(S)$ be the set of all subsets of the set $S$. $L(S)$ is the set lattice (Rasiova, 1974). The ordering determined in the set lattice coincides with the set-theoretical inclusion. It will be said that subset $s_1$ is absorbed by subset $s_2$, that is, $s_1 \leq s_2$, if and only if the inclusion relation is hold between them, that is, $s_1 \subseteq s_2$. Under formation of *STGOOD*, a collection $s$ of indices is stored in *STGOOD* if and only if it is not absorbed by any collection of this set. It is necessary also to delete from *STGOOD* all the collections of objects that are absorbed by $s$ if $s$ is stored in *STGOOD*. Thus, when the algorithm is over, the set *STGOOD* contains all the collections of objects that correspond to GMRTs and only such collections. Essentially, the process of forming *STGOOD* is an incremental procedure of finding all maximal elements of a partially ordered set. The set *TGOOD* of all the GMRTs is obtained as follows: $TGOOD = \{(s, val(s)), (\forall s) (s \in STGOOD)\}$.

*Table 13. The subtask for the value 'Low'*

| Index of example | Height | Color of hair | Color of eyes | Class |
|---|---|---|---|---|
| 1 | Low | Blond | Bleu | 1 |
| 2 | Low | Brown | Bleu | 1 |

## AN APPROACH TO INCREMENTAL INFERRING GOOD DIAGNOSTIC TESTS

Incremental learning is necessary when a new portion of observations or examples becomes available over time. Suppose that each new example comes with the indication of its class membership. The following actions are necessary with the arrival of a new example:

- Check whether it is possible to perform generalization of an existing GMRTs for the class to which the new example belongs (class of positive examples), that is, whether it is possible to extend the set of examples covered by this GMRTs or not.
- Infer all the GMRTs contained in the new example.
- Check the validity of the existing GMRTs for negative examples, and if it necessary:
- Modify tests that are not valid (test for negative examples is not valid if it is included in a positive example, that is, in other words, it accepts an example of positive class).
- Thus the process of inferring all the GMRTs is divided into the subtasks that conform to three acts of reasoning:
- Pattern recognition or using already known rules (tests) for determining the class membership of a new positive example and generalization of the rules that recognize it correctly (deductive reasoning and increasing the power of already existing inductive knowledge);
- Inferring new rules (tests) that are generated by a new positive example (inductive reasoning a new knowledge);
- Correcting rules (tests) of alternative (negative) classes that accept a new positive example (these rules do not permit to distinguish a new positive example from some negative examples) (deductive and

inductive diagnostic reasoning to modify knowledge).

The first act reveals the known rules satisfied with a new example, the induction base of these rules can be enlarged.

The second act can be reduced to the subtask of the first kind.

The third act can be reduced either to the inductive diagnostic rule and the subtasks of the first kind or only to the subtask of the second kind.

## FUTURE RESEARCH DIRECTIONS

Of course, revealing the connection between machine learning and commonsense reasoning is only the first and, perhaps, timid step in the direction of modeling natural human reasoning in computers. Many methodological questions of the organization of such reasoning arise. All these questions can be grouped into the following basic categories:

1. Organization of interacting between data and knowledge in computers on the new foundations. Data must not simply be accumulated without the interference of knowledge in the process of data assimilation. Data must be introduced into an "intelligent system" under control of knowledge available to this system and must contribute to the immediate development of system knowledge.

2. The form of data representation and knowledge must provide the dynamic formation of commonsense reasoning contexts and the possibility of effective application of algebraic lattice (Galois's lattice) structures for realizing this reasoning.

3. It is necessary to resolve the methodological problems of integrating the technologies of databases and knowledge bases modeling with the contemporary technologies of ontology developing.

4. It is necessary to develop the mechanisms of machine learning in the direction of their larger automation. Currently in the tasks of classification, the semantic interpretation of object classes is determined by the selection of feature system given by a supervisor. It is desirable computer to possess a larger freedom in selecting feature systems, relying on the knowledge existing at its disposal and turning to such sources of knowledge as ontology.

5. The realization of reasoning requires that it would be developed the sophisticated systems for the perception (by computers) of diverse external information somehow speech, image, texts and so on. Perception must be based on the automated analysis of external stimuli, the extraction of their structural elements and their features. Thus far all programs of processing input information are built on the knowledge of man, personified in algorithms and rules of recognition, but not on the systems of knowledge about objects produced in the computer itself.

There is no doubt that the solution of these crucial problems requires efforts and cooperation of the specialists from different fields: mathematics, logic, artificial intelligence, psycholinguistics, the theory of programming, machine learning, knowledge engineering, neurophysiology, biology, and many others.

We hope that this article will contribute to the increase of different specialists' interest toward knowing of the unique human ability to mine knowledge on the basis of commonsense reasoning.

## CONCLUSION

This work is an attempt to transform a large class of machine-learning tasks into a commonsense reasoning process based on using well-known deduction and induction logical rules.

For this goal, we have chosen the task of inferring good classification (diagnostic) tests for a given partitioning on a given training set of examples because a lot of well-known machine-learning problems such as inferring functional, implicative and associative dependencies from data are reduced to this task.

We proposed a unified model for combining inductive reasoning with deductive reasoning in the framework of inferring and using implicative logical rules. The key concept of our approach is the concept of a good diagnostic test. We define a good diagnostic test as the best approximation of a given classification on a given set of examples.

The problem of inferring GDTs serves as the ideal model for inductive reasoning since its very statement requires applying inductive canons discovered in our thinking and stated by British logician John Stuart Mill. We relied upon the theory of algebraic lattices as the mathematical language for constructing good diagnostic tests.

Inferring chains of elements of the interconnected lattices ordered by the inclusion relation is the basis for generating all types of tests. We studied four variants of inductive transition from one element of the chain to its nearest elements in the lattice. We constructed rules for implementing these transitions: rules of generalization and specialization, inductive diagnostic rule and dual inductive diagnostic rule.

We have divided commonsense reasoning rules in two classes: rules of the first type and rules of the second type. The rules of the first type are represented with the use of implicative logical statements. The rules of the second type or reasoning rules (deductive and inductive) are rules with the help of which rules of the first type used, updated and inferred from data. The deductive reasoning rules of the second type are modus ponens, modus ponendo tollens, modus tollendo ponens, and modus tollens). The main inductive reasoning rules of the second type are the following ones: the Method of Agreement, the Method of Difference, the Joint Method of Agreement and Difference. The analysis of the inference for lattice construction allows demonstrating that this inference engages both inductive and deductive reasoning rules of the second type. During the lattice construction, the rules of the first type (implications, interdictions, rules of compatibility) are generated and used immediately.

We have introduced the decomposition of inferring good tests for a given set of positive examples into operations and subtasks that are in accordance with human commonsense reasoning operations. This decomposition allows, in principle, to transform the process of inferring good tests into a "step by step" commonsense reasoning process.

We have given also the algorithm DIAGaRa for inferring GMRTs and an approach to incremental inferring good diagnostic tests.

## ACKNOWLEDGMENT

The author is very grateful to Prof., Dr. E. Triantaphyllou (Louisiana State University, Department of Computer Science) who inspired and supported this work, and to Prof., Dr. R. Nedunchezhian (Sri Ramakrishna Engineering College) for his invariable attention to the author. None of these people bear any responsibility for the content as presented, of course.

## REFERENCES

Agraval, R., & Srikant, R. (1994). Fast algorithms for mining association rules. In *Proceedings of the 20-the VLDB Conference*, (pp. 487-499). Santiago, Chile: Morgan Kaufmann.

Anshakov, O. M., Finn, V. K., & Skvortsov, D. P. (1989). On axiomatization of many-valued logics associated with formalization of plausible reasoning. *Studia Logica*, *42*(4), 423–447. doi:10.1007/BF00370198

Birkhoff, G. (1954). *Lattice theory*. Moscow, Russia: Foreign Literature.

Boldyrev, N. G. (1974). Minimization of Boolean partial functions with a large number of "don't care" conditions and the problem of feature extraction. In *"Discrete Systems", Proceedings of International Symposium* (pp.101-109). Riga, Latvia: Publishing House "ZINATNE

Carpineto, C., & Romano, G. (1996). A lattice conceptual clustering system and its application to browsing retrieval. *Machine Learning*, *24*, 95–122. doi:10.1007/BF00058654

Ceri, C., Gotlob, G., & Tanca, L. (1990). *Logic programming and databases*. New York: Springer-Verlag.

Demetrovics, J., & Vu, D. T. (1993). Generating Armstrong relation schemes and inferring functional dependencies from relations. *International Journal on Information Theory & Applications*, *1*(4), 3–12.

Finn, V. K. (1984). Inductive models of knowledge representation in man-machine and robotics systems. *The Transactions of VINITI, A*, 58-76.

Finn, V. K. (1988). Commonsense inference and commonsense reasoning. *Review of Science and Technique (Itogi Nauki i Tekhniki), Series "The Theory of Probability. Mathematical Statistics. Technical Cybernetics*, *28*, 3–84.

Finn, V. K. (1991). Plausible reasoning in systems of JSM type. *Review of Science and Technique (Itogi Nauki i Tekhniki), Series ". Informatika*, *15*, 54–101.

Finn, V. K. (1999). The synthesis of cognitive procedures and the problem of induction. *NTI* [Moscow, Russia: VINITI]. *Series*, *2*(1-2), 8–44.

Galitsky, B. A., Kuznetsov, S. O., & Vinogradov, D. V. (2007). Applying hybrid reasoning to mine for associative features in biological data. *Journal of Biomedical Informatics, 40*(3), 203–220. doi:10.1016/j.jbi.2006.07.002

Ganascia, J. - Gabriel. (1989). EKAW - 89 tutorial notes: Machine learning. In J. Boose, B. Gaines, & J.G. Ganascia, (Eds.), *EKAW'89: Third European Workshop on Knowledge Acquisition for Knowledge-Based Systems* (pp. 287-296), Paris, France.

Ganter, B. (1984). *Two basic algorithms in concepts analysis. B4-Preprint, No. 831.* Darmstadt: Technische Hochschule.

Giraud-Carrier, C., & Martinez, T. (1994). An incremental learning model for commonsense reasoning. In *Proceedings of the Seventh International Symposium on Artificial Intelligence (ISAI'94)*, (pp. 134-141). ITESM.

Huntala, Y., Karkkainen, J., Porkka, P., & Toivonen, H. (1999). TANE: An efficient algorithm for discovering functional and approximate dependencies. *The Computer Journal, 42*(2), 100–111. doi:10.1093/comjnl/42.2.100

Kuznetsov, S. O. (1993). Fast algorithm of constructing all the intersections of finite semi-lattice objects. *NTI* [Moscow, Russia: VINITI]. *Series, 2*(1), 17–20.

Kuznetsov, S. O., & Obiedkov, S. A. (2001). Comparing performance of algorithms for generating concept lattices. *Journal of Experimental & Theoretical Artificial Intelligence, 14*(2-3), 183–216.

Lavraĉ, N., & Džeroski, S. (1994). *Inductive logic programming: techniques and applications.* Chichester, UK: Ellis Horwood.

Lavraĉ, N., & Flash, P. (2000). *An extended transformation approach to Inductive Logic Programming. CSTR – 00 -002* (pp. 1–42). Bristol, UK: University of Bristol, Department of Computer Science.

Lavraĉ, N., Gamberger, D., & Jovanoski, V. (1999). A study of relevance for learning in deductive databases. *The Journal of Logic Programming, 40*(2/3), 215–249. doi:10.1016/S0743-1066(99)00019-9

Lisi, F., & Malerba, D. (2004). Inducing multilevel association rules from multiple relations. *Machine Learning, 55*, 175–210. doi:10.1023/B:MACH.0000023151.65011.a3

Mannila, H., & Räihä, K.-J. (1992). On the complexity of inferring functional dependencies. *Discrete Applied Mathematics, 40*, 237–243. doi:10.1016/0166-218X(92)90031-5

Mannila, H., & Räihä, K.-J. (1994). Algorithm for inferring functional dependencies. *Data & Knowledge Engineering, 12*, 83–99. doi:10.1016/0169-023X(94)90023-X

Megretskaya, I. A. (1988). Construction of natural classification tests for knowledge base generation. In Y. Pecherskij (Ed.), The Problem of the expert system application in the national economy: Reports of the Republican Workshop (pp. 89-93). Kishinev, Moldava: Mathematical Institute with Computer Centre of Moldova Academy of Sciences.

Michalski, R. S. (1983). A theory and methodology of inductive learning. *Artificial Intelligence, 20*, 111–161. doi:10.1016/0004-3702(83)90016-4

Michalski, R. S., & Larsen, I. B. (1978). Selection of most representative training examples and incremental generation of VL1 hypotheses: the underlying methodology and the description of programs ESEL and AQII. *Report No. 78-867.* Urbana, IL: Dep. of Comp. Science, Univ. of Illinois at Urbana-Champaign.

Michalski, R. S., & Ram, A. (1995). Learning as goal-driven inference. In Ram, A., & Leake, D. (Eds.), *Goal-Driven Learning.* Cambridge, MA: MIT Press/Bradford Books.

Mill, J. S. (1900). The system of logic. Moscow, Russia: Russian Publishing Company "Book Affair".

Naidenova, X. A. (1992). Machine learning as a diagnostic task. In Arefiev, I. (Ed.), *Knowledge-Dialogue-Solution, Materials of the short-term scientific seminar* (pp. 26–36). Saint-Petersburg, Russia: State North-West Technical University.

Naidenova, X. A. (1996). Reducing machine learning tasks to the approximation of a given classification on a given set of examples. In *Proceedings of the 5-th National Conference at Artificial Intelligence* (Vol. 1, pp. 275-279), Kazan, Tatarstan.

Naidenova, X. A. (1999). The data-knowledge transformation. In Soloviev, V. (Ed.), *Text Processing and Cognitive Technologies, Issue 3* (pp. 130–151). Pushchino, Russia.

Naidenova, X. A. (2001). Inferring good diagnostic tests as a model of commonsense reasoning. In *"Knowledge-Dialog-Solution"* []. Saint-Petersburg, Russia: State North-West Technical University.]. *Proceedings of the International Conference, 2*, 501–506.

Naidenova, X. A. (2006). An incremental learning algorithm for inferring implicative rules from examples. In Triantaphillou, E., & Felici, G. (Eds.), *Data Mining and Knowledge Discovery Approaches Based on Rule Induction Techniques* (pp. 90–146). New York: Springer. doi:10.1007/0-387-34296-6_3

Naidenova, X. A., & Ermakov, A. E. (2001). The decomposition of algorithms of inferring good diagnostic tests. In A.Zakrevskij (Ed.), *Proceedings of the 4-th International Conference "Computer – Aided Design of Discrete Devices (CAD DD'2001),* (Vol. 3, pp. 61-69). Minsk, Belarus: Institute of Engineering Cybernetics, National Academy of Sciences of Belarus.

Naidenova, X. A., Plaksin, M. V., & Shagalov, V. L. (1995b). Inductive inferring all good classification tests. In J. Valkman (Ed.), *"Knowledge-Dialog-Solution", Proceedings of International Conference in two volumes* (Vol. 1, pp. 79 - 84). Jalta, Ukraine: Kiev Institute of Applied Informatics.

Naidenova, X. A., & Polegaeva, J. G. (1986). An algorithm of finding the best diagnostic tests. In Mintz, G. E., & Lorents, P. P. (Eds.), *The Application of mathematical logic methods* (pp. 63–67). Tallinn, Estonia: Institute of Cybernetics, National Acad. of Sciences of Estonia.

Naidenova, X. A., & Polegaeva, J. G. (1991). SISIF – the system of knowledge acquisition from experimental facts. In Alty, J. L., & Mikulich, L. I. (Eds.), *Industrial Applications of Artificial Intelligence* (pp. 87–92). Amsterdam, the Netherlands: Elsevier Science Publishers B.V.

Naidenova, X. A., Polegaeva, J. G., & Iserlis, J. E. (1995a). The system of knowledge acquisition based on constructing the best diagnostic classification tests. In J. Valkman. (Ed.), *"Knowledge-Dialog-Solution"*, Proceedings of International Conference in two volumes (Vol. 1, pp. 85-95). Jalta, Ukraine: Kiev Institute of Applied Informatics.

Nguifo, M. E., & Njiwoua, P. (1998). Using lattice based framework as a tool for feature extraction. In C.Nedellec, & C. Rouveirol (Eds.), *Proceedings of the 10th conference on Machine Learning* (ECML-98), (LNCS 1398, pp. 304-309). Chemnitz, Germany: Springer.

Nourine, L., & Raynaud, O. (1999). A fast algorithm for building lattices. *Information Processing Letters, 71*, 199–204. doi:10.1016/S0020-0190(99)00108-8

Ore, O. (1944). Galois connexions. *Transactions of the American Mathematical Society, 55*(1), 493–513. doi:10.2307/1990305

Ore, O. (1980). *Theory of graphs*. Moscow, USSR: Nauka.

Piaget, J. (1959). *La genèse des structures logiques elémentaires*. Neuchâtel, Switzerland: Delachaux & Niestlé.

Rasiova, H. (1974). An algebraic approach to non-classical logic (Studies in Logic, Vol. 78). Warsaw & Amsterdam: PWN – Polish Scientific Publishers & North-Holland Publishing Company.

Riguet, J. (1948). Relations binaires, fermetures, correspondences de Galois. *Bulletin des Sciences Mathématiques, 76*(3), 114–155.

Salzberg, S. (1991). A nearest hyper rectangle learning method. *Machine Learning, 6,* 277–309. doi:10.1007/BF00114779

Schmidt-Schauss, M., & Smolka, G. (1991). Attributive concept descriptions with complements. *Artificial Intelligence, 48*(1), 1–26. doi:10.1016/0004-3702(91)90078-X

Stumme, G., Taouil, R., Bastide, Y., Pasquier, N., & Lakhal, L. (2000). Fast computation of concept lattices using data mining techniques. In M.Bouzeghoub, M.Klusch, W. Nutt, & U.Sattler (Eds.), *Proceeding of the 7th International Workshop on Knowledge Representation Meets Databases* (KRDB 2000) (Vol. 29, pp. 129-139). Berlin, Germany: CEUR-WS.org.

Stumme, G., Wille, R., & Wille, U. (1998). Conceptual knowledge discovery in databases using formal concept analysis methods. In Principles of Data Mining and Knowledge Discovery (LNCS 1510, pp. 450-458). Berlin: Springer.

Vinogradov, D. V. (1999). Logic programs for quasi-axiomatic theories. *NTI* [Moscow, Russia: VINITI]. *Series, 2*(1-2), 61–64.

Wille, R. (1992). Concept lattices and conceptual knowledge system. *Computers & Mathematics with Applications (Oxford, England), 23*(6-9), 493–515. doi:10.1016/0898-1221(92)90120-7

Zakrevskij, A. D. (2006). A common logic approach to data mining and pattern recognition problem. In Triantaphyllou, E., & Felici, G. (Eds.), *Data Mining and Knowledge Discovery Approaches Based on Rule Induction Techniques* (pp. 1–42). New York: Springer. doi:10.1007/0-387-34296-6_1

## ADDITIONAL READING

Aros, D. C., Chambrin, M. C., & Pomorski, D. (2001). From local trend extraction to symbolization of time - series. [Publisher: IOS Press.]. *Intelligent Data Analysis, 5*(1), 41–57.

Cimiano, Ph. (Ed.). (2006). *Ontology learning and population from text. Algorithms, evaluation and applications*. Karlsruhe, Germany: Springer.

Dau, F., Mugnier, M.-L., & Stumme, G. (Eds.). (2005). *Conceptual structures: common semantics for sharing knowledge, Proceeding of the 13th International Conference on Conceptual Structures* (ICCS 2005). Kassel, Berlin/Heidelberg, Germany: Springer.

Fanizzi, N., Claudia d'Amato, C., & Esposito, F. (2008). *Conceptual clustering and its application to concept drift and novelty detection*. Presented at: 5th European Semantic Web Conference (ESWC2008). Retrieved from http://dx.doi.org/10.1007/978-3-540-68234-9_25.

Hadjmichael, M. (2009). A fuzzy expert system for aviation risk assessment. *Expert systems with application, 36*(3), 6512-6519.

Huang, S., Wunsch, D. C., II, Levine, D. S., & Kang-Hyun Jo, K.-H. (Eds.). (2008). *Advanced intelligent computing theories and applications with aspects of contemporary intelligent computing techniques, Proceedings of the 4th International Conference on Intelligent Computing (ICIC 2008), Series: Communications in Computer and Information Science*. Springer.

Kao, A., & Poteet, S. R. (Eds.). (2007). *Natural language processing and text mining*. London, UK: Springer-Verlag. doi:10.1007/978-1-84628-754-1

Kononenko, I. (2001). Machine learning for medical diagnosis: history, state of the art and perspectives. *Artificial Intelligence in Medicine, 23*(1), 89–109. doi:10.1016/S0933-3657(01)00077-X

Kotsianti, S. B. (2007). Supervised machine learning: a review of classification technique. *Informatica, 31*, 249–268.

Kuznetsov, S. (2007). On stability of a formal concept. *Annals of Mathematics and Artificial Intelligence, 49*, 101–115. doi:10.1007/s10472-007-9053-6

Kuznetsov, S., Obiedkov, S., & Roth, C. (2007). *Reducing the representation complexity of lattice-based taxonomies*. Paper presented for publication in the Proceedings of the 15th International Conference on Conceptual Structures (Sheffiled, UK), Lecture Notes in Artificial Intelligence, Springer.

Li, N., Wang, R., Zhang, J., Fu, Z., & Zhang, X. (2009). Developing a knowledge-based early warning system for fish disease/health via water quality management. *Expert systems with application 36*(3), 6500-6511.

Michalski, R. S., Kaufman, K., Pietrzykowski, J., Wojtusiak, J., Mitchell, S., & Seeman, W. D. (2006). *Natural induction and conceptual clustering: A review of applications. Reports of the Machine Learning and Inference Laboratory, MLI 06-3*. Fairfax, VA: George Mason University.

Naidenova, X. A. (2009). Machine learning as a commonsense reasoning process. In Ferraggine, V. E., Doorn, J. H., & Rivero, L. C. (Eds.), *Handbook of Research on Innovations in Database Technologies and Applications: Current and Future Trends* (*Vol. 2*, pp. 605–611). Hershey, PA: IGI Global.

Naidenova, X. A. (2009). *Machine learning methods for commonsense reasoning processes. Interactive models*. Hershey, New York: Inference Science Reference.

Nezamabadi-pour, H., & Kabir, E. (2009). Concept learning by fuzzy K-NN classification & relevance feedback for efficient image retrieval. *Expert systems with application, 36*(3), 5948-5954.

Nguifo, E. M., & Njiwoua, P. (2001). IGLUE: A lattice-based constructive inductive system. [IOS Press.]. *Intelligent Data Analysis, 5*(1), 73–91.

Nigro, H. O., & Cisaro, S. E. G. (2009). Ontologies application to knowledge discovery process in databases. Viviana E. Ferraggine, Jorge H. Doorn, & Laura C. Rivero (Eds.), Handbook of Research on Innovations in Database Technologies and Applications: Current and Future Trends (Vol. 2, pp. 509-516). Hershey, PA: IGI Global.

Obiedkov, S. and Duquenne, V. (2007). *Attribute-incremental construction of the canonical implication basis*. The paper accepted for publication in Annals of Mathematics and Artificial Intelligence.

Obiedkov, S., & Roth, C. (Eds.). (2007). Social network analysis and conceptual structures: exploring opportunities. *Proceedings of the ICFCA 2007 Workshop*. Clermont-Ferrand, France.

Priss, U. (2000a). Lattice-based information retrieval. *Knowledge Organization, 27*(3), 132–142.

Priss, U. (2000b). Knowledge discovery in databases using formal concept analysis. *Bulletin of the American Society for Information Science, 27*(1), 18–20. doi:10.1002/bult.186

Priss, U. (2005). Linguistic applications of formal concept analysis. In B. Ganter, G. Stumme, & R. Wille (Eds.). Formal Concept Analysis: Foundation and Applications (LNAI 3626, pp. 149-160). Publisher: Springer-Verlag.

Priss, U., & Old, L. J. (2004). Modeling lexical databases with formal concept analysis. *Journal of Universal Computer Science, 10*(8), 967–984.

Priss, U., & Old, L. J. (2007). Bilingual word association networks. In Priss, Polovina, & Hill (Eds.), *Proceedings of the 15th International Conference on Conceptual Structures* (ICCS'07), (LNAI 4604, pp. 310-320). Publisher: Springer-Verlag.

Qi, Ch., & Sun, J. Cui, Sh. (2006). *A new formal concept analysis method and its construction algorithm. IEE Computer Society*: CS Digital Library. Retrieved Oct. 20-Oct. 21. from http://www2.computer.org/portal/web/csdl/doi/10.1109/ICICTA.2008.

Savinov, A. (2005). Concept as a generalization of class and principles of the concept-oriented programming. *Computer Science Journal of Moldova, 13*(3), 292–335.

Savinov, A. (2006). Query by constraint propagation in the concept-oriented data model. *Computer Science Journal of Moldova, 14*(2), 219–238.

Savinov, A. (2007a). Two-level concept-oriented data model. *Technical Report RT0006*, Institute of Mathematics and Computer Science, Academy of Sciences of Moldova.

Savinov, A. (2007b). An approach to programming based on concepts. *Technical Report RT0005*, Institute of Mathematics and Computer Science, Academy of Sciences of Moldova.

Savinov, A. (2008). Concepts and concept-oriented programming. *Journal of Object Technology, 7*(3), 91–106.

Savinov, A. (2009). Concept-oriented model. In Ferraggine, V. E., Doorn, J. H., & Rivero, L. C. (Eds.), *Handbook of research on innovations in database technologies and applications: current and future trends* (*Vol. 1*, pp. 171–180). Hershey, PA: IGI Global.

## KEY TERMS AND DEFINITIONS

**Diagnostic or Classification Test:** Assume that we have two sets of objects' examples called positive and negative examples respectively. A test for a subset of positive examples is a collection of attributes' values describing this subset of examples if it is unique, i. e. none of the negative examples is described by it.

**Good Classification Test:** A classification test for a given set of positive examples is good if this set is maximal in the sense that if we add to it any positive example, then the collection of attributes' values describing the obtained set will describe at least one negative example.

**Good Maximally Redundant Test (GMRT):** A good test is a maximally redundant one if extending it by any attribute's value not belonging to it changes its property "to be a good test" into the property "to be test but not a good one".

**Good Irredundant Test (GIRT):** A good test is irredundant if deleting any attribute's value from it changes its property "to be test" into the property "not to be a test".

**Implicative Assertions:** Implications describe the regularities mutually connecting objects, properties and classes of objects. They can be given explicitly by an expert or derived automatically from examples via some learning process.

**Commonsense Reasoning Rules (CRRs):** These are rules with the help of which implicative assertions are used, updated and inferred from examples. The deductive CRRs are based on the use of syllogisms: modus ponens, modus ponendo tollens, modus tollendo ponens, and modus tollens. The inductive CRRs are the canons formulated by J. S. Mill (1900). Commonsense reasoning is based on using the CCRs.

**Inductive Transitions:** These are the processes of extending or narrowing collections of values (objects). They can be smooth and boundary. Upon smooth transition, a certain assigned property of the generated collections does not change. Upon boundary transition, a certain assigned property of the generated collections changes to the opposite one.

**The Subtask of the First Kind:** Assume that we have two sets of positive and negative examples and a positive example. The subtask of the first kind is to find all the collections of attributes' values that are included in the description of this example and correspond to the good tests (GNRTs or GIRTs) for the set of positive examples.

**The Subtask of the Second Kind:** For a given set of positive and negative examples and a non-empty collection of attributes' values such that it is not a test for the set of positive examples, find all GMRTs (GIRTs) containing it.

## APPENDIX A: AN EXAMPLE OF USING ALGORITHM DIAGaRa

The data to be processed are in Table 14 (the set of positive examples) and in Table 15 (the set of negative examples).

*Table 14. The set of positive examples R(+)*

| Index of example | R(+) |
|---|---|
| 1 | $A_1A_2A_5A_6A_{21}A_{23}A_{24}A_{26}$ |
| 2 | $A_4A_7A_8A_9A_{12}A_{14}A_{15}A_{22}A_{23}A_{24}A_{26}$ |
| 3 | $A_3A_4A_7A_{12}A_{13}A_{14}A_{15}A_{18}A_{19}A_{24}A_{26}$ |
| 4 | $A_1A_4A_5A_6A_7A_{12}A_{14}A_{15}A_{16}A_{20}A_{21}A_{24}A_{26}$ |
| 5 | $A_2A_6A_{23}A_{24}$ |
| 6 | $A_7A_{20}A_{21}A_{26}$ |
| 7 | $A_3A_4A_5A_6A_{12}A_{14}A_{15}A_{20}A_{22}A_{24}A_{26}$ |
| 8 | $A_5A_6A_7A_8A_9A_{13}A_{14}A_{15}A_{19}A_{20}A_{21}A_{22}$ |
| 9 | $A_{16}A_{18}A_{19}A_{20}A_{21}A_{22}A_{26}$ |
| 10 | $A_2A_3A_4A_5A_6A_8A_9A_{13}A_{18}A_{20}A_{21}A_{26}$ |
| 11 | $A_1A_2A_3A_7A_{19}A_{20}A_{21}A_{22}A_{26}$ |
| 12 | $A_2A_3A_{16}A_{20}A_{21}A_{23}A_{24}A_{26}$ |
| 13 | $A_1A_4A_{18}A_{19}A_{23}A_{26}$ |
| 14 | $A_{23}A_{24}A_{26}$ |

*Table 15. The set of negative examples R(-)*

| Index of example | R(-) | Index of example | R(-) |
|---|---|---|---|
| 15 | $A_3A_8A_{16}A_{23}A_{24}$ | 32 | $A_1A_2A_3A_7A_9A_{13}A_{18}$ |
| 16 | $A_7A_8A_9A_{16}A_{18}$ | 33 | A$_1$ A5 A6 A8 A9 A19 A20 A22 |
| 17 | $A_1A_{21}A_{22}A_{24}A_{26}$ | 34 | A2 A8 A9 A18 A20 A21 A22 A23 A26 |
| 18 | $A_1A_7A_8A_9A_{13}A_{16}$ | 35 | A1 A2 A4 A5 A6 A7 A9 A13 A16 |
| 19 | $A_2A_6A_7A_9A_{21}A_{23}$ | 36 | A1 A2 A6 A7 A8 A13 A16 A18 |
| 20 | $A_{10}A_{19}A_{20}A_{21}A_{22}A_{24}$ | 37 | A1 A2 A3 A4 A5 A6 A7 A12 A14 A15 A16 |
| 21 | $A_1A_{20}A_{21}A_{22}A_{23}A_{24}$ | 38 | A1 A2 A3 A4 A5 A6 A9 A12 A13 A16 |
| 22 | $A_1A_3A_6A_7A_9A_{16}$ | 39 | A1 A2 A3 A4 A5 A6 A14 A15 A19 A20 A23 A26 |
| 23 | $A_2A_6A_8A_9A_{14}A_{15}A_{16}$ | 40 | A2 A3 A4 A5 A6 A7 A12 A13 A14 A15 A16 |
| 24 | $A_1A_4A_5A_6A_7A_8A_{16}$ | 41 | A2 A3 A4 A5 A6 A7 A9 A12 A13 A14 A15 A19 |
| 25 | $A_7A_{13}A_{19}A_{20}A_{22}A_{26}$ | 42 | A1 A2 A3 A4 A5 A6 A12 A16 A18 A19 A20 A21 A26 |
| 26 | $A_1A_2A_3A_6A_7A_{16}$ | 43 | A4 A5 A6 A7 A8 A9 A12 A13 A14 A15 A16 |
| 27 | $A_1A_2A_3A_5A_6A_{13}A_{16}$ | 44 | A3 A4 A5 A6 A8 A9 A12 A13 A14 A15 A18 A19 |
| 28 | $A_1A_3A_7A_{13}A_{19}A_{21}$ | 45 | A1 A2 A3 A4 A5 A6 A7 A8 A9 A12 A13 A14 A15 |
| 29 | $A_4A_7A_4A_6A_7A_8A_{13}A_{16}$ | 46 | A1 A3 A4 A5 A6 A7 A12 A13 A14 A15 A16 A23 A24 |
| 30 | $A_1A_2A_3A_6A_{12}A_{14}A_{15}A_{16}$ | 47 | A1 A2 A3 A4 A5 A6 A8 A9 A12 A14 A16 A18 A22 |
| 31 | $A_1A_2A_5A_6A_{14}A_{15}A_{16}A_{26}$ | 48 | A2 A8 A9 A12 A14 A15 A16 |

*Table 16. The set SPLUS of the collection splus(A) for all A in Tables 14 and 15*

| SPLUS = {splus($A_i$): $s(A_i) \cap s(+)$, $A_i \in T$}: | |
|---|---|
| splus($A_*$) → {2,8,10} | splus($A_{22}$) → {2,7,8,9,11} |
| splus($A_{13}$) → {3,8,10} | splus($A_{23}$) → {1,2,5,12,13,14} |
| splus($A_{16}$) → {4,9,12} | splus($A_3$) → {3,7,8,10,11,12} |
| splus($A_1$) → {1,4,11,13} | splus($A_4$) → {2,3,4,7,10,13} |
| splus($A_5$) → {1,4,7,10} | splus($A_6$) → {1,4,5,7,8,10} |
| splus($A_{12}$) → {2,3,4,7} | splus($A_7$) → {2,3,4,6,8,11} |
| splus($A_{18}$) → {3,9,10,13} | splus($A_{24}$) → {1,2,3,4,5,7,12,14} |
| splus($A_2$) → {1,5,10,11,12} | splus($A_{20}$) → {4,6,7,8,9,10,11,12} |
| splus($A_+$) → {2,3,4,7,8} | splus($A_{21}$) → {1,4,6,8,9,10,11,12} |
| splus($A_{19}$) → {3,8,9,11,13} | splus($A_{26}$) → {1,2,3,4,6,7,9,10,11,12,13,14} |

*Table 17. The sets STGOOD and TGOOD for the examples of Tables 14 and 15*

| STGOOD | TGOOD |
|---|---|
| {2,3,4,7} | $A_4 A_{12} A_4 A_{24} A_{26}$ |
| {1,2,12,14} | $A_{23} A_{24} A_{26}$ |
| {4,6,8,11} | $A_7 A_{20} A_{21}$ |

We begin with $s^* = S(+) = \{\{1\}, \{2\}, ..., \{14\}\}$, $t^* = T = \{A_1, A_2, ....., A_{26}\}$, $SPLUS = \{$splus$(A_i): A_i \in t^*\}$ (see SPLUS in Table 16). In Tables 16, 17, $A_*$ denotes the collection of values $\{A_8, A_9\}$ and $A_+$ denotes the collection of values $\{A_{14}, A_{15}\}$ because splus$(A_8) = $ splus$(A_9)$ and splus$(A_{14}) = $ splus$(A_{15})$.

We use the algorithm DIAGaRa for inferring all the GMRTs having a weight equal to or greater than WMIN = 4 for the training set of the positive examples represented in Table 14.

Please observe that splus$(A_{12}) = \{2,3,4,7\}$ and (splus$(A_{12})$, val($\{2,3,4,7\}$)) is a test, therefore, $A_{12}$ is deleted from $t^*$ and splus$(A_{12})$ is inserted into *STGOOD*.

Then $W(A_*)$, $W(A_{13})$, and $W(A_{16})$ are less than WMIN, hence we can delete $A_*$, $A_{13}$, and $A_{16}$ from $t^*$. Now $t_{10}$ is not a test and can be deleted.

After modifying splus($A$) for $A_5$, $A_{18}$, $A_2$, $A_3$, $A_4$, $A_6$, $A_{20}$, $A_{21}$, and $A_{26}$ we find that $W(A_5) = 3$, therefore, $A_5$ is deleted from $t^*$.

Then $W(A_{18})$ turns out to be less than WMIN and we delete $A_{18}$, this implies deleting $t_{13}$. Next we modify splus($A$) for $A_1$, $A_{19}$, $A_{23}$, $A_4$, $A_{26}$ and find that splus$(A_4) = \{2,3,4,7\}$. $A_4$ is deleted from $t^*$. Finally, $W(A_1)$ turns out to be less than WMIN and we delete $A_1$.

We can delete also the values $A_2$, $A_{19}$ because $W(A_2)$, $W(A_{19}) = 4$, (splus($A_2$), val(splus($A_2$)), (splus($A_{19}$), val(splus($A_{19}$))) are not tests and, therefore, these values will not appear in a maximally redundant test $t$ with $W(t)$ equal to or greater than 4.

After deleting these values we can delete the examples $t_9$, $t_5$ because $A_{19}$ is essential in $t_9$, and $A_2$ is essential in $t_5$. Next we can observe that splus($A_{23}$) = {1,2,12,14} and (splus(1,2,12,14), val({1,2,12,14}) is a test; thus $A_{23}$ is deleted from $t^*$ and splus($A_{23}$) is inserted into *STGOOD*. We can delete the values $A_{22}$ and $A_6$ because $W(A_{22})$ and $W(A_6)$ are now equal to 4, (splus($A_{22}$), val(splus($A_{22}$)) and (splus($A_6$), val(splus($A_6$))) are not tests, and these values will not appear in a maximally redundant test with weight equal to or greater than 4. Now $t_{14}$ and $t_1$ are not tests and can be deleted.

Choose $t_{12}$ as a subtask because now this example is essential in splus($A_{21}$) and in splus($A_{24}$). By resolving this subtask, we find that $t_{12}$ does not produce a new test. We delete it. Then splus($A_{21}$) is equal to {4,6,8,11}, (splus(4,6,8,11), val({4,6,8,11}) is a test, thus $A_{21}$ is deleted from $t^*$ and splus($A_{21}$) is inserted into STGOOD. We can also delete the value $A_{24}$ because (splus($A_{24}$), val(splus($A_{24}$))) is the GMRTs already obtained.

We can delete the value $A_3$ because $W(A_3)$ is now equal to 4, (splus($A_3$), val(splus($A_3$))) is not a test and this value will not appear in a maximally redundant test with weight equal to or greater than 4. We can delete $t_6$ because now this example is not a test. Then we can delete the value $A_{20}$ because (splus($A_{20}$), val(splus($A_{20}$))) is the GMRTs already obtained.

These deletions imply that all of the remaining rows $t_2$, $t_3$, $t_4$, $t_7$, $t_8$, and $t_{11}$ are not tests.

The list of the GMRTs with the weight equal to or greater than WMIN = 4 is given in Table 17.

# Chapter 13
# A Human–Machine Interface Design to Control an Intelligent Rehabilitation Robot System

**Erhan Akdoğan**
*Marmara University, Turkey*

**M. Arif Adlı**
*Marmara University, Turkey*

**Ertuğrul Taçgın**
*Marmara University, Turkey*

**Nureddin Bennett**
*Technical University of Kaiserslautern, Germany*

## ABSTRACT

*The demand for rehabilitation increases daily as a result of diseases, occupational and traffic accidents and population growth. In the present time, some important problems occur regarding the rehabilitation period: the transportation of patients, the acquisition and storage of treatment data and the need to support the physiotherapists with intelligent devices. In order to overcome these challenges, the authors hereby propose a human machine interface to control an intelligent rehabilitation robot system designed for the lower limbs. The human machine interface has a structure that is created with a rule-based intelligent controlling structure, combined with conventional controller and an easy-to-use graphical user interface. By means of this interface, the rehabilitation sessions can be stored and members of the rehabilitation team can reach to this stored data via internet. Additionally, the patient can receive treatment in his house. One physiotherapist is able to treat several patients at a time by utilizing this system. The system's capacity has been elaborated through the test results.*

## INTRODUCTION

The growing world population and the increasing number of problems people have with their limbs have intensified the need for rehabilitation particularly for lower limbs. Reestablishing and improving the limb functionality and strength are major issues. Furthermore, it is most important to help patients to return to society, to reintegrate them into social life and thus to improve the patients'

DOI: 10.4018/978-1-60566-814-7.ch013

quality of life. Injuries in extremities like arms and legs are caused mainly due to old age, work and traffic accidents. The role of the rehabilitation process is to restore functionality of previously damaged limbs. Throughout the therapy, physical exercises for extremities like arms and legs have a key role in the recovery of the patient. Therapeutic exercises consist of active or passive physical movements of the patient, carried out through the physiotherapist (PT), or of movements carried out by the patient with the assistance of the physiotherapist, depending on the condition of the patient. Among them, the performing of resistive exercises is particularly difficult and exhausting for physiotherapists. For rehabilitation either the patient has to go to a healthcare center, or the physiotherapist has to come to the patient. Considering the often time-consuming process of rehabilitation, this is difficult and cost-intensive for both patient and physiotherapist, and demands a high amount of patience of all parties involved. Furthermore, a physiotherapist can only fully attend one patient at a time. Another important issue is to record the treatment period of the patient and to provide the members of the rehabilitation team- physiotherapist, occupational therapist etc- with fast and easy access to these records. By means of this access, the rehabilitation period can proceed well and a database can be formed for patients with similar conditions. The progress of a patient can be therefore monitored and compared to other patients. To achieve this aim and therefore to increase the efficiency of the rehabilitation process, the following issues have to be solved:

- The patient's condition should be monitored and recorded throughout the treatment period. The monitoring information should be saved on the database of the medical center and must be easily accessible.
- Computerized mechanisms, capable of performing therapeutic exercises, are needed to support physiotherapists

- Intelligent human-machine and human-computer interfaces are needed to enable the physiotherapists to control these mechanisms.
- To overcome the problem of transporting patients to the medical center, internet-based rehabilitation methods should be developed for remote operation and treatment.

## BACKGROUND

Over the last decade, the number of studies about robots in rehabilitation has increased. Studies carried out in near past have proved that rehabilitation robots have many advantages compared to classic therapy methods (Lum et al., 2002). In addition, robotic therapy provides better possibilities to acquire and store information such as the therapy response of the patient (Richardson, Brown, & Plummer, 2000). A number of studies – as part of the general studies made about rehabilitation robots – in which particularly conventional control techniques stand out, have hitherto been carried out. Lum and others (1995 & 1997) introduced an assisted rehabilitation system for arms. Krebs and others (1998 & 2003) have developed and have clinically evaluated a robot-aided neuro rehabilitation system called MIT-MANUS. This device provides multiple-degree of freedom exercises of upper extremities for stroke patients. Rao, Agrawal and Scholz (1999) introduced another system using a Puma 240 robot for active and passive rehabilitation of upper extremities. Richardson and others developed a 3 DOF (degree of freedom) pneumatic device for rehabilitation of upper extremities using PD control and impedance control methodologies (Richardson et al., 1999, 2000, & 2003). Reinkensmeyer and others (2000) developed a 3 DOF system called ARM Guide (Assisted Rehabilitation and Measurement Guide) for rehabilitation of upper extremities. Another system with 3 DOF, called GENTLE/s, is developed in England for the rehabilitation of upper extremities, controlled by the admittance control method (Loueiro et al., 2003). The robots and methods developed in these studies generally realize specific tasks or assist the patient throughout rehabilitation.

However, some researchers have applied more intelligent techniques as well. Lee and others developed a robotic system for rehabilitation of upper limbs of paralyzed patients using an expert system (Lee, Agah, & Bekey, 1990). Utilizing two industrial robots, the REHAROB project serves for the rehabilitation of upper extremities. A knowledge base is formed by the sensing force and position during manually conducted rehabilitation sessions. Industrial robots then repeat the same procedure using this knowledge base (REHAROB Project, 2000). Okada et al. (2000) employed impedance control methodologies in a 2 DOF robotic system for lower limbs rehabilitation. Position and force information are received and recorded for the robotic system to reproduce the corresponding motion. The REHAROB Project and Okada's robotic mechanism both deal with the reproduction of the physiotherapist's exercise motions.

These studies for rehabilitation robots generally have a limited exercise capacity and stand out on account of their control techniques. Furthermore, they have a limited capability with regard to having soft computing techniques, an internet-based study environment, data storage and the ease of a user-friendly graphical user interface (GUI).

In this study, a human-machine interface (HMI) is developed for the control of a three degrees of freedom robot manipulator (RM) designed for the rehabilitation of the lower limbs. With the developed HMI, the rehabilitation robot system can perform all active and passive exercises as well as learn specific exercise motions and perform them without the physiotherapist. With this feature, the system differentiates itself from the current rehabilitation robot systems. The HMI

possesses a rule-based intelligent control structure merged with conventional control techniques and a practical GUI. Moreover, the entire treatment period of the patient can be stored in the database. At the same time the HMI has a flexible software structure that makes the system suitable for remote online operation. The preliminary experimental results of this study have been published Akdoğan E., Taçgın E., Adlı M.A. (2009).

## REHABILITATION ROBOT SYSTEM

The following exercises are performed by therapeutic devices or physiotherapists during hip and knee rehabilitation:

- Moving the patient's limb passively (passive exercise)
- Assisting the motion of the patient's limb (active assistive exercise)
- Resisting the motion of the patient's limb (resistive exercise)
- Opening the patient's limb with force despite reaction from the patient (stretching)

The exercises that are given above are procedures that can also be described and modeled as position and force control. The position and force relations and sequences are clear and have no complex uncertainties. With the developed HMI, the rehabilitation robot system (see Figure 1) is able to work as a therapeutic exercise device. It can generate and apply necessary position and force sequences to the patient's limb. The rehabilitation robot system is able to model the physiotherapists' movements and experiences and is therefore enabled to behave like a physiotherapist.

Because of the reasons mentioned above, the developed system has the required features for the rehabilitation of the lower limbs. It can perform six different types of exercises which results in six working modes. These exercise types are of the following kinds:

*Figure 1. Rehabilitation robot system*

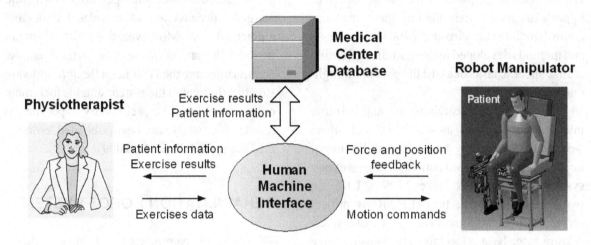

- passive
- isotonic
- isometric
- isokinetic
- active assistive
- manual

The passive, isotonic, isometric and isokinetic exercises can be done with the assistance of the physiotherapist, using some tools such as constant weight, spring or devices such as CPM (continuous passive motion). All these exercises are resistive except for the passive ones. However, the active assistive and manual exercises are done manually only by physiotherapist. A method called *robotherapy* has been developed to model the manual exercises. Robotherapy operates in two modes: teaching mode and therapy mode. The physiotherapist performs the necessary exercise motion on the patient with the robot manipulator. In the therapy mode, the system applies the therapy to the patient with the RM using the data that was obtained during the teaching mode (the position and force data applied by physiotherapist, their limit values and therapy time).

For this mode, two different sub modes have been developed: direct therapy and reactive therapy. Direct therapy imitates the physiothera-

pist completely. The reactive mode models the physiotherapists' stretching motions. Namely, the patient's limb is stretched with force to certain limits in accordance with the patient's muscular condition. These limits are determined in the teaching mode. The detailed explanations of the exercise modes are given in the next section.

The system consists of three basic components. These are the physiotherapist, the human-machine-interface and the robot manipulator.

The physiotherapist has the role of preparing and adjusting the system for the patient. He decides the necessary exercises and teaches the exercise movements to the RM. The physiotherapist inputs the patient's information using the graphical user interface of the HMI. The information needed for input is age, height, weight, and foot size of the patient. For active and passive exercise modes such as passive, isometric, isotonic and isokinetic, the physiotherapist inputs the information on the type of the exercise and the information for that specific exercise (number of repetitions, exercise duration, range of motion, angles and velocity). In the robotherapy mode, he selects the teaching mode for the manual exercises. The patient then performs the necessary exercise movements with the help of the robot manipulator. Next, the physiotherapist selects the therapy mode from

*Figure 2. The structure of the HMI*

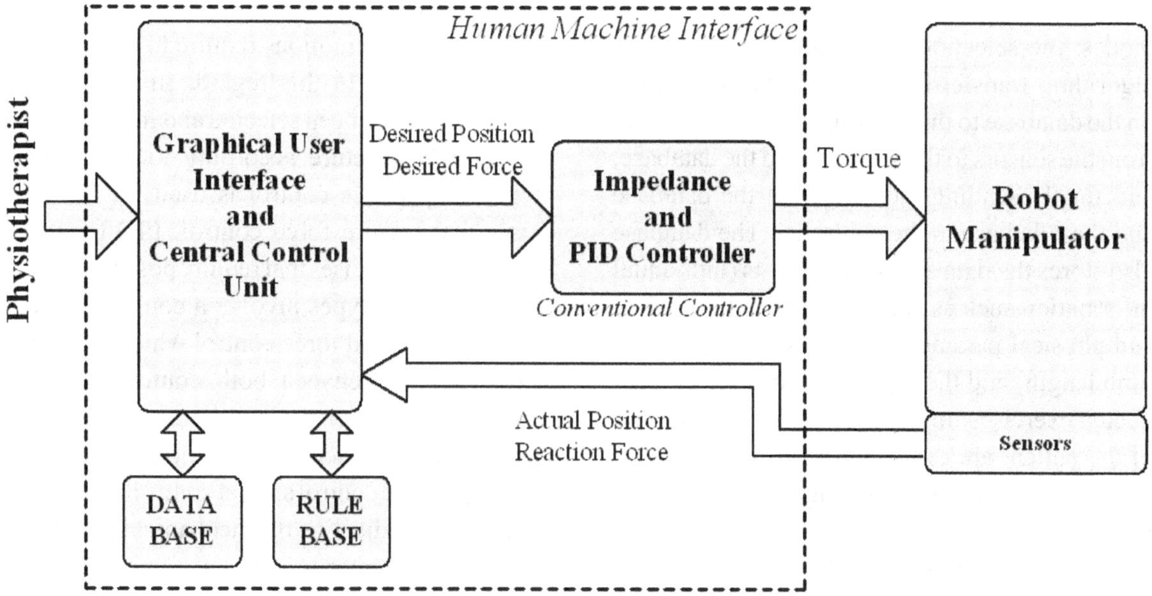

the GUI and the robot manipulator performs the exercise movements with the patient without the physiotherapist.

The robot manipulator's design is suitable for both left and right knees and hips. The mechanism can be adjusted for different body and limb lengths. The manipulator can perform flexion – extension motion for knee rehabilitation and flexion – extension as well as abduction-adduction motion for hip rehabilitation. It has position and force sensors to acquire feedback from the patient. For deeper information refer to (Akdoğan, Taçgın, & Adlı 2009). The robot manipulator is controlled by closed-loop control algorithms based on PID or impedance control depending on the exercise. For PID control, control parameters are proportional, integral and derivative coefficients. For impedance control, the control parameters are inertia ($M_d$ [kg]), stiffness ($K_d$ [N/deg]) and damping coefficients ($D_d$ [Ns/deg]).

The HMI has the key role for the rehabilitation robot system. All communication is performed amongst the system's elements through the HMI. Selecting the proper conventional technique and

determining the control parameters are realized by the HMI in accordance with the exercise type. In the next section, a detailed explanation of HMI will be given.

## HUMAN-MACHINE INTERFACE IMPLEMENTATION

The human-machine interface has been developed using MATLAB/Simulink and the graphical user interface toolbox. The Real Time Windows Target Toolbox is used for realtime control and signal processing. The HMI was developed in a way that allows an internet-based use. It consists of the central control unit, a conventional controller (impedance and PID controller), a data base, a rule base and the GUI (see Figure 2).

As the appropriate control technique must be selected, a database has been realized to store the control parameter values for the upcoming exercise. The communication between all HMI units is provided by a central control unit. The functions of these units are given in Table 1 according to exercise modes. Additionally, the central control unit performs the following tasks for all exercise modes: the selection of the appropriate control algorithm, transferring the patients' parameters on the database to the algorithm, sending the data from the sensors to the rule base and the database, and finally sending the data from the database and the rule base to the controller. The database also stores the data about the patients (individual information such as name, gender and birth date and physical parameters such as length, height, limb length) and the exercise results for all conducted exercises. In this system, exercise results of the patient are evaluated in terms of the mechanical parameters' (joint angle, torque, velocity) index. This index has two different evaluation versions – a patient index and an error index. The patient index reflects patient performance only, while the error index shows the differences between patient performance and commands from the system. In the patient index, three scores are computed or measured: the instant values over time, the time average value for each trial and the overall average value for all trials. For the instant values over time, mechanical parameters are calculated or measured and stored on the database. At the same time, these parameters are shown on the display to the therapist or patient during the rehabilitation session. With the time average value for each trial, the patient and therapist can understand the evaluation results after each session. Using the overall average value for all trials, the patient and the therapist can check changes in the index depending on the day, and compare values before and after training. The aim of the error index is to evaluate the patient's performance. The index consists of the success rate and the mean value of error in tasks. The success rate is computed from the rate of patient motion, while task commands and the mean error come from differences between the patient's motion and the system/therapist commands. For future work, EMG parameters index will be added to the database as well. The usage of the HMI units in

accordance with exercise modes are given in the following part of this section.

The exercise motions require to control position and force. In this regard, suitable control techniques have been selected and integrated into the HMI's structure according to the exercise types. Impedance control is used for the exercises that require force control. PID control is used for the exercises that require position control. Some exercise types involve a combined use of both position and force control which is realized by switching between both controller modes. Table 2 shows an overview about which controller is used for which exercise mode.

Impedance control aims at controlling position and force by adjusting the mechanical impedance of the end-effector to external forces generated by contact with the manipulator's environment. Mechanical impedance is roughly an extended concept of the stiffness of a mechanism against a force applied to it. It is accepted to be the most appropriate control technique for physiotherapy and is used in many rehabilitation robot applications (Culmer et al., 2005, Krebs et al., 1998, & 2003, Tanaka, Tsuji, & Kaneko, 2000). The robot manipulator can apply resistance to the treated limb at the required level of smoothness and stiffness by changing the impedance control parameters. In addition, the physiotherapist can have the patient perform the exercise motions with a high level of ease and with no degree of vibration.

## HUMAN-MACHINE INTERFACE EXERCISE MODES

In this section, the algorithms regarding the exercise modes will be explained in detail.

*A) Passive Exercise Mode:* This type of exercise is specifically applied to patients with little or no muscle contraction (e.g. paralyzed patients). The limb of the patient is moved around the range of motion without resistance. The therapist inputs the angles of the ROM, the number of repetitions

*Table 1. HMI functions*

| Exercise Mode | Central Control Unit | Data Base | Rule Base |
|---|---|---|---|
| **Passive** | - According to extension and flexion angles, repetition number and velocity, determination of motion trajectory and sending this information to data base<br>- Transfer of trajectories to PID controller throughout the exercise. | Storage of exercise trajectory | Not used |
| **Active assistive** | - According to information that come from force sensor, transferring of opposite force data to rule base. | Storage of minimum impedance parameter values | If there is an opposite force on the force sensor, running of PID controller |
| **Isotonic** | - According to selected resistance level, receiving of proper impedance parameter values from data base<br>- Calculation the number of repetitions using position data and sending it to the rule base. | Not used | - Therapy is stopped when repetition numbers completed<br>- Proper impedance values are determined according to resistance level |
| **Isometric** | Sending of weight, duration and limb length values that have been received from data base to the controller | Storage of patient's limb length | Determination of impedance parameter values according to resistance level |
| **Isokinetic** | Sending of velocity data to the controller | Not used | Not used |
| **Teaching** | Detection of limit values of teaching mode and sending them to data base | Storage of position-force data and maximum values of them | Not used |
| **Direct therapy** | Sending of teaching position-force data that have been received from data base to the controller | Recall teaching mode position and force data | Not used |
| **Reactive Therapy** | -Updating of rule base using maximum position and force data in data base<br>-Sending of these data to conventional controller<br>- Using maximum position data and patient's weight, finding and sending of proper desired position and force data in data base to conventional controller<br>- Sending of actual position and force data to rule base in order to control patient reaction and safety | Storing of maximum position and force data during the teaching mode, teaching time and desired position and force data that will be applied to patient | - Determining of data file according to patients limb weight and maximum position value.<br>- In the case of exceeding of limit values, switching on PID controller according to real time data that come from central controller unit |

*Table 2. Exercise modes and control techniques*

| Exercise Mode | Control Method |
|---|---|
| Passive | PID Position Control |
| Active assistive | PID Position Control + Impedance Control |
| Isometric | Impedance Control +Torque Control |
| Isotonic | Impedance Control |
| Isokinetic | Impedance Control |
| Robotherapy | Impedance Control + PID Position Control |

*Figure 3. Flow charts of exercise modes (from left to right): Passive, Active Assistive, Isotonic*

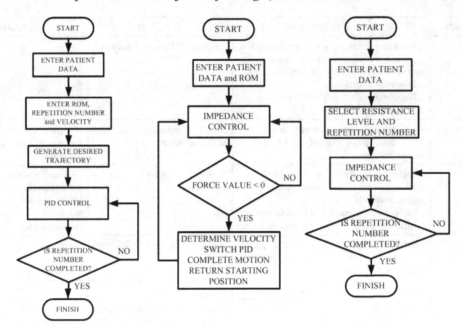

and the movement velocity through the GUI. The passive exercises basically require position control. Therefore, the robot manipulator makes its moves using the PID position control method for the passive exercises in this system. The desired trajectory of the exercise is generated by the HMI according to the ROM and velocity input by the GUI. The trajectory data is saved on the database. The HMI runs the PID algorithm using the desired trajectory when the exercise starts. The flow chart of this process is shown in Figure 3.

*B) Active Assistive Exercise Mode:* The active-assistive exercise is a type of exercise performed by physiotherapist and patient together. In this type of exercise, the patient moves his limb to the extent he is capable of. The patient is helped to move the limb to the required extent by the robot manipulator, which now replaces the physiotherapist, from the position that the patient is unable to move the limb any further. It is applied to patients with a muscle degree of 2 and 3 (The degree of muscles are evaluated with a scale that has six levels. This test is done by physiotherapist as manual. For deeper information refer to (Sarı,

Tüzün, & Akgün, 2002). The GUI input parameters are the range of motion values.

The patient's limb weight is eliminated by the system via a compensation of the gravity effects using impedance control, while always remaining within the patients' range of motion. This way the patient is enabled to move his limb to this level easily despite his muscle weaknesses. In the selection of the impedance control parameters, issues such as enabling the patient to move his limb at the lowest possible level of resistance and eliminating any possibility of causing vibration in the mechanism during the motion have been considered. These parameter values were determined experimentally and are stored in the database. With the evaluation of the force sensor signals it is determined when the patient cannot move his limb any further during the exercise. This force value arising in the opposite direction of the movement is detected by the HMI, which in turn activates the PID position control algorithm for the completion of the motion. Then, the patient's limb is moved to the limit of the range of motion with constant velocity and then brought back to the starting position also at constant velocity. For the flow diagram of this mode refer to Figure 3.

*C) Isotonic Exercise Mode:* It is used for patients with a muscle degree of four and has the purpose of strengthening remaining muscles. A constant resistant force is applied to the patient throughout the entire duration of the movement. The robot manipulator is controlled using impedance control with parameters optimized to the resistance level to be applied. For the isotonic exercise, four different resistance levels have been determined: *low, medium, high, and very high.* When the physiotherapist selects the resistance level in the user interface, the appropriate impedance parameter values are selected respectively from the rule base. There is a total of eight rules for this mode in the rule base. The knee controller has one DOF and performs flexion-extension. The rules for the knee controller are:

- **Rule1**<*If Resistance Level is**Low**then* $M_d=4$, $K_d=20$, $D_d=0$>
- **Rule2**<*If Resistance Level is**Medium**then* $M_d=5$, $K_d=60$, $D_d=0$>
- **Rule3**<*If Resistance Level is**High**then* $M_d=8$, $K_d=40$, $D_d=0$>
- **Rule4**<*If Resistance Level is**Very High**then* $M_d=10$, $K_d=100$, $D_d=1$>

The hip controller is a 2 DOF system and performs flexion-extension as well as abduction-adduction simultaneously. The rules for the hip controller are:

- **Rule1**<*If Resistance Level is**Low**then* $M_{dx}=10$, $K_{dx}=5000$, $D_{dx}=5000$, $M_{dz}=10$, $K_{dz}=5000$, $D_{dz}=100000$>
- **Rule2**<*If Resistance Level is**Medium**then* $M_{dx}=10$, $K_{dx}=5000$, $D_{dx}=5000$, $M_{dz}=500$, $K_{dz}=50000$, $D_{dz}=5000$>
- **Rule3**<*If Resistance Level is**High**then* $M_{dx}=10$, $K_{dx}=5000$, $D_{dx}=5000$, $M_{dz}=500$, $K_{dz}=50000$, $D_{dz}=100000$>

- **Rule4**<*If Resistance Level is**Very High**then* $M_{dx}=10$, $K_{dx}=5000$, $D_{dx}=5000$, $M_{dz}=1000$, $K_{dz}=100000$, $D_{dz}=5000$>

The x and z subscripts in the hip-controller rules represent the axes where motion occurs. The isotonic exercise modes' flow diagram is shown in Figure 3.

*D) Isometric Exercise Mode:* It is applied to patients with a muscle degree of four in order to strengthen them just as in the isotonic exercise. The exercise is realized with the application of constant resistance to the patient again staying within the range of motion. Isometric and isotonic exercise can be applied to the patient in a single exercise mode. The patient can perform isotonic and isometric exercises on the robot manipulator, which is one of the novelties of this system. A device that can perform this type of exercise has not been found in the literature. The GUI parameters are the resistance level of the isotonic and isometric exercise, the number of repetitions and the duration of the isometric resistance.

The patient moves his limb with a counter resistance force according to the resistance level that has been selected. The application of this counter resistance occurs as follows: the central control unit receives the impedance parameter values which have been determined according to the selected resistance level and sends them to the conventional controller. So the patient performs the isotonic exercise during the movement. The torque value that corresponds to the opposite torque input by the robot manipulator in the position of the limb is applied to the patient for the duration of the determined time. If the patient fails to maintain his position against the applied resistance, the HMI detects the situation with data from the sensor values, and switches to impedance control, consequently enabling the patient to easily convey his limb to the beginning position. This mode' flow diagram is shown in Figure 4.

*E) Isokinetic Exercise Mode:* The aim of this type of exercise is to facilitate the exercise by

Figure 4. Flow chart of isometric mode

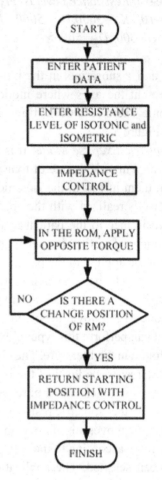

Figure 5. Flow chart of isokinetic mode

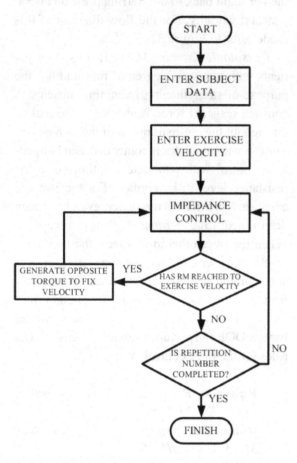

countering the maximum resistance and by keeping the movement velocity of the patient's limb at a stable level (Sarı, Tüzün, & Akgün, 2002). For this exercise, the therapist inputs the movement velocity through the user interface. The flow diagram of this mode is shown in Figure 5. When the exercise is started, the impedance control starts operating and the patient moves his limb. The movement velocity of the limb is continuously inspected by the HMI. If the movement velocity reaches the velocity value determined by the physiotherapist, an equal level of counter resistance is generated for the limb movement by calculating the force value detected by the HMI via force sensors. Doing so, the force generated in the reverse direction of the limb helps to main-

tain the movement velocity at the same level, even if the patient tries to accelerate the limb movement.

*F) Robotherapy:* This mode allows to model the physiotherapist's manual exercises in a very intuitive way. It is the most important novelty of the developed system. Robotherapy has two modes of operation, teaching mode and therapy mode. For the therapy mode, two different sub modes - free manual exercise movements and stretching exercises - have been developed in order to model the physiotherapist's movement.

In the *Teaching mode*, the physiotherapist assists the patient manually to perform the required motion with the patient on the robot manipulator as seen in Figure 6. In this mode, resistive effects of the mechanics of the robot manipulator are

*Figure 6. Robotherapy teaching mode (Akdoğan, Taçgin, & Adli 2009)*

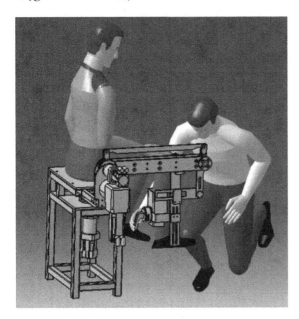

*Figure 7. Teaching mode block diagram*

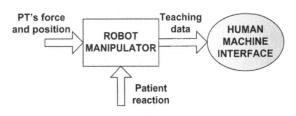

*Figure 8. Flow chart of teaching mode*

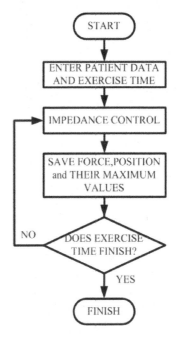

compensated by impedance control to an extent, that the limb of the patient can be moved freely. Force and position values as well as limits the time history are recorded to the data base by the HMI while the therapist is conducting the exercise with the patient. This information is later on used to reproduce the behavior of the physiotherapist by the robot manipulator.

In the case of the patient's reaction to the physiotherapist's movement, the saved force and position values also include the patient's reaction since the physiotherapist has eliminated this reaction during the exercise. Because of this, the saved limit values of position and force will be the limit values of the exercise in the therapy mode and the system will not apply an effect to the patient above the values in question. This situation provides the required safety for the patient which is of crucial importance in rehabilitation. The teaching mode block diagram is shown in Figure 7. The flow diagram of teaching mode is shown in Figure 8.

In the *therapy mode* the robot manipulator reproduces the therapy independent of the phys-

iotherapist using the information recorded during the teaching mode session. The Therapist is no longer required to be present at this point anymore. Therapy mode has two sub modes itself, direct therapy and reactive therapy.

In *direct therapy* mode, the robot manipulator simply repeats the previously recorded motion of the therapist. The recorded teaching data is retrieved by the central control unit and is used as the desired input data of the impedance controller. The robot manipulator performs the exercise according to this data. The flow diagram of this mode is shown in Figure 9.

*Reactive therapy* is used for patients whose limb cannot be opened due to muscle contraction.

*Figure 9. Flow chart of direct therapy mode*

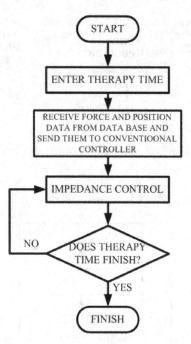

*Figure 10. Flow chart of reactive therapy mode*

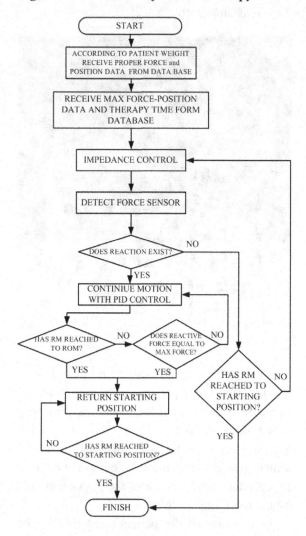

The traditional situation would be that the physiotherapist forces the limb to open. This is called *stretching*. This exercise mode aims to model these stretching exercises. The therapist eliminates the patient's reaction to a certain extent by applying force. The level of this force is in proportion with the therapist's personal experience. How the reactive therapy is applied in the system is systematically explained in the following.

The physiotherapist selects and starts *reactive therapy* mode via the GUI. The central control unit realizes the necessary process in order to determine the limit values of the exercise mode. In other words, the *physiotherapist's experience* is transferred to the system. These are the limit values to be considered and the robot manipulator won't exceed these limits. If the patient's reaction approaches these limit values, the HMI stops the robot manipulator. The flow diagram of this mode is shown in Figure 10.

At this point, the database already contains the force and position values previously gathered for each range of motion from six healthy subjects

with their mass ranging from 67 to 86 kilos (at every 10 degrees on a scale of 75 degrees). The physical specifications of subjects are given in Table 3. The amount of the data from the subjects recorded on the database can be increased due to the flexible structure of the HMI.

While filing the data from the healthy subjects, folders were formed according to the nick name of each subject (such as A, B, C…) and the files in these folders were also named accordingly, such as "1, 2, 3…". The file names with respect to the ROM interval are given in Table 4. Then, the folder name that consists of the proper subject

*Table 3. Subjects' physical specifications*

| Subject | Weight [kg] | Height [cm] | Foot Length [cm] | Leg length [cm] | Age |
|---------|-------------|-------------|------------------|-----------------|-----|
| A | 67 | 174 | 27 | 92 | 21 |
| B | 74 | 175 | 27 | 95 | 22 |
| C | 75 | 175 | 25 | 105 | 23 |
| D | 80 | 174 | 27 | 95 | 21 |
| E | 81 | 175 | 28 | 93 | 21 |
| F | 86 | 175 | 24 | 105 | 24 |

*Table 4. File names according to range of motion intervals*

| File Name | Range of Motion Interval |
|-----------|--------------------------|
| 1 | $0 \leq$ ROM $< 15$ |
| 2 | $15 \leq$ ROM $< 25$ |
| 3 | $25 \leq$ ROM $< 35$ |
| 4 | $35 \leq$ ROM $< 45$ |
| 5 | $45 \leq$ ROM $< 55$ |
| 6 | $55 \leq$ ROM $< 65$ |
| 7 | $65 \leq$ ROM $< 75$ |
| 8 | $75 \leq$ ROM $< 85$ |
| 9 | $85 \leq$ ROM $< 95$ |
| 10 | $-30 \leq$ ROM $< 0$ |

data files and the file name selected in line with the data regarding the maximum stretching position in the teaching mode are determined in the rule base according to the patient's weight. The determined data are received from the database by the HMI and sent to the RM. There are 70 rules in the rule base and the sample rules are given as follows:

< **Rule:** *if BW is bigger than 75 kg. or equal and less than 80 kg. and MXP bigger than 15 degree or equal and less than 25 degree, then Folder is C File is 2>*
...
< **Rule:** *if BW is bigger than 81 kg. or equal and less than 86 kg. and MXP bigger than 65 degree or equal and less than 75 degree, then Folder is E File is 7>*

The therapy continues with this data unless the patient shows a reaction of some kind. In the event the patient reacts, the HMI activates the PID control and the robot manipulator conveys the patient's limb to the range of motion limit that was determined in the teaching mode and then brings it back to the starting position. The HMI detects the patient's reaction continuously in real-time with the system wide used sampling time of 1 ms.

## GRAPHICAL USER INTERFACE

The graphical user interface of the HMI enables the user to communicate with the HMI. The main menu, as shown in the first screen of Figure 11, is used to input the patient's data. This data is used in order to calculate several mechanical parameters. The body limb, which is to be exercised, and the exercise type are selected from the main menu as well. Results from carried out exercises can be accessed from the main menu and are visualized graphically. The graphics display the patients' range of motion numerically and the patient's limb trajectory during the exercises session together with the corresponding forces (the last screen of Figure 11). These results are stored in the database and can be printed out optionally.

*Figure 11. GUI main menu and exercise results screen*

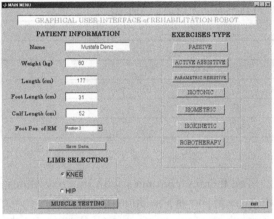

GUI main menu

Exercise Results Screen

## EXPERIMENTAL RESULTS

In the following some experimental results of the robotherapy modes including both direct and reactive therapy are shown. For experimental of the other modes of operation results refer to (Akdoğan, 2007).

Figure 12 illustrates a sample teaching mode sequence, and the corresponding "direct therapy mode" for knees. In this figure, from the top, teaching position ($p_{teach}$), therapy position ($p_{ther}$) and position error ($p_{teach}$ - $p_{ther}$) between teaching and therapy position are shown. As seen from this figure, the robot manipulator can perfectly repeat the motion of the physiotherapist the way it was learned during the teaching mode.

In Figure 13, the teaching mode sequence and the direct therapy mode results on the hip flexion-extension movement are given. The graph titled "Link 1" shows the position data on Link 1 (hip link), the graph titled "Link 2" shows the position data on Link 2 (knee link). The dashed line shows the position of the links during the teaching mode while and the solid line shows the position of the links during the therapy mode.

The teaching mode sequence and direct therapy mode results for the abduction-adduction movement are shown in Figure 14. The abduction-adduction movement is realized by the actuator that moves the hip about the vertical $z$-axis of the robot manipulator. In Figure 14, from the top, teaching position, therapy position and position error between teaching and therapy position are shown. Both Figure 13 and Figure 14 show a successful performance of the hip movement previously taught by the physiotherapist.

Figure 15 illustrates a sample "reactive therapy mode" for the knee of a test person with a weight of 80 kg up to a limit position of 75°. As seen in this figure, when the position is above 10°, the reaction force becomes negative indicating that the patient is resisting against motion. It may be caused by reflexes or disabilities. The subject applies just above 20N reaction force for the position of 75°, and then the rest of the motion is completed by means of the robot manipulator by forcing the patient's knee within possible limits. The reactive therapy mode for the hip movements will be realized in the following studies.

*Figure 12. An example of direct therapy for knee flexion-extension movement (Akdoğan, Taçgin, & Adli 2009)*

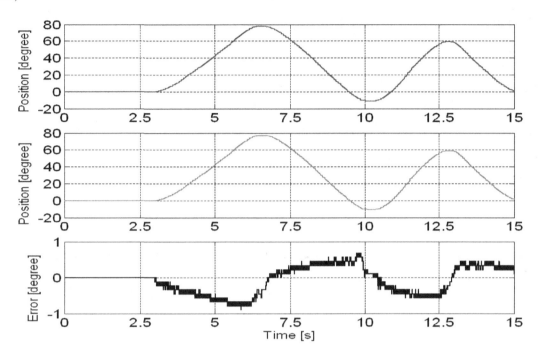

*Figure 13. An example of direct therapy for hip flexion-extension movement*

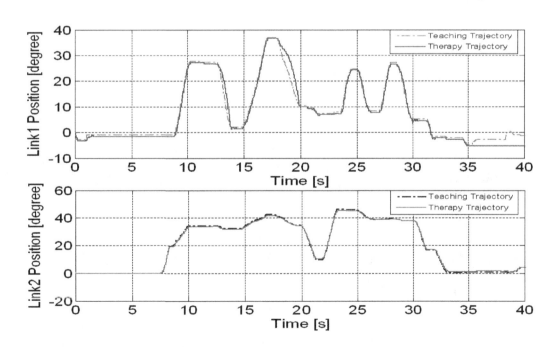

*Figure 14. An example of direct therapy for hip abduction-adduction movement*

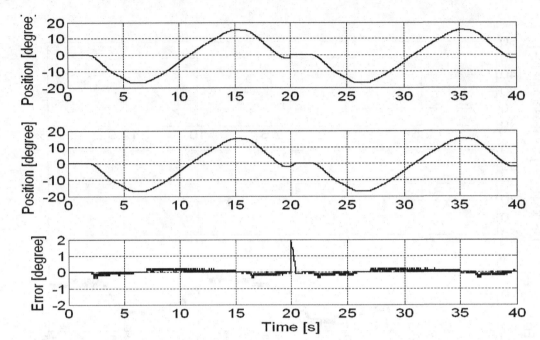

*Figure 15. Knee position and reaction force in reactive therapy (Akdoğan, Taçgin, & Adli 2009)*

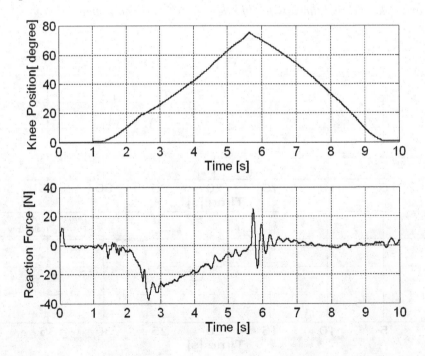

## CONCLUSION AND FUTURE WORK

In this study, a human-machine interface (HMI) was proposed to control a developed robot manipulator (RM) that has three-degrees of freedom for the rehabilitation of the lower limbs. The HMI has a structure created with a rule-based intelligent controller structure, combined with conventional control algorithms of the type impedance and PID control. It also has an easy-to-use, user friendly GUI. With the developed HMI, the progress and the current state of a patient's rehabilitation can be stored on the database. Furthermore, its flexible structure is suitable for internet-based use. With the use of this system, some common problems such as the transportation of patients, storage of data and availability of data of the progress of patients' rehabilitation, and the lacking support of physiotherapists with intelligent devices can be diminished.

The developed HMI can not diagnose the status of patients. If it is able to realize muscle testing like a physiotherapist before the rehabilitation session, it will able to design a treatment period in order to help physiotherapists. On the other hands, human body signals such as EMG signals reflect the real status of patients. Because of this, evaluating of EMG signals will provide important benefits. EMG pattern recognition though is a highly complex process. Especially the neural networks theory, which is one of the soft computing techniques, appears to be suitable for the interpretation of EMG signal patterns. For future work, we are planning to study on these two aspects using effective soft computing techniques.

## ACKNOWLEDGMENT

This work was supported by The Scientific and Technological Research Council of Turkey (TUBITAK) under the Grant Number 104M018. The authors would like to thank Ph.D. PT H. Serap İnal for her valuable advice and suggestions.

## REFERENCES

Akdoğan, E. (2007). *Intelligent position and force control of a robot manipulator for rehabilitation*. Doctoral dissertation, Marmara University, Istanbul, Turkey.

Akdoğan, E., Taçgın, E., & Adlı, M. A. (2009). Knee rehabilitation using an intelligent robotic system. *Journal of Intelligent Manufacturing*, *20*(2), 195–202. doi:10.1007/s10845-008-0225-y

Culmer, P., Jackson, A., Levesley, M. C., et al. (2005). An admittance control scheme for a robotic upper-limb stroke rehabilitation system. In *Proceedings of the 2005 IEEE Engineering in Medicine and Biology 27th Annual Conference*.

Krebs, H. I., Hogan, N., Aisen, M. L., & Volpe, B. T. (1998). Robot aided neurorehabilitation. *IEEE Transactions on Rehabilitation Engineering*, *6*(1), 75–87. doi:10.1109/86.662623

Krebs, H. I., Palazzolo, J. J., Volpe, B. T., & Hogan, N. (2003). Rehabilitation robotics: performance based progressive robot assisted therapy. *Autonomous Robots*, *15*(1), 7–20. doi:10.1023/A:1024494031121

Lee, S., Agah, A., & Bekey, G. (1990). An intelligent rehabilitative orthotic system for cerebrovascular accident. In *Proceedings of IEEE International Conference on Systems, Man and Cybernetics Conference*, (pp. 815-819).

Loueiro, R., Amirabdollahian, F., Topping, M., Driessen, B., & Harwin, W. (2003). Upper limb mediated stroke therapy – GENTLE/s approach. *Autonomous Robots*, *15*, 35–51. doi:10.1023/A:1024436732030

Lum, P. S., Burgar, C. G., Shor, P. C., Majmundar, M., & Van der Loos, M. (2002). Robot assisted movement training compared with conventional therapy techniques for the rehabilitation of upper – limb motor function after stroke. *Physical Medicine and Rehabilitation, 83*(7), 952–959. doi:10.1053/apmr.2001.33101

Lum, P. S., Burgar, G., & Van Der Loos, M. (1997). The use of robotic device for post stroke movement therapy. In *Proceedings of the International Conference on Rehabilitation Robotics,* (pp. 79-82).

Lum, P. S., Lehman, S., Steven, L., & Reinkensmeyer, D. J. (1995). The Bimanual Lifting Rehabilitator: An adaptive machine for therapy of stroke patient. *IEEE Transactions on Rehabilitation Engineering, 3*(2), 166–173. doi:10.1109/86.392371

Okada, S., & Sakaki, T. (2000). TEM: A therapeutic exercise machine for the lower extremities of spastic patient. *Advanced Robotics, 14*(7), 597–606. doi:10.1163/156855301742030

Rao, R., Agrawal, S. K., & Scholz, J. P. (1999). A robot test-bed for assistance and assessment in physical therapy. In *Proceedings of the International Conference on Rehabilitation Robotics,* (pp. 187-200).

REHAROB Project. (2000). Retrieved March 2007 from http://www.reharob.manuf.bme.hu

Reinkensmeyer, D. J., Kahn, L. E., Averbuch, M., McKenna-Cole, A. N., Schmit, B. D., & Rymer, W. Z. (2000). Understanding and treating arm movement impairment after chronic brain injury: progress with the ARM Guide. *Journal of Rehabilitation Research and Development, 37*(6), 653–662.

Richardson, R., Austin, M. E., & Plummer, A. R. (1999). Development of a physiotherapy robot. In *Proceedings of The International Biomechatronics Workshop,* (pp. 116-120).

Richardson, R., Brown, M., Bhakta, M., & Levesley, M. C. (2003). Design and Control of a Three Degree of Freedom Pneumatic Physiotherapy Robot. *Robotica,* (21): 589–604. doi:10.1017/S0263574703005320

Richardson, R., Brown, M., & Plummer, A. R. (2000). Pneumatic Impedance Control for Physiotherapy. In *Proceedings of The EUREL International Conference on Robotics,* (Vol. 2).

Sarı, H., Tüzün, S., & Akgün, K. (2002). *Hareket sistemi hastalıklarında fiziksel tıp yöntemleri.* Istanbul, Turkey: Nobel Tıp Kitabevleri.

Tanaka, Y., Tsuji, T., & Kaneko, M. (2000). A bio-mimetic rehabilitation aid for motor-control training using time base generator. In *Proceedings Industrial Electronics Society, IECON 2000 26th Annual Conference of the IEEE,* (vol.1, pp. 114-119).

## KEY TERMS AND DEFINITIONS

**Data Base:** A collection of information which is organized using a computer program to be accessible, manageable and updatable.

**Human-Machine Interface:** Platforms which provide a connecting interface between a machine, ie a robot manipulator, and a user.

**Impedance Control:** A control method in order to control position and force by adjusting the mechanical impedance of the end-effector to external forces generated by contact with the manipulator's environment.

**Intelligent Control:** Control technique which adopts itself or its parameters to changing control situations to runtime.

**Internet-Based Rehabilitation:** A novel rehabilitation concept that allows patients to be rehabilitated at their homes.

**Rehabilitation Robot:** Robotic devices in order to support daily activities of the people who have not sufficient motion capability and rehabilitate the patients who need motor recovery.

**Soft Computing:** A computing method which aim is to model human behavior for special purposes where it is not easy or impossible to realize a mathematical model such as traffic control, weather estimation and so on.

## APPENDIX: RULES OF HMI

< **Rule 1:** *if BW is bigger than 67 kg. or equal and less than 70 kg. and **MXP** bigger than 0 degree or equal and less than 15 degree, then **Folder** is A **File** is 1>*

< **Rule 2:** *if BW is bigger than 67 kg. or equal and less than 70 kg. and **MXP** bigger than 15 degree or equal and less than 25 degree, then **Folder** is A **File** is 2>*

< **Rule 3:** *if BW is bigger than 67 kg. or equal and less than 70 kg. and **MXP** bigger than 25 degree or equal and less than 35 degree, then **Folder** is A **File** is 3>*

< **Rule 4:** *if BW is bigger than 67 kg. or equal and less than 70 kg. and **MXP** bigger than 35 degree or equal and less than 45 degree, then **Folder** is A **File** is 4>*

< **Rule 5:** *if BW is bigger than 67 kg. or equal and less than 70 kg. and **MXP** bigger than 45 degree or equal and less than 55 degree, then **Folder** is A **File** is 5>*

< **Rule 6:** *if BW is bigger than 67 kg. or equal and less than 70 kg. and **MXP** bigger than 55 degree or equal and less than 65 degree, then **Folder** is A **File** is 6>*

< **Rule 7:** *if BW is bigger than 67 kg. or equal and less than 70 kg. and **MXP** bigger than 65 degree or equal and less than 75 degree, then **Folder** is A **File** is 7>*

< **Rule 8:** *if BW is bigger than 67 kg. or equal and less than 70 kg. and **MXP** bigger than 75 degree or equal and less than 85 degree, then **Folder** is A **File** is 8>*

< **Rule 9:** *if BW is bigger than 67 kg. or equal and less than 70 kg. and **MXP** bigger than 85 degree or equal and less than 95 degree, then **Folder** is A **File** is 9>*

< **Rule 10:** *if BW is bigger than 67 kg. or equal and less than 70 kg. and **MXP** bigger than -30 degree or equal and less than 0 degree, then **Folder** is A **File** is 10>*

< **Rule 11:** *if BW is bigger than 70 kg. or equal and less than 74 kg. and **MXP** bigger than 0 degree or equal and less than 15 degree, then **Folder** is B **File** is 1>*

< **Rule 12:** *if BW is bigger than 70 kg. or equal and less than 74 kg. and **MXP** bigger than 15 degree or equal and less than 25 degree, then **Folder** is B **File** is 2>*

< **Rule 13:** *if BW is bigger than 70 kg. or equal and less than 74 kg. and **MXP** bigger than 25 degree or equal and less than 35 degree, then **Folder** is B **File** is 3>*

< **Rule 14:** *if BW is bigger than 70 kg. or equal and less than 74 kg. and **MXP** bigger than 35 degree or equal and less than 45 degree, then **Folder** is B **File** is 4>*

< **Rule 15:** *if* ***BW*** *is bigger than 70 kg. or equal and less than 74 kg. and* ***MXP*** *bigger than 45 degree or equal and less than 55 degree, then* ***Folder*** *is B* ***File*** *is 5>*

< **Rule 16:** *if* ***BW*** *is bigger than 70 kg. or equal and less than 74 kg. and* ***MXP*** *bigger than 55 degree or equal and less than 65 degree, then* ***Folder*** *is B* ***File*** *is 6>*

< **Rule 17:** *if* ***BW*** *is bigger than 70 kg. or equal and less than 74 kg. and* ***MXP*** *bigger than 65 degree or equal and less than 75 degree, then* ***Folder*** *is B* ***File*** *is 7>*

< **Rule 18:** *if* ***BW*** *is bigger than 70 kg. or equal and less than 74 kg. and* ***MXP*** *bigger than 75 degree or equal and less than 85 degree, then* ***Folder*** *is B* ***File*** *is 8>*

< **Rule 19:** *if* ***BW*** *is bigger than 70 kg. or equal and less than 74 kg. and* ***MXP*** *bigger than 85 degree or equal and less than 95 degree, then* ***Folder*** *is B* ***File*** *is 9>*

< **Rule 20:** *if* ***BW*** *is bigger than 70 kg. or equal and less than 74 kg. and* ***MXP*** *bigger than -30 degree or equal and less than 0 degree, then* ***Folder*** *is B* ***File*** *is 10>*

< **Rule 21:** *if* ***BW*** *is equal to 74 kg. and* ***MXP*** *bigger than 0 degree or equal and less than 15 degree, then* ***Folder*** *is B* ***File*** *is 1>*

< **Rule 22:** *if* ***BW*** *is equal to 74 kg. and* ***MXP*** *bigger than 15 degree or equal and less than 25 degree, then* ***Folder*** *is B* ***File*** *is 2>*

< **Rule 23:** *if* ***BW*** *is equal to 74 kg. and* ***MXP*** *bigger than 25 degree or equal and less than 35 degree, then* ***Folder*** *is B* ***File*** *is 3>*

< **Rule 24:** *if* ***BW*** *is equal to 74 kg. and* ***MXP*** *bigger than 35 degree or equal and less than 45 degree, then* ***Folder*** *is B* ***File*** *is 4>*

< **Rule 25:** *if* ***BW*** *is equal to 74 kg. and* ***MXP*** *bigger than 45 degree or equal and less than 55 degree, then* ***Folder*** *is B* ***File*** *is 5>*

< **Rule 26:** *if* ***BW*** *is equal to 74 kg. and* ***MXP*** *bigger than 55 degree or equal and less than 65 degree, then* ***Folder*** *is B* ***File*** *is 6>*

< **Rule 27:** *if* ***BW*** *is equal to 74 kg. and* ***MXP*** *bigger than 65 degree or equal and less than 75 degree, then* ***Folder*** *is B* ***File*** *is 7>*

< **Rule 28:** *if* ***BW*** *is equal to 74 kg. and* ***MXP*** *bigger than 75 degree or equal and less than 85 degree, then* ***Folder*** *is B* ***File*** *is 8>*

< **Rule 29:** *if* ***BW*** *is equal to 74 kg. and* ***MXP*** *bigger than 85 degree or equal and less than 95 degree, then* ***Folder*** *is B* ***File*** *is 9>*

< **Rule 30:** *if BW is equal to 74 kg. and MXP bigger than -30 degree or equal and less than 0 degree, then Folder is B File is 10>*

< **Rule 31:** *if BW is equal to 75 kg. and MXP bigger than 0 degree or equal and less than 15 degree, then Folder is C File is 1>*

< **Rule 32:** *if BW is equal to 75 kg. and MXP bigger than 15 degree or equal and less than 25 degree, then Folder is C File is 2>*

< **Rule 33:** *if BW is equal to 75 kg. and MXP bigger than 25 degree or equal and less than 35 degree, then Folder is C File is 3>*

< **Rule 34:** *if BW is equal to 75 kg. and MXP bigger than 35 degree or equal and less than 45 degree, then Folder is C File is 4>*

< **Rule 35:** *if BW is equal to 75 kg. and MXP bigger than 45 degree or equal and less than 55 degree, then Folder is C File is 5>*

< **Rule 36:** *if BW is equal to 75 kg. and MXP bigger than 55 degree or equal and less than 65 degree, then Folder is C File is 6>*

< **Rule 37:** *if BW is equal to 75 kg. and MXP bigger than 65 degree or equal and less than 75 degree, then Folder is C File is 7>*

< **Rule 38:** *if BW is equal to 75 kg. and MXP bigger than 75 degree or equal and less than 85 degree, then Folder is C File is 8>*

< **Rule 39:** *if BW is equal to 75 kg. and MXP bigger than 85 degree or equal and less than 95 degree, then Folder is C File is 9>*

< **Rule 40:** *if BW is equal to 75 kg. and MXP bigger than -30 degree or equal and less than 0 degree, then Folder is C File is 10>*

< **Rule 41:** *if BW is bigger than 76 kg. or equal and less than 80 kg. and MXP bigger than 0 degree or equal and less than 15 degree, then Folder is D File is 1>*

< **Rule 42:** *if BW is bigger than 76 kg. or equal and less than 80 kg. and MXP bigger than 15 degree or equal and less than 25 degree, then Folder is D File is 2>*

< **Rule 43:** *if BW is bigger than 76 kg. or equal and less than 80 kg. and MXP bigger than 25 degree or equal and less than 35 degree, then Folder is D File is 3>*

< **Rule 44:** *if BW is bigger than 76 kg. or equal and less than 80 kg. and MXP bigger than 35 degree or equal and less than 45 degree, then Folder is D File is 4>*

< **Rule 45:** *if BW is bigger than 76 kg. or equal and less than 80 kg. and MXP bigger than 45 degree or equal and less than 55 degree, then Folder is D File is 5>*

< **Rule 46:** *if BW is bigger than 76 kg. or equal and less than 80 kg. and MXP bigger than 55 degree or equal and less than 65 degree, then Folder is D File is 6>*

< **Rule 47:** *if BW is bigger than 76 kg. or equal and less than 80 kg. and MXP bigger than 65 degree or equal and less than 75 degree, then Folder is D File is 7>*

< **Rule 48:** *if BW is bigger than 76 kg. or equal and less than 80 kg. and MXP bigger than 75 degree or equal and less than 85 degree, then Folder is D File is 8>*

< **Rule 49:** *if BW is bigger than 76 kg. or equal and less than 80 kg. and MXP bigger than 85 degree or equal and less than 95 degree, then Folder is D File is 9>*

< **Rule 50:** *if BW is bigger than 76 kg. or equal and less than 80 kg. and MXP bigger than -30 degree or equal and less than 0 degree, then Folder is D File is 10>*

< **Rule 51:** *if BW is equal to 81 kg. and MXP bigger than 0 degree or equal and less than 15 degree, then Folder is E File is 1>*

< **Rule 52:** *if BW is equal to 81 kg. and MXP bigger than 15 degree or equal and less than 25 degree, then Folder is E File is 2>*

< **Rule 53:** *if BW is equal to 81 kg. and MXP bigger than 25 degree or equal and less than 35 degree, then Folder is E File is 3>*

< **Rule 54:** *if BW is equal to 81 kg. and MXP bigger than 35 degree or equal and less than 45 degree, then Folder is E File is 4>*

< **Rule 55:** *if BW is equal to 81 kg. and MXP bigger than 45 degree or equal and less than 55 degree, then Folder is E File is 5>*

< **Rule 56:** *if BW is equal to 81 kg. and MXP bigger than 55 degree or equal and less than 65 degree, then Folder is E File is 6>*

< **Rule 57:** *if BW is equal to 81 kg. and MXP bigger than 65 degree or equal and less than 75 degree, then Folder is E File is 7>*

< **Rule 58:** *if BW is equal to 81 kg. and MXP bigger than 75 degree or equal and less than 85 degree, then Folder is E File is 8>*

< **Rule 59:** *if BW is equal to 81 kg. and MXP bigger than 85 degree or equal and less than 95 degree, then Folder is E File is 9>*

< **Rule 60:** *if BW is equal to 81 kg. and MXP bigger than -30 degree or equal and less than 0 degree, then Folder is E File is 10>*

< **Rule 61:** *if BW is bigger than 81 kg. or equal and less than 86 kg. and MXP bigger than 0 degree or equal and less than 15 degree, then Folder is F File is 1>*

< **Rule 62:** *if BW is bigger than 81 kg. or equal and less than 86 kg. and MXP bigger than 15 degree or equal and less than 25 degree, then Folder is F File is 2>*

< **Rule 63:** *if BW is bigger than 81 kg. or equal and less than 86 kg. and MXP bigger than 25 degree or equal and less than 35 degree, then Folder is F File is 3>*

< **Rule 64:** *if BW is bigger than 81 kg. or equal and less than 86 kg. and MXP bigger than 35 degree or equal and less than 45 degree, then Folder is F File is 4>*

< **Rule 65:** *if BW is bigger than 81 kg. or equal and less than 86 kg. and MXP bigger than 45 degree or equal and less than 55 degree, then Folder is F File is 5>*

< **Rule 66:** *if BW is bigger than 81 kg. or equal and less than 86 kg. and MXP bigger than 55 degree or equal and less than 65 degree, then Folder is F File is 6>*

< **Rule 67:** *if BW is bigger than 81 kg. or equal and less than 86 kg. and MXP bigger than 65 degree or equal and less than 75 degree, then Folder is F File is 7>*

< **Rule 68:** *if BW is bigger than 81 kg. or equal and less than 86 kg. and MXP bigger than 75 degree or equal and less than 85 degree, then Folder is F File is 8>*

< **Rule 69:** *if BW is bigger than 81 kg. or equal and less than 86 kg. and MXP bigger than 85 degree or equal and less than 95 degree, then Folder isF File is 9>*

< **Rule 70:** *if BW is bigger than 81 kg. or equal and less than 86 kg. and MXP bigger than -30 degree or equal and less than 0 degree, then Folder is F File is 10>*

# Chapter 14
# Congestion Control Using Soft Computing

**T. Revathi**
*Mepco Schlenk Engineering College, India*

**K. Muneeswaran**
*Mepco Schlenk Engineering College, India*

## ABSTRACT

*In the recent Internet era the queue management in the routers plays a vital role in the provision of Quality of Service (QoS). Virtual queue-based marking schemes have been recently proposed for Active Queue Management (AQM) in Internet routers. In this chapter, the authors propose Fuzzy enabled AQM (F-AQM) scheme where the linguistics variables are used to specify the behavior of the queues in the routers. The status of the queue is continuously monitored and decisions are made adaptively to drop or mark the packets as is done in Random Early Discard (RED) and Random Early Marking (REM) algorthms or schemes. The authors design a fuzzy rule base represented in the form of matrix indexed by queue length and rate of change of queue. The performance of the proposed F-AQM scheme is compared with several well-known AQM schemes such as RED, REM and Adaptive Virtual Queue (AVQ).*

## INTRODUCTION

The demand for the quality of service (QoS) is increasing day by day in this recent Internet era. The QoS is decided by many factors such as the resources available, the techniques used, and the control on the traffic. As a result of heavy demand for image and video data, the rate of congestion increases leading to poor QoS. In high-speed networks with large delay bandwidth products, gateways are likely to

be designed with correspondingly large maximum queues to accommodate transient congestion. But there is always an objective function to be fulfilled for major categories of applications to increase the throughput and decrease the delay. With moderate sized queue in the gateway, due to the heavy and burst traffic, the gateways encounter packet loss causing congestion. Hence the need of the day is to avoid congestion to possible extent. Dropping the packets during overflow of queue is an undesirable feature leading to poor user satisfaction. Either the packets must be dropped in a controlled manner

DOI: 10.4018/978-1-60566-814-7.ch014

*Figure 1. Simple network without any feedback from the network*

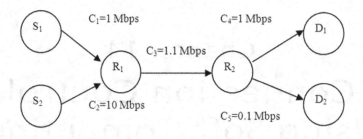

or arrangements have to be made to inform the sources to reduce or control the traffic.

Basically there are two approaches for handling the congestion: reactive and proactive. In the reactive mechanism, the TCP transport protocol detects congestions as the packet traverses through the congested network experiencing a loss. But the congestion will be detected only after a packet is dropped at the gateway. However, it would be undesirable to have large queues (possibly on the order of a delay bandwidth product) that were full in most of the time; this would significantly increase the average delay in the network. Therefore, with increasingly high-speed networks, it is increasingly important to have mechanisms that keep throughput high but average queue sizes low. In the absence of explicit feedback from the gateway, transport-layer protocols could infer congestion from the estimated bottleneck service time or from changes in throughput or end-to-end delay, as well as from packet drops. In proactive method, some initiatives are taken so that congestion can be avoided.

## IMPACT OF CONGESTION

There are two approaches for handling congestion. First one is congestion control, which starts acting after the network is congested or it is overloaded. Second one is congestion avoidance where the network starts playing before the network is overloaded.

## Causes and Effect of Congestion

Consider a network where many sources sending the data at a rate limited only by the source capabilities. It is assumed that the only resource to allocate is link bit rates and if the offered traffic on some link '$l$' exceeds the capacity $c_l$ of the link, then all sources see their traffic reduced in proportion of their offered traffic under First In First Out (FIFO) queue.

Consider the network shown in Figure 1, sources $S_1$ and $S_2$ send traffic to destination nodes $D_1$ and $D_2$ respectively and are limited only by their access rates. There are five links labeled $C_1$ through $C_5$ with capacities shown on the figure. Assume that the sources are limited only by their first link, without feedback from the network. Call $r_i$ the sending rate of source $i$, and $r_i'$ the outgoing rate. For example, with the values given on the Figure 1 it is found that $r_1 =$ 1Mbps and $r_2 =$ 10Mbps, but r1' and r2' are only 0.1Mbps, and the total throughput is 0.2Mbps. Source 1 can send only at 0.1 Mbps because it is competing with source 2 on link 3, which sends at a high rate on that link; however, source 2 is limited to 0.1 Mbps because of link 5. If source 2 would be aware of the global situation, and if it would cooperate, then it would send at 0.1Mbps only already on link 2, which would allow the

*Figure 2. A network exhibiting congestion collapse if sources are not regulated with their traffic*

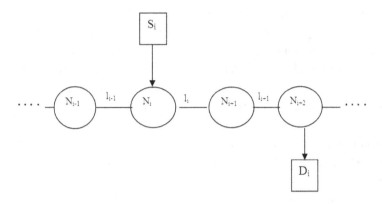

source 1 to send at 1Mbps, without any penalty for source 2. The total throughput of the network would be1.1*Mbps*. Even for this simple network it has shown some inefficiency. For a complex network, this may lead to a form of instability known as congestion collapse. Consider another network shown in Figure 2, $S_i$ refers to the source of data and $D_i$ is the destination for the data, $N_i$ is the node through which data is transmitted and $l_i$ is the link associated with node $N_i$, $c_i$ is the link capacity, $r_i$ is the data rate injected at $S_i$ and $r_i$' is the achieved rate at the link i.

Hence the achieved data rate at each link is:

$$r_i' = \min\left(r_i, \frac{c_i}{r_i + r_{i-1}'}r_i\right)$$

$$r_i'' = \min\left(r_i', \frac{c_{i+1}}{r_i' + r_{i+1}}r_i'\right) \quad (1)$$

For simplicity, symmetric cases are assumed where $r_i = r$, $c_i = c$ for all i. Then $r_i' = r_i$ and $r_i'' = r_i'$. Also if $r = c/2$, then there is no loss and $r'' = r' = r$. Therefore from the equation (1)

$$r' = \frac{cr}{r + r'} \quad (2)$$

The value of r' can be solved from the polynomial equation of order 2 to get the solution:

$$r' = \frac{r}{2}\left(-1 + \sqrt{1 + 4\frac{c}{r}}\right)$$

$$r'' = \frac{cr'}{r + r'}$$

and $r'' = c - \frac{r}{2}\left(\sqrt{1 + 4\frac{c}{r}} - 1\right) \quad (3)$

Using the limited development as applicable for u tends to 0:

$$\sqrt{1 + u} = 1 + \frac{1}{2}u - \frac{1}{8}u^2 + o\left(u^2\right)$$

Hence:

$$r'' = \frac{c}{r^2} + o\left(\frac{1}{r}\right) \quad (4)$$

From equation (4), it is observed that as the payload to the network increases towards infinity, the achieved throughput tends to zero. Hence in the perception of efficiency, sources should limit their sending rate by taking into consideration the state of the network. Ignoring this may put the network into congestion collapse. One objective of congestion control is to avoid such inefficiencies. Congestion collapse occurs when some resources are consumed by traffic that will be later discarded.

Apart from achieving the throughput for a given source, it is essential to look into the aspects of fairness among competing sources of data. From the example given in Figure 1, the throughput achieved at node i for the source $S_i$ is obtained in terms of the capacity of the link i and the sources of data coming from the other sources. Let r be the rate of data at node i and $r_{i-1}$ be the consolidated data from other nodes. Then the throughput at the link i is shared among the competing sources of data. Hence maximizing network throughput for a given source as a primary objective may lead to gross unfairness. In the worst case, some sources may get zero throughput, which is probably considered unfair by these sources. Hence the objective of congestion control is to provide both efficiency and some form of fairness.

## Fairness

Fairness is represented in its variety of forms as:

- Max-Min fairness
- Proportional fairness
- Utility approach to fairness

*(D. Bertsekas & R. Gallager,* 1992) have defined Max-Min fairness as: A feasible allocation of rates $\vec{x}$ is "max-min fair" if and only if an increase of any rate within the domain of feasible allocations must be at the cost of a decrease of some already smaller rate. Formally, for any other feasible allocation $\vec{y}$, if $y_s > x_s$ then there must exist some s' such that $x_{s'} \leq x_s$ and $y_{s'} > y_s$.

The Max-Min fairness puts emphasis on maintaining high values for the smallest rates. This may be at the expense of some network inefficiency. *(Mazumdar R., Mason L.G. & Douligeris C.,* 1991) have proposed an alternative definition of fairness in the context of game theory. The definition of proportional fairness is given as:

An allocation of rate $\vec{x}$ is proportionally fair if and if only, for any other feasible allocation $\vec{y}$, the following inequality holds well:

$$\sum_{s=1}^{S} \frac{y_s - x_s}{x_s} \leq 0 \tag{5}$$

In other words, any change in the allocation must have negative average change.

Proportional fairness is an example of a more general fairness concept, called the *utility* approach, which is defined as: Every source *s* has a utility function $u_s$ where $u_s(x_s)$ indicates the value to source *s* having rate $x_s$. Every link *l* (or network resource in general) has a cost function $g_l$, where $g_l(f)$ indicates the cost to the network for supporting an amount of flow *f* on link *l*. Then, a utility fair allocation of rates is an allocation which maximizes $H(\vec{x})$, defined by equation:

$$H\left(\vec{x}\right) = \sum_{s=1}^{S} u_x\left(x_x\right) - \sum_{l=1}^{L} g_l\left(f_l\right) \tag{6}$$

with $f_l = \sum_{s=1}^{S} A_{l,s} x_x$ over the set of feasible allocations, where S is the number of sources and $A_{l,i}$ is the fraction of traffic from source *i* which uses link *l*. Proportional fairness corresponds to $u_s = \ln(x_s)$ for all *s*, and $g_l(f) = 0$ for $f < c_l$, $g_l(f) = +\infty$ for $f \geq c_l$. Rate proportional fairness corresponds to $u_s(x_s) = w_s \ln(x_s)$ and the same choice of $g_l$. Computing utility fairness requires solving constrained optimization problems and is given by (*PeterWhittle,* 1971).

## DIFFERENT TYPES OF CONGESTION CONTROL

In general there are three types of solutions for congestion control. They are: Rate based; Hop by Hop; and End-to-End.

**Rate Based:** Sources know an explicit rate at which they can send. The rate may be given to the source during a negotiation phase. In such cases, the network is configured with reservation. Alternatively, the rate may be imposed dynamically to the source by the network; this is the case for the Available Bit Rate (ABR) class of ATM. In such cases the network offers a best effort service (since the source cannot be sure of how long a given rate will remain valid), with explicit rate. In Figure 1 source $S_1$ would obtain a rate not exceeding 0.1Mbps.

**Hop by Hop:** A source needs some feedback from the next hop in order to send any amount of data. The next hop also must obtain some feedback from the following hop and so on. The feedback may be positive (credits) or negative (backpressure). In the simplest form, the protocol is stop and go. In the example given in Figure 1, node $R_1$ would be prevented by node $R_2$ from sending source $S_2$ traffic at a rate higher than 0.1Mbps; source $S_2$ would then be throttled by node $R_1$. Hop by hop control is used with full duplex Ethernets using 802.3x frames called *Pause* frames.

**End-to-end:** A source continuously obtains feedback from all downstream nodes it uses. The feedback is piggybacked in packets returning towards the source, or it may simply be the detection of a missing packet. Sources react to negative feedback by reducing their rate and to positive feedback by increasing it. The difference with hop by hop control is that the intermediate nodes take no action on the feedback; all reactions

to feedback are left to the sources. Referring to Figure 1, node $R_2$ would mark some negative information in the flow of source $S_2$ that would be echoed to the source by destination $D_2$; the source would then react by reducing the rate, until it reaches 0.1Mbps, after which there would be no negative feedback. Alternatively, source $S_2$ could detect that a large fraction of packets is lost, reduce its rate, until there is little loss. This is the method invented for *Decnet,* which is now used after some modification in the Internet.

## Congestion Control Algorithms of TCP

In this section the theory of congestion control for best effort network is analyzed. Even in best effort network it is found necessary to control the amount of traffic sent by sources. A congestion collapse is due to the combination of factors, some of them are the absence of traffic control mechanisms and in addition, there are other aggravating factors, which led to *avalanche* effects.

- **IP fragmentation**: If IP datagrams are fragmented into several packets, the loss of one single packet causes the destination to declare the loss of the entire datagram, which will be retransmitted. This is addressed in TCP by trying to avoid fragmentation. With IPv6, fragmentation is possible only at the source and for UDP only.

- **Go Back *n* at full window size**: If a TCP sender has a large offered window, then the loss of segment *n* causes the retransmission of all segments starting from *n*. Assume only segment *n* was lost, and segments $n + 1,..., n + k$ are stored at the receiver; when the receiver gets those segments, it will send an *ack* for all segments up to $n + k$. However, if the window is large, the *ack* will reach the sender too late preventing the retransmissions. This has been addressed in current versions of TCP where all timers are reset when one expires.

In general, congestion translates into larger delays because of queue buildup. If nothing is done, retransmission timers may become too short and cause retransmissions of data that was not yet acknowledged, but was not yet lost. This has been addressed in TCP by the round trip estimation algorithm. Congestion control has been designed right from the beginning in Wide Area public networks (most of them are connection oriented using X.25 or Frame Relay), or in large corporate networks such as IBM's SNA. It came as an afterthought in the Internet. In connection-oriented network, congestion control is either hop by hop or rate based: credit or backpressure per connection (ATM LANs), hop by hop sliding window per connection (X.25, SNA), rate control per connection (ATM). They can also use end-to-end control, based on marking packets that have experienced congestion (Frame Relay, ATM). All connectionless Wide Area Networks rely on end-to-end control. In the Internet, the principles are the following:

- TCP is used to control traffic
- Adjusting the window size controls the rate of a TCP connection
- Additive increase, multiplicative decrease principle is used
- The feedback from the network to sources is packet loss. Thus it is assumed that packet loss for reasons other than packet dropping in queues is negligible. In particular, all links should have a negligible error rate.

RFC 2001 describes it in detail. One implication of these design decision is that only TCP traffic is controlled. The reason is that, originally, UDP was used only for short transactions. Applications that do not use TCP have to either be limited to LANs, where congestion is rare (example: NFS) or have to implement in the application layer appropriate congestion control mechanisms (example: audio or video applications). Only long lasting flows is the object of congestion control. There is no congestion control mechanism for short-lived flows.

## Congestion Window

With the use of sliding window protocol concept (used by TCP), the window size $W$ (in bits or bytes) is equal to the maximum number of unacknowledged data that a source may send. Consider a system where the source has infinite data to send; assume the source uses a FIFO as send buffer, of size $W$. At the beginning of the connection, the source immediately fills the buffer, which is then dequeued at the rate permitted by the line. Then the buffer can receive new data as old data is acknowledged. Let $T$ be the average time one needs to wait for an acknowledgement to come back, counting from the instant the data is put into the FIFO. This system is an approximate model of a TCP connection for a source, which is infinitely fast and has an infinite amount of data to send. By Little's formula applied to the FIFO, the throughput $\theta$ of the TCP connection is given by:

$$\theta = \frac{W}{T} \qquad (7)$$

The delay $T$ is equal to the propagation and transmission times of data and acknowledgement, plus the processing time, plus possible delays in sending acknowledgement. If $T$ is fixed, then controlling $W$ is equivalent to controlling the connection rate $\theta$. This is the method used in the Internet. However, in general, $T$ depends also on the congestion status of the networks, through queuing delays. Thus, in periods of congestion, there is a first, automatic congestion control effect: sources reduce their rates whenever the network delay increases, simply because the time to get acknowledgements increases. This is however

*Figure 3. Phases in slow start and congestion avoidance*

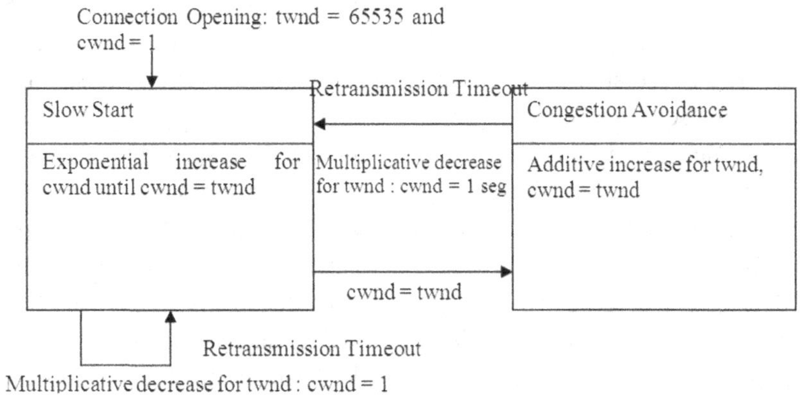

a side effect, which is not essential in the TCP congestion control mechanism. TCP defines a variable called congestion window 'cwnd' and the window size $W$ is then given by

$W = \min(\text{cwnd}, \text{offeredWindow})$

where *offeredWindow* is the window size advertised by the destination. In contrast, *cwnd* is computed by the source. The value of *cwnd* is decreased when a loss is detected, and increased otherwise. The following section describes the details of the operation. A TCP connection is, from a congestion control point of view, in one of three phases.

- Slow start: after a loss detected by timeout
- Fast recovery: after a loss detected by fast retransmit
- Congestion avoidance: in all other cases.

The variable *cwnd* is updated at phase transitions, and when useful acknowledgements are received. Useful acknowledgements are those, which increase the lower edge of the sending window.

## Slow Start and Congestion Avoidance

This section describes a system with only two phases: slow start and congestion avoidance. This corresponds to a historical implementation (TCP Tahoe) where losses are detected by timeout only (and not by the fast retransmit heuristic). Figure 3 shows the phases in the slow start and the congestion avoidance phases.

According to the Additive Increase, Multiplicative Decrease (AIMD) principle, the window size is divided by 2 for every packet loss detected by timeout. In contrast, for every useful acknowledgement, it is increased according to an additive increase. However, there are two small subtleties. First, the principle of AIMD assumes a stationary network. In reality, network conditions vary. Second, bursts of data might be transmitted at the beginning of the connection, or after a timeout if the TCP implementation strictly follows the Go Back *n* principle. In order to avoid this, a supplementary variable, called the target window *twnd* (it is called *ssthresh* in RFC 2001) is introduced. Thus, it is necessary to test carefully whether equilibrium can be reached before using the value of target window *twnd*. At the beginning of the connection, or after a timeout, *cwnd* is set to 1 and a rapid increase based on acknowledgements follows, until *cwnd* reaches *twnd*. This forces the source to avoid sending bursts. The procedure for computing *cwnd* is shown on Figure 3. At connection opening, *twnd* has the maximum value (64KB by default, more if the window scale option is used), and *cwnd* is one segment. During slow start, *cwnd* increases according to the exponential increase. Slow start ends whenever there is a packet loss detected by timeout or *cwnd* reaches *twnd*. During congestion avoidance, *cwnd* decreases according to the Multiplicative Decrease. When a packet loss is detected by timeout, *twnd* is divided by 2 and slow start is entered or re-entered, with *cwnd* set to 1. It is to be noted that *twnd* and *cwnd* are equal in the congestion avoidance phase.

Figure 4 shows an example built with data (*L. Brakmo & L. Petersen*, 1995). Initially, the connection congestion state is in slow start. Then *cwnd* increases from one segment size to about 35 KB, (time 0.5) at which point the connection waits for a missing non-duplicate acknowledgement (one packet is lost). Then, at approximately time 2, a timeout occurs, causing *twnd* to be set to half the current window, and *cwnd* to be reset to 1 segment size. Immediately after, another timeout occurs, causing another reduction of *twnd* to 2 × segment size and of *cwnd* to 1 segment size. Then, the slow start phase ends at point A, as one acknowledgement received causes *cwnd* to equal *twnd*. Between A and B, the TCP connection is in the congestion avoidance state. *cwnd* and *twnd* are equal and both increase slowly until a timeout occurs (point B), causing a return to slow start until point C. The same pattern is repeated. It has to be noted that some implementations do one more multiplicative increase when *cwnd* has reached the value of *twnd*. The slow start and congestion avoidance phases use three algorithms for decrease and increase, as shown in Box 1.

## Fast Recovery

The full specification for TCP involves a third state, called Fast Recovery when a loss is detected by

timeout, the target congestion window size *twnd* is divided by 2 (Multiplicative Decrease for *twnd*) but it also goes into the slow start phase in order to avoid bursts of retransmissions. However, this is not very efficient if an isolated loss occurs. Indeed, the penalty imposed by slow start is large; it will take about log *n* round trips to reach the target window size *twnd*, where *n = twnd/segment size*. This is severe if the loss is isolated, corresponding to a mild negative feedback. Now with the current TCP, isolated losses are detected and repaired with the Fast Retransmit procedure. Therefore, a different mechanism is added for every loss detected by Fast Retransmit. The procedure is as follows:

- when a loss is detected by Fast Retransmit (triplicate *ack*), then run Multiplicative Decrease for *twnd*
- Then enter a temporary phase, called Fast Recovery, until the loss is repaired. When entering this phase, temporarily keep the congestion window high in order to keep sending. Indeed, since an *ack* is missing, the sender is likely to be blocked, which is not the desired effect:

  cwnd = twnd + 3 * seg /* exponential increase */

  cwnd = min(cwnd, 65535)

  retransmit missing segment (say n)

- Then continue to interpret every received ack as a positive signal, at least until the loss is repaired, running the exponential increase mechanism:

  duplicate ack received ->

  > cwnd = cwnd + seg /* exponential increase */

  > cwnd = min(cwnd, 65535)

  > send following segments n+k+1 if window allows ack for segment n received ->

  > go into congestion avoidance

*Figure 4. Behavior with slow start and congestion avoidance phases*

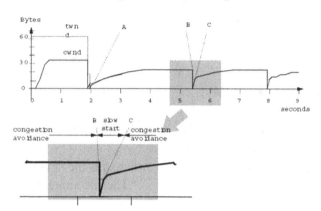

*Box 1.*

| Algorithm for multiplicative decrease for *twnd* |
|---|
| *twnd = 0.5 \* min (current window size)* |
| *twnd = max (twnd, 2 \* segment size)* |
| **Algorithm for Additive Increase for *twnd*:** |
| *for every useful acknowledgement received:* |
| *twnd = twnd + (segment size) \* (segment size) / twnd* |
| *twnd = min (twnd, maximum window size)* |
| **Algorithm for Exponential Increase for *cwnd*:** |
| *for every useful acknowledgement received:* |
| *cwnd = cwnd + (segment size)* |
| *if (cwnd == twnd) then move to congestion avoidance* |

## CONGESTION AVOIDANCE

In normal FIFO queue based routers, packets are simply dropped when their buffers overflow, which is called "tail drop" policy. However it has three drawbacks:

- **Synchronization**: Assume there is a queue buildup in the buffer. Then all sources using the buffer reduce their sending rate and will slowly increase again. The time it takes for sources to reach their maximum rate is in general much larger than the round trip time. As a consequence, after a queue buildup at a router buffer, there may be a long period of reduced traffic. This is an example of global synchronization. The negative effect is to reduce the long-term average utilization. It would be better to spread packet drops more randomly between sources.

- **Bias** against bursty sources: During a queue buildup period, a bursty source may suffer several consecutive drops. In that case, the effect of TCP is a dramatic reduction in throughput. After all, we might think that it is good to penalize bursty sources since bursty traffic uses more resources in any queuing system. However, there are many cases where an initially smooth source becomes bursty because of multiplexing effects.

- **Queuing delay**: In the presence of bursty sources, efficient utilization of the links requires a large buffer (several thousands of packets). This in turn may induce a large delay jitter (delay jitter is due to the random nature of queuing times). Delay jitter is not very good for TCP applications (it increases the RTT estimate) and is very bad for interactive audio flows. It would be good to have smaller buffers, but then bursty sources would suffer a lot. Further, a large average queuing delay implies a smaller throughput for TCP connections, due to TCP's bias against large round trip times.

In order to overcome these problems, it was introduced the concept of Active Queue Management (AQM), which is also called as *packet admission control*.

## Active Queue Management (AQM)

The idea of this technique is to replace tail drop by an intelligent admission decision for every incoming packet, based on a local algorithm. The algorithm uses an estimation of the long term load, or queue length; in contrast, tail drop bases the dropping decision on the instantaneous buffer occupancy only. The specific Active Queue Management algorithm used in the Internet is called Random Early Detection (RED). Various researchers propose many Active Queue Management (AQM) techniques.

## Random Early Detection (RED)

(*Sally Floyd & Van Jacobson*, 1993) presented a technique called Random Early Detection (RED) in gateways for congestion avoidance in packet switched networks. The gateway detects incipient congestion by computing the average queue size. The gateway could notify condition of congestion either by dropping packets arriving at the gateway or by setting a bit in packet headers. When the average queue size exceeds a preset threshold, the gateway drops or marks each arriving packet with a certain probability, where the exact probability is a function of the average queue size. RED gateways keep the average queue size low while allowing occasional bursts of packets in the queue. During congestion, the probability that the gateway notifies a particular connection to reduce its window is roughly proportional to that connection's share of the bandwidth through the gateway. RED gateways are designed to accompany a transport-layer congestion control protocol such as TCP. The RED gateway has no bias against burst traffic and avoids the global

synchronization of many connections decreasing their window at the same time.

For every incoming packet, an estimation *avg* of the average queue length is computed. It is updated at every packet arrival, using exponential smoothing:

$$avg := q * \text{measured queue length} + (1 - q) * avg$$

where q is the target drop probability

The incoming packet is randomly dropped, according to:

if $avg < min_{th}$ accept the packet
else if $min_{th} < avg < max_{th}$ drop packet
with probability p that depends on avg
*else if $max_{th} <= avg$ drop the packe*t

where $min_{th}$ and $max_{th}$ are thresholds on the buffer content. By default, data is counted in packets. The drop probability $p$ depends on a target drop probability $q$, which is itself defined by the function of *avg*.

Simulations of a TCP/IP network were carried out to illustrate the performance of RED gateways with dropping and marking computed as:

$$p_b = \max_p (avg - min_{th})/(max_{th} - min_{th})$$

$$p_b = p_b packetSize/MaximumPacketSize$$

$$p_a = p_b/(1 - count.p_b)$$

where $p_b$ is the packet marking probability which ranges from 0 to $max_p$; $p_a$ is the current packet marking probability $min_{th}$ and $max_{th}$ are the minimum and maximum threshold for queue

## Stabilized RED (SRED)

(*T. J. Ott, T. V. Lakshman & L. H.Wong*,1999) have developed a method called Stabilized RED (SRED). SRED also pre-emptively discards packets with a load-dependent probability when a buffer in a router seems congested. SRED has an additional feature that over a wide range of load levels helps it stabilize its buffer occupation at a level independent of the number of active connections. SRED does this by estimating the number of active connections or flows. This estimate is obtained without collecting or analyzing state information on individual flows. The same mechanism can be used to identify flows that may be misbehaving, i.e. are taking more than their fair share of bandwidth.

## Explicit Congestion Notification (ECN)

RED starts dropping packets before buffer overflows. Explicit Congestion Notification (ECN) (*S. Floyd*, 1994) is another technique used to inform the sources of traffic about the congestion in the network enabling the sources to control their traffic. On detecting congestion at an early stage, a bit in the TCP packet header is set which reaches the source in the form of acknowledgement packet for the previously transmitted successful packet. The source immediately responds to this marked bit by reducing the traffic assuming as if the packet was lost. By means of this early marking, the queue associated with the link avoids dropping the packet enhancing the good put. Using ECN technique the routers select the packets for marking to inform the source that there is incipient congestion. The Active Queue Management (AQM) schemes either mark or drop packets depending on the policy implemented at the router.

## Random Early Marking (REM)

Random Early Marking (REM) consists of a link algorithm, that probabilistically marks packets inside the network, and a source algorithm, that adapts source rate to observed marking. The marking probability is exponential in a link congestion measure, so that the end--to--end marking probability is exponential in a path congestion measure. Marking allows a source to estimate

its path congestion measure and adjusts its rate in a way that aligns individual optimality with social optimality. Because of the finer measure of congestion provided by REM, sources do not constantly probe the network for spare capacity, but settle around a globally optimal equilibrium, thus avoiding the perpetual cycle of sinking into and recovering from congestion. (*S. Athuraliya, D. E. Lapsley & S. H. Low,* 1999) and (*R. J. Gibbens & F. P. Kelly,*1999) had implemented REM.

## BLUE

(*Wu-chang Feng, Kang G. Shin, Dilip D. Kandlur & Debanjan Saha,* 2002) have shown that RED like AQM techniques are ineffective in preventing high loss rates. The inherent problem with these queue management algorithms is that they use queue length as the indicator of the severity of congestion. A fundamentally different AQM algorithm, called BLUE, was proposed, implemented, and evaluated by them. BLUE used packet loss and link idle events to manage congestion. Using both simulation and controlled experiments, BLUE was shown to perform significantly better than RED, both in terms of packet loss rates and buffer size requirements in the network. As an extension to BLUE, a novel technique based on Bloom filters was described for enforcing fairness among a large number of flows. Also they proposed and evaluated Stochastic Fair BLUE (SFB), a queue management algorithm, which could identify and rate-limit non responsive flows using a very small amount of state information. They have demonstrated the inherent weakness of current Active Queue Management algorithms, which used queue length in the algorithms.

## ADAPTIVE VIRTUAL QUEUE (AVQ)

The AVQ being one of adaptive queue management scheme maintains a virtual queue whose capacity (called *virtual capacity*) is less than the actual capacity of the link. When a packet arrives in the real queue, the virtual queue is also updated to reflect the new arrival. Packets in the real queue are marked or dropped when the virtual buffer overflows. The virtual capacity at each link is then adapted to ensure that the total flow entering each link achieves a desired utilization of the link. The marking probability in AVQ is implicit, no marking probability is explicitly calculated. This was originally proposed in (*S. Kunniyur*, 2000, 2003) as a rate-based marking scheme. In the absence of feedback delays, it was shown in (*S. Kunniyur*, 2001) that a fluid-model representation of the above scheme, along with the congestion-controllers at the end-hosts, was semi-globally asymptotically stable when the link adaptation is sufficiently slow. An appealing feature of the AVQ scheme is that, in the absence of feedback delays, the system is fair in the sense that it maximizes the sum of utilities of all users in the network. The AVQ algorithm and the model for stability analysis are described in (*S. Kunniyur*, 2004).

## FUZZY LOGIC

Fuzzy logic is a branch of Computational Intelligence (CI). CI (*J. C. Bezdek*, 1994; *W. Pedrycz*, 1998) is an area of fundamental and applied research involving numerical information processing (in contrast to the symbolic information processing techniques of Artificial Intelligence). Nowadays, CI research is very active and consequently its applications are appearing in many of the end user products. CI exhibits the properties: Computationally adaptive; Computational fault tolerance; Speed approaching human-like turnaround; Error rates that approximate human performance. The major building blocks of CI are artificial neural networks, Fuzzy logic, and evolutionary computation. While these techniques are not a panacea (and it is important to view them as supplementing proven traditional techniques), a lot of interest from the academic

research community (*A. Sekercioglu, A. Pitsillides & A. Vasilakos*, 2001), and industry (*B. Azvine & A. Vasilakos*, 2000) is seen. Fuzzy logic Controllers (FLCs) may be viewed as an alternative, non-conventional way of designing feedback controllers where it is convenient and effective to build a control algorithm without relying on formal models of the system and control theoretic tools. The control algorithm is encapsulated as a set of commonsense rules. FLCs have been applied successfully (*S. Yasunobu & S. Miyamoto*, 1985; *E. Morales, M. Polycarpou, N. Hemasilpin, & J. Bissler*, 2001) for controlling systems in which analytical models are not easily obtainable or the model itself, if available, is too complex and highly nonlinear. In recent years, a number of research papers have been published using Fuzzy logic investigating solutions to congestion control issues, especially to Asynchronous Transfer Mode (ATM) networks. A detailed survey is given in (*A. Sekercioglu, A. Pitsillides & A. Vasilakos*, 2001). This chapter explains the application of Fuzzy logic to congestion control for wired networks.

## Fuzzy Enabled AQM (F-AQM)

An AQM scheme based on Fuzzy rule base (F-AQM) is proposed. The motivation behind this F-AQM algorithm is to design an AQM scheme that results in a low-loss, and high utilization operation at the link. The marking or dropping probability is calculated by measuring the length of the queue and the rate at which the queue changes.

The F-AQM algorithm maintains a Fuzzy Rule Matrix (FRM) to decide the dropping probability. FRM is indexed by queue length and rate of change of queue length. A variant of the scheme was proposed in (*S. Kunniyur*, 2000, 2003) as a rate-based marking scheme. In the proposed method the features of F-AQM are brought out and it is demonstrated how it outperforms the existing methods. Also the performance of the proposed method is compared with Adaptive Virtual Queue

*Figure 5. Fuzzy based AQM*

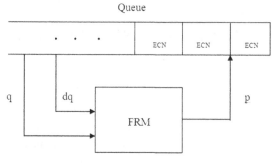

'q' – queue length
'dq' – rate of change of queue length
'p' - drop/mark probability

(AVQ) which was proved to be better than RED and its variants.

The queue parameter ranges and its effect on the congestion control are represented in linguistic variables and they model the real world representation.

## Congestion Control of AQM using Fuzzy logic

In RED, minimum threshold and maximum threshold of the queue size are initially fixed. The probability of dropping a packet is computed based on the threshold values. Then a random number is generated to decide the dropping of packets. In general, RED implementations with fixed thresholds could not provide good results for dynamic network changes (eg:- the number of active sources). Hence the proposed F-AQM method as shown in Figure 5 uses Fuzzy Rule Matrix (FRM). FRM is indexed by two queue parameters: queue length (q) and change in queue length (dq). The matrix contents are nothing but dropping probabilities similar to that of RED. Here mark or drop probability is dynamically calculated based on 'q' and 'dq'. Usually multiple inputs can offer better ability to linguistically describe the system dynamics. The dynamic way of calculating the mark or drop probability from FRM comes

from the fact that considering 'dq', 'q' and using appropriate fuzzy rules, the queue behavior is adapted to control the congestion. Hence the probability is calculated more dynamically than the conventional RED method.

## Construction of FRM

The queue parameters ('q' and 'dq') are represented using linguistic variables. Queue size 'q' is rated as *empty, moderate* and *full* by specifying the ranges in percentage of queue capacity. The typical ranges are: empty (0-33%); moderate (34-66%) and full-(67-99). The change in queue length (dq) is specified as: *decrease in queue length, no change in queue length, and increase in queue length.*

Table 1 shows a typical FRM for finding the probability of dropping or marking a packet. FRM reflects the dynamic state of the queue and provides high-level inference mechanism to take decisions. By appropriately choosing the entries in the table, FRM can be very well used to have control over the congestion in the network. The tuning of FRM is based on desired optimization criterion such as maximization of throughput. Also FRM can be constructed using any of the Fuzzy membership model such as Mamdani. Here the matrix entries are selected in a heuristic manner so as to cover the various possibilities of queue. Selection of matrix entries can be standardized by better methods and it can be future work. The working of F-AQM scheme is shown in Figure 6. Here for every arrival of new packet at the router, the drop or mark probability is obtained by indexing FRM using q and dq. Then the packet is dropped or marked for drop probabilistically and the queue status is updated accordingly.

## SIMULATION SETUP

In this section the experimental set up for evaluating the performance of the proposed method is

*Table 1. A typical fuzzy rule matrix (FRM)*

| | | Change in queue length (dq) | | |
|---|---|---|---|---|
| | | Decrease in queue length | No change in queue length | Increase in queue length |
| **Queue length (q)** | Empty (0-33%) | 0 | 0 | 0 |
| | Moderate (34-66%) | 0 | 0 | 0.25 |
| | Full (67-99%) | 0.25 | 0.5 | 1.0 |

*Figure 6.*

```
A lg orithm   F − AQM   (Q , M , P )
// Q − Queue ; M − FRM
// P − Arriving    Packet
begin
        q = Q  →  length
        dq = q − q_prev
        p = M (q , dq )
        n = rand  (  )
        if ( p ≥ n )
                if ( ECN  == 1 )
                        P_marked   = TRUE
                else
                        FREE  ( P ) )
                end
        end
        q_prev  = q
        Q  →  update  _ length  ()
end
```

described and comparison is made with AVQ. The simulation is carried out using the recent version of NS-2 (http://www.isi.edu/nsnam/ns/). The experimental set up is shown in Figure 7. Here 'N' number of sources and 'N' number of destinations are considered. All these sources are connected to an edge router. The edge router is connected to a core router, which in turn is connected to another edge router. The second edge router is connected with 'N' destinations. The connection between the first edge router and the core router is treated as bottleneck link for the experimentation in the perspective of congestion control. The bandwidth and latency delay between source/destination and edge routers are chosen to be 10Mbps and 1ms respectively. The bottleneck link is assigned with the lower bandwidth of 4.5 Mbps and latency de-

lay of 5ms. For having a predictable response, all sources are configured to generate TCP traffic in predictable time as against random time followed in many experimental setups. Each source node is configured to have 80 TCP flows and each flow is designed to send 3 packets of 512 bytes data and the number of sources is increased from 1 to 20. These experiments are conducted for AVQ and F-AQM. The total number of packets transmitted, the number of packets dropped in the bottleneck queue are noted and tabulated. The number of packets dropped in the observed queue indicates the performance of the proposed and the existing queuing techniques.

## RESULTS AND OBSERVATIONS

The simulation results for proposed experimental setup are tabulated in Table 2 to Table 5. Table 2 shows the simulation results with the number of packets transmitted (throughput), number of packets dropped and the number of packets received at the other end of the queue (good put) for AVQ. The experiments are conducted for different queue sizes i.e. 50,100, and 140. Also the effect of setting Explicit Congestion Notification (ECN) bit is shown in Table 3. It is observed from Figure 7 that the number of dropped packets is less for larger queue size. The effect of setting the ECN bit is shown in Figure 8 in a graphical form. By setting the ECN bit, the congestion is notified to the sources of data thereby controlling the rate of traffic to avoid congestion and hence less number of packets is dropped.

*Figure 7. Simulation setup*

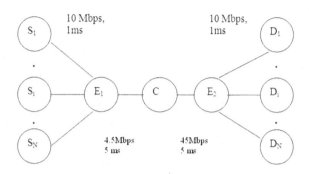

*Table 2. AVQ with increasing number of sources of 80 flows each (ECN – 0)*

| No. of Sources | Queue limit 50 | | | | Queue limit 100 | | | | Queue limit 140 | | | |
|---|---|---|---|---|---|---|---|---|---|---|---|---|
| | Through put | Good put | Drops | Marks | Through put | Good put | Drops | Marks | Through put | Good put | Drops | Marks |
| 1 | 271 | 240 | 31 | 0 | 240 | 240 | 0 | 0 | 240 | 240 | 0 | 0 |
| 2 | 616 | 481 | 135 | 0 | 534 | 482 | 52 | 0 | 485 | 480 | 5 | 0 |
| 4 | 1437 | 965 | 472 | 0 | 1297 | 965 | 332 | 0 | 1175 | 960 | 215 | 0 |
| 8 | 3347 | 1931 | 1416 | 0 | 3214 | 1935 | 1279 | 0 | 3038 | 1925 | 1113 | 0 |
| 12 | 5487 | 2900 | 2587 | 0 | 5245 | 2909 | 2336 | 0 | 5097 | 2898 | 2199 | 0 |
| 16 | 7714 | 3873 | 3841 | 0 | 7550 | 3870 | 3680 | 0 | 7344 | 3876 | 3468 | 0 |
| 20 | 10027 | 4847 | 5180 | 0 | 9826 | 4848 | 4978 | 0 | 9678 | 4834 | 4844 | 0 |

*Table 3. AVQ with increasing number of sources of 80 flows each (ECN – 1)*

| No. of Sources | Queue limit 50 | | | | Queue limit 100 | | | | Queue limit 140 | | | |
|---|---|---|---|---|---|---|---|---|---|---|---|---|
| | Through put | Good put | Drops | Marks | Through put | Good put | Drops | Marks | Through put | Good put | Drops | Marks |
| 1 | 249 | 240 | 9 | 31 | 240 | 240 | 0 | 0 | 240 | 240 | 0 | 0 |
| 2 | 553 | 488 | 65 | 102 | 480 | 480 | 0 | 44 | 480 | 480 | 0 | 5 |
| 4 | 1223 | 970 | 253 | 334 | 1110 | 962 | 148 | 237 | 1036 | 961 | 75 | 171 |
| 8 | 2920 | 1934 | 986 | 1243 | 2514 | 1923 | 591 | 868 | 2373 | 1935 | 438 | 612 |
| 12 | 4821 | 2898 | 1923 | 2546 | 4286 | 2883 | 1403 | 1889 | 3888 | 2895 | 993 | 1445 |
| 16 | 6937 | 3863 | 3074 | 414 | 6168 | 3843 | 2325 | 3262 | 5653 | 3855 | 1798 | 2544 |
| 20 | 9126 | 4828 | 4298 | 6028 | 8199 | 4803 | 3396 | 4912 | 7609 | 4815 | 2794 | 4028 |

Table 4 and Table 5 show the results from the simulation setup configured with the bottleneck link queue controlled by our proposed method using FRM. The experiments that are conducted for AVQ are repeated for F-AQM also and the results are tabulated. From Figure 10.a and Figure 10.b, it is obvious that the number of packets dropped is very less by applying the proposed fuzzy enabled queue management schemes.

*Table 4. F-AQM with increasing number of sources of 80 flows each (ECN – 0)*

| No. of Sources | Queue limit 50 | | | | Queue limit 100 | | | | Queue limit 140 | | | |
|---|---|---|---|---|---|---|---|---|---|---|---|---|
| | Through put | Good put | Drops | Marks | Through put | Good put | Drops | Marks | Through put | Good put | Drops | Marks |
| 1 | 297 | 247 | 50 | 0 | 274 | 244 | 30 | 0 | 254 | 240 | 14 | 0 |
| 2 | 647 | 517 | 130 | 0 | 599 | 509 | 90 | 0 | 578 | 505 | 73 | 0 |
| 4 | 1377 | 1036 | 341 | 0 | 1360 | 1022 | 338 | 0 | 1300 | 1014 | 286 | 0 |
| 8 | 3054 | 2086 | 968 | 0 | 3020 | 2065 | 955 | 0 | 2998 | 2046 | 952 | 0 |
| 12 | 4841 | 3123 | 1718 | 0 | 4899 | 3083 | 1816 | 0 | 4845 | 3088 | 1757 | 0 |
| 16 | 6829 | 4152 | 2677 | 0 | 6799 | 4138 | 2661 | 0 | 6637 | 4165 | 2472 | 0 |
| 20 | 8852 | 5193 | 3659 | 0 | 8794 | 5190 | 3604 | 0 | 8723 | 5186 | 3537 | 0 |

*Table 5. F-AQM with increasing number of sources of 80 flows each (ECN – 1)*

| No. of Sources | Queue limit 50 | | | | Queue limit 100 | | | | Queue limit 140 | | | |
|---|---|---|---|---|---|---|---|---|---|---|---|---|
| | Through put | Good put | Drops | Marks | Through put | Good put | Drops | Marks | Through put | Good put | Drops | Marks |
| 1 | 249 | 240 | 9 | 56 | 240 | 240 | 0 | 29 | 240 | 240 | 0 | 14 |
| 2 | 553 | 488 | 65 | 151 | 480 | 480 | 0 | 111 | 480 | 480 | 0 | 77 |
| 4 | 1223 | 970 | 253 | 433 | 1110 | 962 | 148 | 316 | 1036 | 961 | 75 | 262 |
| 8 | 2899 | 1934 | 965 | 1382 | 2514 | 1923 | 591 | 1033 | 2373 | 1935 | 438 | 789 |
| 12 | 4776 | 2898 | 1878 | 2716 | 4268 | 2883 | 1385 | 2104 | 3878 | 2895 | 983 | 1669 |
| 16 | 6840 | 3863 | 2977 | 4327 | 6133 | 3843 | 2290 | 3488 | 5630 | 3855 | 1775 | 2845 |
| 20 | 9013 | 4828 | 4185 | 6194 | 8102 | 4803 | 3299 | 5208 | 7573 | 4815 | 2758 | 4353 |

*Figure 8. Effect of queue size*

*Figure 9. Effect of ECN bit*

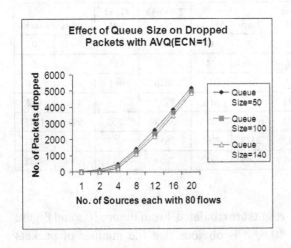

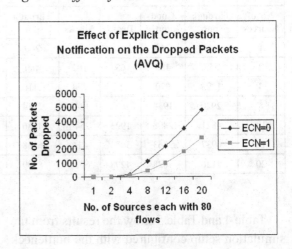

*Figure 10. Comparison of F-AQM with AVQ*

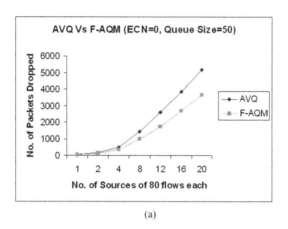

(a)

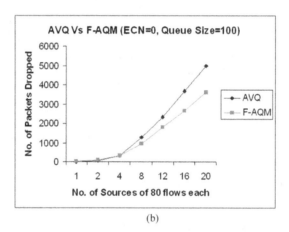

(b)

## FUTURE RESEARCH DIRECTIONS

Selection of FRM entries can be enhanced by extending the range of parameter values to have desired number of linguistic variables. Further scope for this work is to consider the traffic of various preferential levels and implementing the F-AQM mechanism in all link queues.

## CONCLUSION

The proposed congestion control technique addresses the influence of the queuing behavior in handling the traffic in the network. Many techniques such as Drop tail, RED, REM, AQM,

and AVQ control the behavior of the queue. The proposed Fuzzy enabled Active Queue (F-AQM) Management scheme is experimented with a simulation setup for varying number of sources of data and is shown that it outperforms the existing methods such as AVQ which have been stated that their behavior is better than other methods such as Drop tail, RED. Also the effect of queue size is studied. The sensation of received packets exceeding the capacity of the queue is monitored and dropped or marked. Setting of ECN bit enables the marking of packets rather than dropping them. The marking of packets notifies the sources of data about the incipient congestion in the network there by adjusting the flow rate to avoid congestion. It is observed that the number of dropped packets is reduced when ECN bit is set. Except the bottleneck link queue, all other queues are treated as Drop tail queues where the bandwidth is sufficient to handle all the incoming packets. Hence soft computing technique is found more suitable for congestion control in wired networks.

# REFERENCES

Athuraliya, S., Lapsley, D. E., & Low, S. H. (1999). Random early marking for Internet congestion control. In *Proc. IEEE Globecom,* (pp. 1747–1752).

Azvine, B., & Vasilakos, A. (2000). *Application of soft computing techniques to the telecommunication domain* (pp. 89–110). ERUDIT Roadmap.

Bertsekas, D., & Gallager, R. (1992). *Data Networks*. Englewood Cliffs, NJ: Prentice-Hall.

Bezdek, J. C. (1994). What is Computational Intelligence. In Zurada, J. M. (Ed.), *Computational Intelligence: Imitating Life* (pp. 1–12). Washington, DC: IEEE Press.

Brakmo, L., & Petersen, L. (1995). *Tcp Vegas*. IEEE Trans. on Networking.

Feng, W. G., Shin, K., Kandlur, D. & Saha, D. (2002). The BLUE Active Queue Management Algorithms. *IEEE/ACM Transactions On Networking, 10*(4), 513-528.

Floyd, S. (1994). TCP and Explicit Congestion Notification. *ACM Comput. Commun. Rev., 24,* 10–23. doi:10.1145/205511.205512

Floyd, S. & Jacobson, V. (1993). Random Early Detection Gateways for Congestion Avoidance. *IEEE/ACM Transactions on Networking, 1*(4), 397-413.

Gibbens, R. J., & Kelly, F. P. (1999). Distributed connection acceptance control for a connectionless network. In *Proc. 16th Int. Teletraffic Congr.,* (pp. 941–952).

Kunniyur, S., & Srikant, R. (2004). An Adaptive Virtual Queue (AVQ) Algorithm for Active Queue Management. *IEEE/ACM Transaction on Networking, 12*(2), 286-299.

Kunniyur, S., & Srikant, R. (2000). End-to-end congestion control: Utility functions, random losses and ECN marks. In *Proc. IEEE INFOCOM,* (pp. 1323–1332).

Kunniyur, S., & Srikant, R. (2001). A time-scale decomposition approach to adaptive ECN marking. In *Proc. IEEE INFOCOM,* (pp. 1330–1339).

Kunniyur, S., & Srikant, R. (2003). End-to-end congestion control: Utility functions, random losses and ECN marks. *IEEE/ACM Trans. Networking, 11,* 689–702. doi:10.1109/TNET.2003.818183

Mazumdar, R., Mason, L. G., & Douligeris, C. (1991). Fairness in network optimal flow control: Optimality of product form. *IEEE Transactions on Communications, 39,* 775–782. doi:10.1109/26.87140

Morales, E., Polycarpou, M., Hemasilpin, N., & Bissler, J. (2001). Hierarchical Adaptive and Supervisory Control of Continuous Venovenous Hemofiltration. *IEEE Transactions on Control Systems Technology, 9*(3), 445–457. doi:10.1109/87.918898

Network Simulator. (n.d.). *NS-2 Homepage*. Retrieved from http://www.isi.edu/nsnam/ns/

Ott, T. J., Lakshman, T. V., & Wong, L. H. (1999). *Sred: Stabilized red* (pp. 1346–1355). IEEE INFOCOM.

Pedrycz, W. (1998). *Computational Intelligence: An Introduction*. Boca Raton, FL: CRC Press.

Sekercioglu, A., Pitsillides, A., & Vasilakos, A. (2001). Computational intelligence in management of ATM networks. *Soft Computing Journal, 5*(4), 257–263. doi:10.1007/s005000100099

Whittle, P. (1971). *Optimization under Constraints*. New York: Wiley and Sons.

Yasunobu, S., & Miyamoto, S. (1985). Automatic Train Operation by Predictive Fuzzy Control. In Sugeno, M. (Ed.), *Industrial Applications of Fuzzy Control* (pp. 1–18). New York: Elsevier Science Publishers.

## KEY TERMS AND DEFINITIONS

**Congestion:** Congestion is a problem that occurs on shared networks when multiple users contend for access to the same resources (bandwidth, buffers, and queues).

**Active Queue Management (AQM):** Active Queue Management is a technique in which routers actively drop packets from queues as a signal to senders that they should slow down.

**Random Early Drop (RED):** RED is an Active Queue Management scheme that provides a mechanism for congestion avoidance. RED keeps track of an average queue size and drops packets when the average queue size grows beyond a defined threshold. The average size is recalculated every time a new packet arrives at the queue.

**ECN (Explicit Congestion Notification):** The problem with RED is that it drops packets. A more efficient technique would be for a router to set a congestion notification bit in a packet, and then send the packet to the receiver. The receiver could then inform the sender to slow down via a message in the ACK. All the while, the receiver gets its packet and we avoid using packet drops to signal congestion.

**Random Explicit Marking (REM):** An extension to RED is to mark the IP header instead of dropping packets (when the average queue size is between $min_{th}$ and $max_{th}$). ECN bit is used for this purpose. Cooperating end systems would then use this as a signal that the network is congested and slow down.

**Adaptive Virtual Queue (AVQ):** The AVQ algorithm maintains a virtual queue whose capacity (called *virtual capacity*) is less than the actual capacity of the link. When a packet arrives in the real queue, the virtual queue is also updated to reflect the new arrival. Packets in the real queue are marked/dropped when the virtual buffer overflows. The virtual capacity at each link is then adapted to ensure that the total flow entering each link achieves a desired utilization of the link.

**Packets Dropped:** Loss is one of Quality Of Service (QoS) parameters of a network. It is the percentage of packets dropped in the network.

**Fuzzy Logic:** Fuzzy logic is a form of multi-valued logic derived from fuzzy set theory to deal with reasoning that is approximate rather than precise.

# Compilation of References

Abraham, A. (2001). Neuro-fuzzy systems: State-of-the-art modeling techniques. In *proceedings of the 6th International Work-Conference on Artificial and Natural Neural Networks: Connectionist Models of Neurons, Learning Processes and Artificial Intelligence* (pp.269-276). Granada, Spain.

Agraval, R., & Srikant, R. (1994). Fast algorithms for mining association rules. In *Proceedings of the 20-the VLDB Conference*, (pp. 487-499). Santiago, Chile: Morgan Kaufmann.

Akdoğan, E. (2007). *Intelligent position and force control of a robot manipulator for rehabilitation*. Doctoral dissertation, Marmara University, Istanbul, Turkey.

Akdoğan, E., Taçgın, E., & Adlı, M. A. (2009). Knee rehabilitation using an intelligent robotic system. *Journal of Intelligent Manufacturing, 20*(2), 195–202. doi:10.1007/s10845-008-0225-y

Alizadeh, A. A., Eisen, M. B., Davis, E. E., Ma, C., & Lossos, I. S. (2000). Different types of diffuse large B-cell lymphoma identified by gene expression profiles. *Nature, 403*, 503–511. doi:10.1038/35000501

Alon, U., Barkai, N., Notterman, D. A., Gish, K., Ybarra, S., Mack, D., & Levine, A. J. (1999). Broad patterns of gene expression revealed by clustering analysis of tumor and normal colon tissues probed by oligonucleotide arrays. *Proceedings of the National Academy of Sciences of the United States of America, 96*, 6745–6750. doi:10.1073/pnas.96.12.6745

Altman, D. (1994). Fuzzy Set Theoretic Approaches for Handling Imprecision in Spatial Analysis. *International Journal of Geographical Information Systems, 8*(3), 271–289. doi:10.1080/02693799408902000

Alwan, A. A., Ibrahim, H., & Udzir, N. I. (2008). Integrity Constraints Checking in Distributed Databases with Complete, Sufficient, and Support Tests. In *Proceedings of the IADIS International Conference Applied Computing,* (pp. 49-58).

An, A., Shan, N., Chan, C., Cercone, N., & Ziarko, W. (1996). Discovering Rules for Water Demand Prediction: An Enhanced Rough-Set Approach. *Engineering Applications of Artificial Intelligence, 9*(6), 645–653. doi:10.1016/S0952-1976(96)00059-0

Anshakov, O. M., Finn, V. K., & Skvortsov, D. P. (1989). On axiomatization of many-valued logics associated with formalization of plausible reasoning. *Studia Logica, 42*(4), 423–447. doi:10.1007/BF00370198

Arkin, E., Chew, P., Huttenlocher, D., Kedem, K., & Mitchel, J. (1991). An efficiently computable metric for comparing polygonal shapes. *IEEE Transactions on Pattern Analysis and Machine Intelligence, 13*(3), 209–215. doi:10.1109/34.75509

Arkoumanis, D., Terrovitis, M., & Stamatogiannakis, L. (2002). Heuristic Algorithms for Similar Configuration Retrieval in Spatial Databases. In *proceeding of the 2nd Hellenic Conference on Artificial Intelligence (SETN)*, Thessalonica, Greece.

Athuraliya, S., Lapsley, D. E., & Low, S. H. (1999). Random early marking for Internet congestion control. In *Proc. IEEE Globecom,* (pp. 1747–1752).

Azvine, B., & Vasilakos, A. (2000). *Application of soft computing techniques to the telecommunication domain* (pp. 89–110). ERUDIT Roadmap.

Bäck, T. (1995). *Evolutionary algorithms in theory and practice*. New York: Oxford University Press.

Baker, J. E. (1985). Adaptive selection methods for genetic algorithms. In *Proceedings of the International Conference on Genetic Algorithms and Their Applications,* (pp. 100-111).

Baker, J. E. (1987). Reducing bias and inefficiency in the selection algorithm. In J. J. Grefenstette (Ed.), *Proceedings of the 2 nd International Conference on Genetic Algorithms* (pp. 14-21). San Francisco: Morgan Kaufmann.

Baker, M. (2000). The Roles of Models in Artificial Intelligence and Education Research: A Prospective View. *International Journal of Artificial Intelligence in Education*, (11): 122–143.

Bangert, A. W. (2004). The Seven Principles of Good Practice: A framework for evaluating on-line teaching. *The Internet and Higher Education*, *7*(3), 217–232. doi:10.1016/j.iheduc.2004.06.003

Bankscope. (2007). *Bureau van Dijk*. Retrieved from https://bankscope.bvdep.com

Barbara, D., & Garcia-Molina, I. I. (1992). The Demarcation Protocol: A Technique for Maintaining Linear Arithmetic Constraints in Distributed Database Systems. In *Proceedings of the Conference on Extending Database Technology (EDBT'92)*, (pp. 373-388).

Beaubouef, T., Ladner, R., & Petry, F. (2004). Rough Set Spatial Data Modeling for Data Mining. *International Journal of Geographical Information Science*, *19*, 567–584.

Bernstein, P. A., & Blaustein, B. T. (1981). A Simplification Algorithm for Integrity Assertions and Concrete Views. In *Proceedings of the 5th International Computer Software and Applications Conference (COMPSAC'81)*, (pp. 90-99).

Bertsekas, D., & Gallager, R. (1992). *Data Networks*. Englewood Cliffs, NJ: Prentice-Hall.

Beynon, M. (2001). Reducts Within the Variable Precision Rough Sets Model: A Further Investigation. *European Journal of Operational Research*, *134*, 592–605. doi:10.1016/S0377-2217(00)00280-0

Beynon, M. J. (2004). The Elucidation of an Iterative Procedure to $\beta$-Reduct Selection in the Variable Precision Rough Sets Model. In S., Tsumoto, R., Slowinski, J. Komorowski, & J., W. Grzymala-Busse, (Eds.), *Rough Sets and Current Trends in Computing - Fourth International Conference on Rough Sets and Current Trends in Computing*, Uppsala, Sweden, (pp. 412-417). Berlin: Springer-Verlag.

Beynon, M., J., Clatworthy, M., A. & Jones, M., J. (2004). A Prediction of Profitability Using Accounting Narratives: A Variable Precision Rough Set Approach. *International Journal of Intelligent Systems in Accounting Finance & Management*, *12*, 227–242. doi:10.1002/isaf.256

Bezdek, J. C. (1994). What is Computational Intelligence. In Zurada, J. M. (Ed.), *Computational Intelligence: Imitating Life* (pp. 1–12). Washington, DC: IEEE Press.

Birkhoff, G. (1954). *Lattice theory*. Moscow, Russia: Foreign Literature.

Blakemore, M. (1984). Generalization and Error in Spatial Databases. *Cartographica*, *21*(2/3), 131–139.

Blaustein, B. T. (1981). *Enforcing Database Assertions: Techniques and Applications*. PhD Thesis, Harvard University, Cambridge, MA.

Blickle, T., & Thiele, L. (1995). A mathematical analysis of tournament selection. In L. J. Eshelman (Ed.), *Proceedings of the 6th International Conference on Genetic Algorithms* (pp. 9-16). San Francisco: Morgan Kaufmann.

Blickle, T., & Thiele, L. (1997). A comparison of selection schemes used in genetic algorithms. In Evolutionary Computation, (pp. 361-394).

Bodenhofer, U., Hüllermeier, E., Klawonn, F., & Kruse, R. (2007). Special issue on soft computing for information mining. *Soft Computing, 11*, 397–399. doi:10.1007/s00500-006-0105-3

Bogàrdi, I., Bárdossy, A., & Duckstein, L. (1990). Risk Management for Groundwater Contamination: Fuzzy Set Approach. In Khanpilvardi, R., & Gooch, T. (Eds.), *Optimizing the Resources for Water Management* (pp. 442–448). ASCE.

Boldyrev, N. G. (1974). Minimization of Boolean partial functions with a large number of "don't care" conditions and the problem of feature extraction. In *"Discrete Systems", Proceedings of International Symposium* (pp.101-109). Riga, Latvia: Publishing House "ZINATNE

Bonissone, P. P. (1998). Soft Computing: The Convergence of Emerging Reasoning Technologies. *Soft Computing, 1*, 6–18. doi:10.1007/s005000050002

Bordogna, G., Lucarella, D., & Pasi, G. (1999). A Fuzzy Object-Oriented Data Model Managing Vague and Uncertain Information. *International Journal of Intelligent Systems, 14*(7), 623–651. doi:10.1002/(SICI)1098-111X(199907)14:7<623::AID-INT1>3.0.CO;2-

Brakmo, L., & Petersen, L. (1995). *Tcp Vegas*. IEEE Trans. on Networking.

Brameier, M., & Banzhaf, W. (2007). *Linear Genetic Programming*. Berlin: Springer.

Breiman, L., Friedman, J. H., Olshen, R., & Stone, R. (1984). *Classification and Regression Trees*. New York: Wadsworth.

Brindle, A. (1981). *Genetic algorithms in search, optimization*. Technical Report No. TR81-2, Department of Computer Science, University of Alberta, Canada.

Brown, D. G. (1998). Mapping Historical Forest Types in Baraga County Michigan, USA as Fuzzy Sets. *Plant Ecology, 134*, 97–111. doi:10.1023/A:1009796502293

Buckles, B. P., & Petry, F. E. (1985). Uncertainty Models in Information and Database Systems. *Information Sciences, 11*, 77–87. doi:10.1177/016555158501100204C

haudhry, N., & Moyne, J., E.A. & Rundensteiner, E.A. (1999). An Extended Database Design Methodology for Uncertain Data Management. *Information Sciences, 121*, 83–112. doi:10.1016/S0020-0255(99)00066-3

Buckley, J. J., & Eslami, E. (2002). *An Introduction to Fuzzy Logic and Fuzzy Sets*. Advances in Soft Computing. Physica-Verlag.

Burrough, P. A. (1996). Natural Objects with Indeterminate Boundaries. In Burrough, P. A., & Frank, A. U. (Eds.), *Geographic Objects with Indeterminate Boundaries* (pp. 3–28). Boca Raton, FL: Taylor & Francis.

Burrough, P. A., van Gaans, P. F. M., & Macmillan, R. A. (2000). High-Resolution Landform Classification Using Fuzzy k-Means. *Fuzzy Sets and Systems, 113*, 37–52. doi:10.1016/S0165-0114(99)00011-1

Carpineto, C., & Romano, G. (1996). A lattice conceptual clustering system and its application to browsing retrieval. *Machine Learning, 24*, 95–122. doi:10.1007/BF00058654

Castellano, G., Castiello, C., & Fanelli, A. M. (2006). Visual Image Retrieval by Shape Matching. In *Proceeding of ISMIS 2006* (pp. 208–217). VIRMA.

Castiello, C., Castellano, G., Caponetti, L., & Fanelli, A. M. (2003). Classifying image pixels by a neuro-fuzzy approach. In *Proceeding of International Fuzzy Systems Association World Congress (IFSA 2003)*, (pp. 253-256).

Ceri, C., Gotlob, G., & Tanca, L. (1990). *Logic programming and databases*. New York: Springer-Verlag.

Ceri, S., Fraternali, P., Paraboschi, S., & Tanca, L. (1994). Automatic Generation of Production Rules for Integrity Maintenance. *ACM Transactions on Database Systems, 19*(3), 367–422. doi:10.1145/185827.185828

Chakravarthy, U. S. (1990). Logic-Based Approach to Semantic Query Optimization. *ACM Transactions on Database Systems, 15*(2), 162–207. doi:10.1145/78922.78924

Chan, H., & Darwiche, A. (2004). Sensitivity analysis in Bayesian Networks: From single to multiple parameters. In *Proceedings of the 20th conference on uncertainty in Artificial Intelligence (UAI),* (pp. 67-75).

Chaudhry, N., Moyne, J., & Rundensteiner, E. (1994). A Design Methodology for Databases with Uncertain Data. In *7th International Working Conference on Scientific and Statistical Database Management, Charlottesville,* VA, (pp. 32-41). (www.mitexsolutions.com).

Chen, G. Q. (1998). *Fuzzy Logic in Data Modeling, Semantics Constraints, and Databases Design.* Amsterdam: The Kluwer International Series on Advances in Database Systems.

Chen, G. Q., & Kerre, E. E. (1998). Extending ER/EER Concepts Towards Fuzzy Conceptual Data Modeling. *IEEE International Conference on Fuzzy Systems, 2,* 1320-1325.

Chen, G., Ren, M., Yan, P., & Guo, X. (2007). Enriching the ER model based on discovered association rules. *Information Sciences, 177,* 1558–1566. doi:10.1016/j.ins.2006.07.001

Chen, L.-H. & Chiou, T.-W. (1999). A fuzzy credit-rating approach for commercial loans: a Taiwan case. *OMEGA - International Journal of Management Science, 27,* 407-419.

Chen, Y., & Wang, J. Z. (2002). A region based fuzzy feature matching approach to content based image retrieval. *IEEE Transactions on Pattern Analysis and Machine Intelligence, 24*(9), 1252–1267. doi:10.1109/TPAMI.2002.1033216

Chen, Z., He, Y., Chu, F., & Huang, J. (2003). Evolutionary Strategy for Classification Problems and its Application in Fault Diagnosis. *Engineering Applications of Artificial Intelligence, 16*(1), 31–38. doi:10.1016/S0952-1976(03)00027-7

Chen, Z., Wenyin, L., Zhang, F., Li, M., & Zhang, H.-J. (2001). Web Mining for Web Image Retrieval. *Journal of the American Society for Information Science American Society for Information Science, 52*(10), 831–839.

Cheng, T., Molenaar, M., & Lin, H. (2001). Formalizing Fuzzy Objects from Uncertain Classification Results. *International Journal of Geographical Information Science, 15,* 27–42. doi:10.1080/13658810010004689

Clementini, E., & Di Felice, P. (1996). A Model for Representing Topological Relationships between Complex Geometric Features in Spatial Databases. *Information Sciences, 90*(1-4), 121–136. doi:10.1016/0020-0255(95)00289-8

Clementini, E., & Di Felice, P. (1996). An Algebraic Model for Spatial Objects with Indeterminate Boundaries. In Burrough, P. A., & Frank, A. U. (Eds.), *Geographic Objects with Indeterminate Boundaries* (pp. 153–169). Boca Raton, FL: Taylor & Francis.

Clementini, E., & Di Felice, P. (2001). A Spatial Model for Complex Objects with a Broad Boundary Supporting Queries on Uncertain Data. *Data & Knowledge Engineering, 37,* 285–305. doi:10.1016/S0169-023X(01)00010-6

Codd, E. F. (1990). *The Relational Model for Database Management.* Reading, MA: Addison-Wesley Publishing Company, Inc.

Cohen, D., & Prusak, L. (2001). *In good company: How social capital makes organizations work.* Cambridge, MA: Harvard Business School Press.

Cohn, A. G., & Gotts, N. M. (1996). The 'Egg-Yolk' Representation of Regions with Indeterminate Boundaries. In Burrough, P. A., & Frank, A. U. (Eds.), *Geographic Objects with Indeterminate Boundaries* (pp. 171–187). Boca Raton, FL: Taylor & Francis.

Collet, P., & Louchet, J. (2009). Artificial Evolution and the Parisian Approach: Applications in the Processing of Signals and Images. In Siarry, P. (Ed.), *Optimization in Signal and Image Processing, iSTE.* Chichester, UK: John Wiley & Sons. doi:10.1002/9780470611319.ch2

Collet, P., Louchet, J., & Lutton, E. (2002). Issues on the optimization of evolutionary algorithms code. In D. B. Fogel, et al. (Eds.), *Proceedings of the 2002 Congress on Evolutionary Computation* (pp. 1103-1108). Washington, DC: IEEE Press.

Collion, M. H. (1989). Strategic planning for national agricultural research systems: An Overview. *Working Paper, 26*. Retrieved November 24th 2008 from http://www.ifpri.org/divs/isnar.htm

Conati, C., Gertner, A., & VanLehn, K. (2002). Using bayesian networks to manage uncertainty in student modeling. *User Modeling and User-Adapted Interaction, 12*(4), 371–417. doi:10.1023/A:1021258506583

Cooper, G. F., & Herskovits, E. (1992). A Bayesian method for the induction of Probabilistic networks from data. *Machine Learning, 9*(4), 309–347. doi:10.1007/BF00994110

Cordon, O., & Herrera, F. (2003). Author's reply. *IEEE Transactions on Fuzzy Systems, 11*(6), 866–869.

Cordon, O., Moya, F., & Zarco, C. (2002). A new evolutionary algorithm combining simulated annealing and genetic programming for relevance feedback in fuzzy information retrieval systems. *Soft Computing, 6*, 308–319. doi:10.1007/s00500-002-0184-8

Coupé, V. M. H., & Van der Gaag, L. C. (1998). Practicable sensitivity analysis of Bayesian belief networks. In M. Huskova, P. Lachout, & J.A. Visek (Eds.), *Proceedings of the Joint Session of the 6th Praque Symposium of Asymptotic Statistics and the 13th Praque Conference on Information Theory, Statistical Decision Functions and Random Processes*, (p.81-86). Prague: Union of Czech Mathematicians and Physicists.

Cramer, N. L. (1985). A representation for the adaptive generation of simple sequential programs. In *Proceedings of the International Conference on Genetic Algorithms and Their Applications* (pp.183-187).

Cremers, A. B., & Domann, G. (1983). AIM – An Integrity Monitor for the Database System INGRES. In *Proceedings of the 9th International Conference on Very Large Data Bases (VLDB 9)*, (pp. 167-170).

Culmer, P., Jackson, A., Levesley, M. C., et al. (2005). An admittance control scheme for a robotic upper-limb stroke rehabilitation system. In *Proceedings of the 2005 IEEE Engineering in Medicine and Biology 27th Annual Conference*.

Damiani, E., Oliboni, B., & Tanca, L. (2001). Fuzzy Techniques for XML Data Smushing. In B. Reusch (Ed.), 7th Fuzzy Days on Computational Intelligence, Theory and Applications, (LNCS 2206, pp. 637-652). Berlin: Springer Verlag.

Daniel, B. K. Zapata-Rivera, D. J., & McCalla, G. I. (2003) A Bayesian computational model of social capital. In Huysman, M. Wenger, E. and Wulf, V. (Eds.). Communities and technologies (pp. 287-305). London: Kluwer Publishers.

Daniel, B. K., & Zapata-Rivera, J. D & McCalla, G.I. (2005, November). Computational framework for constructing Bayesian belief network models from incomplete, inconsistent and imprecise data in E-Learning (Poster). In *The Second LORNET International Annual Conference, I2LOR-2005, November 16 to 18*. Vancouver, Canada.

Daniel, B. K., McCalla, G. I., & Schwier, R. A. (2005). Data mining and modeling social capital in virtual learning communities. *Proceedings of the 12th International Conference on Artificial Intelligence in Education*, Amsterdam, 18-22 July, 2000-2008.

Daniel, B. K., McCalla, G., & Schwier, R. (2003). Social capital in virtual learning communities and distributed, communities of practice. *The Canadian Journal of Learning Technology, 29*(3), 113–139.

Daniel, B. K., O' Brien, D., & Sarkar, A. (2003). A design approach for Canadian distributed community of practice on governance and international development: A preliminary report. In Verburg, R. M., & De Ridder, J. A. (Eds.), *Knowledge sharing under distributed circumstances* (pp. 19–24). Enschede, The Netherlands: Ipskamps.

Daniel, B. K., Zapata-Rivera, J. D., & McCalla, G. I. (2007). A Bayesian Belief Network approach for modelling complex domains. In Mittal, A., Kassim, A., & Tan, T. (Eds.), *Bayesian Network Technologies: Applications and Graphical Models* (pp. 13–41). Hershey, PA: IGI Publishing.

Darwin, C. (1859). *On the origin of species by means of natural selection or the preservation of favored races in the struggle for life*. London: John Murray.

Davies, J., & Graff, M. (2005). Performance in e-learning: online participation and student grades. *British Journal of Educational Technology*, *36*(4), 657–663. doi:10.1111/j.1467-8535.2005.00542.x

De Caluwe, R. (Ed.). (1997). *Fuzzy and Uncertain Object-Oriented Databases, Concepts and Models. Advances in Fuzzy System – Application and Theory, 13*. Singapore: World Scientific.

De Gruijter, J., Walvoort, D., & Vangaans, P. (1997). Continuous Soil Maps-a Fuzzy Set Approach to Bridge the Gap between Aggregation Levels of Process and Distribution Models. *Geoderma*, *77*, 169–195. doi:10.1016/S0016-7061(97)00021-9

Deb, K., & Agrawal, R. B. (1995). Simulated binary crossover for continuous search space. *Complex Systems*, *9*, 115–148.

Deb, K., Agrawal, S., Pratab, A., & Meyarivan, T. (2000). A Fast Elitist Non-Dominated Sorting Genetic Algorithm for Multi-Objective Optimization: NSGA-II, (LNCS Vol 1917, pp. 849-858). Berlin: Springer.

DeJong, K. (2005). *Evolutionary computation: A unified approach*. Cambridge, MA: MIT Press.

Del Bimbo, A., & Pala, P. (1997). Visual image retrieval by elastic matching of user sketches. *IEEE Transactions on Pattern Analysis and Machine Intelligence*, *19*, 121–132. doi:10.1109/34.574790

Dembczyński, K., Greco, S., Kotłowski, W., & Słowiński, R. (2007). *Statistical Model for Rough Set Approach to Multicriteria Classification* (pp. 164–175). Knowledge Discovery in Databases.

Demetrovics, J., & Vu, D. T. (1993). Generating Armstrong relation schemes and inferring functional dependencies from relations. *International Journal on Information Theory & Applications*, *1*(4), 3–12.

DeOliveria, J. V. (1999). Semantic constraints for membership function optimization. *IEEE Transactions on Systems, Man, and Cybernetics. Part A, Systems and Humans*, *29*(1), 128–138. doi:10.1109/3468.736369

Derviz, A. & Podpiera., J. (2004). *Predicting Bank CAMELS and S&P Ratings: The Case of the Czech Republic*. Working Papers Series of the Czech National Bank.

Dilo, A., de By, R. A., & Stein, A. (2007). A System of Types and Operators for Handling Vague Spatial Objects. *International Journal of Geographical Information Science*, *21*(4), 397–426. doi:10.1080/13658810601037096

Djeraba, C. (2002). Content-based multimedia indexing and retrieval. *IEEE MultiMedia*, *9*(2), 18–22. doi:10.1109/MMUL.2002.998047

Doherty, W. (2006). An analysis of multiple factors affecting retention in Web-based community college courses. *The Internet and Higher Education*, *9*(4), 245–255. doi:10.1016/j.iheduc.2006.08.004

Doulamis, A. D., Doulamis, N. D., & Kollias, S. D. (1999). Relevance feedback for content-based retrieval in video database: a neural network approach. In *Proceeding of International Conference on Electronic Circuit and Systems*, (Vol. 3, pp. 1745-1748).

Druzdzel, M. (1996). Qualitative verbal explanations in bayesian belief networks. *Artificial Intelligence and Simulation of Behaviour Quarterly*, *9*(4), 43–54.

Druzdzel, M. J., & Gaag, L. C. (2000). Building probabilistic networks: "Where do the numbers come from?" Guest editor's introduction. *Data Engineering*, *12*(4), 481–486. doi:10.1109/TKDE.2000.868901

Druzdzel, M. J., & Henri, J. S. (1994). *Relevance in probabilistic models: "backyards" in a "small world."* In Working notes of the AAAI-1994 Fall Symposium Series: Relevance, New Orleans, LA, (pp. 60-63).

Druzdzel, M. J., & Henrion, M. (1993). Efficient reasoning in qualitative probabilistic networks. In *Proceedings of the 11th National Conference on Artificial Intelligence*, (pp. 548-553).

Dubois, D., & Prade, H. (1996). What are fuzzy rules and how to use them. *Fuzzy Sets and Systems, 84,* 169–185. doi:10.1016/0165-0114(96)00066-8

Dubois, D., & Prade, H. (1998). Soft Computing, Fuzzy Logic, and Artificial Intelligence. *Soft Computing, 2,* 7–11. doi:10.1007/s005000050025

Dudoit, S., Fridlyand, J., & Speed, T. P. (2002). Comparison of discrimination methods for the classification of tumors using gene expression data. *Journal of the American Statistical Association, 97*(457), 77–87. doi:10.1198/016214502753479248

Dutta, S. (1989). Qualitative Spatial Reasoning: A Semi-Quantitative Approach Using Fuzzy Logic. In *1st International Symposium on the Design and Implementation of Large Spatial Databases* (LNCS 409, pp. 345-364). Berlin: Springer Verlag.

Dutta, S. (1991). Topological Constraints: A Representational Framework for Approximate Spatial and Temporal Reasoning. In *2nd International Symposium on the Design and Implementation of Large Spatial Databases* (LNCS 525, pp. 161-180). Berlin: Springer Verlag.

Edwards, G. (1994). Characterizing and Maintaining Polygons with Fuzzy Boundaries in GIS. In *6th International Symposium on Spatial Data Handling* (pp. 223-239).

Egecioglu, O., Ferhatosmanoglu, H., & Ogras, U. (2004). Dimensionality reduction and similarity computation by inner-product approximations. *IEEE Transactions on Knowledge and Data Engineering, 16*(6), 714–726. doi:10.1109/TKDE.2004.9

Egenhofer, M. J. (1994). Spatial SQL: A Query and Presentation Language. *IEEE Transactions on Knowledge and Data Engineering, 6*(1), 86–94. doi:10.1109/69.273029

Eiben, A. E., & Smith, J. E. (2003). Introduction to Evolutionary Computing. In *Natural Computing Series.* Berlin: Springer.

Elmasri, R., & Navathe, S. B. (2000). Fundamentals of Database Systems, (3rd. Ed.). Reading, MA: Addison Wesley.

El-Naqa, I., Yang, Y., Galatsanos, N. P., Nishikawa, R. M., & Wernik, M. N. (2004). A similarity learning approach to content-based image retrieval: application to digital mammography. *IEEE Transactions on Medical Imaging, 23*(10), 1233–1244. doi:10.1109/TMI.2004.834601

Embury, S. M., Gray, P. M. D., & Bassiliades, N. D. (1993). Constraint Maintenance using Generated Methods in the P/FDM Object-Oriented Database. In *Proceedings of the 1st International Workshop on Rules in Database Systems,* (pp. 365-381).

Erwig, M., & Schneider, M. (1997). Vague Regions. In 5th *International Symposium on Advances in Spatial Databases,* (LNCS 1262, pp. 298-320). Berlin: Springer Verlag.

Eshelman, L. J., & Schaffer, J. D. (1993). Real-coded genetic algorithms and interval-schemata. In Whitley, L. D. (Ed.), *Foundations of Genetic Algorithms 2* (pp. 187–202). San Mateo, CA: Morgan Kaufmann.

Eswaran, K. P., & Chamberlin, D. D. (1975). Functional Specifications of a Subsystem for Data Base Integrity. *Proceedings of the 1st International Conference on Very Large Data Bases (VLDB 1), 1*(1), 48-68.

Fayyad, M., U. & Irani B., K. (1992). Technical Note: On the Handling of Continuous-Valued Attributes in Decision Tree Generation. *Machine Learning, 8*(1), 87–102. doi:10.1007/BF00994007

Fayyad, M., U., Piatetsky-Shapiro, G. & Smyth, P. (1996). From Data Mining to Knowledge Discovery in Databases. *AI Magazine, 17*(3), 37–54.

Fayyad, U. M., Piatetsky-Shapiro, G., Smyth, P., & Uthurusamy, R. (1996). *Advances in Knowledge Discovery and Data Mining.* Menlo Park, CA: AAAI/MIT Press.

Feil, B., & Abonyi, J. (2008). Introduction to Fuzzy Data Mining Methods. In J. Galindo, (Ed.), *Handbook of Research on Fuzzy Information Processing in Databases,* (Vol. I, pp. 55-95). Hershey, PA, USA: Information Science Reference. Retrieved from http://www.info-sci-ref.com

Feng, D., Siu, W. C., & Zhang, H. J. (Eds.). (2003). *Multimedia information retrieval and management: Technological fundamentals and applications.* Berlin: Springer.

Feng, W. G., Shin, K., Kandlur, D. & Saha, D. (2002). The BLUE Active Queue Management Algorithms. *IEEE/ACM Transactions On Networking, 10*(4), 513-528.

Figueroa, J. P., Soriano, M. M., & Rojas, S. (2005). A type-2 fuzzy controller for tracking mobile objects in the context of robotic soccer games. In proceedings of the FUZZ-IEEE 2005 (pp.359-364), USA.

Finn, J. (1996). *An introduction to Bayesian networks.* London: University College Press.

Finn, J. T. (1993). Use of the Average Mutual Information Index in Evaluating Classification Error and Consistency. *Int. Journal of Geographical Information Systems, 7*(4), 349–366. doi:10.1080/02693799308901966

Finn, J., & Liang, J. (1994). drHugin: A system for value of information in Bayesian networks. In *Proceedings of the Fifth International Conference on Information Processing and Management of Uncertainty in Knowledge - based Systems (IPMU),* Paris, France, (pp. 178-183).

Finn, V. K. (1984). Inductive models of knowledge representation in man-machine and robotics systems. *The Transactions of VINITI, A,* 58-76.

Finn, V. K. (1988). Commonsense inference and commonsense reasoning. *Review of Science and Technique (Itogi Nauki i Tekhniki), Series "The Theory of Probability. Mathematical Statistics. Technical Cybernetics, 28,* 3–84.

Finn, V. K. (1991). Plausible reasoning in systems of JSM type. *Review of Science and Technique (Itogi Nauki i Tekhniki), Series ". Informatika, 15,* 54–101.

Finn, V. K. (1999). The synthesis of cognitive procedures and the problem of induction. *NTI* [Moscow, Russia: VINITI]. *Series, 2*(1-2), 8–44.

Fitch. (2007). Retrieved from www.fitchratings.com

Fleming, P., & Purshouse, C. (1995). *The Matlab Genetic Algorithm Toolbox.* Sheffield, England: IEE Colloquium on Applied Control Technology Using Matlab.

Fleming, P., & Purshouse, C. (2002). Evolutionary Algorithms in Control Systems Engineering: A survey. *Control Engineering Practice, 10*(11), 1223–1241. doi:10.1016/S0967-0661(02)00081-3

Floyd, S. & Jacobson, V. (1993). Random Early Detection Gateways for Congestion Avoidance. *IEEE/ACM Transactions on Networking, 1*(4), 397-413.

Floyd, S. (1994). TCP and Explicit Congestion Notification. *ACM Comput. Commun. Rev., 24,* 10–23. doi:10.1145/205511.205512

Fogel, D. B. (1992). An analysis of evolutionary programming. In D. B. Fogel & W. Atmar (Eds.), *Proceedings of the 1st Annual Conference on Evolutionary Programming,* (pp. 43-51).

Fogel, D. B. (1998). *Evolutionary computation: The fossil record.* New York: Wiley-IEEE Press.

Fogel, L. J., Owens, A. J., & Walsh, M. J. (1966). *Artificial intelligence through simulated evolution.* New York: John Wiley & Sons.

Fonseca, M. J., & Jorge, J. A. (2003). Indexing high dimensional data for content-based retrieval in large database. In *Proceedings of the Eighth International Conference on Database Systems for Advanced Applications,* Kyoto, Japan.

Fort, G., & Lambert-Lacroix, S. (2005). Classification using partial least squares with penalized logistic regression. *Bioinformatics (Oxford, England), 21*(7), 1104–1111. doi:10.1093/bioinformatics/bti114

Fraser, A. S. (1957). Simulation of genetic systems by automatic digital computers. *Australian Journal of Biological Sciences, 10,* 484–491.

Frawley, W., J., Piatetsky-Shapiro, G. & Matheus, C. (1992). Knowledge Discovery In Databases: An Overview. *AI Magazine, 13*(3), 57–70.

Friedberg, R., Dunham, B., & North, J. (1958). A learning machine: Part II. *IBM Research Journal, 3*(3).

Friedman, G. (1959). Digital simulation of an evolutionary process. *General Systems Yearbook, 4*, 171–184.

Fujishiro, I., et al. (1991). The Design of a Graph-Oriented Schema for the Management of Individualized Fuzzy Data. *Japanese journal of Fuzzy Theory and System, 3*(1), 1-14.

Furey, T. S., Cristianini, N., Duffy, N., Bednarski, D. W., Schummer, M., & Haussler, D. (2000). Support vector machine classification and validation of cancer tissue samples using microarray expression data. *Bioinformatics (Oxford, England), 16*(10), 906–914. doi:10.1093/bioinformatics/16.10.906

Galindo, J. (Ed.). (2008). *Handbook of Research on Fuzzy Information Processing in Databases*. Hershey, PA: Information Science Reference. Retrieved from http://www.info-sci-ref.com

Galindo, J., Medina, J. M., Cubero, J. C., & García, M. T. (2001). Relaxing the Universal Quantifier of the Division in Fuzzy Relational Databases. *International Journal of Intelligent Systems, 16*, 713–742. doi:10.1002/int.1032

Galindo, J., Urrutia, A., & Piattini, M. (2006). *Fuzzy Databases: Modeling, Design and Implementation*. Hershey, PA: Idea Group Publishing.

Galitsky, B. A., Kuznetsov, S. O., & Vinogradov, D. V. (2007). Applying hybrid reasoning to mine for associative features in biological data. *Journal of Biomedical Informatics, 40*(3), 203–220. doi:10.1016/j.jbi.2006.07.002

Ganascia, J. - Gabriel. (1989). EKAW - 89 tutorial notes: Machine learning. In J. Boose, B. Gaines, & J.G. Ganascia, (Eds.), *EKAW'89: Third European Workshop on Knowledge Acquisition for Knowledge-Based Systems* (pp. 287-296), Paris, France.

Ganter, B. (1984). *Two basic algorithms in concepts analysis. B4-Preprint, No. 831*. Darmstadt: Technische Hochschule.

George, R., Srikanth, R., Petry, F. E., & Buckles, B. P. (1996). Uncertainty Management Issues in the Object-Oriented Data Model. *IEEE Transactions on Fuzzy Systems, 4*(2), 179–192. doi:10.1109/91.493911

Gibbens, R. J., & Kelly, F. P. (1999). Distributed connection acceptance control for a connectionless network. In *Proc. 16th Int. Teletraffic Congr.*, (pp. 941–952).

Giraud-Carrier, C., & Martinez, T. (1994). An incremental learning model for commonsense reasoning. In *Proceedings of the Seventh International Symposium on Artificial Intelligence (ISAI'94)*, (pp. 134-141). ITESM.

Glover, F. (1977). Heuristics for integer programming using surrogate constraints. *Decision Sciences, 8*, 156–166. doi:10.1111/j.1540-5915.1977.tb01074.x

Glover, F. (1989). Tabu search—part I. *ORSA Journal on Computing, 1*(3), 190-206.

Glover, F. (1990). Tabu search—part II. *ORSA Journal on Computing, 2*(3), 4–32.

Goldberg, D. E. (1989). *Genetic algorithms in search, optimization and machine learning*. Boston: Addison-Wesley.

Goldberg, D., & Deb, K. (1991). *A comparative analysis of selection schemes used in genetic algorithms* (pp. 416–421). Foundations of Genetic Algorithms.

Goldman, R., & Charniak, E. (1990). Dynamic Construction of Belief Networks. In *Proceedings of the Sixth Conference on Uncertainty in Artificial Intelligence*, (pp. 90-97).

Golub, T. R., Slonim, D. K., Tamayo, P., Huard, C., Gaasenbeek, M., & Mesirov, J. P. (1999). Molecular classification of cancer: class discovery and class prediction by gene expression monitoring. *Science, 286*, 531–537. doi:10.1126/science.286.5439.531

Gonzalez-Garcia, A. C., Sossa-Azuela, J. H., Felipe-Riveron, & E. M., Pogrebnyak, O. (2007). Image retrieval based on Wavelet transform and neural network classification. *Computation Y Systemas, 11*(2), 143-156.

Gorzalczany, M. B. (1987). A method of inference in approximate reasoning based on interval-valued fuzzy sets. *Fuzzy Sets and Systems*, *21*, 1–17.

Grefen, P. W. P. J. (1990). *Design Considerations for Integrity Constraint Handling in PRISMA/DB1. Prisma Project Document* (p. 508). Twente, The Netherlands: University of Twente.

Grefen, P. W. P. J. (1993). Combining Theory and Practice in Integrity Control: A Declarative Approach to the Specification of a Transaction Modification Subsystem. In *Proceedings of the 19th International Conference on Very Large Data Bases (VLDB 19)*, (pp. 581-591).

Güting, R. H. (1988). Geo-Relational Algebra: A Model and Query Language for Geometric Database Systems. In *International Conference on Extending Database Technology*, (pp. 506-527).

Gunadi, W. N., Shamsuddin, S. M., Alias, R. A., & Sap, M. N. (2003). Selection of defuzzification method to obtain crisp value for representing uncertain data in a modified sweep algorithm. *Journal of Computer Science & Technology*, *3*(2), 22–28.

Gunasekaran, A., McNeil, R., & Shaul, D. (2002). E-learning: research and applications. *Industrial and Commercial Training*, *34*(2), 44–53. doi:10.1108/00197850210417528

Gupta, A. (1994). *Partial Information Based Integrity Constraint Checking*. PhD Thesis, Stanford University, Stanford, CA.

Gutwin, C., & Greenberg, S. (1998). Design for individuals, design for groups: Tradeoffs between power and workspace awareness. In *Proceedings of the ACM Conference on Computer Supported Cooperative Work* (pp. 207-216). New York: ACM Press.

Gyseghem, N. Van, & De Caluwe, R. (1997). The UFO Model: dealing with Imperfect Information. In Fuzzy and uncertain Object-oriented databases, concepts and Models, (Advances in Fuzzy Systems: Vol. 13, pp. 123-185). Singapore: World Scientific Publishing Co. Pte. Ltd.

Haddaway, P. (1999). An overview of some recent developments in Bayesian problem solving techniques. *AI Magazine*, (Spring Issue).

Hammer, M. M., & McLeod, D. J. (1975). Semantic Integrity in a Relational Data Base System. In *Proceedings of the 1st International Conference on Very Large Data Bases (VLDB 1)*, *1*(1), 25-47.

Han, J., & Kamber, M. (2006). *Data Mining: Concepts and Techniques*. San Francisco: Morgan Kaufmann.

Han, J., & Ma, K. (2002). Fuzzy Colour Histogram and its Use in Colour Image Retrieval. *IEEE Transactions on Image Processing*, *11*(8), 944–952. doi:10.1109/TIP.2002.801585

Hansen, N., Müller, S. D., & Koumoutsakos, P. (2003). Reducing the time complexity of the derandomized evolution strategy with covariance matrix adaptation (CMA-ES). *Evolutionary Computation*, *11*(1), 1–18. doi:10.1162/106365603321828970

Hart, W. E., Krasnogor, N., & Smith, J. E. (2005). *Recent advances in memetic algorithms*. Berlin: Springer. doi:10.1007/3-540-32363-5

Harvey, I. (1993). Evolutionary robotics and saga: The case for hill crawling and tournament selection. *Artificial Life III. Santa Fe Institute Studies in the Sciences of Complexity*, *XVI*, 299–326.

Hassanien, A.-E., & Jafar, A. (2003). Image classification and retrieval algorithm based on rough set theory. [SACJ]. *South African Computer Journal*, *30*, 9–16.

Hassanien, A.-E., Abraham, A., Kacprzyk, J., & Peters, J. F. (2008). Computational Intelligence in Multimedia Processing: Foundation and Trends. [SCI]. *Studies in Computational Intelligence*, *96*, 3–49. doi:10.1007/978-3-540-76827-2_1

Heckerman, D. (1996). *A tutorial on learning with Bayesian networks*. Retrieved 22-06-06 from [ftp://ftp.research.microsoft.com/pub/tr/tr-95-06.pdf]

Heckerman, D., & Horwitz, E. (1998). Inferring informational goals from free-text queries: a bayesian approach. In *Proc 14th Conf on Uncertainty in AI*, (pp. 230-238).

Hendricks Franssen, H., van Eijnsbergen, A., & Stein, A. (1997). Use of Spatial Prediction Techniques and Fuzzy Classification for Mapping Soil Pollutants. *Geoderma, 77*, 243–262. doi:10.1016/S0016-7061(97)00024-4

Henschen, L. J., McCune, W. W., & Naqvi, S. A. (1984). Compiling Constraint-Checking Programs from First-Order Formulas. *Advances in Database Theory, 2*, 145–169.

Herrera, F., Herrera-Viedma, E., & Martinez, L. (2000). A fusion approach for managing multi-granularity linguistic term sets in decision making. *Fuzzy Sets and Systems, 114*(1), 43–58. doi:10.1016/S0165-0114(98)00093-1

Herrera-Viedma, E., Martin-B, M. J., Guadarrama, S., Sobrino, A., & Olivas, J. A. (2005). Soft Computing for Information Retrieval in the Web. *Eusflat-FLA 2005.*

Hildebrand, L. (2005). Hybrid Computational Intelligence Systems for Real World Application. In *Studies in Fuzziness and Soft Computing, 179* (pp. 165–195). Berlin: Springer.

Hinterding, R., Gielewski, H., & Peachey, T. C. (2000), On the Nature of Mutation in Genetic Algorithms, In L. Eshelman (Ed), *Genetic Algorithms, Proceedings of the 6th International Conference*, (pp. 65-72). Morgan Kaufmann, San Francisco CA.

Holland, J. H. (1975). *Adaptation in natural and artificial systems*. Ann Arbor: University of Michigan Press.

Hopfield, J. J. (1982). Neural networks and physical systems with emergent collective computational abilities. *Proceedings of the National Academy of Sciences of the United States of America, 79*(8), 2554–2558.

Hsu, A., & Imielinski, T. (1985). Integrity Checking for Multiple Updates. In *Proceedings of the 1985 ACM SIGMOD International Conference on the Management of Data*, (pp. 152-168).

Huntala, Y., Karkkainen, J., Porkka, P., & Toivonen, H. (1999). TANE: An efficient algorithm for discovering functional and approximate dependencies. *The Computer Journal, 42*(2), 100–111. doi:10.1093/comjnl/42.2.100

Ibrahim, H. (2002). A Strategy for Semantic Integrity Checking in Distributed Databases. In *Proceedings of the Ninth International Conference on Parallel and Distributed Systems (ICPADS 2002)*, (pp. 139-144). Washington, DC: IEEE Computer Society.

Ibrahim, H. (2002). Extending Transactions with Integrity Rules for Maintaining Database Integrity. In *Proceedings of the International Conference on Information and Knowledge Engineering (IKE'02)*, (pp. 341-347).

Ibrahim, H., Gray, W. A., & Fiddian, N. J. (1996). The Development of a Semantic Integrity Constraint Subsystem for a Distributed Database (SICSDD). In *Proceedings of the 14th British National Conference on Databases (BNCOD 14)*, (pp. 74-91).

Ibrahim, H., Gray, W. A., & Fiddian, N. J. (1998). SICSDD – A Semantic Integrity Constraint Subsystem for a Distributed Database. In *Proceedings of the 1998 International Conference on Parallel and Distributed Processing Techniques and Applications (PDPTA'98)*, (pp. 1575-1582).

Ibrahim, H., Gray, W. A., & Fiddian, N. J. (2001). Optimizing Fragment Constraints – A Performance Evaluation. *International Journal of Intelligent Systems – Verification and Validation Issues in Databases. Knowledge-Based Systems, and Ontologies, 16*(3), 285–306.

Ichihashi, H., Shirai, T., Nagasaka, K., & Miyoshi, T. (1996). Neuro-fuzzy ID3: a method of inducing fuzzy decision trees with linear programming for maximising entropy and an algebraic method for incremental learning. *Fuzzy Sets and Systems, 81*(1), 157–167. doi:10.1016/0165-0114(95)00247-2

Ilczuk, G., & Wakulicz-Deja, A. (2007). Selection of Important Attributes for Medical Diagnosis Systems. In Peters, F. J., & Skowron, A. (Eds.), *Transactions on Rough Sets, 7* (pp. 70–84). Berlin: Springer-Verlag. doi:10.1007/978-3-540-71663-1_5

Ishibuchi, H., & Nakashima, T. (1999). Improving the performance of fuzzy classifier systems for pattern classification problems with continuous attributes. *IEEE Transactions on Industrial Electronics, 46*(6), 1057–1068. doi:10.1109/41.807986

Ishibuchi, H., & Nakashima, T. (2001). Effect of rule weights in fuzzy rule-based classification systems. *IEEE Transactions on Fuzzy Systems, 9*(4), 506–515. doi:10.1109/91.940964

Ishibuchi, H., Nozaki, K., & Tanaka, H. (1992). Distributed representation of fuzzy rules and its application to pattern classification. *Fuzzy Sets and Systems, 52*(1), 21–32. doi:10.1016/0165-0114(92)90032-Y

Ishikawa, Y., Subramanya, R., & Faloutsos, C. (1998). Mindreader: Query Databases Through Multiple Examples. In *Proceeding of the 24th VLDB Conference*, New York, USA, (pp. 218–227).

Israel, G. D. (2007). *Determining Sample Size. Institute of Food and Agricultural Sciences*. Gainesville, FL: University of Florida.

Jacobs, D. W., Weinshall, D., & Gdalyahu, Y. (2000). Classification with nonmetric distances: Image retrieval and class representation. *IEEE Transactions on Pattern Analysis and Machine Intelligence, 22*(6), 583–600. doi:10.1109/34.862197

Jang, R. (1992). *Neuro-fuzzy modeling: Architectures, analyses and applications*. PhD Thesis, University of California, Berkeley, CA.

Janikow, C. Z. (1998). Fuzzy decision trees: Issues and methods. *IEEE Transactions of Systems. Man and Cybernetics Part B, 28*(1), 1–14. doi:10.1109/3477.658573

Jeon, J., Lavrenko, V., & Manmatha, R. (2003). Automatic image annotation and retrieval using crossmedia relevance models. In *Proceedings of the 26th Annual International ACM SIGIR Conference on Research and Development in Information Retrieval*, Toronto, Canada.

John, R. I., & Coupland, S. (2007). Type-2 fuzzy logic: A historical view. *IEEE Computational Intelligence Magazine, 2*, 57–62.

John, R., & Birkenead, R. (Eds.). (2001). *Developments in Soft Computing*. Heidelberg, Germany: Physica Verlag.

Johnson, R., & Wichern, D. (2007). *Applied Multivariate Statistical Analysis*. Upper Saddle River, NJ: Pearson.

Jolion, J. M. (2001). Feature similarity. In Lew, M. S. (Ed.), *Principles of Visual Information Retrieval* (pp. 122–162). London: Springer-Verlag.

Jones, P., & Beynon, M. J. (2007). Temporal Support in the identification of e-learning efficacy: an example of object classification in the presence of ignorance. *Expert Systems: International Journal of Knowledge Engineering and Neural Networks, 24*(1), 1–16. doi:10.1111/j.1468-0394.2007.00417.x

Karnik, N. N., & Mendal, J. M. (1998). Introduction to type-2 fuzzy logic systems. In *proceedings of the IEEE World Congress and Computational Intelligence* (pp.915-920), AK.

Karnik, N. N., & Mendal, J. M. (2001). Centroid of a type-2 fuzzy sets. *Information Sciences, 132*, 195–220.

Kato, S., & Iisaku, S.-I. (1998). An Image Retrieval Method Based on a Genetic Algorithm. In *proceedings of the 13th International Conference on Information Networking (ICOIN '98)*.

Katzberg, J. D., & Ziarko, W. (1996). Variable Precision Extension of Rough Sets. *Fundamenta Informaticae, 27*, 155–168.

Kecman, V. (2001). *Learning and Soft Computing: Support Vector Machines, Neural Networks, and Fuzzy Logic*. London: MIT Press.

Keijzer, M., Merelo, J. J., Romero, G., & Schoenauer, M. (2002). Evolving objects: A general purpose evolutionary computation library. In P. Collet, E. Lutton, M. Schoenauer, C. Fonlupt, & J.-K. Hao (Eds.), *Artificial Evolution '01* (pp. 229-241). Berlin: Springer (LNCS 2310).

Keller, C., & Cernerud, L. (2002). Students' perceptions of e-learning in university education. *Journal of Educational Media, 27*(1-2), 55–67. doi:10.1080/0305498032000045458

Kerre, E. E., & Chen, G. (1995). An Overview of Fuzzy Data Models. In Bosc, P., & Kacprzyk, J. (Eds.), *Studies in Fuzziness: Fuzziness in Database Management Systems* (pp. 23–41). Heidelberg, Germany: Physica-Verlag.

Kerre, E. E., & Chen, G. (2000). Fuzzy Data Modeling at a Conceptual Level: Extending ER/EERConcepts. In Pons, O., Vila, M. A., & Kacprzyk, J. (Eds.), *Knowledge Management in Fuzzy Databases* (pp. 3–11). Heidelberg, Germany: Physica-Verlag.

King, R. (1999). *Computational Methods in Control Engineering.* Amsterdam: Kluwer Academic Publishers.

Kirkpatrick, S., Gellat, C. D., & Vecchi, M. P. (1983). Optimization by simulated annealing. *Science, 220*(4598), 671–680. doi:10.1126/science.220.4598.671

Klimanek, D. (2007). *Detection of a Biased Control Loop Function via Evolutionary Algorithms.* PhD. Thesis, Czech Technical University, Prague, Czech Republic.

Klimanek, D., & Sulc, B. (2005). Evolutionary Detection of Sensor Discredibility in Control Loops, In *Proceedings of the 31ˢᵗ Annual Conference IEEE*, (pp. 136–141).

Klimanek, D., & Sulc, B. (2006). Sensor Discredibility Detection by Means of Software Redundancy. In *Proceedings of the 7ᵗʰ International Carpathian Control Conference*, (pp. 249–252).

Klir, G. J., & Folger, T. A. (1988). *Fuzzy Sets, Uncertainty, and Information.* Englewood Cliffs, NJ: Prentice-Hall.

Klir, J., & Yuan, B. (1995). *Fuzzy sets and fuzzy logic: Theory and applications.* New York: Prentice Hall.

Kohonen, T. (1995). *Self Organizing Maps.* Heidelberg, Germany: Springer-Verlag.

Koller, D., & Pfeffer, A. (1996). Object Oriented Bayesian networks. In *Proceedings of the Thirteenth Conference on Uncertainty in Artificial Intelligence.*

Kollias, V. J., & Voliotis, A. (1991). Fuzzy Reasoning in the Development of Geographical Information Systems. *International Journal of Geographical Information Systems, 5*(2), 209–223. doi:10.1080/02693799108927844

Kononenko, I. (1994). Estimating Attributes: Analysis and Extensions of RELIEF. In *Proceedings of the 1994 European Conference on Machine Learning*, (pp. 171-182).

Korb, K. B., & Nicholson, A. E. (2004). *Bayesian artificial intelligence.* Boca Raton, FL: Chapman & Hall/CRC.

Korbicz, J. (2004). *Fault Diagnosis: Models, Artificial Intelligence, Applications.* Berlin: Springer.

Kosmidou, K., Pasiouras, F., Zopounidis, C., & Doumpos, M. (2006). A Multivariate Analysis of the Financial Characteristics of Foreign and Domestic Banks in the UK. *Omega, 34*(2), 189–195. doi:10.1016/j.omega.2004.10.002

Koushanfar, R. (2003). On-line fault detection of sensor measurements. In. *Proceedings of IEEE Sensors, 2*(8), 974–979.

Kovesi, P. D. (2000). *MATLAB and Octave Functions for Computer Vision and Image Processing.* School of Computer Science and Software Engineering, The University of Western Australia. Available from: http://www.csse.uwa.edu.au/~pk/research/matlabfns/.

Koza, J. R. (1992). *Genetic programming: On the programming of computers by means of natural evolution.* Cambridge, MA: MIT Press.

Koza, J. R. (1994). *Genetic programming II: Automatic discovery of reusable programs.* Cambridge, MA: MIT Press.

Koza, J. R. (1999). *Genetic programming III: Automatic synthesis of analog circuits.* Cambridge, MA: MIT Press.

Koza, J. R. (2003). *Genetic programming IV: Routine human-competitive machine intelligence.* Kluwer Academic.

Krebs, H. I., Hogan, N., Aisen, M. L., & Volpe, B. T. (1998). Robot aided neurorehabilitation. *IEEE Transactions on Rehabilitation Engineering, 6*(1), 75–87. doi:10.1109/86.662623

Krebs, H. I., Palazzolo, J. J., Volpe, B. T., & Hogan, N. (2003). Rehabilitation robotics: performance based progressive robot assisted therapy. *Autonomous Robots, 15*(1), 7–20. doi:10.1023/A:1024494031121

Krishnapuram, R., Mesadani, S., Jung, S. H., Choi, Y. S., & Balasubramaniam, R. (2004). Content based image retrieval based on a fuzzy approach. *IEEE Transactions on Knowledge and Data Engineering, 16*(10), 1185–1199. doi:10.1109/TKDE.2004.53

Kruger F, Maitre, O., & Collet., P. (2010). Speedups between x70 and x120 for a generic local search (memetic) algorithm on a single GPGPU chip. To appear in the *Proceedings of EvoApplications'10*, Istanbul, Turkey.

Kulkarni, S. (2004). Neural-fuzzy approach for content based retrieval of digital video. *Canadian on Electrical and Computer Engineering, 4*, 2235–2238.

Kulkarni, S. (2007). Image retrieval based on fuzzy mapping of image database and fuzzy similarity distance. In *Proceeding of the 6th International conference on computer and information science (ICIS 2007)*.

Kulkarni, S., Verma, B., Sharma, P., & Selvaraj, H. (1999). Content based image retrieval using a neuro-fuzzy technique. In *Proceeding of the International Joint Conference on Neural Networks, 6*, (pp. 4304-4308).

Kunniyur, S., & Srikant, R. (2000). End-to-end congestion control: Utility functions, random losses and ECN marks. In *Proc. IEEE INFOCOM*, (pp. 1323–1332).

Kunniyur, S., & Srikant, R. (2001). A time-scale decomposition approach to adaptive ECN marking. In *Proc. IEEE INFOCOM*, (pp. 1330–1339).

Kunniyur, S., & Srikant, R. (2003). End-to-end congestion control: Utility functions, random losses and ECN marks. *IEEE/ACM Trans. Networking, 11*, 689–702. doi:10.1109/TNET.2003.818183

Kunniyur, S., & Srikant, R. (2004). An Adaptive Virtual Queue (AVQ) Algorithm for Active Queue Management. *IEEE/ACM Transaction on Networking, 12*(2), 286-299.

Kushki, A., Androutsos, P., Plataniotis, K. N., & Venetsanopoulos, A. N. (2002). Fuzzy aggregation of image features in content based image retrieval. In *Proceedings of the IEEE International Conference on Image Processing (ICIP)*, (pp. 115-118).

Kuznetsov, S. O. (1993). Fast algorithm of constructing all the intersections of finite semi-lattice objects. *NTI* [Moscow, Russia: VINITI]. *Series, 2*(1), 17–20.

Kuznetsov, S. O., & Obiedkov, S. A. (2001). Comparing performance of algorithms for generating concept lattices. *Journal of Experimental & Theoretical Artificial Intelligence, 14*(2-3), 183–216.

Lacave, C., & Diez, F. J. (2002). Explanation for causal Bayesian networks in Elvira. In *Proceedings of the Workshop on Intelligent Data Analysis in Medicine and Pharmacology (IDAMAP-2002)*, Lyon, France.

Lagacherie, P., Andrieux, P., & Bouzigues, R. (1996). Fuzziness and Uncertainty of Soil Boundaries: From Reality to Coding in GIS. In Burrough, P. A., & Frank, A. U. (Eds.), *Geographic Objects with Indeterminate Boundaries* (pp. 275–286). Boca Raton, FL: Taylor & Francis.

Latecki, L. J., & Lakamper, R. (2000). Shape similarity measure based on correspondence of visual parts. *IEEE Transactions on Pattern Analysis and Machine Intelligence, 22*, 1–6. doi:10.1109/34.879802

Lavraĉ, N., & Džeroski, S. (1994). *Inductive logic programming: techniques and applications*. Chichester, UK: Ellis Horwood.

Lavraĉ, N., & Flash, P. (2000). *An extended transformation approach to Inductive Logic Programming. CSTR – 00 - 002* (pp. 1–42). Bristol, UK: University of Bristol, Department of Computer Science.

Lavraĉ, N., Gamberger, D., & Jovanoski, V. (1999). A study of relevance for learning in deductive databases. *The Journal of Logic Programming, 40*(2/3), 215–249. doi:10.1016/S0743-1066(99)00019-9

Lee, A., Danis, C., Miller, T., & Jung, Y. (2001). Fostering Social Interaction in Online Spaces. In M. Hirose, (ed.), *Human-Computer Interaction (INTERACT '01) — Eighth IFIP TC.13 Conference on Human-Computer Interaction*, (pp. 59-66). Amsterdam: IOS Press.

Lee, H. K., & Yoo, S. I. (2001). Intelligent Image Retrieval Using Neural Network. *IEICE Transactions on Information and Systems, E84*(12), 1810–1819.

Lee, S., Agah, A., & Bekey, G. (1990). An intelligent rehabilitative orthotic system for cerebrovascular accident. In *Proceedings of IEEE International Conference on Systems, Man and Cybernetics Conference,* (pp. 815-819).

Lew, M. S. (2000). Next Generation Web Searches for Visual Content. *IEEE Computing,* 46-53.

Lew, M. S., Sebe, N., Djeraba, C., & Jain, R. (2006). Content-Based Multimedia Information Retrieval. *ACM Transaction on Multimedia Computing. Communication and Application, 2*(1), 1–19.

Li, X.-L., Du, Z.-L., Wang, T., & Yu, D.-M. (2005). Audio Feature selection based on Rough Set. *International Journal of Information Technology, 11*(6), 117–123.

Linoff, G. (1998). *Which Way to the Mine?* (pp. 42–44). Systems Management.

Lisi, F., & Malerba, D. (2004). Inducing multi-level association rules from multiple relations. *Machine Learning, 55,* 175–210. doi:10.1023/B:MACH.0000023151.65011.a3

Liu, H., & Motoda, H. (2000). *Feature Selection for Knowledge Discovery and Data Mining.* Amsterdam: Kluwer Academic Publishers.

Liu, H., Li, J., & Wong, L. (2002). A comparative study on feature selection and classification methods using gene expression profiles and proteomic patterns. *Gene Informatics, 13,* 51–60.

Liu, Y.-M., & Luo, M.-K. (1997). *Fuzzy Topology. Advances in Fuzzy Systems — Applications and Theory* (*Vol. 9*). Singapore: World Scientific.

Lo, Y. L., & Chen, S. J. (2002). The numeric indexing for music data. In *Proceedings of the 22nd International Conference on Distributed Computing Systems Workshops,* Vienna, Austria.

Louchet, J. (2001). Using an individual evolution strategy for stereovision. *Genetic Programming and Evolvable Machines, 2*(2), 101–109. doi:10.1023/A:1011544128842

Loueiro, R., Amirabdollahian, F., Topping, M., Driessen, B., & Harwin, W. (2003). Upper limb mediated stroke therapy – GENTLE/s approach. *Autonomous Robots, 15,* 35–51. doi:10.1023/A:1024436732030

Lum, P. S., Burgar, C. G., Shor, P. C., Majmundar, M., & Van der Loos, M. (2002). Robot assisted movement training compared with conventional therapy techniques for the rehabilitation of upper – limb motor function after stroke. *Physical Medicine and Rehabilitation, 83*(7), 952–959. doi:10.1053/apmr.2001.33101

Lum, P. S., Burgar, G., & Van Der Loos, M. (1997). The use of robotic device for post stroke movement therapy. In *Proceedings of the International Conference on Rehabilitation Robotics,* (pp. 79-82).

Lum, P. S., Lehman, S., Steven, L., & Reinkensmeyer, D. J. (1995). The Bimanual Lifting Rehabilitator: An adaptive machine for therapy of stroke patient. *IEEE Transactions on Rehabilitation Engineering, 3*(2), 166–173. doi:10.1109/86.392371

Lynch, C., Hagras, H., & Callaghan, V. (2006). Using uncertainty bounds in the design of an embedded real-time type-2 neuro-fuzzy speed controller for machine diesel engines. In *Proceedings of the 2006 IEEE International Conference on Fuzzy Systems* (pp.7217-7224), Vancouver, Canada.

Ma, Z. M., Zhang, W. J., & Ma, W. Y. (2004). Extending Object-Oriented Databases for Fuzzy Information Modeling. *Information Systems, 29,* 421–435. doi:10.1016/S0306-4379(03)00038-3

Ma, Z. M., Zhang, W. J., Ma, W. Y., & Chen, Q. (2001). Conceptual Design of Fuzzy Object-Oriented Databases Using Extended Entity-Relationship Model. *International Journal of Intelligent Systems, 16*(6), 697–711. doi:10.1002/int.1031

Ma, Z.M., & Yan, Li. (2007). Fuzzy XML data modeling with the XML and relation data model. *Data & Knowledge Engineering, 64,* 972–996. doi:10.1016/j.datak.2007.06.003

Maitre, O. Lachiche. N. & Collet., P. (2010). Maximizing speedup of GP trees execution on GPGPU cards for as few as 32 fitness cases. To appear in the Proceedings of EuroGP'10, Istanbul, Turkey.

Maitre, O., & Baumes, L. A. Lachiche. N., Corma. A., & Collet., P. (2009). Coarse grain parallelization of evolutionary algorithms on GPGPU cards with EASEA. *Proceedings of the 11th Annual conference on Genetic and evolutionary computation* (pp. 1403-1410). Montreal, Quebec, Canada.

Mamdani, E. H. (1974). Applications of fuzzy algorithm for control a simple dynamic plant. *Proceedings of the IEEE, 121*(12), 1585–1588.

Mannila, H., & Räihä, K.-J. (1992). On the complexity of inferring functional dependencies. *Discrete Applied Mathematics, 40,* 237–243. doi:10.1016/0166-218X(92)90031-5

Mannila, H., & Räihä, K.-J. (1994). Algorithm for inferring functional dependencies. *Data & Knowledge Engineering, 12,* 83–99. doi:10.1016/0169-023X(94)90023-X

Marques, O., & Furht, B. (2002). *Content-based image and video retrieval.* London: Kluwer.

Maslov, I. V. (2003). Content-based retrieval of distorted images using a hybrid genetic algorithm augmented by a self-organizing network. In Proceeding of Internet Multimedia Management systems, (Vol. 5242, pp. 125-136).

Mazumdar, R., Mason, L. G., & Douligeris, C. (1991). Fairness in network optimal flow control: Optimality of product form. *IEEE Transactions on Communications, 39,* 775–782. doi:10.1109/26.87140

Mazumdar, S. (1993). Optimizing Distributed Integrity Constraints. In *Proceedings of the 3rd International Symposium on Database Systems for Advanced Applications, 4,* 327-334.

McCalla, G. (2000). The fragmentation of culture, learning, teaching and technology: Implications for Artificial Intelligence in Education Research. *International Journal of Artificial Intelligence, 11*(2), 177–196.

McCarroll, N. F. (1995). *Semantic Integrity Enforcement in Parallel Database Machines.* PhD Thesis, University of Sheffield, Sheffield, UK.

McCulloch, W. S., & Pitts, W. (1943). A logical calculus of the ideas immanent in nervous activity. *The Bulletin of Mathematical Biophysics, 5,* 115–133.

McCune, W. W., & Henschen, L. J. (1989). Maintaining State Constraints in Relational Databases: A Proof Theoretic Basis. *Journal of the Association for Computing Machinery, 36*(1), 46–68.

McMillan, D. W., & Chavis, D. M. (1986). Sense of community: A definition and theory. *American Journal of Community Psychology, 14*(1), 6–23. doi:10.1002/1520-6629(198601)14:1<6::AID-JCOP2290140103>3.0.CO;2-I

Megretskaya, I. A. (1988). Construction of natural classification tests for knowledge base generation. In Y. Pecherskij (Ed.), The Problem of the expert system application in the national economy: Reports of the Republican Workshop (pp. 89-93). Kishinev, Moldava: Mathematical Institute with Computer Centre of Moldova Academy of Sciences.

Mendal, J. M. (2007). Type-2 fuzy sets and systems: An overview. *IEEE Computational Intelligence Magazine, 2,* 20–29.

Mesadani, S., & Krishnapuram, R. (1999). A fuzzy approach to content-based image retrieval. In *Proceeding of the 1999 IEEE International Conference of Fuzzy systems,* (Vol. 3, pp. 1251-1260).

Mi, J., Wu, W., & Zhang, W. (2004). Approaches to Knowledge Reduction Based on Variable Precision Rough Set Model. *Information Sciences, 159,* 255–272. doi:10.1016/j.ins.2003.07.004

Michalski, R. S. (1983). A theory and methodology of inductive learning. *Artificial Intelligence, 20,* 111–161. doi:10.1016/0004-3702(83)90016-4

Michalski, R. S., & Larsen, I. B. (1978). Selection of most representative training examples and incremental generation of VL1 hypotheses: the underlying methodology and the description of programs ESEL and AQII. *Report No. 78-867.* Urbana, IL: Dep. of Comp. Science, Univ. of Illinois at Urbana-Champaign.

Michalski, R. S., & Ram, A. (1995). Learning as goal-driven inference. In Ram, A., & Leake, D. (Eds.), *Goal-Driven Learning.* Cambridge, MA: MIT Press/Bradford Books.

Mill, J. S. (1900). The system of logic. Moscow, Russia: Russian Publishing Company "Book Affair".

Miller, J. (2000). Cartesian genetic programming. In R. P. et al. (Eds.), *Proceedings of EUROGP'00* (pp. 121-131). Edinburgh: Springer.

Mitra, S., Pal, S. K., & Mitra, P. (2002). Data Mining in Soft Computing Framework: A Survey. *IEEE Transactions on Neural Networks, 13*(1), 3–14. doi:10.1109/72.977258

Mittal, A. (2006). An Overview of Multimedia Content-Based Retrieval Strategies. *Informatica, 30,* 347–356.

Morales, E., Polycarpou, M., Hemasilpin, N., & Bissler, J. (2001). Hierarchical Adaptive and Supervisory Control of Continuous Venovenous Hemofiltration. *IEEE Transactions on Control Systems Technology, 9*(3), 445–457. doi:10.1109/87.918898

Motro, A. (1995). Management of Uncertainty in Database System. In W. Kim, (Ed.), Modern Database System the Object Model, Interoperability and Beyond. Reading, MA: Addison-Wesley publishing Company.

Mühlenbein, H. (1989). Parallel genetic algorithms, population genetics and combinatorial optimization. *Proceedings of the 3rd International Conference on Genetic Algorithms* (pp. 416-421).

Mühlenbein, H., & Paass, G. (1996). From recombination of genes to the estimation of distributions. *Parallel Problem Solving from Nature, 1411,* 178–187.

Mühlenbein, H., & Schlierkamp-Voosen, D. (1993). The science of breeding and its application to the breeder genetic algorithm (BGA). *Evolutionary Computation, 1*(4), 335–360. doi:10.1162/evco.1993.1.4.335

Naidenova, X. A. (1992). Machine learning as a diagnostic task. In Arefiev, I. (Ed.), *Knowledge-Dialogue-Solution, Materials of the short-term scientific seminar* (pp. 26–36). Saint-Petersburg, Russia: State North-West Technical University.

Naidenova, X. A. (1996). Reducing machine learning tasks to the approximation of a given classification on a given set of examples. In *Proceedings of the 5-th National Conference at Artificial Intelligence* (Vol. 1, pp. 275-279), Kazan, Tatarstan.

Naidenova, X. A. (1999). The data-knowledge transformation. In Soloviev, V. (Ed.), *Text Processing and Cognitive Technologies, Issue 3* (pp. 130–151). Pushchino, Russia.

Naidenova, X. A. (2001). Inferring good diagnostic tests as a model of commonsense reasoning. In *"Knowledge-Dialog-Solution"* []. Saint-Petersburg, Russia: State North-West Technical University.]. *Proceedings of the International Conference, 2,* 501–506.

Naidenova, X. A. (2006). An incremental learning algorithm for inferring implicative rules from examples. In Triantaphillou, E., & Felici, G. (Eds.), *Data Mining and Knowledge Discovery Approaches Based on Rule Induction Techniques* (pp. 90–146). New York: Springer. doi:10.1007/0-387-34296-6_3

Naidenova, X. A., & Ermakov, A. E. (2001). The decomposition of algorithms of inferring good diagnostic tests. In A. Zakrevskij (Ed.), *Proceedings of the 4-th International Conference "Computer – Aided Design of Discrete Devices (CAD DD'2001),* (Vol. 3, pp. 61-69). Minsk, Belarus: Institute of Engineering Cybernetics, National Academy of Sciences of Belarus.

Naidenova, X. A., & Polegaeva, J. G. (1986). An algorithm of finding the best diagnostic tests. In Mintz, G. E., & Lorents, P. P. (Eds.), *The Application of mathematical logic methods* (pp. 63–67). Tallinn, Estonia: Institute of Cybernetics, National Acad. of Sciences of Estonia.

Naidenova, X. A., & Polegaeva, J. G. (1991). SISIF – the system of knowledge acquisition from experimental facts. In Alty, J. L., & Mikulich, L. I. (Eds.), *Industrial Applications of Artificial Intelligence* (pp. 87–92). Amsterdam, the Netherlands: Elsevier Science Publishers B.V.

Naidenova, X. A., Plaksin, M. V., & Shagalov, V. L. (1995). Inductive inferring all good classification tests. In J. Valkman (Ed.), *"Knowledge-Dialog-Solution"*, *Proceedings of International Conference in two volumes* (Vol. 1, pp. 79 - 84). Jalta, Ukraine: Kiev Institute of Applied Informatics.

Naidenova, X. A., Polegaeva, J. G., & Iserlis, J. E. (1995). The system of knowledge acquisition based on constructing the best diagnostic classification tests. In J. Valkman. (Ed.), *"Knowledge-Dialog-Solution"*, Proceedings of International Conference in two volumes (Vol. 1, pp. 85-95). Jalta, Ukraine: Kiev Institute of Applied Informatics.

Naisbitt, J. (1984). *Megatrends: Ten New Directions Transforming Our Lives*. London: Macdonald & Co.

Nauck, D. (1995). Beyond neuro-fuzzy: Perspective and directions. In *proceedings of the 3rd European Congress on Intelligent Techniques and Soft Computing* (pp.1159-1164), Aachen, France.

Nauck, D., & Kruse, R. (1995). NEFCLASS, A neuro-fuzzy approach for the classification of data. In *Proceedings of 1995 ACM Symposium on Applied Computing* (pp.461-465), New York.

Neapolitan, R. E. (2004). *Learning Bayesian Networks*. London: Prentice Hall.

Nepal, S., Ramakrishna, M. V., & Thom, J. A. (1998). A fuzzy system for content based retrieval. IEEE International conference on Intelligent Processing System, Gold Coast, (pp. 335-339).

Network Simulator. (n.d.). *NS-2 Homepage*. Retrieved from http://www.isi.edu/nsnam/ns/

Nguifo, M. E., & Njiwoua, P. (1998). Using lattice based framework as a tool for feature extraction. In C. Nedellec, & C. Rouveirol (Eds.), *Proceedings of the 10th conference on Machine Learning* (ECML-98), (LNCS 1398, pp. 304-309). Chemnitz, Germany: Springer.

Nicolas, J. M. (1982). Logic for Improving Integrity Checking in Relational Data Bases. *Acta Informatica*, *18*(3), 227–253. doi:10.1007/BF00263192

Niedermayer, D. (1998). *An introduction to Bayesian networks and their contemporary applications*. Retrieved 6th January, 2006 from http://www.niedermayer.ca/papers/bayesian/

Nourine, L., & Raynaud, O. (1999). A fast algorithm for building lattices. *Information Processing Letters*, *71*, 199–204. doi:10.1016/S0020-0190(99)00108-8

Oelericha, A., & Poddig, T. (2006). Evaluation of Rating Systems. *Expert Systems with Applications*, *30*(3), 437–447. doi:10.1016/j.eswa.2005.10.004

Okada, S., & Sakaki, T. (2000). TEM: A therapeutic exercise machine for the lower extremities of spastic patient. *Advanced Robotics*, *14*(7), 597–606. doi:10.1163/156855301742030

Olaru, C., & Wehenkel, L. (2003). A complete fuzzy decision tree technique. *Fuzzy Sets and Systems*, *138*, 221–254. doi:10.1016/S0165-0114(03)00089-7

Oliboni, B., & Pozzani, G. (2008). *An XML Schema for managing fuzzy documents*. Technical Report RR 64/2008, Department of Computer Science of the University of Verona, Italy. Retrieved on December 2008 at http://profs.sci.univr.it/~pozzani/pub.html

Oliboni, B., & Pozzani, G. (2008). Representing Fuzzy Information by using XML Schema. In *Proc. 19th Int. Conference on Database and Expert Systems Application*, (pp. 683-687).

Ore, O. (1944). Galois connexions. *Transactions of the American Mathematical Society*, *55*(1), 493–513. doi:10.2307/1990305

Ore, O. (1980). *Theory of graphs*. Moscow, USSR: Nauka.

Ott, T. J., Lakshman, T. V., & Wong, L. H. (1999). *Sred: Stabilized red* (pp. 1346–1355). IEEE INFOCOM.

Packham, G., Jones, P., Miller, C. & Thomas, B. (2004). E-learning and Retention: Key factors influencing Student withdrawal, *Education + Training*, (6/7), 335-342.

Pal, N. R., & Chakraborty, S. (2001). Fuzzy Rule Extraction From ID3-Type Decision Trees for Real Data. *IEEE Transactions on Systems, Man, and Cybernetics B, 31*(5), 745–754. doi:10.1109/3477.956036

Papadias, D., Mantzourogiannis, M., Kalnis, P., Mamoulis, N., & Ahmad, I. (1999). Content-based retrieval using heuristic search. In *Proceedings of the 22th Annual International ACM SIGIR Conference on Research and Development in Information Retrieval*, (pp. 168-175).

Park, S. B., Lee, J. W., & Kim, S. K. (2004). Content-based image classification using a neural network. *Pattern Recognition Letters, 25*, 287–300. doi:10.1016/j.patrec.2003.10.015

Park, S. S., Seo, K.-K., & Jang, D.-S. (2005). Expert system based on artificial neural networks for content based image retrieval. *Expert Systems with Applications, 29*, 589–597. doi:10.1016/j.eswa.2005.04.027

Pasiouras, F., Gaganis, C., & Zopoundis, C. (2006). The Impact of Bank Regulations, Supervision, Market Structure, and Bank Characteristics on Individual Bank Ratings: A Cross-Country Analysis. *Review of Quantitative Finance and Accounting, 27*, 403–438. doi:10.1007/s11156-006-0045-0

Pauly, A., & Schneider, M. (2004). Vague Spatial Data Types, Set Operations, and Predicates. In 8th *East-European Conference on Advances in Databases and Information Systems,* (pp. 379-392).

Pauly, A., & Schneider, M. (2005). Identifying Topological Predicates for Vague Spatial Objects. In *20th ACM Symposium on Applied Computing*, (pp. 587-591).

Pauly, A., & Schneider, M. (2005). Topological Predicates between Vague Spatial Objects. In *9th International Symposium on Spatial and Temporal Databases,* (pp. 418-432).

Pauly, A., & Schneider, M. (2006). Topological Reasoning for Identifying a Complete Set of Topological Predicates between Vague Spatial Objects. In *19th International FLAIRS Conference* (pp. 731-736).

Pawlack, Z. (1991). *Rough sets – Theoretical aspects of reasoning about data.* Dordrerecht, The Netherlands: Kluwer.

Pawlak, Z. (1982). Rough Sets. Basic Notions. *International Journal of Computer and Information Science, 11*, 341–356. doi:10.1007/BF01001956

Pawlak, Z. (1982). Rough Sets. *International Journal of Computer and System Sciences, 11*, 341–356.

Pawlak, Z. (1991). *Rough Sets: Theoretical Aspects of Reasoning about Data.* Amsterdam: Kluwer Academic Publishers.

Pearl, J. & Verma, T. (1991). A theory of inferred causation, in Principles of Knowledge

Pearl, J. (1988). *Probabilistic reasoning in intelligent systems: Networks of plausible inference.* San Mateo, CA: Morgan Kaufmann.

Pedrycz, W. (1998). *Computational Intelligence: An Introduction.* Boca Raton, FL: CRC Press.

Pennington, N., & Hastie, R. (1988). Explanation-based decision-making: Effects of memory structure on judgment. *Journal of Experimental Psychology. Learning, Memory, and Cognition, 14*(3), 521–533. doi:10.1037/0278-7393.14.3.521

Petrakis, E. G. M., Kontis, K., & Voutsakis, E. (2006). Relevance feedback methods for logo and trademark image retrieval on the web. *SAC, 06*, 23–27.

Petry, F. E., Cobb, M., Ali, D., Angryk, R., Paprzycki, M., Rahimi, S., et al. (2002). Fuzzy Spatial Relationships and Mobile Agent Technology in Geospatial Information Systems. In P. Matsakis & L.M. Sztandera (Eds.), Soft Computing in Defining Spatial Relations (pp. 123-155), volume in series: Soft Computing. Heidelberg, Germany: Physica-Verlag.

Piaget, J. (1959). *La genèse des structures logiques elé-mentaires.* Neuchâtel, Switzerland: Delachaux & Niestlé.

Piatetsky-Shapiro, G. (2000). Knowledge Discovery in Databases: 10 Years After. *SIGKDD Explorations. Newsletter, 1*(2), 59–61.

Plexousakis, D. (1993). Integrity Constraint and Rule Maintenance in Temporal Deductive Knowledge Bases. In *Proceedings of the 19th International Conference on Very Large Data Bases (VLDB 19),* (pp. 146-157).

Polkowski, L. (2003). *Rough sets: Mathematical founda-tion.* Heidelberg, Germany: Physica.

Poon, W., P., H. & Firth, M. (2005). Are Unsolicited Credit Ratings Lower? International Evidence From Bank Ratings. *Journal of Business Finance & Account-ing, 32*(9-10), 1741–1771.

Poon, W., P., H. (2003). Are Unsolicited Credit Ratings Biased Downward? *Journal of Banking & Finance, 27*(4), 593–614. doi:10.1016/S0378-4266(01)00253-9

Poon, W., P., H., Firth, M. & Fung, H. (1999). A Multi-variate Analysis of the Determinants of Moody's Bank Financial Strength Ratings. *Journal of International Financial Markets, Institutions and Money, 9*(3), 267–283. doi:10.1016/S1042-4431(99)00011-6

Pradhan, M., Provan, G., Middleton, B., & Henrion, M. (1994). Knowledge engineering for large belief networks. In *Proceedings of the Tenth Conference on Uncertainty in Artificial Intelligence,* (pp. 484-490).

Putnam, R. (2000). *Bowling Alone: The Collapse and Revival of American Community.* New York: Simon Schuster.

Qian, X. (1988). An Effective Method for Integrity Constraint Simplification. In *Proceedings of the 4th International Conference on Data Engineering (ICDE 88),* (pp. 338-345).

Qian, X. (1989). Distribution Design of Integrity Con-straints. In *Proceedings of the 2nd International Confer-ence on Expert Database Systems,* (pp. 205-226).

Quinlan, J. R. (1979). Discovery rules from large ex-amples: A Case Study. In Michie, D. (Ed.), *Expert Systems in the Micro Electronic Age.* Edinburgh, UK: Edinburgh University Press.

Quinlan, J. R. (1993). *C4.5: Programs for Machine Learning.* San Mateo, CA: Morgan Kaufmann.

Raju, K., & Majumdar, A. (1988). Fuzzy Functional Dependencies and Lossless Join Decomposition of Fuzzy Relational Database System. *ACM Transactions on Da-tabase Systems, 13*(2), 129–166. doi:10.1145/42338.42344

Rao, R., Agrawal, S. K., & Scholz, J. P. (1999). A robot test-bed for assistance and assessment in physical therapy. In *Proceedings of the International Conference on Re-habilitation Robotics,* (pp. 187-200).

Rasiova, H. (1974). An algebraic approach to non-classical logic (Studies in Logic, Vol. 78). Warsaw & Amsterdam: PWN – Polish Scientific Publishers & North-Holland Publishing Company.

Raymond, R., C. (1966). Use of the Time-sharing Com-puter in Business Planning and Budgeting. *Management Science, 12*(8), B363–B381. doi:10.1287/mnsc.12.8.B363

Rechenberg, I. (1973). *Evolutionstrategie: Optimierung technisher systeme nach prinzipien des biologischen evolution.* Stuttgart: Fromman-Hozlboog Verlag.

REHAROB Project. (2000). Retrieved March 2007 from http://www.reharob.manuf.bme.hu

Reinkensmeyer, D. J., Kahn, L. E., Averbuch, M., McKenna-Cole, A. N., Schmit, B. D., & Rymer, W. Z. (2000). Understanding and treating arm movement im-pairment after chronic brain injury: progress with the ARM Guide. *Journal of Rehabilitation Research and Development, 37*(6), 653–662.

Renooij, S., & Witteman, C. (1999). Talking probabilities: communicating probabilistic information with words and numbers. *International Journal of Approximate Reason-ing, 2,* 169–194. doi:10.1016/S0888-613X(99)00027-4

Representation and Reasoning. Proceedings of the Second International Conference Morgan Kaufmann, San Mateo, CA.

Resnick, P. (2002). Beyond bowling together: socio-technical capital. In J. M. Carroll (Ed), HCI in the new millennium (pp. 247 272). New York: Addison-Wesley.

Reye, J. (2004). Student modelling based on belief networks. *International Journal of Artificial Intelligence in Education, 14,* 63–96.

Richardson, R., Austin, M. E., & Plummer, A. R. (1999). Development of a physiotherapy robot. In *Proceedings of The International Biomechatronics Workshop,* (pp. 116-120).

Richardson, R., Brown, M., & Plummer, A. R. (2000). Pneumatic Impedance Control for Physiotherapy. In *Proceedings of The EUREL International Conference on Robotics,* (Vol. 2).

Richardson, R., Brown, M., Bhakta, M., & Levesley, M. C. (2003). Design and Control of a Three Degree of Freedom Pneumatic Physiotherapy Robot. *Robotica,* (21): 589–604. doi:10.1017/S0263574703005320

Riguet, J. (1948). Relations binaires, fermetures, correspondences de Galois. *Bulletin des Sciences Mathématiques, 76*(3), 114–155.

Rocchio, J. (1971). Relevance Feedback in Information Retrieval. In Salton, G. (Ed.), *The SMART Retrieval System - Experiments in Automatic Document Processing* (pp. 313–323). Englewood Cliffs, NJ: Prentice Hall.

Romano, J., Wallace, T. L., Helmick, I. J., Carey, L. M., & Adkins, L. (2005). Study procrastination, achievement, and academic motivation in web-based and blended distance learning. *The Internet and Higher Education, 8*(4), 299–305.

Ruano, A. E. (Ed.). (2005). *Intelligent Control Systems Using Computational Intelligence Techniques.* London: The IEE Press.

Rumelhart, D. E., Hinton, G. E., & Williams, R. J. (1988). Learning representation of back-propagation errors. *Nature, 323,* 321–355.

Ruspini, E. (1986). Imprecision and Uncertainty in the Entity-Relationship Model. In Prade, H., & Negoita, C. V. (Eds.), *Fuzzy Logic in Knowledge Engineering* (pp. 18–22). Köln, Germany: Verlag TUV Rheinland.

Russell, S., & Norvig, P. (1995). *Solution manual for "artificial intelligence: a modern approach.* Englewood Cliffs, NJ: Prentice Hall.

Rutkowski, L., & Cpałka, K. (2003). Flexible neuro-fuzzy systems. *IEEE Transactions on Neural Networks, 14*(1), 554–574.

Sahajwala, R., & Van den Bergh, P. (2000). Supervisory Risk Assessment and Early Warning Systems. *BASEL Committee on Banking Supervision Working Papers Working papers 4,* Bank for International Settlements.

Sajja, P. S. (2006). A fuzzy agent to input vague parameters into multi-layer connectionist expert system: An application for stock market. *ADIT Journal of Engineering, 3*(1), 30–32.

Sajja, P. S. (2006). Deliberative fuzzy agent for distributed systems. In *Proceedings of the National Seminar on ICT for Productivity,* India.

Sajja, P. S. (2006). Fuzzy artificial neural network decision support system for course selection. *Journal of Engineering and Technology, 19,* 99–102.

Sajja, P. S. (2006). Multi-layer connectionist model of expert system for an advisory system. In proceedings of the National Level Seminar - Tech Symposia on IT Futura, India.

Sajja, P. S. (2008). Type-2 fuzzy user interface for artificial neural network based decision support system for course selection. *International Journal of Computing and ICT Research, 2*(2), 96–102.

Saloky, T., & Piteľ, J. (2005). Adaptive control of heating process with outdoor temperature compensation. 30. *Proceedings of ASR Seminar, Instruments and Control, 51*(2), 113-116.

Salzberg, S. (1991). A nearest hyper rectangle learning method. *Machine Learning, 6,* 277–309. doi:10.1007/BF00114779

Sancho-Royo, A., & Verdegay, J. L. (1999). Methods for the Construction of Membership Functions. *International Journal of Intelligent Systems, 14*, 1213–1230. doi:10.1002/(SICI)1098-111X(199912)14:12<1213::AID-INT3>3.0.CO;2-5

Sarı, H., Tüzün, S., & Akgün, K. (2002). *Hareket sistemi hastalıklarında fiziksel tıp yöntemleri.* Istanbul, Turkey: Nobel Tıp Kitabevleri.

Schaefer, G., Nakashima, T., Yokota, Y., & Ishibuchi, H. (2007). Fuzzy classification of gene expression data. In *IEEE Int. Conference on Fuzzy Systems,* (pp. 1090–1095).

Schmidt-Schauss, M., & Smolka, G. (1991). Attributive concept descriptions with complements. *Artificial Intelligence, 48*(1), 1–26. doi:10.1016/0004-3702(91)90078-X

Schneider, M. (1996). Modelling Spatial Objects with Undetermined Boundaries Using the Realm/ROSE Approach. In Burrough, P. A., & Frank, A. U. (Eds.), *Geographic Objects with Indeterminate Boundaries* (pp. 141–152). Boca Raton, FL: Taylor & Francis.

Schneider, M. (1997). *Spatial Data Types for Database Systems — Finite Resolution Geometry for Geographic Information Systems,* (LNCS 1288). Berlin: Springer-Verlag.

Schneider, M. (1999). Uncertainty Management for Spatial Data in Databases: Fuzzy Spatial Data Types. In *6th International Symposium on Advances in Spatial Databases* (LNCS 1651, pp. 330-351). Berlin: Springer Verlag.

Schneider, M. (2000). Metric Operations on Fuzzy Spatial Objects in Databases. In *8th ACM Symposium on Geographic Information Systems* (pp. 21-26). New York: ACM Press.

Schneider, M. (2001). A Design of Topological Predicates for Complex Crisp and Fuzzy Regions. In *20th International Conference on Conceptual Modeling,* (pp. 103-116).

Schneider, M. (2001). Fuzzy Topological Predicates, Their Properties, and Their Integration into Query Languages. In *9th ACM Symposium on Geographic Information Systems* (pp. 9-14). New York: ACM Press.

Schneider, M. (2003). Design and Implementation of Finite Resolution Crisp and Fuzzy Spatial Objects. *Data & Knowledge Engineering, 44*(1), 81–108. doi:10.1016/S0169-023X(02)00131-3

Schneider, M., & Behr, T. (2006). Topological Relationships between Complex Spatial Objects. *ACM Transactions on Database Systems, 31*(1), 39–81. doi:10.1145/1132863.1132865

Schwartz, D. G. (1985). The case for an interval-based representation of linguistic truth. *Fuzzy Sets and Systems, 17*, 153–165.

Schwefel, H. P. (1995). *Evolution and optimum seeking.* New York: Wiley.

Schwefel, H.-P. (1995). Numerical optimization of computer models (2nd ed.). New-York: John Wiley & Sons.

Schwier, R. A., & Daniel, B. K. (2007). Did we become a community? Multiple methods for identifying community and its constituent elements in formal online learning environments. In Lambropoulos, N., & Zaphiris, P. (Eds.), *User- Evaluation and Online Communities.* Hershey, PA: IDEA Group.

Sekercioglu, A., Pitsillides, A., & Vasilakos, A. (2001). Computational intelligence in management of ATM networks. *Soft Computing Journal, 5*(4), 257–263. doi:10.1007/s005000100099

Sheard, T., & Stemple, D. (1989). Automatic Verification of Database Transaction Safety. *ACM Transactions on Database Systems, 14*(3), 322–368. doi:10.1145/68012.68014

Shen, J., Stepherd, J., & Ngu, A. H. H. (2006). Towards effective content-based music retrieval with multiple acoustic feature combination. *IEEE Transactions on Multimedia, 8*(6), 1179–1189. doi:10.1109/TMM.2006.884618

Shi, W., & Guo, W. (1999). Modeling Topological Relationships of Spatial Objects with Uncertainties. In *International Symposium on Spatial Data Quality* (pp. 487-495).

Shibasaki, R. (1993). *A Framework for Handling Geometric Data with Positional Uncertainty in a GIS Environment. GIS: Technology and Applications* (pp. 21–35). Singapore: World Scientific.

Shubin, N. (2008). *Your inner fish: a journey into the 3.5-billion-year history of the human body.* New York: Pantheon Books.

Simon, E., & Valduriez, P. (1987). Design and Analysis of a Relational Integrity Subsystem. MCC *Technical Report DB-015-87.*

Soumya, B., Madiraju, P., & Ibrahim, H. (2008). Constraint Optimization for a System of Relational Databases. In *Proceedings of the IEEE 8th International Conference on Computer and Information Technology (CiT 2008),* (pp. 155-160).

Spears, W. M., & De Jong, K. A. (1990). An analysis of multi-point crossover. *Proceedings of the Foundations of Genetic Algorithms Workshop.*

Stahl, G. (2000). A Model of collaborative knowledge-building. In B. Fishman & S. O'Connor-Divelbiss, (Eds.), *Fourth International Conference of the Learning Sciences* (pp.70-77). Mahwah, NJ: Erlbaum.

Statnikov, A., Aliferis, C., Tsamardinos, I., Hardin, D., & Levy, S. (2005). A comprehensive evaluation of multicategory classification methods for microarray expression cancer diagnosis. *Bioinformatics (Oxford, England), 21*(5), 631–643. doi:10.1093/bioinformatics/bti033

Stemple, D., Mazumdar, S., & Sheard, T. (1987). On the Modes and Measuring of Feedback to Transaction Designers. In *Proceedings of the 1987 ACM-SIGMOD International Conference on the Management of Data,* (pp. 374-386).

Stergiou, C., & Siganos, D. (1996). *Neural Networks.* Retrieved November 6, 2008 from http://www.doc.ic.ac.uk/~nd/surprise_96/journal/vol4/cs11/report.html#Introduction to neural networks

Stumme, G., Taouil, R., Bastide, Y., Pasquier, N., & Lakhal, L. (2000). Fast computation of concept lattices using data mining techniques. In M.Bouzeghoub, M.Klusch, W. Nutt, & U.Sattler (Eds.), *Proceeding of the 7th International Workshop on Knowledge Representation Meets Databases* (KRDB 2000) (Vol. 29, pp. 129-139). Berlin, Germany: CEUR-WS.org.

Stumme, G., Wille, R., & Wille, U. (1998). Conceptual knowledge discovery in databases using formal concept analysis methods. In Principles of Data Mining and Knowledge Discovery (LNCS 1510, pp. 450-458). Berlin: Springer.

Sugano, N. (2001). Colour Naming System using Fuzzy Set Theoretical Approach. In *Proceedings of 10th IEEE International Conference on Fuzzy Systems,* (Vol. 1, pp. 81-84).

Sulc, B., & Klimanek, D. (2006). Enhanced Function of Standard Controller by Control Variable Sensor Discredibility Detection. In *Proceedings of the WSEAS International Conferences: ACS06, EDU06, REMOTE06, POWER06, ICOSSSE06,* (pp. 119–124).

Syswerda, G. (1987). Uniform crossover in genetic algorithms. In J. Schaffer (Ed.), *Proceedings of the 3 rd International Conference on Genetic Algorithms* (pp. 2-9). San Mateo: Morgan Kaufmann.

Takagi, T., & Sugeno, M. (1985). Fuzzy identification of systems and its applications to modeling and control. *IEEE Transactions on Systems, Man, and Cybernetics, 15*(1), 116–132.

Tanaka, Y., Tsuji, T., & Kaneko, M. (2000). A bio-mimetic rehabilitation aid for motor-control training using time base generator. In *Proceedings Industrial Electronics Society, IECON 2000 26th Annual Conference of the IEEE,* (vol.1, pp. 114-119).

Tang, X., & Kainz, W. (2002). Analysis of Topological Relations between Fuzzy Regions in a General Fuzzy Topological Space. In *Joint International Symposium on Geospatial Theory, Processing and Application.*

Tay, F., Shen, L., & Cao, L. (2003). *Ordinary Shares, Exotic Methods: Financial Forecasting Using Data Mining Techniques.* Singapore: World Scientific. doi:10.1142/9789812791375

The World Bank. (1999). *Social capital research Group.* Retrieved from http://www.worldbank.org/poverty/scapital/

Tilove, R. B. (1980). Set Membership Classification: A Unified Approach to Geometric Intersection Problems. *IEEE Transactions on Computers, C-29,* 874–883. doi:10.1109/TC.1980.1675470

Tran, K. D. (2005). Content-based Retrieval using a multi-objective genetic algorithm. In *proceeding of Southeast Conference,* (pp. 561-569).

Tsakonas, A., Dounias, G., Vlahavas, I. P., & Spyropoulos, C. D. (2002). Hybrid computational intelligence schemes in complex domains: An extended review. *Lecture Notes in Computer Science, 2308,* 494–511. doi:10.1007/3-540-46014-4_44

Tschichold-Gürman, N. N. (1995). Generation and improvement of fuzzy classifiers with incremental learning using fuzzy RuleNet. In proceedings of the ACM symposium on Applied computing (pp. 466-470), Nashville, TN.

Turksen, I. B. (1995). Fuzzy normal functions. *Fuzzy Sets and Systems, 69,* 319–346.

Turksen, I. B. (2002). Type-2 representation and reasoning for CWW. *Fuzzy Sets and Systems, 127,* 17-36. Retrieved November 6, 2008 from http://en.wikipedia.org/wiki/Frank_Rosenblatt

Umano, M., & Fukami, S. (1994). Fuzzy Relational Algebra for Possibility-Distribution-Fuzzy-Relation Model of Fuzzy Data. *Journal of Intelligent Information Systems, 3,* 7–28. doi:10.1007/BF01014018

Umano, M., Okamoto, H., Hatono, I., Tamuri, H., Kawachi, F., Umedzu, S., & Kinoshita, J. (1994). Fuzzy decision trees by fuzzy ID3 algorithm and its application to diagnosis systems. In *Proc. of 3rd IEEE International Conference on Fuzzy Systems,* Orlando, FL, (pp. 2113-2118).

Urrutia, A., Tineo, L., & Gonzalez, C. (2008). FSQL and SQLf: Towards a Standard in Fuzzy Databases. In J. Galindo (Ed.), *Handbook of Research on Fuzzy Information Processing in Databases,* (Vol. I, pp. 270-298). Hershey, PA: Information Science Reference (http://www.info-sci-ref.com).

Usery, E. L. (1996). A Conceptual Framework and Fuzzy Set Implementation for Geographic Features. In Burrough, P. A., & Frank, A. U. (Eds.), *Geographic Objects with Indeterminate Boundaries* (pp. 71–85). Boca Raton, FL: Taylor & Francis.

Van der Gaag, L. C., Renooij, S., Witteman, C., Aleman, B. M. P., & Taal, B. G. (1999). How to elicit many probabilities. In. *Proceedings of Incertainty in Artificial Intelligence, UI99,* 647–654.

Van Gyseghem, N., De Caluwe, R., & Vandenberghe, R. (1993, March). UFO: Uncertainty and Fuzziness in an Object-Oriented Model. In *Proc. IEEE 2nd. International Conference Fuzzy Systems,* San Francisco, CA, (pp. 773-778).

Van Roy, P. (2006). Is There a Difference Between Solicited and Unsolicited Bank Ratings and if so, Why? *National Bank of Belgium, Research Series,* 200603-1.

Vandenberghe, R. M. (1991). An Extended Entity-Relationship Model for Fuzzy Databases Based on Fuzzy Truth Values. In *Proceeding of 4th International Fuzzy Systems Association World Congress, IFSA'91,* Brussels, (pp. 280-283).

VanLehn, K., Niu, Z., Siler, S., & Gertner, A. S. (1998). Student modeling from conversational test data: A bayesian approach without priors. In *ITS'98: Proceedings of the 4th International Conference on Intelligent Tutoring Systems,* (pp. 434–443).

Venkatasubramanian, V., & Rengaswamy, R. (2003). A Review of Process Fault Detection and Diagnosis. *Quantitative Model-based Methods. Computers & Chemical Engineering, 27*(3), 293–311. doi:10.1016/S0098-1354(02)00160-6

Vereb, K. (2003). On a hierarchical fuzzy content image retrieval approach. In *Proceeding of VLDB 2003 (Vol. 76)*. Berlin, Germany: PhD Workshop.

Vert, G., Morris, A., Stock, M., & Jankowski, P. (2000, July). Extending Entity-Relationship Modelling Notation to Manage Fuzzy Datasets. In *8th International Conference on Information Processing and Management of Uncertainty in Knowledge-Based Systems, IPMU'2000*, (pp. 1131-1138), Madrid, Spain.

Vert, G., Stock, M., & Morris, A. (2002). Extending ERD Modeling Notation to Fuzzy Management of GIS Data Files. *Data & Knowledge Engineering, 40*, 163–179. doi:10.1016/S0169-023X(01)00049-0

Vertan, C., & Boujemaa, N. (2000). Embedding fuzzy logic in content based image retrieval. In Proceeding of CIR'2000, Brighton, UK.

Vinogradov, D. V. (1999). Logic programs for quasi-axiomatic theories. *NTI* [Moscow, Russia: VINITI]. *Series, 2*(1-2), 61–64.

Vinterbo, S. A., Kim, E.-Y., & Ohno-Machado, L. (2005). Small, fuzzy and interpretable gene expression based classifiers. *Bioinformatics (Oxford, England), 21*(9), 1964–1970. doi:10.1093/bioinformatics/bti287

Vomlel, J. (2004). Bayesian networks in educational testing. *International Journal of Uncertainty, Fuzziness and Knowledge Based Systems, 12* (Supplementary Issue 1), 83–100.

Wang, D., & Ma, X. (2005). A Hybrid Image Retrieval System wit User's Relevance Feedback Using Neuro-computing. *Informatica, 29*, 271–279.

Wang, F. (1994). Towards a Natural Language User Interface: An Approach of Fuzzy Query. *International Journal of Geographical Information Systems, 8*(2), 143–162. doi:10.1080/02693799408901991

Wang, F., & Hall, G. B. (1996). Fuzzy Representation of Geographical Boundaries in GIS. *International Journal of Geographical Information Systems, 10*(5), 573–590.

Wang, F., & Hall, G. B., & Subaryono. (1990). Fuzzy Information Representation and Processing in Conventional GIS Software: Database Design and Application. *International Journal of Geographical Information Systems, 4*(3), 261–283. doi:10.1080/02693799008941546

Wang, X. Y. (1992). *The Development of a Knowledge-Based Transaction Design Assistant*. PhD Thesis, University of Wales College of Cardiff, Cardiff, UK.

Wang, X., Chen, B., Qian, G., & Ye, F. (2000). On the optimization of fuzzy decision trees. *Fuzzy Sets and Systems, 112*, 117–125. doi:10.1016/S0165-0114(97)00386-2

Wang, Y., Ding, M., Zhou, C., & Hu, Y. (2006). Interactive relevance feedback mechanisms for image retrieval using rough set. *Knowledge-Based Systems, 19*, 696–703. doi:10.1016/j.knosys.2006.05.005

Wei, C.-H., & Li, C.-T. (2005). *Content-Based Multimedia Retrieval* (pp. 116–122). Hershey, PA: Idea Group Inc.

Weiss, S. M. & Kulikowski, C., A. (1991). Computer Systems that Learn: Classification and Prediction Methods from Statistics, Neaural Nets, Machine Learning, and Expert Systems. San Francisco: Morgan Kaufmann.

Wellman, M. P. (1990). Fundamental concepts of qualitative probabilistic networks. *Artificial Intelligence*, (44): 257–303. doi:10.1016/0004-3702(90)90026-V

Whitley, D. (1989). The GENITOR algorithm and selection pressure: Why rank-based allocation of reproductive trials is best. In J.D. Schaffer (Ed.), *Proceedings of the 3 rd International Conference on Genetic Algorithms* (pp. 116-121). San Francisco: Morgan Kaufmann.

Whittle, P. (1971). *Optimization under Constraints*. New York: Wiley and Sons.

Wilhelm, W. B., & Charles, C. (2004). Course selection decisions by students on campuses with and without published teaching evaluations. *Practical Assessment. Research Evaluation, 9*(16).

Wille, R. (1992). Concept lattices and conceptual knowledge system. *Computers & Mathematics with Applications (Oxford, England), 23*(6-9), 493–515. doi:10.1016/0898-1221(92)90120-7

Witczak, M. (2003). *Identification and Fault Detection of Non-Linear Dynamic Systems*. Poland: University of Zielona Gora Press.

Witczak, M. (2006). Advances in model-based fault diagnosis with evolutionary algorithms and neural networks. *International Journal of Applied Mathematics and Computer Science*, *16*, 85–99.

Witczak, M. (2009). *Modelling and Estimation Strategies for Fault Diagnosis of Non-Linear Systems*. Berlin: Springer.

Witczak, M., Obuchowicz, A., & Korbicz, J. (2002). Genetic Programming Based Approaches to Identification and Fault Diagnosis of Non-linear Dynamic Systems. *International Journal of Control*, *75*(13), 1012–1031. doi:10.1080/00207170210156224

Wong, S. K. M. (2001). The Relational Structure of Belief Networks. *Journal of Intelligent Information Systems*, *16*(2), 117–148. doi:10.1023/A:1011237717300

Worboys, M. (1998). Computation with Imprecise Geospatial Data. *Computers, Environment and Urban Systems*, *22*(2), 85–106. doi:10.1016/S0198-9715(98)00023-4

Wu, H., & Mendal, J. M. (2002). Uncertainty bounds and their use in the design of interval type-2 fuzzy logic system. *IEEE Transactions on Fuzzy Systems*, *10*(5), 622–639.

Wu, L., Sycara, K., Payne, T., & Faloutsos, C. (2000). FALCON: Feedback Adaptive Loop for Content-Based Retrieval. In *Proc. 26th VLDB Conf.*, Cairo, Egypt, (pp. 297–306).

Wu, Y., Han, J., Li, H., & Li, M. (2007). Features Extraction and Selection Based on Rough Set and SVM in Abrupt Shot Detection. In *Proceeding of Intelligent Systems and Knowledge Engineering (ISKE 2007)*.

Yan, J., Ryan, M., & Power, J. (1994). *Using fuzzy logic*. New York: Prentice Hall.

Yasunobu, S., & Miyamoto, S. (1985). Automatic Train Operation by Predictive Fuzzy Control. In Sugeno, M. (Ed.), *Industrial Applications of Fuzzy Control* (pp. 1–18). New York: Elsevier Science Publishers.

Yazici, A., & George, R. (1999). Fuzzy Database Modeling. New York: Physica-Verlag (Studies in Fuzziness and Soft Computing).

Yazici, A., & Merdan, O. (1996). Extending IFO Data Model for Uncertain Information. In *4th International Conference on Information Processing and Management of Uncertainty, IPMU'96*. (vol. III, pp. 1283-1282), Granada, Spain.

Yazici, A., Buckles, B. P., & Petry, F. E. (1999). Handling Complex and Uncertain Information in the ExIFO and NF2 Data Models. *IEEE Transactions on Fuzzy Systems*, *7*(6), 659–675. doi:10.1109/91.811232

Ye, H., & Xu, G. (2003). Fast search in large scale image database using vector quantization. In *Proceedings of the 2nd International conference on image and video retrieval* [London: Springer-Verlag.]. *Urbana (Caracas, Venezuela)*, *IL*, 477–487.

Yoo, H.-W., & Cho, S.-B. (2007). Video scene retrieval with interactive genetic algorithms. *Multimedia Tools Application*, *3*(3).

Yu, C.-S., & Li, H.-L. (2001). Method for solving quasi-concave and non-cave fuzzy multi-objective programming problems. *Fuzzy Sets and Systems*, *122*(2), 205–227. doi:10.1016/S0165-0114(99)00163-3

Yuan, Y., & Shaw, M. J. (1995). Induction of fuzzy decision trees. *Fuzzy Sets and Systems*, *69*, 125–139. doi:10.1016/0165-0114(94)00229-Z

Zadeh, L. A. (1965). Fuzzy Sets. *Information and Control*, *8*, 338–353. doi:10.1016/S0019-9958(65)90241-X

Zadeh, L. A. (1973). Outlined of a new approach to the analysis of complex systems and decision processes. *IEEE Transactions on Systems, Man, and Cybernetics. Part A, Systems and Humans*, *SMC-3*, 28–44.

Zadeh, L. A. (1975). The concept of linguistic variable and its application to approximate reasoning. *Information Sciences*, *8*, 199–249.

Zadeh, L. A. (1978). Fuzzy sets as a basis for a theory of possibility. *Fuzzy Sets and Systems*, *1*, 3–28. doi:10.1016/0165-0114(78)90029-5

Zadeh, L. A. (1999). From computing with numbers to commuting with words-from manipulation of measurement to manipulation of perceptions. *IEEE Transactions on Circuits and Systems. I, Fundamental Theory and Applications, 45*, 105–119.

Zadrożny, S., de Tré, G., De Caluwe, R., & Kacprzyk, J. (2008). An Overview of Fuzzy Approaches to Flexible Database Querying. In J. Galindo (Ed.), *Handbook of Research on Fuzzy Information Processing in Databases,* (Vol. I, pp. 34-54). Hershey, PA, USA: Information Science Reference (http://www.info-sci-ref.com).

Zakrevskij, A. D. (2006). A common logic approach to data mining and pattern recognition problem. In Triantaphyllou, E., & Felici, G. (Eds.), *Data Mining and Knowledge Discovery Approaches Based on Rule Induction Techniques* (pp. 1–42). New York: Springer. doi:10.1007/0-387-34296-6_1

Zapata-Rivera, J. D. (2002). cbCPT: Knowledge engineering support for CPTs in Bayesian networks. In *Canadian Conference on AI*, (pp. 368-370).

Zapata-Rivera, J. D. (2003) *Learning environments based on inspectable student models.* Ph.D. Thesis, University of Saskatchewan, Department of Computer Science, Canada.

Zeidler, J., Schlosser, M., Ittner, A., & Posthoff, C. (1996). Fuzzy Decision Trees and Numerical Attributes. *IEEE International Conference on Fuzzy Systems, 2*, 985-990.

Zhan, B. F. (1997). Topological Relations between Fuzzy Regions. In *ACM Symposium on Applied Computing* (pp. 192-196). New York: ACM Press.

Zhan, B. F. (1998). Approximate Analysis of Topological Relations between Geographic Regions with Indeterminate Boundaries. *Soft Computing, 2*, 28–34. doi:10.1007/s005000050032

Zhang, S., & Salari, E. (2005). Image denoising using a neural network based on non linear filter in wavelet domain Acoustics, speech and signal processing. In *Proceeding IEEE on international Conference ICASSP'05,* (Vol. 2, pp. 989-992).

Zhao, G., Kobayashi, A., & Sakai, Y. (2002). Image information retrieval using rough set theory. In. *Proceedings of the International Conference on Image Processing, 1*, 417–420.

Zhao, G., Kobayashi, A., & Sakai, Y. (2005). Group-based relevance feedback for interactive image retrieval. In proceeding of Databases and Applications.

Ziarko, W. (1993). Variable Precision Rough Set Model. *Journal of Computer and System Sciences, 46*, 39–59. doi:10.1016/0022-0000(93)90048-2

Ziarko, W. (1993). Analysis of Uncertain Information in the Framework of Variable Precision Rough Set. *Foundations of Computing and Decision Sciences, 18*, 381–396.

Ziarko, W. (2003). Evaluation of Probabilistic Decision Tables. In G. Wang, et al. (Eds.), *Rough Sets, Fuzzy Sets, Data Mining, and Granular Computing, 9th International Conference, RSFDGrC'03* (189-196). Berlin: Springer-Verlag.

Zighed, D. A., Rabaséda, S., & Rakotomalala, R. (1998). FUSINTER: A method for Discretization of Continuous Attributes. *International Journal of Uncertainty. Fuzziness and Knowledge-Based Systems, 6*(3), 307–326. doi:10.1142/S0218488598000264

Zinn, D., Bosch, J., & Gertz, M. (2007). Modeling and Querying Vague Spatial Objects Using Shapelets. *International Conference on Very Large Data Bases,* (pp. 567-578).

Zitzler, E., Laumanns, M., & Thiele, L. (2001). Spea2: Improving the strength pareto evolutionary algorithm. *Technical Report 103*, Gloriastrasse 35, CH-8092 Zurich, Switzerland.

Zorn, T. E. & Taylor, J., R. (2003). Knowledge Management and/as Organizational Communication. In D. Tourish & O. Hargie (eds.), Key Issues in Organizational Communication. London: Routledge.

Zvieli, A., & Chen, P. (1986). ER Modeling and Fuzzy Databases. In *2nd International Conference on Data Engineering,* (pp. 320-327).

# About the Contributors

**Kalirajan Anbumani** obtained his Bachelor of Engineering degree from the University of Madras (1962), Master of Engineering degree from the University of Pune (1967), and Ph.D degree from the Indian Institute of Science, Bangalore – all in India. Initially, he served in the industry for 2 years. Subsequently, he took up engineering teaching in government and private engineering colleges, Bharathiar university, and Karunya University. After holding his last position as the Director, School of Computer Science and Technology, Karunya University, he has recently taken time off to engage in writing a book. Prof. Anbumani has many research publications, including chapters in books, in areas such as information security, data mining, data compression, multimedia information retrieval, soft-computing, object-oriented methodology, real-time systems, and control. He has completed many funded projects and has conducted a number of conferences and chaired conference sessions. Current interest of Prof. Anbumani covers security, including data hiding in multimedia.

**Raju Nedunchezhian** is currently working as the Vice-Principal of Kalaignar Karunanidhi Institute of Technology, Coimbatore, TamilNadu, India. Previously, he served as Research Coordinator of the Institute and Head of Computer Science and Engineering Department (PG) at Sri Ramakrishna Engineering College, Coimbatore. He has more than 17 years of experience in research and teaching. He obtained his BE(Computer Science and Engineering) degree in the year 1991, ME(Computer Science and Engineering) degree in the year 1997 and Ph.D(Computer Science and Engineering) in the year 2007. He has guided numerous UG, PG and M.Phil projects and organized a few sponsored conferences and workshops funded by private and government agencies. Currently, he is guiding many Ph.D scholars of the Anna University, Coimbatore, and the Bharathiar University. His research interests include knowledge discovery and data mining, Soft Computing, distributed computing, and database security. He has published many research papers in national/international conferences and journals. He is a Life member of Advanced Computing and Communication Society and ISTE.

\*\*\*

**Mehmet Arif Adli** was graduated from Mechanical Engineering Department, Middle East Technical University (METU), Ankara, Turkey, in 1986. He got his MSc. and Dr. Eng. degrees both in Mechanical Engineering (Robotics Division) in 1990 and 1993 from Ritsumeikan University, Kyoto, Japan. After completing his Dr. Eng. degree he worked as a frontier researcher from 1993 to 1996 at Bio-Mimetic Control Research Center, affiliated with "The Institute of Physical and Chemical Research (RIKEN)", Japan. In June 1997 he joined Marmara University in Istanbul, teaching at Mechanical Engineering Department. Since March 2006 he is with "The Scientific and Technological Research Council of Turkey, TÜBİTAK". From March 2006 to September 2007 he worked at the Science Fellowships and Grant Programmes Department as an advisor to the president. He was the director of Academic Research Funding Program Directorate from August 2007 to November 2008. On November 26, 2008 he was appointed as Vice President of TÜBİTAK, responsible from Academic Research Funding, and Science Fellowships and Grant Programmes. Dr. Adli has authored/coauthored over fourty articles in scientific journals and proceedings in the field of redundantly actuated parallel manipulators, human-robot inter-action, bi-manual manipulation and rehabilitation robotics.

**Erhan Akdoğan** received a B.S. degree in electronics and communication engineering from Yıldız Technical University, Istanbul, Turkey in 1999, and M.S. and Ph.D. degrees from Marmara University, Istanbul, in 2001 and 2007, respectively. From 2008 to 2009, he was a visiting researcher at Hiroshima University Graduate School of Engineering's Biological Systems Engineering Laboratory. He has worked as a research assistant at Marmara University's Vocational School of Technical Sciences since 1999. His current research interests include rehabilitation robotics, impedance force control and human-machine interfaces. Dr. Akdoğan is member of the Institute of Electrical and Electronics Engineers and the Chamber of Electrical Engineers of Turkey.

**Maria Alessandra** received the "Laurea" degree in Computer Science from the University of Bari, Italy, in 2004. In 2008 she received the Ph.D in Computer Science from the Department of Computer Science at the University of Bari by discussing a thesis titled "Web Intelligence: a neuro-fuzzy Web personalization system". She is a contract researcher at the Department of Computer Science of the University of Bari and she currently teaches "Computer Architectures" for the 3-year laurea course in "Informatics" at the Science Faculty of the University of Bari, Italy. Her research interests include: neural networks, fuzzy systems, neuro-fuzzy modelling, computational web intelligence.

**Nureddin Bennett** received a Diploma Degree in Mechanical Engineering from University of Applied Sciences of Bingen, Germany in 2006. From 2006 to 2008, he worked for the ITB gGmBH (Institute for Innovation, Transfer and Consultation). Since August 2008, he is working as research assistant at the chair of design in mechanical engineering at Technical University of Kaiserslautern. His current research interests include commercial vehicle automation and simulation of hydraulic and mechanical systems.

**Malcolm J. Beynon** is Professor of Uncertain Reasoning in Business/Management in Cardiff Business Cardiff at Cardiff University (UK). He gained his BSc and PhD in pure mathematics and compu-tational mathematics, respectively, at Cardiff University. His research areas include the theoretical and application of uncertain reasoning methodologies, including Dempster-Shafer theory, fuzzy set theory and rough set theory. Also the introduction and development of multi-criteria based decision making and classification techniques, including the Classification and Ranking Belief Simplex. He has published over 140 research articles. He is a member of the International Rough Set Society, International Opera-tions Research Society and the International Multi-Criteria Decision Making Society.

**Giovanna Castellano** received the "Laurea" degree in Computer Science from the University of Bari, Italy, in 1993. From 1993 to 1995 she was a fellow researcher at the Institute for Signal and Image Processing (CNR-Bari) with a scholarship under a grant from the "Consiglio Nazionale delle Ricerche."

In 2001 she received the Ph.D in Computer Science from the Department of Computer Science at the University of Bari, where she became Assistant Professor in 2002. She is currently teacher of "Computer Architectures" and "Multimedia Publishing" for the 3-year laurea course in "Informatics and Digital Communication" at the Science Faculty of the University of Bari, Italy. Her research interests include: neural networks, fuzzy systems, neuro-fuzzy modelling, knowledge-based neurocomputing, granular computing, computational web intelligence, fuzzy image processing. Within these research areas, she has published about 150 papers on scientific journals and international conference proceedings.

**Pierre Collet.** After a PhD thesis of the French Orsay University in Computer Aided Surgery through Virtual Reality between 1994 and 1997, Pierre Collet discovered artificial evolution and genetic programming through a post-doc in the Fractales Project of INRIA Rocquencourt. From 2000 to 2003, he was researcher in the EEAAX team of the Center of Applied Maths of the French école Polytechnique (CMAPX), as a member of the DREAM (Distributed Resource Evolutionary Algorithm Machine) European Project. In Feb. 2003, he became assistant Professor at the Université du Littoral Côte d'Opale in Calais, and defended an habilitation thesis in June 2004. In Sept. 2007, he was appointed full tenured Professor as head of the Data-Mining and Theoretical Bioinformatics team of the LSIIT lab of the University of Strasbourg where the team is now among the world leaders in evolutionary computation on Graphic Processing Units.

**Ben K. Daniel** is a researcher and an interim manager for Research and Innovation with the Office of the Associate Vice President Research-Health (University of Saskatchewan)/Vice President of Research and Innovation at Saskatoon Health Region, (Saskatoon, Canada). Dr. Daniel also lectures on statistics, research methods and communication technologies at the University of Saskatchewan—Canada. Dr. Daniel is an eclectic scholar with a vast array of training and experiences drawn from many disciplines, some of which include graduate training in computer science, educational and training systems design, philosophy, statistics and communications technologies. Dr. Daniel has extensively published over fifty peer-reviewed conference papers, six international and national journal articles and 10 book chapters on variety of topics in advanced learning technologies. He reviews for half a dozen international conferences and journals on advanced learning technologies and knowledge management. His research has won two major national and international awards and was nominated for a couple of international awards. In the past, he held numerous undergraduate and graduate fellowships, awards and was a Dutch NUF-FIC University Fellow at the University of Twente, Enshede, the Netherlands. Dr. Daniel has recently developed curiosity in e-health systems. He is interested in exploring new techniques and opportunities for extending virtual communities and social networking systems to the domain of e-health.

**Anna Maria Fanelli** is Full Professor of Computer Science at the Department of Computer Science of the University of Bari, Italy. She received the "Laurea" degree in Electronic Physics from the University of Bari, Italy, in 1974. From 1975 to 1979, she worked as full time researcher at the Physics Department of the University of Bari where she became Assistant Professor in the area of "Electronic Computers" in 1980. In 1985 she joined the Department of Computer Science at the University of Bari, as Associate Professor in the area of "Electronic Computers". She is Director of the Computer Science Department at the University of Bari and chair of the CILAB (Computational Intelligence Laboratory) at the same Department. Her research activity concerns Knowledge-Based Neurocomputing, Granular

Computing, interpretable fuzzy classifiers and recommendation fuzzy systems. On the above topics, she published more than 200 papers on international journals and proceedings of international conferences.

**José Galindo** is PhD in Computer Science from the University of Granada (Spain) and professor of Computer Science on School of Engineering at University of Málaga (Spain). He is author of several didactical and research books and papers on computer science, databases, information systems and fuzzy logic. He is co-author of the book "Fuzzy Databases: Modeling, Design and Implementation" (2006) and the editor of "Handbook of Research on Fuzzy Information Processing in Databases" (2008). Research interest: Fuzzy logic, fuzzy databases and ethical issues in the technological age. He is a member of IDBIS research group (Spain) and the Ibero-american research net RITOS-2.

**Benjamin Griffiths** received his PhD from Cardiff Business School at Cardiff University (UK) in Spring 2009, having previously graduated with a Joint honours BSc is Mathematics and Computer Science from the Department of Computer Science at Cardiff University (in 2002). His PhD investigated software development surrounding the technique variable precision rough set theory (VPRS). Additional research work includes feature selection for VPRS and the impact of imbalanced data sets within the VPRS re-sampling environment.

**Hamidah Ibrahim** is currently an associate professor at the Faculty of Computer Science and Information Technology, Universiti Putra Malaysia. She obtained her PhD in computer science from the University of Wales Cardiff, UK in 1998. Her current research interests include databases (distributed, parallel, mobile, bio-medical, XML) focusing on issues related to integrity constraints checking, cache strategies, integration, access control, transaction processing, and query processing and optimization; data management in grid and knowledge-based systems.

**Paul Jones** is currently Divisional Head of Enterprise and Economic Development at the University of Glamorgan Business School and has worked in higher education for over 17 years. He has a degree in Business Studies from Swansea Metropolitan University, an MSc in Computing from Cardiff University and a PhD from the University of Glamorgan. His areas of research interest include information technology usage in the small enterprise sector, entrepreneurship education, business incubation and e-learning. He has published over 80 research articles. He is a member of the British Academy of Management, Institute of Small Business and Entrepreneurship and United Kingdom Association of Information Systems.

**David Klimanek**: Master degree in Control Systems and Instrumentation he obtained at the VŠB – Technical University of Ostrava, Czech Republic in 2001. Then, he continued in the Doctoral Study Program at the Czech Technical University in Prague and in 2007 he obtained a PhD degree after a successful defense of the PhD Thesis at the Department of Instrumentation and Control Engineering. During the postgraduate study, his research activities were oriented towards problems of the sensor software redundancy in application to process control. The work, aimed at evolutionary algorithm methods suitable for the sensor discrediblity detection, was supported by Czech Scientific Foundation within several research projects under supervision of Professor Bohumil Sulc. Currently he works at the Higher Professional School of Information Services in Prague where he responsible for tuition in the Business Information System Program provided by the Prague University of Economics.

**Gordon I. McCalla**, PhD, is a Professor in the Department of Computer Science at the University of Saskatchewan in Saskatoon, Canada. His research interests are in applied artificial intelligence, focussed particularly on user modelling and artificial intelligence in education (AIED). Working with colleagues and students in the ARIES Laboratory at the U. of S., Gord has explored many issues, including granularity in learning and reasoning, educational diagnosis, learner modelling, tutorial dialogue, instructional planning, peer help, learning object repositories. A current focus is a data-centric approach to e-learning called the "ecological approach". Gord is a former President of the International AIED Society.

**K. Muneeswaran** is currently working as Professor & Head in Computer Science & Engineering Department of Mepco Schlenk Engineering College, Sivakasi, Tamilnadu. He has rich teaching experience of 24 years. He published 7 papers in International Journals and 47 papers in various National/ International Conferences. His research interests include Grid Computing, Network Security , Image Processing and Neural networks. He obtained Ph.D. in Image Processing in the year 2006 from Manonmaniam Sundaranar University, Tirunelveli, Tamilnadu, India. Currently he is guiding 7 research scholars. He is involved in a AICTE sponsored research project on Grid Computing for biometric application.

**Tomoharu Nakashima** gained his BS, MS, and Ph.D. degrees of engineering from Osaka Prefecture University in 1995, 1997, and 2000, respectively. He became a research associate at Osaka Prefecture University in 2000 and an assistant professor in 2001. Currently he works as an associate professor since 2005. His research area includes fuzzy rule-based systems, pattern classification, multi-agent systems, and RoboCup.

**T. Revathi** is currently working as Professor & Head in Information Technology Department of Mepco Schlenk Engineering College, Sivakasi, Tamilnadu. She has rich teaching experience of 23 years. She published 3 papers in International Journals and 27 papers in various National/International Conferences. Her research interests include AdHoc Networks, Peer to Peer computing and sensor networks. She obtained Ph.D. in Computer Networks in the year 2008 from Manonmaniam Sundaranar University, Tirunelveli, Taminadu, India.

**Priti Srinivas Sajja** (b.1970) joined the faculty of the Department of Computer Science, Sardar Patel University, India in 1994 and presently working as a Reader. She received her M.S. (1993) and Ph.D (2000) in Computer Science from the Sardar Patel University. Her research interests include knowledge-based systems, soft computing, multiagent systems, semantic web, and software engineering. She has more than 60 publications in books, book chapters, journals, and in the proceedings of national and international conferences. Two of her publications have won best research paper awards. She is co-author of book 'Knowledge-Based Systems' published by Jones & Bartlett Publishers, USA. She is member in editorial board of four international science journals and served as program committee member for many international conferences.

**Gerald Schaefer** gained his BSc. in Computing from the University of Derby and his PhD in Computer Vision from the University of East Anglia. He worked at the Colour & Imaging Institute, University of Derby (1997-1999), in the School of Information Systems, University of East Anglia (2000-2001), in the School of Computing and Informatics at Nottingham Trent University (2001-2006), and in the School of Engineering and Applied Science at Aston University (2006-2009) before joining the Department of Computer Science at Loughborough University in May 2009. His research interests are mainly in the areas of colour image analysis, content-based image retrieval, medical imaging and computational intelligence. He has published extensively in these areas with a total publication count exceeding 200.

**Markus Schneider** is an Associate Professor of Computer Science at the University of Florida and holds a doctoral degree from the University of Hagen in Germany. His research interests are databases in general as well as advanced databases for new, emerging applications, spatial databases, fuzzy spatial databases, and spatiotemporal and moving objects databases. He is coauthor of a textbook on moving objects databases, author of a monograph in the area of spatial databases, author of a German textbook on implementation concepts for database systems, and has published about 80 articles, conference papers, and book chapters on database systems.

**Bohumil Šulc** has been engaged since 1966 in Department of Automatic Control, Mechanical Engineering Faculty at the Czech Technical University in Prague; presently as a professor in Machine and Process Control in the Department of Instrumentation and Control Engineering. Dr. Šulc has published 10 textbooks, almost 100 papers in international journals and conferences and several chapters in books published in English. He is an active reviewer of conference papers submitted for the various events organized by IFAC, IEEE, WSEAS, WMSCI, CCC. He is also a member of the Editorial Board of the leading Czech professional journal "Automatizace". For more than 10 years he has been working in the Technical Committees "Power Plant and Power Systems" and "EDCOM" of the International Federation of Automatic Control (IFAC). More details are available on web pages bohumil.sulc.cz and in Marquis "Who is Who".

**Ertuğrul Taçgın** received BSc degree in Mechanical Engineering from Istanbul Technical University in 1984. He carried out his graduate study in the fields of robotic research in Birmingham University and artificial intelligence applications in University of Wales in United Kingdom. Dr. Taçgın received his PhD degree in 1990. He become associate professor in1993 and full professor in 1999. He worked as lecturer in Marmara University as full professor until 2006. Dr. Taçgın was appointed a chair as dean in 2006 and as rector in 2008 as sabbatical duty in International University of Sarajevo, Bosnia-Herzegovina. He is currently working at Mechanical Engineering Department in Marmara University.

**Angelica Urrutia** is an associate professor at the Maule Catholic University, Chile, in the Computer Science Department. She is member of the Chilean Computer Science Society and RITOS-2 (Red iberoamericana de tecnologías del software para la década del 2000) working group of CYTED and integrant the project 506AC0287-COMPETISOFT The CYTED. She is the founder and president of the Chilean Workshop on Databases. In 2003, she obtained her PhD in computer science at the Castilla-La Mancha University, Spain. Dr. Urrutia has authored several original scientific papers on fuzzy databases and information systems and author the book "Fuzzy Databases: Modeling, Design and Implementation" published by Idea Group Publishing (Hershey) in 2006.

**Naidenova Xenia** was born at Leningrad (Saint-Petersburg) in 1940. She graduated from Lenin Electro-technical Institute of Leningrad (now Saint-Petersburg Electro-technical University) in 1963 and received the specialty of computer engineering. From this institute, she obtained her doctor's degree (Ph.D.) of Technical Sciences in 1979. She has been an invited professor at the University of Paris-Sud,

ORSAY, FRANCE, Research Laboratory of Information Sciences under the head of Dr. N. Spyratos, March, 1991. In 1995, she started to work as senior researcher at the Scientific Research Centre of Saint-Petersburg Military Medical Academy where she is engaged in developing knowledge discovery and data mining systems to support solving medicine and psychological diagnostic tasks. Her research interests include computation methods and algorithms for machine learning, data mining, especially, modeling natural human thinking on computers. Under Xenia Naidenova, some advanced knowledge acquisition systems based on machine learning original algorithms have been developed including a tool for adaptive programming applied diagnostic medical systems and Diagnostic Test Machine for solving supervised machine learning problems. She is also the author of more than 100 scientific articles and a member of the Russia Association for Artificial Intelligence founded in 1989. She is a member of Program Committee of the International Knowledge – Dialog –Solution (KDS) – conferences.

**Juan-Diego Zapata-Rivera**, PhD, is an associate research scientist in the Research & Development Division at Educational Testing Service in Princeton, NJ. He obtained a bachelors' degree in computer science from EAFIT University in Colombia in 1995. In 2003, he earned a Ph.D. in computer science (with a focus on artificial intelligence in education) from the University of Saskatchewan in Canada. His current research interests include the design, development, and evaluation of innovative assessment-based learning environments, Bayesian student modeling and the use of inspectable student models as communication tools and as mechanisms to gather and share assessment information with students, teachers, and parents.

# Index